# GREAT EVENTS FROM HISTORY

# Great Events from History

## Worldwide
## Twentieth Century Series

## Volume 1
### 1900-1945

*Edited by*
FRANK N. MAGILL

*Associate Editor*
Edward P. Keleher

SALEM PRESS, Incorporated
Englewood Cliffs, New Jersey

LIBRARY OF CONGRESS CATALOG CARD NUMBER: 72-86347

Complete Set: ISBN 0-89356-116-9
Volume 1: ISBN 0-89356-113-4

FIRST EDITION
First Printing

PRINTED IN THE UNITED STATES OF AMERICA

# PREFACE

The Worldwide Twentieth Century Series is the fourth three-volume set of GREAT EVENTS FROM HISTORY to appear. The Ancient and Medieval Series was first published in 1972; that set was followed in 1973 by the Modern European Series and in 1975 by the American Series. The work in hand becomes an integral part of the overall development of the twelve-volume survey of scholarly literature concerned with twelve hundred events, beginning in 4000 B. C., that have proved to be of major significance in the history of man.

That these three additional volumes are necessary can be attributed in part to the fact that the tempo of development and change taking place in a human life span today far exceeds that of only a hundred years ago. Indeed, the enormous increase in world population in the twentieth century and the fantastic growth of knowledge dissemination to even the remote parts of the world have created action/reaction syndromes of explosive proportions that cannot now be stilled by the wave of a scepter from London or the dispatch of a gunboat from Washington. Such methods of control, formerly applied to less developed states, have been negated through the marvels of instant worldwide communication and globe-circling rapid transportation—the former assuring parity in information, the latter opening to all the opportunity for wide access to trade in goods and ideas.

When the original sets were developed, Volume Three (1900-1969) of both the Modern European and the American Series was simply overloaded, and many important events had to be selectively omitted. The new Worldwide Twentieth Century Series reinstates many of the unfortunate omissions to the project and brings to the reader an in-depth report on some of the most intriguing happenings in the history of mankind—from "Quantum Physics Research" to "Birth of the First Human Conceived *in Vitro*." Thus, the fourth series in the project is not a mere supplement; it has a life of its own, dealing with events as noteworthy as those found in any of the volumes of the first three series.

Although, as stated above, these three volumes are not a supplement to the earlier project, they are the latest volumes to be added. Therefore, in addition to its own standard six-part Index, to provide continuity the editors have deemed it appropriate to reprint in Volume Three—following the text and index of this Series—the complete Index material carried in the three earlier Series as a convenience for those users who may wish to refer to an earlier related event, a previous personage, or even some of the eight thousand reviewed or annotated titles listed in the recommended reading sections of the three previous series.

The style of the articles is consistent throughout all series. Each article consists of four sections: reference material at the beginning showing type of event, time, locale, and principal personages involved if applicable; the Summary of Event, a journalistic account of the occurrence describing the basic facts of what took place and some of the causes and effects; the Pertinent Literature, wherein two or more original essay-reviews of scholarly works written about the event are presented; and an Additional Recommended Reading list which annotates several other works that the student or researcher might profitably examine if interested in an in-depth study of the event. The critical evaluations referred to above provide a review of the immediate and long-range effects of an occurrence and should enable the reader to view objectively the forces that sparked the event.

The primary objective of the editors has been to present an individual discussion and analysis of twelve hundred significant happenings whose consequences have changed the course of history in the Western world. Events considered in addition to the conventional political and military groups include those dealing with intellectual, scientific, literary, sociological, and cultural achievements as well as various other civilizing forces. A major purpose also has been to make available, along with the narrative summaries of the occurrences themselves, scholarly evaluations of representative literature dealing with the events.

GREAT EVENTS FROM HISTORY is not a compilation of reprinted historical material; all the material it contains was newly written expressly for this set by some two hundred history professors and scholars from more than seventy campuses throughout the United States. Reports of the events themselves average more than one thousand words in length while individual reviews of the literature run about six or eight hundred words each. Events are presented in chronological order in the text of each series.

At the beginning of each volume there appears a chronological list of events for that volume. Volume Three includes these six indexes: Alphabetical List of Events, Key Word Index for Events, Category Index for Type of Event, an alphabetized listing of Principal Personages, a listing by author of the Pertinent Literature Reviewed, and a listing by author of the Literature for Additional Recommended Reading. Since, unlike book titles, not all events lend themselves to a specific title universally applied, as do "Battle of . . ." or "Establishment of . . ." articles, the Key Word Index should enable the user to locate many events more readily than would an alphabetical index of events whose first word was arbitrarily assigned by the editors.

The two indexes of historical literature provide a reading list of thousands of titles that are pertinent to at least one of the events under examination, and an attempt has been made to cite works of divergent viewpoints especially if an event is controversial. Such extensive coverage of the literature of the discipline offers a convenient source for in-depth research by the student, and a handy reference for course development and class assignments by the instructor.

The contributors to the Worldwide Twentieth Century Series are listed elsewhere in this volume along with their academic affiliations. My sincere appreciation goes to those professors and scholars and to the researchers and assistants whose efforts were so important to the completion of the work. I wish also to call attention to Associate Editor Edward P. Keleher's informative Foreword and Professor Saul Lerner's interpretive Introduction. All of us hope that the work will be useful and stimulating to those whose interest lies in the fascinating field of twentieth century history.

FRANK N. MAGILL

# FOREWORD

GREAT EVENTS FROM HISTORY: Worldwide Twentieth Century Series, in three volumes, is an updating and expansionary supplement to the original nine-volume work, GREAT EVENTS FROM HISTORY, published between 1972 and 1975 and composed of three series: Ancient and Medieval, American, and Modern European. The new set, arranged chronologically, includes one hundred and ninety major events and developments in world history from the beginning of the twentieth century to the present. As such, this set accomplishes two purposes. First of all, it not only covers major events in American and Modern European history that have taken place since the publication of the original work; it also covers many important events which, because of space limitations, were not included in the American and Modern European Series at the time of their publication. Second, the new work contains events touching the so-called "Third World," that is, Asia, Africa, and Latin America. In keeping with the supplement's "world view," many of the events defy classification by geographic reference to the United States, Europe, or the Third World. Thus, developments in nuclear physics, medical science, and communications have an impact that is truly global in scope.

Most of the events here can be grouped around several major themes which have contributed much to the shaping of the world during the twentieth century. These themes are: (1) the shift in basic human values, (2) the struggle for human rights, (3) the movements to establish independent states, (4) environmentalism, (5) economic upheavals and the continual problem of adequate energy, (6) advances in communication, (7) man's interest in the cosmos, (8) the evolution of United States foreign policy, and (9) the continual problem of war and threats of war.

The first five themes cited above are closely related inasmuch as they deal with fundamental aspects of the human condition and the basic quality of human life. The shift (some would say the decline) of human values embraces several events, actually trends, including "Changing Attitudes Toward Religion in America," "Changing Patterns in Education," "The Demise of the Puritan Ethic in America," "The Changing Social Contract," and "The Emergence of the Drug Culture." One theme, in particular, which cuts across many of the events in this set is the worldwide struggle for human rights. Several essays under this theme cover civil wars in China, Mexico, Nigeria, Angola, Lebanon, Cyprus, and Iran. Others analyze the struggle for civil rights on the part of the American and South African blacks, the American Indians, the Catholics in Northern Ireland, and the dissidents in the Soviet Union. These freedom movements parallel the efforts, examined in several essays, of the peoples of the Habsburg Monarchy, British India, Bangladesh, Southeast Asia, and Israel to establish independent states. The immediate background of some of these independence movements can be traced to events in World War II, among them, Hitler's efforts to destroy the Jews and the Japanese conquest of Indochina.

Within this group of related themes, environmentalism is treated in several essays beginning with Rachel Carson's publication of *Silent Spring* in 1962 through the enactment a few years later of legislation in a number of countries designed to eliminate some of the ecological threats mentioned in Carson's celebrated book. Similarly, the theme of economic upheavals and the continual problems of energy can be studied in "Devaluation of the Dollar," "Reform of the International Monetary System," "Arab Oil Embargo and the Energy Crisis," and "Establishment of the Organization of Petroleum Exporting Countries (OPEC)," among others.

Other themes in this set embrace events which show man at his creative best. Advances in communication may be studied in essays dealing with such major events as the "Development of Radar," "The Opening of the St. Lawrence Seaway," "The Impact of Television on Society," "Communications and Meteorological Satellites," and the invention of the jet engine, xerography, the teletype, and the transistor. Mankind's interest in the cosmos is examined in "Attempts to Contact Intelligent Beings in Space," and "Philosophical Efforts Toward an Objective View of Planet Earth." Other articles cover the discovery of quasars, pulsars, as well as the investigation into the nature of "Black Holes." The exploration of space is also analyzed in essays dealing with the successful efforts of the United States in putting a man in space, landing two *Viking* explorer packages on Mars, and dispatching two *Voyager* probes to study the outer planets of the solar system. The great American strides in space technology since 1960 are to a considerable extent the result of continuing competition in space exploration with the Soviet Union.

This competition touches the area of United States foreign policy, the evolution of which can be traced in essays dealing with events of the Eisenhower-Dulles era of the 1950's through the decade of the 1970's, a period marked by America's *détente* with the Soviet Union and *rapprochement* with the People's Republic of China. Improved relations between the United States and these major powers will reduce, it is hoped, the possibility of the outbreak of further great wars in this century. Under the theme of the continual problem of war and rumors thereof, a number of articles in the new work examine major battles and turning points in both World Wars, the Korean War, and the Vietnam conflict.

Many of the articles in this fourth series of GREAT EVENTS FROM HISTORY reflect a number of paradoxes in man's development during the twentieth century. Thus, man has learned much about his origins ("Research into the Origins of Man") while at the same time discovering methods of destroying human life on planet earth ("Explosion of the First Hydrogen Bomb"). As man looks beyond his own world for evidence of life on others ("Attempts to Contact Intelligent Beings in Space"), it is hoped that he will master those forces which may someday destroy earth ("Worldwide Attempts at Nuclear Disarmament and Nonproliferation," "The Nuclear Test Ban Treaty Signed," and the "Strategic Arms Limitation Talks (SALT) with the Soviet Union").

In an effort to shed some light on this paradox, sixty-five authors have written essays on one hundred and ninety major events and developments that have occurred since 1900. These authors believe that the latest three volumes of GREAT EVENTS FROM HISTORY will enable the reader to understand better man's triumphs and tragedies during the twentieth century.

EDWARD P. KELEHER
Associate Professor of History
Purdue University Calumet

# INTRODUCTION

Contemporary culture is very much a reflection of how it is perceived. In the years since World War II, intellectuals have viewed culture through the eyes of Friedrich Nietzsche, who said in his *Genealogy of Morals* (1887), "Ever since Copernicus man has been rolling down an incline, faster and faster, away from the center—whither? Into the void? Into the 'piercing sense of his emptiness'?" In a distinctly apocalyptic mood that characterizes most analyses of contemporary culture, critics allege that culture reflects fragmentation, and most cite an oft-quoted passage from Yeats:

> The falcon cannot hear the falconer,
> Things fall apart; the centre cannot hold;
> Mere anarchy is loosed upon the world.
> The blood-dimmed tide is loosed . . .
> The best lack all conviction, while the worst
> Are full of passionate intensity.

Fragmentation is seen by critics and pundits as inherent in all aspects of culture—the arts, literature, philosophy, and society. Merely a listing of some recent titles on contemporary society and culture reveal the belief that a dissolution is taking place. A. Hacker's *The End of the American Era* (1968), R. Vacca's *The Coming Dark Age* (1978), Ronald Stromberg's *After Everything* (1975), J. Lukacs' *The Passing of the Modern Age* (1970), A. Wheelis' *The End of the Modern Age* (1971), and many others fill readers with a sense of foreboding.

This dissolution began decades earlier as part of the dominant nineteenth century intellectual movements—Romanticism, Darwinism, Freudianism, Marxism, Nihilism, and Positivism. These movements all brought in their wake ideas that served as corrosives to the beliefs in a rational world, standards of value and morality, concepts of truth and objectivity, specific views of the nature of man and society as related to the term "civilized," and the idea of progress.

Late nineteenth century scientific and technological changes had contributed significantly to the modification of philosophy, art and culture, society, and economic and political attitudes. Medical advances, including the germ theory of disease, generated a growing interest in sanitation in the cities of Europe and the United States. Preventive medicine and improved sanitary conditions reduced mortality from cholera, typhoid, and smallpox and resulted in a rapid increase of population growth. The emphasis on sanitation led, in the United States, for example, to the establishment of sanitary or health boards and commissions in such metropolitan communities as New York City. These commissions assumed authority to make significant changes in living habits and ushered in the growth and development of bureaucratic government. Increasing concentration of people in metropolitan areas to work in the developing industries confronted these cities with massive social problems that could only be resolved by government intervention. For various nonpolitical reasons, therefore, the traditional European and American political conceptions of individualism or libertarianism were forced gradually to give way to other political, economic, and social doctrines by the late nineteenth and the early twentieth centuries.

These political, social, and economic issues of the period were accompanied by the growth of literacy and the development of the mass circulation press. Such a press manipulated public taste by the publication of salable literature and by political appeals to which the public responded. Thus in the United States, for example, the need of politicians to placate public opinion became evident as in the late nineteenth century more and more European citizens were enfranchised. Literature became divided between those, such as Arthur Conan Doyle and H. G. Wells, who appealed to the popular taste and those who wrote for a more restricted audience. There developed a distinction, which would widen through the years, between art for the masses and its artists and the art that concerned itself less with the public's appreciation and sought, instead, technical and philosophical distinction. In music, for example, the popular appeal of Sigmund Romberg, Franz Lehar, and Victor Herbert may be contrasted with the works of Arnold Schoenberg, Igor Stravinsky, Alban Berg, and Anton von Webern. The public could hardly appreciate, let alone understand, Schoenberg's *Theory of Harmony* (1911). Even the traditional advocates of classical music were affronted by Stravinsky's *Firebird* (1910) and *Petrushka* (1911). Critics and pundits regarded such works as fundamentally destructive of the classical tradition in music.

Equally destructive of tradition in painting were the late nineteenth century French Impressionists. Changes in technique and subject matter on the part of the Impressionists had brought much criticism in the art world. Not only were techniques of the application of color modified, but the subject of art had become popular. In the United States such a popularization of theme may be seen in the development of the Ashcan school of painting, which included William Glackens, Robert Henri, John Sloan, George Bellows, and others. Through their paintings these "Apostles of Ugliness," were criticizing American art, in the words of Everett Shinn, as "merely an adjunct of plush and cut glass," and were attempting to rectify the situation through such works as *Brutal* (1917) by Bellows, *The Laundress* (1903) by Shinn, and *The Green Car* (1910) by Glackens. Out of such challenge to conventional standards of art emerged experimentation in an increasingly abstract manner.

In Europe growing abstraction was manifested in the works of Pablo Picasso and Georges Braque, Vasily Kandinsky and Franz Marc. A continuing evolution of *avant-garde* artists developed so that European and American painting in the early years of the twentieth century went through a series of movements each of which rejected its predecessor and emphasized the need for technical and philosophical change. The result, however, was that art became increasingly abstract and incomprehensible to the public. Altogether in literature and the arts, the early twentieth century manifested a flouting of traditional standards, methods, purposes, subjects, and philosophies of art.

The major changes of this period had been in the sciences. Much intellectual debate had followed Darwin's publication of *On the Origin of Species* (1859). In 1871 his *The Descent of Man* had made somewhat clearer the philosophical implications of the materialism that he was positing. By the beginning of the twentieth century Gregor Mendel had been rediscovered and William Bateson, Hugo De Vries, Carl Carrens, and Erich Tschermak confirmed his work. Mendelism supported Darwin, and by the beginning of World War I work had been advanced on mutation theory by De Vries in Europe and by T. H. Morgan in the United States. Much of this scientific effort was borrowed by the eugenics movement early in the century and eventually helped to provide a pseudoscientific justification for racism. The history of racism is a long and sad story that is detailed in such works as G. L. Mosse's *Toward the Final Solution* (1978) and which contributed significantly to Adolf Hitler's organizing and carrying out of the Holocaust. The biological sciences, however, were occupied in the early twentieth century with the gradual elaboration and development of varying aspects of Darwinian evolution through genetic research—a process that would eventually lead to the discovery in 1953 by Francis Crick and James D. Watson of the structure of DNA.

While the major impetus for change in biology came in the nineteenth century, in physics it came in the twentieth century through the work of Albert Einstein. By the latter part of the nineteenth century the classical world of Newtonian physics required increasing explanation and complication. The discovery in 1895 by Konrad Röntgen of X rays, Henri Becquerel's discovery of similar rays in uranium, and the identification of the radioactive nature of polonium and radium by Marie Curie brought attempts to describe the atom. Ernest Rutherford and J. J. Thompson prior to World War I offered specific suggestions concerning the atom's structure. In 1914 Niels Bohr provided a clearly superior structure based on an earlier formulation by Max Planck. Planck had challenged the classical conception of continuity of energy by suggesting that energy was emitted in quanta or discontinuous particles, and by establishing a constant for the amount or quanta of energy. This was supported in 1905 by Albert Einstein in his famous paper setting forth his special theory of relativity. The paper focused on three issues: the nature of space-time; the relativity of all measurements save the constancy of the velocity of light; and the famous Einstein equation describing the reciprocal convertibility of energy and mass. By 1915-1916 Einstein had developed his general theory of relativity and had completely revised Newtonian physics. The nature of space-time had been elaborated, gravitation had been explained according to the new perspective, non-Euclidean geometry was established as the key to the description of the universe, and Einstein was able to discard many of the discrepancies and problems required by Newtonian physics. By the beginning of World War I, the Newtonian universe had collapsed and the physicists of the period after World War I were involved in an elaboration of the newly established conception of the universe. In the natural sciences, the early twentieth century had been truly revolutionary.

In philosophy during the late nineteenth century under the influence of Nietzsche there had been much criticism of prevailing philosophy. The tendency was to focus on processes and methods. Henri Bergson's *Creative Evolution* (1906) saw reality as a process in which a "life force" infused and gave direction to all matter. Such a conception of life as a process would subsequently be developed in the writings of Alfred North Whitehead and others. Meanwhile dissatisfaction with traditional philosophy had resulted in an emphasis on pragmatism in Europe and in the United States. The European tradition was emphasized by Hans Varhinger (*The Philosophy of "As If,"* 1911) and in the United States by William James, John Dewey and others. According to these pragmatists, truth was defined as what was useful. Absolute standards of right and wrong, truth or falsity, could hardly be maintained with this view. The dissatisfaction with absolutes led pre-World War I philosophers, such as G. E. Moore and Bertrand Russell, into empirical philosophies concerned with the precision of language. Analytic philosophy evolved out of this concern. By World War I philosophy could no longer maintain a unified view. The world of absolutes was being abandoned and fragmentation characterized the discipline.

While philosophy was abandoning absolutes, organized religion was being severely belabored by criticism. Albert Schweitzer's *The Quest of the Historical Jesus* (1906) set a tone among Protestant thinkers that focused less on formal theology than on human relationships. While organized Protestantism was undergoing internal reevaluation, it was being assaulted by the materialism of science or attempting to adjust itself to evolutionary theory. In some cases, as with the American John Fiske or the European Ernst Haeckel, some synthesis was devised, but the effort was clearly defensive and compromised the traditional theology of Protestantism. Both Protestantism and Catholicism were beginning to come to grips in the early twentieth century with the social problems of the cities, but the efforts were late and a reaction long after the fact. Residents of cities increasingly looked to politics, rather than to religion, for the solution of their problems. Meanwhile many believers were turning to revivalism or newer beliefs, such as Theosophy and Christian Science. Altogether, religion was confused and defensive in the early twentieth century.

In an analysis of the totality of European and American society and culture in the early twentieth century, the view of most historians is that of society in the midst of change, traditions in the process of collapse, a value system severely weakened and much uncertainty about the direction of the future. That perceptive observer, George Santayana, in *Winds of Doctrine* (1913) described the situation in the following way:

> . . . the shell of Christendom is broken. The unconquerable mind of the East, the pagan past, the industrial socialistic future confront it with their equal authority. Our whole life and mind are saturated with the slow upward filtration of a new spirit. . . .

Santayana was not quite certain of the outcome of the change confronting Western civilization. That that outcome has still to be resolved and remains uncertain has been the result of the profound and tragic events of the twentieth century.

The intellectual movements that helped to undermine the nineteenth century value and belief structure were augmented by the furious and devastating attacks on value and belief inflicted by the monumental catastrophes of the twentieth century—World War I; the Great Depression; World War II; totalitarianism and Nazi barbarism; and the scientific, social, and technical changes since World War II. These phenomena have had such a horrendous and shattering effect on the intellect, on societies, and on life in the contemporary world that most intellectuals have only been able to see fragmentation as the characteristic view of the period since 1900.

The end of World War I brought a general feeling of disillusionment as Europeans and Americans alike were forced by the filth of trench warfare, the slaughter on the battlefields, and the dissatisfaction with the Treaty of Versailles to recognize that theirs was not a heroic venture in behalf of virtue and democracy, but a matter of mixed motives, missed opportunities, and confused results. But if this were so, in the words of George Kennan as he wrote in *Soviet-American Relations, 1917-1920* (1956),

> . . . then the struggle had to be regarded as a tragedy, with muddled beginnings and probably a muddled end, rather than as a simple heroic encounter between good and evil; and it had to be fought, then, not in blind righteous anger but rather in a spirit of sadness and humility at the fact that western man could involve himself in a predicament so unhappy, so tragic, so infinitely self-destructive.

This sense of tragedy gripped the intellectual and social communities of Western Europe and the United States in the 1920's and 1930's and conveyed an atmosphere of fragmentation and disillusionment.

Such feelings were characteristic of the literature of the period. In the United States, the 1920's ushered in the "Jazz Age"—the time of "flaming youth" when observers contended that young people sought in alcohol, jazz music, and illicit sex the forgetfulness and hedonistic pleasure that identified the period. American literature in the 1920's reflected this. The fascinating autobiography of Henry Adams, *The Education of Henry Adams*, was published posthumously in 1918 (though privately printed in 1907). Filled with remorse over America's lost youth and a decline of spirituality and gentility before the rising forces of materialism and industrialism, this volume conveyed to many young writers of the 1920's a sense of self-pity and dissatisfaction with American life—a feeling that they were members of a "lost generation." The youth of this period regarded F. Scott Fitzgerald as the symbol of their generation, of their life style, and of their problems. His *This Side of Paradise* (1920) described the values and attitudes of the young people of his time, while *The Great Gatsby* (1925) dramatized the inadequacy of money, hedonism, and glamor. Fitzgerald's own life, ending in extravagance, the squandering of his wealth, and alcoholism, was almost as good an example as were his novels of what was wrong with American society in the 1920's and 1930's.

Ernest Hemingway described the feeling of the meaninglessness of life in his portrayal of the life of the expatriate in *The Sun Also Rises* (1926). His *A Farewell to Arms* (1929) depicted the horrors of war. The concern of his writings with violence and brutality indicated a dissatisfaction with contemporary living. The work of Sinclair Lewis, one of the most popular novelists of the 1920's, described small-town provincialism and bigotry, the flaws of "boosterism," and the pettiness of the American middle class in such novels as *Main Street* (1920), *Babbitt* (1922), *Arrowsmith* (1925), and *Elmer Gantry* (1927). His attack on the American way of life was precise, vitriolic, and devastating. His being awarded a Nobel Prize in 1930 indicated both popular and critical acclaim.

Continuing the critique of American life, John Dos Passos published his trilogy, *U.S.A.* (1930-1936). Relying on realism, Dos Passos presented an incisive and cold critique of American society. The Great Depression of the 1930's focused the attention of American writers. John Steinbeck's *The Grapes of Wrath* (1939) was an outstanding portrayal of the bewilderment and exploitation of the poor. Steinbeck also demonstrated his sympathy for the downtrodden in *Tortilla Flat* (1935) and the short stories of *The Long Valley* (1938). While poverty in America had produced much confusion and unhappiness in Steinbeck's works, Thomas Wolfe, in a series of novels (*Look Homeward, Angel*, 1929; *Of Time and the River*, 1935; *The Web and the Rock*, 1939; and *You Can't Go Home Again*, 1940) expressed the confusion and despair of life in urban America resulting from the frantic, frenetic, and undirected pace of life. The castigation of American culture and society was equally significant in William Faulkner's novels, *The Sound and the Fury*, *As I Lay Dying*, *Sanctuary*, and *Light in August*, all published between 1929 and 1932. Faulkner depicted the ways in which Americans were invariably limited in their frantic pursuit of high ideals by their inadequacies and the pressure of their surroundings. Altogether, United States literature in the 1920's and 1930's was particularly critical of life and tradition on this side of the Atlantic and in the context of the Depression revealed a sadness that so little had eventuated from America's historic promise.

In European literature and art during the late 1920's and 1930's, in the words of Michael D. Biddiss, author of *The Age of the Masses* (1977), "images of disease, decay, and putrefaction exerted an ever stronger hold." Having published *The Waste Land* in 1922, a depiction of the lack of moral and cultural substance in the period, *Murder in the Cathedral* (1935), and *Four Quartets* (1935-1943), T. S. Eliot recognized the destruction of traditional values that had come in the wake of World War I.

Manifesting a shift to Marxism, Bertolt Brecht and Kurt Weill's *The Threepenny Opera* (1928) and *Mahagonny* (1929) equated capitalism with criminality. Having exiled himself to Switzerland, Hermann Hesse offered an alternative to the growing materialism of the German state in his publication of the mystical *Steppenwolf* (1927). Man's alienation and loneliness were most conspicuous in the hallucinatory world that Franz Kafka created in the short story *Metamorphosis* (1915) and in the unfinished novels *The Trial* (1925) and *The Castle* (1926). The phantasmagoric world of Kafka soon attained reality in the totalitarian regimes of the period between World War I and World War II. The confusion of reality and dream could be seen also in James Joyce's *Finnegans Wake* (1939), in which language itself was distorted into incomprehensibility. The reader could hardly distinguish between dream and reality, between sense and nonsense, between meaning and meaninglessness. Such literary confusion of reality and unreality paralleled the development of surrealistic painting. Indeed, the very literary and verbal traditions of Western civilization, the reality of Western culture and life, were under attack in the 1920's and 1930's.

The writings of Thomas Mann were critical of life between the wars in another sense. Only in the 1920's was there a growing appreciation of the works of Mann. In *The Magic Mountain* (1924), the central figure, Hans Castorp, represented Western civilization. The rationalistic traditions of Western enlightenment were under attack by the forces of terrorism, brutality, irrationality, totalitarianism, and cults of personality in the period between the world wars. Mann's novella, *Mario and the Magician* (1930), a critique of demagoguery, brought Nazi dissatisfaction and eventually Mann was forced to leave Germany. In the United States where he wrote his *Joseph* trilogy (1933-1943), Mann became a symbol of anti-Nazi resistance and a supporter of the ideals of Western civilization.

The growth of totalitarianism in the 1930's significantly affected culture and ideas during the period. Communist and Fascist dictatorships alike attempted to shape art and culture on the Procrustean bed of ideological orthodoxy. In the 1930's, stylistic experimentation was severely limited as art became a tool of propaganda, confined itself to the expression of messages, and was reduced to philistinism. In the Soviet Union, Boris Pasternak ceased publishing until the 1940's; the free expression of such filmmakers as Sergei Eisenstein was severely limited; and even as creative an artist as Dimitri Shostakovich encountered difficulties from the Soviet leaders for his music. In Nazi Germany culture was purged of its Jewish influence; world-renowned artists, scientists, and intellectuals were forced to flee either because they were Jews or because they would not accept Nazi dictation, and an ideological standardization was mandated.

Even amid the Western nations which had not fallen under dictatorial control, literature and art in the 1930's became increasingly ideological. In reaction against Fascism, some English writers, such as Stephen Spender, were attracted to the political left, while others who were dissatisfied with Communist dictatorship, such as William Butler Yeats and T. S. Eliot, supported the political right. Frequently writers were both attracted to and repelled by particular ideologies because of the political regimes that were based on the ideologies. For example, Ignazio Silone started as a Communist, became disgusted with Stalin's tyrannical methods, and eventually dissociated himself from the Communist Party. In the meantime he wrote such fine novels as *Fontamara* (1933) and *Bread and Wine* (1936). A similar pilgrimage took place in the career of Arthur Koestler, author of *Darkness at Noon* (1940). George Orwell, sympathetic to socialism during the Spanish Civil War, recognized the dangers of totalitarian socialism in *Animal Farm* (1945) and *Nineteen Eighty-Four* (1949). Perhaps the disillusionment of the literary community of the 1930's can best be summed up in two works. Jean-Paul Sartre's publication of *Nausea* in 1938 was a shockingly negative indictment of Western life. In viewing life, a feeling of absurdity developed that filled all thought with a pervasive nausea. *Mind at the End of Its Tether*, published in 1946 by H. G. Wells, described a world totally beyond redemption and conveyed a denial of the perfectibility of man. Here was the outcome among the literary community of the feelings of disillusionment, decline of traditional standards, and sense of fragmentation that characterized the 1920's and 1930's. These feelings were equally pervasive in the philosophy and religion of the time.

Many members of the literary community had, through their writings, been engaged in what they regarded as a moral revolt against tradition in religion and philosophy. In the United States, for example, such writers as F. Scott Fitzgerald, Sinclair Lewis, Theodore Dreiser, and others had attacked what they spoke of as "Puritanism," a term which they applied to anything that, in their view, inhibited freedom. Therefore, organized religion was regarded as outmoded, prudish, fraudulent, and nonmodern. Although highly pessimistic, these writers portrayed a self-indulgent hedonism which they advocated and which was reflected in the "Roaring Twenties," when many Americans were pleased to adopt and practice such ideas. This hedonistic attitude created an atmosphere that affected the organized religion of the period in several ways.

One reaction to the hedonism of the 1920's and 1930's was the growth of Protestant fundamentalism which denied that religion should make any accommodation with modern life. Insistence on biblical authority and the fundamentals was greeted, however, with ridicule by H. L. Mencken and other members of the American literary community, particularly during and after the Scopes trial of 1925.

Organized religion, in contrast to fundamentalism, had increasingly been adjusting itself to the life of the 1920's. This shift was reflected in the decline of emphasis on such historic and traditional concepts as the literal interpretation of the Bible and Original Sin, in the weakening of church discipline, and in the increasing concern of the churches with social problems. By the 1920's revivalism had become in the work of Billy Sunday little more than an effort to attract numbers of people rather than to effect long-lasting conversions. Such huckstering of religion disturbed many Americans and raised serious questions. These aspects of religion in America also brought great concern among religious leaders and theologians that religion and morality were rapidly declining and that, in the absence of traditional religion, Americans were aimlessly drifting with no sense of direction or purpose.

Fear that Americans no longer had religion to guide them was expressed in such publications as H. R. Niebuhr's *The Kingdom of God in America* (1937), Joseph Haroutunian's *Piety Versus Moralism* (1932), Reinhold Niebuhr's *Moral Man and Immoral Society* (1932), and other such works. Assuming a neo-Calvinist view, these writers described what they saw as a decline in religion and morality that had occurred throughout the course of American history. H. R. Niebuhr's *The Kingdom of God in America* and Haroutunian's *Piety Versus Moralism* described seventeenth century America as a time when religion was the very heart of society and gave meaning and purpose to life. The religious content of American society was gradually diminished until Americans had been left without direction, purpose, or guidance. Haroutunian, for example, saw the change as "the faith of the fathers ruined by the faith of their children." Niebuhr argued that the theological changes necessitated by the weakening of religion in the course of American history had produced a religion in which "a God without wrath brought men without sin into a kingdom without judgment through the ministrations of a Christ without a cross." Scholars of American religion by the 1930's had become convinced of a decline of religion and morality.

This belief in a weakening religious tradition was also reflected in European attitudes toward philosophy and religion in the 1920's and 1930's. The cruelest indictment against European religion in the 1930's was the unwillingness of organized religion to protest the barbarism of the Nazis. In September, 1933, Pius XI had negotiated a Concordat with Adolf Hitler. The refusal, for whatever reason, of the Pope and the Catholic Church to oppose Nazi extermination of the Jews and to condemn the Nazis publicly weakened Papal credibility. German Protestantism did not react any more compassionately than did the Catholic Church. This unfortunate posture of official Protestantism and Catholicism toward the Nazis weakened respect for these religions in the 1930's and has continued to do so since World War II.

Traditionalism was also weakened by changes in philosophy in the period between World War I and World War II. The two major streams of European philosophy during the first half of the twentieth century were analytic philosophy and existentialism. Each, in its own way, attacked the dominant philosophical orientation of the nineteenth century. Existentialism was less a philosophy than a lamentation of the human condition. Emerging from the ideas of Edmund Husserl (*Ideas: General Introduction to Pure Phenomenology*, 1913) the existentialists borrowed heavily from Dostoevski, Nietzsche, Kierkegaard, and Bergson. They included among their ranks Martin Heidegger (*Being and Time*, 1927), Karl Jaspers (*Man in the Modern Age*, 1931), Jean-Paul Sartre (*Nausea*, 1938), and Albert Camus (*The Stranger*, 1942; *The Myth of Sisyphus*, 1942; and *The Rebel*, 1951). Because the existentialists denied an essence of man independent of the actions of mankind, they placed upon each man full responsibility for his actions. Moreover, every man in each of his actions was acting in behalf of all mankind. Sartre, in his essay on *Existentialism and Humanism* (1946) said, "Everything happens to every man as though the whole human race had its eyes fixed upon what he is doing and regulated its conduct accordingly." Such "complete and profound responsibility" was placed on man for whom traditional values were uncertain. Sartre and other existentialists insisted that each man must act out his life as if he were legislating for all mankind, but not knowing how to act. This responsibility filled man with anguish, fear, and despair—they were feelings which constantly plagued the existentialists, convinced as they were of the absurdity and meaninglessness of life. Thus, perpetually unhappy with man's lot and denying the relevance of traditional values and standards, the existentialist of the 1930's and 1940's insisted on the performance of genuine and authentic actions while refusing to articulate a standard of value on which to base such action. While Jaspers, Sartre, and Camus opposed Nazi dictatorship, Heidegger's existentialism supported the actionism and relativism of the Nazis and made clear the ability of existentialists to justify any act. Here was one source of the fragmentation of Western philosophy and culture that would continue after World War II and have a particularly profound impact on philosophy and literature after 1945. A second source of such fragmentation was analytic philosophy which would also continue to be important after the war.

Concerned with linguistic analysis, the analytic philosophers sought a language common to science and philosophy. One of the most important of the analytical philosophers was Rudolf Carnap (*The Logical Structure of the World*, 1928; *The Logical Syntax of Language*, 1934; and *Philosophy and Logical Syntax*, 1935), who proved to his satisfaction that "The proper task of philosophy is logical analysis"; that "metaphysical propositions have no sense because they do not concern any facts"; and that "only the propositions of mathematics and empirical science have sense and . . . all other propositions are without sense." Thus would Carnap attempt to restrict philosophy to his definition.

Alfred Ayer (*Language, Truth and Logic*, 1936) held that philosophers had only to correct their language for agreement to emerge among them. Equally concerned with language in the 1920's and 1930's was Ludwig Wittgenstein (*Tractatus Logico-Philosophicus*, 1921) who attempted to resolve all philosophic or metaphysical problems through analyses of language, but by the 1930's was coming to realize that a resolution of all philosophical problems was not so easy. This effort to reduce philosophy to linguistics or mathematics would continue after World War II, but its result was only to undermine philosophy and metaphysics and not to resolve their problems. Dismissing metaphysics with the claim that it was senseless, and seeking to confine philosophy to mathematics or linguistics, weakened philosophy and helped to render irrelevant the answers, standards, and values that it had historically provided as the solutions to Western man's problems.

The experience of science in the 1920's and 1930's also helped to denigrate Western intellectual and cultural traditions, to produce a dissolution of Western values, and to encourage the trend toward relativism. By the mid-1920's, problems had developed in Niels Bohr's proposed structure of the atom. A series of changes was proposed by Louis de Broglie, Erwin Schrödinger, Werner Heisenberg, and Paul Dirac, who addressed themselves to the question of whether electrons were waves or particles. While de Broglie and Schrödinger argued that electrons could be either, depending on the context, Dirac and Heisenberg emphasized mathematical representation. Out of this speculation came Heisenberg's principle of indeterminacy (1927). According to this principle, observation could be made either of the motion or of the position of an electron, but not both. The act of observation resulted in uncertainty of accurate measurement. The concepts of cause and effect were made uncertain. The idea of indeterminancy was subsequently used, along with relativity, developed earlier by Einstein, to undermine certainty. Vulgarization of these ideas contributed to an attack on traditional values and objective truth as the term "relativism" achieved great popularity among social scientists and among the middle classes. Relativity was employed to justify almost any interest or viewpoint. There was a pervasive relativism that characterized much of the sociology and psychology of the period. Cultural relativism was stressed in the writings of such authors as Ruth Benedict, Margaret Mead, Karen Horney, Bronislaw Malinowski, and others. Given the orientation of their writings, it became ever more difficult to universalize the standards and values of Western civilization.

The belief that Western society was destroying the very cultural and intellectual traditions that sustained it was a popular theme of the pre-World War II period. Jan Huizinga's *In the Shadow of Tomorrow* (1936), and *The Revolt of the Masses* (1930) by José Ortega y Gasset argued that the rise of democracy had brought mass culture which undermined the standards and traditions of the nineteenth century. This view was supported after World War II with the argument that the dictatorships of the Nazis and of the Communists were a legacy of the masses and of a relativistic philosophical and religious orientation. Hitler, then, was the reflection of the society he dominated as well as its leader. In such a leader, the characteristics, according to José Ortega y Gasset, of the mass man were combined. Those characteristics—mass man's desire to have everything and his dissatisfaction with everything he received—resulted in barbarism. This problem of Western civilization producing the ideas to destroy itself was dealt with sociologically.

Max Horkheimer and Theodor W. Adorno addressed this issue in their study of *The Authoritarian Personality*, begun in 1944 when they came to the United States as exiles from Hitler's persecution. Completed in 1950, their study argued that a "fascist potential" existed in mass societies, such as that of the United States. Writing from the perspective of what Hitler had done to Europe, this volume served as a warning about the dangers of mass society. The Horkheimer-Adorno assumptions were revealed in an earlier work, *Dialectic of Enlightenment*, begun in 1941. They sought to comprehend why Western civilization was "sinking into a new barbarism" and why the heritage of enlightenment was dying. They argued that enlightenment was primarily designed to undermine superstition with knowledge; anyone could manipulate that tool and thereby control a society. In this sense, the State could utilize and manipulate any mythology that it chose in behalf of its objectives as Hitler had used anti-Semitism to support his objectives. Western enlightenment, in the view of Horkheimer and Adorno, would no longer protect against barbarism but could, itself, support that very barbarism. The searching reality of Adolf Hitler, of Nazi Germany, of the persecution and extermination of the Jews, of the migrations of intellectuals out of Germany to the West, all had a profound effect on the Western intelligentsia and tragically affected their view of Western culture after World War II.

World War II and the experience of the Holocaust convinced most intellectuals of the existence of a bottomless pit of savage barbarism in civilized man as well as dangers inherent in the development of a rational and ordered civilization. Anne Frank's *Diary of a Young Girl*, Ignazio Silone's *Fontamara*, Arthur Koestler's *Darkness at Noon*, George Orwell's *Nineteen Eighty-Four*, and other such works spelled out these lessons in unforgettable scenes that were burned deeply into the popular consciousness of the postwar period. So profound has been the impact of the Holocaust that it has spawned an important and continuing literature, including A. D. Morse's *While Six Million Died* (1968), R. Hochhuth's *The Deputy* (1964), T. DePres's *The Survivor* (1976), L. Davidowicz's *The War Against the Jews, 1933-1945* (1975), A. Lustig's *A Prayer for Katerina Horovitzova* (1973), and the whole body of literary, philosophical, historical, psychological, and sociological literature that has grown around this tragic theme.

The distrust of government has been strengthened by the popularity of a body of anti-Utopian literature, the most outspoken of which is George Orwell's *Nineteen Eighty-Four*. What can be said of a government whose goal is graphically depicted as, "If you want a picture of the future, imagine a boot stamping on a human face—forever"? Such tyranny could only evoke terror on the part of readers whose recent experience had been that of the Holocaust. Orwell, in speaking of the tyranny of the modern state said,

Crime follows crime, one ruling class replaces another, the Tower of Babel rises and falls, but one mustn't resist the process—indeed, one must be ready to applaud any piece of scoundrelism that comes off—because in some mystical way, in the sight of God, or perhaps in the sight of Marx, this is Progress.

In a host of authors from Arthur Koestler in *Darkness at Noon* to Alexander Solzhenitsyn in *The Gulag Archipelago* (1973), writers have been preoccupied with the horrors perpetrated by government. Thus, the post-World War II generation of writers was strongly moved to stress the individual against government.

There was as well a recognition that the tyranny of government was not identified with one or another ideology, but characterized all governments. There was, in fact, a belief in the 1950's that the West was witnessing, in the words of Daniel Bell, "the end of ideology." There was condemnation of government in general, regardless of ideology. This antigovernment tendency has been strengthened by the popularity of existentialism. The writings of Sartre, Camus, Kierkegaard, Jaspers, Heidegger, and others stressed the hopelessness and absurdity of life; the dehumanization and alienation of individuals in modern society and government; and the need for restoring man's wholeness and centrality as opposed to the specialization and bureaucratization of the postwar world. Existentialists believed that, in the absence of absolute values and the undesirability of adopting the values imposed by government or society, each individual must act according to the values that he creates for himself. Moreover, validating each act with personal authenticity reveals a radical individualism and subjectivism in existentialism. Because one must act and choose in an absurd world with no guide to action or choice, save the self, and being continually suspicious of the ideologies and abstractions of others, the emotional posture of existentialism was invariably that of despair, nausea, loneliness. While setting an emotional tone for the post-World War II thinkers, existentialism could provide no guidance, save the conclusion that each person must act authentically and despairingly according to his own judgment.

Nor did the analytic side of philosophy provide answers and direction for the postwar world. Concerned as they were with logical analysis or linguistic analysis, analytic philosophers, like existentialists, refused to serve as guides to Western culture. It made little difference whether the philosopher was an existentialist or an analytical philosopher, philosophy no longer represented a central vision—an attempt to provide orientation for the fragmentation of our time. Philosophy has, in fact, become one of the examples of that fragmentation. In his book *Ideas Have Consequences* (1948), Richard Weaver's was a lonely voice in the wilderness of philosophy crying out for a central vision, for an attempt at the answers to life's major questions, and for an effort to supply meaning and purpose to life.

Nor does art represent a central, cultural vision. In the post-World War II period, the fine arts have become an enormous industry. Alvin Toffler documented this in his book *The Culture Consumers* (1965). The proliferation of art works and artists has permitted a great expansion of techniques. Moreover, the nature of the *avant-garde*, as described in Renato Poggioli's *The Theory of the Avant-Garde* (1968), has precluded domination by an intractable artistic establishment. Experimentation has been a requirement of art for the present, almost, in the words of Poggioli, "in a scientific rather than an aesthetic sense." This may be illustrated in Tom Wolfe's book *The Painted Word* (1975), an amusing attempt to portray the technical experimentation of post-World War II artists and to illustrate the ways in which such artists seek to support and respond to theories and interpretations of art by art critics. Wolfe contended that by rejecting the whole history of Western art, contemporary artists and critics have focused on a self-indulgent flouting of the public and its tastes. Wolfe humorously depicted the modern artistic scene in a manner reminiscent of the children's story "The Emperor's New Clothes," as artists and critics alike sought to make "much ado about nothing." Poggioli identified what he regarded to be the characteristics and concepts of contemporary artists:

> These concepts of activism, antagonism and nihilism, agonism and futurism, antitraditionalism and modernism, obscurity and unpopularity, dehumanization and iconoclasm, voluntarism and cerebralism, abstract and pure art. Almost all have been summed up in the central formula of alienation, as reflected in one or another of the variants of that alienation: social and economic, cultural and stylistic, historical and ethical.

Such characteristics have much in common with nineteenth century Romanticism, but are so widespread in our time that they have come to characterize not only the lives of artists, but the lives of the "beat generation" of the 1950's and the younger generation of the 1960's and 1970's. The sense of alienation, despair, and lack of direction that have been aspects of the fragmentation of the fields of philosophy, literature, and the arts have also affected the young and their drug-oriented, "rock and roll" counterculture. Combining with the demise of faith in political processes and the ability of government to solve national problems, the feeling of alienation was profoundly deepened by the devastating events of the 1960's—the assassination of President John F. Kennedy, the war in Southeast Asia, and the Black Revolution. In the words of Herbert I. London in *The Overheated Decade* (1976), "The optimism that the young shared with the government during the Kennedy Administration had in fifteen years become a pessimism about the will and ability of existing institutions to serve their needs."

In the absence of faith in government, individualism and decentralization have been emphasized. In *The Making of a Counter Culture* (1969), Theodore Roszak wrote that:

> The prevailing spirit of New Left politics remains that reflected in the SDS motto, "One man, one soul." The meaning of the phrase is clear enough: at whatever cost to the cause or the doctrine, one must care for the uniqueness and dignity of each individual and yield to what his conscience demands in the existential moment.

Preserving individual uniqueness could be accomplished only through governmental decentralization. Roszak, Charles Reich, Paul Goodman, and others contributed works that sought to support individualism and decentralization and served as ammunition for the onslaught against the political, economic, educational, and social establishment in the 1960's and 1970's. In such 1960's works as *Compulsory Mis-education and the Community of Scholars* (1964), *Like a Conquered Province* (1967), *People and Personnel* (1965), and *Growing Up Absurd* (1960), Paul Goodman focused his criticism on government, academic institutions, and the economic system that, in his view, formed a rigid interlocking establishment. In that establishment, individual freedom was curtailed or eliminated, meaningful work was prevented, and education had ceased to educate. Goodman supported a radical decentralization that would permit community control of those aspects of government, the economy and education that related to the individual. Government, in the view of Goodman and others, should be curtailed and controlled at the local level, work should be made meaningful, and education should be made relevant. Such changes would solve all of the problems facing the younger generation. Decentralization became the solution to most problems in the 1960's.

The efforts at community control by minority groups were frequently undertaken at the expense of the establishment and occasionally at the expense of other minority groups. Hostility developed, particularly in New York City, between blacks and Jews as blacks sought to control black schools and dismiss Jewish teachers and as blacks attempted to seize political control over districts previously controlled by Jews.

Pursuit of community control was also related to liberation movements in the 1960's and 1970's. Black liberation or Black Power, Latino liberation, and women's liberation have all been movements seeking more freedom and fewer restrictions than historically were imposed by race, color, or sex. While analysts have recognized the many changes wrought in contemporary society by these liberation movements, some have seen them as manifestations of the much larger process of individualism. Andrew Hacker, in *The End of the American Era* (1970), has argued that individualism has been supported in many differing ways since World War II. The result has been "that the egos of 200 million Americans have expanded to dimensions never before considered appropriate for ordinary citizens." The magnitude of privileges and material goods available to Americans has increased expectations for more of the same and has inflated egos and produced an ever-expanding self-indulgence. In *The Revolt of the Masses* (1930), Ortega y Gasset has described mass man as manifesting the two characteristics of a spoiled child. Mass man expects everything and is satisfied with nothing that he receives. This analysis comes close to that of Andrew Hacker.

As each American sought his idiosyncratic goals and objectives, Hacker contended that no one any longer was willing to sacrifice his own goals to those of the family, the community, or the nation. The very existence of society, however, depends on a willingness to sacrifice the self for the benefit of society. Hacker argued, therefore, that the self-indulgent egotism that has come increasingly to prevail since World War II was dissolving the very cement that held society together and rendering the United States incapable of undertakings of a scope beyond the self-gratification of its inhabitants. As he explained it,

> . . . the United States no longer has the will to be a great international power, just as it is no longer an ascending nation at home. We have arrived at a plateau in our history: the years of middle age and incipient decline. We are now at that turning-point ancient philosophers called *stasis*, a juncture at which it becomes pointless to call for rehabilitation or renewal. Such efforts would take a discipline we do not have, a spirit of sacrifice which has ceased to exist.

And what of the future? Hacker predicted that "America's history as a nation has reached its end. The American people will of course survive; and the majority will continue to exist quite comfortably, at least in the confines of their private lives. But the ties that make them a society will grow more tenuous with each passing year." Here is fragmentation carried to its logical conclusion.

The interpretation of the absence of social discipline in a permissive and self-indulgent society has, in the view of contemporary social commentators, permitted individuals and groups to push antisocial behavior, the pursuit of private goals, and personal freedom to extremes. In contrast to much of the history of philosophy and theology, the contemporary definition of freedom has become "the right to do whatever one wishes." This is the traditional definition of "license." In the absence of any enforced or generally accepted standard, social commentators have concluded that contemporary freedom has become indistinguishable from license. A few illustrations will suffice, although examples could be multiplied.

Karl Menninger, in his book *Whatever Became of Sin?* (1973), has thoughtfully urged the need for the establishment of standards of personal responsibility. He had been troubled by the ways in which personal responsibility for sinfulness has disappeared from our society. Moreover, lawyers, social scientists, and psychologists have eliminated personal responsibility from crime by identifying crime with social deviation. Since many lawyers, psychologists, and social scientists assume that social deviation results from the failure of society to socialize satisfactorily, society and not the deviant is seen as ultimately responsible for criminal behavior. Menninger disagreed. Where responsibility is diffused and general, everyone is responsible and, therefore, no one is responsible. Menninger argued in behalf of the restoration of a sense of personal responsibility to society. The fact of Menninger's argument, however, reflects the popular view that contemporary society has strayed from a common code of morality and individual responsibility for maintaining that common moral standard.

Another example that is commonly cited as reflecting a fragmented moral code and self-indulgent individualism is what is frequently referred to as the sexual revolution. While publishers and filmmakers have vied with each other to make obscenity profitable and commonplace, legal libertarians have supported the purveyors of such films and publications by weakening or destroying obscenity laws. First Amendment freedoms are assumed to support sexually oriented literature. The availability of such literature, magazines, and films, combined with sex education classes at all academic levels and the public discussion in the media of sex-related topics, have been perceived as contributing to a weakening of traditional sexual mores and standards. The availability of sexual information and literature has been hailed by psychologists and social scientists as reducing inhibitions and tensions, and denounced by religious fundamentalists and others for producing immorality and unhealthy obsession. Regardless of the consequences, the availability of such sexually oriented materials has permitted more public expression—and hence greater public toleration—of sexual behavior than in previous generations. The range of individual freedom has been greatly expanded in this area.

Still another example often cited of self-indulgent freedom and a decline of morality is frequently spoken of as "Rock Culture." The musical phenomenon known as "rock" has for a number of years rested on the desire to shock the older generation and overturn the popular musical orientation of the 1950's and early 1960's. Practitioners of rock have attempted to shock through outlandish costumes, antiestablishment lyrics (often supporting consumption of drugs and promiscuous sex), a sheer volume of sound that is physically painful, and a style of life blatantly antagonistic to that of conventional society. Rock culture seeks innovation for its own sake; egocentricity and fragmentation have been carried to their extremes.

Even religion since World War II has reflected fragmentation. In 1968 and 1969, Beacon Press published two annual assessments of the religious situation which reflected the growth of a wide variety of movements both inside and outside organized religion. The movements were illustrative of a growth of emotion and the desire for personal fulfillment in religion. Religion was to be tested with the litmus of relevance. For example, the Death of God school in its various forms represented an antiestablishment attempt to focus religion directly on man rather than on theology, the organizational structure, or the edifices of the churches. This desire for relevance was seen in the writings of theologians such as Gabriel Vahanian and Harvey Cox.

In *The Feast of Fools* (1969), Harvey Cox attempted to justify belief in the death of God, radical antiestablishmentarian militancy, charismatic religious movements, radical theology, and whatever anyone chose to call religious as representing appropriate religious experiences. Any quasireligious experience could be justified as long as it was relevant to its practitioners and participants. Cox believed that ecstasy, playfulness, joy, and enthusiasm were the most important religious experiences, and movements that conveyed such feelings were religious. The very term "religion" was modified to include almost anything that someone cared to include.

Gabriel Vahanian, in *The Death of God* (1961), responded to the popularity of existentialism and radical individualism. That popularity among the young, academicians, and members of the clergy was, in the view of Vahanian, proof of the death of God and of Christianity, because existentialism was fundamentally atheistic. Vahanian contended that the individual responsibility that is an important feature of existentialism precludes the concept of organized Christianity. Existentialism "originates in the decay and death of Christianity" and "presupposes the death of God."

The ideas that Cox and Vahanian stressed in a number of publications—that religion must be relevant for each believer; that it must involve personal commitment; that it requires an emotional experience; and that true religion is to be found outside of organized religion—became very popular in the 1960's and 1970's. Ved Mehta in *The New Theologian* (1965) described the impact and popularity of such ideas among theologians and religious leaders in England and the United States. The ideas have resulted in the multiplication of religious and quasireligious organizations and cults in the 1960's and 1970's. Oriental mysticism, the occult, witchcraft, and manifestations of pseudoscientific charlatanry such as numerology, astrology, scientism, and others have abounded as well. Religious fundamentalism has also grown in importance among Catholics, Protestants, and Jews. Charismatic and Pentecostal movements among Catholics and Protestants have been paralleled among the Jews by the growing interest in Hasidism and Jewish mysticism. Altogether, religious enthusiasm, experimentalism, revivalism, and the desire for relevance have characterized recent times.

The changes that have taken place in religion have resulted, in part, from a general feeling that politics and government have not provided and cannot provide satisfactory answers to national problems. In the absence of political solutions, many have sought religious answers. In a similar manner, religion has proved an alternative answer to science and technology. The end of World War II brought an enormous expansion of science and technology, along with a feeling of great unease that accompanied the expansion. In 1956 Jacob Bronowski published *Science and Human Values*, which responded to two types of complaints about the sciences. One problem was expressed in 1947 by Alfred North Whitehead as a fear arising from the logical structure of science "lest a rigid system be imposed upon mankind and that fragile quality, his capacity for novel ideas, for novel aspects of old ideas, be frozen . . . until he and his society reach the static level of insects." Such a rigid system devoid of humanistic values and dedicated to quantifiable objectives had been seen in Auschwitz, Theresienstadt, Buchenwald, and other butcheries of the Nazi state. Science and technology have utilized a methodology that is distinctly rational or logical and involves reducing problems to component parts that are independently solved. When this methodology is applied to political, academic, military, and corporate bureaucracies, it can make those structures too rational, too objective, too passionless, and, consequently, too much lacking in human qualities. In his book *The Human Use of Human Beings*

(1970), Norbert Wiener warned,

> When human atoms are knit into an organization in which they are used, not in their full right as responsible human beings, but as cogs and levers and rods, it matters little that their raw material is flesh and blood. *What is used as an element in a machine, is in fact an element in the machine.*

Thus, one criticism with which Bronowski attempted to deal in *Science and Human Values* was the potentially nonhumane and antidemocratic methodology or logic of science and technology. The second popular criticism of science was articulated by Bronowski when he used a popular song title of the period, "Is You Is Or Is You Ain't Ma Baby," to ascertain whether science was responsible for the horrendous results of Hiroshima and Nagasaki. In recent times a similar question might be asked about experimentation with recombinant DNA and scientific and technological contributions to industry that have an adverse effect on the environment. Bronowski's answers to these important questions were that science possessed humanistic values; that "dissent, freedom of thought and speech, justice, honor, human dignity and self-respect" are all properties of science; that the development of science since the Renaissance has brought these values to Western civilization; and that the world's problems arise not because of too much science, but because scientific values have not yet penetrated the conduct of states. Politicians and not scientists are responsible for the evil uses of science. This answer may have satisfied Bronowski, but it did not satisfy the many scientists and non-scientists who continue to raise these questions.

In an increasingly technologized society, many Americans, both scientists and nonscientists, have perceived great dangers from science and technology. In addition to the issues discussed by Bronowski, fears have been fed by the concern over environmental problems. Such concern became national soon after World War II when atmospheric nuclear tests in the 1950's and 1960's resulted in increased radiation distributed over large areas of the northern hemisphere. Troubled nuclear and other scientists began a partially successful campaign to ban open-air testing of nuclear weaponry. On another front, the publication of Rachel Carson's *Silent Spring* in 1962 alerted many Americans to the consequences of environmental pollution. Out of the effort to curb atmospheric nuclear testing and in the wake of the furor over Rachel Carson's book, the environmental movement was launched. It has subsequently called into question many aspects of our industrial-technological society and has manifested a distinctly apocalyptic bent.

Robert and Leona Rienow's book *Moment in the Sun* (1967) was written from the perspective that the United States had experienced a golden age in the history of the world, the zenith of which was the period of the late 1960's— when the Rienows wrote their book. From that point, the future led downward as material growth and high living standards continued to destroy the environment. High standards of living had been the result of industrial and technological growth, but that growth was now polluting the air and water, and natural resources were rapidly being used up. The only way to preserve America's golden age would be to curtail voluntarily the consumption of material goods and to accept a lower standard of living. Acceptance of a lower living standard would in turn require adoption of a nonmaterial value system. Salvation for America lay in a rejection of greed, materialism, and growth. This theme was reiterated again and again by environmentalists in the 1960's and 1970's. Barry Commoner in *Science and Survival* (1966) and *The Closing Circle* (1971) also supported a curtailment of economic growth as the cure for environmental problems. This was precisely the conclusion of *The Limits to Growth* (1972) by D. Meadows, *Mankind at the Turning Point* (1974) by Mesarovic and Pestel, *The Invisible Pyramid* (1970) by Loren Eiseley, and many other works.

Based on the growing popularity of the idea of limiting growth, the term "post-industrial" has become a popular term among writers, such as Robert Heilbroner in *An Inquiry into the Human Prospect* (1974), Roberto Vacca in *The Coming Dark Age* (1973), Daniel Bell in *The Coming of Post-Industrial Society* (1973), and others who argue that the United States and the Western world are entering a new phase of social and economic development that marks an end to industrialism as the central economic ingredient of Western society. Antiestablishmentarianism has, thereby, taken the form of arguments supporting the inevitable end to the industrial-technological society. What will replace the establishment?

E. F. Schumacher, in *Small Is Beautiful* (1973), argued that small industries, locally controlled and operated, should replace the present industrial system. Small factories would permit the individual expression and autonomy that are not possible in today's massive industrial plants. Assembly-line techniques and top-down direction should be replaced by a harmonious and cooperative economy in which business would come to serve the public interest. As with other aspects of contemporary life, environmentalism and evaluations of the economy have led to a desire for modification of the economy along the lines of an emphasis on individualism and a rejection of the present economic establishment. Here is another example of the quest for fragmentation that has haunted the writings of many commentators on contemporary culture.

The obsessive concern with fragmentation means, in the words of Ronald Stromberg, author of *After Everything* (1975), that

> . . . it may now be impossible to write history about contemporary culture. For we do not find movement, development, but only random change. It is as if a river whose course one could follow ended in a swamp or in innumerable rivulets going off in all directions. One can follow out each of these trickles, but the river as a whole has ceased to have a determinate direction. Perhaps it has ended in a sea where all waters mingle confusedly together. There are all kinds of currents, but the sea, containing everything, is not moving anywhere. We can describe a particular area of it, but this is not "history"!

Thus Stromberg was convinced that fragmentation had so profoundly altered society that there was no discernible whole, save the ongoing process of fragmentation itself. The cultural heritage that existed prior to World War II—belief in a rational world, standards of value and morality, concepts of truth and objectivity, specific views of the nature of man and society as related to the term "civilized," and the idea of Progress—had, the author believed, been replaced by fragmentation.

Finally, it is important to note that social critics both write about and are members of the society that they evaluate; they share the prejudices and opinions of the cultures of which they are a part. Contemporary critics are obsessed with fragmentation, and in adhering to this view they may be contributing to and reflecting the process. Even so, however, it would be difficult to deny the importance of modern man's awareness of fragmentation and dissolution.

Saul Lerner
Professor of History
Purdue University

# LIST OF EVENTS IN VOLUME ONE
## Worldwide Twentieth Century Series

| | | |
|---|---|---|
| 1900-1925 | Development of the Teletype . . . . . . . . . . | 1 |
| 1900-1940 | Genetic Research . . . . . . . . . . . . . | 7 |
| 1901, 1907 | The Formation of the Commonwealth of Australia and the Dominion of New Zealand . . . . . . . | 14 |
| 1902 *ff* | Publication of the Cambridge Histories . . . . . | 24 |
| 1902 | John A. Hobson Publishes *Imperialism: A Study* . . | 31 |
| 1904-1905 | Max Weber Publishes *The Protestant Ethic and the Spirit of Capitalism* . . . . . . . . . . . . . | 38 |
| 1905-1911 | The Moroccan Crises . . . . . . . . . . . . | 46 |
| 1907 | Friedrich Meinecke Publishes *Cosmopolitanism and the National State* . . . . . . . . . . . . | 54 |
| 1909-1911 | Polar Explorations . . . . . . . . . . . . | 63 |
| 1910's | The Mexican Revolution . . . . . . . . . . | 69 |
| 1910-1913 | Bertrand Russell and Alfred North Whitehead Publish *Principia Mathematica* . . . . . . . . . . | 79 |
| 1910 | Establishment of the Union of South Africa . . . . | 87 |
| 1911 | The Chinese Revolution of 1911 . . . . . . . . | 92 |
| 1914 | Russia Invades East Prussia . . . . . . . . . | 101 |
| 1915-1916 | The Great Armenian Massacre . . . . . . . . | 107 |
| 1915 | Japan Presents China with the Twenty-One Demands | 121 |
| 1915-1916 | The Gallipoli Campaign . . . . . . . . . . | 129 |
| 1915 | Italy Enters World War I . . . . . . . . . . | 138 |
| 1917 *ff* | The Continuing Search for Peace in the Middle East . | 145 |
| 1918-1921 | The Great Russian Civil War . . . . . . . . . | 152 |
| 1918 | The Dissolution of the Habsburg Monarchy . . . . | 158 |
| 1920's | Quantum Physics Research . . . . . . . . . | 166 |
| 1920-1940 | Mohandas K. Ghandi Leads the Nonviolent Indian Reform Movement . . . . . . . . . . . . . | 175 |
| 1920 | Treaty of Trianon . . . . . . . . . . . . . | 181 |

| | | |
|---|---|---|
| 1925-1926 | Adolf Hitler Publishes *Mein Kampf* . . . . . . | 188 |
| 1925 | The Locarno Conference . . . . . . . . . . | 197 |
| 1927-1930 | Vernon Louis Parrington Publishes *Main Currents in American Thought* . . . . . . . . . . . | 205 |
| 1927-1949 | The Civil War in China . . . . . . . . . . | 211 |
| 1928 *ff* | Research into the Origins of Man . . . . . . . | 218 |
| c. 1928 | The Reform Program of Mustafa Kemal . . . . . | 225 |
| 1929 | The First Major Arab Attack on the Jews in Palestine | 231 |
| 1930-1944 | Antitotalitarian Literature of the 1930's and Early 1940's . . . . . . . . . . . . . . . | 241 |
| 1930-1945 | Atomic Research . . . . . . . . . . . . | 246 |
| 1930-1950 | Existentialism in Literature . . . . . . . . | 252 |
| 1930 *ff* | The United States Establishes the Good Neighbor Policy Toward Latin America . . . . . . . . . | 260 |
| 1931-1933 | The Manchurian Crisis and the Rise of Japanese Militarism . . . . . . . . . . . . . | 269 |
| 1932-1934 | The Geneva Disarmament Conference . . . . . | 276 |
| 1932 | Chadwick Discovers the Neutron . . . . . . . | 283 |
| 1932-1935 | The Chaco War . . . . . . . . . . . . | 289 |
| 1933-1939 | Emigration of European Intellectuals to America . . | 295 |
| 1933-1939 | Nazi Persecution of the Jews . . . . . . . . | 303 |
| 1933 | Hitler Comes to Power in Germany . . . . . . | 311 |
| 1933 | The United States Establishes Diplomatic Relations with the Soviet Union . . . . . . . . . | 319 |
| 1934-1945 | Development of Radar . . . . . . . . . . | 324 |
| 1934-1954 | Arnold Toynbee Publishes *A Study of History* . . . | 329 |
| 1934 | Stalin Begins the Purge Trials . . . . . . . | 336 |
| 1935 | Germany Renounces the Versailles Treaty . . . . | 342 |
| 1936 | Germany Remilitarizes the Rhineland . . . . . | 348 |
| 1937 | Invention of the Jet Engine . . . . . . . . | 355 |
| 1937-1945 | Japanese Military Campaigns in China . . . . . | 361 |
| 1938-1941 | The United States Establishes a Two-Ocean Navy . . | 368 |
| 1938 | Hitler Establishes Control of the Diplomatic and Military Hierarchy . . . . . . . . . . . . | 375 |
| 1938 | Invention of Xerography . . . . . . . . . | 382 |
| 1939-1942 | Decision by the United States to Construct an Atomic Bomb . . . . . . . . . . . . . . | 389 |
| 1939-1945 | Nazi Extermination of the Jews . . . . . . . | 396 |
| 1939-1945 | The Battle of the Atlantic . . . . . . . . . | 404 |

| | | |
|---|---|---|
| 1939 | Great Britain Issues the 1939 White Paper Restricting Jewish Emigration to Palestine . . . . . . . | 411 |
| 1939 | John Steinbeck Publishes *The Grapes of Wrath* . . . | 418 |
| 1939 | The Synthesis of DDT for Use as an Insecticide . . | 425 |
| 1940-1941 | The Battle of Britain . . . . . . . . . . . | 430 |
| 1940-1941 | Japan Occupies Indochina . . . . . . . . . | 438 |
| 1941 | Germany Invades the Balkans . . . . . . . . | 444 |
| 1941 | German Invasion of Russia . . . . . . . . . | 450 |
| 1941-1945 | Japan Occupies the Dutch East Indies, Singapore, and Burma . . . . . . . . . . . . . . . . | 457 |
| 1941 | Germany and Italy Declare War on the United States | 465 |
| 1942 | The Battle of Midway . . . . . . . . . . | 472 |
| 1944-1945 | Soviet Invasion of Eastern Europe . . . . . . . | 479 |
| 1944 | The First Superfortress Bombing Raid on Japan . . | 487 |
| 1944-1945 | Formation of the Arab League . . . . . . . . | 494 |
| 1945 *ff* | Cellular Research . . . . . . . . . . . . | 501 |
| 1945 *ff* | Changing Attitudes Toward Religion in America . . | 507 |
| 1945 *ff* | Changing Patterns in Education . . . . . . . | 513 |
| 1945 *ff* | The Crisis in Railroad Transportation . . . . . . | 520 |
| 1945 *ff* | The Demise of the Puritan Ethic in America . . . | 526 |

# MEMBERS OF THE WRITING STAFF
Worldwide Twentieth Century Series

---

| | GRADUATE SCHOOL | ACADEMIC AFFILIATION |
|---|---|---|
| **J. Stewart Alverson** Ph.D. | Case Western Reserve University | University of Tennessee |
| **Paul Ashin** M.A. | Stanford University | Stanford University |
| **Terry Alan Baney** M.A. | University of Dayton | Post College at Waterbury |
| **Meredith William Berg** Ph.D. | Tulane University | Valparaiso University |
| **James A. Berlin** Ph.D. | University of Michigan | Wichita State University |
| **Anita O. Bowser** Ph.D. | University of Notre Dame | Purdue University |
| **John R. Broadus** M.A. | University of Chicago | University of Chicago |
| **Henry H. Bucher, Jr.** Ph.D. | University of Wisconsin | University of Wisconsin |
| **Jack L. Calbert** Ph.D. | Indiana University | |
| **John C. Carlisle** Ph.D. | University of Michigan | Purdue University |

| | | |
|---|---|---|
| **Frederick B. Chary** Ph.D. | University of Pennsylvania | Indiana University Northwest |
| **Ronald J. Cima** M.A. | American University | The Library of Congress |
| **Charles E. Cottle** Ph.D. | Kent State University | University of Wisconsin |
| **Thomas D. Crouch** Ph.D. | Ohio State University | Smithsonian Institution |
| **E. Gene DeFelice** Ph.D. | University of Chicago | Purdue University |
| **Tyler Deierhoi** Ph.D. | Duke University | University of Tennessee |
| **Daniel D. DiPiazza** Ph.D. | University of Missouri | University of Wisconsin |
| **Rand Edwards** M.A. | University of Chicago | |
| **Barry Faye** M.A. | University of Chicago | Blackburn College |
| **Elizabeth Fee** Ph.D. | Princeton University | Johns Hopkins University |
| **George J. Fleming** Ph.D. | Catholic University | Calumet College |
| **Jonathan M. Furdek** Ph.D. | Purdue University | Purdue University |
| **Roger A. Geimer** Ph.D. | Northwestern University | Purdue University |
| **Leonard H. D. Gordon** Ph.D. | University of Michigan | Purdue University |

| | | |
|---|---|---|
| **Alan G. Gross**<br>**Ph.D.** | Princeton University | Purdue University |
| **Manfred Grote**<br>**Ph.D.** | University of Maryland | Purdue University |
| **John R. Hanson, II**<br>**Ph.D.** | University of Pennsylvania | Texas A&M University |
| **Jean Harber**<br>**Ph.D.** | University of Wisconsin | University of Wisconsin |
| **James J. Herlan**<br>**M.A.** | University of Quebec | University of Maine at Orono |
| **Cabot C. Holmes**<br>**M.A.** | Purdue University | Elston High School |
| **Charles W. Johnson**<br>**Ph.D.** | University of Michigan | University of Tennessee |
| **Edward P. Keleher**<br>**Ph.D.** | Saint Louis University | Purdue University |
| **Clive Kileff**<br>**Ph.D.** | Rice University | University of Tennessee |
| **Thomas R. Koenig**<br>**Ph.D.** | Louvain University Belgium | Purdue University |
| **Richard L. Langill**<br>**Ph.D.** | The American University | Blackburn College |
| **Saul Lerner**<br>**Ph.D.** | University of Kansas | Purdue University |
| **Paul D. Mageli**<br>**Ph.D.** | University of Chicago | |
| **Anne Millbrooke**<br>**Ph.D.** | University of Pennsylvania | University of Pennsylvania |

| George R. Mitchell<br>Ph.D. | University of Wisconsin | Purdue University |
|---|---|---|
| Paul Monaco<br>Ph.D. | Brandeis University | University of Texas |
| Gordon R. Mork<br>Ph.D. | University of Minnesota | Purdue University |
| John H. Morrow, Jr.<br>Ph.D. | University of Pennsylvania | University of Tennessee |
| Lincoln R. Mui<br>Ph.D. | University of Notre Dame | Tennessee Technological University |
| Victor Namias<br>Ph.D. | Carnegie Institute | Purdue University |
| John C. Neeley<br>Ph.D. | Oregon State University | Purdue University |
| John R. Phillips<br>Ph.D. | Harvard University | Purdue University |
| Doris F. Pierce<br>J.D. | University of Oklahoma | Purdue University |
| Philip R. Popple<br>Ph.D. | Washington University | University of Tennessee |
| James W. Pringle<br>Ph.D. | University of Illinois | Purdue University |
| Anne C. Raymer<br>M.S. | Palmer Graduate Library School | Lake County Public Library |
| John D. Raymer<br>Ph.D. | Ohio University | Purdue University |
| Richard Rice<br>Ph.D. | Harvard University | University of Tennessee |

| | | |
|---|---|---|
| **Richard H. Sander** B.A. | Harvard University | Woodstock Institute |
| **Margaret S. Schoon** M.L.S. | Indiana University | Purdue University |
| **Walter Schultz** M.S. | Purdue University | St. Francis De Sales High School |
| **Jane R. Shoup** Ph.D. | University of Chicago | Purdue University |
| **Thomas M. Smith** Ph.D. | University of Wisconsin | University of Oklahoma |
| **Leon Stein** Ph.D. | New York University | Roosevelt University |
| **Carol Whyte Talabay** M.S. | Purdue University | Purdue University |
| **David Talabay** M.S. | Purdue University | Hammond Technical-Vocational High School |
| **Jonathan G. Utley** Ph.D. | University of Illinois | University of Tennessee |
| **Stuart Van Dyke, Jr.** D.E.A. | Paris Institute of Political Studies | Roosevelt University |
| **Edward A. Zivich** Ph.D. | State University of New York | Calumet College |

# INITIALS IDENTIFYING CONTRIBUTORS OF SIGNED ARTICLES

| | | | |
|---|---|---|---|
| *A.C.R.* | Anne C. Raymer | *J.R.B.* | John R. Broadus |
| *A.G.G.* | Alan G. Gross | *J.R.H.* | John R. Hanson, II |
| *A.M.* | Anne Millbrooke | *J.R.P.* | John R. Phillips |
| *A.O.B.* | Anita O. Bowser | *J.R.S.* | Jane R. Shoup |
| *B.F.* | Barry Faye | *J.S.A.* | J. Stewart Alverson |
| *C.C.H.* | Cabot C. Holmes | *J.W.P.* | James W. Pringle |
| *C.E.C.* | Charles E. Cottle | *L.H.D.G.* | Leonard H. D. Gordon |
| *C.K.* | Clive Kileff | *L.R.M.* | Lincoln R. Mui |
| *C.W.J.* | Charles W. Johnson | *L.S.* | Leon Stein |
| *C.W.T.* | Carol Whyte Talabay | *M.G.* | Manfred Grote |
| *D.D.D.* | Daniel D. DiPiazza | *M.S.S.* | Margaret S. Schoon |
| *D.F.P.* | Doris F. Pierce | *M.W.B.* | Meredith William Berg |
| *D.W.T.* | David W. Talabay | *P.A.* | Paul Ashin |
| *E.A.Z.* | Edward A. Zivich | *P.D.M.* | Paul D. Mageli |
| *E.F.* | Elizabeth Fee | *P.M.* | Paul Monaco |
| *E.G.D.* | E. Gene DeFelice | *P.R.P.* | Philip R. Popple |
| *E.P.K.* | Edward P. Keleher | *R.A.G.* | Roger A. Geimer |
| *F.B.C.* | Frederick B. Chary | *R.E.* | Rand Edwards |
| *G.J.F.* | George J. Fleming | *R.H.S.* | Richard H. Sander |
| *G.R.M.* | George R. Mitchell | *R.J.C.* | Ronald J. Cima |
| *G.R.M.* | Gordon R. Mork | *R.L.L.* | Richard L. Langill |
| *H.H.B.* | Henry H. Bucher, Jr. | *R.R.* | Richard Rice |
| *J.A.B.* | James A. Berlin | *S.L.* | Saul Lerner |
| *J.C.C.* | John C. Carlisle | *S.V.D.* | Stuart Van Dyke, Jr. |
| *J.C.N.* | John C. Neeley | *T.A.B.* | Terry Alan Baney |
| *J.D.R.* | John D. Raymer | *T.D.* | Tyler Deierhoi |
| *J.G.U.* | Jonathan G. Utley | *T.D.C.* | Thomas D. Crouch |
| *J.H.* | Jean Harber | *T.M.S.* | Thomas M. Smith |
| *J.H.M.* | John H. Morrow, Jr. | *T.R.K.* | Thomas R. Koenig |
| *J.J.H.* | James J. Herlan | *V.N.* | Victor Namias |
| *J.L.C.* | Jack L. Calbert | *W.S.* | Walter Schultz |
| *J.M.F.* | Jonathan M. Furdek | | |

# GREAT EVENTS FROM HISTORY

# DEVELOPMENT OF THE TELETYPE

*Type of event:* Technological: invention of products in the area of communication
*Time:* 1900-1925
*Locale:* The United States and Europe

*Principal personages:*

JEAN MARIE EMILE BAUDOT, the inventor of the five-pulse letter code

CHARLES AND HOWARD KRUM, the father and son who developed the Morkrum teleprinter

JOY MORTON (1855-1934), member of the Morton Salt family whose financial backing made the Morkrum Company possible

KENT COOPER, Associated Press wire service administrator who saw the practical value of the teletype for transmitting news during World War I

THOMAS ALVA EDISON (1847-1931), the inventor of the market "ticker"

## Summary of Event

The nineteenth century origins of the teletypewriter proved to be historically less important than its twentieth century technical development, which brought it into worldwide use. The machine was a typical product of the engineering-development tradition that took form during the hundred years from 1850 to 1950 in Europe and the United States. It started as a design concept and the subject of numerous patent claims on both sides of the Atlantic for nearly three quarters of a century, before it became a practical device that was found to be increasingly essential to special business, government, and social communication needs. Scarcely in use by the second decade of the twentieth century, it was in heavy use by the middle of the century for all those occasions when electronic signals need to be transformed automatically into the printed word.

As Samuel F. B. Morse conceived of the telegraph when he developed it in the middle of the nineteenth century, it would incorporate a machine that converted electric pulses coming in over the telegraph wire into written dots and dashes that a human operator could translate at leisure to letters and words. Morse's plan was superseded by the dexterity of early telegraphers, who could get ahead of the recording machine by recording directly as letters the dots and dashes they heard coming in over their "Morse sounders." However, before the beginning of the twentieth century the traffic volume of information being conveyed in pursuit of financial, commercial, administrative, governmental, general news, and private social affairs revived the need for both a practical machine to record

1

incoming messages directly in letter form and a transmitting machine that would itself convert letters to electric pulses to be telegraphed. Although the need was recognized, a general solution was not immediately at hand at the time.

Instead, there were alternative, partial solutions that subsequently would be brought together by 1914 to produce a practical message-sending-and-receiving system using teletypewriters. One of the first of these partial solutions was the duplex technique of transmitting two messages simultaneously, in opposite directions, over the same wire. First put into practice in the United States in 1872, it was followed in 1874 by Thomas Edison's quadruplex system. In that same year in Europe, Jean Marie Emile Baudot devised his five-pulse code, later modified by Donald Murray, which was used by Edison in his famous glass-domed stock market "ticker" that came into special use from 1870 on, reporting stock market quotations in a coded pattern of punched holes in paper tape.

The five-pulse code could be structured into thirty-two different patterns, either by omitting one or more pulses in the sequence of the group of five generated within a fraction of a second, or by reversing the polarity of one or more of the pulses. Twenty-six of these patterns were assigned to the alphabet, while the others were used for such functions as introducing spaces between words or conveying numbers, question marks, and the like. The pulse patterns were punched into paper tape, where they could either be deciphered by trained eyes or fed into a machine that would re-spond to the patterns by typing the corresponding letters.

But the state of the art of typewriter engineering and design was not sufficiently advanced until the turn of the century to provide practical keyboard machines that would utilize the five-pulse code or the later seven-pulse code, introduced by Charles L. Krum, that added clarity between transmitter and receiver by using the first and last pulses as "pattern-start" and "pattern stop" symbols to keep the sender and the receiver synchronized on the same message. Letter-wheel and letter-hammer machines were tried without practical success at first. In 1900 the idea of using a typewriter to send and receive telegraph messages was still a dream of inventors.

Then Joy Morton of the Morton Salt family provided financial backing to Krum, a mechanical engineer, who brought his son Howard into the enterprise. The Morkrum Company was organized under Howard Krum's engineering leadership early in the 1900's and produced a number of encouraging teletype designs using at the start the five-pulse code, a rotating type-wheel, and a stationary roller to hold the paper. The success of the Morkrum machines caused the Morkrum Company to combine with the Kleinschmidt Electric Company in 1923 and form the Teletype Company which was later acquired by the American Telephone and Telegraph Company.

In the meantime, the Morkrum teletypewriter had come into limited use. Practical experience with the "Morkrums" led Kent Cooper, Traffic Manager of the Associated Press wire news service in 1914, to begin installing teletypewriters in newspaper offices in large urban centers such as New York and Washington, where significant news was being made.

The teletype was economical only where there was a sufficient volume of message traffic over the wires. In consequence, although practical teleprinters were available by 1915, the demand remained relatively small. But telegraph and telephone communications traffic continued to grow. For awhile (1910-1914) the Western Union telegraph company was taken over by American Telephone and Telegraph Company, until the government forced the latter to divest itself of Western Union in order to provide competition and avert potential monopolistic control. But whether independent or part of a larger organization, Western Union began to use the teletype and by 1927 had more than six thousand machines on line. Also during the 1920's, Britain's nationalized telegraph and postal service began using British-built Creed teleprinters, expanding their use rapidly between 1929 and 1935 as part of an effort to head off shrinking use of the telegraph as the telephone grew more popular.

The role of the teletype in the communications field in Europe and the United States was influenced by the growing popularity of the telephone and by the economics of the private (in the United States) and the public (in Europe) communications industry, while wire, cable, wireless, and automatic-circuit systems continued to multiply during the second quarter of the twentieth century. The effect upon the teletype of these economic and technical developments during this period was to extend its use to major centers of news and of business and government activities worldwide. In 1931 American Telephone and Telegraph Company introduced in the United States the teletypewriter Exchange Service (TWX), which enabled subscribers to link up their teletypes by telephone lines. In 1932, Western Union introduced a TELEX network utilizing the telegraph lines, and Europe had its own TELEX, which spread worldwide after World War II. By 1940, nearly fifteen thousand American teletype stations were tied together by the TWX network. By 1950, there were over twenty-eight thousand. During the 1960's the number passed fifty thousand, and service was extended to Canada. In 1962, TWX converted to automatic dialing, and subsequently TELEX absorbed TWX to provide a global network.

The inventors' dream of 1900 had demonstrated its practicality to all doubters before 1925. By midcentury it was the major vehicle for written-message transmission and was being incorporated into computer-controlled information networks. Speeds that had reached an early plateau of sixty words per minute rose to one hundred words per minute and then moved into the higher magnitudes afforded by computerized operation. Although the teletypewriter had originated as a communications machine in its own right, subsequently it became one of the components, along with the telephone, the teletypesetter, the television screen, and the computer data bank, of the numerous and increasingly elaborate world-

3

wide, integrated electronic communications systems that arose during
the third quarter of the twentieth century.

## Pertinent Literature

Fagen, M. D., ed. *A History of Engineering and Science in the Bell System: The Early Years, 1875-1925*. Murray Hill, N.J.: Bell Telephone Laboratories, 1975.

Since this book is devoted to the first fifty years of telephone technology as seen from the point of view of the Bell Telephone Laboratories, the teletype is treated as only one item among many. Nevertheless, in Chapter 7, "Non-Voice Communications," there is considerable technical information (layman level) on the teletype, its historical and technical background, its incorporation into communication systems and transmission networks, and related achievements into the 1930's. This information is all made part of the massive engineering success story of "the Bell System" that this one-thousand-page book was intended to relate; fortunately, though, because much of the discussion is on mildly technical matters, the writers' biases provide only small, recognizable distortions that can easily be taken into account. Thus, the startling originality of Baudot's conception pales beside the practical significance of the "multiplex printing-telegraph system" later developed (after 1912) by Western Electric engineers who employed Murray's modification of the Baudot code. And the reader is not told that a trial system set up between New York and Chicago failed; it was simply "discontinued" in 1918. Subsequent "regular service" instituted in 1920 finally convinced the com-

pany by 1923 that this was the most economical way to handle a large volume of messages. (The Associated Press had reached its own practical conclusion nearly a decade earlier.)

The reader who cares enough to pore back and forth over this chapter will find such technological tidbits as the undocumented pioneering use of an Essick typewriter tied into a telephone line in 1891, or the 1868 German patent of an automatic keyboard perforator by Siemens, or the 1915 efforts of the Morkrum, Cardwell, and Kleinschmidt companies to sell teletype machines of their own manufacture. But in addition to the profusion of details that such a survey of past technology often presents, there are also interpretive generalizations, such as the judgment that wire transmission problems, combined with design limitations in nineteenth century precursors of the teletype, prevented the machine from coming into general use at that time.

The wealth of information presented in the book is better appreciated by the reader already familiar with the general story and the technical problems involved, but the novice will find it a stimulating springboard into the wider literature, and the bibliography at the end of the book will prove useful for the more technically curious reader.

Shannon, Claude E. and Warren Weaver. *The Mathematical Theory of Communication*. Urbana: The University of Illinois Press, 1949.

The two papers contained in this small book comprise an oft-reprinted classic. Written during the 1940's, they review the abstract mathematics which constitute the basic theoretical scientific understanding underlying the elaborate integrated teletype networks that came into being after the 1930's. Further, these papers remind us that the teletype became less important as a machine in its own right as the years passed, and more important as a component integrated into a network system developed to transport messages in ever more massive quantities with increasing rapidity between growing numbers of possible points. The teletype both provoked and responded to these developments, but such developments would not have come to pass had there not also occurred the mathematical modeling described by Shannon and Weaver.

Weaver's short paper is a nonmathematical summary and introduction to Shannon's longer and mathematically sophisticated paper. The import of the authors' treatment of the practices carried out when teletyped messages are sent is that mathematical analysis will tell the engineer what can and cannot be accomplished by any message network he designs. To paraphrase Shannon, point-to-point communication of a message is the engineer's central problem. Whatever meaning the message may contain is irrelevant to the engineering task of providing for selection of any two possible points between which any one of a possible set of messages

may be sent. To accomplish this task is to design and build a communication system, and in order to produce such a system, one begins, says Shannon, by transforming the proposed physical components into ideal mathematical entities and recognizing that there are two kinds of systems, plus a third that is a mix of the first two. Radio and television are examples of *continuous* systems that transmit signals and messages as continuous functions, while the dot-dash and pulse-code systems of the telegraph and teletype transmit the signals and the messages as discrete symbols in a *discrete* system of communication. Shannon then proceeds to describe, analyze, and construct these systems in abstract, generalized mathematical terms.

Weaver sees the communication problem as one to be examined on three levels: how accurately may the symbols be transmitted, how accurately do they convey the precise meaning, and with what effectiveness does the conveyed meaning appropriately affect subsequent conduct (since the aim of communicating a message is to affect the conduct and knowledge of the person receiving it)? Weaver argues that Shannon's mathematics, while it focused upon the first of the three levels, also can be fruitfully applied to the other two.

Shannon and Weaver have no interest in the teletype *per se*, but their treatment of general communication theory, when placed alongside the historical development of the teletype, reminds the reader that the

5

story of the teletype is part of the larger story of modern scientific research and engineering development. The practical success of the teletype resulted from the fact that abstract science and engineering technology had developed a technique of playing leapfrog with each other in order to explore the unknown and bring it into the realm of human understanding, exploitation, and technical and social control. The continuing technical progress of the teletype from nineteenth century dream to twentieth century fact was a consequence of the merging of the separate tradition of impractical science with the older tradition of practical technology. — *T.M.S.*

## Additional Recommended Reading

Martin, James. *Telecommunications and the Computer*. Englewood Cliffs, N. J.: Prentice-Hall, 1976.

——————— . *Teleprocessing Network Organization*. Englewood Cliffs, N. J.: Prentice-Hall, 1970. These two books give extensive, technically elementary descriptions of transmission techniques and practices in electronic communications systems worldwide, and place the teletype in historical and technical perspective.

Kieve, Jeffrey. *The Electric Telegraph in the U. K.* New York: Barnes and Noble, 1973. A social and economic history of the British telegraph system.

Harlow, Alvin F. *Old Wires and New Waves*. New York: D. Appleton-Century, 1936. A classic history of the American telegraph, useful for its anecdotes and "local color."

Herring, James M. and Gerald C. Gross. *Telecommunications, Economics and Regulation*. New York: McGraw-Hill Book Company, 1936. Examines the controlling business and governmental factors that established the communications utilities in which the teletype became a minor yet essential component.

Gramling, Oliver. *AP: The Story of News*. New York: Farrar and Rinehart, 1940. The story of the first enterprise, after the stock market, to make significant use of the teletype.

Mott, Frank L. *The News in America*. Cambridge, Mass: Harvard University Press, 1962. Examines the technological, ethical, and professional factors of the mass communications system made practical by electronics and the teletype.

# GENETIC RESEARCH

*Type of event:* Scientific: development of classical genetic concepts
*Time:* 1900-1940
*Locale:* Worldwide, but mainly the United States

*Principal personages:*

THOMAS HUNT MORGAN (1866-1945), first geneticist to receive Nobel Prize (1933), mentor of the "Morgan school" at Columbia University

CALVIN BLACKMAN BRIDGES (1889-1938) and

ALFRED H. STURTEVANT (1891-1971), geneticists and students of Morgan

HERMANN JOSEPH MULLER (1890-1967), a geneticist and student of Morgan who received the Nobel Prize in 1946

SERGEI S. CHETVERIKOV (1880-1959), Russian naturalist and a founder of population genetics

SEWALL WRIGHT (1889-      ), mathematical geneticist

RONALD A. FISHER (1890-1962), British statistician and biometrical geneticist

J. B. S. HALDANE (1892-1964), British theoretician

## Summary of Event

The observations of an Austrian monk, published in an obscure journal in 1866, mark the origin of modern genetics. Gregor Mendel's principles of segregation and independent assortment made little impression upon his contemporaries and lay unnoticed until the turn of the century, when they were verified in a variety of plant and animal species. In this thirty-four-year period many developments in biology, most importantly A. Weismann's theory (1887) of chromosome behavior during reduction division (meiosis) and fertilization, had paved the way for the rediscovery of Mendel's work as well as for the significant discoveries of the 1920's and 1930's.

In 1902, Walter S. Sutton, C. Correns, and Theodor Boveri independently recognized the close parallel between chromosome behavior on the one hand and Mendelian segregation and independent assortment on the other. By 1905, the mechanism of sex determination had been discovered by Edmund B. Wilson. Sex-linked inheritance in the fruit fly, *Drosophila melanogaster*, notably white-eye, was described and interpreted in 1910 by Thomas H. Morgan, the first investigator to associate a specific gene with a specific chromosome. Calvin B. Bridges, working with Morgan, reported nondisjunction of sex chromosomes as proof of the chromosome theory of heredity in 1916. Alfred H. Sturtevant, a student of Morgan at Columbia University, contributed the conception of a linear arrangement of genes and constructed the first chromosome map in 1913. In 1919, Morgan summarized

7

the rapid developments of this period in *The Physical Basis of Heredity* and codified his Nobel Prize-winning theory of linkage. Information developed by the "Morgan school," which dominated the field from 1910 to well into the 1920's, led to the conclusion that during meiosis homologous chromosomes exchange genetic material (cross over). Evidence from crossing over suggested that genes are arranged (linked) in a linear order and that the strength of this linkage between genes is inversely proportional to the frequency of recombination between them.

Development and refinement of chromosome maps in *Drosophila* occupied the Morgan school, particularly under the leadership of Bridges, during the 1920's and 1930's. Study of chromosome aberrations, such as duplications, deficiencies, inversions, and translocations, provided valuable insights into the normal behavior and function of chromosomes. L. V. Morgan, the wife of Thomas Morgan, discovered in 1922 an unusual specimen in her *Drosophila* culture; this fly carried a Y-chromosome and two X-chromosomes attached by their centromere ends. Genetic and cytological analysis of attached-X stocks verified the mechanism of sex-linked inheritance and demonstrated that each of the meiotically paired chromosomes is bipartite at the time of crossing over and that each crossover event involves only two of the four strands.

Hermann J. Muller, also a student of Morgan, concentrated his attention during this period on the nature of the gene, specifically its mutability, or ability to change at a low rate

(from as many as five hundred to fewer than one mutant per million gametes). He noted that genes even within the same organism show differential mutability, that genes can mutate at any stage of the life cycle, and that an entire spectrum of mutation exists, ranging from lethal to minutely visible. His most important contribution (Nobel Prize, 1946) was the demonstration in *Drosophila* (1927) that X-rays increase the mutation frequency several thousand percent, a phenomenon independently verified by L. J. Stadler in barley in the same year. Through the 1930's radiation was a dominant tool in work on the gene concept.

Another productive avenue of research was the cytological study of chromosomes which began to flourish in the 1930's. H. B. Creighton and B. McClintock in 1931 demonstrated the simultaneous occurrence of genetic crossing over and physical exchange of material between homologous chromosomes in maize. C. Stern achieved comparable results in *Drosophila* in the same year.

As early as 1881 giant structures had been described in the nuclei of salivary glands of larval dipterans (flies). In 1933, E. Heitz and H. Bauer recognized the chromosomal nature of these structures and in 1934, T. S. Painter pointed out their great value in genetic analysis in *Drosophila*. One of the early uses of giant chromosomes was in the clarification of the nature of the Bar mutant in *Drosophila*. Bar eye (reduced number of facets) had long been known as a dominant mutant located at 57.0 on the X-chromosome. It was found that about one in sixteen hundred offspring in a Bar culture carry the B+ (wild type) allele, and a similar proportion have a more extreme reduction in facets (double-Bar). Double-Bar stocks may also revert to Bar or to wild type. Sturtevant (1935) showed that these reversions accompanied recombinations between marker genes on opposite sides of the Bar locus. He interpreted this phenomenon to be the result of "unequal crossing over": occasionally one chromosome breaks just to the left of Bar and its homolog just to the right of Bar, yielding two crossovers, one with no Bar (reversion to wild type) and the other with double-Bar. This interpretation was subsequently confirmed cytologically (1936) in salivary gland chromosomes by Bridges; specifically, the Bar mutant results from a duplication of the 16A region of the X-chromosome.

The foregoing events in development of the classical gene concept during the first quarter of the twentieth century resulted in a reevaluation and amplification of the theory of evolution by natural selection presented by Charles Darwin in 1859. Hereditary variation was one of the assumptions of Darwin's theory; but like most of his contemporaries, he assumed a blending mode of inheritance, a process which would have resulted in the rapid loss of variation in a population, leaving little, if any, material upon which natural selection could operate. The establishment of Mendelian laws showing that inheritance is particulate ultimately made possible the resolution of this conflict.

In 1908, G. H. Hardy, a British mathematician, and W. Weinberg, a German physician, independently recognized that because Mendelian inheritance is binary (in a given individual each gene locus has two alleles which segregate and recombine in the offspring), a binomial expression will characterize the distribution of alleles in a population. The algebraic expansion of this binomial expression became known as the Hardy-Weinberg Equilibrium ($p^2 + 2pq + q^2 = 1$). It represents genotype frequencies in a hypothetical population in the absence of mutation and selection.

The Russian naturalist Sergei S. Chetverikov in an essay in 1927 recognized that mutation supplied an abundance of genetic variation within natural populations and that Mendelian inheritance made possible the maintenance of this variability. Unfortunately, Chetverikov's work was not translated into English until 1961, and because of the suppression of genetics in the Soviet Union during the tragedy of Lysenkoism (1925-1960), his important contributions to the birth of population genetics were not available in the West until recently.

In the late 1920's and early 1930's, geneticists Sewall Wright, Ronald A. Fisher, and J. B. S. Haldane demonstrated mathematically how, considering the great age of the earth, relatively low mutation rates in the presence of very slight selective advantage could account for the gradual accumulation of adaptive characteristics. In the 1940's biologist Julian Huxley, geneticist T. Dobzhansky, paleontologist G. G. Simpson, and ornithologist E. Mayr all wrote major works showing the compatibility of

Darwinism and Mendelism.

During the first forty years of the twentieth century, the attention of most geneticists was upon the dynamics of gene transmission in individuals and populations. Several experiments, however, foreshadowed the breakthroughs of the 1940's, 1950's, and 1960's on the mechanism of gene action. In 1902 British physician A. E. Garrod described an inherited disease, alkaptonuria, as an "inborn error of metabolism" caused by the action of a single recessive gene. W. Bateson, E. R. Saunders, and R. C. Punnett in 1905 suggested that flower color in sage, *Salvia horminum*, is regulated by two genes acting sequentially. As a result of transplantation experiments, G. W. Beadle and B. Ephrussi postulated in 1935 that eye color pigments in *Drosophila* result from a gene-controlled sequence of biochemical reactions. These works led to the Nobel Prize-winning experiments of Beadle and E. L. Tatum on the pink bread mold *Neuorospora crassa* (1941), culminating in the "one gene, one enzyme" theory of genetic control, which, with subsequent refinements, is the cornerstone of modern physiological genetics.

## Pertinent Literature

Carlson, Elof Axel. *The Gene: A Critical History*. Philadelphia: W. B. Saunders, 1966.

This volume traces the development of the gene concept from the rediscovery of Mendel's laws to its refinement in the early 1960's. Carlson adopts a thematic rather than a narrative approach, exploring experimental methods and philosophical viewpoints of the proponents of conflicting hypotheses.

Mendel's law of segregation states that one member of each allelic gene pair is distributed to each gamete. This phenomenon corresponds to the behavior of homologous chromosomes during meiosis, directly observed in the microscope as early as 1888 by T. Boveri. The second law, however, the principle of independent assortment, implies that an organism could have only as many gene pairs as chromosomes. This implication was, within the first decade of the twentieth century, contradicted by numerous observations. Consequently, revision and reinterpretation of Mendel's second law was necessary. W. Bateson and R. C. Punnett in 1906 published experiments on sweet peas in which they found that certain gene combinations tended to remain associated during the formation of gametes, giving $F_2$ (second filial generation) ratios significantly different from the classical 9:3:3:1. To explain this deviation Bateson proposed the "reduplication hypothesis" (subsequently discredited by lack of numerical verification in other experimental organisms), which postulated that segregation occurs, not during meiosis but somewhat earlier, and not necessarily at the same time for each gene pair. The cells that are finally produced, Bateson believed, each with a single set of genes, multiply at different rates to give the observed ratios.

In 1910, Morgan proposed an alternative interpretation of the phenomena observed by Bateson and others; namely, that genes are organized in a specific linear sequence within the chromosome. Genes which lie within the same chromosome would be expected to remain associated (linked) with one another during gamete formation, while genes on non-homologous chromosomes would assort independently as postulated by Mendel. Morgan provided the first test of this interpretation with experiments in 1911 on *Drosophila* in which he showed that several sex-linked mutants are associated with the behavior of sex chromosomes. Subsequent data thoroughly confirmed this work and Morgan expanded and refined his "linkage hypothesis" to include the idea that the strength of linkage depends upon the distance between linked genes in the chromosome. Morgan of course ultimately enjoyed the credit (including the Nobel Prize in 1933) for development of modern gene theory.

Another lively debate on the nature of the gene involved the Morgan school. W. E. Castle, studying inheritance of coat color in rats at Harvard, proposed the "contamination hypothesis," which suggested that genes ("unit characters") are unstable. This hypothesis resulted from his experiments on hooded rats (white, with a colored area on the head and back). Castle selected, for mating, rats with increased pigmentation ("plus" line) and rats with decreased pigmentation ("minus" line). Selection was effec-

tive, yielding, after a number of generations, extremes in pigmentation (or lack thereof) greater than the variability within the original stock. When extreme plus or extreme minus were crossed back to wild type ("self-colored") rats, they produced all wild type in the $F_1$ and 3:1 wild type to hooded in the $F_2$. Castle argued that this was attributable to a change or "contamination" of the hooded gene. This view was challenged vigorously by Sturtevant and Muller, both of the Morgan school. Castle himself performed additional experiments. When the two selected lines (plus and minus) were crossed separately to wild type and the hooded $F_2$ rats were back-crossed twice more to wild type, the two lines were nearly identical and Castle reluctantly concluded that the effects of selection were due primarily to modifying genes at loci other than hooded. He conceded that single genes are stable rather than subject to fluctuation.

Clearly "the fly lab" at Columbia University was a remarkably fertile environment. Sturtevant viewed the Morgan school as the ideal of scientific cooperation, with little concern among the group as to the origin of new interpretations. Muller was less sanguine, perhaps harboring some jealousy because Morgan was credited with ideas contributed by his students. Muller's influence on the Morgan school is heavily emphasized by Carlson, probably because Carlson was one of Muller's brightest students at Indiana University. Muller's application of radiation to genetic analysis in 1927 resulted in the development of a vast body of knowledge within the next thirty years.

In the last half of the book Carlson traces the development of biochemical and molecular genetics. It is important to recognize that this modern work rests upon forty years of painstaking and often brilliant research, largely on *Drosophila*, by a number of investigators.

Carlson's book contains an extensive bibliography and is especially recommended to readers with some background in genetics.

Sturtevant, A. H. *A History of Genetics*. New York: Harper & Row Publishers, 1965.

This book is a brief (170 pages) history of genetics from the pre-Mendelian period through post-*Drosophila* developments. Much of the material is derived from lectures the author delivered at the California Institute of Technology and the Universities of Washington, Texas, and Wisconsin.

Sturtevant was an influential member of the Morgan school at Columbia, contributing significantly for more than fifty years with his own studies and with suggestions for research by other workers. His style is highly readable and intensely personal. The book consists of twenty-one chapters, a chronology through 1946, an "intellectual pedigree" of selected biologists, and a bibliography.

Sturtevant emphasizes the discovery of the classic genetic principles: mutation, linkage and crossing over, linear arrangement of genes, gene interaction, multiple alleles, sex linkage, and chromosome aberrations. It is interesting to note that although the first evidence of several of these phenomena was from observations on other organisms, the critical evidence for most of them came from the fly lab at Columbia. Clearly, the contributions of Morgan (linkage), Sturtevant (chromosome maps), Bridges (chromosomes carrying genes), and Muller (radiation-induced mutation), were central to the development of modern genetics.

In the last six chapters Sturtevant discusses immunology, biochemical genetics, population genetics, protozoan genetics, maternal effects, and human genetics, selecting rather arbitrarily those discoveries that he considers to be most important.

The author comments in conclusion that, contrary to a "widespread view that scientific discoveries are more or less inevitable," the contributions of effective researchers result in making the time ripe for their ideas. He believes, for example, that had Mendel's paper (1866) been published in a widely read journal, it would have been appreciated well before 1900. — *J.R.S.*

## Additional Recommended Reading

Sturtevant, A. H. and G. W. Beadle. *An Introduction to Genetics*. New York: Dover Publications, 1962. A corrected but not updated republication of the 1939 Saunders edition, intended as a text for students who have had an introductory course in biology; it outlines the important genetic concepts developed through 1939.

Gabriel, Mordecai L. and Seymour Fogel, eds. *Great Experiments in Biology*. Englewood Cliffs, N.J.: Prentice-Hall, 1955. An anthology including important genetics papers from Mendel (1866) through Beadle and Tatum (1941), a chronology of events, and introductory remarks.

Crew, F. A. E. *The Foundations of Genetics*. London: Pergamon Press, 1966. The historical development of genetics and its ramifications, emphasizing classical genetic theory.

Lerner, I. Michael and William J. Libby. *Heredity, Evolution, and Society*. Berkeley, Calif.: W. H. Freeman, 1976. Chapter 3 on Darwinism and Chapter 13 on population genetics provide background for the synthesis of evolution and genetics.

# THE FORMATION OF THE COMMONWEALTH OF AUSTRALIA AND THE DOMINION OF NEW ZEALAND

*Type of event:* Political: constitutional development leading to self-governing status
for British colonies
*Time:* 1901, 1907
*Locale:* Australia, New Zealand, and Great Britain

*Principal personages:*

SIR HENRY PARKES (1815-1896), politician in the colony of
New South Wales who served a number of times as Premier
until 1891, and the first prominent politician to advocate
Australian Federation

ALFRED DEAKIN (1856-1919), politician in the colony of
Victoria and one of the most effective propagandists for
the Federal cause

SIR EDMUND BARTON (1849-1920), spokesman for Federal
movement in New South Wales, Chairman of constitution-
drafting committee at the Convention of 1897-1898, and
first Prime Minister of the Australian Federation

SIR GEORGE HOUSTON REID (1845-1918), Premier of New
South Wales, 1894-1899; a key figure in constitutional debates of 1897-1898 and in the referendum campaign of 1898-
1899

WILLIAM PEMBER REEVES (1857-1932), New Zealand politician and early literary spokesman of New Zealand nationality

RICHARD JOHN SEDDON (1845-1906), Premier of New Zealand, 1893-1906

SIR JOSEPH GEORGE WARD (1856-1930), Premier of New
Zealand, 1906-1912; secured "Dominion" status for New
Zealand

JOSEPH CHAMBERLAIN (1836-1914), British Secretary of State
for the Colonies, 1895-1903

VICTOR ALEXANDER BRUCE (NINTH EARL OF ELGIN) (1849-
1917), British Secretary of State for the Colonies, 1905-
1908

VICTORIA (1819-1901), Queen of England, 1837-1901

## Summary of Event

The formation of the self-governing federal Commonwealth of Australia in 1901, and the granting of
Dominion status to New Zealand in
1907, were both milestones in the
gradual transformation of the old
British Empire into a free association
of self-governing states: the British
Commonwealth of Nations. The roots
of this development lay deep in the

14

experiences of previous generations in wrestling with the problem of reconciling colonial autonomy with Imperial unity.

In the eighteenth century, the attempt by the British government to reassert its authority over the thirteen North American colonies had led to the armed rebellion of the colonists, and Britain's humiliation in being forced to grant them their independence. During the nineteenth century, successive British governments, mindful of this lesson, pursued a policy of granting autonomy to those colonies whose populations were of white settler stock. One such colony after another was given "responsible government," in which the governing Ministry, although appointed by the British governor, was responsible to the majority of the popularly elected house of the local legislature. The Canadian colonies, which united to form the Dominion of Canada in 1867, were the first beneficiaries of this new policy. The formation of the Commonwealth of Australia in 1901, and of the Dominion of New Zealand in 1907, can be seen as a result not only of the political maturity of the local communities, but also of the liberality and far-sightedness of Britain's policy towards her settler colonies across the seas.

When, in 1788, Great Britain took control of what is now Australia, it was inhabited only by wandering bands of aborigines. The first settlers were English and Irish convicts who had been punished by being transported from their homes. The discovery of gold in 1851, brought a burst of prosperity, enticing large numbers of Britons to migrate to the island continent of their own free will. By 1889, there were six colonies in what is now Australia: Victoria, New South Wales, Queensland, South Australia, Tasmania, and Western Australia. The first five of these colonies received responsible government as early as the 1850's; the latter, sparsely inhabited, did not receive responsible government until 1890.

At first, these colonies, secure under the protective mantle of the British Navy, saw no reason to federate. By the mid-1880's the apparent foreign threat presented by the German occupation of northeastern New Guinea prompted some colonial politicians to call for closer ties among the Australian colonies. Yet, federation, while seen by some as desirable, was nowhere regarded as urgent. It would take long years of hard political struggle to transform the federal idea into a reality.

It was in the latter half of 1889 that the idea of federation received its first powerful push forward. Sir Henry Parkes, the venerable Premier of the colony of New South Wales, wrote to his fellow colonial Premiers urging them to take action aimed at the creation of an Australian federal constitution. As a result of Parkes's efforts, a Conference of Premiers met in February, 1890, in Melbourne. Here, the Premiers reached agreement on the general desirability of federation. In March, 1891, the first Australasian Convention, its members having been chosen by the colonial legislatures, met at Sydney, under the presidency of Parkes. Here they adopted, in April, a draft constitution for a federal system of government and submitted the document to the colonial legislatures for their approval.

Suddenly, however, the federation movement momentarily faltered. In October, 1891, Parkes, the leader of the movement, resigned the Premiership of New South Wales after having lost the confidence of the legislature, which at this point was unenthusiastic about union. Thereafter, the various colonial legislatures refused to take any action on the draft proposal. It would be six years before a new constitutional convention would meet.

The reasons for the failure of the first constitutional draft were many. Representatives of the growing trade union movement criticized the draft for giving too much power to the Upper House, while defenders of local autonomy feared that it would take too many powers away from the individual colonies. The constitution-makers had ignored the knotty question of colonial tariffs and trade regulations, which would have to be resolved if Australia were to be truly unified.

Even after 1891, however, there were those who still strove to keep the idea of federation alive. Two of the most eloquent spokesmen for the cause of Australian unity were Alfred Deakin, a prominent politician of the colony of Victoria, and Edmund Barton, a leading figure in the politics of New South Wales. In the colony of Victoria, the Australian Natives' Association spread profederation propaganda; and in every one of the colonies, "Federal Leagues" began to spring up.

In 1894, the movement for Australian federation began to gather momentum once again. In August of that year, the new Premier of New South Wales, George Houston Reid, announced his support for a new constitutional convention, and took steps to arrange for an intercolonial conference of Premiers to discuss the matter. This conference, which met in Hobart, Tasmania, in January, 1895, decided that the delegates to the constitutional convention would be elected by the people in each of the six colonies. The constitution drafted by the convention would be submitted to a popular referendum in each colony. Once a sufficient number of colonies had approved the draft, it would be submitted to the British government for final approval.

Most of the colonial legislatures proved willing to cooperate, and elections for delegates to the convention were held in every colony except Queensland. The first session of the federal constitutional convention was held on March 22, 1897, in the city of Adelaide; the final session was held on March 17, 1898, in Melbourne. Edmund Barton, who had done so much to spread the gospel of federation in New South Wales, served as chairman of the constitution-drafting committee of the convention.

The dominant issue at the constitutional convention was the rivalry among the various colonies. The smaller, less populous colonies insisted on the creation of a Senate with equal representation for all states, so that their interests would be safeguarded against encroachment by the larger states. The small colonies also insisted on restricting the powers of the future federal government as much as possible. The two large, populous colonies, Victoria and New South Wales, were arrayed against the smaller colonies on these and other issues. The oldest, richest, and most populous colony, New South Wales, was especially afraid that, under a federal government, it would be exploited by the smaller and poorer colonies. It was, therefore, only with great difficulty that a draft constitution was finally hammered together and submitted to the voters of each colony for their approval.

Many people in New South Wales, however, were unhappy with the draft constitution. In the series of referenda held in June, 1898, most of the colonies approved the constitution by decisive majorities. In New South Wales, however, the draft constitution, while supported by a narrow majority, failed to win the statutory minimum number of votes necessary for approval.

Premier Reid now sought to get the draft constitution amended in such a way as to make it more palatable to the people of his colony. Reid's efforts resulted in the convening in Melbourne, from January 29 to February 3, 1899, of a conference of colonial Premiers. The Premiers signed a document, released to the press, which unanimously recommended certain changes in the draft constitution. One change made a simple majority of both Houses necessary for breaking deadlocks between Senate and Lower House, instead of the three-fifths majority required by the 1898 draft; while another amendment ensured that the future capital of the Australian Federation would be located in the territory of New South Wales.

In June, July, and September, 1899, all of the colonies except Western Australia held new referenda, in which the amended constitutional draft was approved by decisive majorities. Following the approval of the constitution by the voters, each of the five colonial legislatures voted for an Address to the Queen, asking for the enactment of the Constitution into law. On March 11, 1900, a delegation of Australian politicians, chosen by the colonial legislatures, had arrived in London for talks with the British Colonial Secretary, Joseph Chamberlain.

The delegates represented an Australia where, despite the growth of local nationalism, a sense of loyalty to the British Empire was still strong. There was, it is true, a current of Anglophobe nationalism in Australia, whose chief organ was the *Sydney Bulletin*, but the extreme sentiments of this newspaper by no means represented the opinions of the majority of Australians. In 1900, thousands of ordinary Australians of military age were volunteering to serve on Britain's side in the war against the Boers in South Africa. Such men as Alfred Deakin, the prominent Victoria advocate of federalism and a delegate to the London conference, shared Colonial Secretary Chamberlain's belief that some form of Imperial supremacy was both necessary and compatible with Australian autonomy. British officials, on their part, had looked with favor on the movement for Australian federation.

In the course of the negotiations, Chamberlain objected to the provision of the new Australian constitution forbidding Australian appeals to the British Privy Council. At first, it seemed as if neither the Australian side nor the British side would give way, but on May 17, a compromise was reached. Appeals to the British Privy Council would be permitted, but not in those legal disputes which involved Federal-state relationships within Australia.

This problem having been disposed of, Chamberlain proceeded to introduce the necessary legislation into the British Parliament, and, on July 9, 1900, shortly after the departure of the Australian delegation, Britain's Queen Victoria signed into law "an Act to constitute the Commonwealth of Australia." Three weeks later, Western Australia decided to join the federation. Accordingly, on January 1, 1901, with the swearing-in of the first Governor-General and the appointment of Edmund Barton as the first Prime Minister, the Commonwealth of Australia was officially born.

The Federation, like the colonies before it, enjoyed "responsible government" in which the Prime Minister was accountable to the majority in the Lower House of the legislature. After 1901, the government of the Federation would, contrary to the expectations of most Australian politicians prior to that date, steadily gain power at the expense of the states.

The path by which New Zealand gained full autonomy was much smoother and simpler than that of Australia. As early as the 1830's the two islands of New Zealand, whose aboriginal inhabitants were Maoris (a people akin to the Polynesians), had received a steady trickle of British settlers who were mostly traders, adventurers, and shipwrecked sailors. In 1840, Great Britain formally annexed the two islands. In 1843 and again in 1860, however, the native Maoris launched wars against white colonization, and it was not until 1870 that the British Army finally crushed their resistance.

Throughout the 1840's and 1850's, immigrants from overpopulated Britain flocked to New Zealand, with its fertile lands and mild climate, but the population would always remain small in comparison to that of Australia. From 1856 onward, the government of the colony, although appointed by the British governor, was responsible to a majority of the popularly-elected House of the legislature. In 1876, the provincial governments lost their authority, and New Zealand acquired a unitary system of administration. New Zealand now enjoyed full internal self-government.

At first, most of the white New Zealanders considered themselves to be Britons, pure and simple; but a spirit of local nationalism gradually developed. Sir William Pember Reeves, the New Zealand scholar and politician, first gave literary expression to this sense of separateness in his book *The Long White Cloud*, published in 1898. This new New Zealand sense of national identity did not involve any antagonism towards Britain, but it did involve an assertion of local rights and interests.

The growing New Zealand sense of national identity was expressed in the political arena as well as in the sphere of literature. In 1870, the New Zealand government sent an Agent-General to London to represent New

Zealand's commercial interests there. As early as 1887, the government of New Zealand, at a conference of self-governing colonies held in London, claimed for New Zealand the right to negotiate her own commercial treaties with foreign states. In 1901, Premier Richard ("King Dick") Seddon proclaimed New Zealand's annexation of the Cook Islands. By sending a New Zealand contingent to fight on Britain's side in the Boer War of 1899-1902, Seddon hoped to win a greater voice for New Zealand in the affairs of the Empire as a whole. In 1905, New Zealand received a further enhancement of her political status when the title of her Agent-General in London was changed to that of High Commissioner, and he was empowered to represent the political as well as the economic interests of New Zealand.

After Seddon's death in 1906, the New Zealand drive for autonomy was continued under his successor, Sir Joseph Ward. At the Imperial Conference of 1907, a gathering of Premiers of the self-governing British colonies which met in London from April 15 to May 14 of that year, Premier Ward pressed the British government to change the official status of New Zealand from that of a "colony" to that of a "Dominion."

Victor Alexander Bruce, Lord Elgin, who was British Colonial Secretary at this time, had no objections to granting Ward's request. The British had no reasons to fear that New Zealand would ever grow hostile or indifferent to Britain's vital interests; for, by sending troops to fight on Britain's side in the Boer War, the New Zealanders had already demon-strated their continuing fidelity to the Imperial connection. When Ward returned home, the New Zealand Parliament gave its formal approval to the change in name, and, from that time onward, New Zealand has been officially known as "the Dominion of New Zealand." Dominion status had been obtained without any bitter argument or conflict whatsoever, since the granting of it merely gave legal recognition to the broad autonomy which New Zealand had already enjoyed for a long time.

The two milestone dates of 1900 and 1907 did not mark the sudden end of all ties of loyalty between Australia and New Zealand on the one hand and Great Britain on the other. Both countries fought on the side of Great Britain during both World War I and World War II.

Yet there has been, ever since 1914, a slow but steady erosion of those chains of dependency and loyalty which once bound these countries so closely to Mother Britain. After World War II, in which American troops protected both Pacific countries against the threat of a Japanese invasion, Australia and New Zealand ceased to rely any longer on Great Britain for military protection. Ever since 1945, the United States has been the principal military shield of both Australia and New Zealand. The entry of Great Britain into the European Common Market in 1973, and the tariff barriers which she was thus compelled to erect against Antipodean farm products, cut the long-standing economic ties between Australia and New Zealand and their Mother Country. Today, the only links between Great Britain and these two Pacific nations are the ties of a common culture and a common language; the "British Empire" is but a fading memory.

## Pertinent Literature

La Nauze, John Andrew. *The Making of the Australian Constitution*. Carlton, Australia: Melbourne University Press, 1972.

La Nauze, who has been a Professor of History at the University of Melbourne since 1955, has written, in *The Making of the Australian Constitution*, the first major study of the origins of Australian Federation. By his own admission, this is not a complete history of the movement for federation in late nineteenth century Australia, but it is certainly a first step towards the writing of such a history.

In Chapters One through Six, La Nauze makes clear just how many false starts occurred before the federal constitution-making process really got moving. In the first chapter, he shows that the idea of Australian federation, although first put forward by a British official in 1847, did not become a spur to action until the 1880's. In Chapters Two through Six, he traces the history of the Federation movement from the first proposals of Henry Parkes in 1889, to the first session of the constitutional convention in 1897.

Throughout the book, La Nauze reminds the reader that Australian federation, however inevitable it might seem to have been in hindsight, did not seem at all inevitable to the Australian politicians of the 1890's. Until the last moment, there were often times when it appeared as if the dream of so many decades would once more be stymied. As late as November, 1897, La Nauze points out, at least one delegate to the constitutional convention believed that federation in the near future was "not much more than a possibility."

In Chapters Seven through Sixteen, La Nauze gives a detailed account of how the Constitution was hammered out in debate after debate at the Convention of 1897-1898, was amended by the Conference of Premiers in 1899, and was finally approved by the voters in a referendum held in each colony. The burning issue at the Convention and in the referenda, the author makes clear, was not that of capital *versus* labor, or of liberalism *versus* conservatism; it was that of states' rights. The framers of the constitution, La Nauze reminds the reader, saw that document as "a treaty between States."

When he discusses the issue of states' rights at the constitutional convention, La Nauze's prose is sometimes tinged with irony, for, once the Commonwealth had been established, this particular issue would rapidly fade in significance. Today, Australians vote along party lines, not along lines of regional loyalty. Even voting in the Australian Senate, established to protect small states against oppression by large states, has tended to reflect party differences rather than regional ones. Although the constitution-makers intended to limit strictly the powers of the future federal government, these powers now dwarf those of the Australian states. To the "mocking imp of hindsight," La Nauze concedes, all these developments might seem inevitable, yet only one of the constitutional fathers, Alfred Deakin, was able to predict the ultimate fading of the states' rights issue. La Nauze concludes that all the intricate concessions to the anxieties of the individual colonies, while of little significance for the future of Australia, were absolutely necessary to get the Federal Constitution approved by the voters.

La Nauze's discussion of the Anglo-Australian negotiations of 1900 over the constitution are particularly enlightening for an American reader. The existence of initial differences between the two sides led not to confrontation, but to compromise. Difficulties could be resolved, the author points out, because the British Co-

lonial Office officials and the Australian delegates agreed both on the need for some sphere of Imperial supremacy and on the desirability of a self-governing Australian Federation.

The principal sources of La Nauze's work are the unpublished papers and correspondence of the leading figures of the 1897-1898 convention and the published records of both that convention and of earlier Federal conferences and conventions. La Nauze's delightful word portraits of the leading politicians of the 1890's are supplemented by twenty-one photographic illustrations. The book also contains an appendix which reproduces key published documents of the period. There are, however, no maps; and the footnotes are placed at the back of the book, making it inconvenient for the reader to consult them.

Sinclair, Keith. *Imperial Federation: A Study of New Zealand Policy and Opinion, 1880-1914.* London: University of London, Athlone Press, 1955.

The constitutional history of New Zealand up to 1907 is the story of the aggressive and successful pursuit of full autonomy by a colony whose people professed themselves to be ardently loyal to the Mother Country. Such a story is particularly difficult for Americans, with their heritage of 1776, to understand. This extremely short but scholarly monograph, whose organization is topical rather than chronological, is the only existing study of the process by which New Zealand came to achieve Dominion status.

Sinclair describes in detail how,

during the Imperial Conferences of 1887, 1897, 1902, 1907, and 1911, the government of New Zealand repeatedly urged that the organization of the British Empire be reformed. The New Zealanders wished to see greater cooperation between the self-governing colonies and Great Britain, a stronger British naval commitment to defend such colonies, and a greater voice for such colonies in Empire-wide decisionmaking. It was at one such Imperial Conference, that of 1907, that New Zealand Premier Joseph Ward asked for and received the formal change in New Zealand's status from that of "colony" to that of "Dominion."

Looking at this record, historians have often argued that, during the three decades prior to World War I, successive governments of New Zealand consciously and consistently pursued the goal of "Imperial Federation": the creation of an Imperial Cabinet and an Imperial Parliament, in which all of the self-governing colonies would be represented. Such historians further argue that this goal enjoyed the enthusiastic support of the overwhelming majority of New Zealanders.

Sinclair, however, disputes this thesis. Most New Zealanders, he asserts, were concerned about the bread-and-butter issues above all else. They were neither enthusiastic for, nor hostile to, the goal of Imperial Federation; instead, they were indifferent to it. Even those few New Zealand politicians and journalists who did express verbal support for the concept of "Imperial Federation" were often unable to define exactly what the concept would mean in practice.

The absence of strong opinions in New Zealand about Imperial Federation resulted, the author contends, from the absence of any internal enemy for Imperial Federationists to attack. In colonies such as Canada and Australia, Sinclair points out, the goal of Imperial Federation was supported with special ardor by the pro-British elements because of the challenge to Imperial loyalty presented by the existence of Anglophobe nationalism within their countries. In Canada, the large minority of French Canadians disliked the tie with Britain. Even Australia, which was much more ethnically homogeneous, had a vocal, albeit tiny, minority of Anglophobe nationalists, whose principal sounding board was the *Sydney Bulletin*. In New Zealand, no such hostility to Britain existed among any group in the population; but neither did any strong feeling of New Zealand nationalism. For, the author makes clear, it was only after 1880 that such thinkers as the scholar and politician William Pember Reeves began to grapple with the question of New Zealand's national identity.

Thus, Sinclair resolves the paradox. New Zealand politicians, lacking any inherited tradition of hostility to Britain, found it quite easy to combine Imperial loyalty with New Zealand patriotism. Such politicians did try to limit the powers of British governors, to gain for New Zealand the right to make commercial treaties with foreign states, and to annex as many South Pacific islands as possible. Yet such men, fully aware of their own country's weakness, chose to rely on the British Navy for the defense of New Zealand against foreign aggression. By seeking a greater voice for the self-governing colonies in Imperial decisionmaking, Premiers Richard Seddon and Joseph Ward were not only trying to tighten the bonds linking New Zealand to the Mother Country; they were, Sinclair argues, also trying to increase the importance of New Zealand on the world stage. This was the publicly proclaimed motive of Premier Ward in seeking to have Dominion status conferred upon his country: "to raise the status of New Zealand."

The principal sources of *Imperial Federation* are the records of the New

Zealand Parliamentary debates, English and New Zealand newspapers and periodicals, the papers of the New Zealand scholar and politician, William Pember Reeves, the verbatim reports of the Imperial Conference of 1897 and 1902, and a contemporary account, written by the English publicist Richard Jebb, of the crucial Imperial Conference of 1907. *Imperial Federation* does not have any index, bibliography, maps, or illustrations. The footnotes, however, are placed at the bottom of the page, making it convenient for the reader to consult them. — *P.D.M.*

## Additional Recommended Reading

Ward, John M. *Colonial Self-Government: The British Experience, 1759-1856.* Toronto: University of Toronto Press, 1976. Argues that the British decision to grant responsible government to Canada in the 1840's, and to the Australian colonies in the 1850's, resulted more from British awareness of changing constitutional practice in Britain itself than from pressure for self-government from the colonists.

La Nauze, John Andrew. *Alfred Deakin: A Biography.* 2 vols. Carlton, Australia: Melbourne University Press, 1965. The first volume of La Nauze's biography, which concentrates on the Australian statesman's career up to 1901 and shows how crucially important this man's tireless efforts were in winning the colony of Victoria for the cause of Australian Federation.

Gordon, Donald C. *The Dominion Partnership in Imperial Defense, 1870-1914.* Baltimore, Md.: The Johns Hopkins University Press, 1965. Shows that Alfred Deakin, in his stance on questions of Imperial defense, shunned the Anglophobia of the *Sydney Bulletin*, seeking instead to reconcile Australian national self-assertion with loyalty to the British Empire as a whole.

Norris, R. *The Emergent Commonwealth: Australian Federation, Expectations and Fulfilment, 1889-1910.* Carlton, Australia: Melbourne University Press, 1975. Demonstrates how the course of political events during the decade after 1901 made the Federal government much stronger, and the state governments much weaker, than the Fathers of the Constitution had originally expected.

Gollan, Robin. *Radical and Working Class Politics: A Study of Eastern Australia, 1850-1910.* Carlton, Australia: Melbourne University Press, 1960. Argues that, while neither the Australian labor parties nor the Australian trade union movement played a major role in the movement for Australian federation, both did much to ensure that the federal constitution was more democratic than it might otherwise have been.

Dalziel, Raewyn M. *The Origins of New Zealand Diplomacy: The Agent-General in London, 1870-1905.* Wellington, New Zealand: Price Milburn, 1975. The author shows that the change in title of New Zealand's representative in London from that of Agent-General to that of High Commissioner reflected the change in New Zealand's status from that of colonial subordination to that of full autonomy and equal partnership with Great Britain.

# PUBLICATION OF THE CAMBRIDGE HISTORIES

*Type of event:* Intellectual: continuing and comprehensive series of books that covers the history of the world
*Time:* 1902 to the present
*Locale:* Cambridge, England

*Principal personages:*

LORD JOHN EMERICH EDWARD DALBERG-ACTON (FIRST BARON ACTON) (1834-1902), general editor

SIR ADOLPHUS WILLIAM WARD (1837-1924), Acton's assistant, later an associate editor

GEORGE WALTER PROTHERO (1848-1922), an associate editor

STANLEY LEATHES (1830-1900), an associate editor

SYNDICS OF CAMBRIDGE UNIVERSITY PRESS

## Summary of Event

In 1896, when the Syndics of Cambridge University conceived the idea to publish a universal history of the world, the man to whom they turned was the newly appointed Regius Professor of History at Cambridge University, a historian who had yet to publish a complete book. That professor, John Emerich Edward Dalberg-Acton, although he died before the first volume appeared in print, was the guiding genius for the first Cambridge history, which was ultimately scaled down to cover the five hundred years since the Renaissance period.

At first thought, Lord Acton seems a strange choice for general editor, despite his reputation as "the most learned Englishman" then alive, a man who allegedly had read twenty thousand volumes, according to one of his recent biographers. Acton is also known as the author of the best book never written because his planned study of the history of liberty was left unfinished at his death. Despite his failure to complete this or

any other book, he did contribute a sizable number of shorter articles to various historical journals; his complete bibliography covers thirty-two pages in Robert Schuettinger's 1976 biography. Working against his general editorship of the project was his inability to delegate responsibilities and his lack of organizational talents. His voluntary work as fund-raiser and publicity director for the series, according to G. N. Clark, a recent Regius Professor of Modern History, "weighed him down" and was ultimately responsible for the paralytic stroke which felled him in April of 1901, while the first volume was being set in type. Associate editors Adolphus William Ward, Acton's assistant; G. W. Prothero; and Sir Stanley Leathes saw the project through to its publication.

It is, however, universally accepted that the original series, *The Cambridge Modern History*, would not be the monument it is had it not been for Acton. Acton welcomed the task, recognizing the rare opportunity of promoting his own ideas of the study of history. The success of the project is attested by the continuing publication of various series of Cambridge histories, the latest volume of which, Volume XIII, "Companion Volume" of *The New Cambridge Modern History*, was issued in 1979.

Acton's training in Germany under the eminent German historian Johann von Döllinger well suited him intellectually for the task. He was one of the most staunch believers in the scientific method in the study of history. He emphasized to the contributors his belief in the impartiality of the historian and their obligation to analyze and evaluate all the new archive material being made available for the first time. He feared that the inundation of records and materials then being released to scholars would be a deterrent to the cultivated layman in his study of history, and that specialists were needed to sort out and evaluate the myriad documents hitherto inaccessible. Thus, a team of specialists would be required to produce the kind of work he envisioned. His stated goals for the series were threefold: *The Cambridge Modern History* was to be universal, it was to be a history of ideas, and, above all, it was to be impartial and objective.

In his division of the topics covered in the twelve volumes of text among one hundred and sixty historians of the day, Acton tried to apply his theory of impartiality in not outlining a strict chronological sequence of the individual national histories, but rather in treating important topics and introducing the individual nations as they came into prominence. For example, a country such as Ireland is not treated in the first two volumes which deal with the Renaissance and the Reformation; but in Volume III, "The Wars of Religion," Chapter 18 considers "Ireland to the Settlement of Ulster," bringing that nation up to the present by going back to the beginning of the sixteenth century and filling in the necessary background. Likewise, the second volume devotes five consecutive chapters to the significant aspects of the Reformation in Germany because of that nation's important involvement; and, of course, France comes in for extensive coverage in Volumes VIII and IX, devoted to "The French Revolution" and "Napoleon."

Acton's interest in combining the intellectual spirit of the times with the prevailing political forces is evident in the several chapters detailing the important or influential literature of the period, contributed by renowned literary scholars rather than historians. In addition, some volumes end with summations of the thought of the times, such as "Tendencies of European Thought in the Age of the Reformation" and "Political Thought in the Sixteenth Century." The final volume of text, "The Latest Age," closes with a chapter summation of "The Growth of Historical Science," written by G. P. Gooch. Gooch's research for this chapter led to his book, *History and Historians in the Nineteenth Century*. The entire series was concluded with Volume XIII, "Tables and General Index," and Volume XIV, "Atlas," published respectively in 1911 and 1914.

From its original appearance, the series met the newly awakened interest in history of the British population. Since its publication *The Cambridge Modern History* has become the most influential history dealing with that period, and has been considered a standard reference by many. The inclusion of extensive bibliographies was an important aspect of its usefulness. The work remains an important monument to its age despite the shortcomings inherent in its division into individual chapters written independently of one another. The work has been criticized for inadequate editorial control which resulted in repetition and overlapping areas of coverage. The attempt at impartiality often results in a lack of judgment. Perhaps the most severe criticism is aimed at the unevenness of the contributors' efforts. Some of England's best historians are included, although several prominent ones were unable or unwilling to complete their task, but the Continent and the United States are poorly represented. The work as a whole lacks a basic thematic unity; some of the writers contradict one another, and many are guilty of dullness. Nonetheless, the book remains one of the best of its kind, and its model has been adhered to in subsequent series.

Encouraged by the success of the original landmark series, the Syndics of Cambridge University have commissioned further studies on the same principle of associate general editors commissioning eminent historians to contribute chapters on their specialty. The next selection was obvious, one that would bring history up to the period of the Renaissance. *The Cambridge Medieval History* was issued in the years 1911 to 1936; this was augmented by *The Cambridge Ancient History*, published from 1923 to 1939. The publication of *The Cambridge History of Poland* was interrupted by World War II; the second volume was issued first in 1941, and the first volume was held up until 1950. As would be expected in such ambitious collaborative ventures, the general editors and contributors were often deceased before the completion of their project.

In addition to these, specialized histories were sponsored by the Syndics, including such titles as *The Cambridge Economic History of Europe*, *The Cambridge History of British Foreign Policy 1783-1919*, *The Cambridge History of the British Empire*, *The Shorter Cambridge Medieval History* in two volumes, and finally, a complete revision of the original work entitled *The New Cambridge Modern History* which was begun in 1957, the final volume of which was issued in 1979. The general acceptance of these histories is evidenced by an almost constant stream of reprintings and revision. The system devised by Lord Acton assures a comprehensive if not exhaustive coverage of the topic according to the latest historical research, and retains the flexibility of constant updating of the material. The overall final estimate of the influence and importance of these histories is incalculable.

## Pertinent Literature

Clark, G. N. "The Origin of the Cambridge Modern History," in *The Cambridge Historical Journal*. VIII (1945), pp. 57-64.

Forty-three years after the publication of the original volume of *The Cambridge Modern History*, G. N. Clark claimed it was still one of the indispensable books of the century and a "monument of a stage in English historical studies." Against Toynbee's charge that the project represents an example of "the baneful influence of 'industrialism' on historical studies," Clark defends the work on the grounds that virtually all historical writing is dependent on cooperative endeavors. Besides the case of several subordinates working under one guiding author, there are joint authors as well as the requisite "perpetual commerce with other minds" in discussions, proofreading and editorial adjustments and corrections of any writers. At any rate, Clark finds that the thoroughness of the work surmounts any of the weaknesses of the collaborative effort. He points out that up to 1945 "no other modern general history on anything like the same scale has been written or even projected," and that there never has been a single individual with the linguistic facility not to mention the familiarity with the substance of history and the latest advances necessary to complete such a task.

The author recounts the propitious intellectual climate in England at the turn of the century when historical studies were in the ascendancy. Lord Acton, influenced by the German school of scientific historiography, believed the new history to be more impartial and scientific than had ever been the case in the past, and the universities and general history reading public were swept along in this new enthusiasm. It was to meet this new demand that the Syndics of the University Press planned to issue a "Universal History." In their consultation with Acton, they indicated their desire for an original work rather than a "serious compilation," and they scaled down their original plan to treat only of modern history.

Clark goes through the correspondence between Acton and the Syndics, showing the gradual process in which the history took form. By October, the detailed plan was ready, showing the pages and arrangement of Acton's plan, including his intention of enlisting the greatest number of competent writers possible. Acton also detailed his theory of history. He felt that a universal history is "not the sum of all particular histories," but that it should be considered "in its distinctive essence, as Renaissance, Reformation, Religious Wars, Absolute Monarchy, Revolution, etc." The individual nations should be considered as they "feed the main stream." When a nation came into prominence, a retrospect of its past was to be given, and when one dropped out, a "prospective sketch" was to be given. Acton planned to combine the moral, intellectual, and political sphere by including chapters on the various branches of literature when they influence the age. His plan was accepted and he was appointed general editor on October 21, 1896.

Acton himself communicated with the many contributors to the history, often in person. In all, one hundred and sixty writers are represented in the final work, but many of those originally contacted did not contribute. Acton's assistant, Adolphus William Ward, the grandnephew of Thomas Arnold, gradually became more and more influential until he was appointed assistant editor in 1897, and at Acton's resignation because of illness in 1901, Ward was appointed associate editor with G. W. Prothero and Sir Stanley Leathes, who saw the publication through to its completion.

"Acton and the *C. M. H.*: Republication and Reassessment," in *The Times Literary Supplement*. LXX (February 19, 1971), pp. 195-198.

Upon the republication of the original *Cambridge Modern History* in 1970, the anonymous author of the present article reevaluated the work, finding it a landmark "both in the history of historiography and of culture, and a monument to a civilization's view of itself." The immense success of the original series is recounted and attributed to its being more comprehensive and up to date in both scholarship and coverage than had ever been previously attempted. The reviewer finds its main value today to be its "comprehensive utility."

The virtues and flaws of the work are attributed to its organizer and chief architect, Lord Acton, whose view of history as well as choice of topics and contributors reflected a concept of a stable society in which "fundamental disturbance was unlikely." Acton's theory optimistically assumed a steady progress in human affairs. He felt that this progress was "above all, the history of state forms and the history of religious struggles." Consequently, his world view envisions two main themes: freedom of the individual and "the organization of national states." This unified design, according to the reviewer, is conveyed more by what the histories omit rather than what they include, and it does not dominate the work or even "emerge naturally and clearly."

The editors are criticized for setting aside art and culture except as they have a "direct bearing on politics, economics and social life," although the reviewer concedes that the greatest strides in art and cultural history have been made in general since 1911. He feels, for example, that though the volume dealing with the Renaissance in the *New Cambridge Modern History* is shorter, it contains more information on early printing, the conditions of literary production, and special forms of education. He is critical, however, of the newer series for its omission of bibliographies.

One of Acton's goals was complete impartiality. To this end he warned his contributors that the specifics of their nationalities, religion, or political affiliations should not be evident in their writing. He insisted on what he termed a universal history rather than a "compilation of national histories." Nonetheless, the ideal was unattainable and there are vast differences in style and tone. In some areas, the reviewer feels, no one took the editorial responsibility of making a unified, coherent whole of the many chapters. Much of the writing is found to be dull, and some of it even incompetent, and, as is inevitable in such an enterprise, some chapters are overlapping and even contradictory. Finally, the reviewer opines that Acton's insistence upon impartiality "paralyses the judgement."

The reviewer briefly recounts the basic conflict of historical method confronting Acton—the belief in the innate historical importance of certain events as opposed to an egalitarian view which assumes an importance in every event and presupposes the necessity of a historical mindedness to evaluate everything. Acton had pointed out that the study of history was threatened by the flood of archive materials that had become available to scholars. He felt specialists were needed to sort and interpret their historic importance. In his preface to Volume I of *The Cambridge Modern History*, Mandell Creighton expanded on Acton's idea by pointing out that old materials needed reevaluation according to the changing concepts of significance.

An example of this reevaluation of the past is the choice of the beginning date for a study of modern history. Mandell Creighton agreed with Acton at placing this date at 1450, at which time man began to cope with problems similar to our own, and man shared aspirations and ideas in common with our own. The reviewer comments that this point of view tends to emphasize the religious struggles and the development of state forms leading to the present. He states that modern history by its nature emphasizes the differences of the past as contrasted to the present.

In spite of the criticisms voiced, the reviewer stresses the importance and value of the work, pointing out that its success led to the launching of many further series of Cambridge histories based on the same format. He also points out that the animating idea behind the first history was that of being the final word, in contrast to Sir George Clark's comment in *The New Cambridge Modern History* that the modern historian expects to be "superseded again and again."
— *R.A.G.*

## Additional Recommended Reading

Himmelfarb, Gertrude. *Lord Acton: A Study in Conscience and Politics*. Chicago: University of Chicago Press, 1952. Though dated, this "biography of a mind" is still the standard study of Acton, showing the development of his ideas of history and his involvement in the publication of *The Cambridge Modern History*.

Schuettinger, Robert L. *Lord Acton: Historian of Liberty*. La Salle, Ill.: Open Court, 1976. A more recent biography of Acton, largely derivative from Himmelfarb's book and published sources; helpful in its extensive bibliography covering virtually every printed work by and about Acton.

Gooch, George P. *History and Historians in the Nineteenth Century*. London: Longmans, Green and Company, 1913. Assesses and summarizes the achievements of historical research and production of important historians of the nineteenth century; considered by many to be still the best treatment of the subject.

Ward, A. W., G. W. Prothero and Stanley Leathes, eds. *The Cambridge Modern History, Planned by Lord Acton*. Cambridge: Cambridge University Press, 1902-1912. Preface to Volume I and Introductory Note by Mandell Creighton discuss the task of putting the work together; the last chapter of Volume XII by G. P. Gooch details the growth of historical science.

Potter, G. R., *et al.*, eds. *The New Cambridge Modern History*. Cambridge: Cambridge University Press, 1957-1979. General Introduction to Volume I by George Clark recounts the historical plan and principles of the original work of Acton as well as the present edition; Chapter I of Volume XIII by Peter Burke deals with the concepts of continuity and change as they confront the modern historian.

Sills, David L., ed. *International Encyclopedia of the Social Sciences*. New York: The Macmillan Company, 1968. Excellent articles on Lord Acton by Gertrude Himmelfarb; "Historiography: The Rhetoric of History" by J. H. Hexter; and several articles on various aspects and types of history.

# JOHN A. HOBSON PUBLISHES *IMPERIALISM: A STUDY*

*Type of event:* Intellectual: influential work on economics as related to imperialism
*Time:* 1902
*Locale:* London

*Principal personage:*
JOHN ATKINSON HOBSON (1858-1940), a journalist, economist, teacher, and social activist

## Summary of Event

In 1899, the *Manchester Guardian* newspaper hired John Hobson as a correspondent to go to South Africa and report on the war that Great Britain was fighting against the Boers. After he returned, Hobson declared that his experiences in that war were the turning point of his career and an "illumination to my understanding of the real relations between economics and politics." It was the war that inspired the writing of *Imperialism: A Study* three years later.

Hobson was the son of a liberal newspaper editor of Derby, England. As a young journalist himself, John Hobson wrote profusely for different liberal newspapers and periodicals for a dozen years or so before taking the assignment to report on the South African war. His various writings before 1899 reflect a growing disbelief and rejection of the social, religious, and especially the economic principles of classical nineteenth century liberalism. He was, as he says, moving intellectually in the direction of socialism, or, as he preferred to call it, "economic humanism." He had joined several reformist organizations, done voluntary teaching in the provinces for the Oxford University Extension Movement, and formed friendships with such people as Prince Kropotkin, the Russian anarchist, Thorstein Veblen, the American economist and sociologist, and Graham Wallas, one of the leading lights of the socialistic Fabian Society.

Upon returning to England in 1900, Hobson contemplated the origins and meaning of the Boer War. In several articles and a book written before *Imperialism: A Study*, he concluded that the war had resulted from greed and economic exploitation by such men as Cecil Rhodes. The Boer War was just another chapter in the story of imperialist aggrandizement by British capitalists.

At the same time, Hobson formulated his broader theory of capitalistic oversaving and underconsumption. This theory held, in essence, that it is in the nature of private capitalism to increase its capital through excessive savings taken from profits. Those savings are then invested to make additional profits for the capitalists. This results in lowered wages for industrial workers and therefore lessened consumption by the workers. The resulting distortion of oversaving and underconsumption contributes to the cyclical economic depressions, unemployment, and social distress that are endemic in the capitalist market economy.

Bringing these concepts together, and augmenting his conclusions with statistical data, Hobson then offered his polemic against capitalist aggrandizement, *Imperialism: A Study*. At the outset of the book, he informs the reader that he has no intention of presenting a balanced critique which gives both sides of the case equally. Economic imperialism is a condition of "social pathology and no effort is made to disguise the disease." His task is to analyze the origin and nature of what he regards as a social illness.

First he differentiates between colonialism and imperialism. The former is defined as the planting of nationalities on noncontiguous territories, as the British have done in Canada or Australia since the eighteenth century, while imperialism, especially as it emerged in the nineteenth century, is a perversion of colonialism. It is not true colonialism, but the imposition of alien rule by one people over another. Using maps and charts, Hobson then demonstrates the global extent of nineteenth century imperialism and shows that expansion has almost wholly involved the political absorption of tropical or subtropical lands by Europeans, lands heavily occupied by what the British imperialists call the "lower races."

The occupation of those new territories in Africa, Asia, and elsewhere, unlike the earlier colonialism, has been by only a handful of white men—traders, industrial organizers, government officials, and military forces. These few whites have gained control of the greater numbers of the native populations and treat those natives haughtily, often brutally. Unlike the white colonies, the native people in the new territories are regarded as incapable of self-government, and certainly not as being equal to their imperialist masters.

Defenders of British imperialism have argued that placing of the new territories under the British flag could serve as outlets for Britain's surplus population. This has not materialized, Hobson asserts. By means of additional statistics, he shows that emigration from Britain since the 1880's has been mostly to regions of temperate climate. There has been no true British settlement in the tropical territories, nor is there likely to be, since few white men will settle with their families in those places.

Hobson then goes on to consider the economic gains and losses from the new imperialism. Basing his conclusions on both official and unofficial data, he finds that between the 1850's and 1900 the external trade of Great Britain has diminshed in proportion to the internal trade; that external trade with British possessions has diminished in proportion to trade with foreign countries; and that trade with the new tropical possessions has been the smallest, least progressive, and most fluctuating in quantity of any British markets. Both in terms of trade and of settlement, then, the new Empire has proved quite barren of returns for the British people.

But if the new imperialism has brought scant returns for Britain as a whole, it has been good business for certain groups. These groups Hobson calls the "economic parasites" of imperialism: the suppliers of munitions and military equipment, dealers in certain export products,

# John A. Hobson Publishes Imperialism: A Study

engineers, miners, ranchers, plantation owners, and even Christian missionaries. These are the beneficiaries of British imperialism, not the British nation, while behind all are the greatest of the parasites, the financiers and bankers. It is they who are the recipients of the oversaving in the home country, much of which they have invested in the overseas territories. Furthermore, the economic parasites have persuaded British governments to spend tax revenues on military expenditures to open up additional territories for trade and industrial development, and further expenditures for the maintenance of civil governments in those imperialist holdings. The people pay, fight, and die to increase "British red" on the maps of the world, and then have little to show for it.

The new imperialists do not admit their primary motive is economic aggrandizement. They, and their apologists, claim in noble phrases that their intentions are to "extend the area of civilization and elevate the lower races" or "extirpate slavery" or "promote Christianity." Some businessmen who mouth such phrases may indeed have a desire to attain those ends; nevertheless, it is the profit motive which impels them fundamentally. As Hobson says, the true attitude of the imperialists was summed up by Cecil Rhodes when he referred to Her Majesty's Flag as the "greatest commercial asset in the world." A German critic of British imperialism put Hobson's premise even more succinctly: "When the British say they are bringing Christianity, they mean they are bringing cotton."

In the chapter called "The Economic Taproot of Imperialism," Hobson presents the gist of his argument. He first observes that after about 1870, British monopoly of world markets for certain types of goods was much impaired by the rise of other nations, particularly the United States and Germany, to industrial and commercial importance. That circumstance, in the view of British imperial expansionists, made it most urgent that Britain find new markets in undeveloped countries. At the same time larger savings had been built up in Britain, but the domestic returns from investments of those savings was shrinking. Higher profits could presumably be gotten from overseas investments. The expansionists argued that although imperialism may be costly, even dangerous, it was necessary for the continued existence of the nation. Britain must expand or die. Without expansion the supplies of food and raw materials would diminish to levels inadequate to support the population. Imperialism, said its defenders, was not even a matter of choice; it was a necessity for survival.

To which Hobson responds with the Latin phrase "cui bono," for whose good, for whose survival has imperialist expansion taken place. He answers in one word: the investor. Modern British foreign policy, he asserts, has been largely a struggle to find markets for profitable investment. Public policy, the public purse, and public force have been increasingly employed to extend the field of private investment and to protect those investments in the territories that have been annexed.

The new imperialism is, moreover, a constant menace to peace. It tends to embroil nations in imperialist rivalries which have, and will, lead to national wars; it stimulates militarism within each nation, as well. A large amount of the national resources and national energies are expended on military preparation. Furthermore, because imperialists favor political tyranny and social authority, the "spirit, policy and methods" of imperialism have proved contrary to the institutions of popular self-government.

Thus Hobson laid out his indictment and bill of particulars against imperialism. Undoubtedly he hoped that his study would inspire an alteration in British public opinion and policies, so that energies and resources consumed in imperialist ventures might be redirected toward the improvement of social conditions for the British people at home.

What Hobson did accomplish by *Imperialism: A Study* was to redirect thinking about imperialism as a term and a process. Henceforth, when people thought of imperialist expansion, they would stress the economic and financial factors as fundamental motivations.

## Pertinent Literature

Lenin, V. I. *Imperialism, the Highest Stage of Capitalism: A Popular Outline*. New York: International Publishers, 1939.

Although John Hobson was a socialist, he was not a Marxist. He could not subscribe to a number of the fundamental tenets of Marxist economic thought: the labor theory of value and the theory of class conflict, primarily. Marxist historians and philosophers, however, have drawn from Hobson's work much material to fortify their criticisms of capitalism. This pamphlet by Lenin, first published at Zurich, Switzerland, in 1916, is undoubtedly the best-known example of the incorporation of Hobson's ideas into Marxist idealogy.

*Imperialism, the Highest Stage of Capitalism: A Popular Outline* is, like Hobson's book, a polemic, and it follows much the same scheme of analysis as the earlier work. Beginning with an examination of the transformation of capitalist competition into a monopoly economy in Germany, Britain, and the United States, Lenin then goes on to explain the dominance of financiers and bankers in the development of that monopoly capital in those countries. Although Lenin, as a Marxist, emphasizes the labor theory of value as the basic contributory factor in the formation of capital, he does join with Hobson in condemning the oversaving of the financiers and "rentiers," with the concomitant underconsumption of the working class. "It is characteristic of capitalism in general that the ownership of capital is separated from the application of capital to production . . . and that the rentier who lives entirely on income produced from money capital, is separated from the entrepreneur."

Moving on to the topic of how the

earth is being divided up by the capitalist trust and cartels, Lenin shows an almost palpable agitation. He not only heaps scorn on the capitalist monopolists. but also on the "reformist, revisionist" un-Marxist socialists who would justify and explain away the phenomenon of the capitalist world market. The theoretical analyses of imperialism by such nominal socialists as Karl Kautsky are, in Lenin's estimation, "absolutely irreconcilable with Marxism."

Lenin then gives his own "correct" analysis of imperialism. It has, he says, five essential features: the concentration of production and capital to such a high level that monopolies are created; the merging of bank capital with industrial capital to create finance capital; the export of capital for investment as distinguished from the export of commodities; the formation of international monopolies which divide and share the markets of the earth among themselves; and the culmination of the territorial division of the earth among the capitalist powers. In the briefest possible definition, "imperialism is the monopoly stage of capitalism."

And yet, as Marx had once contended, the capitalist monopolists are digging their own graves. Lenin, in calling imperialism the highest stage of capitalism, implies that it marks the apex of capitalist aggrandizement, and can only be followed by decay and ultimate collapse, according to Marxist dialectic. In time, the rentier, financier, monopolist class will disintegrate, the working class will recognize its true interests and reject the "opportunists" and the bourgeois liberals who would accommodate to capitalist imperialism. Imperialist rivalries must lead to colonial wars, and those, in turn, will lead to wars between the imperialist powers themselves, even as was then going on in 1916. That Great War, Lenin confidently expects, will usher in world revolution to bring an end to capitalism and imperialism.

Fieldhouse, D. K. "Imperialism: An Historiographical Revision," in *The Economic History Review*. Second Series, XIV, no. 2 (1961).

Criticisms and revisions of Hobson's study began to appear shortly after the book was published, and those criticisms have continued to the present. One of the ablest of the critics is D. K. Fieldhouse of the Institute of Commonwealth Studies, London, who brings out in this article and in other writings some of the arguments both for and against Hobson's thesis.

Fieldhouse first points out that Hobson wrote his study at a time when the British public was much disillusioned by the South African war, and receptive to a condemnation of that war as an imperialistic venture. Yet, it is a curious fact that *Imperialism: A Study* is not concerned primarily with the Boer War, or even with imperial problems. Hobson's chief concern, Fieldhouse contends, was with the social and economic problems of Britain, and the study was primarily intended to publicize Hobson's theory of underconsumption. It is not, therefore, a serious study of imperialism, but rather a socialist tract filled with incomplete data, half-truths, and simplistic conclusions.

Taking the matter of overseas investments, Fieldhouse claims that in his statistical tables Hobson performed an intellectual conjuring trick by making almost no differentiation among the areas where British investment was placed, and assuming that the newly acquired territories received a high proportion of British investment. This, as it turns out, was not the case; the bulk of British investment went to the established colonies or to foreign nations, such as the United States, in the period after 1870. "The sums invested in tropical areas, whether newly annexed or not, were quite marginal to the total overseas investment," Fieldhouse asserts.

Regarding the new territories, Fieldhouse doubts it can be proved that the search for lucrative investment opportunities was a primary motivation for their acqustion. Taking a random selection, he suggests that it is ludicrous to say that such places as Fiji, British New Guinea or Upper Burma were annexed to protect any large British investments or even were taken as areas for subsequent investment. More to the point, the annexation of the Transvaal in 1899 was not, on purely economic grounds, a necessity; British mine owners were already making huge profits under the Boer government there.

Using more recent studies than Hobson's Fieldhouse then goes on to suggest that the export of British capital did not weaken the domestic economy and reduce the living standards of British workers, as Hobson believed. Rather, capital export created new markets for British products, reduced unemployment, moderated profits, and maintained wage levels. Indeed, "it was foreign investment that pulled Britain out of most depressions before 1914."

If,then, Hobson's thesis regarding the economic motivations for post-1870 imperialism is only a half-truth, as Fieldhouse thinks it is, what other motives were there for that territorial aggrandizement? The play of European power politics offers a more basic explanation: "until the end of the century, imperialism may best be seen as the extension into the periphery of the political struggle in Europe." Imperialism after 1870 should be regarded as part of the effort to redress the balance of power by the European states. The acquisition of colonies would serve as "sources of diplomatic strength, prestige-giving accessions of territory, and hope for future economic development." The new imperialism was continuous with, and similar in its motivations to, the older imperialism, not a new phenomenon as Hobson—and even more so, Lenin—believed it to be.

But the new imperialism did not include an ingredient that Hobson overlooked: what Fieldhouse calls "social hysteria." The thrust of later nineteenth century imperialism should be attributed less to any sinister influence by the capitalist financiers and their parasites than to the irrational pressures of aggressive nationalism, notions of racial superiority and related hysterias. Those, not the calculations of the financial counting houses, offer a better explanation for the "forward" policies of the Euro-

*John A. Hobson Publishes* Imperialism: A Study

pean nations. — *J.W.P.*

## Additional Recommended Reading

Cohen, Benjamin J. *The Question of Imperialism: The Political Economy of Dominance and Dependence*. New York: Basic Books, 1973. A revisionist of Hobson, Cohen rejects the primacy of economic interests in determining imperialist policies, holding that the older power politics is a more reliable key to understanding nineteenth century expansionism.

Court, W. H. B., ed. *British Economic History, 1870-1914: Commentary and Documents*. Cambridge: Cambridge University Press, 1965. A collection of documents with editorial commentary dealing with many aspects of the British economy in the period, useful as a background for the study of Hobson's book.

Koebner, Richard and Helmut Dan Schmidt. *Imperialism: The Story and Significance of a Political Word, 1840-1960*. Cambridge: Cambridge University Press, 1964. Using the semantic approach, this book shows how imperialism was transformed from an admired word and doctrine to a derogatory concept.

Lichtheim, George. *Imperialism*. New York: Frederick A. Praeger, 1971. Written by an anti-Leninist democratic socialist, this account traces Western imperialism from the Roman "imperium" to the Third World antiimperialism of the present.

Thornton, A. P. *The Imperial Idea and Its Enemies: A Study in British Power*. Garden City, N.Y.: Doubleday & Company, 1968. Discusses the meaning of empire to British leaders and the British public from the later nineteenth to the mid-twentieth century, and how British attitudes toward empire changed through the writings of Hobson and others.

Winks, Robin W., ed. *The Age of Imperialism*. Englewood Cliffs, N.J.: Prentice-Hall, 1969. A collection of documents, letters, reminiscences, and commentary illustrating the impact and effects of imperialism on Europeans and the colonial peoples.

# MAX WEBER PUBLISHES *THE PROTESTANT ETHIC AND THE SPIRIT OF CAPITALISM*

*Type of event:* Intellectual: appearance of one of the great works of modern social thought
*Time:* 1904-1905
*Locale:* Germany

*Principal personages:*

MAX WEBER (1864-1930), German Professor of Sociology at the University of Munich

WERNER SOMBART (1863-1941), German economic historian

JOHN CALVIN (1509-1564), Swiss Protestant reformer

RICHARD BAXTER (1615-1691), English Protestant divine

KARL MARX (1818-1883), German social philosopher

FRIEDRICH WILHELM NIETZSCHE (1844-1900), German philosopher

## Summary of Event

In 1904-1905, Max Weber published two large articles entitled *Die Protestantische Ethik und der Geist des Kapitalismus* (*The Protestant Ethic and the Spirit of Capitalism*). They were followed by a closely related third article, *Die Protestantischen Sekten und der Geist des Kapitalismus* (*The Protestant Sects and the Spirit of Capitalism*) in 1906. These writings were intended as the first part of a projected larger study on the sociology of religion. Almost immediately, *The Protestant Ethic and the Spirit of Capitalism* became Weber's most widely read, most famous, and most discussed work. Along with Karl Marx and Emile Durkheim, Max Weber was a founder of modern sociology; he largely defined the content, problems, and methods of modern social science.

Weber was born in central Germany of a family of mercantile and pious Protestants. After teaching law at Freiburg and economics at Heidelberg, Weber ended his career as Professor of Sociology at the University of Munich. A national liberal who believed in German greatness, he nevertheless criticized the ruling classes and became interested in social reform. After suffering a nervous breakdown in 1897, he visited America, then returned to Germany to found the influential *Archiv fuer Sozialwissenschaft und Sozialpolitik* (*Archives for Social Science and Social Policy*); it was in this journal that his famous essay was published. In 1919 he founded the German Democratic Party, and was a consultant for the constitutional commission of the early Weimar Republic. He died in 1930 as a result of the influenza epidemic that swept over Europe.

One of Weber's major interests was the exploration of the origins of modern society. As early as 1902 he began to develop a new method of social analysis which synthesized the ideas of the positivists and the idealists, particularly the methods of Karl Marx and Friedrich Nietzsche. From the German idealist tradition, Weber took the theory that ideas, habits, attitudes, and beliefs were the primary forces in shaping social values; in addition, he adopted the idealist position that history was the key to social science. Weber developed the concept of the "ideal type." An ideal type, such as "capitalism" and "Protestantism," was an abstraction that represented a tool of analysis for explaining social forces. Ideal types also represented social values and ways of life. From the German philosopher Friedrich Nietzsche, Weber came to appreciate the importance of irrational forces and beliefs in human affairs, and he became particularly interested in religion as a force in social development.

From the nineteenth century positivists, Weber learned to stress meticulous scholarship, scrupulous use of evidence, a striving for objectivity, and an ultimate belief in human reason. The impact of the social philosopher Karl Marx on Weber's thought was manifest in two ways. First, Weber agreed with Marx that the key to modern Western civilization was the development of capitalism. Second, in the light of Weber's reading of Nietzsche and the psychologist Sigmund Freud, Weber set out to revise Marx's theory that material conditions alone determine the ideas and values of a society. He sought to prove that the opposite could equally be true: that the values of a society could exert a decisive influence upon the economic forces of history. Prior

to Weber's essay, German economic historian Werner Sombart had argued that there was a "spirit of capitalism," but it was Weber who developed the theory.

*The Protestant Ethic and the Spirit of Capitalism* was a truly seminal work, for it set out to explore the central issues of man and society. Weber sought to define the relationship between man's noneconomic spiritual beliefs and his social and economic behavior, and to define the spiritual conditions that made modern rationalistic capitalism possible. In his essay, Weber cut across the disciplines of history, economics, sociology, theology, and psychology in an attempt to develop a synthetic analysis of the origins of modern society. He was deliberately reserved on some points, saying that he did not wish to prove that Protestantism "caused" capitalism or that material forces were unimportant, but merely to illustrate certain aspects of the relationship between religious ethics and economic life.

It was no accident, Weber argued, that capitalism flourished in countries that had become Protestant. This was particularly true of areas that had adopted the ideas of the sixteenth century Protestant reformer, John Calvin. These countries included seventeenth century Holland, the American colonies, and parts of Switzerland and France. Above all, Weber used seventeenth century Puritan England as his prime example of an area where Protestantism and capitalism were most closely related. Weber's major argument was that certain Protestant ideas and values contributed attitudes favorable to a "spirit" of capitalism. Protestantism created a positive social mythology around capitalism that legitimatized capitalist values such as profit; it made moneymaking respectable and even ethically desirable. The crux, and perhaps the irony, of the matter was that the rational, technological capitalism of the modern world was in part an unintended consequence of seventeenth century Protestantism. The Protestants, said Weber, did not set out to create capitalism, yet they contributed greatly to its development.

At the outset of his study, Weber drew a connection between the rational economic techniques necessitated by capitalism and the values of ascetic Protestantism. He contrasted the modern spirit of capitalism with that of medieval capitalism. Though trade and banking had developed in the Middle Ages, medieval spiritual values had frowned upon such practices. Modern capitalism, on the other hand, derived from a combination of the profit motive on the one hand and attitudes of religious self-denial on the other. Weber analyzed the religious elements that were relevant to capitalism in the following manner. With the disappearance of the priesthood in Protestant countries, the conception of the "calling" to God's service made business and labor as noble in the sight of God as the religious life. Indeed, the conscientious performance of productive worldly activities became inseparable from spiritual life. Moreover, John Calvin's doctrine of predestination specified than man could no longer depend upon a priesthood for salvation. It followed that Protestants had to dedicate their lives in this world to the greater glory of God. Weber concluded that Protestants had to prove their faith and their worthiness in active avoidance of sin, in which honest work and trade occupied an important part. He attempted to illustrate that in the nineteenth century, the proportion of German tradesmen and industrialists was higher among Protestants than Catholics. He pointed out that the seventeenth century English and Dutch had realized that Protestants had a propensity for business activities.

The attitudes of the English Puritans were of particular importance to Weber in his study of the shaping of capitalism. He refers to the Westminster Confession of 1647 and the influential writings of the divine, Richard Baxter, to illustrate the Puritan role in the spirit of capitalism. Baxter urged that one must strive to be "rich for God" rather than for oneself. For Weber, this implied that Protestants were exhorted to pursue their specialized callings and to reinvest rather than spend their profits sinfully. This teaching constituted an important element in the emergence of a rational capitalism, the "spirit" of which revolved around ceaseless activity in labor and business in order to glorify God in the world. Certitude of election through grace could only come from the Protestant values of discipline, work, and worldly success—all elements of importance in capitalism. Wealth, then, received a religious value if it was honestly and humbly acquired. Rational economic conduct on the basis of the ethic of the religious calling was, Weber believed, the essence of the "spirit of capitalism."

With the end of the seventeenth century, however, moneymaking no longer became a religious means to salvation; it became an end in itself. Capitalist rationality became devoid of spiritual meaning. There ensued a merciless bureaucratization and mechanization of life, as the commitment of the calling degenerated into the drudgery of the job; and modern life became meaningless. This was Weber's pessimistic diagnosis of later capitalism, and he believed that the only way out of this ultrarational "iron cage" was the development of new systems of ideas by charismatic spiritual leaders.

*The Protestant Ethic and the Spirit of Capitalism* immediately resulted in a ferment of debate on the problems raised by Weber. His work was praised, criticized, and "corrected"; a large amount of work continues to appear on the subject of the "Weber thesis." This is not surprising, for the study of *The Protestant Ethic and the Spirit of Capitalism* is essential to an understanding of how we have come to be what we are.

## Pertinent Literature

Samuelsson, Kurt. *Religion and Economic Action*. Edited by D. C. Coleman. Translated by E. Geoffrey French. Stockholm, Sweden: Svenska Bokförlaget, 1961.

This is a sharply critical analysis of *The Protestant Ethic and the Spirit of Capitalism* by a Swedish economic historian and newspaper editor which sums up many of the criticisms that have been leveled at Weber's essay. Samuelsson's broad attack is two-pronged. First, he questions the way in which Weber handled historical evidence, asking whether there was indeed any relationship between Protestantism and capitalism. He concedes that the Protestant ethic might have fostered such traits as diligence and thrift, but as an economic historian, he maintains that speculation, risk-taking, luck, and innovation were far more important than hard work or thrift in the development of capitalism.

Second, Samuelsson sharply questions Weber's ability to write comparative history. He criticizes Weber's failure to compare the ethos of Catholic capitalist countries, such as Belgium, with that of their counterparts in England and Holland. Weber was mainly concerned with comparing the activist Protestant ethic of the West with the passive religions of the East, such as Taoism, believing that the worldly emphasis of Protestantism encouraged the development of a modern economy, while the Eastern religions remained traditionalist and otherworldly. Samuelsson points out that Weber would have been far more illuminating had he compared Protestant England with Catholic Belgium, which, by the nineteenth century, had become one of the leading capitalist nations of the world—a development which can hardly be attributed to the Protestant ethic.

Samuelsson mounts a more general attack on Weber and the English economic historian, R. H. Tawney, accusing them of "loose thinking" in their attempts to correlate Protestant attitudes with capitalist practices. He shows that the widely read Protestant work, John Bunyan's *Pilgrims Progress*, was actually hostile to the values of trade and profit-making. He even questions whether the Calvinist concepts of the calling and predestination can be linked to the values of hard work and worldly success. The idea of the calling was basically religious, not economic; it exhorted Christians to remain humbly in their social places rather than scrambling up the economic ladder. Calvin, argues Samuelsson, never sanctified capitalist values in the process of predestination. Weber never specified whether the Protestants considered success a sign or a means of predestined salvation.

Moreover, Samuelsson finds that Protestant values were often contradicted by actual practice. Diligence and thrift were preached in seventeenth century Catholic France by Jean Baptiste Colbert, the mercantilist minister of Louis XIV. At the same time, many Protestant Dutch, English, and German capitalists lived in opulent splendor, a style of life hardly in keeping with the austere ethic preached by the Calvinists. Even had these capitalists practiced thrift, says Samuelsson, this would not have enabled them to grow rich: real capitalist advances depend upon speculation and a willingness to take risks.

Weber had tried to show that more German Protestants than Catholics were drawn to business careers. In his own statistical investigations, Samuelsson finds instead that more German Protestants than Catholics chose careers in the army and bureaucracy—vocations hardly in keeping with a capitalist ethic. What might explain the inclination of Protestants for trade was not their "spiritual peculiarity," as Weber would have it, but simply the fact that they lived in large cities where capitalism was developing.

Samuelsson finds much to criticize in Weber's method. He accuses Weber of failing to distinguish between "original" and "later" Calvinism, and, above all, of failing to distinguish between the true capitalism studied by economists and the "spirit" of capitalism he sought to distill. Samuelsson next criticizes Weber's general construct of the "ideal type," which he evaluates as a simplistic generalization based upon complex historical and economic forces. The "ideal type" of Protestantism was simplistically viewed by Weber as ultimately rationalistic, while that of Catholicism was explained away, in spite of the fact that the virtues of thrift were preached in Catholic Belgium as well as in Protestant England. Samuelsson believes that capitalism cut across religious lines, and that Weber distorts history when he isolates some subsidiary traits of Protestantism, such as the calling and the work ethic, and loosely correlates these traits with an entire economic system.

Samuelsson finds much to criticize in Weber's use of America as a test case for *The Protestant Ethic and the Spirit of Capitalism*. Weber cited the writings of Benjamin Franklin as a good example of the relationship between Protestant and capitalist values, yet, by Weber's own admission, Franklin was an eighteenth century deist rather than a New England Puritan. Such modern primers of the "spirit" of capitalism as the novels of Horatio Alger reveal much more than simply a work ethic: Alger's characters receive inheritances. Captains of American industry such as Andrew Carnegie were primarily astute technocrats and organizers. The Protestant ethic served to rationalize the "stewardship" of Carnegie's wealth more than it helped him to acquire it.

*Religion and Economic Action* aspires to be the definitive, full-scale attack on Weber's thesis. In addition to some of its serious criticisms, however, it oversimplifies some of Weber's original intentions. As his defenders continue to point out, Weber never viewed Protestantism as the sole cause of capitalism; instead, he selected those characteristics of Prot-

estantism that seemed to contribute to the "spirit of capitalism." Nor did he argue that there was a mechanical relationship between religious and economic forces, realizing that the seventeenth century attitudes of capitalism preceded the full-blown economic system of the nineteenth century. Above all, Weber wished to call attention to the problem of the interaction of religious values and economic practices. He urged the need for further studies, such as an investigation of the effect of capitalism upon the rise of the Protestant ethic. The appearance of critical studies of Samuelsson and others shows that, whatever its limitations, Weber's essay successfully posed one of the vital questions of social thought.

Mitzman, Arthur. *The Iron Cage: An Historical Interpretation of Max Weber*. New York: Alfred A. Knopf, 1970.

The title of this brilliant psychological and intellectual profile of Weber is taken from a passage in *The Protestant Ethic and the Spirit of Capitalism*. Toward the end of his study, Weber remarks that the concern for external goods that was a peripheral concern of the Protestants has become an "iron cage" in the twentieth century. Mitzman views this cage as the stern housing of Weber's parental influences which involved both capitalist and Protestant forces. In his *The Protestant Ethic and the Spirit of Capitalism*, Weber provided not only a key work on the sociology of knowledge, but indirectly probed into the sources of his own being. Mitzman argues that Weber achieved this in a scientifically objective way which en-

abled him to transcend his Protestant-capitalist background, his own "iron cage."

Mitzman first analyzes the development of Weber's thought from the standpoint of family relationships. Weber's father was an authoritarian, and a merchant capitalist who later became a magistrate; his mother was a pious, ascetic Calvinist who intensely disliked sex and levity. The stifling business ethic of his father and the ascetic piety of his mother became the "iron cage" which Weber had to understand before he could escape it. Weber loved his mother more than his father. The scholar Hermann Baumgarten became a substitute father for him, and he eventually married Baumgarten's daughter, Marianne. Mitzman maintains that Weber's views of the world before 1897 were an attempt to deal with the challenge presented by his father.

Weber's attitude toward his father was ambivalent. On the one hand, he identified his father with the rationalistic attitudes of the middle class, which, Weber believed, fulfilled a positive rational and liberal historical role. On the other hand, Weber also identified his father with the aristocratic, militaristic Junker class that actually ruled Germany. This group of ardent nationalists decried the values of moneymaking, while at the same time they became landed capitalists and hired Slavic laborers. Weber's dislike of the Junkers was motivated by the fact that the German middle class looked up to them and appropriated many of their values. These mores had nothing to do with the spirit of capitalist rationality; the ethos of the Junkers was militaristic and ultranationalistic. Perhaps Weber realized that Germany was the only highly developed capitalist nation in Europe where the middle class failed to overthrow either the power or the values of the aristocracy. For Weber, this prevented a real modernization of the German economy and a liberalization of the political structure. He thus became interested in social reform. Weber ultimately sided with his social-minded mother. In 1897, Weber angrily broke with his father, who died shortly thereafter. The guilt that resulted from his action led to Weber's nervous breakdown.

Mitzman poses the interesting hypothesis that Weber wrote *The Protestant Ethic and the Spirit of Capitalism* to reconcile the capitalist spirit of his father with the pious Calvinist ethos of his mother. According to Mitzman, Weber had an unresolved Oedipus complex which resulted in a sexless marriage and took the form of an obsession with work—itself an expression of the "Protestant ethic." When Weber recuperated from his nervous breakdown in 1902, he remained a rationalist and a follower of scientific methods, but he also emerged disenchanted with the suffocating "iron cage" of modern bureaucracy, mechanization, and soulless utilitarianism of modern life. His writing of *The Protestant Ethic and the Spirit of Capitalism* stemmed from Weber's need for personal reintegration, which had its intellectual counterpart in his need to find a new method to understand social and economic behavior.

From his studies in law and economics, Weber turned to an intense study of social science after 1902. He was stimulated by the writings of Karl Marx on the economic origins of capitalism. At the same time, his study of Nietzsche, Freud, and the American pragmatist philosopher William James, convinced him that nonrational and religious feelings had important effects for social life. He attempted to relate nonrational Protestant ideas to a social, capitalist context. Mitzman shows that Weber's greatness lay in his striving to present the relationship between Protestantism and capitalism in an objective manner. Weber only lapses into value judgments when he implies that the "iron cage" of modern rationality holds great dangers in store for the modern world. It is to Weber's great credit that he freely admits that these are "judgments of value and of faith," rather than conclusions reached by painstaking scholarship.

Mitzman views Weber's *The Protestant Ethic and the Spirit of Capitalism* as a major work of history and social analysis, and a model study of the functional role of ideas. In addition, he values Weber as an early pioneer of social psychology, since in his work he laid bare some of the unconscious motives and contributions of the Protestants as they related to the development of a spirit of capitalism. In so doing, he greatly expanded man's understanding of the relationship between morals and society. Through his brilliant contribution to an objective understanding of his own cultural and economic background, and of the nature of his society, Weber had broken out of his "iron cage." — *L.S.*

## Additional Recommended Reading

Bendix, Reinhard. *Max Weber: An Intellectual Portrait*. Garden City, N.Y.: Doubleday & Company, 1960. An excellent, detailed analysis of Weber's ideas which views *The Protestant Ethic and the Spirit of Capitalism* as a work about the mutual influence of society and ideas.

Tawney, R. H. *Religion and the Rise of Capitalism: A Historical Study*. London: John Murray, 1926. This well-known classic agrees with some elements of Weber's thesis, but attempts to correct it in certain matters of emphasis and detail.

Robertson, H. M. *Aspects of the Rise of Economic Individualism: Criticism of Max Weber and His School*. Cambridge: The University Press, 1933. This early criticism of the Weber thesis maintains that Protestantism was only one of the many (primarily economic) forces that aided the development of capitalism.

Hughes, Henry Stuart. *Consciousness and Society: The Reorientation of European Social Thought, 1890-1930*. New York: Vintage Books, 1961. This fine study of European social scientists considers Weber's work a masterly balance of material and spiritual forces.

Freund, Julien. *The Sociology of Max Weber*. Translated by Mary Ilford. New York: Pantheon Books, 1968. An excellent overview and synopsis of Weber's ideas that includes a useful historical summary of the debate about the "Weber thesis" among American scholars.

Hyma, Albert. *Renaissance to Reformation*. Grand Rapids, Mich.: Eerdmans, 1951. A historian of the Reformation period criticizes Weber for omitting a discussion of Calvin's hostility to usury, as well as for overlooking the fact that Calvinism developed in noncapitalist Hungary.

# THE MOROCCAN CRISES

*Type of event:* Diplomatic: attempt by Germany to secure an African colonial empire
*Time:* 1905-1911
*Locale:* Morocco

*Principal personages:*
WILLIAM II (FRIEDRICH WILHELM VIKTOR ALBERT) (1859-1941), Emperor of Germany, 1888-1918
PRINCE BERNHARD VON BÜLOW (1849-1929), Chancellor of Germany, 1900-1909
THEOBALD VON BETHMANN-HOLLWEG (1856-1921), Chancellor of Germany, 1909-1917
FRIEDRICH VON HOLSTEIN (1837-1909), Under Secretary of the German Foreign Ministry
ALFRED VON KIDERLEN-WÄCHTER (1852-1912), German Foreign Secretary

## Summary of Event

In 1904, Great Britain and France concluded the Entente Cordiale, which settled a number of long-standing colonial disputes between the two countries, including those relating to North Africa. Britain achieved a free hand in Egypt under the terms of the accord, while France received similar rights in Morocco. The French also secured the consent of Italy and Spain to the Moroccan arrangement. This settlement was very alarming to Germany, since her colonial ambitions in North Africa were now being disposed of by two powers increasingly ill-disposed toward her world ambitions. France had generally been anti-German in stance since her defeat by Prussia in the war of 1870, out of which the modern German Empire had arisen, while Britain felt increasingly menaced by Kaiser Wilhelm II's naval building program and by the German economy's world dynamism.

German response to the Anglo-French North African settlement was formulated by Friedrich von Holstein, a politician important in German foreign affairs since the 1870's, and in 1905 Under Secretary of the German Foreign Ministry. Holstein's policy attempted to test the depth of the Anglo-French understanding in order to try to split up the arrangement, turn the tables, and form a Continental bloc against England; if this were not possible at least a "price" could be extracted for Germany's acceptance of the North African agreements. Accordingly, the Kaiser embarked on a cruise to Morocco to call on the Sultan there, and on March 31, 1905, he gave a bombastic speech in Tangier wherein he expressed Germany's concern for Moroccan independence.

Chancellor Bernhard von Bülow followed up the Tangier speech by raising the specter of war with France over Morocco. Berlin calculated that Russia—then at war with Japan—would not be able to come to the aid of her French ally under the terms of their Dual Entente of 1894. The French Foreign Minister, Théophile Delcassé, was alone in the French cabinet in insisting that Bülow was bluffing, and Bülow was able to force Delcassé's resignation under the threat of war. France then agreed to Germany's demand for an international conference on the Moroccan question, but French public opinion greatly resented this intrusion into French domestic affairs. Bülow was awarded the title of Prince by the Kaiser for his achievements at this stage of the Moroccan crisis, indicating that the latter felt Germany to be on the way to a successful conclusion of the problem.

The international conference at Algeciras, Spain, which took place from January to April, 1906, turned out to be a gathering in which Germany found herself to be surprisingly isolated; the German leadership determined that never again would they use this vehicle as a means of settling international disputes to which they were a party. Germany's allies in the Triple Alliance were of little help; Austria-Hungary was not interested in supporting German adventures in Morocco, while Italy took France's side against Germany. Spain took little part in the deliberations, since France had already made arrangements guaranteeing her rights in Morocco. Russia, now extricated from her war with Japan, moved to support the French position; the former was moving toward a colonial settlement with Britain concerning long-disputed central Asian regions and consequently was turning her attentions back to the Balkans against Ger-

many's ally Austria-Hungary. The United States, represented for the first time at such an international gathering by the expansionist administration of Theodore Roosevelt, failed to split with Britain, as the Germans had assumed would happen, and instead supported the Anglo-French accord. The Act of Algeciras closing the conference upheld France in Morocco, and the Anglo-French accord emerged strengthened, not weakened as Bülow's intimidations had intended. The fermenter of the crisis, Under Secretary Holstein, was dismissed by the Kaiser toward the close of the conference.

Joint Anglo-French military discussions began in earnest in 1906, and in 1907 an Anglo-Russian convention ended British and Russian quarrels over central Asia. A Triple Entente of England, France, and Russia was taking shape against German expansionism. A Franco-German colonial agreement was signed on February 9, 1909, wherein France got a free hand in northern Morocco; Germany was confined to the southern part of the country. Germany also was to get help from France in constructing a railroad from the German Cameroons to East Africa across the French and Belgian Congos. However, no part of this agreement ever materialized.

Bülow resigned as Chancellor in 1909 and was replaced by Theobald von Bethmann-Hollweg, a professional civil servant, administrator, and bureaucrat, indicating that the chancellorship was now largely the captive of the Kaiser and the circles surrounding him. Bethmann-Hollweg appointed Alfred von Kiderlen-

Wächter as Foreign Secretary in the summer of 1910, and it was Kiderlen-Wächter who handled the next phase of the Moroccan question which emerged in 1911. The new Foreign Secretary argued that the government needed a success in colonial affairs in order to divert attention from the growth of the Social Democratic Party in the German Reichstag; therefore, a couple of Moroccan ports should be seized and concessions demanded from France. If no concessions were forthcoming, then these ports could be kept. Agadir was mentioned as the best port for seizure, since it was the gateway to Morocco's supposed mineral riches. This scheme was presented to the Kaiser, and he approved it.

Disorders in Morocco resulted in the French advancing into the interior of the country and occupying Fez on May 21, 1911. This intrusion was an open violation of the Algeciras agreement and presented Germany with an opportunity to reopen the entire Moroccan question. Kiderlen-Wächter now had sufficient cause to put his Moroccan plan into operation, and the gunboat *Panther* was dispatched to Agadir harbor. Germany was once again asserting equal claim to Morocco with France.

The Foreign Ministry launched a propaganda campaign in the German press in support of the Moroccan adventure; leading economic, commercial, and expansionist circles were also easily enlisted. German firms in Morocco had signed a "blank check" in advance of the crisis asking for help from the German government, and now virtually the entire nation, excepting the Social Democrats, joined them in a chorus demanding that Morocco's mineral ores be secured.

Despite such an outpouring of support from the German public for the venture, the government found that there was even less support for its position among other nations than had been the case in 1905. Austria-Hungary repeated its stand of the previous crisis indicating that it still had no interest in Moroccan adventures, but that it did have considerable interest in French money markets, which seemed to bear out Bethmann-Hollweg's earlier warning that only if Austria were attacked could Germany be sure of the Dual Alliance holding up. Britain took a stronger stand in support of the French position than she had taken in 1905. Prime Minister David Lloyd George gave his famous Mansion House speech in which he expressed British solidarity with France over Morocco, which was followed by military conversations among the British, French, and Russians in August, 1911.

On July 15, 1911, Kiderlen-Wächter had demanded the whole of the French Congo (French Equatorial Africa with its capital, Brazzaville) as compensation for German renunciation of all claims to Morocco, indicating German interest in a colonial empire in central Africa. On July 17, the French Prime Minister rejected this demand although he was known to be pro-German. Meanwhile the position of the Kaiser had become ambiguous. A council of his closest intimates and advisers concluded against war over Morocco in view of the state of Germany's naval armaments, European alliances, and the position of the Social Democrats. The Kaiser consequently decided against war, and Bethmann-Hollweg was instructed to arrange a negotiated settlement. The Moroccan fever went on to reach its zenith in Germany during the second week of September, 1911, with international bankers generally supporting the decision of the government to reach a peaceful settlement but with representatives of heavy industry and various expansionist and nationalist groups openly attacking the Kaiser and Bethmann-Hollweg in the press. Even the chief of the German General Staff, Helmuth von Moltke, was openly critical of the Kaiser.

A treaty on Morocco was signed by the French and German governments on November 4, 1911. Germany recognized the French protectorate over Morocco in exchange for equal economic opportunity in that country. As compensation, 270,000 square kilometers in the French Congo with over one million inhabitants were transferred to the German Cameroons, which were thereby expanded by one half their size. Germany received a preemptive right to Spanish Guinea, which was now completely surrounded by German territory. Thus Germany won the "sleeping Congo," so named because of its swampy terrain and the endemic presence of the sleeping sickness disease.

During the crisis German public opinion had developed along more belligerent lines than the government had expected or intended. The public and the press generally were outraged by British support of France in the crisis and saw the entire episode as evidence that Britain was intent upon stopping Germany's colonial and economic development. They were not satisfied with the central African compensation, and many wanted war. The Kaiser was openly attacked in the Pan-German press for his weakness in the affair. Matters reached a stormy postmortem in the November, 1911, debates in the Reichstag, where nationalist, expansionist, navalist, colonialist, and Pan-German groups furiously berated Bethmann-Hollweg and Kiderlen-Wächter for their timidity. In a speech of November 9, 1911, Bethmann-Hollweg tried to mollify this angry public opinion by saying that nothing more could have been accomplished without war. He argued that Germany had won "free competition" in mining in Morocco, had secured an opening to the Congo and Ubangi rivers in central Africa, and that the crisis had cleared the atmosphere between Britain and Germany. He asserted that it was his policy that Germany first of all remain strong in Europe and that she not undertake foolish overseas adventures that would ultimately destroy her position at home. Many political parties and groups and large sections of the press still were not satisfied and insisted that Germany had been insulted by the outcome of the Moroccan affair; they insisted that the Kaiser and his regime prepare for war in the future.

## Pertinent Literature

Rich, Norman. *Friedrich von Holstein: Politics and Diplomacy in the Era of Bismarck and Wilhelm II*. 2 vols. Cambridge: Cambridge University Press, 1965.

Friedrich von Holstein, the "Grey Eminence of the Wilhelmstrasse" (the street where the German foreign office was located), exercised an uncanny influence over German foreign policy from the 1870's on through the first Moroccan crisis of 1905-1906. Throughout his career he operated as something of a man of mystery: that is, he occupied subordinate positions and declined high office while still exercising great influence. He lasted in this role until his handling of the first Moroccan crisis resulted in his dismissal by the Kaiser.

Holstein was born into the Prussian upper class in 1837, was well educated by private tutors on his family's estate in Pomerania, and traveled extensively abroad as a youth, thereby learning several languages. His first employment was with the Prussian legal bureaucracy, where his career advanced rapidly with the help and support of the first German Chancellor, Otto von Bismarck, whose Prussian estates bordered those of Holstein's family. Later he switched to the Prussian diplomatic service, where he set a pattern in his career by declining high office and working instead from subordinate positions in the style of an intriguer.

Holstein's extremely individualistic personality eventually led him to break with Bismarck over the latter's attempts to continue an alliance with Russia; Holstein felt that Germany would be better served by arrangements with Austria-Hungary and England. Bismarck was eventually retired by the new Kaiser, Wilhelm II, who seemed to want to speed up the former's dangerous diplomatic juggling acts. Germany began to drive for overseas colonies and the construction of a naval fleet, which resulted in an Anglo-German naval race and the failure of negotiations with the British for an Anglo-German alliance. These policies and failures appeared to Holstein to be largely rooted in the Kaiser's world ambitions, and he therefore concluded that some constitutional changes should be made in order to save the Empire from the Kaiser's leadership. Holstein favored placing power in the hands of the bureaucracy and reducing the Kaiser's role to something like that of a formal head of state, but of course these ideas had no chance of implementation.

The Kaiser's foreign policy did result in the end of the Russian alliance, but Holstein could not get sufficient control of policy to effect a British one as replacement. Isolated, Russia slipped into an alliance with Germany's enemy, France. Austria-Hungary, Germany's only real ally, kept making bigger demands as the price of its friendship. By the middle of the first decade of the twentieth century, when England and France joined together to divide the spoils of North Africa, Germany was isolated and ignored; even Italy and Spain were brought into the Anglo-French North African arrangements. Holstein was then assigned the unhappy task of attempting to break up the Anglo-French Entente Cordiale, so he created a crisis over Morocco. This crisis ended in an international conference at Algeciras, Spain, which confirmed Germany's diplomatic isolation; Holstein, the instigator of the crisis, was then dismissed by the Kaiser for his failure.

Holstein lived for three years following Algeciras, during which time he continued, unsuccessfully, his attempts to exert influence over German foreign policy. The loss of Morocco only led to new gambles on the part of the German leadership. The Kaiser and his circles had set Germany on the path to isolation and World War I, and the efforts of an obscure bureaucratic intriguer could not turn things around.

Fischer, Fritz. *War of Illusions: German Policies from 1911 to 1914.* Translated by Marian Jackson. New York: W. W. Norton and Company, 1975.

Fritz Fischer is the originator of the so-called "Fischer Controversy" in West Germany; he asserts in his books that German policy in the years prior to World War I and during the war itself amounted to a "grab for world power." *War of Illusions* examines the details of this policy as it took firm shape in the three years preceding the outbreak of the World War in 1914, and it includes an analysis of the Moroccan crisis of 1911.

Much has been written about Germany's worsening situation in the alliance system that took hold of European politics and diplomacy from the latter nineteenth century to the outbreak of war in 1914. By the time of the Moroccan crisis of 1905, Germany lacked any reliable friends among the powers, and the Algeciras conference of 1906 confirmed this predicament before the entire world. Fischer takes all this for granted and proceeds to tell the story of German diplomacy prior to World War I, which he sees as a determination to escape from an isolated posture.

German policymakers knew that the odds were against them in the system of alliances that had emerged in Europe; their policy was to test these alliances, to try and break them up, and to reconstitute them around a German continental bloc. At the same time they wished to acquire overseas possessions, particularly in Africa where Germany had largely missed out on the partitioning of the late nineteenth century. When the twentieth century opened, Germany's attentions, along with those of France, were fixed on Morocco, which despite its proximity to Europe was one of the least-known countries of the world. It was thought, however, to be a place of vast mineral riches awaiting development, and Germany counted on securing her share of that country's resources; hence the decision in 1905 to take a stand against the encircling alliance system, which had been tightened by the Anglo-French Entente Cordiale (1904), and to demand her rights in North Africa.

All that emerged for Germany at the Algeciras conference of 1906 was confirmation of encirclement and a shaky position in Morocco. However, in 1911, new Moroccan disturbances allowed the matter to be reopened, and virtually the entire German people demanded that Germany get her share of Morocco. Fischer goes to great lengths to demonstrate that German expansionism was not just something promoted by the German ruling classes, but that it had a very broad basis of support among the

German public, which was riddled with expansionist ideas. Indeed, when the Kaiser and the Chancellor finally failed in 1911 to deliver Morocco, the public turned on them with a vengeance. Henceforth, the government would have to consider carefully the consequences of another failure in foreign policy.

When it became clear that Germany would not be able to establish her influence in Morocco, German policymakers tried to salvage an empire in central Africa as compensation. This was definitely of second-rate importance in comparison to Morocco, but it was still important to the Germans because they long had dreamed of a continuous empire in central Africa. What they finally got is usually referred to in textbooks as "minor compensation," but according to Fischer it was the nucleus of a German central African empire projected eventually to cover the center of the entire continent.

Fischer's emphasis on Germany's desperate attempts to get something first in Morocco and then in central Africa, fed by the force of German public opinion pushing for overseas territory, suggests a picture of an expansionist people with ambitions that went far beyond the European continent. His other books develop this point on through World War I, during which he accuses Germany of plotting the domination of both Europe and Africa. — *J.L.C.*

## Additional Recommended Reading

Albertini, Luigi. *The Origins of the War of 1914*. 3 vols. Translated and edited by Isabella M. Massey. London: Oxford University Press, 1952-1957. The definitive work on this subject which blames Germany for the outbreak of the war; the Moroccan crises are covered in Volume One.

Albrecht-Carrié. René. *A Diplomatic History of Europe Since the Congress of Vienna*. New York: Harper & Row Publishers, 1973. The standard college textbook on recent European diplomatic history; the Moroccan crises are given ample treatment.

Anderson, Eugene Nelson. *The First Moroccan Crisis, 1904-1906*. Chicago: University of Chicago Press, 1930. The only monograph on the 1904-1906 crisis; its style is dated, and its author did not have access to some source materials now available, but its basic narrative and interpretations remain sound.

Barlow, Ima Christina. *The Agadir Crisis*. Chapel Hill: University of North Carolina Press, 1940. Although this work suffers some defects from being almost forty years old, it is unlikely that anyone will produce a replacement.

Lee, Dwight E. *Europe's Crucial Years: The Diplomatic Background of World War I, 1902-1914*. Hanover, N.H.: University Press of New England, 1974. A synopsis of old and recent literature on this subject including material on the Moroccan crises.

Remak, Joachim. *The Origins of World War I, 1871-1914*. New York: Holt, Rinehart and Winston, 1967. A short, readable general survey of the background of the war including the Moroccan crises.

Ritter, Gerhard. *The Sword and the Scepter: The Problem of Militarism in Germany*.

4 vols. Translated by Heinz Norden. Coral Gables, Fla.: University of Miami Press, 1969-1973. These volumes were written by the leader of the opposition to Fritz Fischer within the German historical community and constitute an "answer" to Fischer's work: that is, Ritter argues that Germany had no prewar expansion plans. The Moroccan crisis is covered in Volume Two.

Taylor, A. J. P. *The Struggle for Mastery in Europe, 1848-1918*. Oxford: Clarendon Press, 1954. A provocative treatment of this period which weaves in the Moroccan crises.

# FRIEDRICH MEINECKE PUBLISHES
## *COSMOPOLITANISM AND THE NATIONAL STATE*

*Type of event:* Intellectual: appearance of a new kind of influential historical work
*Time:* 1907
*Locale:* Germany

*Principal personages:*
FRIEDRICH MEINECKE (1862-1954) and
LEOPOLD VON RANKE (1795-1886), German historians
GEORG WILHELM FRIEDRICH HEGEL (1770-1831), German philosopher
FREDERICK WILLIAM IV (1795-1861), King of Prussia, 1840-1861
COUNT OTTO (EDUARD LEOPOLD) VON BISMARCK-SCHÖNHAUSEN (1815-1898), Minister-President of Prussia, and First Chancellor of the German Empire, 1871-1890

### Summary of Event

In 1907, Friedrich Meinecke, Professor of History at the University of Freiburg, published an important work of history entitled *Weltbürgertum und Nationalstaat (Cosmopolitanism and the National State)*. The book was immediately hailed by both German and European scholars as a milestone in modern European history writing. It was the first major historical work of what Meinecke called "*Geistesgeschichte*"—the history of spiritual and intellectual forces in political life. The important German political historian Hans Delbrück and intellectual historian Wilhelm Dilthey praised the work as original in method and true to Prusso-German traditions. The neo-Hegelian Italian historian Benedetto Croce considered the book a model of the new "ethico-political" intellectual history. Social scientists Max Weber and Ernst Troeltsch, who themselves were greatly interested in the connection between cultural and political forces in history, congratu-lated Meinecke on a great achievement.

Meinecke published *Cosmopolitanism and the National State* in his forty-fifth year. Before then he had been an archivist and editor of the prestigious historical journal, the *Historische Zeitschrift*; he had entered the teaching profession in middle age. The publication of *Cosmopolitanism and the National State* helped establish his reputation as Germany's foremost and most influential historian of the first half of the twentieth century. The book was so successful that it went through seven editions between 1907 and 1928.

The methods and values of Meinecke as exemplified in *Cosmopolitanism and the National State* were a blend of many currents of late nineteenth and early twentieth century German political and intellectual life. Meinecke was a product of a typical small-town, middle-class, Prussian, Lutheran, and conservative German background. He admired the universal genius of Johann Wolfgang von Goethe and the ideas of the Prussian reformers of the Wars of Liberation against Napoleon in the period 1806-1819. But he was guided most of all by nationalist and statist writers such as Georg Wilhelm Friedrich Hegel and Leopold von Ranke. He was greatly influenced by Hegel's view of the nation-state as an instrument of the divine spirit and by Ranke's idea of the nation-state as a unique cultural and political individuality that abided by its own nature and interests.

Meinecke's historical approach was formed by the "Prussian school" of German historians. He was impressed by Johann Gustav Droysen, who had advocated that the politician be the historian in practice, that is, that statesmen should realize the goals discovered by historians. Meinecke accordingly hoped that his discovery of the principles of German unification and his advocacy of some reforms would be heeded by statesmen. Meinecke viewed with favor the most popular German chauvinist historian of the later nineteenth century, Heinrich von Treitschke. Treitschke had praised Prussian militarism and authoritarianism as essential to the health of the German spirit. Meinecke was also influenced by the important intellectual historian, Wilhelm Dilthey, who had pioneered the study of the evolution of ideas among individual thinkers. Meinecke went one step further: he analyzed groups of ideas and illustrated how ideas both shaped and responded to political developments. For example, Meinecke showed how conservative writers influenced the German statesman Otto von Bismarck.

Above all, Meinecke was a statist. He believed that the strong nation-state represented the basic unit of modern civilized life and the culmination of human history. He was a moderate constitutional liberal to the extent that he believed that reforms were valuable if they strengthened the state. For this reason he approved of the Prussian liberals of the Napoleonic era. By the turn of the twentieth century Meinecke became a follower of the social-minded monarchist, Friedrich Naumann, who sought to rally the masses behind a reformed Prusso-German monarchy. Again, Meinecke hoped that this would strengthen the state. Despite his moderate constitutionalism, Meinecke ultimately approved of the conservative authoritarian solution of Otto von Bismarck. He saw Bismarck as a man of genius who translated ideas into action and synthesized the Prussian state power with the German national spirit. The German Empire as created by Bismarck provided for Meinecke what seemed up until 1918 to be the form for a lasting German nation-state.

The writing of *Cosmopolitanism and the National State* had several objectives and served a number of purposes. First, it developed a new method of writing and understanding history. Meinecke referred to himself as a historicist. By this he meant that he believed the unique creations of history alone have provided truth, meaning, and value. Hence, if the unique national state had been successfully forged by history, one had to view the phenomenon as an absolute value in itself. Further, Meinecke drew on the German idealist tradition of Immanuel Kant that saw in history a dichotomy between spirit and power, culture and politics, the spirit of Weimar and the spirit of Potsdam. *Cosmopolitanism and the National State* attempted to show that by the turn of the twentieth century a synthesis had been achieved between the idealism of German national culture and Prussian state power in the new German Empire.

Meinecke's new method of historical analysis studied the mutual influence of ideas and politics. He traced the changing views of German philosophers, literary figures, and political theorists together with the changes in Prusso-German political evolution from cosmopolitanism to nationalism. However, he made no attempt to analyze the role of economic and social forces in the process of nation-building.

Second, *Cosmopolitanism and the National State* set out to prove and to justify that the development of German unity from 1815 to 1870 was made possible only by the emancipation from cosmopolitan values and practices. It portrayed modern German history as the triumph of nationalism and the power state over the cosmopolitanisms of both the Enlightenment and Romanticism. At the outset of his work, Meinecke claims that the German nation-state was the result of the spirit of national genius, geography, and power rather than abstract natural laws and a social contract (which were the values of the Western Enlightenment). Despite his views of the romantics as impractical, Meinecke approved of the romanti-

cist idea of history as the development of such unique creations as the nation-state.

Meinecke judges persons and ideas mainly to the extent to which they contributed to the goal of German unification under Prussian leadership. For him, only the power state of Prussia could have unified, furthered, and protected the national genius of Germany. He begins his account during the Napoleonic era, when many German geniuses such as the political theorists Wilhelm von Humboldt and Johann Gottlieb Fichte turned to the Prussian power state for the salvation of Germany from the repressive cosmopolitanism of Napoleon. In Meinecke's judgment, the Prussian and German reformers of 1806-1819 and the Southern German revolutionary intellectuals of 1848 were wrong when they wished to absorb the invaluable political individuality of Prussia into Germany. The conservative romantics, who included King Frederick William IV of Prussia, were also mistaken for the opposite reason: they wished to preserve Prussia intact merely as the head of a new German Confederation in place of Austria. Meinecke concludes that Prussian hegemony in Germany was the only "natural" way to create a German nation-state in the face of French and Austrian opposition. This was accomplished by Otto von Bismarck with the only available solution—military force. The result was a "complex but viable" compromise between monarchy and constitutional government, centralism and federalism.

Finally, Meinecke's work presented the optimistic outlook that the structure of the second German Empire could be perfected and reformed. In his preface to the edition of 1915, Meinecke expressed the hope that the forces of patriotism unleashed by World War I would result in a reform of the suffrage and landholding system. In the 1921 edition of his book, he added an entire chapter advocating the strengthening of the new Republic through reform.

The German disaster of World War I forced Meinecke to alter somewhat the optimistic assumptions of *Cosmopolitanism and the National State*. His book on the history of *Machiavellianism* (1924) showed that power and culture were often opposed to each other rather than representing two sides of the same coin. When,

toward the end of his life, Meinecke reflected on the Nazi experience in *The German Catastrophe* (1946), he was forced to admit that German power had run amok while German culture had degenerated into barbarism. Yet, by characterizing Nazism as "un-German" and asserting that "the work of Bismarck had been destroyed," he side-stepped the possibility that Nazism might itself have been an extreme reaction against cosmopolitan values.

In the last analysis, *Cosmopolitanism and the National State* stands as a model of a new and influential work of history. But it also remains a dated period piece whose absolute nationalist and statist principles Meinecke never quite overcame.

## Pertinent Literature

Sterling, Richard W. *Ethics in a World of Power: The Political Ideas of Friedrich Meinecke*. Princeton, N.J.: Princeton University Press, 1958.

Richard W. Sterling studied with Friedrich Meinecke. His book is the result not only of an analysis of Meinecke's works, but also of many conversations with the author himself. Sterling did not intend his study to be a formal biography, but rather an analysis of Meinecke's lifelong quest to reconcile the historical forces of ethics and political power. Meinecke emerges in this book both as an important historian and as a political philosopher.

Sterling's initial assumption is that Meinecke's supreme value was the national state. Young Meinecke entered his profession in the 1880's and 1890's when the second German Empire had recently taken form. For him

the nation-state was both a lofty idea and a practical reality; it was the basic unit of civilization. Sterling devotes considerable time to exploring Meinecke's views of the relationship between ethical values and political realism.

*Cosmopolitanism and the National State* represents for Sterling the summation of Meinecke's political thinking up to World War I and as the foundation for his later works. Above all, Meinecke sought to illustrate and achieve a multitude of syntheses of opposing forces in German history in *Cosmopolitanism and the National State*—cosmopolitanism and nationalism, ethics and power, Prussia and Germany, conservatism and reform,

Immanuel Kant and Otto von Bismarck.

Meinecke was primarily a statist, a nationalist, and a conservative, says Sterling. *Cosmopolitanism and the National State* was intended to celebrate the triumph of the Bismarckian solution for the German nation-state. Yet Meinecke also admired the reformers of the period from 1806 to 1819. These high-minded men, such as Baron vom Stein, Wilhelm von Humboldt, and Johann Gottlieb Fichte, sought to turn Prussia into a powerful yet humane state that would lead the rest of Germany. Unfortunately, their values were much too impractical and cosmopolitan and did not realistically appreciate the uniqueness of the Prussian power state. They wished to obliterate Prussian identity for the sake of German culture—an impossible and erroneous goal. They did not realize that a powerful state was needed to realize their own noble cultural ideals.

It was left for Georg Friedrich Hegel, Leopold von Ranke, and Otto von Bismarck to understand forces at work in Prussia, Germany, and Europe. Hegel saw the progressive development of the nation-state as the theme of history, while Ranke viewed the nation-state as a cultural spiritual entity in itself. Bismarck, the realistic man of action, used force to impose the genius of the Prussian state system upon the greatness of the German national community. Sterling concludes that Meinecke singled out the conservative tradition in modern German history as the worthy maker of national unity and considered the Germany of 1907 as the best of all possible worlds at the time.

For Meinecke, then, Germany had overcome the debilitating cosmopolitanism of the French Enlightenment and its universal monarchy of Napoleon. It had also emerged victorious over the reactionary Christian romanticism of the Holy Alliance that threatened German unity. Both revolution and reaction were cosmopolitan extremes for Meinecke. King Frederick William IV of Prussia was himself a conservative romantic who could not break away from the tradition of a German Confederation of states. Only a synthesis of Prussianism and German nationalism could encourage and preserve the spiritual individuality of the nation.

Despite Meinecke's glorification of a powerful nation-state, Sterling views his subject as a humanist, arguing that he sought to retain the cosmopolitan values of liberty and individuality within the unique confines of Prussia-Germany. This is somewhat at variance with Sterling's other judgments of Meinecke as a statist, an elitist, and a conservative who believed in a strong executive. Meinecke's very theory of individuality was that the state was "man writ large." Moreover, Sterling illustrates how Meinecke theorized that force, self-preservation, and state egotism were most desirable in international relations. It was mainly for these reasons that Meinecke felt it necessary to defend Prussian militarism. In Meinecke's scale of values in 1907, Bismarck took precedence over Goethe: power must prevail to protect the very existence of national genius. Sterling skillfully shows that Meinecke's view of the nation-state as the supreme value could justify the power strivings of Prussia-Germany in World War I.

Meinecke professed a relativism that allowed room for the existence of a plurality of nations to represent the variety of human cultures. Here was a needed survival of eighteenth century cosmopolitanism. Yet, Meinecke's assertions of German superiority would violate his attempt to salvage something from the Enlightenment.

It was only with the tragic defeat of Germany in World War I and the bankruptcy of the monarchy that Meinecke began slowly to reevaluate his faith in the second German Empire. After 1919, he moved away from a theory of the synthesis of ethics and power to a dualistic view of a conflict between ethics and political power.

Sterling maintains that because of the horrifying experience of the Nazi regime, the aged Meinecke moved away from his belief in the national power state as an absolute value. The old scholar sought after 1945 to stress the ethical elements in a world of power, and, by the end of his life, elevated the cosmopolitan Goethe to a place in German history perhaps even higher than that of Bismarck. Sterling's conclusion is that by 1946 Meinecke had accepted the logical implications of his theory of historical individuality—that the nation-state could be eclipsed by new historical forms of political and international life. Thus, Sterling concludes that Meinecke ultimately abandoned the rigid categories of history of *Cosmopolitanism and the National State*.

Sterling provides a lucid exposition of Meinecke's impressive intellectual and moral ability to alter his views on the development of the German national state. Meinecke had learned to accept the flaws of the German nation-state created by Bismarck. Yet Sterling leaves the impression that Meinecke substituted no real theory of the nation-state to replace that of *Cosmopolitanism and the National State*. Meinecke's 1907 synthesis of ethics and power had broken down, and nothing could replace it.

Pois, Robert A. *Friedrich Meinecke and German Politics in the Twentieth Century*. Berkeley: University of California Press, 1972.

This recent critical analysis of Friedrich Meinecke is concerned with the political ideas of the German historian and with the relationship of these ideas to the abrupt changes of twentieth century German politics. The major concern of Robert A. Pois lies in the intellectual and political implications of *Cosmopolitanism and the National State*: what were the core ideas of the work, and how did Meinecke modify these ideas in the light of German developments after 1918?

Pois maintains that *Cosmopolitanism and the National State* summed up Meinecke's pre-World War I historical rationalizations of the Prussian solution to German unification. Meinecke felt that Germany needed a strong state to protect its individuality and its interests, and he went on to show that the acceptance of the state "idea" developed in tandem with political conditions in Germany.

In order for a unified Germany to prevail, cosmopolitan rationalist and romantic ideals had to be discarded by thinkers and politicians.

Pois claims that neither Otto von Bismarck nor Georg Wilhelm Friedrich Hegel should be considered the real heroes of *Cosmopolitanism and the National State*; the key figure of the book is Leopold von Ranke. It was Ranke who divinized the state itself, rather than viewing the state merely as an instrument of a higher divine purpose, as did Hegel. With Ranke the nation became an instrument of the individual, self-seeking state, especially in the area of foreign policy.

This study is the only one in English that provides an in-depth discussion of Meinecke's attempts to reform the second German Empire (1871-1918). Meinecke became associated with Friedrich Naumann, a social reformer who sought to build a "Peoples' State" (Volkstaat) by reforming the constitution, encouraging a social-minded monarchy, and integrating the working classes into the system. However, the purpose of these reforms was a social-liberal means to a higher conservative end— the strengthening of the German power state (Machtstaat) in the world as traced in *Cosmopolitanism and the National State*. Moreover, the masses were to be led by the educated bourgeoisie of which Meinecke was a part. The result was to be a moderate statist nationalism rather than the extreme racial nationalism advocated by the social Darwinists of the time. *Cosmopolitanism and the National State* was therefore an optimistic work that believed in the ultimate perfectibility of the Prusso-German nation-state.

The shattering defeat of Germany in 1918 exposed the inadequacies of the system and the brutal power drives of the German ruling classes. Pois shares the opinion of most scholars that Meinecke turned away from the optimistic synthesis of power state and culture state he thought Germany had achieved in his work of 1907, and instead posited a dualistic struggle between power and ethics. The author provides a probing criticism of Meinecke's dichotomy of power and culture from the following standpoints. First, by compartmentalizing power as demonic and culture as humanistic, Meinecke continued in the idealist footsteps of *Cosmopolitanism and the National State*. In Meinecke's "confused psyche," the historian ended up absolutizing both political and cultural life without realizing that power could be controlled. Second, Meinecke modified but never abandoned the statist beliefs of his work of 1907. Though he became committed to the survival of the Weimar Republic, he drew close to the right-wing ideas of corporativism and statism.

Pois provides the important insight that the vestiges of statism in Meinecke left from the pre-1918 period prevented him from understanding the real nature of the Nazi revolution. Meinecke responded to the tremendous crisis of Nazism by viewing the movement as an extreme of demonic state power, but he was incapable of recognizing the connections between Nazi power drives and world views— views that had some roots in Meinecke's own statist and nationalist outlook. Pois argues that Meinecke's interpretation of the Nazi revolution as merely an explosion of nihilistic power elements in the equivalent of placing the blame for Nazism on original sin. Meinecke sidestepped the unique circumstances and forces that made German National Socialism possible. Thus, Meinecke emerges as a theologian in the same degree as a historian. His *German Catastrophe* of 1946 provides a negative rationalization for Nazism just as *Cosmopolitanism and the National State* of 1907 had provided a positive rationalization for German unity under Prussian leadership.

In the course of his long life, Meinecke moved from cosmopolitanism to nationalism in the early twentieth century, and back to cosmopolitanism by the mid-twentieth century. Pois views Meinecke's late cosmopolitanism as "archaic," "facile," and "not entirely genuine." This is because Meinecke's return (or escape) to the Olympian cosmopolitan spirit of Goethe was entirely lacking in political applications. Thus, Meinecke's rejection of the nationalist statism of *Cosmopolitanism and the National State* created more problems than it solved. The power-culture synthesis of 1907 was abandoned, while the falsely separate concepts of state and culture were continued, thus preventing any meaningful understanding of their relationship in twentieth century German history. For Pois, Meinecke's conceptual and political failures represented the more general failure of the educated German bourgeoisie in the first half of the twentieth century.

What is particularly tragic about Meinecke's career is that in spite of his intelligence and his humaneness, he was culturally and emotionally unwilling to question the course of German cultural history. The assumptions of *Cosmopolitanism and the National State* were modified, but never replaced by a new system of analysis. According to Pois, Meinecke's stature as one of Germany's greatest intellectual historians must be balanced by a stern appraisal of his intellectual and spiritual inadequacies and weaknesses.

The usefulness of this probing study of Meinecke is enhanced by the "Postscript" of the book, which contains a brief summary of the debates about Meinecke among the German and American historians. — *L.S.*

## Additional Recommended Reading

Iggers, Georg G. *The German Conception of History: The National Tradition of Historical Thought from Herder to the Present*. Middletown, Conn.: Wesleyan University Press, 1968. A fine survey of German historical thought which contains a highly critical treatment of Meinecke indicating that even at the end of his life he was unable to face the tragic consequences of the values of 1907—that is, his belief that the state was a spiritual end in itself.

Antoni, Carlo. *From History to Sociology: The Transition in German Historical Thinking*. Translated by Hayden V. White. Detroit, Mich.: Wayne State University Press, 1959. An important survey of major German historians which views *Cosmopoli-*

*tanism and the National State* as a key work on the importance of ideas in history, but criticizes Meinecke for failing to explore the relationships between German political and intellectual history.

Snyder, Louis L. *German Nationalism: The Tragedy of a People*. Harrisburg, Pa.: Stackpole Company, 1952. While praising Meinecke's skill as a scholar, Snyder views the historian as a conservative nationalist, statist, and militarist trapped by his outlook.

Hughes, Henry Stuart. *Consciousness and Society: The Reorientation of European Social Thought, 1890-1930*. New York: Vintage Books, 1961. This major analysis of European social scientists evaluates *Cosmopolitanism and the National State* as a pioneering work of modern European intellectual history in which Meinecke attempted to bring the spiritual and political elements of history into a precarious synthesis.

Gilbert, Felix. *History: Choice and Commitment*. Cambridge, Mass.: Harvard University Press, 1977. Maintains that *Cosmopolitanism and the National State* advocated constitutional reforms for the German Empire as well as putting its blessing on the Prusso-German solution for Germany.

Anderson, Eugene Nelson. "Meinecke's *Ideengeschichte* and the Crisis in Historical Thinking," in *Medieval and Historiographical Essays in Honor of James Westfall Thompson*. Edited by James Lea Cate and Eugene Nelson Anderson. Chicago: University of Chicago Press, 1938. Mildly criticizes *Cosmopolitanism and the National State* as lacking a satisfactory social and economic framework.

# POLAR EXPLORATIONS

*Type of event:* Scientific: exploration into uncharted regions of the world
*Time:* 1909-1911
*Locale:* The Arctic and the Antarctic

*Principal personages:*

ROBERT EDWIN PEARY (1856-1920), an American explorer who was first to reach the North Pole

ROALD E. AMUNDSEN (1872-1928), a Norwegian explorer who was first to navigate a Northwest Passage and first to reach the South Pole

ROBERT FALCON SCOTT (1868-1912), a British explorer who reached the South Pole just after Amundsen and who died on the return journey

ERNEST HENRY SHACKLETON (1874-1922), a British explorer who came nearest to the South Pole before Amundsen's success

## Summary of Event

The first decade of the twentieth century saw the culmination of centuries of striving toward human domination of the two poles. For hundreds of years men had ventured to the Arctic ice in the hope of discovering a passage through the frozen seas of the North Pole to the spices of the Orient. Such a lucrative Northwest Passage remained illusive until generations of explorers had garnered enough knowledge of the shifting ice floes and irregular weather patterns to cope with such a harsh and unpredictable environment. The Antarctic, on the other hand, presented a completely reverse set of problems, for it is a rugged and mountainous land mass surrounded by water. Man's desire for mastery over these challenging areas has played a significant part in his motivation toward polar discoveries, as have patriotic competitiveness among explorers from different countries and man's thirst for scientific knowledge. All of these factors combined near the end of the nineteenth century and led, in the early twentieth century, to numerous polar expeditions and to a mood of romantic popular excitement.

Not all of the expeditions had as their goal the discovery of the North or South Pole; many explorers journeyed forth simply to see what they could find, while others were commissioned by various groups to gather specific data. Many of the thrill seekers found themselves ill-equipped for the situations they encountered, sometimes with tragic results; but the group of professional explorers which developed had specific goals which gave their missions focus.

One such professional with a specific mission was Roald Amundsen, who set out in 1903 to navigate a Northwest Passage through the Arctic seas. It was far from a whim of fate that brought Amundsen to his quest. He had studied seamanship in sailing vessels, since they were far more practical for years-long polar voyages than were vessels that had to be refueled. He had enlisted with a Belgian expedition to the Antarctic in 1897 which was the first group to winter over in such a harsh environment, in order to gain practical knowledge of scientific exploration. He had also studied terrestrial magnetism at Hamburg expressly because there were organizations that would grant funds to polar expeditions which would gather information on such topics. It was with this background that, in 1903, Amundsen sailed the *Gjøa*, a cutter equipped with an auxiliary motor, north to the southeast end of King William Island. He and his crew spent nineteen months, including two winters in Gjøahavn, studying magnetism, but more particularly learning about sleds, the feeding and handling of sled dogs, and many other Eskimo practices. They did successfully navigate a Northwest Passage, and sailed on to the Pacific Ocean in 1906 after a third winter. Such a navigation was not to be repeated by a commercial vessel until the *S. S. Manhattan*, an icebreaking oil tanker, managed it in 1969.

While many groups were active in Arctic exploration, it is to Robert E. Peary that the distinction of discovering the North Pole has been given. Peary was another professional explorer, an engineer who was more interested in perfecting the techniques and equipment for Arctic travel than in scientific investigations. In the late 1880's and early 1890's, he had made several expeditions to Green-

land, and in 1899 and again in 1902 he attempted unsuccessfully to reach the North Pole. Nevertheless, these trips taught Peary that not only must his sleds be very lightweight but also that they could cross the ice more smoothly during the dark Arctic winter when the ice was more solidly frozen than in the brighter summer months. He encountered less open water between ice drifts in the winter months; increased stability made his return path much easier to mark for at least a short time.

That Peary learned from his experiences heartened his financial backers, a group of wealthy New Yorkers who formed the Peary Arctic Club to raise the money to outfit him for another trip. After another false start in 1905, Peary and five companions finally reached the North Pole on April 6, 1909.

Peary was by no means the only explorer hard at work. Ernest H. Shackleton led a private expedition aboard the *Nimrod* to Antarctica in 1907 and established his base on Ross Island. Some members of his party scaled Mt. Erebus, while Shackleton and another group came within ninety-seven miles of the South Pole, on January 9, 1909, before dwindling provisions forced them to turn back. News of Shackleton's successes accelerated other preparations for Antarctic expeditions on the part of Roald Amundsen for Norway; Wilhelm Filchner for Germany; Robert Scott for Britain; Douglas Mawson for Australia; and Nobu Shirase for Japan. The closest contenders were Robert Scott and Roald Amundsen.

Robert Scott had been to Antarctica with a previous expedition (1901-

1904) before he, in addition to Shackleton and others, made the first deep land penetrations. Scott's philosophy differed from Amundsen's, however, in his form of transportation. Amundsen used dogs pulling sledges to transport his supplies. As the journey progressed and the load became lighter, fewer dogs were needed, so the Norwegians killed the now-surplus dogs and used them for fresh meat. Scott refused to participate in this practice and transported by means of ponies. Scott's group reached the South Pole on January 17, 1912, to discover that Amundsen's group had arrived there one month and three days earlier. Scott's party suffered from a lack of provisions, very bad weather, and several accidents during their return journey, and the entire polar party perished.

Roald Amundsen's journey to the South Pole was far from easy, but he pursued his goal with a cold, professional determination. His group wintered over in Antarctica in 1911, preparing the base camp, working to make the equipment as lightweight as possible, and conducting scientific experiments. His party of five men finally set out in the warm spring weather ($-22°F$) of mid-October for the South Pole. They took the journey in stages, resting at each depot that they established but nevertheless averaging fifteen miles per day. They used dog sleds to transport the supplies while the men traveled on skis. Although they were forced to detour around numerous large crevasses and to climb several mountain ranges, they reached the South Pole very close to their planned date, on December 14, 1911. On the return trip, the group had fairly good weather, as well as ample provisions. Amundsen arrived back at his winter camp in January, having covered an average of twenty-two miles each day.

## Pertinent Literature

Peary, Robert Edwin. *The North Pole, Its Discovery in 1909 Under the Auspices of the Peary Arctic Club*. New York: Frederick A. Stokes, 1910.

That polar exploration enjoyed great public support and appealed to the discerning layman is evident in this narrative of Peary's great adventure, and is reflected in the introduction by Theodore Roosevelt.

Peary's account begins with a summary of the factors which he felt contributed most to his success, particularly careful planning and a solid knowledge of Eskimo ways. He describes at length Eskimo home life and practices such as igloo building in a separate early section of the book.

His narrative of the expedition itself is detailed, although written in the pompous and overblown style typical of the times. Many of the less pleasant details are glossed over as a function of this style, although sufficient particulars remain to humanize the events for the reader. He mentions, for instance, the importance of many of the smaller elements of the adventure, such as the perfection of a system for bringing water to a boil rapidly in order to speed along each day's preparation of tea.

The sections on how Peary chose the twenty-two men for the expedition provide good background sketches of the participants as well as clear photographs. Peary chose to make his equipment as lightweight and efficient as possible, although he enumerates many "crank" letters which he received regarding motorcars, sawmills, and all manner of other trinkets, the proponents of which guaranteed his success should he only use their ideas. His final list of provisions nonetheless included such entries as sixteen thousand pounds of flour and nearly four thousand gallons of kerosene, to name just two.

The "Peary system" that insured success for their expedition is expounded at length. Since the North Pole is in the middle of an ice-capped sea, Peary found it imperative to sail his ship as far north through the ice as possible to minimize the amount of foot travel necessary. Peary's group included many Eskimos, and he freely adapted as many of their survival and travel techniques as he could.

From previous experience in the Arctic region Peary knew that travel was less hazardous over the more stable ice pack in the winter even though the sky was always dark and the temperatures particularly cold. Even during these months, however, the ice could drift, so he determined that leaving well-stocked depots along more than one return route was wise.

At the end of Peary's narrative there are three appendixes. The first is a summary of the scientific observations made by the group, particularly those regarding the tides. The second contains facsimiles of the original data as recorded in the notebooks. The third is the report of the Sub-Committee of the National Geographic Society which investigated the claims of Dr. Frederick A. Cook to have reached the North Pole before Peary. The subcommittee found Peary's claim to have more credence.

Amundsen, Roald. *The South Pole: An Account of the Norwegian Antarctic Expedition in the "Fram", 1910-1912*. Translated by A. G. Chater. 2 vols. London: John Murray, 1912.

Roald Amundsen was a highly skilled professional explorer, and the account he presents in these volumes is written in a simple, straightforward style that can be understood by readers at many levels. It is a chronological account with the freshness of a well-kept journal.

The Antarctic is a rugged land mass with different problems of exploration from that of the Arctic. Travel is best accomplished in the bright and relatively warmer summer months, although blizzards can still occur. There are mountain ranges up to ten thousand feet high to traverse as well as many perilously deep crevasses to avoid. In such conditions it is possible to mark a path with a series of depots without encountering the Arctic problem of depots changing positions. Amundsen's party set up three primary depots at the start of their expected route, with a total of three tons of provisions. They marked their path by constructing snow beacons, man-sized towers made of blocks of snow topped with flags designed to be visible against the blinding white of the snow. Flags were also placed four miles to the east and west of the depots in case the polar party wandered off their north-south course.

Amundsen's base camp was set up with equal care. The tents, workshops, larder, and the like were all connected so that there was no need for the men to go outside in particularly bad weather as they waited out the winter working on their equipment and performing scientific experiments. The sled dogs upon which the party would depend were kept in kennels with connecting igloos and tents to protect them from the harshest weather.

The account of the polar party actually begins as spring breaks, and Amundsen notes their progress day by day. They set up small depots all along their route, resting themselves and the dogs at each. They detoured around deep crevasses, climbed mountains, encountered blizzards and marched over terrain where they could not use their skis. Nonetheless, they averaged fifteen miles per day

and reached the South Pole on December 14, 1911. The party remained at the Pole for several days before returning over the same dangerous path to their base camp.

Included in these volumes are a detailed map of Amundsen's trek drawn by Amundsen himself, as well as a wealth of other illustrations. In the appendixes are diagrams of their ship's construction, charts of their meteorological, astronomical, and oceanographic observations, and explanations of the instruments which were used to obtain them. In the second volume there is a lengthy report, written by Lieutenant K. Prestrud, of the group from Amundsen's party that made a concurrent eastward trek while the polar party went south.

The text of both volumes is sprinkled with observations—such as what pleasure the explorers took in the middle of the day to stop for a cup of hot chocolate from a vacuum bottle, or how difficult it can be to concentrate after staring at snow glare for a few hours—that bring home to the reader what an enormously uncomfortable and heroic effort polar exploration really was. — *M.S.S.*

### Additional Recommended Reading

Byrd, Richard E. *Alone*. New York: G. P. Putnam's Sons, 1938. An introspective account of Byrd's solitary manning of a scientific experiment station in Antarctica which describes his physical and mental reactions to the harsh environment.

Kirwan, Laurence P. *A History of Polar Exploration*. New York: W. W. Norton and Company, 1960. A history of the various polar explorers and their motives, starting with the Greeks, with particular emphasis on Shackleton's Antarctic achievements rather than on Amundsen's.

Shackleton, Ernest H. *The Heart of the Antarctic: Being the Story of the British Antarctic Expedition, 1907-1909*. London: William Heineman, 1911. A marvelous narration by the leader of the expedition that came within a hundred miles of attaining the South Pole; also contains many fine black and white plates which give

the reader a good idea of the true conditions which the explorers encountered.
Scott, Robert Falcon. *Scott's Last Expedition: The Journals of Captain R. F. Scott.*
Boston: Beacon Press, 1957. Scott's diaries and notebooks, which were found with
his body and those of his companions on the Ross Ice Shelf in Antarctica.

# THE MEXICAN REVOLUTION

*Type of event:* Political: national conflict which results in a constitutional government
*Time:* The 1910's
*Locale:* Mexico

*Principal personages:*
PORFIRIO DÍAZ (1830-1915), President of Mexico, 1876-1880 and 1884-1911
FRANCISCO INDALECIO MADERO (1873-1913), precipitator of the Mexican Revolution; and President of Mexico, 1911-1913
VICTORIANO DE LA HUERTA (1854-1916), Provisional President of Mexico, 1913-1914
ÁLVARO OBREGÓN (1880-1928), a major figure in the Constitutionalist Movement; and President of Mexico, 1920-1924
VENUSTIANO CARRANZA (1859-1920), leader of the Constitutionalist Movement; and President of Mexico, 1914-1920
FRANCISCO (PANCHO) VILLA (DOROTEO ARANGO) (1877-1923), a popular revolutionary leader in northern Mexico
EMILIANO ZAPATA (1877?-1919), a popular revolutionary leader in southern Mexico
ADOLFO DE LA HUERTA (?-1955), a political leader in Sonora and ally of Obregón; and Provisional President of Mexico, 1920
PLUTARCO ELÍAS CALLES (1877-1945), a political leader in Sonora and ally of Obregón; and President of Mexico, 1924-1928

## Summary of Event

The second decade of the twentieth century included three significant revolutions which have affected world history. These were the Chinese Revolution led by Sun Yat-sen against the Manchu Dynasty; the Russian Revolution led by Vladimir Lenin against the Romanov Monarchy; and the Mexican Revolution precipitated by Francisco Madero against the regime of Porfirio Díaz. In some ways these revolutions had strong similarities. Each was a reaction to an authoritarian ruler who had lost contact with the people. Each was a revolt against a highly centralized but essentially weak regime. Each was a movement to broaden political participation. Each was a rejection of the socioeconomic system which caused a maldistribution of the wealth of the country. Finally, although there might be some nationalistic fervor in the Russian experience, it is clear that in China and Mexico a strong antiforeign sentiment pervaded the revolutionary movement.

In 1876 Mexico had come under

69

the governance of Porfirio Díaz, whose motto had been the restoration of constitutional government. Although his administration was constitutional in the literal sense, there is general agreement that the Mexican government during his reign was autocratic, arbitrary, and repressive. Except for a brief "retirement" from office (1880-1884), Porfirio Díaz ruled Mexico until 1911. His program might be described as one of "scientific" development of Mexico, and he accepted the suppression of the political rights and the denial of the economic rights of large sections of the Mexican society.

To bring about the development of Mexico, Díaz invited the investment of foreign capital under extremely favorable conditions. Foreign investors, especially Americans, happily accepted the invitation. Their economic penetration occurred in the areas of railroads, mining, and, more significantly from the perspective of the Mexican Revolution, in petroleum and land.

Simple figures can best explain the extent of foreign control of the Mexican economy. Between the 1870's and 1910, American investments increased from a few million dollars to over one billion dollars, while the capital investment of other groups approached about one half of that of the United States. At the time of the beginning of the Revolution, investment in petroleum amounted to something in the vicinity of fifteen million dollars. However, petroleum exploitation was the fastest developing sector of the economy, rising in production from about ten thousand barrels in 1901 to more than 12,500,000 barrels in 1911. Moreover, it was an industry which was virtually tax exempt during the Díaz era. Foreign individuals and companies also invested in land, establishing large haciendas, some of which exceeded millions of acres. Despite the economic development and its social ramifications, however, the Mexican Revolution began as a reaction to the suppression of political rights. As such, one could describe the revolution in its initial stage as liberal in character.

As the Díaz regime aged, it became subject to much criticism, particularly for its authoritarian political nature. Whether he believed it or not, as the 1910 election approached, Díaz gave an interview to an American journalist in which he declared that Mexico was ready for a system which included political opposition. In the north, Francisco Madero took the President at his word and declared his candidacy. The Madero family was an established upper-class group which had in the early Díaz years benefited from that regime. However, the Madero family, like others, had become disfranchised and was embittered by that experience. Francisco Madero was a peculiar man. He was very intense—almost a mystic—and obviously took himself seriously. Without question, he wanted to be president. In 1910, he had published a book entitled *Presidential Succession* in which he criticized the Díaz regime and made particular reference to the repeated reelection of the president. The criticism of this practice became a political tenet which is honored to this day: presidents cannot succeed themselves and, since 1929, are permitted to serve only once.

Madero's challenge to Díaz in the election of 1910 can be said to have begun the Mexican Revolution because, when Madero lost, he called the election fraudulent and declared himself in revolt under the Plan of San Luis Potosí, claiming that the people sought political freedom and not bread. The Madero act opened the gates to full-scale opposition to Díaz. In 1911 the regime collapsed, and Díaz went into exile; Francisco Madero was elected the new president. Madero's presidency was ineffectual, in part because his moderate policies satisfied neither the *porfiristas* (supporters of Díaz) nor those intent upon a more comprehensive revolution. In his reluctance to move swiftly, Madero retained and relied upon many of the members of the previous regime. As a result, the Madero presidency did not bring peace and stability, and rebellions occurred throughout his brief administration. Finally, reactionary elements led by General Victoriano Huerta plotted a successful *coup d'état* in February, 1913, in which Madero and his Vice President were murdered.

General Huerta, in his attempt to reestablish the old regime, caused immediate reaction in several sections of the country. The most significant of these were the Zapata revolt in the south, the Villa-led uprising in the north, and the Constitutionalist revolt in the north which ultimately assumed legitimate power in Mexico. Indeed, the reaction to Huerta was so universal that, at one time, more than two hundred "Revolutionary" groups claimed to be the legitimate government of Mexico.

The armed uprisings against Huerta can only loosely be called coordinated. Each leader or group had his or its own ambitions and plans. Emiliano Zapata, who remains a mythical figure in Mexico, issued his Plan of Ayala which called for major agrarian reform. This revolt was centered in the southern state of Morelos, and was essentially an Indian- and peasant-based action, although some of its leaders were influential in the Carranza government after the death of Zapata. Francisco Villa, better-known as "Pancho," led his personal revolt from the northern Mexican state of Chihuahua. Although he fought along with Venustiano Carranza, the leader of the Constitutionalists, Villa was actually associated with the *Carrancistas* rather than allied with them. Carranza, who led the third important group, issued the Plan of Guadalupe, which called for the restoration of constitutional government in keeping with Madero's Plan of San Luis Potosí.

Together, these three men reflect the roots of the enormous struggle which is called the Mexican Revolution. Zapata was of Indian extraction, and his family had long played a leadership role in their community. Villa, whose real name was Doroteo Arango, was of mixed blood and uncertain of his origins. Although he is often described as a bandit, he had a personal magnetism and ambition which caused him to join forces with other revolutionists in an attempt to seize political power. Carranza, a man of Spanish extraction from the upper class, was above all else an ardent Mexican nationalist. His followers possessed the most talent and organizational skill of any revolutionary group.

These revolutionary forces worked to overthrow Huerta, and with the aid of the lifting of the arms embargo by the United States, they were successful, and collectively took over the government in August, 1914. But within a short time, the leaders of these factions began to fight among themselves. Although they cannot be said to have joined forces, for a time Villa and Zapata acted against Carranza and, for a short period from December, 1914, to January, 1915, occupied Mexico City.

However, Carranza and the Constitutionalists were to prevail because of two factors. One was the extraordinary talent of Carranza's ally Álvaro Obregón. As a military leader, Obregón was responsible for the defeat of Villa in April, 1915, and became known as the Hero of Celaya. He also had enormous political skills which he used to influence such groups as the emerging Mexican labor movement to join with the Constitutionalists. The other decisive factor in Carranza's success was the decision of the Woodrow Wilson Administration to extend *de facto* recognition to his regime in October, 1915. This latter action has been cited as the cause of the notorious Villa raid on Columbus, New Mexico, which led to the famous Pershing Expedition of 1916-1917. It is safe to say, however, that the defeat of Villa at Celaya and the recognition of Carranza by the United States mark the ascendancy of the Constitutionalists and therefore the turning point in the Mexican Revolution.

Carranza, who never exercised authority throughout all of Mexico, did proceed to consolidate his power. Most spectacularly, in the autumn of 1916, he authorized the calling of a constitutional convention to translate the Plan of San Luis Potosí into a basic law and program for Mexico. The Constitutional Convention went well beyond the plan and incorporated some of the more revolutionary ideas, including land reform, labor reform, reform of the extractive industries, anticlerical reform, and ardent nationalism. This new constitution, which took effect in May, 1917, went well beyond the claim of Madero that all Mexicans wanted was political freedom. It established the first major modern socioeconomic instrument for the transformation of society.

Among the more significant provisions of the Constitution of 1917 are Article 27, which dealt with many of the basic socioeconomic demands of the Revolution, and Article 123, which dealt with the rights of labor. It has been claimed that the radical nature of the new constitution was the work of members closely associated with Obregón. There is ample evidence, however, that Carranza, despite his association with much of the reform, was not committed to the realization of many of the radical goals incorporated into the Constitution. He was criticized for not fulfilling many of the promises which he had made since 1913; and he was also blamed for the lack of stability and order in the country, as civil war, banditry, and corruption continued in the country throughout his administration. Carranza can be called a true follower of

Madero, unlike persons such as Obregón and Zapata, the latter having originally revolted against Madero because of the president's failure to carry out agrarian reform.

Carranza had other difficulties as well. Villa and Zapata remained armed challengers of his authority, and the President did not have the assistance of Obregón and Plutarco Calles, who had left his government and retired to Sonora. In 1919, Carranza "solved" the Zapata problem by permitting Zapata's assassination at the hands of his lieutenants; the elimination of the Villa problem had to await a new regime.

Carranza also suffered strong opposition from reactionary elements led by Felix Díaz, a nephew of Porfirio Díaz. These elements worked to attempt to overthrow Carranza and reestablish order as known in the pre-1910 period. But Carranza was intent upon resisting all opposition and upon retaining political power. However, since the Constitution prohibited presidents to succeed themselves, Carranza selected a surrogate in Ignacio Bonillas, Mexico's Ambassador to the United States; he planned to have Bonillas succeed him on December 1, 1920.

This decision was a tragic error. The logical candidate for the presidency was Álvaro Obregón. Here was a national hero known in Mexico as a "genius in war and peace." Obregón had announced his own candidacy in June, 1919. In an attempt to frustrate that candidacy, Carranza ordered federal troops to move into Sonora, which was the base of Obregón's power; as a result, within two days a new revolutionary movement emerged. Led by the so-called "Sonora Clique" of Obregón, Calles, and Adolfo de la Huerta, who was Governor of Sonora, a political program was drawn up.

Known as the Plan of Agua Prieta and proclaimed on April 23, 1920, the program declared that Carranza was attempting to impose a president upon the Mexican people by use of force and that he had violated the sovereignity of the states of Mexico. He was declared unfit for office; the revolutionaries moved to seize power and appoint a provisional president to serve until elections could be held. The Plan of Agua Prieta achieved wide support and immediate success. Carranza fled the capital and was killed by pursuing forces on May 21, 1920. Adolfo de la Huerta was installed as provisional president until November 30, 1920; it was he who made an accommodation with Villa which brought an end to the latter's antigovernment activities.

Meanwhile, Obregón, who was then forty, was elected president and formally assumed the office on December 1, 1920. He had great natural ability and was greatly respected by his contemporaries. His election marked the end of the Mexican Revolution; his government brought calm to the country and compliance to the purposes of the Revolution. The tasks of the Obregón Administration were not simple or easy: pacification of the countryside; reform of the society; consolidation of power; and attaining the recognition of his government by the United States. When he left office in 1924, Obregón could claim a great deal of success. The political threat to the new stability of the regime was eliminated by the defeat of the de la Huerta uprising and the assassination of Pancho Villa in 1923; and the United States extended recognition to his government in that same year. Although the fundamental reforms had not been fully accomplished, a base had been established from which future administrations might and did take major actions.

The Revolution, which began with the attempt of Madero to succeed Díaz as president of Mexico, unleashed a reform movement which led to the socioeconomic and political reorganization of Mexico. Although there is some question as to the degree of success of the Revolution in transforming Mexican society, there were some evidences of real change. The government of Mexico had been popularized; the heirs to power were those of the middle class represented by Obregón. Political authority was transferred from those of Spanish extraction to the Mexican of Mestizo background. Land was redistributed most dramatically by Lázaro Cárdenas, who was President from 1934 to 1940.

The nationalism which was so important to Mexico was the Revolution's greatest achievement. In the Constitution of 1917, Mexico attempted to rid itself of the claim that it was "Mother to the foreigner and step-mother to the Mexican." This change was accomplished in steps, the latest being the expropriation of the oil industry in 1938. Therefore, while the political aspects of the Revolution of 1910 can be said to have come to an end in 1920, the socioeconomic aspects took longer to be realized. Indeed, there are some in Mexico and elsewhere who claim that the Revolution of 1910 has not yet ended.

## Pertinent Literature

Cumberland, Charles Curtis. *Mexican Revolution: The Constitutionalist Years*. Austin: University of Texas Press, 1972.

Charles Cumberland had no responsibility for the title of this book, which was chosen by David Bailey, who completed the work after Cumberland's death. A more appropriate title might have been *The Mexican Revolution: Prosecution Under Carranza*. This work lacks any analysis of the Villa movement, the Zapata Revolt, or even the reactionary efforts of Felix Díaz. It is difficult to believe that Cumberland would not have returned to the period to study the other movements which have done so much to shape modern Mexico.

Cumberland began his work by examining the forces which reacted to the overthrow of Porfirio Díaz. The victor, Francisco Madero, could not overcome the four most powerful interest groups which had supported the previous dictator: the landed groups, the military, the entreprenurial class, and foreigners—symbolized by Americans. All these factions worked to overthrow Madero. Finally, the army under Victoriano Huerta removed the government and General Huerta became president.

Among his major opponents was Venustiano Carranza, whose opposition to Huerta seemed ambiguous. Cumberland's book suggests that it was a delaying tactic to allow Carranza to collect his scattered forces and gather needed money to support his fight.

The following four chapters deal with various aspects of the resistance to Huerta. Military efforts against Huerta were centered in the north of Mexico; the author argues that Zapata in the south was not central to the Revolution. The true hero was Álvaro Obregón, and the villain was Huerta, who was doomed because he failed militarily. On the political front, Huerta was unsuccessful in establishing a legal government; he climaxed a series of unpopular moves by dissolving the Congress. Perhaps the major cause for the demise of the Huerta regime was the refusal of President Wilson to recognize his government; Wilson wanted Huerta out of office, and he helped the rebellion by lifting the arms embargo.

Huerta's demise might have occurred sooner if the American occupation of Vera Cruz had not helped to keep Huerta in power for a few more months. In the end, the success of the Constitutionalists, particularly under Obregón, whom Cumberland calls the greatest military mind in Mexican history, was assured. Huerta resigned and fled the country, and on August 20, 1914, Carranza entered Mexico City.

The arrival of Carranza in Mexico City began the "Constitutionalist" years. Almost immediately, the war of the winners began; the main contestants were Villa and Zapata against Carranza. At Aguascalientes, a convention was called which ultimately declared Carranza to be in rebellion. Some revolutionary leaders joined the Conventionists, but Obregón stayed with Carranza. After defeating Zapata's forces, Obregón turned to deal with Villa. In April, 1915, Obregón was victorious in the battles at Celaya, and Villa's military and political powers began their steady decline. The resolution of the conflict was slow. Opposition forces tended to fade away, and the Constitutionalists emerged as the power.

In Chapter Seven, Cumberland attempts to describe the real revolution which had occurred. There were six areas of major change in this period. First was the issue of Church and state. Clergymen were persecuted; Church lands were confiscated; the religious were exiled or executed; and the Church was to be excluded from education. A second change was in land tenure. All leaders were interested in land reform, particularly regarding the subsoil question as it affected petroleum. Related to this question was the foreign influence problem and the problem of national control. Major changes also took place in labor, education, and politics. Constitutionalists accepted a labor program for political reasons. Education was to be national and freed of all foreign influence. In the political realm the real revolution came in the arrival of the middle class, exemplified by Obregón, which assumed political power.

Cumberland next examines the search for recognition of the Carranza government, particularly by the United States. Carranza did everything he could to assure Americans that their interests would be protected, but his nationalist fervor created difficulty. Despite attempts to find other solutions, President Wilson extended *de facto* recognition to Carranza in October, 1915.

In June, 1916, Carranza called for a constitutional convention in which the selection process favored those allied with Carranza or Obregón. Only the *Porfiristas* were excluded; the *Obregónistas* controlled the committees that wrote the constitution. The six major areas of change mentioned above were included in their final draft. Most significantly, the constitution accepted a positive role for government in social and economic affairs.

The final chapter deals with Carranza's inability to live with the Constitution of 1917. Carranza tried to frustrate the realization of change in the six major areas. The real problem was the presidential succession in 1920: Carranza wanted his own man, although Obregón was the logical choice. In an effort to remove Obregón as a candidate, Carranza tried to destroy his political base, and in so doing, revived the rebellion. The year 1920 marks the end of the Revolution and the end of the "Constitutionalist Years." Obregón was elected president of Mexico and proceeded with the resolution of his country's major problems.

Brenner, Anita. *The Wind That Swept Mexico: The History of the Mexican Revolution, 1910-1942.* Austin: University of Texas Press, 1971.

This extraordinary work by Anita Brenner and George Leighton was originally published in 1943. Most impressive is the collection of 184 photographs of the revolutionary period by George Leighton, which are accompanied by individual commentaries that effectively tell the story of the Mexican Revolution as interpreted by the authors. To call this work an amazing pictorial history does not diminish the text which is an integral part of the work. Text and photographs tell a complete and fascinating story, while the photographic collection reflects the generally accepted interpretation of the origins of the Mexican Revolution. Although the title suggests a starting date of 1910, the photographic essay begins well before during the regime of Porfirio Díaz and then proceeds to complement the textual narrative to 1942.

Brenner's text follows an accepted American interpretation of the Mexican Revolution which finds its major causes in the philosophy and policy of the Díaz regime, which favored progress at all costs. There are, however, some interesting variations in interpretation. The author emphasizes economic issues and their consequent social effects; she places great responsibility upon the foreign influence in Mexico and upon the "scientific" management of public policy which made Mexico the reputed mother of foreigners and the stepmother of Mexicans; and she emphasizes the socioeconomic dislocations which were enforced by ruthless police power. Neither anticlericism nor antimilitarism appear to her to have been precipitating forces.

Brenner sees in the course of the Revolution the myths of ancient Indian culture being invoked; one example is the sign of the gods' dissatisfaction given by the eruption of a volcano. The author sees a great chasm between the myths of the Díaz regime and those of the great masses of Mexicans, and believes that in the end, it was the collapse of the new myths rather than the strength of the old myths which brought on the Revolution.

In relating the actual events of the Revolution, Brenner follows a traditional narrative approach. She identifies four men as the principal actors, including Francisco Madero, Pancho Villa, and Emiliano Zapata. Brenner does not view Madero as truly revolutionary, but instead believes the Maderos to have been selfishly motivated to protect certain economic interests of their family. Villa is credited with playing a dominant military role at least until the battles at Celaya in 1915. In the south, Brenner focuses on the revolution led by Zapata, in which she sees a real revolutionary movement. She emphasizes the intellectual influence upon Zapata of Andrés Molina Enríquez, who wrote the single most significant political tract of the Revolution: *Los Grandes Problemas Nacionales* (1909). The last "actor" is really a compound of Venustiano Carranza and Álvaro Obregón.

All these men struggled to defeat Díaz and then continued the struggle against one another until Carranza won. Brenner does not see Carranza as a truly revolutionary figure and feels that his demise offered a chance for the Revolution to succeed.

At this point, the author takes an interpretive position which has been a center of controversy. Some suggest that the Revolution ended in 1920, but Brenner takes the position that the Revolution was an ongoing phenomenon. Therefore, she views the political history of Mexico from 1920 to 1942 in terms of the principles of the Revolution. She sees progress as uneven, and identifies the major frustrator of the Revolution as Plutarco Calles, who was President from 1924 to 1928 and who attempted to wield power even after he left office. The major contributor to the goals of the Revolution was Lázaro Cárdenas, who was President from 1934-1940. In each case, Brenner's judgment is based on how each president dealt with the economic and antiforeign issues.

Mexican leaders repeatedly claimed that the Revolution was over. Brenner argues that they were wrong, since new leaders took up the cause. Finally, Brenner finds in the Mexican experience a democratic cause to which the United States should be sympathetic and supportive.
— *D.D.D.*

## Additional Recommended Reading

Cumberland, Charles Curtis. *Mexican Revolution, Genesis Under Madero*. Austin: University of Texas Press, 1952. A scholarly and well-documented companion to *Mexican Revolution: The Constitutionalist Years* which examines the sources of the Revolution in the Díaz Regime and the reactionary "tiger" unleashed by Madero which precipitated the Civil War of 1910-1920.

Womack, John. *Zapata and the Mexican Revolution*. New York: Alfred A. Knopf, 1969. A compelling and persuasive history of the Mexican Revolution in the south.

Beals, Carleton. *Porfirio Díaz, Dictator of Mexico*. Philadelphia: J. B. Lippincott Company, 1932. Beals' study remains the best, most objective biography of Díaz; the negative tone of the work reflects the general assessment of Díaz among scholars in the United States.

Quirk, Robert E. *The Mexican Revolution, 1914-1915: The Convention at Aquascalientes*. Bloomington: Indiana University Press, 1960. An excellent study of a very critical event in the Mexican Revolution.

Ross, Stanley R., ed. *Is the Mexican Revolution Dead?* Philadelphia: Temple University Press, 1975. Argues that the Mexican Revolution never achieved its purposes.

Clendenen, Clarence C. *The United States and Pancho Villa: A Study in Unconventional Diplomacy*. Ithaca, N.Y.: Cornell University Press, 1961. Claims that Villa was a friend of the United States up to the time of Carranza's recognition by Wilson; Villa is portrayed as an intelligent, true revolutionary who joined the Madero revolution for the good of Mexico.

Rouveral, Jean. *Pancho Villa: A Biography*. Garden City, N.Y.: Doubleday & Company, 1972. A popular study, favorable to Villa, which argues that Villa was loyal to the Revolution.

Meyer, Michael C. *Huerta: A Political Portrait*. Lincoln: University of Nebraska Press, 1972. An attempt to present an objective view of Victoriano Huerta; Meyer seems to overreact in his effort to counterbalance his subject's historical reputation.

# BERTRAND RUSSELL AND ALFRED NORTH WHITEHEAD PUBLISH *PRINCIPIA MATHEMATICA*

*Type of event:* Intellectual: attempt to recast the concept of mathematical relations
*Time:* 1910-1913
*Locale:* England

*Principal personages:*

BERTRAND ARTHUR WILLIAM RUSSELL (1872-1970), British mathematician, philosopher, and author

ALFRED NORTH WHITEHEAD (1861-1945), Anglo-American teacher and philosopher

## Summary of Event

The *Principia Mathematica* is one of the most respected intellectual achievements of the twentieth century; yet, almost all of its conclusions were challenged within a decade of its publication, and few scholars agree with its ideas today. The three volumes of the *Principia Mathematica* rank among the most admired mistakes in history. Bertrand Russell and Alfred North Whitehead have awed academics not through what they accomplished, but through what they set out to accomplish. They sought to reorder the fundamental premises of mathematics and to tie logically these premises to the abstract structure of philosophy. The reasons which led them to make this ambitious attempt, and which doomed their project to failure, are not interesting only to the logician. They also tell us a great deal about the age in which Russell and Whitehead lived.

The Victorian age is commonly regarded by the sophisticated present as a period of restraint, dullness, and morality. To most nineteenth century writers, however, the dominant mood of the time was the ongoing sensation of forward movement—of "progress." Then, as now, there was evident and rapid advancement in technology: the inventions of locomotive, telegraph, sewing machine, mass-produced steel, typewriter, telephone, and light bulb followed one another with increasing speed. But in nineteenth century England, in contrast to modern society, technological progress was overshadowed by economic, social, and political progress. The Industrial Revolution was in full swing, rapidly transforming England from a rural to an urban nation, and, toward the end of the century, visibly raising the general standard of living. English society became more and more open as the vestiges of feudal practices dropped away and those without aristocratic blood succeeded in joining the governing class. Disabilities and discrimination against Protestant dissenters, then Catholics, and then Jews, were abolished one by one. In a series of climactic "Reform Bills," parliament gradually extended the right to vote and restricted the power of the House of Lords.

There were many throughout this

79

period who insisted that this progress was not progress at all, but a rapid disintegration of tradition and stability that would push the country to disaster. Widespread revolutions throughout continental Europe seemed to justify their fears. But in England itself, change seemed only to enhance the nation's stability and expand the power of the British Empire. Liberal, "forward-thinking" people were convinced that theirs was the best of times, and that it would become steadily better.

This faith in improvement pervaded the sciences. In almost every field, steady advances foreshadowed the appearance of new, overarching theories which brought mankind closer to understanding the order of the universe. In chemistry, the rise of atomic theory seemed to provide an important part of this order. By assuming that all matter was composed of tiny, indivisible atoms, it was possible to explain in precise terms any chemical transformation—such as the change of burning wood into ashes and carbon dioxide. In physics, the Victorian period brought rapid new advances in electricity, magnetism, and mechanics. James Clerk Maxwell and others developed exciting new theories which seemed to tie these fields together; by the end of the nineteenth century, most physicists in England had concluded that all important questions in physics would soon be quite definitively solved. In biology, the new Darwinian theories seemed to solve many of the most basic riddles behind life itself, and brought a public awareness of the advances of science.

Such was the environment in which rising young scholars were reared and instructed; the "advancement of science" became their universal goal. One of the most promising of the young scholars was Alfred North Whitehead, who was born in a rural corner of western England in 1861—two years after the publication of Darwin's *On the Origin of Species*. His father was a vicar and local schoolmaster; in earlier times Whitehead probably would have followed in this path, but his early years showed the new possibilities of English society. Through hard work, he achieved entrance into a good school, and eventually he won a scholarship to Trinity College at Cambridge University—one of the most prestigious centers of learning in England. At Cambridge Whitehead was again successful, and upon graduation he became a Fellow of the College and a respected professor. In his early career, Whitehead's main interest was teaching; he particularly sought to bring out hidden talents in his students. In the fall of 1889, he administered the math scholarship exams for entrance to Trinity. Only one scholarship was available, and one of the students had clearly superior marks. But Whitehead was intrigued by another student, who was poorly prepared but seemed to have a better mind. Whitehead finally decided in favor of the second student, and Bertrand Russell was thus admitted to Cambridge University.

Russell's background was wildly different from that of Whitehead. Grandson of a Prime Minister and Earl, Russell was orphaned at the age of four and reared in a wealthy but isolated environment, tutored at home and substituting the pursuit of math for friendships. At Cambridge, Russell slowly blossomed from a shy boy to a brilliant young thinker. He studied under a wide variety of mathematicians and philosophers and formed a strong friendship with Whitehead. Russell also was made a Trinity Fellow, and the two men both began serious mathematical work in the mid-1890's.

They were puzzled by the course of mathematical thought in the nineteenth century. Unlike the other sciences, math theories had not become steadily more simple and all-embracing; if anything, the field was becoming complex and even irrational. Non-Euclidean geometry, for example, showed that the simple, commonsense principles of geometry were relevant only to one specific set of assumptions about space. If one assumed instead that the shortest distance between two points was *not* a line, then an entirely new set of axioms and geometric theories resulted which could be neither proven nor disproven. Several mathematicians were developing a new field around the concept of the "infinite," which they maintained had a different set of properties from those applied to anything which could be assigned a number, however large. An array of findings such as these were exciting, since they threw new perspective on old problems, but they seemed to be moving mathematics not in the direction of progress, but in the direction of the bizarre. As such, the field posed a challenge to the Victorian mind.

Whitehead and Russell accepted the challenge. Although both men were mathematicians, they were also drawn to philosophy. They noticed that philosophers were developing sophisticated methods for linking various philosophical questions through logic, and they suspected that logical analysis might be the best tool for developing a broad mathematical theory. Russell's first mathematical work, *An Essay on the Foundations of Geometry*, followed these lines, brilliantly examining the philosophical assumptions underpinning geometric thought. For several years, the two men continued to exchange letters and papers expanding upon this type of thinking.

In July, 1900, Russell and Whitehead attended a Paris conference of European philosophers. In the course of the conference discussions, Russell observed that Guiseppe Peano, an eminent Italian mathematician, seemed to get the better of any argument upon which he embarked. Russell suspected that Peano was successful because of his system of logical notation, of which Russell had heard but which he had not mastered. Upon returning to England, Russell quickly read all of Peano's works. He was delighted; here was just the sort of system that Whitehead and he had been looking for—a method for rebuilding the foundations of mathematics. He drafted some of the possible applications of the method and communicated these to Whitehead, and the two men quickly agreed to embark upon a major work: the *Principia Mathematica*, a work which they hoped would recast the entire field of mathematics and put it on an equal footing of progress with the other sciences.

The method for this ambitious effort was based upon an elaboration of Peano's logical system, and was called by Russell the "logic of relations." It maintained that the various ideas of mathematics could be thought of in terms of classes, and that these classes could be logically related to one another. For example, the ideas represented by numbers (such as one, two, and three) could be expressed as classes; the number "three" represented "the class of all classes with three members." A sequence of numbers could be presented as one of many classes with a particular order. By applying these principles to much more complex ideas, an analysis of mathematical relations was feasible.

Or at least it *seemed* feasible. In mid-1901, Russell encountered a paradox in the method which threatened to destroy the entire system. One day, almost by accident, Russell casually considered the application of "class" analysis to classes themselves. All classes, he knew, could be divided into two groups: those classes which are members of themselves (such as the class of classes with at least one member), and those classes—the great majority—which are not members of themselves (such as the class of all people). This second group of classes could be logically expressed as "the class of all classes which are not members of themselves." Suddenly, Russell posed to himself an insoluble question: was this class a member of itself, or not? Either a "yes" or a "no" answer was self-contradictory; and the more Russell tried to solve the paradox, the more he realized that it could invalidate the whole method of class analysis.

Russell, with Whitehead's assistance, ultimately found a makeshift way around the contradiction, but other difficulties continued to crop up. The project dragged on for another twelve years, and in the enormous, sustained effort of making their theory comprehensive, Whitehead and Russell placed themselves under incredible strain. Russell occasionally contemplated suicide to escape the work; Whitehead would scribble logical equations for hours on sheet after sheet of paper, completely oblivious to anything around him. In the end, both men were somewhat skeptical of their own conclusions. Other mathematicians found the specifics of the *Principia Mathematica* dazzling and ingenious, but its general structure of mathematical thought never received very wide support. It was generally decided that *no* general system of mathematical analysis was possible.

The *Principia Mathematica* was not the only work which suffered from increasing skepticism. In 1900, when Russell and Whitehead began their analysis, their attempt symbolized the steady and confident advance of thought in every field. By 1913, when the final volume of the *Principia Mathematica* was published, its disappointing reception epitomized a series of developments in many fields. Eight years before, Albert Einstein had published his first work on relativity, which threw doubt upon the entire structure of physics and suggested (and later proved) that the Laws of Motion developed by Newton were not entirely correct. In 1911, Ernest Rutherford and other physicists showed that most of the space occupied by atoms was "empty," and that atoms were not indivisible at all, but were composed of protons, electrons, and other particles. Immediately, the comprehensive structure of chemistry was also thrown into doubt. The work of Russell and Whitehead seemed to be yet another confirmation that the Victorian confidence in unlimited progress was unjustified and that the limits to man's understanding would eventually be reached.

As science and society shared in the rapid sense of progress in the nineteenth century, so they shared the disillusion of the twentieth. The beginning of World War I in 1914 shattered hopes of permanent peace and reason between nations; the Depression showed the dangers of dependence on an industrial economy and dampened hopes of permanent economic growth. The outcome of the *Principia Mathematica* was, perhaps, foreordained by the circumstances in which the work was written; for as men lost their faith in progress, they lost the sublime confidence which made the search for underlying truths possible.

## Pertinent Literature

Whitehead, Alfred North. *Science and the Modern World*. New York: The Macmillan Company, 1925.

When the *Principia Mathematica* was finally completed in 1913, both Whitehead and Russell felt they had made their major career contribution to knowledge. Strangely enough, both men were wrong. Perhaps because of the effort and the disappointments of their mathematical work, Whitehead and Russell each turned to other subjects in later life and won renown for the unusual breadth of insight they brought to these areas.

By the end of World War I, Whitehead was in his late fifties, and he was surprised to receive an offer from Harvard University to come and teach in the United States. He reluctantly accepted an appointment of a few years, but soon found that the new appointment gave him opportunity to explore various philosophical questions which had long interested him. He eventually decided to remain in America, and lived on for a full twenty-five years, dying in 1945 at the age of eighty-four. The first major product of his years at Harvard became his most famous book, widely influencing not only scholars but also the general public. The work was called *Science and the Modern World*, and it arose from a series of lectures Whitehead gave in the spring of 1925 on the nature of scientific thought.

*Science and the Modern World* addresses a great many complex issues, but two aspects of the book are very interesting in the context of Whitehead's work on the *Principia Mathematica*. First is the nature of the book itself, which is philosophical rather than mathematical. Though Whitehead attempts to explain and relate various ideas, he no longer attempts to do so through the precise notation and logical analysis used in his earlier work. There is a sense in *Science and the Modern World* that

Whitehead has concluded that there are sharp limits to what can be precisely known, and that wisdom is more attainable through flashes of intuitive insight than through the rigors of deductive logic.

The second interesting feature of the book is Whitehead's objectivity. He evaluates such subjects as God, social progress, and the value of science with remarkable detachment, expressing an opinion but carefully explaining a number of other opinions as well. Moreover, he examines how mankind's conceptions have changed from one period to another, and the direction in which they seem to be moving in the twentieth century. This approach is a departure from the attitude behind the *Principia Mathematica*, in which Whitehead and Russell showed a willingness and a confidence to compress a multitude of ideas into a single, logical system. In *Science and the Modern World*, Whitehead instead shows a careful delicacy in handling various points of view, and there is at times a sense that he considers each view, under its circumstances, equally valid. Since the time of Whitehead's lectures, such objectivity and such candid acceptance of the subjectivity of knowledge have become nearly universal among writers. Indeed, society's current tolerance of diverse religious, political, and theoretical thought has become one of the most widespread characteristics of our time. Whitehead's work thus has a special relevance, for, just as the *Principia Mathematica* was a culmination of the thinking of one age, so *Science and the Modern World* was a forerunner of the thinking of the next.

Russell, Bertrand. *Mysticism and Logic.* New York: W. W. Norton and Company, 1929.

The later career of Bertrand Russell was perhaps even more distinguished than that of Whitehead; it was certainly more tumultuous. Whereas the writing of the *Principia Mathematica* influenced Whitehead's intellectual direction, it radically changed Russell's entire approach to life.

In the course of working on the system of logical analysis, Russell developed at once a sense of the absolute need for making such intellectual efforts, but also a realization that his life as a quiet academic was completely irrelevant to the larger problems of the world. These changes led him to fall out of love with his wife, Alys Russell, and to drift gradually into political activism. With the outbreak of World War I in 1914, he became a fervent pacifist and the leader of the antiwar movement in England; he was first fined and then jailed for writing antiwar pamphlets.

After the war he remarried, traveled to the new Soviet Union and the Republic of China, and began writing a series of books on social issues in which he advocated such then-scandalous ideas as agnosticism, premarital sex, nonclassical education, and redistribution of wealth. With his second wife, Dora Black, he established an experimental school in southwest England. During this period Russell was, in comparison with his earlier life, a social outcast. He was no longer welcome at Cambridge University, where he had lived and taught for so many years; many of his old friends now rejected him; his income was dependent upon producing a steady stream of popular articles.

*Mysticism and Logic* was one of Russell's few works during this difficult period that dealt with mathematical issues. It is also an eloquent statement of resolute independence. Part of the work was a restatement and defense of Russell's earlier mathematical ideas. Another portion dealt with the problem of objective thought which had been raised by Whitehead and other philosophers. Russell conceded that logic could not deal with all questions: it could not resolve ethical issues, nor could it show the purpose of human effort. Mysticism and intuition must be relied upon for those questions. But Russell insisted that "scientific" philosophy—that is, philosophy which avoided moral questions and used logical methods— could come "nearer to objectivity than any other human pursuit." But the underlying problem remained in the disillusioned years of the 1920's: why pursue objectivity at all?

In another chapter of *Mysticism and Logic*, Russell attempted to answer this question. "The Free Man's Worship" is an intuitive probing of some of the most fundamental questions of life. Suppose, asks Russell, that logic is true and scientific investigation valid. The world that science presents to man is completely devoid of purpose. It suggests "that Man is the product of causes which had no prevision of the end they were achieving; that his origin, his growth, his hopes and fears, his loves and his beliefs, are but the outcome of accidental collocations of atoms. . . ." If all this is true, then what reason or meaning is there in the "progress" of science? For many, this observation is sufficient reason to turn from science and entrust one's fate and purpose to God. For Russell, however, the findings of science are not so easily avoided; they must be dealt with through a mysticism that is consistent with logic.

The free man's worship, then, is stolid resolution in the face of apparent purposelessness. It is the admission that man's role in the universe is tiny and perhaps irrelevant, but that man can nonetheless understand his environment, and thus, at least partly, free himself from the heedless march of time. Though Russell and his ideas became popular and fashionable in the decades after World War II, he always felt that continual searching and questioning were the only real guarantees of civilization. — *R.H.S.*

## Additional Recommended Reading

Kasner, Edward and James Newman. *Mathematics and the Imagination*. New York: Simon and Schuster, 1940. A lively and well-written discussion of mathematical problems, understandable to the layman but concerned with fairly complex issues, including many of the ideas involved in the *Principia Mathematica*.

Lawrence, Nathaniel. *Alfred North Whitehead*. New York: Twayne Publishers, 1966.

Provides a brief biography of Whitehead and considers some of his philosophical works.

Russell, Bertrand. *The Autobiography of Bertrand Russell*. 3 vols. Boston: Little, Brown and Company, 1967-1969. Russell's three-volume autobiography is one of the best ever written: fair, eminently readable, witty, and full of observations about the times and places in which Russell lived.

——————— . *Introduction to Mathematical Philosophy*. London: George Allen and Unwin, 1919. A clear but complex discussion of mathematical philosophy and logical analysis.

Strachey, Lytton. *Eminent Victorians: Cardinal Manning, Dr. Arnold, Florence Nightingale, General Gordon*. New York: Modern Library, 1918. An interesting and entertaining book about the people and culture of Victorian England.

# ESTABLISHMENT OF
# THE UNION OF SOUTH AFRICA

*Type of event:* Political: creation of a white supremacist state in South Africa
*Time:* 1910
*Locale:* South Africa

*Principal personages:*

SIR ALFRED MILNER (1854-1925), Great Britain's High Commissioner for South Africa

GENERAL HORATIO HERBERT KITCHENER (EARL KITCHENER OF KHARTOUM AND OF BROOME) (1850-1916), British Commander in Chief in the Boer War and negotiator for Britain in the postwar period

JOSEPH CHAMBERLAIN (1836-1914), Great Britain's Secretary of State for the Colonies

LOUIS BOTHA (1862-1919), Prime Minister of the Transvaal and cofounder of *Het Volk* in 1904

JAN CHRISTIAN SMUTS (1870-1950), State Attorney for the Cape Colony and cofounder of *Het Volk*

J. T. JAVABU, one of the first black leaders in the Native Convention (later the African National Congress)

## Summary of Event

The two most serious problems within South Africa in the nineteenth century were political unity between the whites, and what the whites (South Africans of English and Dutch descent) called "native policy." The end of the Boer War in 1902 (or what the Boers called the Second War of Freedom and the Africans called "the White Man's War") left Britain as victor in a double bind. How was victory to promise British supremacy in a land where Africans outnumbered whites, and where Afrikaners, now the vanquished, outnumbered whites of English origin? Furthermore, both parties in Great Britain agreed that established white communities in the British Empire should run their own affairs.

Britain's High Commissioner for South Africa, Sir Alfred Milner, had a solution: namely, "a self-governing white Community, supported by well-treated and justly governed black labour from Cape Town to Zambesi." In order to assure that white South Africans remained loyal to the British Empire, Milner proposed massive British immigration to the South African gold fields and the "denationalization" of the Afrikaners. Whereas General Horatio Herbert Kitchener, the British Commander in Chief in the Boer War, and Secretary of State for the Colonies Joseph Chamberlain wanted to treat both the Boers (Afrikaners) and the Africans (Blacks and Coloreds) more liberally, the views of British High Commissioner for South Africa Alfred Milner momentarily prevailed at the Treaty of

Vereeniging in 1902. However, because of the postwar recession, little British immigration materialized, and the treaty with its accompanying diplomacy had the effect of making the Afrikaners even more nationalistic than before. Hence, the British government adopted a conciliatory policy of Anglo-Dutch equality. But even so, a new Afrikaner emerged in the postwar period: the war hero-progressive farmer with education and political savvy.

Louis Botha was such a man; so was Jan Smuts. Both were guerrilla leaders turned politicians. Botha, the progressive farmer, differed from Jan Smuts, the cosmopolitan intellectual lawyer. But they complemented each other and became the twin architects of their policy of conciliation epitomized in the founding in 1905 of *Het Volk* (*The People*) which stood for Afrikaner self-government within the context of conciliation to be realized on four levels. First, Afrikaners were to be reconciled to one another, and second to citizens of British descent. Third, regional disputes would be solved by joining the British colonies of Cape and Natal with the Boer colonies of Transvaal and the Orange Free State into a union based on the principles of conciliation. The fourth level dealt with external relations and was aimed at South African national fulfillment within a liberalized empire.

By 1908, Botha and Smuts had almost convinced leaders of the South African colonies that conciliation could be politically rewarding and morally sound. For some (especially religious conservatives), conciliation was dangerously radical. For the majority of

South Africa's people, however, conciliation was a white solution to a white problem. The most liberal white sentiment in the most liberal colony (the Cape) preferred a modified version of the Cape's own system—"a uniform, colour-blind franchise which would not endanger white supremacy because the vast majority of those who qualified would be white men, but would nevertheless provide a safety valve." Smuts's response to the Cape's solution was prophetic for South Africa's future: "It ought to be the policy of all parties to do justice to the Natives and to take all wise and prudent measures for their civilization and improvement. But I don't believe in politics for them."

Among the white minority, the idea of union had become feasible by 1907, and for many union was given top priority since the economic and political factors (a Zulu rebellion in Natal) encouraged a sense of urgency. Imperialists wanted union to lessen intercolony conflicts and to facilitate positive British influence; they argued that a unified and peaceful South Africa might attract large numbers of Britons and fulfill Milner's dream of a British electoral majority. Antiimperialists in all four colonies, on the other hand, viewed unification as a consolidation of South Africa's white communities against imperial interference.

At last, eight years after the Peace of Vereeniging, the Union of South Africa was formed on May 31, 1910. All four colonies—Natal, the Orange Free State, the Transvaal, and the Cape—joined the Union of South Africa, leaving Britain with the "native territories" of Bechuanaland,

Basutoland, Swaziland, and Northern and Southern Rhodesia.

The principal guarantees of the Act of Union were for the white population, and the hottest controversy that nearly wrecked the convention and almost rendered the Union stillborn was not in relationship to the rights of the majority black population, but over the question of the distribution of power within the white community. The two major problems involved the electoral system and the language question. The decision to treat English and Afrikaans on an equal basis convinced the Afrikaners that their language and culture could be preserved against the onslaught of the largely urban anglicizing forces.

The real price of conciliation and formal unity was the institutionalization of white supremacy. While moderate whites agreed to become the Union of South Africa and become an independent dominion within the British Commonwealth of Nations, the political and economic price was paid, and is still being paid, by the African majority. African political organizations date back to 1882, but the Act of Union jolted the National Native Convention to more open protest resulting in the formation of the African National Congress in 1912 under the leadership of British- and American-trained lawyers and journalists like J. T. Javabu. The ANC remained the chief voice of South African black nationalism until it was banned in 1960 after the massacre of blacks at Sharpeville.

## Pertinent Literature

Wilson, Monica and Leonard Thompson, eds. *The Oxford History of South Africa.* 2 vols. Oxford: Clarendon Press, 1969 and 1971.

These two volumes form the best available history of South Africa in English. Volume One begins with surveys of the history of African peoples before the arrival of the Dutch and English, who are treated in later chapters up to 1870. Volume Two covers the period 1870 to 1966. Both volumes are written to highlight the central theme that South African history is the interaction of peoples of diverse origins, languages, and cultures on South African soil.

Volume Two is the most germane to an understanding of the Act of Union in 1910, and the chapter entitled "The Compromise of Union" is written by Leonard Thompson.

Excellent background and follow-up chapters are written by other well-known scholars: Hobart Houghton, Monica Wilson, Francis Wilson, Donald Welsh, Leo Kuper, Jack Spence, and René de Villiers. Both volumes are copiously footnoted with scholarly references and thorough bibliographies.

The scope of disciplines covered is also impressive. Economic development is traced as a development of technology as well as the growth of peasant communities; agriculture and growth of towns are detailed. But the bulk of Volume Two is devoted to the interaction of Africans and Europeans. The last two chapters treat

African nationalism in South Africa and South Africa's special problems in relating to the modern world.

Both volumes are highly recommended for the scholar, not to be read at one time, but to be used judiciously in research in the long journey that anyone truly interested in South Africa must take to understand the complexities of that unique situation in today's world.

De Kiewiet, C. W. *A History of South Africa, Social and Economic*. London: Oxford University Press, 1957.

Although the author devotes relatively little space to the role of the Cape Colored people and of those of Asian origin, he does focus on South Africa as an integral part of the British Empire. Beginning with the arrival of the first Europeans (Portuguese), De Kiewiet establishes the "foundation of a new society" with the installation of the Dutch in the seventeenth century. With the coming of the English, new ideas and industries developed.

After an excellent section on the Boer War, the author devotes a chapter to the formation of the Union of South Africa. He is frank about the preoccupation of the whites in South Africa with their own problems at the cost of putting off reconciliation with the majority population. He notes: "More bad history was created in a short time than many years of fair-minded study have since been able to disprove." As expected, De Kiewiet's interpretation of history is closely linked to economic factors. He describes the "native proletariat" transferring itself to towns where the industries grew up.

In allowing self-government for the whites in 1910 without regard to the political status of the blacks, Great Britain appeared (although De Kiewiet could not have drawn the comparisons) to be allowing the kind of "Unilateral Declaration of Independence" that Her Majesty's Government so emphatically resisted in Zimbabwe/Rhodesia in 1965. In abandoning her effort to exercise control over black/white relations, Downing Street "had surrendered to the frontier."

The schisms even within Afrikaner society are mentioned, as are divisions within various African societies. But African rebellion against white oppression is a major theme, and behind every rebellion were always found grievances concerning land, taxes, and labor. De Kiewiet concludes the chapter on Union with these words: "It is not given to any people, however wise or rich, to extricate itself simply from the disorders and maladjustments that history has produced in its midst."

The remainder of this useful volume describes gold mining, the role of poor whites and white "civilized labour"; and finally the regulation of industry. This book is an excellent introduction to South African economic and social history. A bibliography aids those who would go deeper into this fascinating and timely subject. — *H.H.B.*

## Additional Recommended Reading

*The Cambridge History of the British Empire.* Vol. VIII: *South Africa, Rhodesia and the High Commission Territories.* London: Cambridge University Press, 1963. An authoritative complement to the Oxford volumes on South Africa.

Carter, Gwendolen M. and Patrick O'Meara, eds. *Southern Africa: The Continuing Crisis.* Bloomington: Indiana University Press, 1979. An excellent update of the present situation with historical background and sources for contemporary Southern Africa.

Engelenburg, F. V. *General Louis Botha.* Pretoria: J. L. van Schaik, 1929. A biography of a Boer War guerrilla fighter and hero (1862-1919) who later became a notable statesman in shaping the destiny of South Africa.

Hancock, W. K. *Smuts: The Sanguine Years, 1870-1919.* London: Cambridge University Press, 1962. A very important biography for background to the Act of Union in 1910.

Stuart, J. *A History of the Zulu Rebellion, 1906, and of Dinuzulu's Arrest, Trial and Expatriation.* London: Macmillan and Company, 1913. Covers one important African resistance that affected the Act of Union.

Thompson, Leonard Monteath. *The Unification of South Africa, 1902-1910.* Oxford: Clarendon Press, 1960. The single best volume focusing on Union and the events surrounding it; includes good bibliography.

# THE CHINESE REVOLUTION OF 1911

*Type of event:* Political: overthrow of the Manchu Dynasty and the creation of the Republic of China
*Time:* October 10, 1911-March 10, 1912
*Locale:* China

*Principal personages:*

SUN YAT-SEN (1866-1925), Chinese revolutionary leader who conspired against the Manchus, 1895-1911

LIANG CH'I-CH'AO (1873-1929), a leading advocate of reform during the last decade of the Manchu Dynasty

YÜAN SHIH-K'AI (1859-1916), military officer under the Manchus; and President of China, 1912-1916

TZ'U-HSI (1835-1908), Dowager Empress and *de facto* ruler of China, 1861-1908

HUANG HSING (1873-1916), Chinese revolutionary conspirator and one of Sun Yat-sen's coworkers

SUNG CHIAO-JEN, Chinese revolutionary conspirator who drafted China's first Republican constitution; assassinated in March, 1913

HENRY P'U-YI (HSÜAN-T'UNG) (1906-1967), the last Manchu Emperor of China, 1908-1912

PRINCE CH'UN (1882-      ), Regent of China, 1908-1912

## Summary of Event

The goal of the Chinese Revolution of 1911 was the revival of national power and the establishment of a democratic form of government. Yet, this revolution inaugurated a long period of internal chaos and foreign interference, which ended only in 1949.

The ultimate cause of the Chinese Revolution of 1911 was the impact of the West on China. Ever since the disastrous Opium War of 1839-1842, the Chinese, who had long believed their civilization to be far superior to all others, had watched helplessly as the Great Powers of the West, and after 1895, the Asian state of Japan as well, steadily chipped away at their sovereignty. Each of these states secured trade concession after trade concession, special privilege after special privilege. It was only the large number of Powers involved in the China concession scramble, and their intense rivalries with one another, which kept China from becoming the colony of any single European Power. The Manchu Dynasty, established in the seventeenth century by invading Manchurians, seemed unable to meet the foreign challenge to China.

After China's defeat in the Sino-Japanese War of 1895, and the suppression of the antiforeign Boxer Rebellion by a multinational Army of the Great Powers in 1900, the cry for change grew louder and louder among thoughtful Chinese, particu-

92

larly among the well-educated young. Some of these restless young men were reformers who wanted change, but within the framework of the Manchu Dynasty; such a man was Liang Ch'i-ch'ao. There were, however, also revolutionaries who believed that the abolition of the monarchy was absolutely necessary for China's salvation. One of the earliest and most prominent of such revolutionaries was Sun Yat-sen.

Sun Yat-sen, born in a village in the South China province of Kwangtung in 1866, had emigrated to Hawaii as a teenager, where he had received a Western education and had been converted to Christianity. Although Sun wanted China to be strong enough to resist Western imperialism, he also wished to see China copy what he regarded as the good aspects of modern Western civilization.

In 1894-1895, Sun founded, in Hawaii and in the British colony of Hong Kong, the Society to Revive China, a tiny group of revolutionaries dedicated to the overthrow of the Manchus. In October, 1895, Sun and his fellow revolutionaries, using Hong Kong as a base, tried to incite a rebellion in Canton, the capital of Kwangtung province. When this revolt was crushed, Sun was forced to leave China. Thus began his long years as a political exile in Japan, Southeast Asia, and the West.

During the decade after 1895, other educated young Chinese also began hatching plots against the Manchus, independently of Sun. One such conspirator was Huang Hsing, who had been forced to flee to Japan in 1903. In the summer of 1905, Sun Yat-sen, Huang Hsing, and other anti-Manchu Chinese founded the Revolutionary Alliance, or T'ung-Meng-hui. Sun now became the leader of a broad revolutionary coalition, uniting all the foes of the Manchu regime. In his attempts to foment revolution from abroad, Sun was now able, for the first time, to obtain substantial financial support from the Overseas Chinese. These were the Chinese who had emigrated to Southeast Asia, and their descendants.

Even after 1905, however, Sun's schemes for revolution were by no means blessed with instant success. Most of his attempts to stir up rebellion against the Manchus within China came to nothing. Although Sun was important as the theoretician and symbol of the Chinese Revolution of 1911, this revolution had other roots besides the ideas of one political exile. For, during the years from 1900 to 1911, the ground for political upheaval was being prepared within China itself.

After 1900, the Manchu Dowager Empress, Tz'u-hsi, who had once strongly opposed both reform and reformers, suddenly embraced their cause. The reforms enacted after 1900 included the establishment of locally elected provincial assemblies, and the promise of constitutional Parliamentary government in the future; the abolition of the practice of selecting public officials through examinations based on the Confucian classics, and their selection, instead, from the ranks of those trained in specific skills; the building of a nationwide railway system; the creation of a new educational system to train future leaders; the sending of selected students abroad for further training;

and the creation of a new and more efficient national Army, based on the European model. The Manchus may have hoped that, through reform, they would prevent revolution; instead, they hastened its coming.

All these reforms enlarged the ranks of potential rebels. The abolition of the examination system made it more difficult for those from families of modest means to rise into the ranks of the bureaucracy; school attendance was far costlier than the part-time study the old system had allowed. Thus, literate, ambitious youths from poor families chose, for the first time, to enter the Army, where they would prove to be a force for anti-Manchu dissidence. The students at the new schools and colleges developed a questioning, rebellious attitude towards the old Manchu system. Finally, the provincial assemblies came to serve as the mouthpiece for the growing desire of local elites for a greater say in their own affairs: a desire for autonomy which would prove incompatible with traditional Manchu centralization. After the death of the Dowager Empress in 1908, there was no strong ruler capable of keeping a lid on the boiling pot of discontent.

Up to 1911, all of the carefully planned uprisings of Sun Yat-sen's revolutionary organization had been easily suppressed by the Manchu government. In the autumn of that year, however, the end of the monarchy came suddenly, almost as if by accident.

The year 1911 had witnessed famine, floods, and economic disaster. In May of that year, the Regent, Prince Ch'un, who governed in the name of the "boy emperor" P'u-yi, had earned much unpopularity by delaying the calling of a parliament, by appointing a cabinet made up mostly of Manchus, and by seeking a foreign loan to finance his planned nationalization of the Chinese railways. The last had aroused protests in part of China. Normally, the Army would have been able to repress dissent; but rebellion would soon spread to its ranks also.

In October, a revolutionary organization was discovered in the garrison of Wuchang, capital of the province of Hubei. Fearful of punishment, the soldiers of the garrison did not humbly submit to discipline; instead, on October 10, 1911, they revolted, kidnaped their commander, and forced him, under threat of death, to assume the leadership of their rebellion against the Manchu Dynasty. This day was the famous "Double Ten" of future Chinese patriots.

The nationwide response to this mutiny was as sudden as it was electrifying. Throughout the country, provincial assembly after provincial assembly, each representing the local elite groups, declared their independence from the Manchu Dynasty. Soon a revolutionary regime was established in the central Chinese city of Nanking. All that remained to the Manchus were the capital, Peking, and several provinces in northern China. Sun Yat-sen returned from exile in December, and on December 29, 1911, he was elected Provisional President of the Republic of China by the Nanking government.

The revolutionary victory was not, however, complete. The able military officer, Yüan Shih-k'ai had come out of retirement to defend the Manchus.

His forces were far too strong for Nanking to defeat, but far too weak to defeat the Nanking regime. After some haggling, the unscrupulous and ambitious Yüan struck a deal with the revolutionaries. Yüan would persuade the Manchus to abdicate; in return, he would become President of China.

On February 12, 1912, the Manchus formally announced the end of their Dynasty. On February 15, 1912, Sun Yat-sen resigned the presidency, recommending that Yüan be named as his successor. This the Nanking provisional Parliament promptly did. On March 10, 1912, Yüan Shih-k'ai was formally sworn in as Provisional President of the Republic of China. On April 1, the provisional Parliament, acting on the urging of Yüan, voted for the transfer of the capital to Peking. China was now both united and a Republic.

Yet liberal democracy was by no means secure. On March 20, 1913, the outspoken liberal Sung Chiao-jen, the drafter of the new constitution, was assassinated under myste-rious circumstances. Soon afterwards, in July and August, Yüan destroyed provincial autonomy and suppressed all organized opposition. Sun Yat-sen was once again forced to flee to exile in Japan. When Yüan tried to make himself Emperor in January, 1916, however, a military uprising broke out, forcing him to give up this plan. After Yüan's death in June of the same year, China soon disintegrated into a host of feuding warlord states. In 1925, Sun Yat-sen died.

In the late 1920's, Chiang Kai-shek, leader of the Chinese Nationalists, was briefly successful in re-uniting China; but soon he was faced with a Japanese threat abroad and a Communist threat at home. Internal peace finally came in 1949, when the Communists, under Mao Tse-tung, secured power over the mainland; Chiang's Nationalists were confined to the island of Taiwan. After 1949, each regime claimed to be the exclusive heir to the glorious tradition of Sun Yat-sen and the Chinese Revolution of 1911.

## Pertinent Literature

Rhoads, Edward J. M. *China's Republican Revolution: The Case of Kwangtung, 1895-1913*. Cambridge, Mass.: Harvard University Press, 1975.

The southern Chinese coastal province of Kwangtung was the home province of that tireless revolutionary, Sun Yat-sen. In this book, Rhoads, who teaches Chinese History at the University of Texas at Austin, studies the process of revolution in Kwangtung from 1895, the year of the Sino-Japanese War, to 1913, the year of Yüan Shih-k'ai's suppression of his political rivals.

Most traditional Chinese historiography on the 1911 Revolution, Rhoads believes, puts far too much emphasis on the role played by Sun Yat-sen in bringing about the overthrow of the Manchus in that year. While not denying the significance of Sun's activities, the author assigns far greater importance to social change within

China itself as a cause of the political revolution of 1911. The reforms carried out in the last years of the Manchu period, he contends, made revolution inevitable by creating a climate of ever-rising expectations which the existing Imperial government could never hope to satisfy.

In the first chapter, Rhoads gives us a picture of Kwangtung province on the eve of the Sino-Japanese War of 1894-1895. He sees Kwangtung as a province where, despite the heavy impact of foreign trade during the preceding fifty years, traditional Chinese culture, with its old habits of "political passivity," had undergone very little change.

It was the shock of two events, Rhoads argues, the defeat of China in the Sino-Japanese War of 1894-1895 and the suppression by foreign Governments of the Boxer Rebellion in 1900, which finally forced the Chinese to try seriously to reform their government and their society. After 1900, the Manchu government reorganized the Army and began to spend much more money on education. Provincial assemblies, dominated by local elites, were set up throughout China. In Chapters Three through Seven, Rhoads traces the course of government-sponsored reform through the early, middle, and final years of what he calls "the post-Boxer decade."

Having briefly discussed Sun Yat-sen's early career as a revolutionary conspirator in Chapter Two, Rhoads deals more fully in Chapter Eight with the man and the organization he founded, the T'ung-Meng-hui. Sun's revolutionary career, the author makes clear, was by no means a steady, painless advance towards the pinnacle of success. On the contrary, the organization Sun had founded actually went into a period of decline during the years 1907 to 1911. By itself introducing reforms, the Manchu regime had stolen much of the revolutionaries' thunder; internal disagreements also hampered the effectiveness of the T'ung-Meng-hui. The uprising of April, 1911, in Canton, the capital of Kwangtung, which the organization had so carefully planned, was easily crushed by the Manchu authorities.

In Chapter Nine, Rhoads emphasizes the rapidity with which a revolutionary situation developed in Kwangtung, and in China as a whole, during the latter half of 1911. Such a situation, he argues, developed not because of the cleverness of Sun Yat-sen, but because of the blunders of the ruling dynasty. A series of government measures, including the appointment of an all-Manchu Cabinet, the nationalization of private railways, and the borrowing of foreign money to finance this nationalization, had deeply shocked elite opinion in Kwangtung. Thus, when the Wuchang mutiny broke out on October 10, 1911, in the province of Hubei, the Kwangtung elite was all too ready to throw in its lot with the Hubei rebels.

In Chapter Ten, Rhoads describes in great detail the Westernizing reforms carried out by the Kwangtung revolutionary regime during its brief period in power. Many people, particularly in the cities, exchanged traditional Chinese clothing for Western-style dress. While somewhat hostile to such old Chinese religions as Taoism, Confucianism, and Buddhism, the Kwangtung regime, which included many Chinese Christians, took a benign attitude towards the preaching of Christianity. Independent political parties flourished, and the number of newspapers multiplied. The city of Canton witnessed, in June, 1912, the birth of a Chinese Women's Rights movement.

In the summer of 1913, however, many of these reforms were terminated. President Yüan Shih-k'ai succeeded in doing away with the autonomy of all the Chinese provinces, including Kwangtung. Having lost the support of the Canton merchant class through its financial ineptitude, the Kwangtung regime was unable to rally local opinion behind it. In August, its forces were quickly defeated by President Yüan's armies.

In his research, Rhoads has relied on the following Chinese-language sources: recently published collections of documents concerning Sun-Yat-sen's revolutionary movement, the memoirs of participants in that movement, the Chinese-language press, and the Chinese Foreign Ministry Archives. All were found in Hong Kong or on Taiwan. In addition, the author has made use of the English-language press of the foreign settlements in China, the English-language *Hong Kong Telegraph*, and the reports of British and American consuls. The British and American consular reports are to be found in the British Foreign Office Archives in London and in the United States State Department records of the National Archives in Washington, D.C., respectively.

Esherick, Joseph W. *Reform and Revolution in China: The 1911 Revolution in Hunan and Hubei*. Berkeley: University of California Press, 1976.

It was in Hubei, an inland province of central China, that the military mutiny which started the Chinese Revolution of 1911 broke out on October 10, 1911. In this scholarly, well-researched book, Esherick, a Professor of History at the University of Oregon, studies the causes and consequences of the revolutionary movement in the two adjoining Chinese provinces of Hunan and Hubei. These two provinces, although administratively separate, together constituted an economic and geographic unit. From this small-scale study, the author tries to draw broader conclusions about the nature of the revolutionary process in China during the first two decades of the twentieth century. Unlike orthodox Chinese historians of the 1911 Revolution, Esherick does not believe that the activities of Sun Yat-sen were of crucial importance in bringing about the Revolution of 1911. Consequently, Esherick focuses his attention not on "the haunts of exiles in Japan, Southeast Asia, and the West," but on "events in China itself."

Esherick sees the roots of revolution in the reforms of the late Manchu period, undertaken to strengthen China in her struggle against foreign encroachments. According to the author, both the reforms of the late Manchu period, and the 1911 Revolution itself, benefited the "urban reformist elite" at the expense of the peasant masses of China. Thus, the Revolution of 1911, Esherick contends, was simultaneously "politically progressive" and "socially regressive."

In the first two chapters, the author describes the activities of the early advocates of reform in the two provinces, from the 1890's onward. These individuals were students, intellectuals, and revolutionary conspirators; they could not change China, however, until a social class had emerged which would demand change in its own interest.

The third chapter offers a portrait of the social class which was to succeed in changing China: "the urban reformist elite." This group consisted of younger members of the traditional degree-holding landlord-gentry elite, who had taken up residence in the growing cities. Although many of this new class were absentee landlords, others were enterprising industrialists and mineowners. The men of this new class, while firmly opposed to Western and Japanese imperialism, were ardent advocates of the thoroughgoing reform of China along Western lines. Thus, they urged China to adopt a Western-style educational system, Western-style private enterprise, and the Western system of constitutional parliamentary government. Using the provincial assemblies as a sounding board for their views, they incessantly criticized the Manchu Dynasty for what they saw as the excessively slow pace of reform. By undermining the authority of the monarchy, they helped to bring about the Revolution of 1911.

Esherick regards many of the reforms sponsored by this new elite as "repressive"; they benefited only a tiny segment of the people, while saddling the peasant majority with a heavy burden of taxation. In the fourth chapter, such incidents as the Changsha rice riots of 1910 are cited as evidence of the widespread opposition among the "masses" to the reforms enacted by the Manchu Dynasty at the behest of the urban reformist elite. In writing the accounts of such incidents of mass violence, Esherick has relied heavily on the contemporary reports of British and Japanese consuls to their home governments.

Chapter Five is an attempt to explain the origins of the fateful Army mutiny of October 10, 1911. The Hubei conspirators had only "tenuous" connections with Sun Yat-sen's organization; their attraction to revolutionary conspiracy arose from their high level of literacy, their concentration in urban centers where discontent with the Manchus was already common, and their poor chances of rising through the ranks.

The sixth chapter contains a blow-by-blow account of the outbreak of military revolt in Hubei, and of its spread to the neighboring province of Hunan. Esherick's account relies heavily on the eyewitness narratives of those who participated in the 1911 Revolution in these two provinces. Some of these narratives have been published separately; some have been preserved in the Kuomintang (Nationalist) archives on the island of Taiwan; while others are included in documentary collections on the 1911 Revolution, published recently by both the Peking and Taiwan regimes. In addition, the author has made use of the contemporary reports of British and Japanese consuls to their home governments. From his investigation of all these sources, Esherick has concluded that, throughout the turbulent months of revolution, the "urban reformist elite" remained fully in control of the course of events in Hunan and Hubei.

In Chapter Seven, Esherick tries to explain why the radical revolution of 1911 was so quickly followed, in 1913, by the reactionary counterrevolution of Yüan Shih-k'ai. The urban elite, he contends, had supported the revolution in 1911 because they had seen it as a means of preserving the existing social structure. By 1913, however, the same urban elite had come to see Yüan Shih-k'ai as the only man who could preserve law and order. A revolt against Yüan, carried out in the name of liberal principles, raised the danger of anarchy. Chinese liberals, now deprived of elite support, were easily defeated when they tried to launch an armed revolt against Yüan's dictatorship. Their cause had little appeal to the Chinese peasant masses, who identified Republican liberalism with oppression by local elite groups.

Esherick's work has generally been praised by his fellow historians. Some scholars, however, have criticized him for exaggerating both the extent of class conflict between the "elite" and the "masses" in the China of 1911, and the degree of cohesion within the "elite" itself at that time.
— *P.D.M.*

## Additional Recommended Reading

Young, Ernest P. *The Presidency of Yüan Shih-k'ai: Liberalism and Dictatorship in Early Republican China*. Ann Arbor: University of Michigan Press, 1977. A reevaluation by an American historian of one of the most hated figures of the early Republican period.

Huang, Philip C. *Liang Ch'i-ch'ao and Modern Chinese Liberalism*. Seattle: University of Washington Press, 1972. A study of the political philosophy of one of the leading advocates of reform within the framework of the Manchu Dynasty.

Yen, Ch'ing-huang. *The Overseas Chinese and the 1911 Revolution*. New York: Oxford University Press, 1976. Stresses the key role of the Chinese communities of Malaya and Singapore in providing financial support for Sun Yat-sen's revolutionary movement during the years from 1906 to 1911.

Schiffrin, Harold Z. *Sun Yat-sen and the Origins of the Chinese Revolution*. Berkeley: University of California Press, 1968. An excellent study of Sun Yat-sen's early career, which carries the story of the revolutionary leader's life up to the year 1905.

Gasster, Michael. *Chinese Intellectuals and the Revolution of 1911: The Birth of Modern Chinese Radicalism*. Seattle: University of Washington Press, 1969. Shows that many of the intellectuals associated with Sun Yat-sen in the T'ung-Meng-hui differed as much among themselves as they did with nonrevolutionary reformers such as Liang Ch'i-ch'ao.

Liew, Kit Siong. *Struggle for Democracy: Sung Chiao-jen and the 1911 Chinese Revolution*. Berkeley: University of California Press, 1971. A biographical study of a prominent Chinese advocate of Western-style Parliamentary liberalism which covers his career as a revolutionary up to 1911, his relationship with Sun Yat-sen, and his struggle against Yüan Shih-k'ai.

# RUSSIA INVADES EAST PRUSSIA

*Type of event:* Military: Russia's entrance into World War I
*Time:* August, 1914
*Locale:* Russia and East Prussia

*Principal personages:*

GENERAL PAVEL KARLOVICH RENNENKAMPF (1854-1918),
Russian Army commander

GENERAL ALEKSANDR VASILIEVICH SAMSONOV (1859-1914),
Russian Army commander

NICHOLAS II (NIKOLAI ALEKSANDROVICH) (1868-1918), Tsar
of Russia, 1894-1917

GENERAL PAUL VON HINDENBURG (PAUL LUDWIG HANS
ANTON VON BENECKENDORFF UND VON HINDENBURG)
(1847-1934), German Army commander

## Summary of Event

On June 28, 1914, Gavril Princip, a member of a Serbian terrorist organization, successfully assassinated Archduke Franz Ferdinand, heir to the throne of Austria-Hungary. The assassination took place in Sarajevo, the capital of Austrian-held and Serbian-populated Bosnia-Hercegovina. Subsequently, Austria-Hungary issued an ultimatum to the Balkan kingdom of Serbia, accusing her of responsibility for the assassination of the Archduke. Serbia, while acknowledging most of Austria-Hungary's demands, found itself at war with the Habsburg state following Austria-Hungary's declaration of hostilities on July 28, 1914. The history of diplomacy in Europe for decades prior to Sarajevo insured a much wider conflict than the showdown over Austria-Hungary's presence in the Balkans. By 1914, the major European powers were divided into two major alliances that had now become "armed camps." The Triple Alliance, formed by secret treaty in 1882, embraced Austria-Hungary,

Germany, and Italy; the Triple Entente, finalized in 1907, included Great Britain, France, and Tsarist Russia. Russia had maintained a long-standing interest in the Balkans throughout the nineteenth century. As part of Russian-inspired Pan-Slavism—attempts to foster unity of Eastern Europe's various Slavic nationalities under "Mother Russia's" influence—Russia had repeatedly intervened in Balkan politics. Russia had centuries-old ties with Bulgarians and had developed strong diplomatic ties with the Serbs as well. By 1900, Serbia was the largest independent Balkan state. Hence the Serbs, "brother Slavs" and "brother Orthodox," commanded geopolitical importance for Russia as relations between Serbia and Austria-Hungary steadily deteriorated after 1903. Russia's decision to support Serbia in the wake of Austria's declaration of war meant that a local Balkan conflict would escalate into a world conflagration. World War I, a conflict unprecedented in violence, size, and scope, had begun.

Russia entered World War I while attempting to rehabilitate her diplomatic and military reputation in keeping with her pretensions to great power status. In two prior military conflicts—the Crimean War (1853-1856) and the Russo-Japanese War (1904-1905)—Russia had suffered serious defeats. World War I presented Russia with numerous opportunities to advance territorially. The Ottoman Empire was clearly leaning toward the Triple Alliance, and indeed would formally join the German war effort by October, 1914. The Russians in this setting could hope to increase greatly their involvement in the Balkans with British and French support. In Central Europe, playing on Pan-Slavic sentiments, Russia would prove able to mobilize other Slavic groups such as the Czechs and Slovaks to fight against their Austro-Hungarian oppressors. In addition, Russia hoped for consolidation of control over Polish lands, some of which were still under German and Austrian control. All in all, the war seemed to promise much for Russia's attempt to recoup diplomatically and militarily.

The Tsar and his Council of Ministers, on July 28, 1914, ordered the first partial mobilization of the Russian Army. By July 30, Nicholas II announced a full-scale general mobilization of Russia's troops. The war effort clearly had widespread support in Russia. Among the political parties, only the Bolsheviks maintained a consistent antiwar position. The other parties from right to left enthusiastically endorsed the war in a special meeting of the Russian parliament, the Duma, on August 8, 1914. Support for war came from key non-Russian nationalities of the Russian Empire as well.

Enthusiasm, however, could not overcome serious difficulties as Russia prepared for its first campaign. Russia's key advantage, its potential manpower, was tempered by many factors. With Russia's huge population, the Russians entered the war with a standing army of more than 1,400,000 men with 3,000,000 in reserve. However, this massive army lacked proper equipment throughout the war. Russia had just begun to industrialize prior to the war, and its small-scale industrial base could not readily produce a mass of war matériel. Rail and other forms of transportation to the Prussian frontier were severely underdeveloped, hampering the movement of weapons and men westward; medical facilities were deficient; Russian military intelligence was weak; troops as well as officers were poorly trained. The Russian general staff could not measure up to any commanders of the other great powers. The personal hatred between Generals P. K. Rennenkampf and A. V. Samsonov, leaders of the campaign into East Prussia, created yet another liability to afflict the East Prussian campaign.

In terms of overall planning, the Triple Entente asked far too much of the Russian Army in planning the invasion of East Prussia. Russia was expected to draw German forces away from France so that the French might be relieved of a massive German assault. To draw off sufficient German companies to the Eastern Front, Russia was required to launch a fateful invasion of East Prussia a mere sixteen days into the mobilization. This forced the Russians to commit 800,000 troops—more than half of the standing army—to the very first campaign of the war. On August 17, 1914, the Russian First Army, under General Rennenkampf, invaded East Prussia from the east. According to plan, on August 19, General Samsonov at the head of the Russian Second Army was to proceed from Warsaw northward into East Prussia. The two Russian armies would thus encircle the German forces in a giant pincers movement. At first, matters went Russia's way, with Rennenkampf winning in his first few encounters with German troops. At this point, however, the German high command became greatly concerned with Rennenkampf's successes and brought General Paul von Hindenburg out of retirement to head the defense of East Prussia. With the entry of Hindenburg into the campaign, Russia's early successes were followed by massive defeats.

Hindenburg, in a calculated risk, decided to focus his first actions against Samsonov's trailing Second Army. Counting on Rennenkampf's hatred of Samsonov, Hindenburg reasoned that Rennenkampf would not come to the aid of Samsonov's forces—a calculation which proved frighteningly true for the Russians. While smaller in number, the Germans used their superior weaponry and staff to surround and massacre Samsonov's Second Army between August 23 and 30 in what came to be known as the Battle of Tannenberg. The bulk of Samsonov's forces were captured or killed, and Samsonov himself committed suicide upon this crushing defeat. As Hindenburg expected, Rennenkampf had failed to support the Second Army. With Samsonov's forces defeated, the Germans then concentrated full force against Rennenkampf's First Army, which was chased from East Prussia by mid-September, 1914. The Russian invasion of East Prussia ended in the total defeat of the Tsar's forces. Russian losses were estimated at 300,000 men and 650 guns. This terrible loss served as the first damper on support for the war in Russia. The East Prussian debacle, coupled with subsequent Russian losses, helped to convert mounting Russian domestic discontent into revolution by 1917.

## Pertinent Literature

Thoumin, Richard. *The First World War*. Edited and translated by Martin Kieffer. New York: G. P. Putnam's Sons, 1964.

There is little in the way of full-length treatments about Russia's general mobilization and abortive invasion of East Prussia available in English. Beyond Russian-language accounts unavailable and inaccessible to the English-speaking reader, the general reader can obtain at best only the most fragmented bits of information on the East Prussian campaign. There are three types of sources that can be consulted by readers interested in the Rennenkampf and Samsonov debacles. First, readers should examine any number of excellent college-level Russian history textbooks, which include coverage of the war. Sidney Harcave, George

Vernadsky, and Michael Florinsky all have produced texts of good quality over the past two decades that contain accounts of the general mobilization, the state of Russia as it entered the conflict, and the terrible setbacks in East Prussia. Second, general readers can obtain more detailed accounts in histories dealing with the fall of tsardom. In these books, coverage of the war is broadened usually to the length of an entire chapter thus increasing what readers can learn of the conflict in East Prussia. Finally, readers should consult any of the many history books written about World War I. These narrative accounts contain descriptions of the so-called Eastern Front of the war, including Russia's ill-fated entrance into the conflict.

The volume under consideration by Richard Thoumin belongs to this latter category. Thoumin was an active participant in the war, serving as an infantry officer for France. The book begins with a useful chronology of the entire conflict for both the Western and Eastern Fronts, then moves into a narrative account that includes extensive first-hand accounts of the war by participant-observers. These richly detailed personal narratives come from individuals including diplomats, generals, and foot soldiers.

Thoumin begins with accounts of the mobilization that affected all of Europe following Princip's action in Sarajevo. In particular, Russia's mobilization was directed on behalf of the Serbs now facing direct Austrian invasion. Russia became the first great power to order a general mobilization, doing so on July 30, 1914.

On July 31, 1914, Germany, aware of Russian troop movements on her East Prussian frontier, issued an ultimatum to Russia, and, receiving no reply, declared war on Russia on August 1, 1914.

Thoumin relies on an account by Maurice Paléologue, French Ambassador to the Russian Court, to describe the euphoria with which Russia entered the conflict. In a "magnificent spectacle," replete with a formal Orthodox liturgy, Tsar Nicholas II issued a manifesto to the Russian people, a direct appeal for a united, unstoppable war effort. From this ceremony in St. George's gallery, the Tsar made an appearance on the balcony of the Winter Palace before a huge crowd carrying posters, banners, and icons. As one, the crowd knelt, singing the national anthem.

Euphoria aside, the opening campaign faced serious drawbacks. In particular, the mobilization was committed to a swift entry into the conflict, an entry that no amount of emotionalism could sustain in terms of training and equiping the Russian troops. Despite Russia's formal commitment against Austria, the bulk of Russia's raw troops were to be pitted against Germany in an Allied move to take pressure off France. The East Prussian debacle was the result. Thoumin includes a vivid account of Russia's defeat at Tannenberg by General Paul von Hindenburg, describing the German "ring of fire" that succeeded in crushing both Rennenkampf's and Samsonov's armies. As the Russian troops were surrounded, many faced the alternatives of death, capture, or drowning in lakes near the battle site. Thoumin concludes his account of East Prussia with a description of the tremendous

demoralization that set in following the defeat.

Charques, Richard. *The Twilight of Imperial Russia*. London: Phoenix House, 1958.

This volume deals with the history of the ill-fated reign of the last Tsar, Nicholas II. In this context, the book contains material dealing with the war, the mobilization, and the East Prussian campaign. The war in its entirety, beginning with the crushing defeat at East Prussia, played a direct role in bringing on the revolution in 1917 that toppled tsardom.

Russia entered the conflict at the behest of the tiny Balkan kingdom of Serbia, which faced Austrian invasion following the assassination of the Austrian Archduke by a Serbian terrorist. The Russian response to the situation was to call for a complete mobilization, the first one ordered by any Entente nation. The call for mobilization was accompanied by an outpouring of patriotic fervor. Unfortunately, Russia entered the conflict with real and serious liabilities. Though Tsarist Russia had begun to modernize and industrialize since the reforms associated with Serge Witte, the Russian economy simply could not sustain a prolonged war. A long conflict (as the war proved to be) would strain Russian productivity beyond its means. In addition to the economic liabilities, there were also important military liabilities. The military drawbacks pointed up by Russia's embarrassing defeat by Japan in the Russo-Japanese War of 1904 had not yet been corrected.

The Army suffered from inadequate staff, inadequate intelligence, inferior supplies, and poor medical care. Its only strong point was numbers, for Russia had a huge population from which to draw. Still, as Charques points out, even the Army's numerical strength could not counter the Army's deplorable organization. In addition, the general mobilization, despite its patriotic fervor, was a hasty affair indeed. Russia's massive fighting force did not have adequate time to train. The Army was pushed into full-scale conflict in a matter of weeks, with a huge number of raw recruits in action. Actual conflict, as the troops in East Prussia learned, could not be sustained by patriotic fervor alone.

The specific East Prussian campaign had its own unique drawbacks. For example, Russia was in effect, being used by the Entente to draw off German forces from France as the war began, with the East Prussian invasion designed to divert several German divisions from the Western to the Eastern Front. To further complicate matters, the two Russian armies were led by two generals, Rennenkampf and Samsonov, who had been bitter personal enemies since a famous fistfight at the Mukden railroad station in 1904. While still bitter rivals, however, these two generals were expected to coordinate their activities and mutually support each other's efforts. Yet, when the Russians, under Samsonov faced the brilliant German general Paul von Hindenburg at the Battle of Tannenberg, Rennenkampf failed to provide support and

Samsonov's forces were crushed. Rennenkampf's forces were then chased from East Prussia by mid-September. The Russian defeat was the beginning of a chain of events leading to Bolshevik triumph. Charques' account, well-written and well-documented throughout, places the East Prussian campaign in the general context of the world war and the coming crisis of tsardom. — *E.A.Z.*

## Additional Recommended Reading

Florinsky, Michael T. *The End of the Russian Empire*. New Haven, Conn.: Yale University Press, 1931. An account by one of the leading *émigré* historians.

Harcave, Sidney. *Russia: A History*. Philadelphia: J. B. Lippincott Company, 1968. Text includes a good chapter on World War I and the East Prussian invasion.

Pares, Bernard. *The Fall of the Russian Monarchy: A Study of the Evidence*. New York: Alfred A. Knopf, 1939. Classic account by a British historian of Rasputin, the war, and the end of tsardom.

Seton-Watson, Hugh. *The Decline of Imperial Russia, 1855-1914*. New York: Frederick A. Praeger Publishers, 1952. Contains a chapter on the impact of the war on Russia.

Von Laue, Theodore H. *Why Lenin? Why Stalin? A Reappraisal of the Russian Revolution, 1900-1930*. Philadelphia: J. B. Lippincott Company, 1964. Provides a good discussion of how the war weakened the Tsarist aristocracy.

# THE GREAT ARMENIAN MASSACRE

*Type of event:* Political: atrocity perpetrated against an ethnic minority
*Time:* 1915-1916
*Locale:* The Ottoman Empire (present-day Turkey and Syria)

*Principal personages:*

MEHMET TALAAT PASHA (1872-1921), a member of the Young Turk triumvirate which ruled the Ottoman Empire from 1913 to 1918

ENVER PASHA (1881?-1922), another Young Turk triumvir

AHMED DJEMAL PASHA (1872-1922), the third triumvir

DJEVDET BEY, Turkish Governor of Van in 1915

ABDUL-HAMID II (1842-1918), Sultan of the Ottoman Empire, 1876-1909

MUSTAFA KEMAL (later, KEMAL ATATÜRK) (1881-1938), founder of the Turkish Republic in 1923

JOHANNES LEPSIUS (1858-1926), German theologian who helped expose the massacre

VISCOUNT JAMES BRYCE (1838-1922), English political theorist who helped expose the massacre

ARNOLD JOSEPH TOYNBEE (1889-1975), Bryce's assistant

THOMAS WOODROW WILSON (1856-1924), twenty-eighth President of the United States, 1913-1921

OTTO LIMAN VON SANDERS (1855-1929), German adviser in the Ottoman Empire, 1913-1918

HANS VON WANGENHEIM, German Ambassador to the Ottoman Empire, 1912-1915

PAUL WOLFF-METTERNICH (1853-1934), German Ambassador to the Ottoman Empire, 1915-1918

HENRY MORGENTHAU, SR. (1856-1946), United States Ambassador to the Ottoman Empire, 1913-1916

JAMES BARTON, American clergyman who headed the American organization which sent relief to Armenian massacre victims

## Summary of Event

The great Armenian massacre of 1915-1916 which so shocked public opinion in the United States and Western Europe was an event of great significance in the political history of the Middle East. The massacre delivered a fatal blow to dreams of erecting an independent Greater Armenia on the ruins of the Ottoman Empire. The ultimate consequences of the massacre were twofold: the annihilation of a large portion of the Armenians of the Ottoman Empire and the exodus of the survivors to the United States, the Soviet Union, and other parts of the world; and the cre-

107

ation, in 1923, of the Republic of Turkey, which would be almost completely Muslim-Turkish in ethnic composition.

The Armenian people, who had been converted to Christianity in the fourth century A.D., had once enjoyed political independence. By the beginning of the twentieth century, however, the lands inhabited by the Armenians were divided among three states: Persia, the Ottoman Empire, and the Empire of the Russian Tsars. In all three of these states, the Armenians constituted an ethnic minority; yet it was in the Ottoman Empire that friction between the Armenian minority and the dominant majority would become most acute.

The Ottoman Armenians lived throughout the eastern half of what is now Turkey in Asia Minor, from the Mediterranean coastal province of Cilicia up to the Russian border. There were also sizable Armenian colonies in the Aegean Seaport of Smyrna, in the Syrian cities of Damascus and Aleppo, and even within the capital city of Constantinople (present-day Istanbul) itself. Thus, any nationalist movement among the Armenians would be a grave threat to the very existence of the Ottoman Empire.

Although the Armenians were almost indistinguishable from their Turkish neighbors in physical appearance, the cultural gap between Turk and Armenian was a wide one. The Turks were Muslim, while the Armenians were Christians, belonging to either the ancient Armenian Gregorian Church or the Protestant Churches founded by nineteenth century American missionaries. The

Muslim Turks were divided into a small bureaucratic-military elite and an illiterate peasant majority. The Armenians, on the other hand, had a flourishing commercial middle class which was the envy of their Muslim neighbors.

During the first three centuries of Ottoman Turkish rule, Armenians and Turks had coexisted fairly peaceably, despite the legal disabilities imposed on the Armenians as a Christian minority. In the second half of the nineteenth century, however, relations between the two peoples changed markedly for the worse. The principal reason for this deterioration was the growth of nationalism among the Ottoman Armenians and the resentment this provoked among the Turks. Quite a few Armenians now came to believe that they should have a state of their own.

Several factors contributed to the flowering of nationalism among the Ottoman Armenians. The successful revolts of the Serbs, Greeks, and Bulgars against Ottoman rule undoubtedly inspired some Armenians to hope that they, too, might, with the help of foreign powers, throw off the Turkish yoke. The annexation in 1828 of parts of Persian Armenia by the Russian Empire, that hereditary Christian foe of the Muslim Turk, created a new base for Armenian cultural development and a new place of refuge for Armenian opponents of Turkish rule. American Protestant missionaries, through their educational efforts, promoted rising expectations of liberty and self-government among Ottoman Armenians, some of whom came to view the United States as a new and powerful foreign guardian. Finally, there was the Treaty of Berlin. This treaty, which revised the treaty ending the Russo-Turkish War of 1877-1878, obliged the Turks to promise fair treatment of the Armenian Christians within their borders, while providing no practical means for enforcing this guarantee. The treaty encouraged the Armenians to become bolder and bolder in demanding their rights, while making the Ottoman authorities more and more anxious and resentful.

A decent Ottoman administration, faithfully protecting the rights of its Armenian subjects, might have dampened the fires of Armenian nationalism. In 1894-1896, however, the despotic Turkish Sultan, Abdul-Hamid II, obsessed with the threat of revolution among the Armenians, had 300,000 of them massacred. Although the massacres aroused a cry of indignation throughout the United States and Western Europe, disagreements among the Great Powers prevented anything from being done to help the victims.

Abdul-Hamid II persecuted not only his Armenian subjects, but also many liberal-minded Muslim Turks. In July, 1908, a military *coup*, carried out by officers loyal to the underground "Committee of Union and Progress" (the so-called "Young Turks") ended the despotism of Abdul-Hamid II. The Sultan was forced to give the Empire a liberal constitution, complete with a representative Ottoman Parliament. In the following year, Abdul-Hamid, having been forced to flee into exile after an unsuccessful attempt at counter-revolution, was replaced by his brother. The latter would be merely a figurehead monarch, with no real power. For a while, it seemed as if Christian Armenian and Muslim Turk might be able to live peacefully together under a common order of liberty and constitutional government.

The Balkan Wars of 1912-1913, however, put an end to this dream. The Young Turks had seen in liberal, constitutional government a means of preserving the integrity of the Turkish Empire. The new Ottoman constitution, with its guarantee of equal rights for all ethnic groups, did not, however, succeed in deterring foreign aggression. In October, 1912, the Balkan states (Greece, Serbia, Montenegro, and Bulgaria), temporarily putting aside their quarrels, launched an unprovoked attack against Turkish territory in Europe. When the fighting was over, the Turks had been stripped of Albania, Macedonia, and Western Thrace. The remainder of Thrace, including the capital city of Constantinople, was all that was left of Turkey in Europe. By the thousands, Turkish Muslim refugees from the lost territories poured into the capital city.

The shock of defeat turned many Young Turks from tolerant liberals into xenophobic nationalists. After the *coup* of January, 1913, in which an Ottoman minister was assassinated for allegedly making too many concessions to the Balkan states at the peace table, the Turkish Cabinet gradually came to be dominated by three young jingoists: War Minister Enver Pasha, Navy Minister Ahmed Djemal Pasha, and Interior Minister Mehmet Talaat Pasha. These three men were all "Young Turks": members of the Committee of Union and

Progress who had fought to topple Abdul-Hamid in 1908-1909.

In the autumn of 1914, this clique committed the Ottoman Empire to war against Russia, Great Britain, and France on the side of Germany. Only in this way, these men believed, could the Turks halt the steady erosion of their Empire; for Germany, of all the Great Powers, seemed to have no designs on Ottoman territory. The Turkish entry into the Great European War would spell the doom of the Armenians of the Ottoman Empire.

The war did not begin well for the Turks. In December, 1914, Turkish armies led by Enver Pasha tried to invade the Russian Caucasus. In January of the following year, the Turkish invasion force was defeated at Sarikamish by a force composed partly of regular Russian troops, and partly of a special corps of Russian-Armenian volunteers. During the months of February and March, 1915, British ships bombarded Turkish forts on the Dardanelles (the Turkish strait linking the Aegean Sea and the Sea of Marmora). On April 25, 1915, a force composed of British, Australian, and New Zealand troops landed near the Turkish town of Gallipoli on the Dardanelles; their goal was the capture of Constantinople. It was only by dint of the most heroic efforts that the local Turkish armies, led by the young officer Mustafa Kemal and the German military commander Otto Liman von Sanders, were able to beat back the assault of the British-led forces, and it was not until the beginning of the following year that the last of the invasion forces finally withdrew.

It was, therefore, at a moment of grave national emergency that the Young Turk ruling clique, dreading military defeat above all else, decided to strike against the group that they had come to see as the enemy within the gates: the Armenian minority. The flight, after the beginning of the war, of a number of prominent Ottoman Armenians to Russia, and the enlistment of some young Ottoman Armenian *émigrés* in the Russian-Armenian volunteer corps, seemed to the Young Turks to provide clinching proof of something they had already suspected; that there was a widespread Armenian conspiracy against the Ottoman Empire, that the conspirators were in league with Russia, and that every Armenian living on Turkish soil was a potential conspirator. To deal with such a conspiracy, the Young Turks concluded, the most extreme measures were necessary.

On April 20, 1915, the Armenians of the town of Van, goaded into fury by the brutality and misgovernment of Governor Djevdet Bey, rose in revolt against the Turkish authorities. On May 16, after long weeks of hard fighting, the Armenian rebels were rescued when the Russian Army captured the town from the Turks.

The revolt of Van was later cited by apologists for the Turks as a justification for Turkish measures of persecution against the Armenians. It was this revolt, such apologists argued, that had finally provoked the Young Turks into taking drastic action. Armenophile writers, however, have asserted that the Turkish authorities had begun to carry out a policy of organized persecution even before the revolt of Van had broken out. There is little doubt that the eruption of this revolt, whether it preceded or followed the initiation of the policy of organized persecution of Armenians, did stiffen the resolve of the Young Turks to carry through the policy to the bitter end.

The policy of persecution, carried out under the direction of Interior Minister Talaat Pasha, took the form of forced deportations. Throughout eastern Anatolia, Armenian men of military age were rounded up, marched off for several miles, and shot. Armenian women, children, and old men were ordered, at bayonet point, to leave their home villages and to move to relocation centers in the Syrian desert. Armenian farms were left unplowed; and the property which the Armenians had labored so long and so hard to accumulate had to be abandoned. Since no attempt was made to provide food, water, or shelter for the forced emigrants, thousands of them dropped dead of hunger, thirst, and exhaustion during the long march to the Syrian desert. Others died of disease. Many were murdered by Kurdish shepherds, Turkish peasants, and even by some of the very police who had been assigned to guard them. Some were shot, while others were drowned. Survivors were sometimes subjected to rape or to forcible conversion to Islam.

The forced deportations began in April in the Mediterranean coastal province of Cilicia. During the months of April through October, the process of deportation was carried through in one Armenian-inhabited province after another. The execution of the policy was made easier by the Turks'

recapture, on August 4, of the town of Van from the Russian Army. The whole deadly operation was carried through with chilling speed and efficiency. Only in Smyrna and in Constantinople were the majority of the Armenians spared. In the latter city, it was only the most prominent Armenian citizens who were subjected, on April 25, to forced arrest, deportation, and execution.

Not all Armenians submitted to the persecutions meekly. In Cilicia four thousand Armenian men, women, and children retreated to the mountain of Musa Dagh, where they held off fifteen thousand Turkish soldiers for fifty-three days. On September 12, 1915, the survivors were rescued by a French ship which had been cruising in the eastern Mediterranean. Isolated acts of resistance such as this, however, were of little avail against the overwhelming force of the Turkish Army and police.

By the beginning of 1916, the deportations had been mostly completed, but sporadic outbursts of violence and brutality against Armenians continued to occur until the Turkish-Allied armistice of October 30, 1918. The exact number of Armenians killed in the course of the deportations and massacres will probably never be known. The conservative estimate, given by apologists for the Turks, is 500,000; the highest number, given by Armenian sources, is 1,500,000. It seems likely that the number of Ottoman Armenians who perished as a result of the Young Turk persecutions was about 1,000,000.

Germany, the ally of the Young Turks, might have been able to help the persecuted Armenians, but she

111

did not. Johannes Lepsius, a German theology professor and long-time expert on the Near East, succeeded to some extent in arousing the German public against the misdeeds of its Turkish ally; but he could not prod the Imperial German government into taking effective action. Neither Ambassador Hans von Wangenheim, who died in October, 1915, nor his successor, Paul Wolff-Metternich, were willing to exert any real pressure on the Ottoman government to stop the massacres. In November, 1916, General Otto Liman von Sanders, the military adviser to the Turkish armies, was able to obstruct a Turkish plan to deport the Armenians of Smyrna; but by then most of the Ottoman provinces had already been cleared of Armenians. At a time when Germany was locked in a titanic struggle with France, Great Britain, and Russia, the German government was unwilling to risk alienating the Turks through overzealous intervention on behalf of a persecuted minority.

No such inhibitions hobbled the American Ambassador to Turkey, Henry Morgenthau, Sr. Morgenthau, who had been appointed Ambassador by United States President Woodrow Wilson, first learned about the massacres from the reports of American Protestant missionaries. Morgenthau could not, however, do anything effective to help the Armenians; his protests to Talaat Pasha were heated, but in vain. The Ambassador did, however, give President Wilson the fullest possible account of the grisly events. After his return to the United States in 1916, Morgenthau became an ardent crusader for the cause of a free Armenia.

Although the United States government had been unable to stop the massacres, the news of the persecutions did encourage the growth of a vocal and influential Armenophile movement among the people of the United States. In the autumn of 1915, American Protestant churchmen set up a national organization, headed by former Near East missionary James Barton, whose goal was to aid the survivors of the Turkish massacres. In their nationwide campaign for Armenian relief, Barton and his colleagues made extensive use of a graphic 684-page British report on the massacre, written by the venerable political theorist Viscount James Bryce with the aid of the youthful classics professor Arnold J. Toynbee, and based primarily on the accounts of American Protestant missionaries. During the years 1915 to 1917, Americans from all walks of life, appalled by tales of violence and destitution in the lands of the Bible, contributed more than $25,000,000 to Barton's organization, the American Committee for Armenian and Syrian Relief. In late 1918, Barton, heartened by such success, helped set up the American Committee for the Independence of Armenia, a lobbying group whose goal was the creation of a state of Greater Armenia on the ruins of the Ottoman Empire.

By the beginning of 1919, the prospects for the emergence of such a state of Greater Armenia looked fairly bright. In May, 1918, several months after the new Bolshevik regime had taken Russia out of the war, the Russian Armenians had organized a tiny independent Republic of their own, with its capital at Erivan. The government of Erivan now looked confidently forward to annexing most of eastern Anatolia. President Wilson, converted to the cause of Armenian independence by Barton's tireless efforts, seemed likely to exert a tremendous influence over the final peace settlement, for it had been American intervention in 1917-1918 which had made possible the victory of the Allies over Germany. On October 30, 1918, the Ottoman Empire had been forced to sue the Allies for an armistice, and Enver Pasha, Djemal Pasha, and Talaat Pasha had been forced to flee to exile in Germany. The Turks were on their knees.

Instead of swiftly imposing a peace treaty on the defeated Turks, the victorious Allies spent more than a year quarreling over the division of the spoils of victory. By the end of 1919, Mustafa Kemal, the hero of the Dardanelles, had emerged as the military and political leader of the Turkish nationalist resistance movement. Kemal and his followers, while willing to renounce the Arab provinces of the Ottoman Empire, staunchly refused to accept the cession of either western Anatolian territory to Greece, or of eastern Anatolian territory to an independent Armenia.

Perhaps armed American intervention might have saved the Armenian nationalist cause. Yet Americans, once so enthusiastic about the Armenians' struggle for freedom, quickly grew indifferent to their aspirations when it became clear that implementing them would require new military exertions. On June 1, 1920, the United States Senate, bowing to a revival of isolationist sentiment among the American people, decisively defeated President Wilson's proposal that the United States undertake the responsibilities of a protectorate, or "Mandate," over Turkish Armenia.

With the American threat removed, Mustafa Kemal found it easy to play off the various powers against one another. The new Bolshevik regime in Russia, smarting under Western ostracism, proved especially willing to aid the Turkish Nationalist leader. In the final months of 1920, the Kemalist forces combined with the Bolsheviks' Red Army to crush the Armenian state. In March, 1921, the Bolsheviks not only recognized Kemal's right to eastern Anatolia, but also ceded to him the Armenian territory of Kars, which had belonged to Russia since 1878. The pitiful rump of Armenia was reabsorbed into the Russian State as a so-called "Soviet Socialist Republic."

Soon France, one of the victorious Allies, was also beginning to help the Kemalists. Angry at the British failure to back the tough French policy towards defeated Germany, the French government decided to defy the Turcophobes of the British Foreign Office by striking a bargain with the Turkish Nationalists. On October 20, 1921, France formally recognized Kemal's right to rule Cilicia, which France had been occupying since the war's end. Soon afterwards, a hundred thousand Armenians were fleeing from the province.

In August, 1922, Kemal's forces, freed from the threat of French intervention, decisively defeated the Greek Army, which had been occupying Smyrna and much of western

Anatolia since May, 1919. The entry of Nationalist troops into Smyrna in September led to the wholesale slaughter of much of that city's Armenian minority, and the panicky exodus of the rest.

By the end of 1923, Mustafa Kemal had achieved most of his foreign policy goals. The Treaty of Lausanne, signed in July of that year by Turkey and the Allied Powers, had finally confirmed Turkish possession of those territories of eastern Anatolia which had once been inhabited by Armenians. In October of the same year, the Republic of Turkey had been proclaimed, with Mustafa Kemal as its first President; the Sultanate was finally dead.

Of the nearly two million Armenians who had once lived in the Empire of the Ottoman Turks, only about forty thousand, all residents of Istanbul (the former Constantino-ple), lived in the Republic of Turkey after 1923. Many of the survivors of the 1915-1916 massacre migrated, after 1921, to Syria and Lebanon, two formerly Turkish-ruled territories governed by France under the Mandate system; other Armenians moved to the new Soviet Armenia; while other Armenians, probably the majority, migrated to that classic refuge of the persecuted, the United States.

If the fate of the Armenian refugees from Turkey, cut off forever from their native land, was indeed a sad one, the fate of the Young Turk triumvirs in exile was no happier. One former triumvir, Enver Pasha, died in 1922 fighting alongside anti-Bolshevik Muslim forces in Russian Central Asia. In 1921, Talaat Pasha was killed by an assassin, and in 1922 the same fate befell Djemal Pasha. In both cases, the assassins were Armenian refugees.

## Pertinent Literature

Grabill, Joseph L. *Protestant Diplomacy and the Near East: Missionary Influence on American Policy, 1810-1927*. Minneapolis: University of Minnesota Press, 1971.

The focus of this book, despite its somewhat misleading title, is on Protestant influence on American policy towards the Ottoman Empire during the years of the Woodrow Wilson Administration, from 1913 to 1921. The author, a Professor of History at Illinois State University at Normal, devotes most of his attention to the entanglement of American Protestant churchmen, and of the American government, in the Armenian question. Grabill makes a valiant attempt to treat this emotion-laden subject in a dispassionate and objective man-ner.

In 1810, the Congregational Church established the American Board of Commissioners for Foreign Missions. In the first two chapters, Grabill traces the history of American Protestant missionary activity in the Ottoman Empire from its beginnings, ten years after the above-mentioned date, up to the beginning of World War I in 1914. In nearly a hundred years of laborious effort, Protestant missionaries not only created a native Protestant Church, by winning away Armenians from their traditional

114

Gregorian Church, but also established a broad network of excellent educational institutions throughout the Ottoman Empire. Grabill sees the missionaries as messengers not only of the Christian gospel, but also of that whole complex of social and political values commonly known as the "American way of life." Prior to 1914, however, the missionaries transmitted such values primarily through preaching, teaching, and personal example; they did not try to make the United States government an instrument of their goals.

During World War I, however, the American Protestant missionary establishment began to take a much more active role in politics. Protestant churchmen created the American Committee for Armenian and Syrian Relief, under the chairmanship of former Near East missionary James Barton, to relieve widespread destitution in the Ottoman Empire. After the war ended, Barton and other Protestant churchmen exerted intense pressure on the United States government to assume responsibility for a protectorate over Turkish Armenia in order to prepare that country for independence. In Chapter Three, Grabill discusses the event that prompted American Protestants to undertake both of these two major initiatives: the Turkish massacre of the Armenians in 1915-1916.

The plan of massacre was, the author believes, first conceived by the Young Turks shortly after the defeat of the Turkish Army by Russian troops and Russian-Armenian volunteers at Sarikamish in the winter of 1914-1915. In the spring of 1915, the Young Turks, "enraged" by the Armenian revolt at Van and by the Russian Army's capture of that city, proceeded to carry out this plan in a systematic fashion.

Grabill tries his best to be fair to the Turks; but he does not accept the argument that the Van revolt provided a justification for the persecution of the Armenians. He also rejects the notion that the uprising at Van was the fruit of some deep-laid Armenian plot against the Ottoman authorities. He points out that the revolt broke out only after the local Turkish governor had murdered a delegation of Van Armenians who had visited him to pledge their loyalty. While conceding that prior to the spring of 1915 some Armenians had become Allied agents, the author insists that the overwhelming majority of Turkish Armenians were innocent of treason.

After a brief but graphic account of how the massacre was carried out, Grabill describes the effect of this tragedy on the missionary enterprise in the Ottoman Empire. The wholesale Turkish persecutions came very close to wiping out the American-founded Protestant Church, most of whose clergy and laity were Armenians. Many Protestant schools and churches were forced to close. In addition, quite a few American missionaries died from epidemics spawned by the deportations, the massacres, and the constant Russo-Turkish warfare in eastern Anatolia. By the end of 1915, the American Board of Commissioners for Foreign Missions had seen their investment in the Ottoman Empire in property and personnel fall to about half its prewar figure.

Grabill's discussion of the Armenian massacre of 1915-1916 relies heavily on the published autobiographies, unpublished diaries, and private papers of American Protestant missionaries in the Ottoman Empire. In addition, he uses a published account by an Armenian survivor of the massacre; the published report on the massacre written by the British Armenophiles Viscount James Bryce and Professor Arnold J. Toynbee; the published memoirs of Ambassador Henry Morgenthau, Sr.; and the private papers of Ambassador Morgenthau. He does not, however, make use of the archives of the German Foreign Ministry, or of any Turkish-language sources.

In the latter part of Chapter Three, and in Chapters Four through Eleven, the author tells the story of James Barton's successful campaign for Armenian relief and of his ultimately unsuccessful campaign for a free Armenia under an American Mandate. He shows how, once the victory of the Kemalists had become obvious, Barton reversed his previous position and publicly called for American reconciliation with Turkey and for ratification of the Treaty of Lausanne. The failure of the United States Senate on January 18, 1927, to ratify the Treaty of Lausanne represented, in the author's opinion, the last victory of an Armenophile lobby which was already rapidly declining in influence. After that date, both the American Protestant mission establishment and the American government were able to achieve a *modus vivendi* with the new Kemalist Turkey.

Throughout the book, Grabill makes a great effort to be strictly impartial, to be both defense attorney and prosecuting attorney. He tries to steer a middle course between moral relativism, on the one hand, and American Protestant ethnocentrism, on the other. To be sure, the author does not condone the Turkish massacre, which he sees as analogous to the Nazi action against the Jews a generation later; but he also finds fault with American Protestant missionaries for what he regards as their excessive self-righteousness and their uncritical identification of Christianity with the American way of life.

Thus, the author, while finding much to admire in the activities of nineteenth century American missionaries, also finds much to criticize. By their educational endeavors among Turkish Armenians and their translation of the Bible into the Armenian language, the missionaries unwittingly encouraged the growth of nationalism among that minority group, thereby laying the basis for its future conflict with the Turks. By permitting the student body in the Protestant schools of Anatolia to become predominantly Armenian, the missionaries showed, in Grabill's opinion, a lamentable "insensitivity" to the legitimate fears of their Ottoman Turkish hosts. The author compares American Protestant educational endeavors among Christian Armenians to a hypothetical foreign Muslim endeavor among black Americans.

If Grabill finds fault with some aspects of Protestant missionary activity prior to 1914, he is even more harshly critical of the "clamorous Armenianism" displayed by American Protestant churchmen during and immediately after World War I. Barton's Armenophile propaganda, the author argues, tried to make the average American believe that the unspeakably wicked Turk could do no right, while the angelically virtuous Armenian could do no wrong. Grabill believes that Protestants like Barton, by championing so enthusiastically the cause of Armenian nationalism, forgot a great truth of the Christian religion: that God is a respecter of all persons.

For, the author insists, the "religiously romantic" view of the Christian Armenian purveyed by Protestant Armenophile propaganda was belied by the facts. Armenians did sometimes commit crimes against Turks. Thus, after the Russian Army had occupied Van in May, 1915, the Armenian inhabitants attacked and killed Turkish civilians. In 1916, after the Russian Army had captured Bitlis and Erzurum, Armenian irregular troops slew thousands of Turkish men, women and children, and destroyed Muslim villages.

Grabill's tendency to equate the occasional acts of violence by some Armenians to the persecutions of the Young Turks has not gone unchallenged by historians. Some scholarly critics have even accused Grabill, a Midwestern American of evangelical Protestant background, of trying so hard to be fair to the Turks that he has actually been unfair to both the Armenians and the American Protestant missionaries. Whatever quarrel one might have with the author's interpretations, however, one cannot deny that his work is a monument to indefatigable scholarly effort. The excellent maps of Armenia and the Near East are a great help to those whose knowledge of Near Eastern history and geography is minimal. The photographs of leading personalities of the time bring this tragic period to life again for today's reader. The extensive bibliographical essay is a treasure trove for future researchers. The footnotes, unfortunately, are located at the back of the book, making it inconvenient for the reader to consult them.

Trumpener, Ulrich. *Germany and the Ottoman Empire, 1914-1918*. Princeton, N.J.: Princeton University Press, 1968.

This book, which treats the whole question of German-Turkish relations during World War I, also contains a good discussion of the Armenian tragedy of 1915-1916. The author, who teaches history at the University of Alberta in Canada, does not give the reader any of the gruesome details of the manifold sufferings inflicted on the Turkish Armenians in the course of the deportations. He does, however, try to examine certain historiographical issues connected with the massacre. In doing so, he rejects contentions put forward by both Allied propagandists during World War I and by present-day Turkish historians.

Throughout his book, Trumpener emphasizes how limited was the influence which the German government was able to exert, during the war, on its Turkish ally; he also shows in great detail how stubbornly independent the Young Turks really were. Thus, the Turkish government successfully frustrated almost all German attempts to win new economic advantages in the Empire. After the military collapse of Russia in 1917, the German government protested in vain against Turkish military encroachments in Transcaucasia. Trumpener sees the Turkish massacre of the Armenians in 1915-1916 as just one more example of the inability of Germany to control the actions of its Turkish ally.

In Chapter Seven, Trumpener traces the response of German officials and diplomats to the massacres, from the beginning of the persecutions in April, 1915, to the early part of 1917, when the pace of persecution finally began to slacken. The author, unlike the Allied propagandists of World War I, does not believe that the German government either "instigated" or "approved of" the deportation and massacre of the Armenians. He does, however, blame the German government for having refrained, "for reasons of political expediency," from trying more energetically to restrain the Turks from killing Armenians. At the same time, he admits that, given the absence of large concentrations of German troops in the Ottoman Empire, there was little the Germans could have done to coerce the Turks into following a more humane policy.

Trumpener is careful to take note of those few Germans whose consciences were aroused by the Armenian horrors. Thus, he has high praise for Otto Liman von Sanders, the German military adviser who halted the deportation of Armenians from Smyrna in November, 1916. Trumpener also singles out for honorable mention the German theologian and philanthropist Johannes Lepsius, who, by his activities among German clergymen, university professors, and journalists, did so much to expose the Turkish atrocities before the bar of German public opinion. Without this man's activities, the author suggests, the German government would have done even less for the Armenians. Yet, the author sees both Liman von Sanders and Lepsius as rare exceptions to the general pattern of German "timidity" and "passivity" in dealing with the Young Turks. It was fear of losing a valuable ally in time of war, Trumpener concludes, that effectively inhibited Germany from exerting more pressure on her Turkish ally.

While criticizing the German government for its sins of omission, Trumpener does not attribute to the Armenians themselves any degree of responsibility for the disaster that befell them; instead, he regards them as innocent victims. Although Trumpener does concede that some Ottoman Armenians did engage in subversion and espionage or desert to the Russians, he insists that the broad majority of them were innocent of "overtly disloyal" activities. He flatly rejects the argument, frequently made by Turkish historians, that the Armenian districts were "teeming with sedition" even before April, 1915. Similarly, Trumpener dismisses as "oversimplified" the view, held by many Turkish historians, that the outbreak of fighting between Turks and Armenians at Van, in April, 1915, resulted from the "rebelliousness" of the Armenian population.

Thus, the author places responsibility for the massacre squarely on the shoulders of the Young Turk leaders. He sees no extenuating circumstances to mitigate their guilt. Whatever provocations the Armenians might have committed, the author does not believe that they justified the kind of countermeasures put into effect by the Ottoman authorities in 1915. Resting his case chiefly on secondary works written by resettled Armenian historians, Trumpener asserts something that Turkish historians vigorously deny: that the young Turks had already decided to commit genocide against the Armenians of their eastern provinces even before April, 1915, and that the fighting in Van was merely a convenient excuse for beginning the work of deportation and extermination.

Trumpener's discussion of the Armenian massacre of 1915-1916 is based primarily on the archives of the German Foreign Ministry, located in Bonn, West Germany. In addition, the author makes use of two contemporary publications by Johannes Lepsius; the contemporary published report of the British Armenophiles, Viscount James Bryce and Professor Arnold J. Toynbee; and certain secondary works written by historians of Armenian origin living in the United States. Trumpener has not, however, been able to obtain access to the Turkish archives. When he does refer to Turkish-language secondary sources which discuss the Armenian deportations, he does so only to refute their arguments defending the Young Turks' actions.

There are no photographs in Trumpener's book, although there are two maps; one of Transcaucasia, the other of the Berlin-to-Bagdad railway project. The appendixes include a list of key personnel of the Ottoman Cabinet for the World War I period and a list of those German Foreign Office officials who played a key role in German-Ottoman relations during this period. There is a full bibliography; and the footnotes are placed at the bottom of each page, making it easy for the reader to consult them. — *P.D.M.*

## Additional Recommended Reading

Arlen, Michael J. *Passage to Ararat*. New York: Farrar, Straus and Giroux, 1975. A work which is part travel account, part the story of a man's search for his ethnic roots, and part a fresh reexamination of what the author views as the twentieth century's first case of organized genocide, this book was written by a staff writer for the *New Yorker* of partly Armenian descent.

Hartunian, Abraham H. *Neither to Laugh Nor to Weep: A Memoir of the Armenian Genocide*. Translated by Vartan Hartunian. Boston: Beacon Press, 1968. An emotionally charged eyewitness account of the deportations and massacres, written by an Armenian Protestant minister who owed his survival to American missionaries.

Shaw, Stanford J. and Ezel Kural Shaw. *History of the Ottoman Empire and Modern Turkey*. Vol. II: *Reform, Revolution, and Republic: The Rise of Modern Turkey, 1808-1975*. New York: Cambridge University Press, 1977. Relies chiefly on Turkish sources to assert that the Young Turks' deportation of the Armenians was an understandable response to Armenian manifestations of disloyalty and rebellion, and that the Young Turks tried to have the deportations carried out in a humane fashion.

Morgenthau, Henry, Sr. *Ambassador Morgenthau's Story*. Garden City, N.Y.: Doubleday, Page and Company, 1919. Contains five chapters packed with grisly details of the Armenian massacre; the former American ambassador argues that the Young Turks' action was inspired by the doctrines and practices of Pan-Germanism.

Djemal Pasha, Ahmed. *Memories of a Turkish Statesman, 1913-1919*. New York: George H. Doran Company, 1922. The former Young Turk triumvir, while conceding that some crimes were perpetrated against the Armenians in the course of the deportations, insists that these deportations were absolutely necessary in order to protect the Turkish Army against the danger posed by an Armenian revolutionary conspiracy.

Nalbandian, Louise. *The Armenian Revolutionary Movement: The Development of Armenian Political Parties Through the Nineteenth Century*. Berkeley: University of California Press, 1963. The author views the formation of Armenian revolutionary nationalist groups in the Ottoman Empire in the latter half of the nineteenth century as an understandable response by the younger and more impatient members of a minority group to the repression and injustice of Turkish rule.

# JAPAN PRESENTS CHINA WITH THE TWENTY-ONE DEMANDS

*Type of event:* Diplomatic: Japanese demands which threaten China's sovereignty
*Time:* January 18-May 25, 1915
*Locale:* Japan, China, Great Britain, and the United States

### Principal personages:

THOMAS WOODROW WILSON (1856-1924), twenty-eighth President of the United States, 1913-1921

SIR EDWARD GREY (1862-1933), Foreign Secretary of Great Britain, 1905-1916

JOHN NEWELL JORDAN, British Minister to China, 1906-1920

PAUL SAMUEL REINSCH (1869-1923), United States Ambassador to China, 1913-1919

HIOKI EKI, Japanese Minister to China, 1914-1918

BARON TAKAAKIRA KATO (1859-1926), Foreign Minister of Japan, 1914-1915

PRINCE ARITOMO YAMAGATA (1838-1922), leading figure among the Japanese "genro," or elder statesmen

YÜAN SHIH-K'AI (1859-1916), President of China, 1912-1916

WILLIAM JENNINGS BRYAN (1860-1925), United States Secretary of State, 1913-1915

ROBERT LANSING (1864-1928), Counselor to United States Secretary of State, 1913-1915; and United States Secretary of State, 1915-1920

ARIGA NAGAO, Japanese adviser to Yüan Shih-k'ai

### Summary of Event

The Twenty-One Demands, presented by the Japanese Minister to China, Hioki Eki, to Chinese President Yüan Shih-k'ai on January 18, 1915, represented the first step in Japan's long march towards confrontation with the Western powers. It was now that Japan set out on a path which would lead, in 1941, to all-out war with Great Britain and the United States, and to defeat and ruin.

The island nation of Japan had originally received much of her civilization from China, and there have always been many racial and cultural similarities between the two countries. The Buddhist religion first came to Japan from China, and the Japanese system of writing is derived from that of China. During the nineteenth century, however, the two countries had responded to the challenge of the West in quite different ways. Under the Manchu emperors, China had stagnated in the traditions of the past, while greedy Western states extorted from her more and more special privileges for their nationals. Japan, on the other hand, had adopted thoroughgoing reforms in her economy, her Army, her educational system, and her administrative system; and

121

she had done so within the traditional Imperial form of government.

By 1895, Japan had become so strong that she was able, in the Sino-Japanese War, to defeat China on the field of battle. As a result of this war, Japan annexed outright the island of Taiwan, and gained a predominant influence over the nominally independent kingdom of Korea. In 1900, Japanese troops joined the soldiers of the Western states, in suppressing that last great Chinese popular antiforeign outburst, the Boxer Rebellion. Such early successes only helped to whet the Japanese appetite for further expansion.

By 1915, China had become an inviting target for further Japanese encroachments. The Republican Revolution of 1911 had not arrested the long decline of China's power; it had, in fact, accelerated it. In January, 1916, President Yüan Shih-k'ai would try to make himself Emperor; but the outbreak of armed rebellion, and the death of Yüan himself in June of the same year, put an end to this plan. Little more than a year after Yüan's death, southern China would set up a rival government, defying the authorities in Peking. Successive Chinese governments, fully aware of their country's weakness and disunity, tried to avoid involvement in the quarrels of Europe. Thus, the Peking regime would not declare war on Germany until August, 1917.

In August, 1914, Takaakira Kato, who had become Foreign Minister of Japan in April of that year, led Japan into the war against Germany on the side of Great Britain, who had been an ally of Japan since 1902. Soon, Japanese forces had quickly overrun the German leasehold in the Chinese province of Shantung.

Kato, a believer in government by political parties, had long wished to get rid of the traditional power of the elder statesmen, or genro, in Japanese politics. The most prominent of the genro was Aritomo Yamagata, who had once served as Minister of War, Prime Minister, and Minister of Home Affairs. This venerable gentleman thoroughly detested Kato. By 1915, however, Kato thought he saw a golden opportunity to win the political struggle at home by gaining a decisive diplomatic victory abroad. All the European powers were preoccupied with World War I; the time was ripe, he believed, for extracting valuable advantages for Japan at the expense of a helpless China.

Thus, on January 18, 1915, the Japanese Minister to China, Hioki Eki, acting on Kato's instructions, presented to Chinese President Yüan Shih-k'ai a series of proposals that came to be known as the Twenty-One Demands. These demands were divided into five groups. In Groups One through Four, the Japanese government demanded that the government of China confirm Japan's recent gains in Shantung and her existing territorial, trade, and railway concessions in Manchuria and Inner Mongolia, while granting her new concessions in the latter territories as well. Furthermore, China was asked to promise never to permit any other power to acquire or lease any harbor, bay, or island along the coast of China.

It was Group Five of the Twenty-One Demands, however, which most seriously threatened China's national sovereignty. In Group Five, the Japanese government demanded that China consult with it before allowing any foreign capital into Fukien province (the coastal Chinese province opposite the Japanese-ruled island of Taiwan), grant Japan new railway concessions in the Yangtze River Valley, and buy at least half of her arms from Japan. In addition, the Chinese government would have been required to hire influential Japanese as political, financial, and military advisers, and to share with Japan the control of the police forces at key points throughout China. If China had accepted Group Five of the Twenty-One Demands, she would have become a *de facto* protectorate of Japan.

President Yüan knew that China, because of her military weakness, was incapable of resisting Japan or any other power singlehandedly; her only hope lay in playing off the Great Powers against one another. Therefore, once negotiations with Japan had begun, Yüan stalled for time, dragging out the talks for as long as possible. Although Hioki had demanded that the Chinese government keep the negotiations secret, Yüan leaked news of the talks to the United States Ambassador to China, Paul Samuel Reinsch, and the British Ambassador to China, John Newell Jordan.

At first, Yüan's tactics seemed to pay off. Reinsch sent telegram after telegram to United States President Woodrow Wilson, urging American intervention to preserve China's territorial integrity. President Wilson was quite disturbed by Japan's bullying of China; it seemed to challenge

the American policy of preventing any single power from dominating that vast country. Robert Lansing, who was Counselor to Secretary of State William Jennings Bryan, seriously questioned Wilson's efforts to block Japanese expansion in China. In any event, on March 13, 1915, the United States government sent a note to Japan expressing its objections to specific proposals of the Twenty-One Demands. When British Foreign Secretary Sir Edward Grey learned from Jordan about Japan's demands, he, too, became alarmed. While Grey wanted to keep Japan as an ally of Great Britain, he did not want to see Japan elbow Britain out of her existing rights in China. On May 3, 1915, the British government, like the American, sent a note to Japan, specifying its objections to some of the Twenty-One Demands.

Yüan also acted to fan dissension within the ranks of the Japanese Cabinet itself. He sent Ariga Nagao, a Japanese adviser of whose loyalty he was certain, to the Japanese capital of Tokyo. When Ariga arrived there, he warned Japanese politicians that Kato's policy had placed Japan in great peril by alienating Great Britain. Many of the Japanese genro, who wielded great influence over the Cabinet, found Ariga's arguments convincing; they still had vivid memories of the days when Japan herself had been a weak State. On May 4, 1915, shortly after Japan had received the warning from Britain, the Japanese Cabinet, prodded by the genro, held an emergency meeting. As a result of this meeting, Kato's China policy was modified. Japan would indeed, submit, on May 6, an ultimatum to China; but the demands of Group Five, which had aroused so much controversy, would not be included in this ultimatum. These demands would be "postponed" for consideration at an unspecified future time. Japan threatened war, however, if China did not agree, by May 9, 1915, to accept the first four groups of the original Twenty-One Demands.

When Yüan received this ultimatum, he knew he could stall no longer. British Ambassador Jordan urged the Chinese President to accept the modified Japanese demands as soon as possible. The Americans, despite their pious wishes, proved equally unwilling to help China. Wilson had by now been diverted from his paternal concern for China by the crisis in German-American relations arising from the sinking of the *Lusitania*. On May 25, 1915, therefore, Yüan Shih-k'ai signed a treaty with Japan, granting all of the first four groups of the Twenty-One Demands.

The treaty did not satisfy the ardent nationalists of Japan. Many Japanese ultrapatriots blamed Britain for keeping Japan from making even larger gains. In August, 1915, Kato, faced with widespread dissatisfaction with his conduct of the talks with China, resigned from the Foreign Ministry; he would never hold office again. Many nationalistic Chinese were enraged by the treaty, which they viewed as a national humiliation; they especially bewailed the loss of effective Chinese control over Manchuria and Inner Mongolia. The Twenty-One Demands had aroused a new wave of antiforeign sentiment in China, one which was directed, for the first time, against the Japanese as well as against the Western powers. Chinese anger against Japan would be inflamed still further when, on May 4, 1919, the Treaty of Versailles confirmed Japan's wartime gains in the province of Shantung.

The Twenty-One Demands marked the beginning of American and British opposition to further Japanese expansion in China. On May 11, 1915, Secretary of State Bryan publicly warned Japan that the United States would not recognize any agreement that impaired the sovereignty of China. True, Bryan's successor as Secretary of State, Robert Lansing, would try to reach a lasting agreement with Japan in 1917; but the seeds of mutual suspicion had already been sown.

In 1923, Great Britain, desiring to please the United States, terminated the alliance between herself and Japan. In March, 1932, Japan, having evicted the Chinese administration by force in the previous September, created a puppet state in Manchuria. In July, 1937, full-scale war erupted between China and Japan; and in December, 1941, Anglo-American opposition to Japanese expansion in China finally resulted in a war between Japan and these two Western countries. It had been twenty-six years earlier, however, that Japan and the United States had taken the very first steps down the long road to Pearl Harbor.

124

## Japan Presents China with the Twenty-One Demands

### Pertinent Literature

Lowe, Peter. *Great Britain and Japan, 1911-1915: A Study of British Far Eastern Policy*. London: Macmillan and Company, 1969.

In this well-written work, Peter Lowe, a Lecturer in History at Manchester University, studies the history of the Anglo-Japanese alliance of 1902 from the time of its renewal in 1911, to the crisis caused by the issuance of the Twenty-One Demands by Japan in 1915. The major theme of the book is the wide divergence which developed during these years between Japan and Great Britain concerning their respective policies in China: "Britain wished to defend her position. Japan wished to expand her position." It was this difference in their approaches to China which, the author implies, finally doomed the alliance, causing it to expire in 1923.

In the first chapter, the author deals with the revision and renewal, in 1910-1911, of the Anglo-Japanese alliance of 1902. In 1910 and 1911 this alliance was still based on the mutual needs and mutual confidence of both countries. Such mutual confidence was not, however, to last very long. In chapters Three to Five, the author shows how Japanese and British policies in China came more and more into conflict with each other during the years between the outbreak of revolution in China in 1911, and the outbreak of war in Europe in August, 1914. By the eve of the European war, Japan was trying to gain new concessions in the Yangtze Valley region of China, which Britain regarded as her own exclusive sphere of influence.

Japan's entry into the war on the side of Britain in August, 1914, did, the author points out in Chapter Six, temporarily gloss over Anglo-Japanese differences over China. With her Navy stretched thin to meet the challenge of the German fleet, Britain could not afford to do without the aid of Japan in the Far East. Yet, in the following year, the sharp differences between the two allies would come to the surface once again.

In the seventh chapter, Lowe treats at length the diplomatic crisis arising from Japan's issuance of the Twenty-One Demands and shows clearly how Japan's conduct of the negotiations with China was adversely affected by the split within the Japanese government between the genro, or elder statesmen, and Foreign Minister Takaakira Kato. Lowe views Kato as a clumsy blunderer, whose attempts to hide Group Five of the Demands from the knowledge of the British government succeeded only in arousing British anger at Japanese duplicity.

The author has high praise for both Chinese President Yüan Shih-k'ai and British Foreign Secretary Sir Edward Grey for their conduct during the crisis of 1915. Lowe stresses Yüan's skill in preventing all of the original Twenty-One Demands from being imposed on China, and emphasizes Grey's adroitness in managing to salvage, at least temporarily, both British rights in China and the Anglo-Japanese alliance. The author also believes, however, that the crisis of 1915, by sowing a profound distrust of Japan within the ranks of the British Foreign Office, did much to render inevitable the termination of the Anglo-Japanese alliance after the war was over.

Lowe's account of the Sino-Japanese negotiations of 1915 is based primarily on the archives of the British Foreign Office and on the published diplomatic documents of the United States. He has also made use of interviews with Captain Malcolm Kennedy, a former Reuters correspondent in Tokyo, and has consulted all available English-language secondary works on the subject. The author has not, however, made use of any Chinese-language or Japanese-language sources. His book is full of useful aids for the nonexpert reader: an ample bibliography, informative maps, and one particularly informative appendix consisting of the biographical data on the British and Japanese diplomats whose names are mentioned in the main body of the book. The rest of the appendixes are complete texts of all key documents, including the Twenty-One Demands. There is an excellent series of photographic illustrations of British and Japanese diplomats which, like the British political cartoons included in the book, bring the period to life for today's reader. As a final aid, the author has placed the footnotes at the bottom of each page so that they can be consulted easily.

Chi, Madeleine. *China Diplomacy, 1914-1918*. Cambridge, Mass.: Harvard University Press, 1970.

Madeleine Chi, a Professor of History at Manhattanville College, has written a short but scholarly study of Sino-Japanese relations during the period of World War I. Throughout these years, Chi contends, Japan followed an aggressive policy of expansion at the expense of China. She shows how, during this period, the efforts of China's diplomats to defend their country against Japanese encroachment were hampered again and again by political disunity at home. Chi also argues that successive Chinese governments, in their efforts to protect China's independence, relied far too much on the benevolence of Great Britain and the United States, and far too little on their own exertions. Thus, the authorities in Peking ignored the crying need for military and administrative reforms, which alone could have made China strong enough to face the Japanese threat.

After having discussed Japan's entry into the war in Chapter One, the author devotes the entire second chapter to a blow-by-blow account of the diplomatic crisis arising from Japan's issuance of the Twenty-One Demands in 1915. The roles played by the United States, Great Britain, and the Japanese elder statesmen (genro) are all treated quite thoroughly.

In her judgment of Yüan Shih-k'ai's conduct of the negotiations of 1915, the author damns the Chinese president with faint praise. She does admit that Japan's gains ". . . were not as extensive as they appeared on paper." She does concede that, given Chinese military weakness, there might be "some justification" in praising Yüan's skill in handling the talks. She also emphasizes, on the other hand, that Yüan was the only Chinese who regarded the results of the negotiations as a diplomatic victory for China; and suggests that the Chinese president was deluding himself in regarding the results that way. Most thinking Chinese, the author points out, viewed the treaty of May 25, 1915, which ended the diplomatic crisis, as a great national humiliation for China. Chi herself believes that the terms of the treaty constituted a "giant stride" towards the Japanese goal of gaining "a paramount position over all China."

In Chapter Three, Chi argues that it was Japanese intrigue, as well as popular disaffection within China, which led to the downfall of Yüan Shih-k'ai in 1916. In Chapters Four and Five, Chi contends that, during the period from May, 1915, to the end of World War I, both Great Britain and the United States demonstrated all too frequently their willingness to sacrifice the rights and interests of China on the altar of good relations with their Japanese ally. In Chapter Six, the author shows that China's declaration of war on Germany, in August, 1917, worsened internal dissensions within the country without assuring her of fairer treatment by the United States, Great Britain, and Japan at the Peace Conference of 1919. She sees in the humiliation suffered by a weak China during these wartime years, and the nationalistic passions which this aroused among the Chinese intelligentsia, the roots of Chinese Communism.

The author's account of the Sino-Japanese negotiations of January-May, 1915, relies heavily on the archives of the Japanese Foreign Ministry and on a published collection of Chinese Foreign Ministry documents for the period. In addition, she makes use of the British Foreign Ministry Archives, the United States State Department Archives, and a published collection of United States diplomatic documents for the period. Although this book has a very full bibliography, it lacks maps or illustrations of any kind. The footnotes are placed at the back of the book, making it inconvenient for the reader to consult them. — *P.D.M.*

### Additional Recommended Reading

Li, T'ien-i. *Woodrow Wilson's China Policy, 1913-1917*. New York: Twayne Publishers, 1952. Views President Wilson's policy towards China in 1915 as having been morally praiseworthy, but impractical.

Beers, Burton F. *Vain Endeavor: Robert Lansing's Attempts to End the American-Japanese Rivalry*. Durham, N.C.: Duke University Press, 1962. Examines the reasons for Robert Lansing's disagreements with President Wilson, in 1915, over American policy towards China.

Reinsch, Paul Samuel. *An American Diplomat in China*. Garden City, N.Y.: Doubleday, Page, and Company, 1922. Chapter Twelve is a first-hand account by the onetime American Ambassador to China of his role in the Sino-Japanese diplomatic crisis of 1915.

Israel, Jerry. *Progressivism and the Open Door: America and China, 1905-1921*. Pittsburgh, Pa.: University of Pittsburgh Press, 1971. Argues that Ambassador Reinsch's strong opposition to Japanese expansion in China was derived from his background as a Wisconsin Progressive and staunch opponent of monopolistic tendencies within the American business world.

Duus, Peter. *Party Rivalry and Political Change in Taishō Japan*. Cambridge, Mass.: Harvard University Press, 1968. Examines in depth the long conflict between believers in oligarchy and advocates of rule by political parties, and shows how the conflict inside Japan affected Japanese foreign policy in 1915.

Young, Ernest P. *The Presidency of Yüan Shih-k'ai: Liberalism and Dictatorship in Early Republican China*. Ann Arbor: University of Michigan Press, 1977. Examines anew the role played by Yüan during the Sino-Japanese crisis of 1915, and concludes that the manner in which the crisis was resolved was a fatal blow to the prestige of his regime.

# THE GALLIPOLI CAMPAIGN

*Type of event:* Military: Allied expedition launched against Turkey
*Time:* February, 1915-January, 1916
*Locale:* The Gallipoli peninsula of Turkey and surrounding waters

*Principal personages:*

SIR WINSTON LEONARD SPENCER CHURCHILL (1874-1965),
British First Lord of the Admiralty, 1911-1915

SIR JOHN ARBUTHNOT FISHER (1841-1920), British First Sea
Lord

VICE-ADMIRAL SIR SACKVILLE HAMILTON CARDEN (1857-
1930), Commander of the British expeditionary fleet

VICE-ADMIRAL JOHN DE ROBECK, Carden's replacement

GENERAL SIR IAN STANDISH MONTEITH HAMILTON (1853-
1947), Commander of the Allied expeditionary army

GENERAL SIR CHARLES CARMICHAEL MONRO (1860-1929),
Hamilton's replacement

HORATIO HERBERT KITCHENER (EARL KITCHENER OF
KHARTOUM AND OF BROOME) (1850-1916), British Secretary of State for War, 1914

ENVER PASHA (1881?-1922), head of the ruling junta in Turkey

MUSTAFA KEMAL (1881-1938), a Turkish commander

GENERAL OTTO LIMAN VON SANDERS (1855-1929), German
adviser to the Turkish Army and commander of Turkish
forces in the Dardanelles

## Summary of Event

Jutting southwestward from European Turkey into the Aegean Sea is the Gallipoli peninsula, a finger of land some sixty miles long and fifteen miles across at its widest. The Gallipoli terrain is rugged; high cliffs rise abruptly from the surroundings, and inland much of the peninsula consists of steep ridges and deep gullies covered with thick scrub growth. Separating the peninsula from Asiatic Turkey to the south is the deep, narrow, Dardanelles Straits which connects the Mediterranean to the entrances to the Black Sea. It was on the Gallipoli peninsula and in the Dardanelles that one of the most important Allied campaigns of World War I took place in 1915.

Allied plans for the campaign emerged not long after Turkey had entered the war on the side of the Central Powers in late 1914. One of the first moves by the Turks on coming into the war had been to close the Dardanelles to Allied traffic. This was done to prevent Russia from receiving munitions from her western allies, Britain and France, and to deny the export of Russian wheat to the west.

As early as December, 1914, British strategists were considering the feasibility of opening the Dardanelles by naval action. As Winston Churchill put it: "are there no alternatives to sending our armies to chew barbed wire in Flanders?" One alternative, suggested by Sir John Fisher, British First Sea Lord, would have been to send the British fleet into the Baltic and link up with the Russians there. Fisher warned that the Dardanelles would be strongly defended, and that as many as twelve ships might be lost in trying to force a passage through those straits.

But Fisher's doubts were overcome by Churchill and the pro-Dardanelles advocates. A successful endeavor would, they argued, bring a host of benefits to the Allied war effort. Forcing the Dardanelles would gain a secure supply line with Russia; an Allied front in the Balkans could be established; Bulgaria would be won to the Allied side; Serbia would be saved; Constantinople could be attacked, which might knock Turkey out of the war. To these advantages, Churchill added that an attack on the Dardanelles was an "ideal method" of defending British interests in Egypt and the water routes to India.

British naval commanders in the Mediterranean were perhaps less confident of the success of such an expedition than Churchill. Vice-Admiral Carden, who would command the proposed attack, judged that the Dardanelles could not be "rushed" but might be forced by means of an extended operation with a large number of ships. Nevertheless, Carden dutifully put forth a plan which he estimated would require about one month to accomplish. The Navy, Car-

den wrote, would destroy the Turkish defenses at the western entrance to the Dardanelles, then move up the forty-mile-long channel. The mine fields would have to be cleared, then the Navy would move up to the Narrows, a tight neck of the channel, only some sixteen hundred feet across and heavily protected by land artillery. If the fleet broke through the Narrows, the ships could move on to bombard Constantinople some sixty miles beyond. It was further expected that, when the British fleet arrived, the Turks in Constantinople would rise up against the pro-German junta of Enver Pasha, and force Turkey out of the war.

The Germans were cognizant of the strategic importance of the Dardanelles. The German Naval Minister, Alfred von Tirpitz, is quoted as saying in 1915: "Should the Dardanelles fall, then the World War has been decided against us." Accordingly, the Turks and their German advisers, had for some six months been busily improving the land defenses on both sides of the straits. By early 1915, some one hundred heavy (up to fourteen-inch caliber) weapons were emplaced in Turkish forts, with lighter guns and howitzers scattered in locations between the several forts located on the Dardanelles shores. The straits waters were heavily sown with a series of mine fields, to which were added antisubmarine nets, searchlights, and torpedoes to hamper or halt the invading Allied ships.

Meanwhile, the French government approved of the Dardanelles expedition and agreed to send a squadron of ships to join the British fleet. Vice-Admiral Carden would command fifteen British battleships, five French battleships, seven Allied cruisers, and sundry smaller vessels in what would be one of the greatest Allied naval efforts of World War I. Many of the ships were obsolescent, but several, particularly *Queen Elizabeth*, were new and armed with fifteen-inch guns.

As planned, the Allied naval bombardment of the western approach forts commenced in the early morning of February 19, 1915. After several hours, the Turkish defenders withdrew from the outer forts, and marines were landed to destroy the abandoned guns. Bad weather delayed further action for about a week. Then, on February 25, the fleet moved forward again, further into the straits. Some thirty miles eastward from the outer forts, the Allied fleet encountered the first lines of exploding mines. Mine-sweeping trawlers were dispatched to clear a channel through the mine fields. The Allied delay gave the Turks the opportunity to regroup and strengthen the forts at the Narrows to resist the passage of the fleet. At that point, ill and exhausted from the strain of command, Vice-Admiral Carden resigned and returned home. Vice-Admiral Robeck assumed command of the fleet and prepared to carry on.

March 5 saw the first attacks on the forts at the Narrows. Robeck decided to launch a major assault against Fort Chanak on the Asiatic side of the Narrows. For two and a half hours the heavy guns of seven British and four French battleships poured their fire on Fort Chanak and on the auxiliary Turkish batteries on the Gallipoli side. Six more British ships were sent to the Narrows, adding their firepower to the smashing of Fort Chanak. By early afternoon on March 5, the Turkish fire had slackened and nearly stopped; it was later revealed that the Turks had virtually run out of ammunition.

Then came a sudden reversal with the main assault launched on March 18. The old French battleship *Bouvet* was struck, and it sank with most of its crew. The British *Irresistible* hit a floating mine and was put out of action. *Gaulois* and *Inflexible* hit mines and heeled over. *Ocean* was fatally damaged by another mine and sank within a few minutes; all hands were lost. Several smaller ships were also sunk or badly damaged. Of the fifty-eight Allied ships in the Narrows engagement, about a dozen were lost in the afternoon of March 5, including six capital ships; also, some two thousand men had died. Such losses, while severe, were not disastrous. Lord Herbert Kitchener, British Secretary of State for War, urged de Robeck to push forward through the Narrows the next day. Churchill added that even heavier losses would justify a successful effort to force the Narrows. The Turks and Germans fully expected that the British would make another attempt, but Robeck decided against a renewed effort and withdrew the fleet from the Narrows. He judged that naval action alone would not be sufficient to gain control of the Dardanelles; the forts would have to be neutralized by the army.

Plans and preparations for landing the army on Gallipoli were already under way. General Ian Hamilton, who had been appointed commander of a projected expeditionary force in

February, was eager to use that force, and Robeck supported him. Lord Kitchener also supported him, and arranged to ship a full division of regular army troops from the western front to Hamilton who also made use of forces drawn from all parts of the British Empire. The French government agreed to send Hamilton a division drawn from its colonial empire. The bulk of those forces was dispatched to Egypt and to the Greek island of Lemnos off the coast of Asia Minor where Hamilton had his headquarters. There was further delay for the assembling of landing craft and for repacking of the transports. The Turks used that period to improve the Gallipoli defenses, erecting barbed wire barricades, digging trenches, and placing field artillery and machine guns along the shores of the peninsula. Enver Pasha and Otto Liman von Sanders, German commander of the Turkish forces in the Dardanelles, raised six divisions and placed them at strategic points on Gallipoli.

Hamilton planned to make landings at several places on the western tip of Gallipoli, consolidate those beachheads, move inland to the heights, and go on to knock out the forts at the Narrows. The first British landings on Gallipoli were made from Lemnos on April 25 at Cape Helles and Ari Burnu. The French landed at Kum-Kale on the Asiatic side of entrance to the Dardanelles. The French landings were a feint intended to confuse the defenders; they were soon withdrawn and joined the British forces on Gallipoli. Turkish artillery located on the Gallipoli heights kept up a heavy fire against the invaders. Several of the landing parties were driven back off the beaches, but other groups were able to hold their beachheads along the southwestern edge of Gallipoli.

By early May, 1915, the Allies had some seventy thousand troops ashore and consolidated on the western end of Gallipoli. They moved eastward toward the village of Krithia, which controlled the only road through the peninsula. The fight for Krithia was very intense until the Allies had to pull back when their ammunition ran out. A week later, resupplied, they made a second attempt to take Krithia, preceded by a heavy bombardment of the area by the naval guns offshore. In the second attempt at Krithia, the British had gained about one-half of the village when a little-known commander of a Turkish reserve brigade, Mustafa Kemal (later leader of the Turkish national revival), led his men to drive the British back again.

Both sides then settled into trench warfare, bombarding each other across the width of the peninsula. The slaughter and the suffering were terrible. For the British there was a scarcity of fresh water, which had to be brought ashore by ships. Malaria and dysentery struck down hundreds; arrangements to remove the wounded and the ill were inadequate; and the Turks constantly attacked. By late May, 1915, British losses on Gallipoli approached fifteen thousand, while Turkish losses were as great, or greater. Advances of a few miles would be made by one side, only to be forced back by the other side. It was a stalemate.

Hamilton decided to break the

deadlock by attempting a landing at Suvla Bay on the north shore of the peninsula which would put his troops behind the Turkish lines and closer to the Narrows forts. The Suvla Bay landings were to be coordinated with new attacks on the Turkish-held heights, in the middle of the peninsula, and with a feint by the Navy at Saros Gulf northeast of Suvla. Hamilton requested more troops for what was to be the major offensive of the Gallipoli campaign. Kitchener obliged with three regular and two territorial divisions. Munitions for Gallipoli were also to be given priority over those for the western front in France.

At Suvla Bay, Anzac (Australian and New Zealand) troops and Indian Ghurkas went in first. They got ashore on August 6 and headed for the twelve-hundred-foot ridges called Sari Bair. To reach Sari Bair, they had to cross a wide salt flat beach upon which the Turkish guns looked down. Unprotected, the Anzacs and the Ghurkas were hit hard, but some of them reached the Sari Bair crests. Then the Turks, led by Mustafa Kemal, counterattacked to drive the Allied forces off the crests. The loss of life was extremely heavy in the fighting for Suvla and Sari Bair; some units on both sides were virtually annihilated. Finally, suffering from those losses as well as from lack of water, the heat, and sickness, the attackers withdrew to the beaches on August 10. The Turks held Sari Bair and the lands beyond. The Allied offensive had failed.

For that failure, General Hamilton was relieved of his command and returned to England in October. Allied armies still held points around the perimeter of Gallipoli, but it was evident that they were too depleted to return to the offensive. When Lord Kitchener visited Gallipoli in November, 1915, the new commander, General Charles Monro, recommended immediate withdrawal of the troops. It would be a humiliating end to a great enterprise, but it had to be done. The phased withdrawal began in December, 1915, and finished in January, 1916. Monro conducted the evacuation with much skill; there was virtually no further loss of life. Nevertheless, it was a total retreat and, for Britain, the worst defeat since Saratoga.

Human costs were enormous in the Dardanelles-Gallipoli campaign. Allied casualties reached more than 250,000 men; Turkish losses were of equal magnitude. Reputations were wrecked or enhanced. Of the British leaders, Churchill was forced out of office, Fisher resigned, Hamilton left the army, and even the fame of the great Lord Kitchener was tarnished by the disaster at Gallipoli. On the Turkish side, Mustafa Kemal was hailed as the "Savior of Gallipoli," and partly based on that reputation, he went on to become the first president of the Turkish Republic.

## Pertinent Literature

Moorehead, Alan. *Gallipoli*. New York: Harper and Brothers, 1956.

This is a fine book, probably the best single volume available on the subject. Moorehead, an Australian journalist, historian, and novelist brings together his skills in those fields to present a graphic story of the tragic Gallipoli campaign.

Particularly striking are his characterizations of the leaders on both sides. The cunning, self-seeking Enver Pasha, the ambitious idealist Mustafa Kemal, and the efficient, determined and temperamental German organizer of victory, Limon von Sanders are compared with the British leaders: Carden, who broke under pressure; Robeck, who was shocked by the losses at the Narrows and had no heart to make another attempt; and Hamilton, the poetic intellectual who proved insufficiently flexible in tactics and who gave his subordinates too much independent authority. Moorehead is less harsh in assessing the role of Winston Churchill than others have been. Churchill, like nearly everyone on the British side, was overly confident about the might of the British Navy. Churchill paid the political price for his optimism, yet the naval campaign that he supported was realistic and feasible. Indeed, new plans to force the Dardanelles in 1919 were being made by others after Churchill had left office.

Moorehead's description of life in the trenches and on the beaches of Gallipoli are gripping. For month after month both sides were pinned down and hammered away at each other. Some of the engagements during June and July, 1915, are starkly summarized. For example: "June 4. Allied attacks in the center. Gain of 25-50 yards on a one mile front. Allies' casualties 6500, Turkish 9000," or "July 5. Turkish attack along the whole line. Nothing gained. Casualties, Turks 16,000. Allies negligible." Battle conditions were hellish for both sides. By July, the heat reached nearly ninety degrees in the shade, and there was no shade. The sun glared down on the men packed in the trenches from four in the morning until eight at night. Canned meat melted in the tins. Fresh water was scarce in the dry hills of Gallipoli; uniforms were woolen and scratchy. But most unbearable were the flies which were everywhere, feeding on garbage, unburied corpses, and the men's food. Malaria and dysentery spread, creating weakness, lassitude, and incapacity to fight. "It all fills me," Hamilton wrote, "with a desperate longing to lie down and do nothing but rest." Yet the battles and the suffering dragged on to the inconclusive end.

Finally came the British decision to disengage, which brought many new problems. Troops were pulled out gradually in limited numbers. All sorts of ruses were used to keep the Turks from suspecting that an evacuation was proceeding and that the British ranks were thinning: no tents were struck, the gunners fired twice as many rounds and kept moving the guns around, barges and small boats took the men off the beaches at night.

By January, 1916, the Turks at last realized that the Allies were departing, and came in for a final kill at Cape Helles. An intense Turkish bombardment of the Allied trenches began on January 7. Previously such bombardments had been followed by a bayonet charge, but that charge never came, and the remaining Allied troops were able to get away from the

# The Gallipoli Campaign

last foothold on Gallipoli. "Decorations were awarded to General Monro and his chief-of-staff who had so firmly insisted on the evacuation. No special medal, however, was given to the soldiers who fought in the Gallipoli campaign."

The bibliography in *Gallipoli*, while not extensive, is excellent, and there are several maps of the campaign sites.

Churchill, Winston S. *The World Crisis*. Vol. II: *1915*. New York: Charles Scribner's Sons, 1923.

In this volume of his memoirs of the Great War, the former First Lord of the Admiralty deals extensively with the planning and execution of the Dardanelles-Gallipoli campaign. He blends personal recollection with memoranda, official orders, private letters, and minutes of meetings to reconstruct the calculation and sentiments that went into making the fateful decisions.

Churchill acknowledges in the preface to this volume that primary responsibility for the Dardanelles campaign was his; but, by implication, he denies that he should be blamed entirely for the failure of the endeavor. As early as January, 1915, he had understood that a joint land-sea operation would be undertaken early that spring. He further understood that the veteran 29th Regular Division would be sent from England to lead the Gallipoli landings. Then in February, Lord Kitchener refused to release the 29th Division for Gallipoli, saying that he feared a German attempt to invade Britain. This, in Churchill's estimation, caused a fatal postponement of the whole undertaking. And when the cautious Kitchener further refused to commit British forces already on the Greek island of Lemnos to an invasion of Gallipoli, Churchill asserted that Kitchener's half-measures marked a change in the whole operation as originally planned, and he disclaimed any responsibility for the consequences.

Nevertheless, the First Lord of the Admiralty continued to press for the commitment of the 29th Division while warning that further delays in beginning a land operation could be most dangerous. He quotes, with satisfaction, the findings of the Royal Commission that investigated the Dardanelles campaign after the war: "We think Mr. Churchill was quite justified in attaching utmost importance to the delays which occurred in dispatching the 29th Division." Finally, in March, 1915, Kitchener relented; the 29th Division would be sent to the Near East after all. Churchill, still optimistic, believed that if landings were begun by late March, Constantinople could be taken within a short time.

Then another factor intervened. Allied planning had anticipated that at least three divisions of the nearby Greek army would be sent to join the British and French in making the landings, and that the Greeks would constitute a substantial proportion of the combined Allied forces. But in March, to Churchill's astonishment, the Russian government informed the British that they would not con-

135

sent to Greek participation in the Gallipoli operation. In the Russian opinion, Greek involvement would lead to "complications," and they were against it. Their opposition was political; they distrusted the pro-German Greek King, Constantine, and did not want his army near Constantinople, which Russia claimed in the event the Allied operation was a success. In any event, Constantine repudiated his government's offer of military assistance to the Allies.

Churchill makes much of the Russian refusal to permit the use of Greek forces, calling it detrimental to the Allied effort. "Whom the gods would destroy, they first make mad," he writes, regarding the Russians. He also quotes from a letter he wrote to Sir Edward Grey, the British Foreign Minister, saying that he would do his utmost to prevent the Russians from having Constantinople.

Despite the delays and the disappointments, the land campaign finally did get under way; during which Churchill might well have recalled another proverb about the mills of the gods grinding slow but exceeding fine. In the wake of the failure to take the Narrows, Lord Fisher resigned his post as First Sea Lord in May, declaring he had never approved of the naval expedition from the beginning. British newspapers, led by Lord Northcliffe, launched a "vile Press campaign" against the Liberal government in general and Churchill in particular for the bogged-down expedition.

Shortly after Fisher's resignation, the Conservative-Unionist leaders informed Prime Minister Asquith that unless their party were included in a coalition government with the Liberals, they would assume the role of active opposition. Asquith acceded; the cabinet was reshuffled with about half the places going to Conservative-Unionists. One of the first to lose his place was Winston Churchill, who was replaced by Arthur Balfour. "I alone," Churchill writes rather plaintively, "was held to blame for the upheaval and its discontents." — *J.W.P.*

### Additional Recommended Reading

Cruttwell, C. R. M. F. *A History of the Great War, 1914-1918.* Oxford: Clarendon Press, 1936. A standard work which includes a sober, detached explanation of the causes and consequences of Gallipoli.

Falls, Cyril. *The Great War: 1914-1918.* New York: Capricorn Books, 1961. A brief, balanced account of the Gallipoli Campaign and its significance within the context of the larger war by the official British historian of World War I.

Horne, Charles F., ed. *Source Records of the Great War.* Vol. III. New York: National Alumni Press, c 1923. Contains accounts of the campaign by participants on both sides.

Marshall, S. L. A. *World War I.* New York: American Heritage Press, 1971. This survey of the Great War includes an extended description of the Gallipoli-Dardanelles fighting which is quite critical of the British commanders.

Masefield, John. *Gallipoli.* New York: The Macmillan Company, 1916. A melodramatic recounting of the campaign by the former Poet Laureate of Britain, apparently intended as a propaganda piece for American readers and a morale builder for Britons; replete with descriptions of British valor under fire and useful for its immediacy.

Morgenthau, Henry, Sr. *Ambassador Morgenthau's Story*. Garden City, N.Y.: Doubleday, Page and Company, 1919. The American Ambassador to Turkey during World War I relates his experiences, especially of the Turkish responses to the Allied attacks as he interpreted them.

Wren, Jack. *The Great Battles of World War I*. New York: Grosset and Dunlap, 1971. Primarily a book of photographs, many of the Gallipoli campaign.

# ITALY ENTERS WORLD WAR I

*Type of event:* Political: Italy's decision to intervene in World War I
*Time:* May, 1915
*Locale:* Rome and London

*Principal personages:*
ANTONIO SALANDRA (1853-1931), conservative head of the
Italian government during World War I
GIOVANNI GIOLITTI (1842-1928), leading liberal-democrat in
Italy's Chamber of Deputies
GABRIELE D'ANNUNZIO (1863-1938), antiestablishment poet
and ardent nationalist
BENITO MUSSOLINI (1883-1945), socialist editor in Italy

## Summary of Event

Aside from the status of Turkey, Italy's position with regard to World War I was perhaps the most uncertain element in Europe's international scene during the early months of the fighting. Diplomats representing both the Triple Entente (France, Great Britain, and Russia) and the Central Powers (primarily Germany and Austria-Hungary) waged a determined competition in Constantinople and Rome to swing the allegiance of Turkish and Italian officials. However, while Turkey seemed likely to convert to the side of Germany because of their prewar friendliness, Italy's lack of commitment until May of 1915 remained a matter for intense speculation.

As a partner with Germany and Austria-Hungary in Otto von Bismarck's original Triple Alliance, Italy was at least technically a member of the Central Powers in 1914. When World War I broke out in the Balkans, however, Italy announced her decision to adopt a position of neutrality. It had been Italy's contention that Austria had not acted in a defensive fashion by declaring virtual war on Serbia, and, as such, Italy was not obligated to join Austria's cause.

Italy's position was announced by the relatively conservative Antonio Salandra government in Rome, and produced a generally favorable response from Italians as a whole. Support for neutrality in Italy came from a broad assortment of politically influential segments, including most of the Socialist Party, the moderate parliamentarians led by the liberal-democrat Giovanni Giolitti, and the potent force of Italy's Catholic clergy. In the case of the Church, opposition to the prospect of Italy's intervention was based on humanitarian grounds, and on the fear that a destructive war might endanger the status of Catholic Austria.

Many of those in Italy who favored a neutral stance nevertheless felt that Italy ought to receive some compensation for this position. Naturally, a neutral Italy would weaken the Central Powers' capacity to wage a successful war in Europe, and there were those in Italy who expected the Entente nations to reward Italy for this gesture. It was to this significant element in Italian politics that British and French diplomats played in the Entente's efforts to sway Italian opinion. A satisfied Italy steadfast in her neutrality was, in the Entente view, preferable to an Italy actively engaged as a combatant with the Central Powers.

The Entente also found a sizable segment of Italian opinion favoring outright intervention in the war on its side. As was the case with the pro-neutral, antiwar factions, the interventionists of Italy represented a number of political views. Old line liberals in Italy had a tendency to view France and Britain as leading the cause of civilized world development, and felt that Italy would be wise to ally herself with them. Both the Italian army and the press favored intervention, including a still little-known socialist editor named Benito Mussolini and a prominent antiestablishment poet and ardent nationalist named Gabriele D'Annunzio.

D'Annunzio's efforts, both as a literary figure and as a political activist, seem to have had a significant effect upon the undecided element of Italian public opinion, especially in Rome. His appeal originally had been directed to those in Italy who felt a measure of discontent with the political system. However, the war brought D'Annunzio's views out into the streets of Rome in the form of mass demonstrations which may very well have been one of the catalysts in swaying the Italian view.

Yet, while domestic politics divided Italy on the war question, Salandra's government busily dickered with En-

tente representatives on the issue of compensation for Italy. In general, the emphasis in these talks was upon concrete gains and territorial acquisitions for Italy once the war itself was concluded. Both the British and the French were willing to provide Italy with a banquet of territorial promises, but essentially these required that Italy abandon neutrality and become an active belligerent in the Entente camp.

As the Entente assurances of territorial gains for Italy were enlarged in scope, Italy's neutrality views ebbed and a prointerventionist stance became more pronounced. The British and French offers included many southeastern European and eastern Mediterranean areas of interest to Italian statesmen. Among these promises were that Italy would receive the Austrian Tyrol as far north as the vital Brenner Pass; Trieste; a broad range of Adriatic regions including northern Albania; and, in the likelihood of a partitioning of Turkey, a slice of Asia Minor. Sweetening these land offerings would be a share for Italy in whatever war reparations monies were levied on the defeated countries.

Virtual guarantees this vast were difficult for Italian leaders to ignore. Essentially, Italy's government could already count on a sizable portion of Italian opinion to support an interventionist position, and the neutrality proponents in the country were certain to be swayed by the lavish territorial prospects.

By spring of 1915, Italy was prepared to take her place among the Entente allies. The only obstacles remaining to such a step were the

Church, the Socialist Party, and the supporters of Giovanni Giolitti in the Chamber of Deputies. Giolitti, the leading Italian liberal-democrat since the turn of the century, remained determined to combat Italian intervention in World War I, but allies willing to stand with him were few. Roman street mobs were already loudly voicing their opposition to his resistance, and both the Church and the Socialists were visibly intimidated by public opinion. The absence of anything approximating a unified opposition to intervention doomed Giolitti's efforts by May of 1915.

On May 18, 1915, Salandra's government offered the Chamber of Deputies a war resolution. In hand already was a secret treaty signed with Great Britain and France in London on April 26, 1915, assuring Italy of her territorial bounty and part of the war indemnity. As such, the war resolution passed easily with only a handful of loyalists of Giolitti voting with the opposition. Five days later, Italy formally entered the war by declaring war on Austria-Hungary.

Ironically, Italy found her position undercut at the end of World War I by the Treaty of Versailles and, more importantly, by the atmosphere of pacificism expressed in President Woodrow Wilson's Fourteen Points. Italy's failure to secure all the territories promised her in the Treaty of London, combined with postwar domestic turmoil, contributed to the rise of Fascism under Benito Mussolini.

## Pertinent Literature

Sprigge, Cecil Jackson Squire. *The Development of Modern Italy*. New Haven, Conn.: Yale University Press, 1944.

Writing this work during the midst of a still unresolved World War II, Cecil Sprigge is understandably enamored with the mysteries behind the emergence of Italian Fascism. Sprigge looks to the impact which the frustrations of World War I had on the aspirations of Italian leaders in order to ferret out the causes of Fascism and the rise of Benito Mussolini. Unlike many of the significant European nations of World War I, Italy's sense of true national identity was still in its infancy. Her political and economic problems impaired the smooth functioning of the constitutional monarchy under Victor Emmanuel III.

Unlike England, whom Italian leaders seemed to admire at least for her preeminent position in European affairs, Italy did not enjoy the stability of two-party government. Italy's political scene more closely resembled that of France with a blinding array of parties that too often functioned more like cliques or factions than responsible, national-minded organizations. And, unlike either the British or the French, Italy had yet to translate her liberalism into genuine economic opportunities for advancement of her public. Liberalism had been grafted upon an economic condition in Italy that lacked the resources to maintain it. Poverty ran deep even in many of the more urbanized centers, and the industrial development of the nation had yet to bear substantial fruit in the midst of the political alterations of the late nineteenth century. Italy remained a predominantly agrarian society where opportunity was more a product of birth and inheritance than expansion of markets.

Italian leaders, however, sensed that the potential for growth was there, particularly once Italy could claim to have a position of respect and identity in European international circles. Accomplishing this would require that Italy carve for herself a share of the European and Mediterranean map. While Italian political figures differed on questions of leadership, there was broad support for the acquisition of territories inhabited by Italian nationals. In particular, Italy coveted the areas to the north which still lay in Austrian hands, and Adriatic Sea communities to the east which would once more place Italy in the position of influencing Mediterranean affairs—something Italy could not claim to have done since the days of the Renaissance.

Italy's entrance into World War I on the side of the Triple Entente allies after months of uncertain neutrality came with some reluctance. Despite considerably demonstrative voices rising out of public mob actions in Rome, the lure of belligerency came more from promises of territorial gains than from any truly combative urge. In purely military terms, Italy's participation on the Entente side came too late to be of any benefit to Russia in the east, and she was too unprepared to offer any serious threat to Germany or Austria from the south. The entry of Bulgaria in the war by October of 1915 as a member of the Central Powers somewhat offset Italy's own intervention, and Italy also proved to be incapable of preventing Rumania from being overrun by German and Austrian forces. Italy's participation in a Balkans campaign failed to provide her with anything remotely approximating a position of international prestige.

Italy's relatively poor performance militarily in World War I was compounded by her equally poor record of genuine territorial compensation at the Paris Peace Conference which concluded the war. Her failure to come away from the conference with the significant land acquisitions to which she felt entitled helped to form the burden of public disillusionment which plagued postwar Italian governments and politics.

Naturally, in seeking the background identity of Italy's Fascist movement, Sprigge has dealt in some depth with these World War I complications. Regretably, in choosing to stress the Fascist angle, he does not deal adequately with the complex panorama of Italy's domestic conditions related to her entry into the war itself. However, in tying together the more obvious strands of Italian society and its aspirations during the first three decades of the twentieth century, Sprigge's book is a valuable tool for the uninitiated.

Salomone, Arcangelo William. *Italian Democracy in the Making: The Political Scene in the Giolittian Era, 1900-1914.* Philadelphia: University of Pennsylvania Press, 1945.

Written during World War II at a time when Italy, although technically out of the war as a Fascist Axis power, was still very much a battleground, Salomone's work seems intent upon reconstructing Italy's political past. The assumption here may be that the author had hoped once again to place Italy in the mainstream of the liberal-democratic Allied nations of the West; yet, regardless of his intentions, he has offered an insightful look at the domestic political scene of Italy from the turn of the century.

Most particularly, Salomone concentrates on the pre-World War I period dominated in Italian politics by the figure of Giovanni Giolitti. In the years running from 1892 to 1914, Giolitti held the prime ministry of Italy's government on four separate occasions and witnessed many of the formative developments which helped to chart Italy's eventual course in the Great War. In this respect, Salomone's work sheds some light not only upon Giolitti's political legacy, but also upon those factors which led Italy into an interventionist course on the Allied side in 1915.

Giolitti's first experience as Italy's Prime Minister during the period from 1892 to 1893 was largely uneventful, although he left the government under the shadow of a financial crisis involving the Bank of Rome and its leading official, Signor Tanlongo, whom Giolitti had appointed. In its aftermath, Giolitti actually left Italy for a brief period of time.

A look at the second and third prime ministries, however, sheds better light on the turbulent nature of Italy's early twentieth century domestic political scene. Between 1903 and 1905, Giolitti came to power at a time when Italy as a whole was experiencing a decidedly leftist turn. Italy's constitutional monarch, Victor Emmanuel III, had a rather liberal outlook, a fact that was augmented by the violent emergence of radical socialism which was breeding a strike atmosphere in the more urbanized centers such as Milan. Pressures from the left brought about three separate changes in the Italian government, including the second ousting of Giolitti during a brief 1905-1906 period.

Returning for a third time in 1906, Giolitti began to establish a closer relationship between the government and the Catholic Church. Over the next three years, he attempted to juggle the government's more secular concerns with the traditional Catholic loyalties of much of the population. In particular, Giolitti successfully promoted the concept of religious education in those communities where the local citizenry had requested it.

Returning to the Prime Minister post for a fourth time between 1911 and 1914, Giolitti continued to democratize the Italian political arena by a vast expansion of suffrage which nearly tripled the number of citizens eligible to vote. Liberals such as Giolitti still held a majority in the 1913 elections, although both the socialists and the more conservative Catholic groups made notable gains.

Giolitti's 1911-1914 Ministry was perhaps even more noteworthy for its foreign policy involvements. Italian nationalists, a potent force on the domestic scene which often cut across party lines, had long sought assurances of an Italian sphere of influence over Turkish-controlled Tripoli in North Africa. In 1911, Italian troops landed and seized the area. The annexation was proclaimed on the somewhat questionable pretext of Turkish interference with Italian interests.

Italian control of Tripoli, however, was not simply a local matter. The Turks refused to be conciliatory on the issue, and the major powers, including Austria, feared that an Italian-Turkish confrontation in the Eastern Mediterranean would upset the already trying conditions in the Balkans. To press their claim, Italy attempted to take the conflict to the Turks by occupying Rhodes and threatening even the Dardanelles. Because of uncertainties in the Balkans, the Turks gave in in 1912, and the Treaty of Lausanne, Switzerland, on October 18, 1912, put an end to the current Italian-Turkish dispute. Tripoli was abandoned *de facto* by the Turks while Italy agreed to restore Dodecanese islands she had recently seized.

Coming as it did on the eve of World War I, the Italian-Turkish crisis helps to illustrate the temperament which prevailed in the Italian government. Expansionist-minded nationalism during the prewar years appeared to be, in Salomone's view, an even stronger ingredient in Italian politics than the democratizing efforts under Giolitti. The relationship of these factors continued to be ap-

parent in 1914 as Giolitti resigned following widespread strikes over taxation brought on by the war with Turkey.

While Giolitti did not head the Italian government during the period when Italy wavered between neutrality and intervention in World War I, he remained a vital force in the makeup of Italy's parliamentary Chamber of Deputies. As an outspoken neutralist, he became the most prominent voice in the government restraining the more interventionist-minded Antonio Salandra government. Any hopes Giolitti and his backers may have had for keeping Italy out of the war were, however, dashed by factionalism in the socialist camp and the reluctance of the Catholic Church to resume an atmosphere of confrontation with the government. On May 23, 1915, Italy formally joined in the war effort as a member of the Triple Entente.

Salomone is primarily concerned here with charting the course of liberalization and democracy-building during Italy's formative decades. Yet he has not ignored the specter of nationalism in Italy's political situation, and he suggests that the democratic expansion of the vote in 1912 may have helped to increase that attitude. As such, his work provides a worthwhile look at a variety of considerations which combined to influence the Italian intervention in 1915. — *T.A.B.*

### Additional Recommended Reading

Chambers, F. P. *The War Behind the War, 1914-1918: A History of the Political and Civilian Fronts*. New York: Harcourt Brace, 1939. Deals broadly with the World War I domestic scene; the Italian topic is only covered thinly.

Halperin, S. William. *Italy and the Vatican at War*. Chicago: University of Chicago Press, 1939. A fine study of the difficulties encountered between the new Italian national state and the conservative hold of the Catholic Church; offers one of the best looks at the Church's stand regarding Italian intervention in World War I.

Croce, Benedetto. *A History of Italy, 1871-1915*. Translated by Ceilia M. Ady. Oxford: Clarendon Press, 1929. A fine history of the early years of the Italian nation up to its entry into World War I.

Taylor, A. J. P. *The Struggle for Mastery in Europe, 1848-1918*. Oxford: Clarendon Press, 1954. In this broadly based work, an established authority on international affairs provides a good overall survey of the trends and events up to, but not including, Versailles; World War I is seen as the climax of half a century's diplomatic sparring.

Smith, D. M. *Italy: A Modern History*. Ann Arbor: University of Michigan Press, 1959. A modern history of Italy which concentrates on the problems Italy faced in adjusting to contemporary times.

# THE CONTINUING SEARCH FOR PEACE
# IN THE MIDDLE EAST

*Type of event:* Diplomatic: seeking a just solution to the problems that have led to
armed conflict
*Time:* 1917 to the present
*Locale:* Primarily the Arab Republic of Egypt, Israel, Jordan, Syria, and Lebanon

> *Principal personages:*
> HENRY ALFRED KISSINGER (1923-      ), United States Sec-
> retary of State, 1973-1977
> JIMMY (JAMES EARL) CARTER (1924-      ), thirty-ninth Pres-
> ident of the United States, 1977-
> ANWAR EL-SADAT (1918-      ), President of the Arab Re-
> public of Egypt since 1970
> YASIR ARAFAT (MOHAMMED ABED AR'OUF ARAFAT) (1929-
>       ), leader of the Palestinian commando group Al Fatah,
> the dominant group in the umbrella structure of the Pal-
> estinian Liberation Organization (PLO)
> MENACHEM BEGIN (1913-      ), a leader of the Zionist com-
> mandos against Britain in Palestine before 1948 and Prime
> Minister of Israel after 1977

## Summary of Event

Today's headlines of the Middle East usually focus on the war between Israel and her neighbors which began before Palestine was divided and which has intensified year by year. A Jew whose relatives perished in Nazi gas chambers or a Palestinian who lost his home and farmlands in 1948 feels a deep bitterness regarding this conflict; his involvement is so intensely personal that there is no room for discussion. Each is convinced of the justice of his position, and each is willing to die for his cause. To understand how people feel is more important than to argue whether their feelings are justified. Although an uninvolved observer might not fully understand the intensity of this long and bitter war, there are six basic points that are helpful to recognize as a base from which most of the is-

sues can be discussed. These six points have remained more or less unchanged through time.

First, the Middle East conflict is not simply a war between Jews and Arabs, since there is no single "Jewish" or "Arab" position. Of some fifteen million Jews in the world, less than three million live in Israel. Some Israeli Jews would seek peace immediately even if that meant allowing thousands of Palestinians to return to their former lands, while others want Israel to remain primarily Jewish. The major link between some seventeen Arab countries is the Arabic language. Arabs do not otherwise compose a united bloc, either politically or philosophically, and they disagree widely over their policies toward Israel. Experiments in Pan-Arabism by small groups of Arabic-speaking nations have, on the whole, failed; Lebanon and Sudan, for example, are as different from each other as Spain is from Peru. And in any case, the seventeen Arab nations are not the crux of the problem so much as are the nationless Palestinians. The conflict, then, is not between Jews and Arabs but between modern Zionism and Palestinian nationalism. Each has its allies in the Middle East and in the world at large.

The second point is the most misunderstood. The conflict is *not* over religion, although religious arguments have been used by all sides. The status of Jerusalem, for example, is a religious aspect of the greater problem: the struggle of two peoples for the same land. Judaism, Christianity, and Islam all hold that worship of God does not depend on a geographical place but on a special relationship between God and man. Jews outside Israel and within Israel are divided over Zionism; so are Christians and Muslims. Culture, religion, and politics are an integral part of ethnicity and group identity in much of the Mediterranean world. Religion is an aspect of the Palestinian-Zionist impasse only in the sense that religion is a part of every aspect of Middle Eastern life.

The third point is obvious to anyone who reads newspapers or watches newscasts on television. Every act of violence in this prolonged war is in "retaliation" to a provocation by the other side. Thus we may hear one day of Israel's "retaliatory raid" against Palestinian *fedayeen* (commandos) who placed a bomb in an Israeli bus the day before. Newspapers in Arab capitals report that this bus bombing was "retaliation" against Israel's leveling of Arab homes in a Palestinian village the day before that. Both sides are correct from their own understanding of history and from their own interpretation of their own rights and destiny. If we trace the chain of retaliations back far enough, we find the Israelis reacting against thousands of years of Western hatred for Jews, as epitomized by Hitler's Germany, and the Palestinians retaliating against the sudden loss of everything they owned in 1948. Terrorism and counterterrorism will continue until the root causes of this conflict are dealt with cooperatively by all sides.

The fourth point underlines the frustrations of any hope for peace: every major argument in the Zionist-Palestinian impasse has a counterargument equal in force and opposite in direction. Whether justified or not, the arguments, supported so intensely by each side, confront each other in hopeless deadlock. Israel does not recognize the existence of the Palestinians; Palestinians do not recognize the existence of Israel. The Israelis believe that the Palestinians, with assistance from other Arabs, will push them into the sea; the Palestinians and their Arab neighbors are just as convinced that Israel's real aim is to expand and push them by force into the desert. Each side has used the hopeless plight of refugees to further their own cause, although many refugees, both Jewish and Palestinian, have suffered by choice because they believed in the rightness of their cause. The Palestinians, with no regular army or modern equipment, resort to terrorist tactics even within areas populated by civilians; the Jewish underground during the British mandate resorted to the same tactics for the same reasons.

The fifth point is that most of the irreconcilable aspects of this conflict emerged from decisions made at conference tables in Europe about lands and people in the Middle East. Most of the Middle Easterners affected were not consulted. Permanent peace must depend primarily on direct negotiations between Israel and all her Arab neighbors, especially the Palestinians.

The sixth and final point deals with the way all sides view their present roles in the Middle East. The Arab states in general see themselves as a part of the Third World and believe that Israel is part of the Western bloc's strategy for manipulating them. Israel, highly dependent on the United States economically, believes that she must make her own decisions and that her skills could be used to modernize the whole Middle East if the Arabs in the region would come to the peace table.

The continuing search for a comprehensive peace in the Middle East is closely related to the civil war in Lebanon (1975-1976) and the intervention of Syria and Israel. The key question, however, remains the future of the Palestinians. The flamboyant and courageous diplomacy of United States Secretary of State Henry Kissinger apparently failed. Egyptian President Anwar el-Sadat's peace initiative, including an unprecedented trip to Israel in November, 1977, surprised the world, but once again the primary roadblocks were the Palestinian question and the future of Arab lands occupied by Israel since 1967. A comprehensive peace is probably impossible without negotiations with Yasir Arafat, head of the Palestinian commando group Al Fatah (part of the Palestinian Liberation Organization), and other key Palestinian leaders.

In September, 1978, President Jimmy Carter of the United States, President Anwar el-Sadat of Egypt, and Prime Minister Menachem Begin of Israel held a summit conference at Camp David, Maryland, where they worked out a framework for peace between Egypt and Israel. After several more months of torturous negotiations, the Israeli and Egyptian leaders met in Washington on March 26, 1979, where they signed the long-sought peace accord. The accord provides for a gradual withdrawal, over a three-year period, of Israeli forces from the Sinai Peninsula seized during the Six Day War of 1967, the establishment of formal diplomatic relations between the two former belligerents, and the opening of negotiations between Egypt and Israel on the Palestinian question. The treaty formally went into effect one month later.

At present, the prospect for peace between Israel and her other Arab neighbors appears dim. Hence, the search continues for a comprehensive and lasting peace settlement in the Middle East.

## Pertinent Literature

Gendzier, Irene L., ed. *The Middle East Reader.* New York: Pegasus, 1969.

The editor of this useful volume provides a historical and ideological guide to the world east of the Mediterranean. Focusing on the contemporary situation, the first group of essays (Parts 1 and 2) discuss the nature and practice of radical change with emphasis on the Arab Republic of Egypt, Syria, Iraq, and Israel. All twelve essays are by outstanding scholars.

Part 3 contains eight essays on Israeli perspectives and on Arab unity. This section is important background for Part 4, which contains the most crucial collection of statements for understanding the Arab-Israeli impasse, or what the editor calls "Squaring the Circle." Chaim Weizmann discusses Palestine's role in the "Solution of the Jewish Problem" (1942). Judah Magnes warns (1946) of the tragedy ahead if force must be used to gain Palestine and calls for a binational state. The Arab Higher Committee Delegation for Palestine explains (1948) why the Arab armies entered Palestine; and Musa Alami, a Palestinian, discusses the lessons of losing Palestine, as does Cecil Hourani. Charles Yost, former United States Ambassador to the United Nations, relates how the June, 1967, Arab-Israeli war began and concludes that the conflict appears to have affected the ability or willingness of the Israelis and Palestinians to follow the advice of major powers. One of the unexpected results of the 1967 war was the realization that the final adjudication of the impasse lies in the hands of Jews and Arabs in general, and specifically in the hands of Israelis and Palestinians.

In a chapter entitled "Arab-Israel Parley," we have one early example (1968) of a meeting between five distinguished Palestinians and Israelis in Jerusalem. Representing divergent political opinions, the five men discussed all eventualities, including what would happen in the event of an Arab victory in a future war. Only one part of the parley is included here: namely, the discussion of how a political settlement might be reached. This may be the most important section in the volume because the ideas it expresses have proved prophetic, and reminds us that the Palestinian/Israeli deadlock is above all a human problem at the local level, whatever its international implications may be.

Also prophetic is the last essay by a Palestinian, Atallah Mansour, entitled "The Future Is the Son of the Past." After a brief impassioned history of what happened in Palestine, Mansour asks: "Is there a way out?" He affirms that there is, believing that both Israeli Jews and Palestinians can share the rich land the way that Switzerland, Holland, and Belgium have done with their pluralistic ethnic situations. The role of the great powers, he suggests, is to apply pressure for an Israeli-Palestinian compromise. After going into more detail, he concludes: "This is my hope and for it I live; for my children's future as well as for the future of all other children." This volume is an important beginning for anyone wishing to understand the continuing search for peace in the Middle East. Besides the extensive footnotes, a good bibliography is provided for each of the four parts.

## The Continuing Search for Peace in the Middle East

Davis, John H. *The Evasive Peace: A Study of the Zionist-Arab Problem.* Cleveland, Oh.: Dillon/Liederbach, 1976.

Written in clear and concise language, this brief account of the long search for peace in the Middle East provides an excellent basic text and a basis for deeper research. Davis' goal is future-oriented: to probe and evaluate the forces and factors that will determine the future of Arab-Israeli relations. The author was Commissioner-General of the United Nations Relief and Works Agency for Palestine Refugees in the Near East for five years, and spent another five years formally studying the question of Arab-Israeli relations.

In discussing the seeds of the conflict (1897-1917), Davis begins with the roots of Zionism, focusing on the more recent political aspects, such as the First Zionist Congress in Basel (1897) at which the World Zionist Organization was established, and on the life of the founder of modern political Zionism, Theodor Herzl.

Herzl was elected the first president of the World Zionist Organization, and his book, *The Jewish State* (1896), became the guide of the organization. In this booklet, Herzl states:

We are one people—our enemies have made us one in our respite, as repeatedly happens in history. Distress binds us together, and, thus united, we suddenly discover our strength. Yes, we are strong enough to form a State, and, indeed, a model State. We possess all human and material resources necessary for the purpose.

Herzl's attempt to secure Palestine from the Ottomans failed, as did efforts to obtain desert areas of Egypt or sections of Uganda from Britain. Before his death in 1904, however, he had set in irreversible motion the idea of a Jewish State, and his followers were quick to resolve uncompromisingly that the Jewish State must be in Palestine.

The birth and solidification of the Zionist idea corresponded in time roughly to the rise of Arab feelings for self-determination. In search of allies against Germany and her Ottoman ally Turkey, Britain negotiated secret terms with Sherif Hussein of Mecca promising independence in return for alliance with Britain in World War I. However, Britain also needed Jewish support for the war, and Dr. Chaim Weizmann, the influential scientist and leader of the Zionist movement in Britain, was able to relate British interests and ambitions in the Middle East to Zionist goals. Weizmann and his associates were pleased with the Balfour Declaration in 1917, which stated:

His Majesty's Government view with favour the establishment in Palestine of a national home for the Jewish people, and will use their best endeavors to facilitate the achievement of this object, it being clearly understood that nothing shall be done which may prejudice the civil and religious rights of existing non-Jewish communities in Palestine, or the rights and political status enjoyed by Jews in any other country.

Davis skillfully summarizes the delicate situation after World War I when Arab hopes for independence were swept aside by the mandate system. He covers the mandate period between the wars and shows the rising tension on both sides. What the Balfour Declaration did for Zionism in 1917, the 1939 White Paper undid; but paper promises were always subject to the facts of the battlefield. Davis outlines the increasing global activities of the Zionists as World War II closed and the resort to terrorism in mandated Palestine by Jewish underground units.

The United Nations General Assembly voted for partition of Palestine on November 29, 1947, which increased the hostilities in Palestine/Israel—hostilities which had already created an Arab refugee problem. From this point on, Davis describes the impasse as a "conflict without end," which he proceeds to chronicle up to 1975. Davis has special chapters on the Palestine refugee problem and on the state of Israel and its special relationship to the World Zionist Organization, a global support group that has no parallel on the Palestinian side of the equation.

In taking stock of the entire situation, Davis presents several facts: first, the State of Israel exists; second, it could not have come into being without pressure and the use of force against the indigenous Arab population; third, the Arab-Israeli conflict as a whole is based on the use of force; and fourth, "Israel, once established, has shown an alarming attitude of aggressiveness towards the Arab people." Davis succinctly describes the growing problems Israel faces in the occupied areas. Davis notes, finally, that the world will in time regard the acts committed against the Palestinians in 1948 and subsequently as "grave injustices which must be rectified in the name of humanity and in the interests of peace."

Given his definition of Israel's dilemma, it is not surprising that Davis' solution calls for Israel to become a conventional state concerned about its own people and the neighboring populations and thus to become an integral part of the Middle East. A modification of Zionist principles and a move toward rectifying past wrongs to the Palestinian Arabs would greatly reduce the incentive for the arms race and would thus be conducive to peace. — *H.H.B.*

### Additional Recommended Reading

Lewis, Bernard. *The Middle East and the West*. New York: Harper & Row Publishers, 1966. One of the best short books available; traces the chief political and intellectual currents of the Middle East for the Western reader.

Hertzberg, Arthur, ed. *The Zionist Idea: A Historical Analysis and Reader*. Garden City, N.Y.: Doubleday & Company, 1959. A rabbi and scholar provides readings on and an investigation into the major contributors to Zionist thought.

Avnery, Uri. *Israel Without Zionists: A Plea for Peace in the Middle East*. New York: The Macmillan Company, 1968. A minority member of Israel's parliament eloquently proposes a Semitic federation of Arabs and Israelis.

Karpat, Kemal H., ed. *Political and Social Thought in the Contemporary Middle East*. New York: Frederick A. Praeger, 1968. A wide representation of the thoughts of well-known political, social, and religious thinkers.

Rodinson, Maxime. *Israel and the Arabs*. Translated by Michael Perl. New York: Pantheon Books, 1968. A French Jewish professor of linguistics analyzes the conflict with criticism for both sides, but with more sympathy for the Arab Palestinian position.

Berger, Elmer. *A Partisan History of Judaism*. New York: Devin-Adair Company, 1951. An American rabbi, long outspoken against Zionism, believes that Jews are truer to their historic faith when they identify themselves with the country of their citizenship.

# THE GREAT RUSSIAN CIVIL WAR

*Type of event:* Political: counterrevolutionary activity aimed at restoring representative
  government
*Time:* 1918-1921
*Locale:* The Soviet Union

*Principal personages:*
VLADIMIR ILICH LENIN (ULYANOV) (1870-1924), Bolshevik
  leader and head of Communist Russia, 1918-1924
GENERAL LAVR GEORGIEVICH KORNILOV (1870-1918),
GENERAL ANTON IVANOVICH DENIKIN (1872-1947), and
GENERAL PËTR NIKOLAEVICH WRANGEL (1878-1928), com-
  manders of White forces in Southern Russia
ADMIRAL ALEKSANDR VASILIEVICH KOLCHAK (1874-1920),
  White commander in Siberia and White "Supreme Ruler,"
  1918-1920
NIKOLAI VASILIEVICH CHAIKOVSKI (1850-1926), Socialist
  Revolutionary Party leader of anti-Soviet movement in
  Northern Russia
GENERAL NIKOLAI NIKOLAEVICH YUDENICH (1862-1933),
  White commander in Northwest Russia
LEON TROTSKY (LEIB DAVYDOVICH BRONSTEIN) (1879-1940),
  Red Army commander and Commissar of War after 1918
MAKHNO, Ukrainian anarchist peasant leader

## Summary of Event

Any revolution that suddenly topples a long-standing regime is likely
to face continued resistance from
remnants of the "old order." Opposition can be centered among embittered *émigrés* who flee to distant ha-
vens of refuge, or opposition can take
the form of open counterrevolution.
When Vladimir Ilvich Lenin and his
well-organized Bolshevik followers
staged their successful *coup* in November (October according to the
Julian Calendar in use in Russia at
the time), 1917, the new Soviet government encountered both types of
residual opposition. Many wealthy
Russians, sensing the seriousness of
Bolshevik expropriations, fled the
country for Paris, New York, and
other Western cities, where they continued to oppose the Bolshevik regime. By far the most serious threat
to the Bolshevik Revolution was a
series of armed uprisings that shook
the edges of Soviet Russia between
1918 and 1921. These uprisings, collectively grouped under the heading
"The Great Russian Civil War," for
a time posed a serious threat to the
infant Soviet state. Lenin's eventual
victory insured the triumph of the
Communist experiment in Russia.

White (anti-Soviet) forces in
Southern Russia centered in a Volunteer Army augmented by Cossack
forces. Led in succession by Generals

Lavr Kornilov, Anton Denikin, and Pëtr Wrangel between 1918 and 1920, the Volunteer Army attempted to maintain both an anti-Soviet and anti-German campaign simultaneously. Politically, the campaign aimed for restoration of an assembly form of government featuring traditional political parties. The southern movement, however, was hampered by a lack of cohesion in its daily operations, which would lead to ultimate defeat.

Another important center of White activity proved to be Siberia. Here fighting erupted in 1918 between Soviet troops and the famous Czechoslovak Legion, which had aided Tsarist forces in assaults on Austria-Hungary during World War I. The Legion was on its way through Siberia for eventual crossing into North America and from there to the Western Front in Europe, when frictions with the Soviets erupted into violence. The Legion, comprising some 35,000 troops, abandoned plans to leave Russia and effectively sealed off the Siberian east, creating a zone where anti-Soviet movements might flourish. Ultimately, the Siberian White movement was led by Admiral Aleksandr Kolchak.

Northern anti-Soviet movements, led by Nikolai V. Chaikovski , relied too heavily on British troops brought in as part of the Allied intervention. So did the White forces in Estonia, where the White movement was under the control of General Nikolai N. Yudenich. At first, these White forces, peripheral though they were, scored some impressive victories, and, indeed, for a time in 1919 threatened the Soviet regime. In the south, General Denikin scored key victories, notably his capture of Kiev in September, 1919. By November, however, the Red Army (Soviet) launched a resounding counteroffensive that drove the remnants of the Volunteer Army into the Crimea, from whence under Pëtr Wrangel they were later evacuated in disarray. In Siberia, Admiral Kolchak began an offensive against key sites near the Volga river. Kolshak rode a wave of military successes through March, 1919, but with the Volga threatened, the Red Army repelled his forces through the month of April. Attempts by northern Whites based in Archangel to link up with Kolchak's troops failed, as did two attacks by Yudenich's forces against Petrograd. By the winter of 1919-1920, impressive White campaigns ceased.

The anti-Soviet crusade was also joined by forces from Russia's minority nationalities, particularly in the Ukraine, where fierce nationalist pride motivated many to use the Civil War as a backdrop for Ukrainian independence. Of great importance in the Ukrainian movement was the peasant leader Makhno, an avowed anarchist, whose politics made Allied action with the White forces very tenuous. By 1920, the Soviets had crushed the Ukrainian independence movement.

Another aspect of the Civil War had more diplomatic than military impact. This was the famous intervention of the Allied armed forces of Great Britain, France, the United States, and Japan in Russia in 1918. Japan, in landing its forces at Vladivostok, had definite territorial aims, a stance which did not characterize the other interventionist powers. British, French, and American troops were sent to Vladivostok and Archangel, but played no direct combat role. Instead, these Western forces acted as suppliers of arms, aid, and advice to the White forces. By 1919, with the end of World War I, the Allied forces were withdrawn, as the rationale of restoring Russia to the Triple Entente no longer mattered.

By 1920, the Civil War was nearing completion with Soviet victory. The Volunteer Army had been chased out of the Crimea, evacuated via Istanbul to the Kingdom of Serbs, Croats, and Slovenes (as Yugoslavia was then known), ending all southern resistance. In Siberia, the tired and demoralized Czechoslovak Legion, which had buttressed the eastern White forces, quit the field and handed Kolchak over to the Soviets, who promptly executed the admiral in February, 1920. With Allied forces gone, the civil uprising was over.

Historians have often wondered how the fledgling Soviet state could win the Civil War. First, it won because of major White flaws. The Soviet forces had the advantage of defending interior lines, while the Whites were fighting the offensive from the periphery of Russia. Transportation and communications had been difficult prior to World War I and the Bolshevik Revolution. It proved exceedingly difficult for the Whites to fight a united war, given their disparate locations. Beyond these tactical difficulties were political difficulties. The White forces, on all fronts, had little in the way of political unity. White sentiments ranged from parliamentary liberals to the reactionary, autocratic Right.

Coupled with White liabilities were some distinct Red Army strengths. First and foremost, there was the brilliant military leadership of Leon Trotsky, who was made Commissar of War by the Lenin government. Trotsky quickly abandoned many Bolshevik concepts of a peoples' army that had held sway since 1917. Discipline of a strict type was restored, as was the practice of conscription. The Red Army did not have to defend far-flung points like those held by the Whites. In addition, the Red Army, quite unlike the Whites, had a unified outlook and program which lifted its morale as the war went on. Finally, the Red Army had the crucial advantage of representing the government in the struggle. Though the Soviet state probably did not command the support of most of its people, it still was the state, and as such, commanded a legitimacy not possessed by the Whites. The government, under a program of "War Communism," obtained the necessary sacrifices from the Soviet populace to secure victory.

## Pertinent Literature

Brinkley, George A. *The Volunteer Army and the Allied Intervention in South Russia, 1917-1921*. South Bend, Ind.: University of Notre Dame Press, 1966.

This volume by George A. Brinkley, part of Notre Dame's International Studies Series, is an important contribution to the sparse scholarly literature available on the Russian Civil War. Its focus on the Volunteer Army is justifiable inasmuch as this fighting force was perhaps the leading anti-Bolshevik movement during the Civil War.

Brinkley begins his narrative with the conditions brought about by World War I. He sees two major factors leading Russia from World War to Civil War. The first factor is what he labels "the disintegration of Russia"—the massive political upheavals that shook that country during 1917, culminating in the Bolshevik *coup* in November. The second factor was the German occupation of areas of South Russia. These two developments led to the formation of the Volunteer Army.

The core of the book contains a narrative account of the rise and fall of this movement. It is clear that the Volunteer Army possessed some advantages in the beginning. It could attract support from all non-Bolshevik factions, particularly after the Bolsheviks dissolved Russia's Constituent Assembly in January, 1918. In addition, it drew strength from the fighting traditions of the Cossacks in South Russia. Third, its string of commanders were trained military leaders, quite unlike the leadership of the Bolshevik Red Army. Finally, it had the potential to draw support from the Ukraine, long a center of nationalist sentiments.

Beyond these advantages, the Volunteer Army received aid from the Allied intervention, which is detailed in three separate chapters in Brinkley's book. In the end, however, the Volunteer Army suffered defeat and expulsion from Russia. The reasons for this ultimate failure involve, first, the political program that evolved among the leaders of the Volunteer Army. The army acquired the reputation of political reaction, seeming to push for a restoration of the monarchy and the pre-1917 autocracy. In addition, the politics of the leadership ultimately alienated Ukrainian support because a return to the tsarist system would mean a reassertion of Great Russian chauvinism. The Ukrainians rallied for a brief time to the independence movement led by the peasant anarchist Makhno, rather than to the Volunteer Army. The Allied intervention came to an end. If the intervention had provided little military hardware for the Civil War, it still had given the Volunteer Army and the other White forces some respectability and international support. Without this support, the Volunteer Army and the White cause in general became a much more isolated effort. In the end, a redisciplined Red Army under Commissar of War Leon Trotsky chased the remnants of the volunteer forces out of Russia via the Crimea.

Brinkley's account is one of the few available in English. It is scrupulously documented and worth the attention of any reader interested in the Russian Civil War.

Chamberlin, William Henry. *The Russian Revolution, 1917-1921.* 2 vols. New York: The Macmillan Company, 1935.

William Henry Chamberlin's study     is the product of twelve years of study and research, mostly carried on in the Soviet Union. From the time he arrived in Moscow in 1922 as a correspondent for *The Christian Science Monitor*, Chamberlin conceived the idea of writing a comprehensive study of the Russian Revolution and its sequel, the Russian Civil War. Chamberlin's work, completed during 1933 and 1934 under a Guggenheim fellowship, is the first one of its kind based on original Russian source material. His book is enhanced by richness of detail; a clear, readable style of writing; and a very helpful table of chronological events covering the period from March, 1917, to March, 1921.

Chamberlin devotes more than half of the forty-one chapters in the book to the Russian Civil War, which broke out in earnest in January, 1918, with the effort of the Bolsheviks to reestablish their control over the rebellious Ukraine. The struggle for the Ukraine was only one of several major contests in which the Bolsheviks found themselves engaged with rival elements over the following three years. During 1918, the Bolsheviks saw the Germans, with whom they had made peace at Brest-Litovsk in March of that year, steadily extend their control over the Ukraine. Simultaneously, on the Middle Volga and in Siberia, the Bolsheviks faced the opposition of the Czech Legion which threw in its lot with local White Forces. Finally, the Bolsheviks had to contend with the intervention of Allied forces in northern, southern, and far-eastern Russia; later, during 1920, they had to block Poland's attempt to extend its control over the Ukraine.

In the face of all these opponents, it is amazing that the Bolsheviks emerged triumphant. The explanations that Chamberlin offers for the Bolshevik success have largely stood the test of subsequent research on the subject of the Russian Civil War. Geographically, the anti-Red forces, scattered around the periphery of the Great Russian heartland, were never able to unite or coordinate their military efforts. Politically, the divided ranks of the anti-Bolshevik foes, embracing conservative pro-tsarist elements and peasant anarchists, allowed no basis for lasting cooperation. Chamberlin makes the interesting point that although several stalwart anti-Bolshevik leaders came to the fore, such as Denikin, Wrangel, and Makhno, none of them could match the appeal which Lenin and Trotsky had with the masses. In short, as Chamberlin puts it, the White movements produced no Mussolini or Hitler.

All factions involved in the Civil War, Chamberlin points out, had trouble in maintaining the loyalty of those peasants under their immediate control. Insurgent peasants on several occasions contributed to serious defeats of the Red Army. But in the critical months of late 1919, when the White forces seemed to be converging for the kill on Bolshevik-held central Russia, Lenin managed to control the peasants in his area. Kolchak and Denikin, on the contrary, owe much of their ultimate failure in the Civil War to their inability to retain the loyalty of their peasant populations at critical moments in the struggle. To many peasants, however bad the Bolsheviks might be, they appeared better than the Whites, who were always associated with the hated prewar regime.

Chamberlin also cites important psychological factors in explaining the victory of the Bolsheviks. The Reds, with all their ignorance and inexperience, displayed the crude strength of a fresh young ruling class that was convinced its revolution was not only Russian but also international in character. The Whites, by contrast, could never escape the charge that they were a decadent group which had had its chance to rule and had failed. Whereas the Whites appeared as the guardians of aristocratic privilege, the Bolsheviks, at least during the Civil War, seemed to afford oppressed peoples, whether Jews, peasants, or workers, the opportunity to rise in the ranks and participate in the building of a new society. Ultimately, the Bolsheviks triumphed because, as Chamberlin puts it, "their will to power, their determination to hold the seats of power which they had gained were stronger than the efforts of the former privileged classes to regain their old position." — *E.A.Z.*

## Additional Recommended Reading

Beneš, Eduard. *My War Memoirs*. Translated by Paul Selver. Boston: Houghton Mifflin Company, 1928. Contains an account of the Czech Legion's role in the Civil War.

Chamberlin, William Henry. *The Ukraine: A Submerged Nation*. New York: The Macmillan Company, 1944. Focus is on the South Russian aspects of the Civil War.

Coates, W. P. and Zelda K. Coates. *Armed Intervention in Russia, 1918-1922*. London: V. Gollancz, 1935. A detailed military history of the Allied intervention.

Denikin, Anton I. *The White Army*. Translated by Catherine Zvegintzov. London: J. Cape and Company, 1930. Memoirs of the prominent White general.

Footman, David. *Civil War in Russia*. London: Faber and Faber, 1961. A recent scholarly account of the total Civil War.

Kennan, George Frost. *Russia and the West Under Lenin and Stalin*. Boston: Little, Brown and Company, 1961. Provides a concise narrative account of the Russian Civil War.

# THE DISSOLUTION OF THE HABSBURG MONARCHY

*Type of event:* Constitutional: end of the oldest European dynastic state
*Time:* November 13, 1918
*Locale:* Austria, Hungary, and Bohemia

*Principal personages:*
FRANCIS JOSEPH I (1830-1916), Emperor of Austria and King
of Hungary
FRANCIS FERDINAND (1863-1914), Archduke of Austria and
heir apparent to the thrones of Austria-Hungary
CHARLES I (CHARLES FRANCIS JOSEPH) (1887-1922), Em-
peror of Austria and King of Hungary
TOMÁŠ GARRIGUE MASARYK (1850-1937), Czech professor;
and first President of Czechoslovakia, 1918-1935
THOMAS WOODROW WILSON (1856-1924), twenty-eighth
President of the United States, 1913-1921

## Summary of Event

At noon on November 11, 1918, Emperor Charles I Habsburg of Austria hastily penciled his resignation, without formal abdication of his powers, as Emperor of Austria. On November 13, he resigned the kingship of Hungary. By these acts Europe's oldest ruling monarchy came to an end. As with most historical events of major significance, the dissolution of the Habsburg monarchy was brought about both by long-term and short-term causes. The underlying problems that hastened its decline were the many unresolved national, political, and social tensions that had built up prior to 1914. The immediate cause of the actual downfall of the monarchy was World War I. The enormous internal and external pressures of war were destructive of what had at least been a "ramshackle realm" in time of peace.

The seven-hundred-year-old house of Habsburg ruled over a multinational dynastic empire. The realm was an anomaly in a world in which the unitary nation-state was fast becoming the standard organization of civilized life. By 1815, the Habsburg monarchy had lost its former control over the Holy Roman Empire, Spain, and Belgium, but it retained its rule over Alpine Austria, Bohemia, Hungary, and parts of Italy, Poland, and the Balkans. At the turn of the twentieth century the Habsburg monarchy of Austria-Hungary had become a primarily Danubian state located in Central and Southeastern Europe. It contained an area about the size of Texas and was inhabited by approximately fifty-two million people who represented a mosaic of about a dozen nationalities with a wide range of social, economic, and cultural systems.

Though the Habsburg Empire had the disadvantage of being a state without a nation, certain supranational forces worked to hold together the diverse lands until the twentieth century. The stabilizing influences were the loyalty of the aristocracies to the dynasty, the army, the bureaucracy, the Catholic Church, the city of Vienna as an administrative and cultural center, and the German language as the lingua franca of the diverse realm. Some historians have argued that, prior to the mid-nineteenth century, Austria had provided a sense of mission and common purpose for the peoples of the Empire. The Habsburgs had led the Counterreformation and the wars against the Turks, pioneered enlightened despotism, and waged the struggle against Napoleon. Moreover, the Empire was able to survive because it had the support of the major European nations in the balance of power system.

By the mid-nineteenth century, however, the monarchy was becoming anachronistic. The rising forces of liberalism, industrialization, and especially nationalism threatened the conservative foundations of the state. The liberal and nationalist revolutions of 1848, although a failure, spanned numerous nationality conflicts which spelled the doom of the Habsburg Empire seventy years later. By 1850, reaction triumphed in the reign of the new Emperor, Francis Joseph I.

In the 1860's and 1870's, the Habsburgs suffered diplomatic and military setbacks when they lost the friendship of Russia and relinquished their foothold in Germany and Italy. The resulting "Compromise of 1867" transformed the former Austrian Empire, formally created in 1804, into the Dual Monarchy of Austria-Hungary. Though the German Austrians and the Magyars constituted a minority among the other nationalities, the two groups exercised the real power in the state.

From 1870 to 1914, Austria-Hungary experienced increasing domestic difficulties. The nationalities problem was the most serious of all. The Czechs and South Slavs demanded autonomy and obtained some concessions, but remained dissatisfied. The Magyars adamantly refused to grant any advantages to the Slovaks and Croats under their control. Many German Austrians and Magyars themselves became intensely nationalistic and resentful of the Habsburgs; one such individual was the young Adolf Hitler, who was living in Vienna just prior to World War I. With the growth of the middle class and the industrial proletariat, liberalism and socialism made headway in the later nineteenth century. The Habsburgs responded by granting universal suffrage in 1907, but then took to ruling by decree, thereby choking off further reforms.

By the early twentieth century, Austria-Hungary's losing struggle to remain a world power took two forms. First, the Habsburg monarchy became increasingly dependent upon the might of the new German Empire, unified in 1871. Second, Austria sought to pursue imperialist ambitions in the Balkans. Her outright annexation (from Turkey) of the heavily Serbian area of Bosnia-Herzegovina in 1908 infuriated the new kingdom of Serbia. Bosnian Serbs wished to be reunited with their conationals, while a pro-Russian Serbia looked upon Bosnia as "unredeemed" territory.

During this time Vienna remained

the cultural leader of Central Europe. But despite the Viennese genius for innovation in literature, philosophy, and music, its cultural creations on the eve of the war were marked by escapism, fragmentation of styles, and a morbid fascination with decay and death. Many intelligent people in the Habsburg realms expressed feelings of impending disaster. The coming of war turned their suspicions into a shattering reality.

In 1914, the seemingly insoluble nationality problem in Austria-Hungary converged with a great diplomatic crisis in Europe. On June 28, 1914, Archduke Francis Ferdinand, heir apparent to the Habsburg throne and reputed to have favored limited autonomy for the Slavs, was assassinated in the Bosnian capital of Sarajevo by a Bosnia-Serbian nationalist, Gavrilo Princip. On July 28, 1914, exactly a month after the assassination, Austria declared war on Serbia; Austria's ally Germany went to war with Russia and France, and World War I began. High officials of the Habsburg monarchy believed that a preventive war with Serbia was the only way to preserve the Habsburg state as a unified entity and a world power. Instead, the war exacerbated the tensions in the Dual Monarchy to the breaking point and resulted in the complete destruction of the Habsburg order.

World War I was both an effect of the problems of the Habsburg monarchy and the major cause of its disintegration. In 1914, the majority of the peoples of the Empire rallied behind the old Emperor Francis Joseph I, but by 1915, the strains of war began to widen the cracks in the system's structure. The state took on the features of a military dictatorship that antagonized many groups within the society. In 1915, radical Czechs and Croats formed National Committees in the West. In October of 1916, Austrian Prime Minister Count Karl von Stürgkh was assassinated by a young socialist.

On November 21, 1916, Emperor Francis Joseph I died after a reign of sixty-eight years. He had been a tragic and hard-working ruler, but he was unimaginative and unresponsive to the needs of his rapidly changing times. He was succeeded by his grand nephew Charles I, a well-intentioned but inexperienced and irresolute man. Charles reconvened the parliament (Reichsrat) and declared an amnesty, but this won him few friends. His inept peace overtures to the Western Allies were negated by his dependence on Imperial Germany. Above all, he balked at granting complete autonomy to the subject nationalities.

Despite many problems, the survival of the Empire seemed secure in 1916. But in 1917, the Russian revolutions and the entry of the United States into the war heightened the demands for reform and insured the military defeat of Germany. Economic hardships in the winter of 1917-1918 resulted in rioting, desertions, and strikes. The Western powers had not been bent on the destruction of the monarchy before 1918; but when the German offensive in the West began in the spring of 1918, the Allies decided to hasten victory by supporting the break-up of the Habsburg monarchy. By May of 1918, the exiled Czech leader Tomáš Garrigue Masaryk, the influential British journalist H. Wickham Steed, and President Woodrow Wilson of the United States all pressed for an end to the monarchy.

The final destruction of the monarchy coincided with its military collapse. By October of 1918, the Czechs, Poles, and South Slavs seceded from the monarchy, while the Austrian and Hungarian parliaments drew up plans for their own independent republics. The interests of the Habsburgs had totally diverged from those of its peoples. Emperor Charles I was not driven from office; his resignation in November of 1918 simply affirmed the realities of the situation. The passing of the monarchy marked the end of an era in both Austrian and European history.

## Pertinent Literature

May, Arthur J. *The Passing of the Habsburg Monarchy, 1914-1918.* 2 vols. Philadelphia: University of Pennsylvania Press, 1966.

This thorough narrative by an expert in the field is based upon the vast manuscript holdings of the *Staatsarchiv* in Vienna and the important newspapers of the time. It is an open-ended account of the fall of the Habsburg Empire devoid of the older deterministic point of view that the state was doomed by 1914.

Arthur J. May begins his story in 1914, when Archduke Francis Ferdinand's plan for Slavic autonomy might have saved the monarchy. The author nicely illustrates the irony of the Archduke's visit to Sarajevo on June 28, 1914. Francis Ferdinand visited the capital of Bosnia because he expected to be warmly welcomed in view of his sympathy for the Slavic peoples of the monarchy; he also hoped to secure a wider acceptance of his morganatic marriage to Sophie Potiorek. Instead, he was assassinated. May agrees with most historians that Austria was determined to punish Serbia. He does well to call attention to the little-known hate campaign waged by newspapers in both Vienna and Belgrade.

The author skillfully illustrates the forces that prevented an end to the war between Austria-Hungary and the Triple Entente. Though the Habsburgs were willing to compromise with the Western powers, the Germans were more rigid and confident. Austria was trapped by her alliance with Germany. In 1915 the Habsburgs were dealt an unexpected blow: Italy, tempted by promises of Trieste, Northern Dalmatia, and South Tyrol, entered the war on the side of the Entente.

May views the influence of such Czech *émigrés* as Tomáš G. Masaryk and British publicists H. Wickham Steed and R. W. Seton-Watson as crucial influences in convincing the Entente to destroy the Habsburg monarchy. He goes so far as to say that of all the leaders of the period, Masaryk was most responsible for the discredit and ruin of the monarchy.

An interesting discussion is devoted to the impact of the war on the intellectual and literary figures of the

Habsburg lands, most of whom became pacifists. Sigmund Freud's *Essay on War* (1915) illustrated that whole peoples could behave in a self-destructive way. The Czech novelist Jaroslav Hašek wrote his masterpiece *The Good Soldier: Schweik*, and the Austrian satirist Karl Kraus composed an important tragedy entitled *The Last Days of Mankind*. These great works were written under the impact of the war.

May ends his first volume with the death of the old Emperor Francis Joseph I in 1916, the accession of the young Emperor Charles, and the failure of peace negotiations. He ascribes the failure of the talks between Premier Jan Smuts of South Africa and Count Albert Mensdorff of Vienna to the increasing domination of Germany over Austria.

Volume Two of this detailed work opens with the author's most important point of the entire book: the Empire could have been preserved as late as the spring of 1918. May illustrates his argument by pointing out that when the United States declared war on Austria-Hungary on December 4, 1917, President Woodrow Wilson stated that his aim was not the destruction of the Habsburg monarchy, but rather its liberation from Germany. Moreover, Wilson's Fourteen Points of January, 1918, called for an independent Poland and an autonomous federation for the nationalities, but it did not advocate the destruction of the Habsburg realm *per se*.

The turning point in the intentions of the Entente toward the Habsburgs came about in March of 1918 for two reasons. First, the Treaty of Brest-Litovsk in early 1918 demonstrated the collaborative rapacity of Germany and Austria towards Russia and Eastern Europe. Second, the March offensive of the Germans in the West convinced the Entente that its support of the independence of the nationalities within the monarchy would speed the end of the war. May argues that contrary to accepted beliefs, Masaryk "exercised no direct influence on Wilson's new course." The decision to dismember Austria-Hungary was a result of military necessity.

The impact of the Bolshevik Revolution and economic hardships caused a massive revolt of workers and returning soldiers by the spring of 1918. By the fall of 1918, one-seventh of the nine million men under arms in the Habsburg Empire had perished. For May, it was the internal and external impact of World War I that decisively settled the fate of the monarchy. A federative union of autonomous peoples advocated by the revolutionaries in 1849 and by desperate Austrian parliamentarians in 1916 would have meant the destruction rather than the salvation of the Habsburg structure. Thus, May disagrees with many historians who maintain that a federation would have been the only reform that could have saved the monarchy. He ends his work with the eloquent argument that peace and peace alone could have saved the Habsburg experiment in Central Europe. Austria's ill-fated mission of self-preservation against Serbia destroyed only Austria. Indeed, World War I was caused partly by the problems of the Austro-Hungarian monarchy. In the long run,

Western civilization paid a great price for the destruction of the Habsburg state, as the subsequent Nazi and Soviet dominations of Eastern Central Europe attest. With these conclu-sions, the author helps lay to rest the myth that revanchist Western statesmen were bent on the dissolution of the Habsburg monarchy.

Zeman, Z. A. B. *The Break-Up of the Habsburg Empire, 1914-1918: A Study in National and Social Revolution*. London: Oxford University Press, 1961.

Z. A. B. Zeman dedicated this balanced and sober study to correct one-sided misconceptions over a whole spectrum of historical opinion. The theme of his account is the multifaceted nature of historical causation as applied to the end of the Habsburg monarchy. To those historians of the 1920's and 1930's who saw the breakup of the Empire as a long process starting in 1866, Zeman argues that World War I alone was decisive in transforming anti-Habsburg radicalism into real national and social revolutions. Against Marxist historians of the present who maintain that the Bolshevik revolution was necessary for the breakup of the state, Zeman maintains that social revolution broke out in Austria and Hungary alone, while movements of national liberation were characteristic of Bohemia, Poland, and the lands of the South Slavs. For those who maintain that the monarchy broke up because of the decisions of the victorious powers at the Paris Peace Conference of 1919, Zeman would reply that the decision to dismember the Empire had already been taken by the spring of 1918.

For Zeman, the major reasons for the demise of the Empire are numerous and connected: the German drive for hegemony in Austria, the Allied defeat of the Central Powers, the radicalization of the nationalities and the working class, and cooperation between the radicals inside the monarchy and political exiles living in the West.

The author adds another significant force usually overlooked in accounts of the subject; the struggle between the military and civilian authorities in Austria during the war. The coming of war increased the power of the army in Austria as it did among all the belligerents. What was especially fatal to the Habsburgs was the heavy-handed treatment of the Slavic nationalities, especially the Czechs, at the hands of Habsburg military commanders. The talented but arrogant Austrian Chief of Staff, Conrad von Hötzendorf, remained in power until February of 1917. His policies included the arrests, trials, and shootings of Czechs and Serbs considered hostile to the regime. The creation of a War Supervisory Office gathered great powers into the hands of the military; in early 1918 mass strikes were brutally suppressed by the army, which alienated the workers and increased the growth of a radical socialist movement against the regime.

For Zeman, as for other historians, the entry of the United States into the war was an important turning point for the end of the monarchy.

Because of American intervention, German domination of Austria increased, while the fate of the Habsburgs became closely tied to the military fortunes of Germany. Zeman provides the astute observation that by May of 1918 the Allies began to use the exiles from the Habsburg monarchy to weaken the state in the same manner as the Germans had used Vladimir Ilych Lenin to weaken the Russian military commitment to the Allies. The decision of the Czechs to break away from Austria was decisive, for Bohemia-Moravia had been a cornerstone of the Habsburg state. Thus, the Entente and the exiles supported the end of the monarchy before the event had actually taken place.

The national movements that proclaimed independence from the Austrians in October, 1918, had little in common with the movements of prewar days. Though the radical secessionists were still in the minority in 1917, mass movements against the Empire were developing. Zeman includes a fascinating discussion of the defection of the Czech Legion from Habsburg military command. Austrian military oppression, hunger and strikes, Hungarian intransigence, Allied support of the national councils, the example of the Bolshevik Revolution—all played a role in radicalizing the masses against the Habsburg regime.

In his concluding remarks Zeman produces one last important reason for the demise of the Habsburg monarchy: the lack of political acumen and resolve by the ruling groups of the state. The last chance for reform came in the spring of 1917 with the opening of the Austrian parliament (Reichsrat). Charles I and his advisers failed to dissociate themselves from the German alliance, grant autonomy to the nationalities, and conduct fruitful peace negotiations. Consequently, the Reichsrat became a forum for anger and sedition rather than a body that could work to save the Habsburgs. The United States and revolutionary Russia were forces of dynamism that greatly overshadowed and discredited the half-hearted efforts of the Habsburgs at reform.

The theme of Zeman's study is that national and social revolution worked hand in hand to topple the monarchy. The Czech middle classes, the Austrian workers, the Polish intellectuals, the South Slav peasants, and thousands of soldiers all had national and social reasons for ultimately rejecting the Habsburgs. This well-documented account is aided by useful maps and well-chosen photographs. Zeman's compact study provides a most useful introduction to a complex and multifaceted subject. — *L.S.*

## Additional Recommended Reading

Valiani, Leo. *The End of Austria-Hungary*. London: Secker and Warburg, 1973. Emphasizes the inability and unwillingness of the ruling classes of the Empire to reform the political and social structure and to prevent the entry of Italy into the war.

Pick, Robert. *The Last Days of Imperial Vienna*. London: Weidenfeld and Nicolson,

1975. A lively account of everyday life in Vienna and the mostly indifferent attitudes of the Viennese toward the break-up of the monarchy.

Taylor, A. J. P. *The Habsburg Monarchy, 1809-1918: A History of the Austrian Empire and Austria-Hungary*. New York: Harper & Row Publishers, 1965. A well-written and insightful volume that provides valuable background for understanding the end of the monarchy; maintains that Tito succeeded where Francis Joseph failed.

Mamatey, Victor S. *The United States and East Central Europe, 1914-1918: A Study in Wilsonian Diplomacy and Propaganda*. Princeton, N.J.: Princeton University Press, 1957. This important study of American policies toward Austria-Hungary argues that America stimulated, but did not necessarily engender, the destruction of the Habsburgs, a demise that was mainly due to internal problems and the defeat of the Central Powers.

Jaszi, Oscar. *The Dissolution of the Habsburg Monarchy*. Chicago: University of Chicago Press, 1961. A massive work by the Hungarian publicist and scholar, first published in 1929, which maintains that World War I was not the cause of the end of the Empire, but was the effect of two hundred years of "organic" decline.

Crankshaw, Edward. *The Fall of the House of Habsburg*. New York: The Viking Press, 1963. A lively narrative account of the Empire from 1848 to 1918 with emphasis on personalities.

# QUANTUM PHYSICS RESEARCH

*Type of event:* Scientific: basic research in pure physics
*Time:* The 1920's
*Locale:* Germany, France, and England

*Principal personages:*
NIELS BOHR (1885-1962), a Danish physicist
ERWIN SCHRÖDINGER (1887-1961), an Austrian physicist
LOUIS VICTOR DE BROGLIE (1892-      ), a French physicist
WOLFGANG PAULI (1900-1958) and
WERNER HEISENBERG (1901-1977), German physicists
PAUL ANDRE MARIE DIRAC (1902-      ), a British physicist

## Summary of Event

The birth of Quantum Mechanics can be traced back to Max Planck's famous lecture on December 14, 1900, before the German Physical Society. Planck's revolutionary idea postulated that the emission and absorption of light by material bodies always took place in discrete bundles of energy, called light quanta. In 1905, Albert Einstein successfully extended Planck's idea to explain the laws of the photoelectric effect (the emission of electrons from metallic surfaces irradiated by ultraviolet light). Eight years later, Danish physicist Niels Bohr achieved the synthesis of Rutherford's planetary model of an atom with Planck's quantum hypothesis. In his papers spanning the years 1913 to 1918, Bohr introduced a set of specific assumptions regarding the stationary states of an atom and the frequency of the emitted radiation when the atom passes from one discrete energy state to another. He succeeded in obtaining a simple interpretation of the laws governing the line spectra of elements and was able to deduce Johann Jakob Balmer's empirical formula, originally advanced in 1885, for the hydrogen spectrum. In spite of its success, however, Bohr's theory proved to be inadequate, as it failed to explain the mechanism of the transition process from one state to another; nor was it able to predict the intensities of the various lines in optical spectra.

In his early papers, Bohr introduced the so-called Principle of Correspondence, and he elaborated further on this topic in his 1920 and 1923 papers. The Principle of Correspondence states that the quantum theory should yield the results of the classical radiation theory in the limit of large quantum numbers (a set of numbers which specify the state of an atom in quantum theory). The research work during the years 1919-1925, which eventually led to the formulation of Quantum Mechanics, was strongly influenced by this correspondence principle.

Meanwhile, an important experiment performed in 1923 by the American physicist Arthur Compton proved the reality of light quanta. Compton

166

studied the collision of X-rays—whose quanta carry large amounts of energy—with electrons bound in lightweight atoms, and showed that the energy and, hence, the frequency of the scattered X-rays would decrease with the increasing scattering angle. The results of this experiment stood in agreement with the theoretical formula derived from conservation of energy and momentum applied to the light quantum and the electron.

In 1925, the French physicist Louis Victor de Broglie published a paper based on his doctoral thesis in which he proposed a novel interpretation of Bohr's quantum orbits. Broglie suggested that the motion of each electron is governed by some kind of mysterious pilot wave whose velocity and wave length depend on the velocity of the electron. He then showed that the various quantum orbits of Bohr were those that could accommodate an integral number of pilot waves. Just as light, generally accepted to be a wave phenomenon, occasionally displays particle features, so electrons, generally accepted as particles, would also exhibit wave properties and, under proper conditions, show diffraction phenomena similar to those characteristic of light. Confirmation of Broglie's brilliant idea was obtained in experiments carried out simultaneously and independently by Sir George Thompson in England and G. Davisson and L. H. Germer in the United States. They discovered diffraction effects in the reflection or transmission of a beam of electrons by a crystal, and the measured wave length coincided exactly with the value predicted by Broglie's formula. Broglie, however,

did not exploit the particle-wave dualism to its full extent.

Shortly thereafter, the Austrian physicist Erwin Schrödinger developed a general equation for the Broglie waves which was capable of describing electrons in all kinds of dynamical situations. The Schrödinger equation is similar to other well-known equations in mathematical physics, except that it contains explicitly the imaginary unit ($i = \sqrt{-1}$). The solution of this equation, called the wave function $\psi$, also turned out, in general, to be complex; its physical interpretation was far from obvious. In particular, it could not directly represent a physical vibration. A real quantity obtained from the wave function $\psi$, namely, the square of its absolute value, appears to have physical significance. It measures the probability at each point and each instant that the associated particle will be observed at this point at that instant. As a result, one cannot, at any given instant, assign a definite position to the particle; one can only say that there is such-and-such a probability of finding it here or there. In the new theory, the classical notions of velocity and trajectory lose their precise meaning and give way to a probabilistic interpretation. The theory based on the Schrödinger equation was called Wave Mechanics.

Almost simultaneously with Schrödinger's paper, there appeared a paper by the German physicist Werner Heisenberg, dealing with the same subject and yielding the same results as Schrödinger's theory. Heisenberg's method started from entirely different physical assumptions and used entirely different mathematical techniques. Heisenberg, who was then only twenty-four years of age, based his theory on the so-called noncommutative algebra, in which a times b is not necessarily equal to b times a. As had been known to mathematicians for quite some time, certain arrays of numbers can be considered as mathematical objects called "matrices"; and, in general, they do not obey the laws of commutative multiplication. Heisenberg's theory thus became known as Matrix Mechanics. Whereas Schrödinger visualized the motion of atomic electrons as being governed by a system of three-dimensional waves, Heisenberg's model considered the atom as being composed of an infinite number of virtual "vibrators" with frequencies coinciding with all those that the atom could emit.

In both theories, it is found that every quantum state can be characterized by a set of three quantum numbers. The first, or principal quantum number, designated n, must be an integer; it specifies the shell in which the electron lies. The energy level of a state depends mainly on the principal quantum number n. The second, or orbital quantum number, designated l, is also an integer; it determines the angular momentum of the electron with respect to the nucleus. The third, or magnetic quantum number, designated $m_l$, is an integer which specifies the possible orientations of the angular momentum vector. Eventually, after the discovery of the spin of the electron, a fourth quantum number, $m_s$, was introduced to account for the two permitted directions of the spin.

In one of his subsequent papers,

Schrödinger demonstrated that, in spite of their widely differing appearances, the two theories were actually quite identical and that one could be derived from the other. Thus, the wave or matrix formulations were simply different interpretations of a more general Quantum Theory.

Many other important discoveries occurred in the remarkable year 1925. Samuel Goudsmit and George Uhlenbeck showed that in order to explain certain details in atomic spectra of elements subjected to strong magnetic fields one had to assume that the electron behaved as a small electrically charged rotating body. It would thus carry an intrinsic angular momentum and, associated with it, a magnetic moment—as if it were a tiny magnet. The German physicist Wolfgang Pauli incorporated these features in the new Quantum Theory. His most significant and far-reaching discovery was the famous Exclusion Principle, which he enunciated in 1925. The Exclusion or Pauli Principle states that in a multielectron system there can never be more than one electron in the same quantum state. This principle led to the understanding of the shell structure of atoms, the periodic table of the elements, and the chemical affinities of elements one for another.

Inherent in the physical structure of the Quantum Theory is the Uncertainty Principle formulated by Heisenberg in 1927. This principle limits the accuracy with which position and velocity (more precisely, the momentum) can be simultaneously ascribed to a particle. It implies that no technical or mathematical method, no matter how ingenious, can ever be devised to obtain an absolutely sharp and accurate account of the physical situation at any given moment.

Finally, one must mention that the feverish years of research which led to the formulation of the Quantum Theory were pervaded by the genius of the British physicist Paul Andre Marie Dirac, whose crowning achievement (1928) was the successful and harmonious merging of the Quantum Theory with the Theory of Relativity. The Dirac equation, which describes the motion of the electron, is relativistically correct. It also yields, without *a priori* assumptions, the spin property and the magnetic characteristics of the electron. Further analysis of the Dirac equation necessitated the interpretation of certain negative energy states which eventually were found to be linked to the existence of the positron, a particle with the same mass as that of the electron but carrying a positive charge. The positron could thus be called an anti-electron, and the interpretation of the solutions of the Dirac equation opened the vast field of antiparticle physics which eventually led to the discovery of the antiproton and many other antiparticles.

## Pertinent Literature

Gamow, George. *Thirty Years That Shook Physics*. Garden City, N.Y.: Doubleday & Company, 1966.

This book offers a comprehensive, accurate, and very entertaining account of the story of Quantum Physics in its formative years, and it expounds the progress of this science in layman's language. As a rule, books that attempt to explain scientific theories in layman's terms do not hold much interest for the specialist; on the other hand, books which are aimed at the specialist are incomprehensible to the layman. Gamow's book is a remarkable exception to this rule. Thanks to his exceptional scientific mastery, combined with an artistic gift for narration and a puckish sense of humor, he has written a book which does appeal to laymen and specialized physicists alike. The author explains the scientific discoveries not as a collection of dry theoretical statements and experiments, but through the thoughts and genial intuition of the scientists who, stone by stone, laid the foundations of the Quantum Theory. He describes the climate of scientific turmoil and excitement which characterized the few fateful years that saw the birth and early growth of the Quantum Theory.

Gamow makes important contributions of his own, explaining the emission of $\alpha$ particles from radioactive materials by means of the newly created wave mechanics. Many of the great architects of the Quantum Theory were his teachers, colleagues, or simply friends. The story is enlivened by the recounting of many anecdotes and amusing details of the personal lives of these great men. The first chapter, entitled "M. Planck and Light Quanta," recalls the state of physics at the turn of the century and introduces Planck's famous assumption that the energy content of a radiation quantum is proportional to the frequency. The photoelectric effect and the Compton effect are explained in detail and with great clarity.

The second chapter, entitled "N. Bohr and Quantum Orbits," discusses Bohr's interpretation of the Rutherford model of the atom and his attempts to solve the problem of light emission and absorption by atoms. His bold intuition that the mechanical energy in atoms must decrease by quantized amounts led to the idea of quantum states of atomic electrons and to the successful explanation of the hydrogen spectrum. This chapter is spiced with numerous anecdotes about Bohr.

The third chapter, entitled "W. Pauli and the Exclusion Principle," begins with a series of colorful anecdotes about Pauli, describing him as a devil of inspiration. The author humorously declares that Pauli was famous in physics on three counts: for the Pauli Principle, which he preferred to call the Exclusion Principle; for the Pauli Neutrino, a particle which he conceived of in the early 1920's and which was only discovered three decades later; and for the Pauli Effect, a mysterious phenomenon according to which something usually broke in the laboratory whenever Pauli stepped across the threshold.

The Exclusion Principle prevents all of the atomic electrons from collapsing into the lowest quantum state. Pauli suggested that only two electrons could occupy a given quantum state (specified by three quantum numbers). After the discovery of the electron spin, the original Pauli principle was reformulated by stating that the two electrons occupying a given quantum state must have spins in opposite directions. Alternatively, the principle states that there can never be more than a single electron in the same quantum state specified by *four* quantum numbers, the fourth quantum number being related to the direction of the spin. Pauli and Bohr used this principle to construct the models for all atoms, from hydrogen to uranium. They explained the periodic changes in atomic volumes, ionization potentials, and other chemical properties, thus providing a sound and rational basis for the empirical classification established by the Russian chemist Dimitri Ivanovich Mendeleev in his periodic system of elements.

The third chapter further discusses Pauli's contributions in the field of nuclear physics. Certain radioactive decay processes are characterized by the emission of electrons which do not have well-defined energies. The energies of the electrons emitted by a given element extend continuously from zero to some maximum value, in apparent contradiction of the law of conservation of energy. Whereas Bohr assumed that this law was violated in these decay processes, Pauli opposed this view and showed that the balance of energy could be restored by assuming the existence of a˙ yet unknown particle, the "neutrino." The existence of this most elusive, zero-charge, zero-mass particle was not established experimentally until thirty years later, by Fred Reines and Clyde Cowan.

The fourth chapter, "L. de Broglie

and the Pilot Waves," begins with an explanation of Broglie's original idea of associated waves fitted to the quantum orbits in Bohr's atom model and their experimental verification in electron diffraction experiments. A short time later, this fundamental idea was developed into a strict mathematical theory by E. Schrödinger, who succeeded in formulating a general equation for the Broglie waves. By using an analogy based on acoustics, the author offers a simple description of the Schrödinger waves in an atom. An electron moving around a proton in the hydrogen atom is somewhat similar to the vibrations of a gas in a rigid spherical enclosure. The wave mechanics based on Schrödinger's equation not only reproduces the results of Bohr's theory of quantum orbits, but also successfully explains the emission of particles by radioactive elements and their penetration into the nuclei of other light elements. The author himself made his first major contribution to the latter theory in 1928.

The fifth chapter is devoted to "W. Heisenberg and the Uncertainty Principle," and begins with a discussion of matrices, those arrays of number which are the cornerstones of Heisenberg's theory. A physical picture of the mathematical theory was provided by an article published by Heisenberg in 1927, in which he attacked the concept of trajectory, which is basic to classical mechanics. The discussion of an ideal experiment to observe the position of an electron led to the famous Uncertainty Principle.

The sixth chapter, entitled "P. A. M. Dirac and Anti-particles,"

begins by exposing the conflict between quantum and relativistic physics. The British physicist Dirac, who achieved the harmonious unification, is introduced by a series of colorful anecdotes revealing his remarkable scientific mind as well as his sense of humor. Dirac's brilliant idea was to linearize the wave equation; that is, to use first derivatives with respect to the space coordinates (instead of second order ones, as in Schrödinger's equation). The interpretation of the solutions of this new equation forces one to consider states with negative total energy which could not be discarded. In relativistic Quantum Theory, all of the normal electrons would then jump from positive energy states to the lower negative energy states. Dirac overcame this difficulty by invoking the Pauli Principle and assuming that all of the negative energy states are already occupied, leaving no room for the positive energy states to jump into. Dirac assumed that this infinite distribution of negative energy electrons (the Dirac Sea) could not be observed. On the other hand, the absence of a negative energy electron or "hole" in the Sea could be observed as a particle with positive electric charge. Dirac overstretched this idea and thought that the positive particle could represent the proton. The correct interpretation surfaced in 1931 when the American physicist Carl Anderson discovered a positively charged particle with the same mass as that of the electron. These positrons behaved exactly as Dirac holes did, and thus were the antiparticle corresponding to the electron. Later, antiparticles of many other known particles were detected experimentally.

The seventh and eighth chapters are devoted to Enrico Fermi's and Hideki Yukawa's achievements after 1930.

Margenau, Henry. *The Nature of Physical Reality: A Philosophy of Modern Physics.* New York: McGraw-Hill Book Company, 1950.

In this book, the author examines in depth the fundamental issues of scientific thought and theory and joins them by means of a philosophical synthesis. The first chapters are discursive and deal with traditional philosophical problems in science, concentrating mainly on the meaning of physical reality. The concepts of space and time and the general framework of physical description are discussed at length.

Chapter XVI, which deals with the breakdown of physical models, is an excellent introduction to the recent history of atomic physics. The author discusses the early efforts by Planck to formulate the quantum hypothesis, together with the postulates of Bohr which heralded the departure from the concepts and methods of classical physics. He then proceeds to develop the wave-particle dualism, reviewing in detail the evidence for assuming that light is either a wave or a corpuscle. A similar discussion is presented in the case of the electron. The wavelike nature of the electrons is examined in the light of Broglie's famous hypothesis and its subsequent experimental confirmation. The wave nature of the electron precludes the simultaneous determination of its position and its velocity (more precisely, its momentum), and the ensuing discussion paves the way for Heisenberg's Uncertainty Principle.

Chapter XVII is devoted to the basic ideas of Quantum Mechanics. The author recalls briefly the historical origin of wave mechanics and matrix mechanics as formulated by Schrödinger and Heisenberg, respectively. A theory general enough to encompass both methods was elaborated by Schrödinger and Dirac. John von Neumann provided a sound basis for this general theory by proving that the elements of matrix mechanics and those of wave mechanics are but a special form of operators constructed in an abstract space called the Hilbert space. This general theory is now commonly known as Quantum Mechanics. After introducing in an elementary fashion the new concepts of operators, eigenfunctions, and eigenvalues, Margenau proceeds to examine in a systematic way the five basic axioms of Quantum Mechanics. An acquaintance with differential and integral calculus is assumed, but all of the arguments are reduced to a form simple enough to make them accessible to a reader who is not particularly skilled in those disciplines.

Chapter XVIII is devoted entirely to the Uncertainty Principle and its implications for the theory of measurements. The principle is demonstrated in a general way with the use of the basic axioms laid out in the previous chapters. Philosophically, the Uncertainty Principle reflects in a rather loose way what has been called the intrinsic haziness of nature;

but its true meaning becomes apparent only when a definite interpretation of the act of measurement is adopted.

In Chapter XIX the concept of causality, that is, the cause and effect relation in natural phenomena, is examined first from the classical point of view as expressed in Laplace's famous statement which is the motto of scientific determinism. In the decade of the great discoveries of Quantum Mechanics, the statement of violation of causal reasoning dramatically described the revolutionary features of the new theory. In Quantum Mechanics, causality had to be reinterpreted; in a more restricted sense, it applies to the evolution of the state functions ψ which describe the system.

Chapter XX is devoted to an in-depth study of the Exclusion Principle, discovered by Pauli in analyzing the motion of electrons. This principle requires that no two electrons (or no two protons, neutrons, or certain other particles) can ever be in the same quantum state at any one time. This principle is first discussed in terms of the four quantum numbers which describe the state of an electron in an atom. Subsequently, the principle is stated in its most general form, which is tantamount to imposing a radical restriction (antisymmetry) on the wave function representing a system of electrons. The author then develops the consequences of this principle and, by means of simple examples, shows that it implies a correlation of the behavior of particles which is rather similar to the effect of forces of nondynamical origin.

This book constitutes an invaluable source of information for the philosopher or the historian of science seeking an authoritative general view of the evolution and progress of the quantum theory. — *V.N.*

## Additional Recommended Reading

Einstein, Albert and Leopold Infield. *The Evolution of Physics.* New York: Simon and Schuster, 1938. The fourth and final chapter dealing with quanta and the Quantum Theory is highly descriptive and requires practically no mathematical knowledge.

Lindsay, Robert B. and Henry Margenau. *Foundations of Physics.* New York: Dover Publications, 1957. Chapter IX, comprising 142 pages, covers the subject of Quantum Mechanics, its foundations and fundamental concepts; mathematical knowledge is required.

Broglie, Louis, Prince de. *The Revolution in Physics: A Non-Mathematical Survey of Quanta.* New York: Noonday Press, 1958. Offers a remarkably clear nonmathematical survey of the evolution and progress of the Quantum Theory and traces its emergence from classical physics.

Van der Waerden, B. L., ed. *Sources of Quantum Mechanics, Classics of Science.* New York: Dover Publications, 1967. A collection of the most important early papers on Quantum Mechanics, many of which are translated from their original language into English and provide an invaluable source of information for both physicists and historians of science.

Andrade e Silva, J. and G. Lochak. *Quanta*. New York: McGraw-Hill Book Company, 1969. A discussion of the origin and development of the Quantum Theory in terms easily comprehensible to the layman.

Cropper, William H. *The Quantum Physicists, and an Introduction to Their Physics*. New York: Oxford University Press, 1970. An interesting account of the development of quantum physics presented through the endeavors of the great physicists who founded it.

Jammer, Max. *The Philosophy of Quantum Mechanics*. New York: John Wiley and Sons, 1974. A detailed analysis of interpretrations of Quantum Mechanics in their historical perspective.

# MOHANDAS K. GANDHI LEADS THE NONVIOLENT INDIAN REFORM MOVEMENT

*Type of event:* Sociological: nonviolent reform movement
*Time:* 1920-1940
*Locale:* India

> *Principal personages:*
> MOHANDAS KARAMCHAND GANDHI (1869-1948), Indian reformer
> JAWAHARLAL NEHRU (1889-1964), a follower of Gandhi who eventually became the first Prime Minister of India
> MOHAMMED ALI JINNAH (1876-1948), Muslim leader determined to rid India of British rule, also a leader of the movement to partition India and establish Pakistan
> LORD IRWIN (EDWARD FREDERICK LINDLEY WOOD) (1881-1959), British Viceroy whom Gandhi opposed with his famous Salt March

## Summary of Event

Mohandas Karamchand Gandhi's leadership of the reform movement during the 1920's and 1930's was inseparably joined with the struggle for Indian independence.

A unique figure in the twentieth century, Gandhi was an able politician who was considered by many to be a Hindu saint. This combination gave him a hold over the Indian masses far greater than any "official" position could have provided. First attracting attention as a champion of Indian immigrants' rights in South Africa, Gandhi returned to India in 1915, bringing with him his tools of the *ashram*, a communal living establishment for himself and his followers, and *satyagraha*, his philosophy of self-improvement and nonviolence.

In 1917 Gandhi achieved his first major reform when the British government abolished indentured emigration, thus ending the source of much of the injustice he had fought against while in South Africa. Soon afterwards, Gandhi, whose reputation as a friend of the poor was growing, was able to persuade the government to end the requirement that three-twentieths of a tenant's land had to be worked for the benefit of the landlord.

One of Gandhi's earliest concerns was the position of the untouchables in Indian society. As members of Hinduism's lowest caste, they were considered fit only for manual labor; they were not allowed to use the common well or to touch those of a higher caste for fear of pollution. Soon after the founding of his *ashram*, Gandhi admitted an untouchable family, and he himself performed tasks that were supposed to be performed only by untouchables.

In taking these actions Gandhi lost the support of some rich Hindu businessmen and was prepared to move his entire community to the untouchable quarter, demonstrating, as he

175

was to do throughout his life, that scorn or personal hardship could not deter him from acting on his convictions. Subsequently, he was saved from this necessity by a large donation from a Muslim. In time, support from Hindus resumed, convincing Gandhi that untouchability had been dealt a severe blow. However, it remained a concern and a subject of his attention for the rest of his life.

With the passage of the Rowlatt Act in 1919, an extension of wartime restraints on free speech, freedom of the press, and the right of assembly, Gandhi's reform efforts became permanently merged with the Indian national movement. He called for a nationwide *hartal*, or general strike. The response was overwhelming. On April 6, 1919, virtually all of India stopped working. Unfortunately, the work stoppage was also accompanied by widespread violence; this dismayed Gandhi, who realized that many of the masses were not ready for his nonviolent methods.

The worst violence, however, occurred when the British garrison at Amritsar fired on a large crowd which was meeting in violation of regulations against public assembly. The resultant "Amritsar Massacre," in which 379 were killed and 1,137 wounded, is judged by many to have been the decisive event of the Indian independence movement. It convinced many that the British could not be trusted and that there was no alternative to independence. As a consequence, Gandhi accepted leadership of the Home Rule League in 1920 and called for noncooperation with British rule, a policy which was adopted by the Indian Congress Party in September of 1920.

As an important example of noncooperation, Gandhi asked people to boycott British-made cloth and to use the spinning wheel to produce homespun. Although many, including Jawaharlal Nehru, considered such economic ideas immature, the ideas carried the kind of appeal which the masses could understand and relate to. All over India the wearing of homespun became a source of pride as well as a detriment to the British economy.

Following an outbreak of violence at Chauri Chaura in February of 1922, Gandhi was arrested and charged with the writing of three seditious articles for his newspaper, *Young India*. Sentenced to six years in prison, he was released on February 5, 1924, after an appendicitis operation. Upon his release, concerned with the growing enmity between Muslims and Hindus, he decided to withdraw from politics and dedicate himself to "constructive work" such as the promotion of the spinning wheel and his work on behalf of the untouchables. More than ever he was convinced that self-rule would come only when the Indians improved or "purified" themselves.

When conditions continued to worsen, Gandhi undertook a twenty-one-day fast beginning on September 18, 1924. The fast was to become his supreme weapon because of the masses' veneration for him, and because no one wanted to be blamed for injury to his health or for his death. Showing his great understanding of the Indian people, Gandhi undertook his fast at the home of the Muslim leader Mohammed Ali Jinnah, who shared his determination to rid India of British rule, but who would later oppose Gandhi and lead the movement to partition India into Muslim and Hindu states. At Jinnah's home, Gandhi was attended to by a Muslim physician and there he was to receive his first bit of food from a Muslim, a matter of great significance to the religious Hindus. By the time the fast had ended, millions of Hindus and Muslims had taken a pledge to keep peace.

To most of the world, Gandhi's best-known reform was that of the salt laws in 1930. Deciding to test the laws which forbade the sale or manufacture of salt, he first wrote the British Viceroy explaining his intentions and asking whether discussions were possible. When no direct answer was received, Gandhi, on March 12, 1930, accompanied by seventy-eight members of his *ashram*, began a march to Dandi on the seacoast. After a twenty-four-day march, Gandhi arrived at the coast and picked up a small handful of salt on April 5, 1930. All over India millions began making and buying and selling salt. Within a month, over sixty thousand persons had been jailed, and Gandhi was arrested on May 5. The campaign was a perfect example of *satyagraha*, or nonviolent civil disobedience. Even when the police resorted to violence, the people made no attempt to defend themselves.

Many Indians supported the campaign by resigning from government positions, further handicapping a government that was already strained to the breaking point with a hundred thousand political prisoners. Realizing the futility of the struggle, the British released Gandhi from jail on January 26, 1931. His release was followed by a series of conversations with the Viceroy, Lord Irwin, the first occasions on which a British official and an Indian spoke as equals. (Winston Churchill recognized this important fact when he commented on the "nauseating and humiliating spectacle of this one time Inner Temple lawyer, non-seditious fakir, striding half-naked up the stairs of the Viceroy's palace, there to negotiate and to parley on equal terms with the representative of the King Emperor.") The resulting Gandhi-Irwin Pact, signed March 7, 1931, provided for the termination of civil disobedience, the release of political prisoners, and the free making of salt along the seacoast.

Gandhi considered his civil disobedience campaign an integral part of the Indian effort to prod Great Britain into granting India dominion status, if not complete independence. He was convinced that once British rule was removed, the Indians could solve the many problems which divided them. The unwillingness of the new Viceroy, the Earl of Willingdon, to negotiate certain issues with Gandhi led him to resume civil disobedience during the early 1930's. Thereafter, Gandhi devoted most of his energy to improving the lot of the untouchables. He remained devoted throughout his life, however, to the dream of an independent Indian nation which would embrace Muslims and Hindus. Hence, his great disappointment in 1947, one year before his death by assassination, when British India was divided into the two independent states of India (mostly

Hindu) and Pakistan (mostly Mus-    lim).

## Pertinent Literature

Boudurant, Joan V. *Conquest of Violence*. Berkeley: University of California Press, 1965.

In this work the author examines the technique of *satyagraha*, Gandhi's term for the nonviolent civil disobedience which he used to further both the reform movement and the Indian national movement during the 1920's and 1930's. *Satyagraha*, however, goes far beyond passive resistance or nonviolence and is often misunderstood.

An understanding of *satyagraha* demands an understanding of three concepts: truth, nonviolence, and self-suffering. Truth, as the term was used by Gandhi, refers to the Hindu belief in the possibility of "ultimate realization of the absolute." His personal goal was to "see God face to face." "To find truth completely is to realize oneself and one's destiny; that is to become perfect. I am painfully conscious of my imperfections, and therein lies all the strength I possess, because it is a rare thing for a man to know his own limitations." In Gandhi's search for the truth, he concerned himself with the means by which he could realize his objective.

Nonviolence, or *ahimsa*, became one of the chief tools for the achievement of Gandhi's truth. Gandhi believed it impossible to reach absolute truth by doing harm to anyone. Therefore, *ahimsa* stood for more than just passive resistance; it became the "supreme value" by which true action could be determined. Self-suffering was not based on cowardice or weakness but on the lack of fear that one who searches after truth and who eschews violence in its pursuit will ultimately possess. Boudurant describes how these three elements combine to produce *satyagraha*, and why this technique is so often misunderstood in the West. The author also comments on the challenge posed by *satyagraha* to Western political theory and explores the relationship between ends and means which she feels is a primary reason for the success of *satyagraha* and for its possible application today.

Brown, Judith M. *Gandhi and Civil Disobedience*. Cambridge: Cambridge University Press, 1977.

This book is an excellent recent source for information on Gandhi's political career between 1928 and 1934, the peak years of his use of nonviolent civil disobedience to achieve both internal reform and independence. It is a continuation of the analysis begun in the author's first volume on the subject, *Gandhi's Rise to Power*, published in 1972.

Brown points out that the civil disobedience movement which began with the Salt March of 1930 marked the peak of Gandhi's political influence. It followed six years (1922-1928) of "stock-taking" which included two years in prison and four years in semipolitical retirement where Gandhi rethought his priorities and the validity of his methods. His conclusions forced him once again into the political arena. In his own words: ". . . I found also that the politics of the day are no longer a concern of kings but they affect the lowest strata of society. And I found through bitter experience that, if I wanted to do social service, I could not possibly leave politics alone."

Sent to prison for his violation of the salt laws, Gandhi was removed from direct leadership of the civil disobedience campaign until his release in 1931. The author traces the campaign during this period, revealing the extensive scope of the movement and its basic adherence to Gandhian principles, even in his absence.

Following the Gandhi-Irwin Pact, Gandhi's efforts were directed toward the establishment of national unity and of the Congress Party's representation of this position. Brown points out that Gandhi's greatest strength, and conversely his greatest weakness, during this period was his lack of a permanent power base. While this lack of identification with any one faction allowed him to appeal to followers of all persuasions, it also handicapped him, as the conflicting demands of his supporters constrained his avenues of action.

Finally, the author deals with the dissipation of Gandhi's political power as the civil disobedience movement began to wane by 1932. Gandhi's most important political contribution was to demonstrate the importance of leaders who place nationwide concerns ahead of those of a particular locale. Through his interest in myriad concerns he was able to attract a following from all walks of Indian life who would eventually need to cooperate to achieve Indian independence. — *C.C.H.*

## Additional Recommended Reading

Brown, Judith M. *Gandhi's Rise to Power: Indian Politics, 1915-1922*. Cambridge: Cambridge University Press, 1972. Examines Gandhi's rise within Indian politics during the years 1915-1922; includes the events in South Africa which shaped his methods.

Chaudhury, P. C. Roy. *Gandhi and His Contemporaries*. New Delhi: Sterling Publishers, 1972. An excellent source for the views of Gandhi's contemporary critics.

Karunakaran, K. P. *New Perspectives on Gandhi*. Simla: Indian Institute of Advanced Study, 1969. A good source for an examination of the relationship between religion and politics with which Gandhi was so involved.

Ramachandran, G. and T. K. Mahadevan. *Gandhi: His Relevance for Our Times*. Berkeley, Calif.: World Without War Council, 1967. A study of nonviolent methods as promoted and used by Gandhi, together with an examination of the influence of Gandhi's ideas, including their effect on the peace and civil rights movements in the United States.

Ray, Sibnarayan, ed. *Gandhi, India and the World: An International Symposium*.

Philadelphia: Temple University Press, 1970. A collection of articles examining Gandhi's philosophy, together with his contributions in several different areas, and discussing the impact of Christianity and Western ideas on the development of Gandhi's thought.

Watson, Francis. *The Trial of Mr. Gandhi*. London: Macmillan and Company, 1969. An excellent study of Gandhi's trial following the violence of 1922 and its implications for his subsequent career.

# TREATY OF TRIANON

*Type of event:* Diplomatic: peace settlement with nation defeated in World War I
*Time:* January 15-June 4, 1920
*Locale:* Paris and Trianon, France

### Principal personages:

ADMIRAL MIKLÓS VON NAGYBÁNYA HORTHY (1868-1957),
Commander of the Hungarian armed forces

COUNT ALBERT GYÖRGY APPONYI (1846-1933), chief of the
Hungarian delegation to the peace conference

COUNT PAUL TELEKI (1879-1941), delegate to the peace conference and Hungarian Foreign Minister after April 19,
1920

COUNT STEPHEN BETHLEN (1874-1947), delegate to the peace
conference

CHARLES HALMOS, lawyer on the Hungarian delegation

MAURICE PALÉOLOGUE (1859-1944), Secretary General of
the French Ministry for Foreign Affairs, 1921-1925

## Summary of Event

The conditions under which peace with Hungary was concluded at the end of World War I arose first from the military occupation of portions of the defeated Habsburg Empire by the Allies and the successor states, and then during formal negotiations with the Allies in connection with the series of peace settlements with the Central Powers. On November 3, 1918, an armistice was reached between the Habsburg monarchy and the Allies; an additional agreement, signed in Belgrade on November 13, 1918, provided for the tentative delimitation of the areas to be held by the various claimants to the Habsburg lands. Croatia and Slovenia were detached from Hungary, while Rumania occupied the Banat and those portions of Transylvania as far as the Maros river. In December the government of the newly constituted Czechoslovakian state claimed Slo-

vakia in a line along the Danube and the eastern tributaries of the Tisza river. In January, 1919, Yugoslavia renewed its advance in the Baranya district north of Slovenia. Further and yet more serious incursions into Hungary took place when the provisional postwar government was overthrown in March, 1919, and a Communist regime seized power in Budapest. In April, Rumania overran the remaining portions of Transylvania, while Czechoslovakia advanced further along the northern borders of Hungary. By August, 1919, the Hungarian Communists had been displaced by a rightist putsch, while the Rumanians occupied Budapest before withdrawing to a line well within the provincial boundaries of Transylvania.

As early as January, 1919, the American delegation to the Paris peace conference had filed a recommendation suggesting that Transylvania and part of the Banat be given to Rumania and Slovakia be allotted to Czechoslovakia. The peace conference also heard representations from Rumanian, Czechoslovakian, and Yugoslav delegates, and reports from territorial commissions that had been designated by the Allies were also considered. On the basis of these deliberations, the Allies were inclined to sustain the territorial claims of Hungary's neighbors, though with some modifications. During the spring and summer of 1919, the Communist government in Hungary was unable to obtain support for its national interests, and no effective presentation of Hungarian claims could be received by the Allies until after the peace conference had recorded the proposals of the successor states.

In Hungary itself, a coalition government was eventually formed after the commander of the Hungarian Army, Admiral Miklós von Nagybánya Horthy, had entered the capital on November 16, 1919. A Hungarian delegation to the peace conference was formed, of which the major delegates were Count Albert Apponyi, for many years a government minister in Habsburg Hungary; Count Paul Teleki, a distinguished scholar and an expert on regional geography and ethnography; and Count Stephen Bethlen, a long-time member of Parliament in Habsburg Hungary. The Hungarian delegation arrived in Paris on January 7, 1920, and eight days later they were presented with a series of memoranda that embodied the territorial and other claims on which the Allies had already dealt with the successor states.

On January 16, Apponyi presented Hungary's case before the Supreme Council of the peace conference. He objected most strenuously to the territorial provisions on the draft treaty, which, he maintained, were unacceptable to the Hungarian people and were entirely out of proportion to any responsibility Hungary may have had in the outbreak of the World War. Pointing out that the proposed peace terms would transfer two-thirds of the territory of prewar Hungary, and one-third of all ethnic Hungarians, to other states, Apponyi called for the territorial integrity of the lands formerly under the Hungarian crown. Though the British and French delegations were impressed by Apponyi's statement of the Hungarian position, they showed little interest in wholesale changes of the proposed treaty.

On February 12, the Hungarian delegation presented a series of notes in which they argued for the revision of frontiers to promote Hungarian ethnic integrity, the arrangement of plebiscites in areas of mixed population, and guarantees for ethnic minorities in areas under the administration of the successor states. With only small gains to show for their efforts, members of the Hungarian delegation contacted individual representatives of the Allied powers in the hope of gradually accumulating support for Hungarian interests. The most ambitious such effort began with the overtures of Charles Halmos, a lawyer on the Hungarian delegation, to Maurice Paléologue, of the French Foreign Ministry. In a note of April 15, 1920, Paléologue indicated France's willingness to use its influence to obtain a modification of the Hungarian-Rumanian frontier as well as satisfaction of other Hungarian claims. In return he raised the possibility of a Franco-Hungarian military alliance. The French, however, had committed themselves only to a certain measure of moral support, and the French Foreign Ministry eventually repudiated Paléologue's initiative in favor of a closer relationship with other East European states.

On May 5, 1920, a final version of the peace treaty was presented to the Hungarian delegation, accompanied by an official reply to the major contentions that had been raised by the Hungarian representatives. The peace conference rejected Hungary's claims for revision of its frontiers with the successor states, and for plebiscites in disputed areas; Transylvania, Slovakia, the Banat, and the area south of the Drava river, along with other outlying portions of Habsburg Hungary, were assigned to the neighboring states, previously mentioned, who already had occupied these lands. In addition, a strip of German-speaking territory in the west, the Burgenland,

was assigned to Austria, a transfer confirmed by a plebiscite in December 1921. While some minor concessions were made on economic and military provisions, the terms of the treaty were essentially the same as those that had been presented in January.

In a speech to the Hungarian Parliament, on May 10, 1920, Count Teleki, who had recently become Foreign Minister, stated openly that he felt the treaty to be very harmful to Hungary. On May 16, Count Apponyi formally resigned as head of the Hungarian delegation in protest against the severity of the treaty. Teleki and his colleagues did, however, empower members of the government to sign the treaty, and the definitive peace between Hungary and the Allies was concluded on June 4, 1920, at the Grand Palace in Trianon, outside Paris. Though widely regarded as a dictated peace, no other alternatives were considered possible in view of the uniform insistence of the Allies and the successor states on Hungarian compliance with the terms established by the peace conference.

## Pertinent Literature

Deák, Francis. *Hungary at the Paris Peace Conference: The Diplomatic History of the Treaty of Trianon*. New York: Columbia University Press, 1942.

This is the most thoroughgoing and detailed work on the peace of Trianon; it furnishes a systematic day-by-day account of the negotiations between Hungary and the Allies, and also discusses, where appropriate, the political background to Hungary's moves on the diplomatic stage. The documentation available at the

time of writing has been utilized on an extensive basis; Deák had the further advantage of conducting interviews with former Hungarian diplomats who had participated in the peace conference.

Beginning with the capitulation of the Austro-Hungarian monarchy in November, 1918, and taking his story through the ratification of the peace two years later, Deák devotes about half of his study to the events leading to the convocation of the peace conference with Hungary, while the remaining portion of his work deals with the actual discussions between Hungarian and Allied diplomats in Paris. Deák's focus is largely on the diplomatic, rather than the social or ethnic-national transactions that eventually led to the peace of Trianon; he does not argue, as later scholars sometimes have done, that ideological considerations, and the contest between Bolshevism and conservative restoration in Eastern Europe, weighed heavily in Allied decisionmaking. At the same time, Deák does maintain that the Western Allies were overly receptive to the claims of their partners in Eastern Europe, notably Rumania and Czechoslovakia, and that Allied interests in the successor states produced a settlement unduly biased against Hungary. Hence Hungary was unable to obtain favorable conditions for independent nationhood; the territories ceded at Trianon deprived the Hungarian state of many of its conationals, and of important economic resources.

Deák's criticism is directed largely against Allied diplomats for their short-sightedness with regard to Hungary and its importance for the stability of East Central Europe, and against the self-interested and sometimes misleading brand of diplomacy practiced by representatives of the successor states. His views, therefore, are essentially those of a moderate Hungarian nationalist who, while not seeking to explain all controversies or complications by reference to

the unfortunate Treaty of Trianon, does raise serious questions regarding the wisdom of the Allies' settlement with Hungary.

On the whole, Deák is inclined to deal favorably with the Hungarian leaders who presented their country's case before the peace conference. In particular, he cites the eloquence and oratorical powers of Apponyi and the diligence and meticulous expertise of Teleki in the preparation of Hungarian arguments on a number of factual matters. He considers the tactics adopted by the Hungarian delegation to have been essentially sound; the decision at the outset to oppose the peace terms in their entirety was successful in conveying to the Allies the indignation of the Hungarian people, while the presentation of more specific objections was reserved for later sessions of the peace conference.

Deák also traces the various diplomatic initiatives pursued with respect to individual states; in addition to serious and prolonged discussions with French leaders, Hungarian representatives pursued possible openings with the British and Polish governments. The Hungarian delegation at the peace conference also managed to win some sympathy from the Italian prime minister, and for a brief period the possibility was explored of combining Italian support for Hungary with Hungarian cooperation on Central European questions that also affected Italy. While these avenues of diplomatic recourse were used with some skill by the Hungarian diplomats, the prior commitment of the Allies to the claims of Hungary's neighbors left few areas in which the Hungarians could have obtained substantial alterations of the peace terms.

In retrospect, the major problem created by the peace of Trianon was that, with the division of much of East Central Europe into small, dependent states, each of which held grievances or suspicions of a nationalistic character against its neighbors, most of the area was left open to the ambitions of larger powers such as Germany. These conclusions were inescapable to Deák and his contemporaries, viewing the

situation twenty-two years after the peace treaties, and in the midst of World War II. Deák does point out, however, that even at the time of the conclusion of the peace some political observers in the Allied nations had forseen this outcome; whatever the effects on individual nations in Eastern Europe, overall political instability was one of the more serious consequences of the peace settlements.

Macartney, Carlile Aylmer. *Hungary and Her Successors: The Treaty of Trianon and Its Consequences, 1919-1937.* London: Oxford University Press, 1937.

The most distinctive and useful feature of this work is its systematic treatment of nationality questions on the lands divided between independent Hungary and the successor states. Written by the leading British authority on modern Hungary, the overall tone reflects the author's greater familiarity with the Hungarian point of view, though the policies of the successor states are also given a sympathetic hearing. Macartney deals first with the history of the nationalities problem in Hungary, and then with the areas of Habsburg Hungary ceded to neighboring states, before returning finally to a reconsideration of Hungary and its position after the peace of 1920.

Many of the nationality questions that surfaced after the collapse of the Habsburg Empire arose from Hungarian administration of the lands they had held as a consequence of partnership in the Austro-Hungarian monarchy; many of the claims against Hungary made by the successor states were based on real and alleged abuses committed under direct Hungarian

rule. As Hungary had been governed by a form of unified centralism, and with the exception of Croatia-Slavenia few special measures were taken for the representation of minorities, Hungarian policy before 1918 had tended on the whole to promote the assimilation rather than the development of other nationalities. With the installation of the successor states on areas of mixed population, the pattern was in a sense reversed: the territorial changes effected at Trianon left a Hungarian minority in each of the four states bordering Hungary, and thus created vast irredenta that had a notable influence on the politics and diplomacy of independent Hungary.

The largest single transfer of ethnic Hungarians to a neighboring state resulted from the settlement with Rumania, which accounted for about one-sixth of the Hungarian population; Czechoslovakia obtained more than one-tenth of all Hungarians, while Yugoslavia received a substantial Hungarian minority on its northern frontiers. A small Hungarian community was also consigned to Austria, while even Italy, with the realization of its claims on the former Habsburg lands, also held small numbers of Hungarians. The cumulative effect, Macartney notes, was to impose losses of territory and population that had a far more severe impact on Hungary than the treaties of 1919-1920 had on Germany, Austria, or the other Central Powers.

This problem arose to a certain extent from the circumstances under which the Treaty of Trianon was negotiated: the Allies, by hearing in turn the presentations of each of Hungary's neighbors, decided on territorial provisions that, in the majority of cases, favored other nationalities. Macartney does point out, however, that in many areas the problems arising from the peace settlement probably could not have been handled in any form without serious inequities on one side or another; the attempt to apply the principle of national self-determination to the lands of Habsburg Hungary would in any event have foundered on the uneven distribution of national communities and economic resources in the regions surrounding the middle Danubian plain.

The problem was most clearly posed in the case of Transylvania, where about 900,000 Hungarians were found in the easternmost districts, while nearly one and one-half million Rumanians occupied the surrounding areas nearest central Hungary. In the Banat and the Voivodina, substantial Hungarian populations existed side by side with Rumanian and South Slav communities, to the extent that even approximate geographical delimitation of nationalities could not have been made without injustice to one or more national groups. Moreover, while during the last years of Habsburg Hungary some attempts had been made to develop a balanced agricultural and industrial economy, the peace settlement of 1920 produced a fragmentation of resources that left independent Hungary with the most extensive and the richest farmland. The great majority of Hungary's forests, as well as most of its mineral resources, were divided between the successor states, and most of Hungary's water power was also lost; thus the raw materials for industrial development were apportioned among several neighboring states, while many of the industrial plants that had been built under the old regime were deprived of the necessary resources.

Though generally critical of the Treaty of Trianon and its consequences, Macartney does not feel that wholesale revision would have been wise; apart from certain frontier districts, there were relatively few areas in which Hungarian claims were clearly more justified than those of the successor states. The fact that all such difficult nationality decisions had gone against Hungary illustrated not merely the depth of national feeling in East Central Europe, but also, in Macartney's view, the advantages of a system of federalism rather than the attempt to divide areas of mixed population according to one version or another of the idea of national self-determination. — *J.R.B.*

## Additional Recommended Reading

Apponyi, Albert. *The Memoirs of Count Apponyi*. London: William Heinemann, 1935. Written by the head of the Hungarian delegation to the peace talks; contains an anecdotal chapter on the author's experiences there.

Bethlen, Stephen. *The Treaty of Trianon and European Peace: Four Lectures Delivered in London in November, 1933*. London: Longmans, Green & Company, 1934. A series of lectures by a former delegate to the peace conference; argues that the Treaty of Trianon was unjust on all counts, and set an unfortunate precedent for the resolution of nationality questions in Europe.

Jaszi, Oscar. *Revolution and Counter-Revolution in Hungary*. London: P. S. King and Son, 1924. A discussion of political developments in postwar Hungary by one of the most acute critics of Hungarian nationality policy.

Low, Alfred D. *The Soviet Hungarian Republic and the Paris Peace Conference*. LIII, part 10. Philadelphia: American Philosophical Society, 1963. New series of transactions of the American Philosophical Society on the diplomacy of the Hungarian Communist regime of 1919, and the resolution of concurrent claims on Hungary in favor of the successor states, which argues that, apart from a general dislike of revolutionary Communism, the Allies had no fixed policy regarding the short-lived Soviet government in Hungary.

Tihany, Leslie Charles. *The Baranya Dispute, 1918-1921: Diplomacy in the Vortex of Ideologies*. New York: Columbia University Press, 1978. Deals with the Yugoslav occupation of a province in Southwestern Hungary and their eventual withdrawal after the Trianon settlement.

Lederer, Ivo J. *Yugoslavia at the Paris Peace Conference: A Study in Frontiermaking*. New Haven: Yale University Press, 1963. Useful for background on the Yugoslav position on negotiations also affecting Hungary.

# ADOLF HITLER PUBLISHES *MEIN KAMPF*

*Type of event:* Sociological: publication of the major work on Nazi ideas and aims
*Time:* July 18, 1925-December 10, 1926
*Locale:* Munich, Germany

*Principal personages:*
ADOLF HITLER (1889-1945), Führer of the National Socialist German Workers' (Nazi) Party
MAX AMANN, Director of Nazi Publishing
WALTHER RICHARD RUDOLF HESS (1894-    ), Hitler's Secretary and Deputy
KARL HAUSHOFER (1869-1946), German Professor of Geopolitics

## Summary of Event

Adolf Hitler wrote *Mein Kampf* (My Struggle) during his comfortable nine-month imprisonment in Landsberg Fortress for his role in organizing the unsuccessful "Beer Hall Putsch" in Munich. Volume One appeared on July 18, 1925; Volume Two was written during a vacation in the Bavarian Alps, and appeared on December 10, 1926. A projected third volume that elaborated the foreign policy ideas of *Mein Kampf* was written in 1928, but was never published. It was discovered thirty years later, and published in English under the title of *Hitler's Secret Book* (1961).

There were many reasons why Hitler wrote *Mein Kampf*. As early as 1922, he had intended to write an autobiographical tract entitled "A Reckoning," probably in the form of a polemic against those enemies responsible for the German defeat in 1918. Max Amann, business manager of Nazi Party publishing enterprises, urged him to write the book as a means of raising some cash to pay Hitler's trial expenses. Hitler agreed, and decided on the title "Four and a Half Years of Struggle Against Falsehood, Folly, and Cowardice," which Amann persuaded him to shorten to *Mein Kampf* (My Struggle). The four-hundred-page Volume One sold for the high price of twelve marks (three dollars), twice the average price for a German book of that period. Ten thousand copies were published in 1925, and nearly all were sold.

In addition to economic reasons, Hitler published *Mein Kampf* as a means of establishing his uncontested position as an original intellectual authority in the Nazi Party; he hoped this would match the dictatorial political position he had already achieved. He also turned to writing because his public speaking appearances had been temporarily banned. Hitler wished to illustrate in his book that the abortive Putsch of 1923 had not been in vain, but rather had paved the way for a regenerated Germany; he accordingly dedicated the book to those who were killed during the affair. Amann, who had hoped for a sensationalized account of the Nazi attempt to take power in Bavaria, was therefore disappointed, since *Mein Kampf* turned out to be a lengthy, rambling work of autobiography, ideology, and tactics. Above all, Hitler intended *Mein Kampf* to be the bible of the Nazi movement, a work that would hold its own among the acknowledged classics of political thinking, and be readily understood by the masses as well.

The sources that went into the making of *Mein Kampf* were a variety of antiliberal, anti-Marxist, racist, and anti-Semitic tracts produced by the radical right in the late nineteenth and early twentieth centuries. They included the anti-Semitic forgery, the *Protocols of the Elders of Zion*, whose theme was that of a worldwide Jewish conspiracy, and numerous works of social Darwinism that stressed history as racial struggle. Hitler also drew on the latest studies of crowd psychology and techniques of propaganda, and on the advice of Professor Karl Haushofer, a geopolitician who stressed the importance of Eastern Europe and Russia as future areas for the German conquest of living space. Hitler made an effort to imitate the bombastic prose style of Richard Wagner, whom he revered for his mythological operas, anti-Semitism, and showmanship.

Hitler dictated *Mein Kampf* to his secretary and later chauffeur Emil Maurice, and to Rudolf Hess, his future deputy. Much editorial work had to be done to make the book fit for publication. The writing contained thousands of grammatical, syntactical, and spelling errors; the German novelist Leon Feuchtwanger claimed to have detected over 164,000 such

mistakes in *Mein Kampf*. Hitler himself admitted that he was a much better orator than writer, believing that the great movements of history were inspired by the spoken word. He nevertheless thought of his book as the definitive statement of Nazi policy and ordered that no major changes be made in subsequent editions.

The prose style of *Mein Kampf* is verbose, difficult, and dull in many places. Hitler's attempt to appear learned and profound resulted in pretentiousness, repetition, mixed metaphors, involved clauses, long words, and flabby substantives. On the other hand, the emotional fanaticism of his vision, his skillful popularization of reactionary ideas, the brilliance of his chapters on tactics, and the fact that his promises were later carried out, all make *Mein Kampf* one of the most important books ever written. Despite the mean-spirited banality of its contents, its actual significance ranks it with such works as *The Prince* by Niccolo Machiavelli and *What Is To Be Done* by Vladimir Ilich Lenin.

The essential contents of *Mein Kampf* can be organized around the following headings: autobiography, ideology, tactics, and ultimate intentions. The idea that ties all these themes together is that of struggle. Hitler's vision, for himself and for Germany, was one of do or die. He believed that either a racially purified Nazi Germany would emerge victorious over its designated enemies— the Marxists, liberals, Slavs, and Jews—or it would perish. Germany would become the battlefield to decide the fate of the entire world. A tone of hatred toward the many enemies of Hitler's making pervades

*Mein Kampf.* Hitler saw history as a Jewish-Bolshevik conspiracy against civilization, and his answer to this imagined conspiracy was the terrifying counterconspiracy that was ultimately carried out by the Nazis. Moreover, a messianic theme of suffering and deliverance for Germany also pervades *Mein Kampf*; Hitler and Germany become the self-appointed ideological and racial saviors of the world from decay and destruction.

It was important for Hitler to present in *Mein Kampf* a stirring autobiography of his life until 1924. He portrayed himself in childhood and adolescence as a sensitive, artistic young person who is awakened to the meaning of history and to his unique role in shaping Germany's future. He reveals that while suffering from poverty during his life in Vienna (1906-1913), he realized what was wrong with the modern world: the liberal-socialist-Jewish disease of cultural modernism and racial corruption. It was in Vienna that he claims to have developed the "granite foundations" of his outlook. He relates stories of his military heroism in World War I, and of his anguish in 1918 caused by the shameful "stab-in-the-back" by Germany's internal enemies and the humiliating Treaty of Versailles. He claims to have dedicated his life in 1919 to founding a mass movement that would avenge the sufferings of Germany and make the nation great again. Many historians have exposed the autobiographical portions of *Mein Kampf* as half-truths, such as Hitler's claim of dire poverty in Vienna.

*Mein Kampf* sets forth all the elements of Nazi ideology. Ideology was crucial for Hitler, for he felt that his correct world outlook would radically reshape the attitudes and behavior of the German people. Ideology was to be the instrument of power. The basic premise that underlies all of *Mein Kampf* was that of a crude and brutal social Darwinism that defines existence as a struggle for survival between superior and inferior races. Hitler believed that the racial principle was the major revolutionary force in history. Progress had been made possible by Aryan victories while decay was caused by racial intermingling. Hitler developed the radical idea that the state was the means to the end of furthering the interests of the race. Hence, he was obsessed with the creation of a powerful state that would purify Germany at home and create living space in the East for his new German Empire. In *Mein Kampf*, his radical conservatism manifests itself in a hatred of Marxism and liberalism; but his greatest hatred is reserved for the Jews. A rabid anti-Semitism is the cornerstone of *Mein Kampf*, which presents the Jew as the root of all evils, past and present, and calls for the destruction of the "Jewish peril."

The portions concerned with propaganda and political tactics are probably the most lucid and astute chapters of *Mein Kampf*; they discuss the use of demagogic oratory, mass meetings, violence, the appeal to peoples' fears, and the "big lie." Hitler also stresses the importance of charismatic, dictatorial leadership; and he never loses sight of the opportunistic pursuit of power by any possible means.

Hitler's actions after coming to

power in 1933 show that he meant to carry out what he wrote in *Mein Kampf*. The pursuit of living space in the East and the elimination of the Jews were put into effect by 1941. The either/or fanaticism of *Mein Kampf* took its final form when Hitler committed suicide in his underground bunker in 1945.

The popularity of *Mein Kampf* was a barometer of Hitler's general political appeal. In 1928, only three thousand copies were sold, but with the coming of economic and political crises, sales reached fifty thousand by 1930 and ninety thousand by 1932. Increased sales, however, reflected the popularity of the Nazis rather than the appeal of the work itself, which many Nazis confessed to never having read. After 1933, *Mein Kampf* became required reading and re-placed the Bible as the customary wedding present. By 1943, sales had soared to about ten million copies, and the book had been translated into sixteen languages. This fact does not imply, however, that *Mein Kampf* was taken seriously at first: it was largely ignored by the German press and by German writers until 1933. Neither Western nor Soviet states-men took it seriously until the out-break of World War II. Perhaps the greatest irony of *Mein Kampf* was that the nearly successful execution of its blueprint was aided by the fact that readers initially either ignored or underestimated the deadly serious-ness of its message.

## Pertinent Literature

Maser, Werner. *Hitler's* Mein Kampf: *An Analysis.* Translated by R. H. Barry. London: Faber, 1970.

Werner Maser is a recognized Ger-man authority on many little-known details of Hitler's life. In addition to providing a useful and thorough anal-ysis of *Mein Kampf*, he has unearthed a number of interesting details about the background and impact of the book. His interpretation of *Mein Kampf* as a banal and unoriginal work is consistent with his attempt to "de-demonize" Hitler both as man and as statesman, by exposing the ordinariness of the man and his ideas.

According to Maser, *Mein Kampf* was the unoriginal product of a self-taught man who rummaged from a grab bag of reactionary and racist books and pamphlets available at the time. The author emphasizes that many of the sources for the work came from Hitler's close associates. For example, the anti-Semitic Die-trich Eckart provided Hitler with a conspiracy theory about the Jews, and was probably the most important single figure who influenced Hitler. Alfred Rosenberg, who later became the chief Nazi ideologist, introduced Hitler to his translation of the *Pro-tocols of the Elders of Zion*. Maser provides the important discovery that Hitler did not restrict his reading to racist pamphlets, but also studied such important works of Western thought as Arthur Schopenhauer's *The World as Will and Idea*. More-over, he was influenced by such rep-utable works of sociology as Gustave

Le Bon's *The Crowd* and William McDougall's *The Group Mind*.

Maser characterizes *Mein Kampf* as, above all, a work of propaganda, or "propagandistic autobiography." He systematically refutes many of Hitler's grandiose assertions about his adolescent years in Vienna, showing, for example, that Hitler was not the poverty-stricken youth in Vienna portrayed in *Mein Kampf*; rather, an adequate inheritance from his mother enabled him to avoid regular work and to attend the opera regularly. Maser effectively exposes *Mein Kampf* as a welter of lies, half-truths, and inaccuracies. He rightly urges that historians not rely exclusively on *Mein Kampf* as a sourcebook on Hitler, but also study Hitler's letters, notes, and wartime "Table Talk" (1941-1944). Moreover, he cautions the reader not to look upon *Mein Kampf* as an absolutely rigid body of doctrine: *Mein Kampf* could never have foreshadowed such Machiavellian moves as the Russo-German nonaggression pact of 1939.

The author offers an interesting reinterpretation of the origins of Hitler's anti-Semitism. Contrary to Hitler's assertion that he became an anti-Semite in Vienna, Maser argues that his hatred of Jews might have been acquired from his father. Maser cites Hitler's childhood friend, August Kubizek, who wrote that Hitler had already become an anti-Semite by 1904, to support his belief that Hitler's views were shaped in Linz, not Vienna.

According to Maser, the most fanatical and important portions of *Mein Kampf* deal with ideology. Hitler had an apocalyptic view of the world, and, however absurd and monstrous his racist and anti-Semitic beliefs might have been, he nevertheless held a coherent world view which he presented in an orderly way. Maser illustrates that the racial laws of Nazi Germany are prefigured in *Mein Kampf*. Hitler's plans for *Lebensraum* (living space) in the East also followed the blueprints of *Mein Kampf* and *Hitler's Secret Book*. Thus, all of Hitler's ideas that deal with race in *Mein Kampf* later materialized into horrifying reality. What was most "radical" about Hitler's biological view of the world was his willingness to use the state to conquer and destroy for the benefit of the race, regardless of the consequences.

Hitler's obsession with the leadership principle (*Führerprinzip*) of National Socialism emerges very clearly in Maser's study. Hitler stubbornly refused to change or to expurgate any portions of *Mein Kampf*. For example, when it was pointed out to him in 1936 that the violently anti-French portions of *Mein Kampf* might be omitted to conform to Germany's diplomatic needs of that year, Hitler refused to change the book. He answered that any changes would be made in the practical area of diplomacy, not in the ideas he had set down in *Mein Kampf*. The only section of the work that Hitler did change related to the strengthening of the leadership principle. In the 1925 first edition of the book, he had laid down the principle that the Nazi Party subleaders were to be elected to conform with "Germanic democracy." In the 1930 edition he advocated that party chairmen should not be elected, but instead appointed by their superiors and invested with unlimited power and authority. This change of emphasis reflected Hitler's absolute dicatorial power by 1930 as well as his belief that history was made by dictatorial great men.

Maser's study is very useful for its documentation of Western reactions to *Mein Kampf*. An abridged and expurgated English translation of *Mein Kampf* appeared in Britain and America in 1933; Danish, Swedish, and Arabic translations came out in 1934; and a Czech edition appeared in 1936. It took until 1939, however, for a French translation to be published. Also in 1939, the first complete and unexpurgated English translation was published. Thus, it was only on the eve of World War II that the English-speaking world be-

gan to take *Mein Kampf* seriously. In 1939, *The Times* printed excerpts from it, referring to it as a "frightening book" that would test the patience of its readers.

Maser concludes that although Hitler's program was available for all to see by 1925, *Mein Kampf* was virtually ignored by the outside world for the next fifteen years. The book was translated only after Hitler came to power and was studied only when it appeared that its author's ideas might materialize. *Mein Kampf* became a legitimization for world war and genocide. Maser powerfully concludes his book with the assertion that the world view of *Mein Kampf* was a major cause of the death of thirty-five million people.

Waite, Robert G. L. *The Psychopathic God: Adolf Hitler*. New York: Basic Books, 1977.

Robert G. L. Waite's major psychological study of Hitler approaches the Führer both as a mentally deranged individual and as a highly intelligent and skillful political leader. Waite characterizes Hitler as a "borderline personality," an individual whose mental state is between neurosis and psychosis. The major characteristic of a "borderline personality" is a split ego caused by great conflicts between contradictory elements within the personality. Thus, Hitler was a masochist who strove to be cruel; he was effeminate and was proud of his brutality; he had great energy but was also lazy. He resolved his inner conflicts by projecting them into a worldwide struggle between good, creative Aryans and evil de-

generate Jews; this technique enabled him to function both ideologically and politically.

The major premise of Waite's fascinating and thought-provoking study is that Hitler's psychological makeup produced crucial historical consequences. Psychologically, the writing of *Mein Kampf* allowed Hitler to justify the failure of his Munich Putsch and provided him with a meaningful pastime during his imprisonment in Landsberg Fortress; in other words, the composition of *Mein Kampf* served, at least in part, a therapeutic function for its author. The book allowed the "terrible simplifier" to find an outlet for his hatreds, imbue them with meaning, and translate them into useful political slogans and programs. Waite agrees with Hitler's major biographer, Alan Bullock, who pointed out that Hitler was an intellectual in the sense that he lived intensely in a world of his own thought. At the same time, he strove to use his words and ideas as the instruments of his power. The Führer emerges as both a fanatical ideologue and a brutal opportunist.

Unlike Werner Maser, Waite believes that none of the sources that went into the making of *Mein Kampf* were drawn from the high culture of Germany. (Waite's subsequent remark that Hitler read the German philosopher Friedrich Nietzsche is thus somewhat contradictory.) He maintains that Hitler's short attention span and his lack of intellectual sophistication led him to such racist, anti-Semitic pamphleteers as Georg Lanz von Liebenfels, Guido von List, and Theodor Fritsch. Waite calls needed attention to a book that is usually overlooked among those works that influenced Hitler: Berthold Otto's *The Future State as a Socialist Monarchy* (1910), which probably helped Hitler to formulate the reactionary concept of a racist, militaristic, biologically oriented society headed by a charismatic leader. The operatic composer Richard Wagner is also cited as an important intellectual influence on Hitler because he shared some personality traits, such as the need to dominate others, with the Führer.

The author effectively illustrates that many of Hitler's personality traits and projections of what he believed himself to be appear in *Mein Kampf*. Hitler's many phobias and sexual obsessions are reflected in *Mein Kampf*; the book is replete with passages reflecting its author's interest in rape, sodomy, sexual perversion, prostitution, syphilis, and contamination of the blood. Hitler portrayed himself in his book as the new messiah who would redeem Germany, and accordingly intended his work to be the new holy scripture of the Third Reich. He saw his enemies (and the enemies of Germany) as the Jews, Marxists, Slavs, and the Western powers. He argued that hatred was an effective means of winning and mobilizing the masses; propaganda, terror, and a charismatic dictatorship were his most powerful weapons. No wonder, then, that Waite refers to the role of hatred in *Mein Kampf* as "axiomatic."

Circumstances surrounding the publication of *Mein Kampf*, such as Hitler's refusal to make major changes in the book from its publication in 1925 to his death twenty years later, reveal for Waite the rigidity and infantilism of the Führer's personality. Hitler adorned the cover of his book with a swastika and signed his name as he would when he later became chancellor: "A. Hitler." Along with other psychohistorians, Waite finds evidence of Hitler's "primal scene trauma" in *Mein Kampf*. He analyzes a passage in which Hitler dramatizes the harshness of working-class life by telling of a three-year-old child who witnesses his father sexually assaulting his mother; the child grows up to despise authority. This is a "thinly disguised autobiographical memoir," says Waite.

Two of Hitler's major pillars of *Mein Kampf*, anti-Semitism and the need for living space in the East, are related to the psychopath in Hitler. Waite sees no reason to argue with Hitler's statement in *Mein Kampf* that the future chancellor became an anti-Semite in his Vienna years (1908-1913). (This strongly contrasts with Rudolph Binion's thesis that Hitler became a rabid anti-Semite during World War I, and is equally at variance with Werner Maser's contention that Hitler became an anti-Semite as a child in Linz.) He agrees with most historians that, whatever its origins, Hitler's anti-Semitism was the central element in Hitler's personality and in his book. His obsession with the German acquisition of living space is ascribed to his obsession with time and death. Hitler felt that time was running out for Germany, and that she must acquire living space or she would die. His intention to reunite Austria with Germany (*Anschluss*) stemmed, according to Waite, from his need to defeat his hated father (Austria) and return to his beloved mother (Germany).

As an intelligent historian, Waite is not content simply to relate Hitler's personality to his ideas and actions. He provides an excellent analysis of the political and cultural milieu that shaped Hitler, and forcefully proves that authoritarianism, social Darwinism, and anti-Semitism pervaded German society and culture. He suggests that in *Mein Kampf*, Hitler skill-fully adopted preexisting ideas to appeal to millions of lower-middle-class Germans who shared many of his hatreds and who were reared in authoritarian family structures similar to his own.

It is questionable, however, whether these millions read *Mein Kampf* before 1933, and Waite's assertion that *Mein Kampf* was a "smashing success" must therefore be qualified. The book did not become a best seller until the depths of the depression in 1932 and Hitler's seizure of power in 1933, suggesting that nonpsychological forces such as economic hardships and political crisis played a significant role in the popularity of *Mein Kampf*. Moreover, the major significance of the work lay not merely in its psychological elements or its popularity, but rather in the fact that its horrifying program was carried out. Waite himself makes this abundantly clear.

Waite concludes that Hitler's psyche was self-destructive and that he courted failure; yet, one must question whether Hitler wanted his ultimate visions in *Mein Kampf* to fail. In that book he laid down for Germany the grim alternative of racial world domination or total destruction. Whether he wished to fail or not, he would remain a prisoner of his elemental vision as presented in *Mein Kampf*. — L.S.

### Additional Recommended Reading

Bullock, Alan. *Hitler: A Study in Tyranny*. New York: Harper & Row Publishers, 1962. One of the first and still one of the best Hitler biographies, although it sometimes relies too heavily on *Mein Kampf* as a credible source for Hitler's life.

Fest, Joachim C. *Hitler*. Translated by Richard and Clara Winston. New York: Harcourt Brace Jovanovich, 1974. A remarkably detailed and well-written study of a "normal" Hitler which aptly characterizes *Mein Kampf* as tract of "eschatological Darwinism": that is, salvation through racial struggle.

Binion, Rudolph. *Hitler Among the Germans*. New York: Elsevier Scientific Publishing Company, 1976. A provocative study of the sources of Hitler's appeal to the Germans which views the wartime trauma of 1918 as the major reason for the writing of *Mein Kampf* and for its appeal.

Jäckel, Eberhard. *Hitler's Weltanschauung: A Blueprint for Power*. Translated by Herbert Arnold. Middletown, Conn.: Wesleyan University Press, 1972. A concise exposition of Hitler's ideas which argues that *Mein Kampf* has a consistent world outlook and a logical sequential structure.

Heiden, Konrad. *Der Fuehrer: Hitler's Rise to Power*. Translated by Ralph Manheim. Boston: Houghton Mifflin Company, 1944. This early survey of Hitler's career by an opponent of Nazism who observed Hitler at close range has withstood the test of time for its remarkable insights into *Mein Kampf*.

Rauschning, Hermann. *The Revolution of Nihilism: Warning to the West*. Translated by E. W. Dickes. New York: Longmans, Green, and Company, 1939. This controversial book by the former Danzig Nazi who later broke with Hitler maintains that Hitler's goals are not to be found in *Mein Kampf*, since the Nazis had no real ideology except power for its own sake.

# THE LOCARNO CONFERENCE

*Type of event:* Diplomatic: France seeks guarantees of her national security
*Time:* October 5-December 1, 1925
*Locale:* Locarno, Switzerland

### Principal personages:
GUSTAV STRESEMANN (1878-1929), German Foreign Minister, 1923-1929
ARISTIDE BRIAND (1862-1932), French Foreign Minister, 1925-1932
SIR AUSTEN CHAMBERLAIN (1863-1937), Great Britain's Conservative Party Foreign Secretary, 1924-1929

## Summary of Event

The post-Versailles Treaty hammered out by European diplomats at Locarno, Switzerland, in October of 1925 served as a commentary both on the past and on the war which would be unleashed some fourteen years later. The "Spirit of Locarno," as it came to be known, highlighted not only the diplomatic temperament of key European nations during the post-World War I period, but also indicated that such foreign policy outlooks were subject to vacillation and uncertainty.

In certain respects, the "Spirit of Locarno" had its more distant origins in the French defeat at the hands of an emerging Germany in 1871. More immediately, the culmination of the Treaty of Versailles in 1919 gave vent to a surge of French paranoia over national security through which the Locarno Pacts can best be seen in perspective.

World War I had left in its wake little distinction between victors and victims. As a vicious war of attrition, World War I had somewhat erased the centuries-old distinction between combatants and noncombatants leav-

ing a death toll of approximately ten million. Psychologically, the impact of human loss, as well as that of property damage and economic dislocation, was felt as strongly in France and Britain as it was in Germany.

For France, their successful defense in World War I was something of a Pyrrhic victory. Although German troops never pushed closer to Paris than eighteen miles, northern France was a devastated region. Significant agricultural and industrial areas were destroyed on a scale unheard of in Europe since the disruption of Germany during the Thirty Years' War (1618-1648). Under these conditions, France's victory was small comfort for her embarrassment at the hands of Prussia in 1871.

At the Versailles peace talks which formally ended World War I, France's determined and embittered leader, Georges Clemenceau, was in no mood for the conciliatory offerings presented by President Woodrow Wilson of the United States. Through a dictated settlement, France managed to secure at Versailles a measure of the satisfaction that the military outcome of the war had not provided. Germany was reduced to the level of a secondary power in world affairs, and the likelihood of Germany ever again posing a threat to French security was substantially lessened.

While unimpressed with the pacific nature of Woodrow Wilson's Versailles positions, France did see potential promise in the concept of a League of Nations. As proposed, the League would offer a more or less permanent international assembly designed to safeguard the future peace. More concretely, the League appeared to France to hold out the prospect of a general and virtually universal collective security arrangement under which nations victimized by aggressors could expect comfort and assistance from an otherwise unaffected world.

Although France had not received all that she had hoped for in the Versailles Treaty, it was clearly the most comprehensive such arrangement for European security since the accords of the Congress of Vienna a century before. Assuming the effectiveness of an operational League of Nations assembly, individualized security treaties such as those which had ushered in World War I would appear to be unnecessary.

For France, however, the effectiveness of the League quickly became a matter for disheartened speculation. The unwillingness of the United States Senate to ratify the Versailles Treaty with the League as an unamended, integral component seriously called into question the collective security of the Western nations. Just as troublesome was the relative inability of the League to deal convincingly with the Greco-Turkish War in 1919-1922. As a result of such insecurities, France entered a prolonged period of apprehension bordering on paranoia regarding her own future security.

After 1924, France sought to arrange for herself the assurances of national security that seemed unfulfilled through the League of Nations. In doing so, France's policies ran counter to the general mood which prevailed in the United States and Great Britain calling for increased efforts towards disarmament in the post-World War I era. Both Great Britain and the United States had become convinced that World War I was at least partially the by-product of armaments competition and conflicting camps of alliances on the part of the European states. Both saw the future peace as best assured through a reduction of such enterprises, and security was viewed as a means by which war could be avoided once again.

For the French, the lessons of World War I had not coincided with the viewpoints drawn by the British and Americans. France tended to believe that a well-armed defense and comforting allies had saved her from defeat at the hands of the Germans. Only a state confident of its national security could entertain talk of disarmament. A staunch circle of allies and a military prepared for the worst could better guarantee the security upon which more conciliatory negotiating could take place.

The economic relief which most nations sought through disarmament, therefore, encountered a stiff barrier in the French position. During 1923 and 1924, efforts were undertaken through the League to draft a "Treaty of Mutual Assistance" catering to the French view that security guarantees must precede any arms reduction agreements. On each occasion, however, the British refused to ratify such broadly based military commitments. In frustration, France instead attempted to win narrower British assurances of a guarantee of her Rhineland border with Germany. Somewhat surprisingly, the French found the British more receptive to this approach, and the seeds of the Locarno Pacts were sown.

In truth, the Locarno Pacts may also be traced to a proposal put forth by a vanquished Germany. As early as 1922, Germany had suggested to France that both agree to refrain from aggressive war on each other for a generation. While the particulars of the German proposal were originally vague, Germany also recommended that Great Britain and Belgium become integral components of the arrangement. Coupled with the French overtures to the British, the negotiations proceeded and eventually considered the demilitarized zone in the Rhineland and the Belgium-Germany borders as well. In addition, Italy became a further element in the collective discussions.

The talks held in Locarno, Switzerland, between October 5 and October 16, 1925, resulted in the establishment of a multipact agreement which was formally signed in London on December 1, 1925. Cordial relationships between the foreign ministers of Great Britain, France, and Germany, respectively, Sir Austen Chamberlain, Aristide Briand, and Gustav Stresemann, made the understanding possible. The Locarno Treaties offered British guarantees of the French-German and Belgian-German borders, treaties of arbitration between Germany and a group of nations including France, Belgium, Poland, and Czechoslovakia, and a mutual assistance pact between France and both Poland and Czechoslovakia. The considerable extent of these pacts gave to France, as well as to much of the rest of Europe, a genuine feeling of security which had been absent through the League of Nations itself.

Oddly, however, the Locarno Pacts were rife with contradictions and seemingly ignored innuendos. The British seemed willing enough to commit themselves to a guarantee of the western borders of Germany, but unwilling to become involved in such assurances in the eastern boundaries which the Germans themselves did not regard as final. France responded by offering such missing guarantees to both Poland and Czechoslovakia, although France was clearly overburdening herself with these assurances in the absence of similar British commitments.

The British had drawn a vague but nonetheless real distinction between their determination to uphold the Versailles border settlements on Germany's western frontier and eastern frontiers. As a result, France could promise to try to fill the void with a series of separate assurances to the Poles and Czechs, but the Versailles Treaty and the overall security of Europe was undermined nevertheless by the suggestion of priorities on the part of Great Britain.

Beyond this came contradictions

which also went ignored. In agreeing to be the guarantor of a French-German nonaggression pact, the British had entered into the curious position of offering their military expertise to the French in the event of German aggression and to the Germans should the French attack. The coordination of defense for both parties relied upon Britain's confidentiality, which undoubtedly could not be effective under both guises.

Not surprisingly, though, such seemingly inherent difficulties in the Locarno Pacts were smoothed over by a general atmosphere of good will. The "Spirit of Locarno" offered for roughly a decade that precious sense of security that France especially sought and that the world as a whole had not found in the aftermath of Versailles.

## Pertinent Literature

Newman, William J. *The Balance of Power in the Interwar Years, 1919-1939.* New York: Random House, 1968.

Few works available today deal with the importance of the Locarno Pacts of 1925 as dynamically as William J. Newman's text. Newman, Professor of Government at Boston University, was a Fulbright Scholar in France and remains a specialist in international relations. His work here may provide the single best study of the intricacies of the Locarno arrangements and the implications of those discussions.

While the scope of this work technically charts all twenty of the years between the World Wars, the determinations arrived at in Locarno in 1925 form the heart of Newman's perspective. Newman holds that, while the Locarno guarantees did provide a measure of diplomatic reason and well-being for Europe, the inability of the statesmen to arrange genuine assurances regarding Eastern Europe undermined the process. Indeed, it was in this very eastern region that Adolf Hitler enjoyed his most far-reaching diplomatic successes as a result of the void created there during the Locarno negotiations.

Newman's book is particularly valuable in that it not only contains the text of the Locarno Pacts themselves, but also deals with these arrangements as part of a broader effort to seek a balance of power in Europe after World War I. Divided basically into three chapters, Newman's treatment deals initially with the notions of a balance of power in fairly abstract terms which he defines as a problem in political science. The second chapter examines in detail the Locarno arrangements themselves as well as German, French, and British personalities responsible for the final agreements.

Understandably, the focus of Newman's account lies in a study of France's perceived need to further guarantee her security. In this regard, France was as vitally interested in the stability of Poland and Czechoslovakia as she was in her own borders with Germany. The French view was essentially that a Germany contained in the east would also lessen the prospects of renewed German ambitions in the west.

However, in her efforts to secure a collective security combination that would ring Germany, France found the British to be unwilling to enter into such a substantial commitment. With Britain hedging and the United States virtually withdrawn on the entire question of Europe, France undertook Czechoslovak and Polish guarantees through her own design.

Adding to France's dilemma was the establishment of the American Dawes Plan (1924), which Newman identifies as a vital ingredient in the growing French paranoia over a resurrected Germany. Newman suggests that the Dawes Plan, designed to foster German financial recovery, was responsible as much as any other single factor for Germany's reentrance into the front ranks of European nations. To be sure, Germany still carried the stigma of defeat and guilt from World War I and Versailles, but her economic recovery was now considered to be worthwhile. More importantly, perhaps, was the understanding that Western opinion would no longer allow Germany's sovereignty as a state to be tampered with. Germany could now be expected to promote the sovereignty issue in the western zones (the Ruhr and the Rhineland), while France was faced with the prospect of an uncertain reaction to such moves on the part of Great Britain.

Ironically for Germany, her efforts to push the sovereignty question with regard to the Rhineland in 1925 may have been responsible for a revitalization of Anglo-French cooperation. Although the British still expressed reluctance to commit themselves to the vast security arrangements France preferred, it was clear that a more limited British participation regarding the sanctity of the Franco-German frontiers was feasible. Once involved in guarantees along these lines at Locarno in 1925, it was a relatively minor addendum for the British also to assure the Belgian-German borders.

While comforted somewhat with respect to her own frontiers with Germany, France found herself essentially alone on the issue of Germany's eastern borders with Czechoslovakia and Poland. The Eastern European map lacked that major nation capable of restraining German interests, a fact made doubly evident by Britain's reluctance to fill the vacuum. Despite French security demands that she attempt to fill this void herself, France had not recovered so substantially from World War I that her economy could easily accept the additional burden. For reasons similar to these, Britain had chosen to place priorities upon her own commitments.

France's attempts to convert the new Poland into a significant Eastern European state included the construction of a Polish army, but the absence of anything approximating a defensible border with Germany was a limitation no military organization could easily overcome. Nevertheless, France remained convinced that an Eastern European collection of nations, armed with a partnership of resolve to safeguard themselves from German encroachment, was essential to the maintenance of a Germany that could not disrupt the security of the Continent.

Curiously, Newman is less critical of the British unwillingness to play an active role as guarantor of Eastern European security than he is of French efforts to construct a patchwork balance of power in Britain's absence. Undoubtedly, French security demands lost for her the sympathy of Western opinion to which she felt entitled, and much of that feeling ironically seemed to transfer to Germany instead. This subtle but genuine fluctuation of opinion remained in force throughout the period from about 1924 to 1936.

Taylor, A. J. P. *The Origins of the Second World War*. New York: Atheneum Publishers, 1962.

In his highly controversial book on the origins of the Second World War, A. J. P. Taylor examines the diplomatic maneuvering of the great European powers which led to the conclusion of the Locarno Pacts in 1925. Taylor's view of the German question is noteworthy for its depiction of the role of Gustav Stresemann as the first significant voice in post-World War I German policy. Stresemann, like any German leader of the period, faced the grim task of living within the dictates and confines of the Versailles Treaty, although German opinion of the provisions was understandably bitter. Unlike most Germans, however, Stresemann did not feel that an abolition of the Treaty's more distasteful articles was essential before Germany could begin to recover a measure of her status in Europe. On the contrary, it was a hallmark of Stresemann's policies to maneuver for the resurrection of the German state within the Treaty's limitations. Only then could the Versailles Treaty be effectively challenged from the German vantage point.

It was a proposal put forth by Stresemann that served as the foundation stone for the Locarno agreements. Stresemann suggested a Franco-German nonaggression pact which Great Britain and Italy could guarantee. To the Italians, such a role was widely welcomed as a step towards greater prestige in European affairs—something Italy had not secured through World War I or the Versailles Treaty. For the British, the Stresemann concept offered new conservative leader Sir Austen Chamberlain an opportunity to acquiesce in the French security overtures while maintaining a general even-handedness. The term "aggressor" was now theoretically applicable to both the Germans and the French through this proposal, and Great Britain would become the safety valve for whomever the victim might be. Although such a notion did not sit well with Chamberlain's more decidedly pro-French leanings, it nevertheless seemed certain that the aggressor label would continue to rest primarily upon Germany. In addition, Chamberlain's views would help to bring about, through the Stresemann proposal, a genuine Anglo-French security arrangement.

While German opinion, although embittered, seemed willing to concede the reality of her Versailles-imposed borders with France, it was far less tolerant of Stresemann's conciliatory mood with regard to Germany's eastern frontiers. While Stresemann made it clear that Germany intended at some future date to adjust or rearrange her borders with Czechoslovakia and Poland, he was willing to imply that this would be accomplished by solely peaceful means. As such, Stresemann offered the notion of arbitration treaties between his Germany and her eastern neighbors.

Chamberlain's British government was more than willing to be of service as a guarantor of France's borders with Germany, but not so anxious to become formally involved in the eastern question. It was, of course, France which elected to assume this role in the east.

Taylor views the agreements reached at Locarno in 1925 as the vital turning point of the interwar years. In his words, "Its signature ended the first World war; its repudiation eleven years later marked the prelude to the second." The Locarno Pacts appeared to offer a reassurance that security in Europe was in everyone's best interests and that whatever outstanding issues might remain (namely, Germany's eastern frontiers) were capable of eventual resolution through peaceful means. Adding to this diplomatic mood of satisfaction may have been the fact that, as Taylor suggests, the Locarno agreements rested more upon moral commitments than hard and fast military obligations. Locarno set a course, or, rather, was the culmination of one, for a European peace after World War I. That it should become a first step towards the appeasement atmosphere of the 1930's seemed in 1925 to be an unlikely prognosis.
— *T.A.B.*

## Additional Recommended Reading

Cameron, E. R. *Prologue to Appeasement: A Study in French Foreign Policy, 1933-1936.* Washington, D.C.: American Council on Public Affairs, 1942. A work written during World War II which offers a somewhat bitter but nonetheless incisive view of the failure of French foreign policy prior to the war itself.

Gilbert, M. and R. Gott. *The Appeasers*. Boston: Houghton Mifflin Company, 1963. Continues the critical evaluation of British and French policies with regard to Germany during the interwar years. Munich is stressed; the Locarno arrangements are also evaluated.

Schuman, F. L. *War and Diplomacy in the French Republic: An Inquiry into Political Motivations and the Control of Foreign Policy.* New York: McGraw-Hill Book Company, 1931. Written during the period of the French Third Republic, this account predates the Munich Conference and basks somewhat in the lingering glow of the "Spirit of Locarno."

Selsam, J. P. *The Attempts to Form an Anglo-French Alliance, 1919-1924.* Philadelphia: University of Pennsylvania Press, 1936. An excellent work from the pre-World War II period which deals with British and French views of how best to insure security and stability for Europe in the aftermath of Versailles.

Wandycz, P. S. *France and Her Eastern Allies, 1919-1925: French-Czechoslovak-Polish*

*Relations from the Paris Peace Conference to Locarno*. Minneapolis: University of Minnesota Press, 1962. A first-rate study of the efforts undertaken by France to create a "Little Entente" in the eastern regions as a safeguard against a revitalized Germany.

# VERNON LOUIS PARRINGTON PUBLISHES
## *MAIN CURRENTS IN AMERICAN THOUGHT*

*Type of event:* Intellectual: study of the American experience
*Time:* 1927-1930
*Locale:* Seattle, Washington

## Summary of Event

Vernon Louis Parrington published the first two volumes of his *Main Currents in American Thought* in 1927, to which was posthumously added in 1930 the final, incomplete volume. Parrington's ambitious effort was, as he explained in his introduction, an attempt "to give some account of the genesis and development in American letters of certain germinal ideas that have come to be reckoned traditionally American— how they came into being here, how they were opposed, and what influence they have exerted in determining the form and scope of our characteristic ideals and institutions." The work was unlike anything that had before appeared in either American history or American literary criticism, and response to the first two volumes was swift and nearly unanimous: they were judged a major contribution to both historical and literary studies of the American experience, and in 1928 the work was awarded the Pulitzer Prize in History. It was the first literary work ever so honored. Publication of the third volume confirmed the justice of this immediate response in the minds of a wide range of critics—conservative as well as liberal, academic as well as journalistic. Twenty-five years later, however, Parrington's *Main Currents in American Thought* was completely rejected by most literary scholars,

and historians were pointing to serious flaws in both its method and conclusions. This period of aggressive reaction has now passed, and today Parrington is regarded as a figure who, for all his imperfections, is of great significance in the development of both literary and historical studies in America.

In the Foreword to *Main Currents in American Thought*, Parrington sets forth the ruling principle of his method: "The point of view from which I have endeavored to evaluate the materials, is liberal rather than conservative, Jeffersonian rather than Federalistic; and very likely in my search I have found what I went forth to find, as others have discovered what they were seeking." Parrington goes on to present American history from the Progressive point of view, and in so doing provides a clear image of the liberal mind at work. This, however, is not the only striking feature of his method. Although his work is ostensibly a history of American literature, Parrington does not limit himself to works of poetry and fiction, but includes numerous works from a wide variety of sources, especially political ones. Parrington's justification is that he is primarily concerned with making political and moral judgments about America's historical development and not with narrower aesthetic evaluations of literature. Thus, literary works are treated as part of the history of ideas—like all other ideas, products of the environment—and of value to Parrington only insofar as they contribute to the understanding of American democracy. In fact, Parrington's main purpose is the depiction of the struggle over democracy which he sees as having been at the heart of America from its beginning to the present: the conflict between democratic and antidemocratic forces. His main device for depicting this battle is the presentation of biographical sketches of characters who represent the opposing positions—seen most clearly in his treatment of Jefferson and Hamilton.

In Volume I, *The Colonial Mind, 1620-1800*, Parrington sees the struggles between democratic and antidemocratic forces as taking place on two fronts: one within New England and one without. The first witnessed the clash of a liberal political philosophy deriving from French and English sources and the reactionary theology of the Puritans. From France and England came the notion of natural rights which replaced the absolute state with the principle of democracy. In New England, however, this principle was challenged by an absolute theology that upheld an arbitrary and absolute divine sovereign, the inherent evil of human nature, and a class division which extended to eternity. At the same time, colonies outside New England attracted immigrants who in the eighteenth century became the farmers who were to determine in large part the development of America for the next hundred years. These colonials embraced French romantic theories that insisted upon the perfectibility of human nature and the necessity of public institutions encouraging good rather than evil. The individual was to be regarded as more important than the state, and agriculture was to be recognized as the only true source of wealth. Opposed to this largely agrarian complex of Jeffersonian thought was the capitalist Hamiltonian theory, centered in the city, which saw human nature as neither good nor bad but simply as acquisitive, and the government as a peacemaker in a free enterprise system. Economic laws alone were to rule society.

In *The Romantic Revolution in America, 1800-1860*, Parrington traces the decline of Jeffersonian liberalism in America. The East, the stronghold of Hamiltonian economics, witnessed the immigration of workers to the factory and the beginning of the movement which was to change America from a rural to an urban society, replacing the farmer with the businessman. In the South, the Jeffersonian heritage faded as expansion came about because of the increased need for cotton in textile manufacturing, and with it the increased exploitation of the black people. Meanwhile, on the Western frontier, Jeffersonianism was defeated by the acquisitive spirit as freedom became the freedom to exploit and equality became the equality of business opportunity. Jacksonian democracy attempted to carry on the spirit of Jefferson but failed because of its inability to understand economic factors. The only authentic voice of liberalism to be found in this period was among the transcendentalists of New England, but they were doomed because of an abstruse metaphysics and the forces of industrialism.

In *The Beginnings of Critical Realism, 1860-1920*, Parrington is concerned with the triumph of industrialism under the leadership of the middle class at the expense of traditional agrarianism, and with the conquest of nature by mechanistic science. Jeffersonian liberalism had been completely defeated, but Parrington saw a new liberalism emerging—a "Critical Realism"—that would challenge the errors of the age. Although the agrarian revolt of the late nineteenth century failed, it gave rise to the Progressive movement, which in turn provided new economic tools for investigating industrialism and the scientific world view. The Progressives revealed the economic basis of politics and showed that there could be no democracy until the economy was made responsive to the common good. For Parrington, the major contribution of the Progressive movement was Charles Beard's *The Economic Interpretation of the Constitution*, a work which showed the undemocratic nature of the American Constitution and its origin in economic interests. Finally, because, un-like the old liberalism, Progressivism was based on facts and not on faith, it provided an effective defense for the tools of scientific investigation.

The effects of *Main Currents in American Thought* were deep and far-reaching. For the next decade and even after, the work was the established text in American literature survey courses and occasionally found its way into history classes. Parrington stimulated interest in American literature at a time when it was ignored by most English departments. He also took the business of literary criticism out of the hands of the right-wing and elitist critics, and in so doing contributed to the reevaluation of American literature. Furthermore, his work was published at a time when there was a renewed interest in American intellectual history, and the work encouraged this interest. Parrington also showed the value of combining the study of literature and history in exploring a national culture and thus reinforced the tendency in the academic world to venture into new and unconventional exploration. Finally, his work has proven to be of enduring value in that it offers an intelligent explanation of the American experience which continues to stimulate and challenge.

## Pertinent Literature

Hofstadter, Richard. *The Progressive Historians: Turner, Beard, Parrington.* New York: Alfred A. Knopf, 1968.

This is the most complete and authoritative evaluation of the meaning and significance of Parrington's work. As his title indicates, Hofstadter places Parrington within the Progressive movement in America and establishes his relation to the two other important Progressive historians, Frederick Jackson Turner and Charles Beard. His treatment of Parrington, however, also does a great deal more. Hofstadter presents considerable biographical information which clears up questions about Parrington's early life and helps explain some features of his work. Parrington's theory of literary criticism is also examined closely and discussed in terms of the dominant theories of the day. Finally, Parrington's value as a historian is carefully considered.

Following the lead of Turner and Beard, Parrington presented history from the liberal point of view. As Hofstadter explains, these historians not only explained the liberal mind to itself, but also presented many of the most important ideas of the first half of the century. In their work, history was made relevant to the political and intellectual issues of the day as they presented the concepts which seemed to their audience the most worthy of studying and evaluating. As a result, the three strongly influenced many young historians, including Hofstadter himself, and encouraged young people to take up history as a profession.

Like Turner and Beard, Parrington's response to history and politics grew in large part out of his Midwestern experience. Parrington's grandfather was a working-class radical who left England after losing his job to a machine; he passed on to his son and grandson an antipathy for the conservatism of England. Parrington was born in Illinois in 1871, but his family moved to Kansas, near Emporia, when he was six. Although his father was a relatively prosperous farmer and politician, Parrington knew the harshness and ugliness of life on the prairie, and this later shaped his

reading of the frontier experience in American history. For a time, Parrington attended the College of Emporia, a small Presbyterian school, and completed his degree at Harvard. His experience with the established order at Cambridge was unpleasant at best, since he felt rejected because of his Midwestern origin. He returned to teach at Emporia, where he came to know the stultifying narrowness of fundamentalist religion and was eventually influenced by the Populist movement. After four years at Emporia, he moved to the University of Oklahoma, where, after ten years of outstanding service, he was summarily dismissed as the result of a shameful political and religious upheaval at the university. He immediately secured a position at the University of Washington, where he was to remain until his death in 1929.

Hofstadter explains in close detail the inevitability of the eventual decline of Parrington's reputation. From the point of view of literary critics, Parrington was employing an approach which was soon to be completely denounced by the New Critics of the 1930's. Parrington's literary criticism focused on the biographical, historical, sociological, and moral features of the work—everything which the New Criticism was to find totally irrelevant in evaluating literature. Furthermore, Parrington tends to regard politics as preeminently important, so that literature is politicized and the aesthetic experience is all but ignored. At the same time, historians have strongly questioned Parrington's method and conclusions. *Main Currents in American Thought* suffers from an ambiguity of intention because of Parrington's inconsistent movement between political and literary documents. His large scope—the whole of American history and literature—also led him to superficiality, vagueness, and false generalizations. His fixing on two historical currents in America—the democratic and antidemocratic—led to oversimplification and the tendency to see ideas not as developing but as simply reoccurring. Parrington's liberal stance and his distrust of fundamentalist religion also led him to unfair and inaccurate judgments of historical characters, and even—as in the case of the Puritans—of whole groups of people. Finally, Parrington overestimated the French influence in the development of American democracy and tended to attribute ideas he liked to the French and ideas he disliked to the English.

In his final chapter, Hofstadter discusses the relationship of the three Progressive historians to the views of history which emerged in the 1950's; this section gives a sense of completeness to the work as a whole. Hofstadter also includes a thorough bibliographical essay on each of the three Progressive historians. In the final analysis, Hofstadter's treatment of Parrington, as well as of Turner and Beard, must be considered a balanced, scholarly effort which succeeds in estimating the ultimate significance of Parrington to the study of American history and literature.

Peterson, Merril D. "Parrington and American Liberalism," in *Virginia Quarterly Review*. XXX (Winter, 1954), pp. 35-49.

Written at a time when Parrington's reputation had nearly reached its nadir, this article is one of the best attempts to arrive at a balanced evaluation of his work. Peterson acknowledges the numerous defects in *Main Currents in American Thought*, yet maintains that these should not obscure its contribution to our understanding of American history. He also offers an intelligent reading of Parrington's scheme of thought which illuminates the power and subtlety of Parrington's understanding of the development of American culture.

Peterson admits that Parrington suffered from the excessive humanitarian enthusiasm of the Progressive mind, that he committed numerous errors in fact and interpretation, and that he displayed too great a moral commitment and too strong an advocacy of a single point of view. Still, he insists, Parrington's work must be regarded as a major synthesis of American culture and a significant statement on the nature of the liberal tradition in America. It is the latter feature which explains how a history written from an avowedly biased viewpoint—liberal and Jeffersonian—could gain such strong acceptance. Furthermore, even though *Main Currents in American Thought* was a reaction against the genteel criticism of New England, it was also an assertion of the value of American literature at a time when both universities and iconoclastic critics, such as H. L. Mencken and Van Wyck Brooks, were denying it. Finally, despite Parrington's flawed design—a structure torn between a history of ideas and a history of literature—his treatment of literature from the point of view of politics, economics, and social development gave life and significance to America's cultural past.

Peterson closes his article with an evaluation of the lesson that modern liberals can learn from Parrington. The main thrust of that lesson is the danger of losing the "humane content" of the Enlightenment—the idealism of liberalism—in the quest for economic prosperity and social control. Parrington's understanding of the nature of the perennial conflict for the liberal in America—the tension between democracy and plutocracy, humanism and economism, Jefferson and Hamilton—is, Peterson declares, as valuable an insight for today as it was for yesterday. Parrington thus continues to be of value to the growth and development of democratic culture. — *J.A.B.*

## Additional Recommended Reading

Smith, Bernard. "Parrington's *Main Currents of American Thought*," in *Books That Changed Our Minds*. Edited by Malcolm Cowley and Bernard Smith. New York: Doubleday, Doan, and Company, 1939, pp. 179-191. An appreciation of Parrington and an accurate account of his reputation in his own time, written by a fellow liberal.

Gabriel, Ralph H. "Vernon Louis Parrington," in *Pastmasters: Some Essays on American Historians*. Edited by Marcus Cunliffe and Robert W. Winks. New York: Harper & Row Publishers, 1969, pp. 145-166. The best available discussion of the contributions of Parrington to the development of the study of American history and literature.

Trilling, Lionel. "Reality in America," in *The Liberal Imagination: Essays on Literature and Society*. New York: The Viking Press, 1950, pp. 3-25. One of the most intelligent criticisms of the flaws in Parrington's approach to evaluating literature.

Higham, John. "The Study of American Intellectual History," in *Writing American History: Essays on Modern Scholarship*. Bloomington: Indiana University Press, 1970, pp. 41-72. An estimate of Parrington's contribution to the history of ideas which, along with its summary of his theory, is generally favorable.

Ruland, Richard. *The Rediscovery of American Literature: Premises of Critical Taste, 1900-1940*. Cambridge, Mass.: Harvard University Press, 1967. A reevaluation, in a brief but thoughtful section, of Parrington's method of literary criticism, which finds some of the charges made against him to be unjust.

Skotheim, Robert Allen. *American Intellectual Histories and Historians*. Princeton, N.J.: Princeton University Press, 1966. An especially perceptive overview of Parrington's method, theory, and major errors.

# THE CIVIL WAR IN CHINA

*Type of event:* Military: conflict between the Chinese Communists and Nationalists
*Time:* March, 1927-October 1, 1949
*Locale:* China

*Principal personages:*

SUN YAT-SEN (1866-1925), leader of the Republican Revolution and the Kuomintang

CHIANG KAI-SHEK (1887-1975), late President of the Republic of China and Nationalist military leader during China's Civil War

CHU TEH (1886-1976), Commander of Chinese Communist forces who helped Mao Tse-tung in 1928 organize the Fourth Red Army and establish the Communist base in Kiangsi

MAO TSE-TUNG (1893-1976), leader of the Chinese Communist Party and founder of the People's Republic of China

CHANG HSÜEH-LIANG (1898-    ), known as the Young Marshal, he became warlord of Manchuria in 1928, and later fraternized with the Chinese Communist forces for which he was arrested by Chiang Kai-shek

GEORGE CATLETT MARSHALL (1880-1959), United States Ambassador to China who led the mission to mediate an end to the Civil War, 1945-1947; and United States Secretary of State, 1947-1949

## Summary of Event

To bring China out of the chaos caused by warlordism in the 1920's, Sun Yat-sen sought to revitalize the Kuomintang (Nationalist Party) and direct a military unification under the Party's leadership. Communists were invited to join the Kuomintang in 1923 and to participate in the Northern Expedition led by Chiang Kai-shek in 1926, a year after Sun had died. While regrouping in the Yangtze Valley in 1927, the Nationalist-Communist alliance grew strained. The Communists' independent action to organize strikes, engage in sabotage, and create mass organizations, all in defiance of Kuomintang policy, led to suspicion and enmity between the two groups. An open break resulted, and the Nationalists and Communists came into conflict.

When the Chinese Communists rejected the Kuomintang alliance, they established rural soviets in South China, beginning in late 1927. In April, 1928, while Chiang Kai-shek's forces were conquering north China, Chu Teh joined Mao Tse-tung to form the Fourth Red Army. The soviets and the Red Army, with its disciplined and indoctrinated troops experienced in guerrilla warfare, became the focal points of Communist strength. They also became the target

211

of Chiang Kai-shek's five "extermination campaigns," from 1930 to 1934. The final target was the large Kiangsi soviet where Mao Tse-tung had risen to prominence but whose position was threatened in 1934 by intraparty struggles. Chiang's strike against the Communist headquarters at Juichin led to the Long March which began with 100,000 Communist troops and officials on October 15, 1934. The difficult trek through inhospitable terrain, harassed by hostile forces, took its toll. When the Communists set up new headquarters at Yenan in Shensi province in December, 1936, only about thirty thousand bedraggled men were left.

A significant event in the Long March occurred during a pause at Tsunyi in northern Kweichow province in January, 1935. At an organizational conference, Mao Tse-tung was made head of the Party's Politburo and Secretariat; and his emphasis on guerrilla strategy and peasant organization would prevail.

Later in the same year, Chinese Communist strategy shifted in accord with Comintern policy, which directed Communist alliances with anti-Fascist groups. In 1936, the Chinese Communists urged a "United Front" among all parties against Japanese encroachment. Chiang Kai-shek was reluctant to cooperate with the Communists; but some of his leading commanders, such as Chang Hsüeh-liang in northeast China, wanted to end the Civil War. Chiang went to Sian in December, 1936, to meet with Chang and the Commander of a Northwest Army to gain their support. In the bizarre sequence that followed, Chang arrested Chiang and demanded an end to the Civil War. When it appeared that the mutinous anti-Chiang troops might widen the internal conflict, the Communists came to mediate at Sian on Chiang's behalf. Chang Hsüeh-liang released Chiang and flew to Nanking with him, whereupon Chiang Kai-shek put his rebellious Commander under house arrest. Reluctantly, Chiang now led a United Front against Japan.

Before the Japanese attack on China in July, 1937, the Communists and Nationalists discussed United Front arrangements. The Communists pledged in part to end sabotage, sovietization, and the confiscation of landlord holdings, and to reorganize the Red Army and place it under the Nationalists' Military Commission. The Communists took advantage of this reprieve from Nationalist attacks by expanding and strengthening their base in northern China. When the Sino-Japanese War came to a virtual stalemate in 1939, tension developed between the Nationalists and Communists, leading to a serious military clash in January, 1941. Periodic negotiations in 1943 and 1944 resulted in Communist demands for a coalition government and more army divisions, followed by a Nationalist refusal. The United Front fell apart in recrimination.

When the war ended in 1945, the Communists were in a stronger position than when it began. They controlled eighteen "liberated areas" in several north China provinces with a population of one hundred million. An estimated one million troops and a larger militia provided security and an attack force that moved quickly at the war's end to take over the Japanese surrender. The Nationalists, far away in the West from strategic areas in north China, tried to get the Japanese not to surrender to the Communists. With American help, Nationalist troops managed to occupy strategic northern cities, while Communist forces concentrated mainly on the countryside, aided by Russian forces occupying Manchuria.

To prevent a civil war from developing out of the scramble for territory, Mao met with Chiang at Chungking, the Nationalists' wartime capital. While Mao was conciliatory and both sides agreed on principles, each side sought control. Disarming the Japanese and control of local affairs in north China were among points of disagreement. In Manchuria, meanwhile, a half million of Chiang's best troops stationed in cities fought a losing battle to Communist guerrillas based in the countryside. When the Soviets left Manchuria in May, 1946, most of the area was occupied by the Chinese Communists.

As the military situation deteriorated for the Nationalists, diplomatic efforts were made for a compromise solution. After Patrick J. Hurley failed in his mission to China, George C. Marshall was sent in December, 1945, to bring about a coalition government of all parties. Marshall's proposals for a ceasefire, convening a Political Consultative Conference, and uniting Nationalist and Communist forces into a national army were favorably received. Mistrust again hindered implementation of an agreement, however, as both sides jostled for advantage and control. When intense fighting broke out in Manchuria in April, 1946, the Marshall mission was doomed. It was extremists on both sides, Marshall believed, who caused the irreparable break. The Nationalists then went their own way and called for a National Assembly to meet in November, 1946, and the Communists refused to participate.

From the summer of 1946 to the summer of 1947, a new Nationalist offensive was succeeding and taking its toll on the Communists in north China. In March, 1947, the Communists had even lost their capital of Yenan, and by June had lost 191,000 square kilometers of land. The summer of 1947, however, was a turning point in the Civil War when the expanded Communist forces took the offensive. Outmaneuvering the Nationalists in Manchuria again, the Communists captured large numbers of Chiang's best troops and considerable American equipment. In the fall of 1948, the Nationalist defense began to crumble rapidly. After more victories in Shantung province in September, 1948, the Communists proceeded south to Nanking. Entire divisions of Nationalists began to surrender. After the Communist occupation of Peking in January, 1949, the Communists refused to negotiate further, as they saw victory near. On October 1, 1949, the Communists proclaimed the establishment of the People's Republic of China. Remaining Nationalists in south China left for Taiwan in December, 1949.

## The Civil War in China

### Pertinent Literature

Johnson, Chalmers A. *Peasant Nationalism and Communist Power: The Emergence of Revolutionary China, 1937-1945*. Stanford, Calif.: Stanford University Press, 1962.

The resistance movement of China's peasant population against Japanese aggression is the subject of this historical inquiry. By examining the Japanese military records, which include captured Communist and Nationalist documents, the author contends that the Chinese Communists were responsible for mobilizing the peasantry, whose successful tactics weakened the Japanese war effort. Moreover, the wartime leadership of the Chinese Communist Party won the sympathy and support of the peasantry that continued into the postwar era, giving the Communists an advantage over the Nationalists in the Civil War.

The author sees the peasant-based Chinese Communist movement in terms of "nationalism." The Japanese threat to Chinese land and life style awakened a latent "China Consciousness" and a need to defend their homeland among the peasantry. Taking advantage of the opportunity, the Chinese Communists mobilized the peasants, who gave mass support. The Chinese Communist Party provided the leadership, organizational techniques, and training in guerrilla tactics, education, and agriculture. The intolerable conditions that existed in rural China began to change under Communist direction.

Japanese tactics, contends Johnson, also contributed directly to the growth of peasant Nationalism. In areas occupied by the Japanese, their use of frequent terrorist harassment made it easier for the Communists to mobilize peasant support. Tactics other than military force also contributed to advantageous conditions for the Communists. Japanese pressure, for example, forced traditional rural elites to leave the peasants disarrayed and leaderless, thus creating a vacuum for the Communists to fill. The Japanese also failed to set up a Chinese government that could gain popular support and maintain friendly relations with Japan. Attempting to weaken the United Front, the Japanese stressed the ulterior motives of the Communists and the opportunism of the Nationalists, a tactic that only made the peasants more defensive. Lastly, the Japanese occupied too large an area to manage securely. In addition to Japanese pressure and Communist sympathy, Nationalist failures, loss of prestige, and combat with the Communists eliminated the Nationalists as a viable alternative and strengthened the Communist hand in winning over the peasantry.

Instrumental in Communist strategies, according to Johnson, was the army. In addition to its military responsibilities, the army spread anti-Japanese propaganda in the villages; and by the end of the war it had set up nineteen "bases," mainly in north China. Military and political training was given to the peasants, from whose ranks regulars, guerrillas, and militia for the Communist cause were recruited. The "New Fourth Army" was especially important in the Communist arsenal. It was created in September of 1937 from Communist survivors of the 1927-1937 phase of the Civil War and clashed with Nationalist troops in January, 1941, permanently damaging the United Front against Japan. Moreover, the peasantry viewed this clash as a hostile act by the Nationalists against the Communist effort to defend the Chinese homeland against Japanese aggression. The Communists were seen as the true "nationalists."

Johnson compares the Communist experience in China with peasant mobilization in wartime Yugoslavia and finds that the same ingredients were present: harassment by the invaders, Communist mobilization of the peasants, blame for trouble placed on the Communists, peasants and Communists drawn together by close organizational work, and guerrilla forces (not foreign troops) taken over from the invaders. Johnson's thesis on this point is that in countries where

the Communists are able to mobilize the peasantry and elicit a nationalistic response, a foreign policy and ideology develops independent of the Soviet Union. In the Chinese experience in the postrevolutionary period, the Communists did not adhere strictly to the Marxian ideal of "proletarian internationalism."

Johnson believes that it was the strength of nationalism among the Chinese people which prevented a foreign authority such as Moscow from dictating policy to China. The Communists in China were advancing the interests of their own country rather than an international movement; the Chinese Communist Party was not so much anti-Russian as it was pro-Chinese. In the final analysis, it was this independence and the nationalism which the Communists encouraged among the peasantry which brought about a military unification of China in 1949.

Pepper, Suzanne. *Civil War in China: The Political Struggle, 1945-1949*. Berkeley: University of California Press, 1978.

Western historians have viewed the Chinese Civil War as a military clash between Nationalists and Communists and have focused on American efforts to contain and influence it. To these historians, the Communist victory is seen as an illegitimate seizure of power and as an American political loss. Suzanne Pepper, in her thorough exploration of political questions not considered by others, examines policy direction and implementation by the Nationalists and Communists and makes a comparative analysis of their respective

programs for dealing with China's social problems.

The author's dual objective is to determine whether the chaos in China after World War II resulted mainly from a "default of authority" by the ruling Nationalist Party, or whether the Chinese Communist Party successfully gained popular support on their merits. The question Pepper asks is, Did the Communists win a genuine mandate to rule, or was their victory due to Nationalist failure and Japanese excesses?

In searching for an answer to this

question, the author first examines the cities where the strength of the Nationalist Party (Kuomintang) was strongest. Among urban intellectuals, Pepper points out, disillusionment in the Nationalist government was widespread after World War II, and accusations of "incompetent" and "corrupt" were commonplace. These charges were substantiated by poorly conceived policies and widespread cheating by officials in the administration of Chinese territory liberated from Japanese occupation. In addition, economic mismanagement resulted in a disastrous inflation. Before long, business, industry, and the general public lost confidence in the Nationalist government. Hoarding and speculation also added to the recession-unemployment cycle. These developments created a seriously discontented urban middle class, yet this class did not desert the Nationalist government until it was defeated militarily.

The attitudes of the intellectuals are thoroughly scrutinized by Pepper. She notes that their options were limited to either bringing about reforms within the Nationalist Party or making a peaceful accommodation with the Communist Party. Intellectuals only had limited reservations about the latter. While sympathetic to Communist programs and policies, intellectuals generally disliked the form of Communist rule. The Communists' credibility and achievements are what attracted intellectual support. Pepper indicates that the Communists had a reputation of implementing their policies and correcting mistakes, while the Nationalists never did. Moreover, in regard to effective administration, integrity, political competence, and their ability to manage economic costs, the Communists surpassed the Nationalists.

Necessity required that the Communists concentrate their efforts in rural China, and it is there that political victory was most decisive. Having allied with the discredited landlords who mistreated the peasantry, the Nationalists lost the support of China's masses. By contrast, the Communist policy of working closely with the peasants in north China during World War II won their allegiance. Employing new techniques, the Communists provided an alternative to Japanese oppression by mobilizing the peasants for guerrilla warfare, redistributing land and wealth, and breaking the corrupt and arbitrary use of political power in the villages. This thesis coincides with that of Chalmers Johnson (above). The Communist program in the north China countryside, moreover, developed solid roots, making it impossible for the Nationalists to compete effectively for popular support.

While the Communists did not win an unqualified mandate for one-party rule in 1949, Pepper contends that the Party's achievements were sufficient to gain popular acceptance of the new Communist government. In addition, she sees importance in the Japanese invasion, the Communist's strong Stalinist organization, socioeconomic conditions in China, and the weakness of the Nationalists. The author does not subscribe to the idea that Japan's invasion made the Communist victory possible by preventing the Nationalists from defeating the Communists. She contends that Communist successes were due to the fact that their program was more closely identified with the people and their problems in the 1940's. — *L.H.D.G.*

## Additional Recommended Reading

Eastman, Lloyd E. *The Abortive Revolution: China Under Nationalist Rule, 1927-1937*. Cambridge, Mass.: Harvard University Press, 1974. Argues that Nationalist shortcomings were due to causes beyond the Kuomintang's control.

Kataoka, Tetsuya. *Resistance and Revolution in China: The Communists and the Second United Front*. Berkeley: University of California Press, 1974. Supports a conservative theory that places stress more on the military as a primary factor in consolidating Communist power and less on peasant revolt.

Rosinger, Lawrence K. *China's Wartime Politics, 1937-1944*. Princeton, N.J.: Princeton University Press, 1944. Sketches briefly some of the major political developments in Nationalist China and how they were affected by the course of the war and the economic upheaval.

Liu, Frederick F. *A Military History of Modern China, 1924-1949*. Port Washington, N.Y.: Kennikat Press, 1972. Traces the development of military and political forces within the Nationalist government, the Kuomintang Party, and the Communist Party.

Melby, John F. *The Mandate of Heaven: Record of a Civil War, China 1945-49*. Toronto: University of Toronto Press, 1968. A diplomat's account of the Chinese Civil War with diary excerpts and narrative explanations.

Selden, Mark. *The Yenan Way in Revolutionary China*. Cambridge, Mass.: Harvard University Press, 1971. An excellent analysis of Mao's revolutionary policies which expanded the Communist following substantially between 1935 and 1947.

Tien, Hung-mao. *Government and Politics in Kuomintang China, 1927-1937*. Stanford, Calif.: Stanford University Press, 1972. Supplements Eastman's book and concentrates on patterns of political development and administration, concluding that the Kuomintang could not have indefinitely stemmed the tide of Communist success.

Van Slyke, Lyman P. *Enemies and Friends: The United Front in Chinese Communist History*. Stanford, Calif.: Stanford University Press, 1967. Traces the United Front theme as it developed in the Chinese Communist Party since 1935, emphasizing Mao's view.

# RESEARCH INTO THE ORIGINS OF MAN

*Type of event:* Scientific: developments in archaeology and anthropology
*Time:* 1928 to the present
*Locale:* Taung, South Africa; Olduvai Gorge, Tanzania; and selected sites around the
world

*Principal personages:*
RAYMOND ARTHUR DART (1893-      ), Australian anatomist
who explored Taung remains in Africa
ROBERT BROOM (1866-1951), Scottish paleontologist who
became a leading figure in the "missing link" debate
LOUIS SEYMOUR BAZETT LEAKEY (1903-1972), British anthropologist (born in Kenya) who led extended excavations
in the fossil-rich Olduvai Gorge

## Summary of Event

The reconstruction of mankind's evolutionary past has taken on an astonishing coherence over the past decade. For most of this century, archaeologists with their discoveries have been mainly engaged in demolishing old beliefs about the descent of man and in announcing "missing links." Recent finds have produced enough such links to create intriguing and supportable theories, and clear pictures have emerged.

Although the early archaeologists who supported Darwin dismissed their critics as narrow-minded, they were not themselves entirely free of nineteenth century prejudices. Most of them had specific and fastidious preconceptions about how civilized *Homo sapiens* had emerged. In the temperate climate of Europe, it was agreed, early man had appeared rather suddenly, perhaps a million years ago, as a "brainy ape," a creature somewhat like a gorilla except for his very large brain. This intelligent animal had then descended from the trees (losing his stooping gait), and begun to eat plants and cooked meat (losing his fangs) and to make tools (developing coordinated hands for better craftsmanship). Gradually, intelligence caused early man to lose his lower primate characteristics and become ready for civilization.

This theory was supported by two widely publicized finds in the early part of this century. One was a skeleton in France near La Chapelle-aux-Saints in 1908. It was readily identified as that of a Neanderthal man, a species whose remains had been found scattered through Europe, and who was thought to have flourished about two hundred thousand years ago. Archaeologists studying the La Chapelle-aux-Saints skeleton proclaimed that although Neanderthal man had a large brain cavity, he was otherwise not far removed from the apes: he walked with a severe stoop, grasped with his toes as well as his fingers, and had a "coarse" brain and a simian expression. The claims of this group were buttressed by the discovery of "Piltdown man" in England, which consisted of a skull and jawbone dated at 50,000 B.C.; the skull was much like that of a human being, while the jaw was apelike. This find suited the generally accepted ideas about human evolution very well, for it suggested that man's development had been sudden, recent, and from the brain down.

The first serious challenge to this orthodoxy came in 1924, when a young amateur archaeologist named Raymond Dart received a crate of fossilized stones in his South African study and found among them a small, nearly complete skull, which at first appeared to be that of an extinct ape. Dart soon realized, however, that the facial bones were remarkably similar to those of a human baby and that the teeth were clearly hominid (that is, prehuman) in formation. Perhaps most intriguing was the juncture with the neck, which suggested that the "Taung baby," although he lived millions of years ago, had walked almost fully erect. Early in 1925, Dart asserted that his discovery was a true intermediate species between human beings and apes; but the idea that the earliest men were not large-brained Europeans was too much for most archaeologists. Dart's ideas were ridiculed, and he largely abandoned his research.

He was soon joined, however, by an eminent paleontologist named Robert Broom. Broom had discovered many of the missing links between reptiles and the early mammals, and he was convinced that the rich fossil beds of South Africa could yield the bones of early men. Over the next generation he built up an impressive collection of skeletal frag-ments, most of them so similar to the Taung baby that a new species was established: *Australopithecus africanus* (African ape-man). The accompanying discoveries of stone tools strengthened the belief in these beings as genuine human forerunners.

While evidence for a new theory of human origins mounted, the finds which supported the orthodox theory crumbled. In 1953, suspicious British scientists realized that the Piltdown head was a clever forgery—the simple combination of a modern human skull and the jaw of an orangutan. Other investigators discovered that the Neanderthal man of La Chapelle-aux-Saints was not a typical specimen: he was rather old and suffering from rickets. More representative Neanderthal skeletons revealed individuals so nearly human that they were included in the species *Homo sapiens*; modern man was assigned to the subspecies *Homo sapiens sapiens*. With these revelations the way was clear for an interpretation of the African evidence.

The problem was that this new body of evidence was by no means unambiguous. Archaeologists were aware of three species of protoapes which had lived some fourteen million years ago, two species of hominids which lived three million years ago, and a clear "early man," *Homo erectus* (discovered in Java, Peking, and Europe over the years), who flourished one million years ago. But no one could account for the transitional periods between these clusters of fossils; nor could anyone fully demonstrate that a particular specimen was definitely a human ancestor.

Credit for solving these puzzles belongs largely to Louis and Mary Leakey, who spent forty years carefully excavating a rich African fossil area in Olduvai Gorge, located in present-day Tanzania. The Leakeys found strong signs of primitive tool use on the part of one of the pro-toapes, *Ramapithecus*, as well as further evidence that this species was not an ancestor of apes at all, but had broken off from the main evolutionary lines to form the ancestry leading to man. They also discovered a third new species: a three-million-year-old hominid that showed clear connections with both *Ramapithecus* and his successor *Homo erectus*. This new type, called *Homo habilus*, also revealed a great deal about the sequence of changes that produced intelligent men.

It now appears that the most crucial factors in human evolution were climatic and environmental, forcing early *Ramapithecus* to abandon the forest (the natural habitat of apes) and seek survival in the open grasslands and savannas of Africa. Adaptation to new sources of food (animal meat and seeds) produced crucial changes: *Ramapithecus* developed a more upright posture for better run-

ning and detection of predators; it exchanged fangs for molars that could grind seeds; and it acquired coordinated hands. Over a period of some ten million years, this species differentiated into several distinct species, all of them rather human in appearance but of varying intelligence. The superior brain of *Homo habilus* enabled it to survive another environmental crisis some two million years ago (the other species did not), and it developed and spread across the world as *Homo erectus*.

Some of the major remaining mysteries concern the last million years of evolution. Both *Homo erectus* and Neanderthal man were successful, populous, and intelligent users of tools who had mastered fire and developed the rudiments of culture. Yet both types completely vanished before the end of the last Ice Age, leaving only one homogenous subspecies to fill the entire earth—*Homo sapiens sapiens*. Based on a very few finds, archaeologists have developed a remarkably complete view of the general evolutionary rise of mankind, but the ecological and social conditions responsible for the changes are still far from being understood.

**Pertinent Literature**

Wilson, Edward O. *Sociobiology: The New Synthesis*. Cambridge, Mass.: Harvard University Press, 1975.

Edward Wilson's massive treatise on sociobiology is one of the few works of this generation that can make a serious claim to classic status. In purely scientific terms, the book is impressive but innocuous: it summarizes the scattered work of

hundreds of scientists and provides a clear and usable statement of one of the most advanced biological theories: Darwin's concept of "group selection," a modification of his theory of natural selection which he developed to explain why some animals live in societies. The larger importance of *Sociobiology* stems from the author's attempt to show that the concept of group selection can be used to explain not only human societies, but also "ethics and ethical philosophers . . . at all depths." In making such an assertion, Wilson threatens to revolutionize man's view of himself more thoroughly than any thinker since Darwin.

Wilson is well aware that he is breaking new and controversial ground, and he proceeds with an almost taunting arrogance. He diagrams the relative importance of the sciences, casually observing that the social sciences are "two orders of magnitude" more complex than the natural sciences, and maintaining (without evidence) that mankind's "ecosystem" will stabilize about A.D. 2100. Even his title betrays a confidence that his theories will soon become the new orthodoxy. Such complacency has led many opponents to reject his work completely; but an objective biologist cannot afford to do so. Most of the book is rigorous analysis, synthesizing thousands of related studies and offering ingenious solutions to long-standing puzzles. The proper question is not so much whether the theories of sociobiology are wrong, but whether Wilson has pushed them too far.

The theory of group selection works most evidently when applied to the insect societies. Natural selection usually works by the relative success individual creatures have in passing on their own genes to descendents. Those who do not propagate disappear. But in a honeybee hive, only the queen bee meets this criterion of

evolutionary success. How did drones and worker bees, willingly refraining from reproduction for the larger good of the group, develop? Darwin solved this problem by pointing out that an insect could sacrifice itself and still enjoy evolutionary success so long as its sacrifice promoted the survival of related insects with very similar gene types. Over millions of generations, groups of insects can develop reciprocal characteristics which permit remarkably interdependent societies while still promoting the genetic success of the individual.

Wilson has elaborated considerably on these ideas, showing the mathematics of gene diffusion and the conditions under which altruistic and social gene traits will successfully survive. Each action which risks the self for the good of the whole must be dictated by hereditary instructions. Hence, it is not surprising that Wilson regards human societies as vast conglomerations of social traits, evolved over millions of years and still changing. These social traits do not simply include language, facial expression, motherly love, and the "herding" instinct, but extend to cultural heritage, aesthetic sense, generosity, morality, and elaborate division of labor. In short, Wilson believes that the chief dynamics governing human thought and social change are genetically based.

Aside from disagreement among biologists and animal behaviorists, Wilson's theories have drawn attacks from a wide spectrum of disciplines. For example, some psychologists have argued that sociobiology underestimates the unique flexibility of human learning; and social scientists have

221

insisted that the theory does not consider the autonomous role that human institutions play in social affairs. But the most earnest of Wilson's opponents are those humanists who intuitively feel that the creativity and independence of the human mind cannot be accounted for through genetic analysis. The author himself admits that people form a certain paradox: the general rule in the animal kingdom is that the greater complexity of the individual, the more difficult it is to attain social cohesion: a pack of wolves lives together less smoothly than a hive of bees. Yet the exceptionally individualistic human race is also exceptionally cohesive. It is not unreasonable to assume that man is the benefactor of special talents, such as consciousness and sympathy, which were not intended by evolution and which free him in some degree from instinctual control. Wilson may not have fully plumbed the complexities of the human soul, as he suggests; but he has at least succeeded in setting old questions about human nature in an intriguing new dimension.

Leakey, Richard E. and Roger Lewin. *Origins*. New York: E. P. Dutton, 1977.

The relationship between a society's intellectual bent and its social development is tenuous but often very suggestive. In the decades after World War II, a series of writers produced very successful and widely discussed books which stressed the innate depravity of man and placed the blame on the fact that human origins are so closely associated with hunting and savagery. Robert Ardrey's *African Genesis* and Desmond Morris' *The Naked Ape* are representative. Even the eminent ethologist Konrad Lorenz warned in his book *On Aggression* that powerful human instincts toward territoriality must find some outlet in modern civilization. The last ten years, however, have seen a marked reversal of this trend. In 1968, anthropologist Ashley Montagu pointed to a number of peaceful and cooperative peoples as evidence that aggression is not inherited and can be avoided. Four years later *The Descent of Woman* appeared, in which Elaine Morgan argued that early men (and, especially, early women) had been quiet, food-gathering individuals; early tools were developed not to slay game but to crack shells. E. O. Wilson's *Sociobiology* stressed the importance of altruistic and cooperative instincts in human evolution.

*Origins* represents, perhaps, a sort of culmination of this trend; and it may become the definitive response to Lorenz. Richard Leakey's reputation as an archaeologist and the book's careful consideration of recent discoveries give the enterprise a solid cast of scientific credibility; and the authors do not hesitate to throw their weight behind a very specific conception of human nature. But they do not offer simply an expression of faith in innate human goodness. Instead, they argue that man's most basic characteristics are neither good nor bad, but flexible; people respond to their environment in ways that are demanded of them.

Leakey and Lewin draw their conclusions from recent work in several fields. In archaeology, they review the most recent finds of Leakey's own archaeological sites, which have yielded considerable evidence that the earliest man, *Homo habilis*, lived quietly on lake shores with several other species of hominid nearly three million years ago. All of these groups apparently evolved into closely knit societies based on hunting and gathering. The crucial advantage for the ancestors of man was their superior social skill; they could keep the society together under more difficult circumstances than their competitors, and thus they survived.

Studies of ape behavior, especially Jane Goodall's observations of chimpanzees, show a similar pattern of evolution. These primates, which are more advanced and intelligent than any others, have developed their intelligence largely as a means of ensuring a stable society. A long childhood and a considerable learning capacity (also found in human beings) are used by chimps to learn the "cul-

ture" of the band: the varying faces and temperaments of other members, social etiquette, and sharing habits. Anthropological studies of hunting and gathering groups of people in Africa reveal a similar emphasis on learning techniques of cooperative social behavior, and on using cultural forms to symbolize and maintain the spiritual unity of the group.

From such sources, Leakey and Lewin weave a careful and interesting argument to show that the basic tenor of human action is not aggressive, but rather the adaptation of social skills to a particular environment. In modern societies, man's surroundings have changed too rapidly and disruptively to permit a proper balance. A better environment, aimed at facilitating cooperative interaction, would lead to a far better society. The optimism of the authors lies in their belief that people have enough wisdom and will, individually and collectively, to make the necessary changes. — *R.H.S.*

## Additional Recommended Reading

Geertz, Clifford. *The Interpretation of Cultures*. New York: Basic Books, 1973. An excellent collection of articles on anthropology, written by one of the field's most imaginative scholars.

Jolly, Alison. *The Evolution of Primate Behavior*. New York: The Macmillan Company, 1972. A survey and discussion of recent findings.

Montagu, Ashley. *The Nature of Human Aggression*. New York: Oxford University Press, 1976. An attempt to explain hostility and violence in man while defending his underlying goodness.

Morgan, Elaine. *The Descent of Woman*. New York: Stein and Day, 1972. An imaginative reworking of scattered biological and archaeological evidence which argues that early man (and woman) evolved for millions of years on the seacoast, thus losing body fur, gaining body fat, learning to stand erect, and developing weblike feet and hands; polemic tone at times.

Pfeiffer, John E. *The Emergence of Man*. New York: Harper & Row Publishers, 1972.

An excellent survey of archaeological and anthropological knowledge of the subject. Wendt, Herbert. *From Ape to Adam*. Indianapolis: Bobbs-Merrill, 1972. An entertaining narrative of archaeological finds from the sixteenth century to the present.

# THE REFORM PROGRAM OF MUSTAFA KEMAL

*Type of event:* Cultural: transformation of Turkish society
*Time:* c. 1928
*Locale:* Turkey

*Principal personages:*
> MUSTAFA KEMAL ATATÜRK (1881-1938), first President of the Turkish Republic, 1923-1938
> ISMET INÖNÜ (1884-1973), Prime Minister of Turkey, 1923-1937
> ALI FETHI OKYAR (1880-1943), Turkish Ambassador to France, founder of opposition Free Republican Party

## Summary of Event

In October, 1927, Mustafa Kemal, President of the infant Turkish Republic, addressed his nation in a radio speech lasting five days. Kemal recounted the story of his rise to power, his successful expulsion of foreign armies from Turkey, his overthrow of the Ottoman Sultanate, and his inauguration of the Turkish revolution which was then in progress and would continue until his death and beyond. In his speech Kemal analyzed the nature of his reform program, which had no less a goal than the complete transformation of Turkey from a backward society lost in medieval Islamic obscurantism to a modern Westernized nation which could proudly take its place among the countries of the twentieth century. Kemal set out to achieve six goals: republicanism, nationalism, populism, revolutionism, secularism, and statism.

Republican reforms involved much more than the removal of the Turkish monarch, which had taken place in 1923. "Popular sovereignty" was a key slogan of the Kemalist republic, and Mustafa wished to end the de-bilitating effect of the old Ottoman bureaucracy at all levels. He wanted the entire Turkish nation to feel that it had a voice in ruling Turkey.

Quite logically, the fostering of Turkish nationalism was related to republicanism as well as to other reforms. Mustafa Kemal hoped to replace the older pan-Islamic and pan-Ottoman sentiments with the modern conception of nationalism as it existed in Europe. Press and schools popularized the role that Turks had played in world history. Some went to extremes, as in the semiofficial "Sun-Language Theory," which maintained that Turkish was the original language of mankind.

The reforms associated with "populism" complemented both those of republicanism and nationalism by emphasizing the unity of the Turkish people. The Ottoman *millets*, the old autonomous religious communities, were dissolved; all Turkish citizens were made equal before the law, regardless of class or creed. Internal administration retained some of the old forms while becoming more streamlined. Kemal also used his Re-

225

publican Popular Party (RPP) to propagandize his reforms among the people. RPP "people's houses" and "people's rooms" in every Turkish city and village served as community centers to spread the ideas of modernization among the populace.

By "revolutionism" Kemal meant the zeal with which he intended his nation to carry out its transformation. This was the underlying philosophy of his reforms, which were indeed not just a repetition of the superficial changes of the nineteenth century Tanzimat, but a complete revolutionary transformation of society.

Through "secularism" Kemal had ended the Caliphate in 1924. Afterwards, religious properties were nationalized. Members of Islamic institutions lost their government subsidies; religious courts were abolished; civil marriage was made mandatory; and education was secularized. Muslim religious restrictions, hitherto part of Turkish law, were now made voluntary or even abolished. Polygamy became illegal; women could now appear in public without veils and could initiate divorce proceedings; and the sale of alcohol was now permitted. Even within the Muslim religion, Kemal brought about changes in accordance with his reform program, Turkish replacing Arabic as the language of ceremony. The secularization program was perhaps Kemal's most important reform. It, more than any other aspect of the revolution, transformed the external face and internal character of the Ottoman Empire into those of modern Turkey.

The last feature of the Kemalist reformation was "statism," which embraced an economic program. Mixing nineteenth century laissez-faire and twentieth century planning, Kemal sought to bring Turkey to the point of economic self-sufficiency. Turkish leaders worked to develop both the agricultural and industrial sectors of the Turkish economy. Land reform, cooperatives, state banks for the granting of credit on easy terms, and agricultural schools and training programs were introduced to help the Turkish farmer. In industry and commerce, the government adopted policies of encouraging native private entrepreneurs through tax credits, tariffs, and the mandatory use of Turkish products by government offices and employees. At the same time Kemal introduced economic planning after the Soviet Union model, with two five-year plans beginning in 1934.

Kemal's reformation program was indeed an amazingly successful genuine revolution which turned the remnants of the decaying and defeated Ottoman Empire into a modern nation-state. Because of Kemal's employment of some harsh measures, he is often pictured as a dictator; however, while there is some truth to the charge, the Turkish leader should be viewed in the context of his goals and the state of the world in the twentieth century. Kemal neither adopted the aggressive foreign policy of other modern dictators nor completely stifled internal opposition to his rule. It is true that he dealt ruthlessly with those persons who engaged in armed rebellion against his reforms; but several times he encouraged the formation of opposition political parties, provided that they adhere to the basic principle of modernization; for example, the Free Republican Party of Ali Fethi Okyar. It must be noted, however, that in the final analysis Kemal could not work under these restrictions; he eventually outlawed the rival parties he had helped to create. Yet the principles of democracy and parliamentarianism took root in Turkey and grew after his death.

Mustafa Kemal stands as a towering figure in the creation of modern Turkey. Only his associate and successor Ismet Inönü approached him among post-World War I Turkish statesmen. With good reason, when he decreed in 1935 that all Turks assume family names in the modern fashion, he himself became Atatürk, father of the Turkish people.

## Pertinent Literature

Lewis, Bernard. *The Emergence of Modern Turkey*. London: Oxford University Press, 1968.

Bernard Lewis is one of the leading authorities on modern Turkish history writing for the English-speaking public. This work serves both as a basic text for modern Turkish history and a thorough analysis of the reforms initiated by Atatürk. In the first half of the volume, Lewis chronicles the history of the Ottoman Empire and Turkey from the nineteenth century to the post-World War II era, emphasizing the decay of the old regime and the developing vigor of the Turkish revolutionary movement under the impact of Westernization. In the latter half of the book, he analyzes various aspects of Turkish society—religion, culture, and ideas of state, government, and national and class identity—both in the old and the new Turkey.

Lewis clearly demonstrates that the Kemalist reforms had their roots in the reformatory and revolutionary traditions of nineteenth century Turkey; but the incisive sagacity and iron determination of Atatürk were the catalysts which brought them about. Lewis presents a detailed picture of

Turkish attitudes and world outlooks both before and after the advent of Kemal. He thus shows how Atatürk changed not only the external face of Turkey, even to the point of replacing the old dress with the modern European, but also the Ottoman belief that nothing in the West could be of value to the superior Islamic culture. This tradition, which the Turks believed that Allah had ordained through the Koran, fell before Kemal's insistence that Turkey adopt Western modes and technology for the good of the republic.

Lewis also draws attention to the fallacy of comparing the Turkish revolution with earlier European revolutions, such as those in France and Russia, and with later revolutions in the Third World. While superficial similarities may exist, Lewis insists fundamental differences distinguish the Turkish experience. Neither the class conflicts of prerevolutionary Europe nor the development of humanism and liberalism in the Renaissance and post-Renaissance age had many counterparts in the Islamic Empire of the sultans. With respect to the Third World, although the Ottoman Empire was an indirect victim of European imperialism, it never became the victim of colonial conquest. Thus, Lewis claims, Turkey's modernization and struggle for national independence and unification differ from those in other modern countries of Asia and Africa. The Turks have striven both for nationalism and Westernization without feeling the two goals to be contradictory.

Lewis states that many Turks see the Kemalist transformation not merely in terms of economic, social, or government changes, but as an elemental process of civilization—another step toward the West, completing a process that began a thousand years before, when the Turks rejected Chinese culture for Islam. Now, he writes, "the replacement of old, Islamic conceptions of identity, authority, and loyalty by new conceptions of European origin was of fundamental importance." Lewis perhaps best summarizes the Turkish transformation in this sentence: "In the theocratically conceived polity of Islam, God was to be twice replaced: as the source of sovereignty, by the people; as the object of worship, by the nation."

Shaw, Stanford J. and Ezel Kural Shaw. *History of the Ottoman Empire and Modern Turkey*. Vol. II: *Reform, Revolution, and Republic: The Rise of Modern Turkey, 1808-1975*. New York: Cambridge University Press, 1977.

This volume completes the authors' general history of Turkey. Their use of original Turkish sources makes it uniquely valuable for English readers. However, its unswerving adulation of everything Turkish and disparagement of non-Turkish and Christian elements within the Ottoman Empire and in Europe constitute a flaw. Although the biased approach may counterbalance past anti-Turkish accounts by European scholars, it reduces the credibility of the Shaws' interpretation. This fault is unfortunate, since much of the onesidedness is confined to Turkish foreign relations or relations between various minorities in the old Ottoman Empire. The Shaws' account of Turkish domestic policy and the development of revolutionary and reformist ideas is presented in a much more temperate if not impartial fashion.

The Shaws emphasize the fundamental soundness and merit of traditional Turkish and Islamic society. They do not admire Kemal the revolutionary and innovator so much as Kemal the national hero, the savior of the Turkish state after the disasters of World War I. The authors stress the aspect of the Kemalist reformation which developed out of the old reform policy (Tanzimat) of the nineteenth century. They also call attention to the peaceful foreign policy of Atatürk. Instead of trying to regain the lost territories of the Ottoman Empire, the reformer wisely decided to build up the republic on the national heartland which remained in Turkish hands, and pursued a policy of friendship with his neighbors and neutrality in European and world affairs.

The viewpoint of the Shaws, honoring Kemal as a Turkish hero and cherishing what was traditional in Turkish society rather than championing the innovations above all else, can be seen in their analysis of the populist and secularist aspects of the Turkish reforms. They defend Kemal's use of dictatorial methods to bring about his revolution as needed by the times and conditions in which he worked. They point out that after Kemal, Turkey remained a democratic republic and did not sink into the totalitarianism of dictators less able than Atatürk.

Secularism as applied by Atatürk, the Shaws insist, was an attempt to release the nation from clerical rule and the individual from the superficial constraints of religious dogma. They believe that Atatürk's critics are wrong when they accuse him of abandoning religion. Islam continued to play an important and meaningful role in the lives of the Turks after the Kemalist revolution. The spiritual values it offered could not be replaced by the worldly ideology of nationalism.

The authors show that because of the country's low state of development, Atatürk did not precisely follow the model of the Soviet planned economy, with its emphasis on capital development. Hence, the five-year plan concentrated on those industries which would directly raise the standard of living. The authors do not view all of Kemal's actions favorably. For instance, they fault the government for failing to change substantially the nineteenth century tax policy. However, while admitting that the economic policy was less successful than was officially claimed, they believe that it was more successful than Atatürk's critics have credited it with being.

The Shaws deplore the Kemalist nationalist reform's overemphasis on the past and the weakening of the Western humanism which had entered Ottoman educational institutions in the nineteenth century. In short, they conclude that the place of Atatürk in Turkish history cannot be denied, while strongly implying that his reforms were part of a process begun by the Sultans and grounded in the great spiritual values of Islam and Ottomanism. — *F.B.C.*

## Additional Recommended Reading

Kemal Atatürk, Mustafa. *A Speech Delivered by Ghazi Mustafa Kemal, President of the Turkish Republic, October 1927.* Leipzig: Koehler, 1929. This official English translation presents Kemal's own version of the Turkish revolution.

Armstrong, Harold C. *Grey Wolf: Mustafa Kemal, an Intimate Study of a Dictator.* London: Arthur Barker, 1932. A balanced critical biography of Atatürk.

Balfour, Patrick (Lord Kinross). *Atatürk: The Rebirth of a Nation.* New York: William Morrow and Company, 1965. A detailed, sympathetic biography.

Fisher, Sidney Nettleton. *The Middle East: A History.* New York: Alfred A. Knopf, 1960. Contains excellent chapters on modern Turkey.

Karpat, Kemal H. *Turkey's Politics: The Transition to a Multi-Party System.* Princeton,

N.J.: Princeton University Press, 1959. A monograph by a respected Turkish scholar on the political effects of the Kemalist revolution.

Edib, Halidé (Adivar). *Turkey Faces West: A Turkish View of Recent Changes and Their Origin*. New Haven, Conn.: Yale University Press, 1930. An insider's interpretation of Kemalist Turkey by the country's most famous woman revolutionary.

# THE FIRST MAJOR ARAB ATTACK
# ON THE JEWS IN PALESTINE

*Type of event:* Sociological: historical friction between Arabs and Jews of Palestine
culminates in Arab riots
*Time:* August 15-29, 1929
*Locale:* Palestine

*Principal personages:*
> SIR HERBERT LOUIS SAMUEL (1870-1963), High Commissioner of the Palestine Mandate, 1920-1925
> FIELD MARSHAL LORD PLUMER (HERBERT CHARLES ONSLOW) (1857-1932), High Commissioner of the Palestine Mandate, 1925-1928
> SIR ROBERT JOHN CHANCELLOR (1870-1952), High Commissioner of the Palestine Mandate, 1928-1931
> DR. CHAIM WEIZMANN (1874-1952), principal spokesman for the Zionist movement during the 1920's
> VLADIMIR JABOTINSKY (1880-1940), the militant leader of the minority "Revisionist" faction among Zionists
> LORD ARTHUR JAMES BALFOUR (FIRST EARL OF BALFOUR) (1848-1930), British statesman, Foreign Minister, and author of the "Balfour Declaration" of November 2, 1917
> HAJJ AMIN AL-HUSAYNI (1893-    ), Grand Mufti of Jerusalem after 1921, and chief leader of the Palestinian Arabs during the period of the British Mandate

## Summary of Event

The Palestinian Arab riots of August, 1929, had far-reaching consequences. They dug a permanent trench between Arab and Jew in Palestine, thus preparing the way for the seemingly endless cycle of Arab-Israeli conflict after Israel became independent in 1948. The roots of the 1929 riots lay deep in the history of both peoples.

The Jews entered Palestine for the first time about 1300 B.C. After A.D. 135, when the Romans crushed the last Jewish rebellion, most of the Jews in the world lived outside Palestine, in the so-called Diaspora.

There, they continued to adhere to their religious tradition. Palestine first became part of the Roman Empire and then of the Byzantine Empire. Ever since the defeat of the Byzantines by the Arabs in A.D. 638, Palestine was, except for the short interval of the Crusades (A.D. 1096 to 1187), under Muslim rule until 1918. In 1517, the Ottoman Turks took the place of the previous Arabic-speaking rulers; but since the Turks were also Muslim, their coming made little difference in the lives of the people of Palestine. By 1517, most of these people, except for the few Jews and

231

the largely urban Christian Arab minority, were Arab Muslim peasants (*fellahin*).

Throughout the long centuries of Muslim rule, a small Jewish population did remain in Palestine; most of these Jews were either Arabic-speaking Sephardic Jews or aged pilgrims from Eastern Europe. The latter spent their last years in the Holy City of Jerusalem, living on alms from their coreligionists in Europe. The resident Jews were too small a group to be a threat to the Arabs of Palestine.

The late nineteenth and early twentieth centuries saw the emergence of a new type of nationalism among both Jews and Arabs. For centuries, the Jews of Christian Europe were an oppressed and often persecuted minority; it was not until the nineteenth century, with the spread of liberalism, that European Jews finally began to enjoy equal rights with their non-Jewish neighbors. Though progress had occurred by the 1890's, the Jews still had not been completely integrated into European society. Those who lived in the vast domains of the Russian Tsar remained subject to severe discrimination and periodic massacres, while even in "civilized" Western Europe, there remained strong undercurrents of political anti-Semitism. The medieval Christian had hated the Jew as an infidel; the nineteenth century nationalist feared him as an alien.

In 1896, the Austrian-Jewish journalist Theodor Herzl, shocked by a recent wave of anti-Semitism in liberal, democratic France, decided that only the creation of an independent Jewish State would solve the Jewish problem once and for all. Under Herzl's leadership, the First World Zionist Congress took place in Basel, Switzerland, in 1897. Herzl's scheme for buying Palestine from the Turks failed utterly, but the World Zionist Organization survived his death in 1904. His message had had a powerful appeal for the oppressed Jews of Eastern Europe.

As early as 1882, tiny groups of Eastern European Jews had tried to create Jewish agricultural settlements in Palestine, and a second wave of Russian-Jewish colonists arrived in Palestine after 1905. These new settlers, most of them young and idealistic, wished to create a self-sufficient Jewish economy in Palestine. Inevitably, their efforts began to cause friction with the local Arabs. By 1914, however, the new Jewish community had finally become firmly established on Palestinian soil.

Meanwhile, the Arabs of the Ottoman Empire had slowly begun to develop a nationalism of their own. Anti-Turkish nationalism had first begun to arise among the Arab Christians of the Empire in the middle of the nineteenth century. Among the Muslim Arabs, anti-Turkish nationalism first began to appear only after 1908, when the government of the "Young Turks" tried to rejuvenate the Empire by centralizing the administration and Turkifying the non-Turkish peoples.

In 1914, World War I broke out, pitting the Central Powers (Germany, Austria-Hungary, and the Ottoman Empire) against the Entente Powers (Great Britain, France, and Russia). The coming of the war opened up new opportunities for both Zionist and Arab nationalism. By 1917, the Polish-born English Zionist leader Chaim Weizmann had persuaded the British Cabinet of Sir David Lloyd George to take a stand in favor of Zionism. Weizmann had been a personal friend of Arthur Balfour, then the British Foreign Minister, since 1906. Balfour and Lloyd George believed that a public British commitment to Zionism would gain Britain the support of world Jewry, thus aiding the British war effort. In addition, they thought that such an act might help atone for the centuries of Christian persecution of the Jews.

The famous Balfour Declaration, issued on November 2, 1917, asserted that the British government would view with favor, and do its best to facilitate, the establishment of "a national home for the Jewish people" in Palestine. The Declaration added, however, that nothing would be done which might "prejudice the civil and religious rights of existing non-Jewish communities in Palestine."

Britain had also made promises to the Arabs. In 1915 and 1916, Sir Henry McMahon, the British High Commissioner in Egypt, had promised Sherif Husayn of the Hejaz (the region around Mecca) that if Husayn would lead an Arab revolt against the Turks, an independent Arab state would be created after the war which would include the greater part of what was called "Syria." Husayn was nominally under the suzerainty of the Turkish Sultan, but he had been growing restless. He took McMahon at his word, and on June 5, 1916, launched a revolt against the Ottoman Empire; Husayn's son Faisal commanded the Arab insurgent forces. While this revolt did not win the support of all Ottoman Arabs, it did make an important contribution to the final British victory over the Turks. Faisal's forces captured the Turkish-held Palestinian Red Sea port of Aquaba in July, 1917. In December, 1917, the British captured Jerusalem, and, in October of the following year, captured Damascus. In October, 1918, the Turks finally signed an armistice.

Whether McMahon had promised Palestine to the future Arab state (as Palestinian Arabs would allege after the war) will always be a matter of dispute. McMahon had used such ambiguous language in his correspondence with Husayn that one could infer from his words almost anything one wished.

The decisions of the Allied Conference of San Remo, in April, 1920, grievously disappointed all nationalist-minded Arabs. Instead of creating the independent Arab state promised by McMahon, the Conference decided to parcel out the non-Turkish parts of the Ottoman Empire into "Mandates" under the guidance and control of the Western Powers. Syria and Lebanon were assigned as Mandates to Britain's wartime ally France, while Palestine (including Transjordan) and Iraq became Mandates of Great Britain. On July 1, 1920, Sir Herbert Samuel was appointed as the first British High Commissioner of Palestine. Arabs in Syria and Palestine bitterly denounced the postwar settlement, severely criticizing Faisal for meekly accepting it. Before 1920, Arab nationalism had been anti-Turkish and pro-British; after 1920, it would become strongly anti-British. A new enemy had also appeared on the scene, against which all Arabs would unite: Zionism.

The British soon made Iraq an independent Emirate under Faisal and made Transjordan an autonomous state under Faisal's brother, Abdullah. In Palestine itself, however, self-government was completely impracticable. Throughout the thirty years of the British Mandate, the political goals of the Zionists and the Palestinian Arabs would remain completely irreconcilable. The Palestinian Arabs were opposed to the Balfour Declaration from the very beginning of the Mandate. They demanded the immediate introduction of a majority-rule government, which the Arabs (then ninety percent of the population) would have been able to dominate. In addition, they urged the British government to put strict limits on further Jewish immigration.

The Zionist leadership, on the other hand, demanded the strict fulfillment of the promises implicit in the Balfour Declaration. They wanted Palestine to be the national home for the Jewish people, to which Jews from all over the world would be free to immigrate. They did not want Palestine to be merely another state ruled by a sovereign non-Jewish majority. To protect what they saw as the special rights of world Jewry in Palestine, the Zionists relied, until 1929, on the benevolent protection of Great Britain.

As early as 1921, there had been anti-Jewish rioting in Palestine; for eight years thereafter, however, a period of calm settled over the land. The rate of Jewish immigration slowed down, especially after a severe eco-nomic slump hit Palestine in 1927, and the Arabs were temporarily lulled into thinking that the Zionist experiment would die a natural death. After 1928, however, the situation once again began to grow tense, as the rate of Jewish immigration increased.

In the hot summer of 1929, a seemingly trivial quarrel over the Wailing Wall in Jerusalem brought the eight-year period of calm to a sudden end. The city of Jerusalem was divided into a new city, built by the immigrants who came after 1905, and the old walled city. Within the walled city there existed the "Wailing Wall," a site which was sacred to both Jews and Muslims. Among religious Jews, the Wailing Wall is revered as the last remnant of the long-buried Temple of Jerusalem, built by King Solomon in 900 B.C. and destroyed by the Romans in the first century A.D. The Jews of Jerusalem worship there on the Sabbath. Among the Muslims, the Wall is venerated as the site where the prophet Mohammed (who founded the Islamic religion in the seventh century) tethered his horse while he ascended to Heaven to appear before Allah (God). In addition, the Wailing Wall adjoins one famous Muslim mosque, the Dome of the Rock, and stands close to another, Al-Aqsa. During the 1920's much effort and expense had been borne by Palestinian Arabs in restoring these shrines.

Throughout 1928 and 1929, it was widely rumored among Palestinian Arabs that the Jews of Jerusalem were planning to rebuild their ancient Temple by destroying the Dome of the Rock and Al-Aqsa. These rumors appear to have been deliberately circulated by Hajj Amin al-Husayni, the Grand Mufti of Jerusalem, and chief leader of the Palestinian Arabs during the period of the British mandate. Hajj Amin al-Husayni, the scion of an old Jerusalem Arab family, had been appointed Grand Mufti by the British High Commissioner in Palestine, Sir Herbert Samuel, in May, 1921. By accepting this post, Hajj Amin al-Husayni became the religious leader of the Palestinian Arabs. Samuel had known this man to have a reputation as a nationalist extremist, but he had hoped that the burden of responsibility would make the young Arab more moderate.

Samuel was wrong. The new Grand Mufti began to feed his flock a potent mixture of Islamic fundamentalism and fanatic Arab nationalism. By the end of the 1920's, the Grand Mufti had become the living symbol of Palestinian Arab resistance to the encroachments of Zionism. Unfortunately for them, the religious Jews of Jerusalem, by their own actions, provided grist for the Mufti's propaganda mill. Because the area in front of the Wailing Wall was controlled by a Muslim religious endowment, Jews had never been permitted to erect permanent structures of worship there. In September, 1928, however, Jewish worshipers insisted on installing both chairs and a partition screen (for separating male and female worshipers) at their Yom Kippur service in front of the Wall. When a British police officer removed the screen, they protested loudly.

In the months that followed, the Jews launched a propaganda campaign demanding additional rights at the Wall, while the Muslims stubbornly refused to make the slightest concession. To the Muslims it seemed that the Jews were trying to change unilaterally, and in their own favor, the rules governing the Holy Sites which had been inherited from the days of the Ottoman Empire. Only a spark was needed to start the violence. On August 15, 1929, a band of militantly Zionist youths from Tel Aviv (a purely Jewish coastal city) marched toward the Wailing Wall, where they sang the Zionist anthem (the Hatikvah) and listened to speakers proclaiming that the Wall belonged to the Jews. The next day, an Arab counterdemonstration took place. On August 17, 1929, a teenage Jewish youth of Jerusalem, who was trying to retrieve a football lost during a soccer game, was stabbed to death by a young Arab. On Friday, August 23, large numbers of Muslim villagers streamed into the city of Jerusalem armed with clubs. Soon they were attacking and killing Jews throughout the city.

On August 24, the contagion of violence spread to the little town of Hebron, south of Jerusalem. Out of the Jewish community of seven hundred, sixty Jews, including children, were slaughtered by armed bands of Arabs. On August 29, Arab rioters in the northern town of Safed murdered twenty Jews, including children, and destroyed more than a hundred houses.

The forces of order were incapable of coping with this unrest. In an economy move the previous year, the British Government had sharply reduced the number of British troops stationed in Palestine; the poorly armed police, many of whom were

Arabs sympathetic with the rioters, were in no position to stop the bloodshed. To suppress the rioting, the Mandatory Administration, now under High Commission Field Marshal Lord Plumer, had to call in British troops from Malta (a British colony) and Egypt (a British protectorate). By the end of August, order had finally been restored. In the course of the riots, 116 Arabs had been killed and 232 wounded, mostly by the forces of order. The Arabs killed 133 Jews and wounded 339. Ironically, many of the Jewish victims (in Hebron, for example) had been members of the long-established Arabic-speaking Sephardic community. Until 1929, these Sephardic Jews had by no means shared in the enthusiastic Zionism of the more recent Eastern European immigrants.

The shock of the 1929 riots aroused bitter disputes among the Zionists over the sorry state of Jewish self-defense in Palestine. In the 1920's most of the Zionists had had pacifist leanings. Vladimir Jabotinsky, (1880-1940), the maverick leader of the "Revisionist" group, was the first Zionist to stress repeatedly the need for a strong Jewish military force in Palestine. The decade of the 1930's, however, saw a marked strengthening of the discipline and effectiveness of the Jewish militia, the Haganah. This militia, whose first units had been organized by Zionist agricultural colonies in the early 1920's, would become the nucleus of the future Israeli Army.

The 1929 riots provoked the first serious rift in the hitherto close relationship between the British Government and the Zionist movement.

After two British Commissions had been sent to investigate the riots, the British Colonial Secretary, Sidney Webb, known as Lord Passfield, issued, on October 21, 1930, a White Paper calling for sharp limitations on further Jewish immigration to Palestine. Chaim Weizmann, after hurriedly consulting with British Prime Minister Sir Ramsay MacDonald, persuaded him to agree not to implement the Colonial Secretary's proposals.

By the late 1930's, however, Weizmann's diplomacy was no longer so effective. By then, British officials had come to think of the Balfour Declaration not as a solemn promise but as an unwelcome burden. After the Arabs revolted in 1936, the British Cabinet decided to make concessions to them. In May, 1939, the Government issued another White Paper, sharply curtailing further Jewish immigration to Palestine. Despite protests from the Zionists, this White Paper was enforced.

Between 1933 and the issuance of the White Paper in 1939, a new wave of Jewish immigrants had come to Palestine from Europe. These Jews were frightened by the ever-growing power of the anti-Semitic Dictator of Germany, Adolf Hitler. Barred from most countries of the world by immigration restrictions, they had been forced to seek refuge in the British Mandate. This massive flight from Hitlerism raised the proportion of Jews in the Palestinian population from ten percent in 1919 to thirty percent in 1939. Even after the Allies (Great Britain, the United States, U.S.S.R.) had defeated Hitler in 1945, the European Jews still attempted to reach Palestine.

The British Government had tried to be fair to both the Arabs and the Zionists and had won the hatred of both sides. In 1947, the frustrated British handed over the whole problem of Palestine to the newly formed United Nations Organization. The United Nations, in November of the same year, decreed the partition of Palestine into two States, one Arab and one Jewish. The Arab States in the United Nations refused to accept this solution.

The 1929 riots had marked a milestone on the road toward greater solidarity between the Muslim Arabs of Palestine and those of other States. The campaign to save the Jerusalem mosques from supposed Zionist encroachments had, by 1929, been sympathetically received far beyond the borders of the Mandate. In December, 1931, a pan-Muslim conference meeting in Jerusalem with representatives from twenty-two countries had adopted a resolution warning against the dangers of Zionism. By March, 1945, the growth of pan-Arab solidarity had culminated in the formation of the League of Arab States.

When the State of Israel declared its independence on May 15, 1948, it was surrounded by a ring of hostile Arab states. These states now tried to snuff out the life of the newborn Jewish State by force of arms; but they failed. In March, 1949, they were forced to sign an armistice, though they never recognized the right of Israel to exist.

Thus, the final legacy of the Arab riots of 1929 has been a seemingly endless cycle of wars between the State of Israel, representing the old Zionist ideal, and the surrounding states of the Arab world determined to champion the cause of Arab Palestine.

## Pertinent Literature

Porath, Yehoshuah. *The Emergence of the Palestinian-Arab National Movement 1918-1929*. London: Frank Cass and Company, 1974.

In this book, Porath traces the development of anti-Zionist nationalism among the Arabs of Palestine from the beginnings of the British Mandate to the riots of 1929. Though the author is an Israeli, a professor at Hebrew University in Jerusalem, his account is nonetheless objective and scholarly. There is no hint of an anti-Arab bias.

In the introduction, Porath explains how Palestine as a whole, and the Jerusalem region in particular, came to be seen as the "Holy Land" by Muslims as well as by Christians and Jews. He sees the period of the Muslim struggle against the Crusaders, in the twelfth century, as the time when Palestine finally achieved this sacred status. The author has to explain all this in order to show precisely why Muslim Arabs became so upset by Jewish worship innovations at the Wailing Wall in August of 1929. In his introduction, Porath also examines the earliest beginnings of Arab-Jewish animosity. He shows that even during the Ottoman period, before 1914, there had been evidence of Palestinian hostility to the new Zionist immigration.

In Chapters One through Six, Porath shows how, after 1918, the Palestinian Arabs developed organizational forms for their struggle against Zionism. In Chapter Four he traces "The Emergence of Al-Hajj Amin al-Husayni," the Grand Mufti of Jerusalem. In Chapters Five and Six, the conflict between the faction led by Amin al-Husayni and the one led by Ragheb Bey Nashashibi is explained. The eighth and final chapter covers "the organizational and social aspects of the development of the movement."

Chapter Two, "From 'Southern Syria' to Palestine," deals at length with the problem of the relationship between Palestinian Arab nationalism and the wider concept of "Pan-Arab" nationalism. In 1918-1920, the Palestinian Arabs supported the Hashemite prince Faisal, who wished to set up an independent Kingdom of Greater Syria which would include Palestine. In 1920, however, the French Army occupied the Syrian Mandate assigned to her by the Allied Powers, bombarded Damascus, and put an end to all dreams of a Kingdom of Greater Syria. It soon became clear, moreover, that the Hashemite prince had attempted to negotiate with the Zionists in an attempt to resolve Arab-Jewish differences. Angry at this apparent betrayal of their interests, the Palestinian Arabs reverted, for a time, to a narrower and purely Palestinian nationalism based on uncompromising opposition to Zionism.

In the seventh chapter Porath gives a careful account of the immediate background of the riots of August, 1929. According to him, these riots did not represent a turning point in the history of relations between the Zionists and the British Mandatory Administration. The British had favored the Zionists in the early, vulnerable stages of the development of the new Jewish settlement (Yishuv), when it had seemed that one financial disaster would be enough to kill it. (Financial disaster almost did kill it in 1927.) The 1929 riots did not make British policy more favorable to the Arabs; only the Arab rebellion of 1936 was able to do that.

The real significance of the 1929 riots, Porath argues, was in its polarization of Jews and Arabs. By stirring up religious antagonism over the Jews' worship at the Wailing Wall, the Grand Mufti had been able to convert anti-Zionism into a popular cause among the Arab Muslim masses of Palestine. By appealing to the religious feelings of Muslims abroad, the Grand Mufti had also been able to win support for the Palestinian cause in Arab countries which had hitherto been indifferent to it.

The major sources of Porath's work are the British Archives, on the one hand, and intelligence reports submitted to the political department of the Zionist organization in Palestine (the Jewish Agency), on the other. He also uses published sources in Hebrew and Arabic. The book contains several numerical tables and an excellent bibliography. The footnotes, unfortunately, are placed at the back of the book. There are no maps, nor are there any photographs of the personalities involved in the events of 1918-1929.

Laqueur, Walter Ze'ev. *A History of Zionism*. New York: Holt, Rinehart and Winston, 1972.

Walter Laqueur is a well-known and prolific historian who has, in the past two decades, concerned himself chiefly with the history of ideas. In this lengthy six-hundred-page work, Laqueur traces the idea of Zionism from its origins in nineteenth century Europe to the founding of the State of Israel in May of 1948.

In the early chapters, Laqueur explains how unlikely and impractical the idea of a Jewish return to Palestine seemed in nineteenth century Western Europe. He also shows how the idea of Zionism first began to gain widespread support among the oppressed and poverty-stricken Jews of Eastern Europe, who had not been able to be assimilated as easily as had their Western cousins. It was from Eastern Europe that most of the early Zionist immigrants to Palestine came.

In Chapter Six, Laqueur describes how the Eastern European intellectual heritage of Marxist Socialism influenced the development of the Zionist experiment in Palestine. Collective farming became widespread among these new immigrants, most of whom had had almost no previous experience in agriculture. "Labor Zionism" became the dominant political tendency among these new immigrants.

Chapters Five and Eight present an in-depth analysis of the origins and consequences of the Arab riots of August, 1929. Laqueur tries to explain the puzzle of the Zionists' seem-ing obliviousness, up to 1929, to the problem of Palestinian Arab opposition to Zionism. Zionists, he argues, did not at first clearly understand that a Jewish National Home in Palestine needed a Jewish State and a Jewish Army if it were to survive; only a few Zionists, such as the "revisionist" Vladimir Jabotinsky, understood this truth. Instead, most Zionists simply relied on the British Mandate to protect their experiment; they at first labored under the delusion that Palestinian Arab nationalism was solely the property of a minority of wealthy Arab landowners, and that working-class cooperation could bridge the gap between Arab and Jew. It took the shock of the 1929 riots to awaken the Zionists from these illusions.

In the final chapters (Nine through Eleven), Laqueur traces the advent of Hitler, who, by impelling masses of European Jews to seek refuge in the Holy Land, hastened the final decision of the Zionists to seek an independent State of Israel.

Laqueur's work is based on published sources in English, German, Russian, Yiddish, and Hebrew, and it contains rare photographs of the leading personalities of the Zionist movement. There are six maps, a glossary of foreign-language terms likely to be unfamiliar to the reader, and an extensive bibliography listing the sources used for each chapter, as well as footnotes in the text itself.
— *P.D.M.*

## Additional Recommended Reading

Allen, Richard. *Imperialism and Nationalism in the Fertile Crescent: Sources and Prospects of the Arab-Israeli Conflict*. New York: Oxford University Press, 1974. A good general account, designed for the nonspecialist reader, of the origins of the Arab-Jewish hostility which first burst into violence in 1929.

Hyamson, Albert Montefiore. *Palestine Under the Mandate*. London: Methuen, 1950. A tracing of the lost opportunities for Arab-Jewish understanding during the years of the Mandate, written by a British-Jewish scholar who served in the Palestine Mandatory Administration.

Marlowe, John. *The Seat of Pilate*. London: Cresset Press, 1959. An impartial history of the British Mandate by a long-time British expert on the Near East.

Sykes, Christopher. *Crossroads to Israel*. New York: The World Publishing Company, 1965. A vividly written account of the Mandate years, somewhat slanted on the side of the British Administration and the Zionists.

Rose, Norman. *The Gentile Zionists*. London: Frank Cass and Company, 1973. A scholarly account of the deterioration of relations between the British Government and the Zionist movement during the years from the Arab Riots of 1929 to the British White Paper of 1939.

Friedman, Isaiah. *The Question of Palestine, 1914-1918: British-Jewish-Arab Relations*. London: Routledge and Kegan Paul, 1973. Though this account of the origins of the Balfour Declaration is scholarly and well-researched, the author's belief that the McMahon Letter excluded Palestine from the promised Arab state is not shared by all scholars.

Quandt, William B., Fuad Jabber and Ann Mosely Lesch. *The Politics of Palestinian Nationalism*. Berkeley: University of California Press, 1973. Contains an essay by Lesch on "The Palestinian Arab Nationalist Movement under the Mandate" which stresses the total inability of the Palestinian Arabs to achieve any one of their major political goals.

Weizmann, Chaim. *Trial and Error: The Autobiography of Chaim Weizmann*. New York: Harper, 1949. A revealing autobiography of the man who was the leading personality of the world Zionist movement during the 1920's.

# ANTITOTALITARIAN LITERATURE OF THE 1930'S AND EARLY 1940'S

*Type of event:* Literary: misery of dictatorial oppressions upon human life is vividly depicted in works of literature
*Time:* 1930-1944
*Locale:* Europe and the United States

*Principal personages:*

LION FEUCHTWANGER (1884-1958), a German author who became obsessed with the violence of pre-World War II Europe and is best remembered for the work *The Oppermanns* (1934)

ROY CORYTON HUTCHINSON (1907-    ), a London-born author who focused his attention upon prewar Germany in his best book *The Fire and the Wood* (1940)

ALDOUS HUXLEY (1894-1963), a British novelist who, in *Brave New World* (1932), equates totalitarian "happiness" with spiritual sterility

IGNAZIO SILONE (1900-1978), Nobel Prize-winning Italian author who focused on both capitalism and Fascism in such works as *Bread and Wine* (1936) and *The Seed Beneath the Snow* (1940)

UPTON BEALL SINCLAIR (1878-1968), an American author best known for his muckraking novel *The Jungle* (1906)

ARTHUR KOESTLER (1905-    ), a Hungarian-born author who depicted the horrors of Joseph Stalin's Russia in his novel *Darkness at Noon* (1940)

ANDRÉ MALRAUX (1901-1976), a French author who explored the topic of life's meaninglessness in Western society in such works as *Man's Fate* (1933) and *Days of Wrath* (1936)

ERNEST HEMINGWAY (1899-1961), an American Nobel Prize winner whose *For Whom the Bell Tolls* (1940) conveys the special contempt in which the author held all things Fascist

THOMAS WOLFE (1900-1938), an American author who deals with the oppressiveness of the Nazi state in prewar Berlin in his novel *You Can't Go Home Again* (1940)

## Summary of Event

The period following World War I witnessed the emergence in Russia, Italy, and Germany of totalitarian dictatorships, each of which was dedicated to the suppression of human freedom in the name of some future holistic society. Whether Communism in Soviet Russia under Joseph Stalin, Fascism in Italy under Benito Mussolini, or worst of all, National

241

Socialism in Germany under Adolf Hitler (and later Francisco Franco's Fascist regime in Spain), all these authoritarian regimes brutalized not only the people in their own countries but those in neighboring lands as well. Among the first to perceive and speak out against the antiintellectualism, racial and class hatreds, and mindless jingoism that typified these police states during the 1930's were a number of distinguished writers representing various countries and viewpoints.

Many writers in this period, perhaps because of their leftist orientation, ignored the abuses of Stalinism. A major exception to this rule was the Anglo-Hungarian writer Arthur Koestler, who, in his *Darkness at Noon* (1940), vividly portrayed the inhuman suffering of prisoners in Stalinist Russia. This novel, one of the century's finest antitotalitarian pieces of literature, describes the misery of Rubashov, ironically a dedicated Communist, from his imprisonment and trial to his confrontation with death.

Foremost in the condemnation of Italian Fascism is Ignazio Silone, especially in his novels *Fontamara* (1934), *Bread and Wine* (1936), and *The Seed Beneath the Snow* (1940). Silone's general subject in each of these novels is the poverty-stricken peasants, their conflict with their wealthy landlords, and their consequent need to assert themselves politically. He elucidates his subject by describing those idealists—the heroes of socialism—who, at great peril to themselves, attempt to help the peasants.

Among those writers who attacked Nazism were native Germans Lion Feuchtwanger, author of *The Oppermanns* (1934) and Thomas Mann, creator of *Mario and the Magician* (1930). Non-Germans who were critical of Hitlerism included Roy Coryton Hutchinson, the Englishman who wrote *The Fire and the Wood* (1940), French theorist André Malraux in his *Days of Wrath* (1935), and Americans Thomas Wolfe and Upton Sinclair, the former in *You Can't Go Home Again* (1940) and the latter in the middle volumes of his monumental "Lanny Budd" series (1940-1949). Two other sharp thrusts at the totalitarian upsurge of the times were Aldous Huxley's *Brave New World* (1932) and Ernest Hemingway's *For Whom the Bell Tolls* (1940).

Lion Feuchtwanger is best recalled as the author of one of the more hard-hitting anti-Nazi novels of the 1930's, *The Oppermanns* (1934), the saga of a Jewish family living in the interwar period when Fascism was only starting to develop in Berlin. Feuchtwanger alarms the reader with nightmarish descriptions of a racist, amoral Germany. Gradually, it becomes apparent that neighbors and former friends are conspiring against the accomplished Oppermanns and that their bucolic life will be rent asunder by Hitler's street bullies and police. The violent atmosphere inevitably leads to a hailstorm of blows against Jews—and some Oppermanns die as a result. Those who do not die find that their lives are irreparably altered and that they must see themselves as Jews rather than as Germans.

Thomas Mann, one of Germany's best-known novelists and a Nobel Prize winner, obliquely deals with the rise of Fascism in his allegorical and symbolic novella, *Mario and the Magician*, an attack upon Hitler-era xenophobia. In *The Fire and the Wood* by Roy C. Hutchinson, English writer and professional soldier, Nazi Germany's horrors are as vividly presented as they are in *The Oppermanns*. Hutchinson demonstrates how a talented young Jewish person—in this case, a researcher and physician—can be ruined by a Fascist government. André Malraux's *Days of Wrath* is a tribute to a Communist hero of artistic sensibility (simply referred to as Kassner) whose dedication to his cause lands him in a German concentration camp. Malraux's ability to depict tellingly Fascist degradation of the spirit is remarkable.

In the "Lanny Budd" novels *Dragon's Teeth* (1942), *Wide Is the Gate* (1943), and *Presidential Agent* (1944) by Upton Sinclair (perhaps best known for *The Jungle* [1906], a novel about Chicago slaughterhouse conditions) readers are provided with a high-minded indictment of Nazi barbarism set in the interwar period. In these novels, the reader senses the tremors that were going through the European psyche during this troubled time. Equally effective is the section of Thomas Wolfe's *You Can't Go Home Again* dealing with Southern American novelist George Webber's sojourn in his beloved Germany during which he is transfixed by the disintegration of an entire nation. Webber's confusion about and sadness over Germany's turn toward Fascism is convincingly portrayed. Unlike

Hemingway's tender antiwar love story, *A Farewell to Arms*, *For Whom the Bell Tolls* celebrates the towering determination of free men to resist to the death the shackles Franco's Fascism would place upon them. Huxley's *Brave New World* presents a veiled warning against surrendering personal freedom to the totalitarian monolith, regardless of how attractive the *soma* life-style may be made to seem.

Though many of the best antitotalitarian novels were written in the interwar period, it would be a mistake to assume that the antitotalitarian strain in literature died out after the early 1940's, for there are many contemporary writers following the same path as Feuchtwanger, Mann, Silone, Huxley, Hutchinson, Wolfe, Hemingway, Sinclair, and Koestler. For instance, Germany's prolific Günter Grass has written several novels about the moral cancer of Nazism, as has his fellow countryman, Heinrich Böll. In America, both Kurt Vonnegut, Jr., and Thomas Pynchon have dealt with Nazi Germany; moreover, Russian exile Alexander Solzhenitsyn, much of whose work has been the depiction of Russian life, is currently writing essays and fiction at his American retreat in Vermont.

Thus, if the twentieth century has been a time of unprecedented butchery and repression, it has also been a time when gifted individuals have spoken out in defense of freedom in their novels. All free people owe much to the antitotalitarian writers of Europe and America.

## Pertinent Literature

Feuchtwanger, Lion. *The Oppermanns*. New York: The Viking Press, 1934.

In *The Oppermanns*, Lion Feuchtwanger takes as his foreword a quotation from the German poet Goethe: "There is nothing the rabble fear more than Intelligence. If they understood what is truly terrifying, they would fear ignorance." Nonetheless, *The Oppermanns* is not merely a pseudosociological study of mob psychology but rather an attempt to answer the one question most often posed to those who knew Nazi Germany: namely, "Why did things get so out of hand in a country respected for its high level of civilization?"

The author had fellow Germans in mind when he wrote *The Oppermanns*, for he repeatedly drives home the notion that the members of the Oppermann family are not cultural "aliens," as the mob would believe, but instead, true Germans in every sense of the word. In the family there are decorated war heroes who served Germany passionately, as well as humanists, scholars, and businessmen, all of whom evinced a sincere love of country. Nevertheless, despite their patriotism and accomplishments, the Oppermanns are accused by their fellow countrymen of being unassimilatable aliens—traitors.

One of the main characters, Martin Oppermann, a Berlin businessman, loses his community standing and sense of personal worth, and finally his nationality, because he is Jewish. His losses accrue gradually as he finds himself slowly sucked into the vortex of Nazi terror and oppression.

To Feuchtwanger, Nazism is a kind of moral contagion that takes hold of a resentful Germany. Nazism is a creeping, insidious thing, manifested in such scenes as Martin Oppermann being taunted in the street by Brown Shirts; the bright student Berthold Oppermann being pushed to despair and then suicide by a sadistic Nazi schoolmaster; and the songs of race hatred reverberating in the German night.

In one of the novel's pivotal episodes, Martin Oppermann, deeply envied by a gentile competitor in the furniture business, Heinrich Wels, is forced to sell his profitable company to Wels simply because the State does not believe Jews fit to be in charge of any operation. With teeth clenched, Oppermann endures excruciating humiliation in Wels's outer office, as client after client sees Wels before him.

*The Oppermanns*, then, is a believable tale of terror, harrowing in its accurate attention to detail. In it one discovers civilization gone mad, a once vital country turned upside down. As a study of the effects that a truly totalitarian state has upon its subjects, the novel has few rivals, and it is unfortunate that it is seldom read today.

Wolfe, Thomas. *You Can't Go Home Again*. New York: Harper & Row Publishers, 1940.

*You Can't Go Home Again*, another of Thomas Wolfe's sprawling creations having as a protagonist a young Southerner in search of his place in time and the world, is in part about Nazi Germany in the prewar period when the horrible features of Hitler's Fascist state were beginning to be noticed by alert foreign observers like the novelist George Webber.

In Book Six, Webber, deciding to return to a fondly recollected Germany, does so only to regret almost immediately his decision. The last time Webber had seen Germany, in the 1920's, he ended his stay in a hospital after having been attacked in a wild beer hall melee of a vaguely political nature. He failed to see in this brawl a portent of things to come.

Time and again, Webber's German friends reassure him about Germany, telling him that "outside agitators" alone are to blame for the violence in the streets. For a time, he is able to believe such explanations and exult in the beauty of Germany's lakes and woodlands. Also, the fact that his novels are still widely read by Germans reassures him, though books by Germans have already been banned.

Because Webber arrives in Germany during the summer of 1936 when the Olympic Games are being staged, he is able to witness the military parades under swastika banners. Webber watches these parades until Chancellor Hitler finally swings into view, saluting in Roman fashion, and the crowd thunders its approval, much to Webber's dismay.

Eventually, of course, it dawns upon Webber that his Germany is teetering on the brink of internal collapse and outward aggression and that he must leave the country to its own madness. Heartsick and despondent over his adopted country's decline, Webber makes his departure, which itself is marred by further evidence of German repression and police state tactics. Like Sir Edward Grey prior to the outbreak of the first world conflict, Webber too sees the lights in his own era going off all over Europe. — *J.D.R.*

### Additional Recommended Reading

Sender, Ramón José. *Seven Red Sundays*. Translated by Sir Peter Chalmers Mitchell. New York: Liveright, 1936. A novel set in revolutionary Madrid against an unsuccessful uprising of Communists, anarchists, and syndicalists.

Jameson, Storm. *In the Second Year*. New York: The Macmillan Company, 1936. A futuristic novel in which a young intellectual emigrates to Norway after returning to a Fascist England of concentration camps, murdered Jews, and a starving population.

Wylie, I. A. R. *To the Vanquished*. Garden City, N.Y.: Doubleday & Company, 1934. The horrors of Hitlerism in Germany exposed through the love story of Wolf von Selteneck, a storm trooper, and Franzle Roth, daughter of a high-minded liberal.

Oppenheim, Edward Phillips. *Last Train Out*. Boston: Little, Brown and Company, 1940. Leopold Benjamin, Viennese philanthropist, escapes Austria on the last train out before the Nazi occupation.

# ATOMIC RESEARCH

*Type of event:* Scientific: circumstances of the dawning of the age of atomic energy
*Time:* 1930-1945
*Locale:* Europe, the United States, and Japan

*Principal personages:*
ERNEST RUTHERFORD (1871-1937), a New Zealand physicist who first speculated on the possible existence of the neutron
JAMES CHADWICK (1891-1974), an English physicist who demonstrated the existence of the neutron
OTTO HAHN (1879-1968), a German physical chemist and atomic experimentalist
LISE MEITNER (1878-1968), a refugee Austrian mathematical physicist who calculated that Hahn had split the uranium atom
ENRICO FERMI (1901-1954), a refugee Italian physicist who saw the possibility of a chain reaction and obtained it in the first atomic pile
NIELS BOHR (1885-1962), a Danish physicist who aided American scientists in 1939 in developing a theory of nuclear fission

## Summary of Event

Between 1930 and 1945, the basic research tradition of atomic physics gave birth unexpectedly to atomic energy technology, the atomic pile, and the atom bomb. From the perspective of theoretical physics research these were incidental applied science "spin-offs," but from the perspective of international power politics dominated by World War II and its aftermath, they dramatically redistributed the balance of world power in favor of the United States.

Two political prerequisites to these developments were the drive for military conquest by Germany and Japan, which provoked World War II, and the oppressive racist policy of Nazi Germany that drove creative European physicists and mathematicians into exile and flight to the United States, where their activities contributed essentially to wartime atomic research. But in 1930 none of these developments was foreseen, least of all by the atomic researchers, who were exploring the little-known nucleus of the atom by shifting back and forth between experimental investigations and abstract mathematical models that would explain what the experiments were discovering. By 1930, physicists understood that atoms possessed protons and electrons and that these alone did not account for all the mass of any of the ninety-one elements heavier than hydrogen. They also had understood since 1911 that atoms of the same element could differ physically in mass, presenting different isotopes of the same element. The most interesting atoms were among the heaviest, such as uranium, radium, and polonium. While Ernest Rutherford in his famous Bakerian Lecture of 1920 had speculated that a third major component of the atom might be an electrically neutral particle composed perhaps of a proton and an electron whose opposite charges would cancel each other, no experimental work gave credence to this idea until James Chadwick in 1932 proposed the "neutron" to explain radioactive data turned up in 1930 by Walter Bothe and H. Becker in Germany and other data obtained in 1932 by Irène Curie and Frédéric Joliot in Paris.

In the meantime, other relevant but independent lines of research were being followed. The behavior of isotopes and the riddle of the internal structure of their atoms posed intriguing problems, especially where radioactive elements were concerned. After 1910-1914, cosmic rays were under study, and their high energy suggested that collision with an atomic nucleus might produce revealing results. In 1932, Carl Anderson in the United States theorized, from studying cloud chamber photographs of cosmic ray impacts, that there existed another nuclear particle equal to the tiny electron in weight but carrying an opposite charge, the positron. This particle enabled Curie and Joliot in January, 1934, to explain their discovery that a nonradioactive element, such as aluminum, could be made temporarily radioactive by exposing it to a bombardment of helium nuclei (alpha particles) spontaneously emitted by polonium; the aluminum then emitted positrons.

The theoretical structure of the atom was growing more complex.

The following April, Enrico Fermi in Rome reported that he too had radioactivated a number of other elements; but he had bombarded them with neutrons. It was possible to produce artificial isotopes and elements heavier than uranium. Meanwhile, still another line of inquiry was being followed in which protons (hydrogen nuclei) accelerated in powerful electromagnetic fields would be used as missiles to smash heavier atoms. Efforts in England and the United States culminated in the cyclotron, developed by Ernest O. Lawrence. By 1939, cyclotron atom smashers were being built in Europe, Japan, Russia, and the United States.

All of these diverse efforts were devoted to exploring the internal structure of the atom and identifying the growing number of components of the nucleus. Thus, Fermi in 1934 found that slow neutrons could penetrate the heaviest element, uranium, and he, Curie, and others speculated that slow-traveling neutrons might be captured by the uranium nucleus, transforming it into a new synthetic isotope or element heavier than any known before, and also radioactive.

Chemical analysis was another indispensable tool in identifying, separating, and analyzing the experimental radioactive materials; it became an established practice to use barium as a carrier of neutron-bombarded uranium in order to accomplish some of these analyses. Otto Hahn and Fritz Strassmann reported from Nazi Germany in January, 1939, that they had produced what they thought was an isotope of radioactive radium, except that it also confusingly had the chemical characteristics of the nonradioactive middle weight element, barium. Lise Meitner, an Austrian mathematician who had once worked with them but was now a refugee in Sweden, speculated with her nephew Otto Frisch that the addition of a neutron to uranium might sometimes cause the uranium nucleus to fracture into two halves, two middle weight elements (such as barium), instead of transforming into a neighboring heavy element or isotope.

Thus in January, 1939, the concept of "atomic fission" was born. It was spread abroad, importantly, by Niels Bohr, the Danish physicist, on a visit to Washington, D.C., that month. Subsequent confirming experiments and calculations in Europe and America led researchers to a further speculation: the fission of a uranium atom should liberate an incredible burst of energy along with the release of two or more neutrons which could be acquired by adjacent atoms, causing *them* to split and release more neutrons and energy—the start of a self-propagating chain reaction. Fermi, now a refugee in the United States, subsequently led the wartime technological project that by December, 1942, had built at the University of Chicago the first atomic pile. It proved capable of a controlled chain reaction, briefly releasing energy in the available form of heat and demonstrating the practicality of the process. Its success opened the way to techniques for fashioning the first atomic bomb.

The political action required to organize the bomb-building technology was instigated in the United States by apprehensive refugee scientists in 1939, but serious American response to their pleas came only after the Japanese attack on Pearl Harbor in December, 1941. The top secret Army "Manhattan Project" was formed to conduct a two-billion-dollar program to develop the atomic bomb. The first "explosive device" was tested successfully in July, 1945, at Alamogordo, New Mexico. It was followed by the dropping of two bombs on Japan in August, while Japan was considering a negotiated surrender. The Hiroshima and Nagasaki bombs precipitated unconditional surrender.

So ended the utterly unpremeditated historical sequence of a half century of atomic research that had begun in 1896 when Henri Becquerel discovered radioactivity. Appreciation of the role of the neutron had begun to emerge early in the 1930's. Finally, five years of intensive technological effort in the United States during World War II had opportunistically applied the basic research knowledge won during the preceding forty-five years, with the result that atomic energy was no longer the abstract mathematical concept first perceived by Albert Einstein in his 1905 equation, $E = mc^2$. Without intending to, fundamental scientific research had given mankind its first "Doomsday weapon" while ushering in the era of atomic energy. As the American physicist who led the Manhattan Project, J. Robert Oppenheimer, pointed out, despite their political innocence as they pursued their eager researches, "the physicists have known sin." The political and social consequences set in motion by their apolitical atomic research activities remain to be historically worked out in the decades to follow.

## Pertinent Literature

Heisenberg, Werner. *Physics and Beyond: Encounters and Conversations*. Edited by Ruth N. Anshen. Translated by Arnold J. Pomerans. New York: Harper & Row Publishers, 1971.

Volume 42 in the "World Perspectives" series, this small book of memoirs and platonic reconstructions by one of the most famous of twentieth century physicists takes the reader swiftly into the intellectual world in which creative atomic research was carried on; and it does so without requiring any prior technical understanding on the part of the reader. One is given an authentic feeling for how the experts were operating on the frontier of atomic knowledge in their specialty, and of how the scientific life of the mind was being carried on by these creative physicists.

Werner Heisenberg is known for his Indeterminacy (or Uncertainty) Principle, which asserts (in nontechnical, hence superficial, terms) that the act of observing such phenomena as nuclear particle behavior requires the observer to interfere with and alter that behavior; consequently, some phenomena and processes of nature we can never hope to experience or appraise or understand in their purely natural state. This circumstance imposed a practical and philosophical limitation upon the extent and depth of scientific knowledge, and Heisenberg clearly saw it as a predicament that the atomic physicists simply would have to live with, stopping well short of the ultimate ideal goal of apprehending nature as it really is.

In this book, whether he is reconstructing a speculative discussion with Rutherford and Bohr (Chapter 13) or recalling the pure scientist's predicament in the middle of the awful distractions of war (Chapter 14) or reflecting upon the moral and social responsibilities suddenly thrust upon the physicists and chemists by their own terrible achievement of unleashing the energy of the atom (Chapter 16), Heisenberg gives the reader an authentic insider's view of a technical realm that most outsiders have long since concluded was accessible only to the initiated few. While the reader does not learn precisely what the scientists did in technical detail, he learns impressionistically how they proceeded, with the result that some of the scientific circumstances of the dawn of the atomic age assume approachable human proportions for the layman.

The European way of creative science is not the American way, Heisenberg's reminiscences remind the reader. American achievements in atomic energy are seen to emerge as the consequence of a meld of European theoretical genius with American pragmatic talent to accomplish the very difficult, costly, and complex task of tapping the energy of the atom.

# Atomic Research

Smyth, Henry DeWolf. *Atomic Energy for Military Purposes: The Official Report of the Development of the Atomic Bomb Under the Auspices of the United States Government, 1940-1945*. Princeton, N.J.: Princeton University Press, 1945.

In its first form this report was issued to press and radio reporters on August 12, 1945, six days after the first atom bomb was dropped on Hiroshima, Japan. This edition is a later version of the historic document released to the public by the United States Government to explain how the awesome weapon had been brought into being. As Major-General Leslie R. Groves, chief of the "Manhattan Project" that developed the bomb, explains in a foreword, no military secrets or appropriate technical details are divulged. Consequently no special technical background is required of the reader.

The "Smyth Report," as it came to be called, is a hybrid; it is an administrative and technical history of the federal government's five-year enterprise to convert the theoretical understanding of atomic fission to practical use as a strategic weapon. Smyth, a physicist, opens the subject with a survey of the state of scientific knowledge of the atom as it was known by 1940 and then proceeds to relate the organizational history of (in Groves's words) the "enormous enterprise of scientists, engineers, workmen and administrators . . . whose prolonged labor, silent perseverance, and wholehearted cooperation have made possible the unprecedented technical accomplishments here described."

As an official report, it of course had to be a sanitized account of a technological success story without precedent in science and industry. But within these limitations the principal threads of the story are laid out: the voluntary retreat of physicists of the Allied Powers into wartime secrecy during 1939; the first cautious moves of the Executive Branch ($6,000 in Army and Navy funds by November, 1940); and the formation, expansion, and reorganization of early governmental committees staffed not with civil servants or public officials but with key scientists and engineers. There was the issue of exchange of information with the British, largely solved when they sent Chadwick to the United States as a representative and administrator. There were the problems of locating and obtaining uranium ore before it was at all clear how much would be needed. There was the gigantic task of planning the laboratories that would be needed, as well as the pilot plants, the technical facilities, the selection and development of key sites at Alamogordo, New Mexico; Oak Ridge, Tennessee; Hanford, Washington; the University of Chicago, and elsewhere.

Most of the action was crowded into the last three and a half years of the war, following the December, 1941, bombing of Pearl Harbor—an act that precipitated the American nation into instant and total participation and guaranteed that the atomic project would have first call on material, human resources and funds. The only commodity that could not be bought was precious time; and as Smyth's account makes clear, it was by no means a foregone conclusion that all the scientific and engineering problems could be solved. Here was a high-risk venture in several dimensions: exploring the physical unknown, marshaling human talent and physical resources, and achieving a practical solution without knowing what form it might take, before Adolf Hitler's atomic scientists—Heisenberg was one of them—could do so. They had to design a reactor pile to see if the theoretical chain reaction could actually be generated, separate out the needed uranium isotope, and develop a novel mechanism that would bring together a critical mass fast enough to explode.

Smyth's account is modulated, low-key, sober, and unspectacular; and because the events, crises, and issues themselves were so huge, his report becomes an understatement in its description of what was achieved. Nevertheless, it remains *the* historic firsthand account of the forced creation of a specific scientific technology that came into being at a time when all other major scientific technologies had "jus' naturally growed," most of them under the tolerant, leisurely circumstances of peacetime research, industry, and commerce. — *T.M.S.*

## Additional Recommended Reading

Hersey, John R. *Hiroshima*. New York: Alfred A. Knopf, 1946. A vivid report of experiences selected by survivors of the first atom bomb attack, August 6, 1945.

Glasstone, Samuel. *Sourcebook on Atomic Energy*. New York: D. Van Nostrand, 1950. Detailed technical and historical survey of essential concepts and discoveries; not a beginner's book but full of authoritative information.

Hecht, Selig. *Explaining the Atom*. A revised edition with four new chapters by Eugene Rabinowitch. New York: The Viking Press, 1954. A lucid beginner's book.

Lamont, Lansing. *Day of Trinity*. New York: Atheneum Publishers, 1965. A lay journalist's "human drama" account of how the scientists in the Manhattan Project organized to build and explode the first test bomb in July, 1945, at "Trinity site" in New Mexico.

Lapp, Ralph E. *Roads to Discovery*. New York: Harper & Row Publishers, 1960. A mildly technical survey of major technical and historical developments in nuclear physics and technology.

# EXISTENTIALISM IN LITERATURE

*Type of event:* Literary: outcome of a philosophical and religious movement
*Time:* 1930-1950
*Locale:* Europe and the United States

*Principal personages:*

JEAN-PAUL SARTRE (1905-    ), a leader and principal spokesperson for the existentialists and a French Marxist philosopher

ALBERT CAMUS (1913-1960), Algiers-born philosopher/novelist and a major voice of French existentialism

MARTIN HEIDEGGER (1889-1976), German philosopher and professor whose writings had a marked influence upon existentialist writers

SÖREN AABYE KIERKEGAARD (1813-1855), Danish theologian and philosopher who is often called the "Father of Existentialism"

SIMONE DE BEAUVOIR (1908-    ), author who worked closely with Jean-Paul Sartre in Paris and a leading exponent of existentialism in Europe

## Summary of Event

Though many nineteenth century literary works, ranging from Georg Buchner's play *Woyzeck* to Fyodor Dostoevski's *The Underground Man*, can be called "existentialist," dealing as they do with the dread-filled, the isolated, and the anxious, existentialism really made its mark on twentieth century literature in Europe and (eventually) in America. Growing in significance through the early decades of this century, its presence became felt especially after World War II, when Jean-Paul Sartre, Albert Camus, and Simone de Beauvoir achieved world fame. Taking its central ideas from the groundbreaking philosophers Sören Kierkegaard, Martin Heidegger, and Friedrich Nietzsche, existentialism came to be regarded as the dominant intellectual approach to literature, philosophy,

and religion. Europeans took the lead in the late 1930's and early 1940's, and later, in the decade or so after World War II, their ideas spread to America, influencing the work of such authors as Ernest Hemingway, John Dos Passos, Richard Wright, Nathanael West, Norman Mailer, and William Faulkner. Sartre's novel *Nausea* (1938) gave the world its first heady exposure to the new concepts of existential dread, *angst* (severe anxiety), authentic being, and the absurdity of existence.

Along with Sartre, Camus, and de Beauvoir, Friedrich Durrenmatt of Switzerland, Rainer Maria Rilke of Germany, and Samuel Beckett of Ireland all portrayed man living in an indifferent, perplexing universe—and suffering as a result. Existentialism led to the absurdist movement in the

252

arts during the postwar period in which Eugene Ionesco, the Rumanian-born French playwright, and the English playwrights John Osborne and Harold Pinter envisioned the world as a cruel and empty joke.

Existentialism arose out of the need for a new vision of the inner life. Intellectuals felt that traditional religion had failed them and that technology and modern warfare had so cheapened life and demeaned the image of man that life appeared at times to be futile. For many of the intelligentsia (though certainly not all), God was, as Nietzsche's madman put it, dead; his "murder" by people of the technological age left man very much on his own. Others, such as Gabriel Marcel and Paul Tillich, retained a belief in God as a living presence; however, their God was not the traditional one, but rather a God who must be found "above" the "false" gods of men. Both atheistic and Christian existentialists find that man is responsible for the sorry condition of his world, since God cannot be counted upon somehow to set things right and eliminate evil. Man is, to paraphrase Matthew Arnold's "Dover Beach," truly alone on a darkened plain full of anguish and terror: the very dread spoken of by Kierkegaard, the Danish theologian whose writings sparked the existentialist movement.

If God is, for all intents and purposes, out of the immediate (earthly) picture, twentieth century man is, according to the existentialists, responsible for his own destiny. No longer is it possible for a thinking person to turn to a higher spiritual authority for direct assistance; man must take charge. If he chooses to do wrong, then that is the destiny he has created for himself. His wrongdoing will create misery and suffering, helping to turn earthly existence into the sort of hell Sartre envisioned in his play *No Exit* (1944), about three persons of opposite natures who find themselves forced to exist together for eternity. For graphic proof of man's potential for choosing an inauthentic and evil destiny, the existentialist of the 1930's and 1940's only had to glance backward at the last world war.

Existentialism provides modern man (who, in the words of critic Richard Kostelanetz, "has neither a universally accepted explanation for the mysteries nor an ethical system universally observed") with a means of expression in the face of an indifferent universe. On the other hand, of course, man can allow himself to be engulfed and destroyed by the absurdity of the universe rather than living as if it had meaning. For Sartre, *authentic* existence had to do with taking a stand against social injustices of all kinds; it meant becoming a leftist who asserts the rights of the common man against the bourgeoisie. Judging what ought to be done from a Marxist-Leninist viewpoint, Sartre gave himself over to writing novels that would (he hoped) reach the laboring masses so often ignored by "elitist" writers. His kind of novel, he maintained, would "take the universe as a whole, with man inside it, and . . . give an account of it from the point of view of nothingness." He would stress "engagement"—that is, commitment to the poor and abused in society.

Like his fellow Frenchman Sartre, Algiers-born Albert Camus believed in commitment, but not to what he considered a prescribed, cut-and-dried formula like that provided by Marxism, a system he thought unrealistic. As he demonstrated in his well-known work *The Rebel* (1951), Camus believed that freedom is the ultimate expression of man's humanity—his one way to rebel against absurdity. This rebellion entails one's not being a member of this or that organization or espousing this or that party line, but in discovering one's own inner self by modestly heeding one's own inner voice. By this, Camus does not imply that man should do anything he chooses; instead, he, like Sartre, feels that a truly free person will not commit acts of evil, choosing rather to be kind to his fellow man. It is through their mutual belief in man's potential for goodness that Sartre and Camus are united. Both believe in "tragic courage"—the courage to behave responsibly in a universe where there are no apprehensible codes of conduct. Characters like Meursault, the antihero of Camus' *The Stranger* (1942), who violates his freedom by killing another person, lose their humanity as well as their freedom, thus giving their lives over to inauthenticity and the void.

Sartre and Camus are usually named whenever literary discussions turn to the subject of existentialism. That is fitting, for they, along with the philosophers Kierkegaard, Heidegger, and Nietzsche, are the preeminent spokesmen for the movement. Yet numerous others have contributed significantly to the body of existentialist literature, among them, W. H. Auden, Antoine de Saint-Éxupery, Franz Kafka, and Max Frisch.

In the 1930's and (especially) the 1940's, American writers read and discussed the novels coming from Europe, absorbing the existentialist outlook on life and art as they did so. Certainly the isolated, tortured heroes and heroines of Hemingway; the brooding, forlorn, characters of Faulkner; the wildly despairing characters frequenting the novels of Baldwin; and the socialistic sensibilities of Steinbeck and the early Dos Passos strongly resemble the characters and sensibilities found in European existentialist literature. Uncertainty about the future and the idea that man is free to choose his destiny also become standard themes in twentieth century American literature. Moreover, it is difficult to imagine writers as diverse as Saul Bellow, Richard Wright, and Nathanael West writing without the cultural context provided by the existentialists; existentialism, simply put, is the predominant philosophical outlook of the century—an influence so pervasive that no writer can escape it.

Hemingway, whose 1926 novel *The Sun Also Rises* catapulted him to literary recognition of the first order, wrote some of his most important novels and short stories during the same period in which the existentialists were doing their best work; from the 1930's and 1940's came a string of works having to do with man *versus* a baffling, indecipherable universe: *Death in the Afternoon* (1932); *Winner Take Nothing* (1933); *The Green Hills of Africa* (1935); and *For Whom the Bell Tolls* (1940). In these works, Hemingway's people are often faced with the choice between taking direct and drastic action, thereby asserting their freedom and making their existence "authentic," or giving in to futility and loss of selfhood. Though these people are often savage to each other, they are also fully capable of showing real concern for each other's pain and anxiety.

Like Hemingway, Faulkner wrote about people in extreme circumstances—often on the verge of ruin, disgrace, madness, or despair. Alienated and alone in a chaotic world jerry-built on the remains of a world forever gone, Faulkner's characters often can—and do—assert themselves and authenticate their existence. Yet many succumb to despair and death, lost in an irrational, violent society of the uprooted. In the 1930's and 1940's Faulkner wrote, among other books, *As I Lay Dying* (1930); *Sanctuary* (1931); *Light in August* (1932); *Absalom, Absalom!* (1936); *The Unvanquished* (1938); and *Go Down, Moses* (1942).

Called "the greatest American novelist of the century" by Jean-Paul Sartre, John Dos Passos, the creator of such analyses of the tumultuous twentieth century world as *The Big Money* (1936); *Journeys Between Wars* (1938); and *Tour of Duty* (1946),

evinced considerable sympathy for the "little guy" whose life is controlled by the venal rich and powerful, as well as by technology. Dos Passos, taking a cue from the European existentialists, depicted the modern era as a painful and confusing time in which old creeds simply do not mean much anymore.

Nathanael West, the creator of the wildly bizarre and revolutionary antinovel *Miss Lonelyhearts* (1933), is best known for his black humor and sardonic, acerbic comments on the helter-skelter perversity, decadence, and horror at the heart of life in postwar America. His main characters are embittered ex-innocents for whom modern life holds no real meaning, embroiled in battles to achieve authentic selfhood; unfortunately, they are destroyed eventually by the cruelly indifferent universe around them before having discovered any sense of authentic selfhood or purpose.

Existentialism was—and remains—an extremely potent intellectual outlook, providing a viable way of looking at man, his fate, and his possibilities. Without the pioneering efforts of Sartre and Camus, American and European literature would have been far different from what it has turned out to be.

## Pertinent Literature

Spanos, William V., ed. *A Casebook on Existentialism*. New York: Thomas Y. Crowell Company, 1966.

This book offers a compendium of well-chosen European existentialist literature as well as a sampling of critical writing by some of the more influential existentialist writers, philos-

ophers, and theologians. Ernest Hemingway, for instance, is represented by his classic tale, "A Clean Well-Lighted Place"; Franz Kafka by the story "A Country Doctor"; Albert Camus by his famous "The Guest"; Jean-Paul Sartre by his retelling of the Orestes story, *The Flies*; Eugene Ionesco by his whimsical play *The Future Is in Eggs or It Takes All Sorts to Make a World*; Miguel de Unamuno by the exemplary story "Saint Emmanuel the Good, Martyr"; Fyodor Dostoevski by his "Legend of the Grand Inquisitor"; and W. H. Auden by "For the Time Being," an oratorio written to celebrate the birth of Christ.

Among the writers who provide contemporary criticism of the above are Sartre ("We Will Write for Our Time"), Kenneth Tynan ("Ionesco and the Phantom"), Ionesco ("Hearts Are Not Worn on the Sleeve"), and Philip Rahv ("The Legend of the Grand Inquisitor"), all supplying a grounding in the tenets of existentialism and the several paths existentialist thought can take. Further insight may be gleaned from the essays of the existentialist philosophers and theologians Blaise Pascal, Kierkegaard, Nietzsche, Heidegger, Sartre, Camus, Karl Jaspers, and Tillich. Also included is an illuminating introductory essay by Spanos entitled "Abraham, Sisyphus, and the Furies," which offers the historical context of the existentialist movement and a helpful, though very circumscribed, selected bibliography.

Actually, of all the critical essays included by Spanos, his own, "Abraham, Sisyphus, and the Furies," is a most accessible overview of existentialism dealing with those concepts most dear to the hearts of Sartre and Camus (among others): dread and how it can be dealt with; *angst* and how it destroys the self by destroying

initiative; and freedom from restrictions that make life "inauthentic." Also, Spanos deals with—and gives answers to—such basic and difficult questions as "What is an existentialist?" "Can existentialism be boiled down to a system of ideas?" and "How can one tell if a certain writer has an 'existential outlook'?" To the query "What is existentialism?" Spanos replies, "It is a philosophy of existence, which attempts to view man in his relationship to the universe in all its concrete plenitude—and problematic complexity." His discussion of the philosophical forebears of contemporary existentialists is particularly useful.

Also helpful are other critical essays, especially Sartre's famous "We Write for Our Own Time," in which he formulates his notion of "engagement" (that is, the writer as participant in the moral and philosophical struggles of his day). "The Broken Center: A Definition of the Crisis of Values in Modern Literature," by Nathan Scott, Jr., constitutes another critical insight, spotlighting as it does the impossibility of the newer (for that time) writers sharing in the feelings of the older writers who developed in a more orderly world prior to World War I—now gone forever. After the mindless terrors of that first war of the century, Scott notes, writers have been confronted with a world where "there is no longer any robust common faith to orient the imaginative faculties of men with respect to the ultimate mysteries of existence." Faced with this "intractable and unpromising reality," the existentialist writer must somehow try to unearth a "commonality" with his readership—a special, shared relationship that may no longer exist.

In terms of the examination of individual works, Stanley Cooperman's "Kafka's 'A Country Doctor': Microcosm of Symbolism" and Philip Rahv's article about Dostoevski's "Legend of the Grand Inquisitor" furnish readers with a close reading of two important works in which anxiety, dread, terror, and a sense of absurdity commingle.

It is suggested that the reader of Spanos' book first study the critical material, then go on to the stories and plays. By so doing, he will acquire a fine sense of what the existentialist movement in literature, philosophy, and religion is all about.

---

Sypher, Wylie. *Loss of the Self*. New York: Random House, 1962.

Wylie Sypher allies himself with mainstream existentialists such as Albert Camus when he states that ". . . a residue of humanism persists, illogically enough, in our world where there is a 'void at the center of things.' " For, as long as people realize that there is a void at the core of existence, "there is some locus for a sort of humanism, even if it be unlike any kind of humanism held in the past by cultures based upon a different world from ours." His central mission in *Loss of the Self*, then, is to determine how a humanistic "residue" can exist when the Western conception of "selfhood" has been, for all intents and purposes, obliterated.

Sypher, a critic-at-large, deals with the changing concept of the self, from that of Romantic writers such as Goethe, Shelley, and Byron, who asserted the potential uniqueness of the individual, to that of such moderns as existentialists Jean-Paul Sartre and Albert Camus, who "carry on a romantic quest for the self and its meaning." Going beyond Sartre and Camus, Sypher discusses latter-day artists such as France's Nathalie Sarraute and Alain Robbe-Grillet, two representatives of the "new novel" school (or, more properly, *nouveau roman*). In the writing of Robbe-Grillet and Sarraute, Sypher detects what he terms a "European subversion of literature" which is at once antiromantic and "desperate" in its attempt to destroy the notion of self.

Samuel Beckett, the Irish dramatist who lives and works in France, is singled out as the one writer who has ushered in "a last phase of anti-literature" with the play *The Unnameable* (1953). Like Sartre, who wrote from a "point of nothingness" and envisioned the terrible void at the center of things, Beckett cannot readily affirm the self—yet, despite all his efforts to destroy the whole idea of selfhood, something of a self remains attached to his characters. Even he, after the self has apparently shriveled, must admit to an essence of humanity hovering over the ruins of personality. Feelings of pain, loss, and rejection on the part of Beckett's characters signal the presence of an irreducible something that defies rational explanation.

For those interested in a lucid and thoughtful account of the existentialist movement as a search for meaning, Sypher offers a satisfying explanation of the existentialist's compulsion to cut through hypocrisy and cant so that he may find the higher truths he seeks. For Sören Kierkegaard and Friedrich Nietzsche, such a search necessarily meant breaking all ties with both traditional Christianity and the accepted pieties of their own society. Their question became the question for later writers: Ortega y Gasset, Unamuno, Sartre, de Beauvoir, Camus—"What is authentic existence?" Materialism having failed to shore up the notion of selfhood, other avenues are explored; finally, existentialists discover that to be living a really "authentic" life, one must take risks, stand up for ideals, and help others in their struggle against the cruelly indifferent world into which they are born.

Sypher makes a clear distinction between the existentialist and his successor, the nihilistic writer who sees life as an entropy-ridden, thoroughly hopeless affair, as intolerable as it is incomprehensible. Among the latter group he lists Sarraute, whose antinovel *Planetarium* concerns a bleak, meaningless world where action has no meaning. Sarraute's characters are appropriately "blurred" and featureless automatons living lives of sterility and boredom. The same could be said about others of this "ashcan" school of writing: Jean Genet, Eugene Ionesco, Robbe-Grillet. Just as he feels that painting has reached a "zero degree" in the latter twentieth century, so Sypher postulates that contemporary novels, plays, and poems—light years removed from existentialist literature—have become so dehumanized that there is

little left to say.

One of Sypher's main beliefs is that the anonymity of setting and character in contemporary literature, so evident in the works of the newer novelists and playwrights, is subversive of Western culture. "Anti-literature," as Sypher terms it, is far removed from the writings of the existentialists, such as Camus and Sartre, basically because in the latter "man has a 'privileged metaphysical condition,' " whereas in the former he does not. The existentialists believe that ". . . as long as man is aware of his existence as being absurd, thwarted, blocked, or irrelevant, a kind of humanism persists, simply through man's awareness of his plight." Theirs is a humanistic verdict, but so is that of Robbe-Grillet and Beckett, who have labored mightily to strip away all of man's meaning, only to end up showing that man does have a "center."

Camus is allowed the last word: "The disease of Europe is to believe in nothing, and to claim to know everything." For Camus, we are all responsible for catastrophes occurring around us which we have explained away as "history." We are responsible for our fate as well as for the fate of mankind; no *deus ex machina* will descend from the heavens to deliver us from evil. We must instead deliver ourselves, and, if possible, others.

As an explanation of literary trends in the twentieth century (up to the 1960's) and as a further word on what the major existentialist writers did that was so revolutionary, Wylie Sypher's *Loss of the Self* is a valuable contribution to scholarship. It is one of those uncommon books that needs to be read by all who appreciate lit- erature. — *J.D.R.*

## Additional Recommended Reading

Heinemann, Frederick. *Existentialism and the Modern Predicament*. New York: Harper & Row Publishers, 1953. An excellent discussion of technology's part in creating the tensions of modern society and how an existentialistic outlook on life is necessary.

Wahl, Jean. *A Short History of Existentialism*. New York: The Philosophical Library, 1949. Incisive introductory analysis of the various major existentialists: Kierkegaard, Jaspers, Heidegger, Sartre, and others.

Bree, Germaine. *Camus and Sartre: Crisis and Commitment*. London: Calder and Boyars, 1974. Bree offers a cogent defense of Albert Camus' writings, finding him a more substantial existentialist theoretician than Sartre.

Glicksberg, Charles I. *Modern Literature and the Death of God*. The Hague: Martinus Nijhoff, 1966. Discussion of the change of consciousness in twentieth century literature brought about by existentialism and the other "-isms."

Kaufmann, Walter A., ed. *Existentialism from Dostoevski to Sartre*. New York: New American Library, 1965. A discussion of how existentialism has "hardened into a sustained protest and preoccupation" in the modern era, and how it has affected literature.

# THE UNITED STATES ESTABLISHES THE GOOD NEIGHBOR POLICY TOWARD LATIN AMERICA

*Type of event:* Diplomatic: fostering the development of a special relationship between the United States and the Latin American countries
*Time:* 1930 to the present
*Locale:* Washington, D.C.

*Principal personages:*
HERBERT CLARK HOOVER (1874-1964), thirty-first President of the United States, 1929-1933
FRANKLIN DELANO ROOSEVELT (1882-1945), thirty-second President of the United States, 1933-1945
HARRY S TRUMAN (1884-1972), thirty-third President of the United States, 1945-1953
DWIGHT DAVID EISENHOWER (1890-1969), thirty-fourth President of the United States, 1953-1961
JOHN FITZGERALD KENNEDY (1917-1963), thirty-fifth President of the United States, 1961-1963
CORDELL HULL (1871-1955), United States Secretary of State, 1933-1944
SUMNER WELLES (1892-1961), United States Assistant Secretary, 1933-1937; and United States Under-Secretary of State, 1937-1942
GEORGE CATLETT MARSHALL (1880-1959), United States Secretary of State, 1947-1949
JOHN FOSTER DULLES (1888-1959), United States Secretary of State, 1953-1959
HENRY ALFRED KISSINGER (1923-    ), United States Secretary of State, 1973-1977

## Summary of Event

The Good Neighbor policy represented a major change in the United States posture toward the other countries of the Western Hemisphere. It is commonly associated with the administration of President Franklin Delano Roosevelt; but its foundation was laid earlier by President Herbert Hoover. The phrase "good neighbor" was not original with either president; it had been used by statesmen on numerous occasions in reference to Western Hemisphere relations.

Hoover applied the term to Latin American affairs in several of his addresses while on his good-will tour in 1928. Roosevelt first used it in his inaugural address in 1933, initially not intending to have it apply solely to Latin American relations. It was more by chance than by intent that it came to be the exclusive label for his new policy toward Latin America.

By 1928, it had become abundantly clear to the policymakers in Washington that the problems and incompatibilities in United States-Latin American relations could be resolved only through a basic reorientation of policy. Latin Americans were resentful and suspicious because of United States efforts at political tutelage. This state of affairs was largely the consequence of the Monroe Doctrine and the corollary promulgated by President Theodore Roosevelt, claiming the right for the United States to intervene freely in Latin American affairs and to function as the hemisphere's "policeman." Under Secretary of State J. Reuben Clark drafted a memorandum on the Monroe Doctrine in 1928, repudiating the Roosevelt Corollary outright. The memorandum became official policy with its publication in 1930. This formal adoption of the doctrine of nonintervention in 1930, therefore, may be considered the beginning of the Good Neighbor policy. The Hoover Administration, furthermore, withdrew United States Marines from Nicaragua and prepared for their withdrawal from Haiti; President Hoover gave notice to American investors that they must exhaust local remedies before they could appeal for diplomatic protection; and he refused to press for settlement of financial obligations to Americans.

Although the Hoover Administration first began to apply the ideal of the Good Neighbor, it failed to spark a significant positive response. Its principal weakness lay in the fact that it appeared to look backward, envisioning a return to times before Theodore Roosevelt and Woodrow Wilson. The Hoover policy did not go beyond wanting to create good will and to provide for the growth of trade

through conventional private channels. This effort was frustrated by the Great Depression, and the Hoover Administration was unable to provide the leadership for any inter-American action to cope with the problems. Indeed, the signing of the Smoot-Hawley tariff act of 1930 made matters worse; it was a measure intensely hated by many Latins. Nevertheless, the foundations of the Good Neighbor policy were laid by Hoover.

Franklin D. Roosevelt and his Secretary of State Cordell Hull adopted and dynamically expanded the policy. Roosevelt outlined his Good Neighbor policy more specifically in his Pan-American-Day address on April 12, 1933, and by December of that year, at the Seventh International Conference of American States in Montevideo, it was already bearing rich fruit. Many of the resentments and suspicions seemed to have vanished, as all topics of interest were freely and openly discussed. Cordell Hull won the friendly cooperation of Argentine Foreign Minister Carlos Saavedra Lamas, one of the leading opponents of the United States. The Latin American republics obtained the full acceptance by the United States of the doctrine of nonintervention, as well as of the so-called Calvo and Estrada doctrines. These latter two meant, respectively, that a state could not be considered responsible for losses incurred by aliens in time of civil war and that a state could not pass judgment on the legitimacy of a particular government in its recognition policy. The Pan-American spirit flourished and served the United States well in the oncoming troubles and threats to the security of the

Western Hemisphere during World War II.

The preeminence of the United States in Latin America expanded continually and reached an all-time high immediately after World War II. American initiatives led to the creation of the inter-American security system (the Rio Treaty of 1947) and the establishment of the Organization of American States (OAS) in 1948. However, this period of viable hemispheric cooperation swiftly deteriorated to a new "low" in United States-Latin American relations. The major cause was the Truman Administration's heavy concentration on the urgent problems of Europe and the allocation of billions of dollars under the Marshall Plan for European rehabilitation, which had vastly heightened the expectations for economic assistance on the part of Latin America. When they were left unfulfilled, the United States not being in a position to commit itself to large-scale economic assistance programs in the Americas, growing numbers of Latin Americans felt that they were being taken for granted. Evidently the Good Neighbor policy had taken on a new meaning for Latin America—the assumption that the United States had an obligation to promote economic well-being in the hemisphere.

President Dwight D. Eisenhower and Secretary of State John Foster Dulles, having inherited a rather strained relationship, promptly asserted that the rebuilding and reinforcing of the spirit of Pan-American cooperation was of the utmost importance. Latin American leaders were particularly pleased to hear Dulles say that the United States would no longer assume that hemispheric solidarity would go on automatically. The President sent his brother, Milton S. Eisenhower, as his personal representative and special ambassador on a lengthy fact-finding tour to Latin America. The resultant Eisenhower Report attracted considerable attention. Dr. Eisenhower had concluded that a pervasive and tragic misunderstanding of the intentions of the United States and its economic capacities clouded United States-Latin American relations. Among the sound, if somewhat conservative, recommendations made by Milton Eisenhower were the pursuit of stable trade policies, price-support systems, incentives for private investment, more substantial public loans, expanded technical assistance, and (in unusual circumstances) food grants. However, the Eisenhower Administration failed to work out a mutually agreeable program for economic development; the continuing, and in some respects heightened, Latin American expectations were gravely disappointed. The vehement expressions of hostility encountered by Vice-President Richard Nixon during his Latin American tour in 1958 were a testimony to the strong anti-American sentiment.

In response to the need for new and dramatic action, President John F. Kennedy proclaimed the "Alliance for Progress" in 1961. This new policy toward Latin America represented a significant departure from earlier ones in its scope and approach. Striking a note of social idealism, the Alliance for Progress proposed a vast cooperative effort to satisfy the basic needs for homes, work, land, health, and schools. The projected ten-year program of the "Alliance for Progress," as established by the Charter of Punta del Este in 1961, envisioned as much as one billion dollars in United States contributions annually.

As a result of the intensified concern in the region, the number of United States government personnel assigned to Latin America increased dramatically and inter-American institutions expanded. The whole process led to an even deeper engagement in the domestic affairs of many Latin American countries. A reversal in the pledge to forswear unilateral military intervention came about when United States troops were used in Santo Domingo in 1965, although this action was retroactively sanctioned by the OAS. The United States had asserted the assumed right to remove from the hemisphere whatever political forces were considered a threat. The surreptitious actions against the Salvador Allende regime in Chile during the Nixon Administration seemed to have been conditioned by this posture.

The increasing assumption of hegemony by the United States was not in harmony with the Good Neighbor policy and intensified anti-American sentiment in Latin America, despite huge United States efforts toward economic development of the region. Irrespective of the differences between themselves, Latin American solidarity regarding the common objective of reducing the United States hegemonic presence grew. It was manifest in the relative decline of the volume of trade, as well as in nationalizations and restrictions placed on enterprises operated by United States citizens. Increasingly self-assertive and confident, the various countries began to act independently of Washington's intentions. The United States response to these developments was to reassert somewhat lamely the spirit of the "Good Neighbor." Secretary of State Henry Kissinger, during the Conference of Tlatelolco at Mexico City in February, 1974, talked of a "new dialogue" and a "new spirit" dedicated to the building of a "new community." He acknowledged major changes in Latin America and the need for the "mutuality of respect and equality" in our dealings with the major nations of the region, but it seemed to be a dialogue unilaterally proclaimed. In the end, all references to "community" were purged from the final communiqué of the conference. The prevailing sentiment in Latin America appeared to be that Pan-American harmony is a myth and that the reality entails fundamental conflicts between the interests of the United States and those of Latin America.

A principal question for United States policymakers may well be whether this country should have a distinct Latin American policy at all. The main problems the United States is likely to face in Latin America are not regional but global in nature; they have to do with the basic problems of the so-called Third World. A list of these problems would include fairer terms of trade; expanding food and energy production; using and conserving resources; curbing military spending; limiting environmental destruction; improving human welfare and protecting fundamental human rights; coping with terrorism; alleviating economic calamities and natural disasters; and building more effective international agencies.

Advocates of a new American approach have recommended a focus on securing the active cooperation of Latin America in dealing with this global agenda. References to "special regional ties" or "bonds of traditional friendship" are insufficient. The proposals which have been made for a more effective United States policy include the admonitions to free ourselves from the legacy of paternalism and interventionism; to face the fact that absolute military security in the hemisphere is no longer possible; to accept cultural and political diversity; to set differing priorities for our relations with the various countries in the region; and to recognize that there are definite limits to what we can achieve in the region.

## Pertinent Literature

Wood, Bryce. *The Making of the Good Neighbor Policy*. New York: Columbia University Press, 1961.

The origin and consequences of the doctrine of nonintervention and abandonment of the use of force by the United States in its relations with Latin America are the major concern of Bryce Wood's extensive and highly respected study. As he notes at the outset, it is not intended to be a history of the Good Neighbor policy as such, but a work about politics among states which have renounced the use of force as the ultimate arbiter. Wood examines a series of policy decisions over a period of time in order to detect patterns which may then be used in an assessment of the Good Neighbor policy as a whole.

From 1898 to 1920, United States Marines entered the territory of Caribbean area states no less than nineteen times, to say nothing of the Army's pursuit of Pancho Villa into Mexico. The frequency of such armed intervention established the view in this country that it was normal and proper for the United States to resort to the use of force for the purpose of upholding principles of international law and preventing chaos. Not until the intervention in Nicaragua in 1927, which was unusually complicated and difficult, was there a serious demand for a reappraisal of policy. The Nicaraguan affair, therefore, was a kind of turning point. The following three decades saw no armed intervention by the United States in the Americas.

Wood argues that the dubious Nicaraguan intervention persuaded American leaders that new principles of action were needed. The Monroe Doctrine, directed to external threats, was not appropriate for changed Latin American conditions. There was no desire for conquest and no need for defense on the part of the United States. The use of force as an instrument of policy merely to protect citizens and property abroad seemed counterproductive and relatively costly. In Wood's assessment, it was essentially the reevaluation along these lines which led to the formulation of the Good Neighbor policy. United

States objectives could be furthered far more advantageously by way of the concept of reciprocity. Simply put, the idea of reciprocity meant that the United States would do what was desired by Latin American states, who would in turn respond by doing what was desired by the United States.

However, for the idea to take hold and work, the United States had to project a genuine neighborly attitude. This was successfully accomplished by Franklin D. Roosevelt. Wood shows how the Roosevelt Administration carefully built its credibility regarding the pledge not to employ force in achieving its objectives. He skillfully analyzes the initial problems of the Good Neighbor policy, especially those caused by the Cuban situation. The United States scrupulously refrained from intervention, but it "intermeddled." Sumner Welles, then the United States Ambassador, had a relatively free hand in applying rather ambiguous instructions and succeeded in getting the unloved General Machado to relinquish the office of the presidency and leave the country. President Roosevelt objected to any requests for direct intervention, wishing to remove all fear of American aggression. If help were to be extended to a Latin American country wracked by strife and internal disorder, it should be done in concert with others, not unilaterally.

The renunciation of force did not mean, of course, the relinquishment of influence over Latin American affairs. As the Good Neighbor policy evolved, the policy of nonintervention was gradually complemented by the policy of noninterference. How-

ever, the distinction as to what constituted "interference" and what did not was difficult to make, and open to varying nuances. "Friendly advice" and "good offices" might be offered, but there was a definite refusal to get directly involved in domestic affairs. How categorically the policy was applied was demonstrated by the cold "hands-off" posture in the Nicaraguan civil war of 1936, which allowed General Anastasio Somoza to gain power. Certain critics, in fact, accused the United States of being a "good neighbor of tyrants." Nevertheless, through the pursuit of the Good Neighbor policy, the United States was able to create the kind of reciprocal obligation it was seeking in regard to equity and reasonable and just treatment of American-owned enterprises.

Wood singles out certain methods or approaches of the Good Neighbor policy for special analysis. One of these was the "principle of discrimination," which was applied against Bolivia and ultimately led to mutually satisfactory settlements of the conflicting claims arising out of the Bolivian action against Standard Oil. Another was the "principle of accommodation." The principle was also tested in the Mexican expropriation of oil companies' properties, and entailed the utilization of a joint commission as a good method for settlement. A third approach, most expressive of the spirit of the Good Neighbor policy, was the "principle of collaboration," which was effectively used in respect to Venezuela's efforts to get a larger share of the oil proceeds. The President, Cordell Hull, and Sumner Welles were persistent and deliberate in their actions to instill genuine confidence in the United States and to generate the proper attitude to obtain adequate reciprocity from Latin America. Wood makes a valuable contribution by emphasizing the importance of this interaction of attitudes and policies. Roosevelt's Good Neighbor policy achieved a well-functioning system of reciprocity. Unhappily, it was not sufficiently institutionalized to assure its continuity through changing times and circumstances.

Burr, Robert N. *Our Troubled Hemisphere: Perspectives on United States-Latin American Relations*. Washington, D.C.: The Brookings Institution, 1967.

This highly informative study by Robert N. Burr, a noted scholar of Latin American history, traces the history of United States relations with the region, then evaluates the American objectives and the instruments for achieving them. Burr shows how the United States was relatively successful in creating a Pan-American system through which American policy objectives could be achieved. At first largely informal and improvisatory, the system became formalized at the very apex of the era of good feeling generated by Roosevelt's Good Neighbor policy. But the sad irony of this development was the fact that the creation of the OAS also came at the very time when fundamental global political changes wrought by World War II had rendered the Western Hemisphere idea itself anachronistic.

The main United States goal was to secure the Western hemisphere against Communist penetration; the primary emphasis was thus on military and political measures. However, as Burr's study reveals, developments in Latin America called for a greater emphasis on economic measures. The political and social revolutions occurring in the region and the seeming unwillingness of the United States to respond to the growing needs inevitably placed a strain on relations with Latin America. The United Nations Economic Commission for Latin America documented the economic plight of the region; and its guidelines regarding economic development gained wide acceptance throughout the hemisphere, except in the United States. The United States government continued to favor private enterprise and eschewed development loans to publicly owned Latin American industrial complexes. The United States retreated from these policies only in the face of a quickly deteriorating relationship and the impact of Fidel Castro's revolution in Cuba. Toward the end of the 1950's, the revised American posture allowed for such measures as the creation of the Inter-American Development Bank; the relaxation of the loan policy of the World Bank through the creation of the affiliated International Development Agency; and the creation of the Latin American Free Trade Association. However, no marked general improvement was achieved. Relations with Cuba came to a breaking point, while that country's leader became a celebrated revolutionary hero and personified the aspirations of the deprived masses of Latin America.

Burr systematically analyzes the importance of Latin America to the United States from a military, economic, and general political perspective. He notes that the region has resources of potential strategic significance; but it is not itself militarily strong. Economically, the region is very important to the United States. Roughly one fourth of our imports and exports come from and go to the region, and investments in the area also add up to about one fourth of the total volume of investments abroad. The region's political importance is also considerable. Notable in this regard would be Latin America's role in the formulation of the basic policies of the Third World and the control of a voting bloc in the United Nations. Burr's general assessment suggests that Latin America is very important to the United States. In order to improve its relations with the region, the United States must change the image of arrogance and superiority it has been projecting. Milton S. Eisenhower had talked about the pervasive misperceptions of the United States in Latin America. Burr, in turn, notes the distorted and faulty perception of Latin America in this country. There has been a woeful absence of accurate and thorough information about Latin America. The media have paid little attention to Latin American affairs, and the misrepresentations which have been allowed to circulate have led to a distorted image of the region. Burr considers this situation to be a major impediment to improved relations.

It is certainly difficult for an outsider to come to grips with Latin American politics. Burr catalogues the diverse aspects of Latin American domestic politics and shows the infinite complexity and subtlety of their politics. Additionally, his detailed survey of United States relations with a number of Latin American countries reveals the degree of American involvement in their domestic affairs. This involvement has tended to cause many citizens to view the United States as an obstacle to economic, social, and political modernization. Yet it is modernization which the United States has been attempting to promote, especially under the Alliance for Progress. In retrospect, Burr has overrated the potential of the Alliance for Progress in furthering American hemispheric interests. In any case, his conclusion that the United States must continue to engage itself on behalf of bringing Latin America into the "mainstream of Western civilization" may have continuing validity. — *M. G.*

## Additional Recommended Reading

Bemis, Samuel Flagg. *The Latin American Policy of the United States*. New York: Harcourt, Brace, 1943. A general history of United States-Latin American relations, including the evolution of the Good Neighbor policy.

Blasier, Cole. *The Hovering Giant: United States Responses to Revolutionary Change in Latin America*. Pittsburgh: University of Pittsburgh Press, 1976. An investigation of United States responses to three stages of revolutionary change in the cases of Mexico, Bolivia, Guatemala, and Cuba.

Connell-Smith, Gordon. *The Inter-American System*. New York: Oxford University Press, 1966. A carefully researched study of the Inter-American system from its beginning in 1890 to the establishment of the OAS and that organization's functioning up to the Dominican crisis of 1965.

DeConde, Alexander. *Herbert Hoover's Latin American Policy*. Stanford, Calif.: Stanford University Press, 1951. Reprinted by Octagon Books, 1970. A portrayal of President Hoover's efforts to implement a policy of good will and friendly cooperation toward Latin America.

Eisenhower, Milton S. *The Wine Is Bitter: The United States and Latin America*. Garden City, N.Y.: Doubleday & Company, 1963. A well-written work on the disturbing conditions in Latin America, in which the author incorporates the insights that he acquired as a presidential representative and special ambassador to Latin America.

Lowenthal, Abraham F. "The United States and Latin America: Ending the Hegemonic Presumption," in *Foreign Affairs*. LV, (October, 1976), pp. 199-213. Persuasively presented proposals for new approaches and directions in United States policy toward Latin America.

May, Ernest R. "The Alliance for Progress in Historical Perspective," in *Foreign Affairs*. XLI (July, 1963), pp. 257-274. President Kennedy's program for Latin America seen in its broader historical context.

Mecham, J. Lloyd. *The United States and Inter-American Security, 1889-1960*. Austin: University of Texas Press, 1961. This comprehensive study of every aspect of security cooperation in the Western Hemisphere includes an excellent chapter on the Good Neighbor policy.

Rangel, Carlos. *The Latin Americans: Their Love-Hate Relationship with the United States*. New York: Harcourt Brace Jovanovich, 1977. A Venezuelan argues that Latin America's failure to achieve political unity, economic prosperity, and social equity cannot be blamed on the United States.

Whitaker, Arthur P. *The Western Hemisphere Idea: Its Rise and Decline*. Ithaca, N.Y.: Cornell University Press, 1954. Insightful sketches of the key stages of the history of the Western Hemisphere idea.

# THE MANCHURIAN CRISIS AND THE RISE OF JAPANESE MILITARISM

*Type of event:* Military: takeover of Manchuria by Japan
*Time:* September 18, 1931-February 24, 1933
*Locale:* Manchuria, principally Mukden

*Principal personages:*

MORI KAKU, Parliamentary Vice Minister of Foreign Affairs under Premier Giichi Tanaka and a major proponent of the policy of continental expansion

COLONEL SEISHIRŌ ITAGAKI (1885-1948), Senior Staff Officer of the Kwantung Army and the prime mover behind the Mukden Incident

LIEUTENANT COLONEL KANJI ISHIHARA (1889-1949), Staff Officer of the Kwantung Army and one of the main promoters of the Manchurian Affair

CAPTAIN SHINTARŌ IMADA, an officer in the Army Special Service Agency of the Kwantung Army and one of the promoters of the Manchurian Affair

MAJOR HANAYA TADASHI, an officer in the Army Special Service Agency of the Kwantung Army and one of the four major promoters of the Manchurian Affair

## Summary of Event

Japanese troops had been stationed in Manchuria since 1905 to guard the South Manchuria Railway. About 10:00 P.M. on September 18, 1931, they created an incident by setting off an explosion on the South Manchuria Railway to the north of the city of Mukden (Shenyang). Fighting between the Japanese railway guards and Chinese troops immediately followed. By the next morning the Japanese Kwantung Army which protected Japanese interests in the leased Manchurian territory of Kwantung had succeeded in occupying the city and the nearby areas. The significance of this incident went beyond the slight damage done to the railroad by the explosion. As a positive manifestation of the

Japanese military's opposition to its government's domestic and external policies, this incident paved the way for the rise of Japanese militarism and the ultimate demise of the civilian government.

The incident was engineered by two senior staff officers in the Kwantung Army: Colonel Seishirō Itagaki and Lieutenant Colonel Kanji Ishihara. It was an initial manifestation of a secret plan to occupy Manchuria already approved by the most influential of the central army authorities. Two conferences early in the summer of 1931 indicated the extent of collaboration between the Kwantung Army in Manchuria and Tokyo. The first meeting took place in June, when Major Hanaya Tadashi of the Mukden Special Service Agency secretly returned to Tokyo to express the strong desire of the Kwantung Army to resort to action in Manchuria in the coming fall. Although there was no unanimous agreement among them, many high-ranking officers at the meeting gave their approval to Hanaya's plea. The second meeting took place when Honjō Shigeru, the newly appointed Commander in Chief of the Kwantung Army, and Miyake Mitsuharu, Chief of Staff of the Kwantung Army, were in Tokyo to attend the Division and Army Commanders' Conference in early August. At a secret meeting after the formal Conference, the two Kwantung Army leaders revealed their preparation for action in the near future to high government and military leaders. Commander Hayashi Senjuro of the Korean Army reportedly expressed determination to come to the aid of the Kwantung Army whenever it was in danger.

In any case, the incident was the product of a well-executed plan that, according to the League of Nations' Lytton Commission, had been laid out in advance. Itagaki and Ishihara instigated the incident, and many high-ranking officials acquiesced in their plan and cooperated with them. They planned to initiate the incident on the night of September 28, immediately after the harvest of the tall sorghum, but they changed the date when Itagaki received a secret telegram from the Director of the Russian Subsection, Hashimoto Kingorō, informing him that the War Ministry was about to deliver letters to Manchuria ordering the Commander in Chief of the Kwantung Army not to take any military action. After some debate, the plotters of the incident decided to advance its date to the night of September 18, in order to force the government to accept a *fait accompli*.

On the night of the predetermined date, Captain Shintarō Imada of the Army Special Service Agency directed the blasting of the railroad at a spot north of Liutiaohu, near Mukden. Since the purpose of the explosion was merely to create an incident, a small bomb producing minimum damage was chosen to do the job, and after the explosion, sentries were posted at the site.

At the time of the explosion, according to the Japanese version, a small guard detachment under First Lieutenant Kawamoto Suemori was patrolling the tracks of the South Manchuria Railway just to the north of Mukden. The detachment reacted immediately by marching toward the site of the explosion, a distance of only two hundred yards; there they were fired upon from the fields to the east of the track. They quickly returned the fire, and, at the same time, sought reinforcement from the Third Company, which was engaged in night maneuvers some 1,500 yards to the north. Also according to this version, the Third Company, under Captain Kawashima Tadashi, arrived on the scene at about 10:15 P.M. Meanwhile, Lieutenant Colonel Shimamoto Masaichi at battalion headquarters in Mukden had ordered the First and Fourth Companies to rush to the aid of the forces already on the scene and sent a hurried call to the Second Company at Fushun, about twenty-five miles due east. Shortly after midnight, the company from Mukden arrived at the scene of the skirmish, increasing the strength of the Japanese troops to approximately five hundred men. Then Shimamoto ordered an attack on the North Barracks, where Chinese soldiers in Mukden were quartered.

Apparently the Chinese troops at the North Barracks were not battle-ready, for the area was still brightly lit when the Japanese troops arrived. The Third Company led the attack by breaking down the left wing of the west wall; the First Company attacked the right wing and the Fourth Company the center portion of the small wall. At 5:00 A.M., after two cannon shells had demolished the gate to the south wall, a detachment under Lieutenant Noda poured through. Although the Chinese soldiers resisted fiercely, in the face of Noda's attack they yielded ground; by 6:00 A.M. the North Barracks was completely in Japanese hands, with the Chinese soldiers retreating through the east gate northeastward toward the village of Erhtaitze.

According to the Japanese version of the Incident, it was not impossible that those Japanese troops could have thought of their actions as self-defence. But the Chinese version revealed the Japanese action as a planned military effort. According to a report by an officer named Liu, a train of three or four coaches without the usual locomotive stopped northwest of the barracks (located only about 250 yards east of the railroad tracks) at 9:00 P.M. An hour later there was a loud explosion, followed by rifle fire. At 10:30 P.M. the roar of distant artillery was heard coming from the southwest and northwest. A general attack on the southwest corner of the barracks came at about 11:00 P.M., and the Japanese effected entry into the walled compound half an hour later.

By midnight, live shells were bursting within the barracks. The main body of Chinese troops evacuated the grounds, building by building, without offering resistance. The only exception was the 620th Regiment, whose path of retreat was cut off at the eastern exit by the Japanese troops. It was there, according to the Chinese account, that their heaviest casualties were sustained.

In Mukden at 10:30 P.M. Colonel Shimamoto informed Colonel Hirata Yukihiro, one of the major instigators, of the bombing and of his intention to send reinforcements. It is not certain that Itagaki gave him a direct order to do so, but at 11:30 P.M. Hirata led his troops in an attack on the walled city in Mukden and captured it by 3:40 the following morning. The only resistance was from the Chinese police, of whom seventy-five were slain. The staff of the Second Division and a part of the Sixteenth Regiment arrived shortly after 5:00 A.M. from Liaoyang, and the arsenal and airfield located to the east of the walled city were captured at 7:30 A.M. The East Barracks, three to four miles northeast of the city, was occupied by 1:00 P.M. Thus, within fifteen hours or so, all important Chinese military installations in and about Mukden were in the hands of the Japanese army.

During the same night, Chinese troops at Antung, Yingkow, Liaoyang, and other smaller towns, were overcome and disarmed without resistance. The attack on Changchun, the northern terminus of the South Manchuria Railway, also began that night, and the city was occupied by 3:00 P.M. the following day. Kirin, approximately seventy miles to the east, was occupied on September 21 without a shot being fired. With lightning speed, the Kwantung Army thus captured much of Manchuria in a very short period of time.

Why did the Mukden Incident occur, and why did the Kwantung Army capture Manchuria? While the questions are not simple, some answers may be elicited from a study of Japan after World War I. Postwar political and intellectual liberalism was not widely accepted in Japan. For the most part, people outside the cities (rural landowners, lower-middle-class residents of the small towns, military officers, and many minor government officials) resented the liberal challenge to established political and social authority. Among the dissidents were Mori Kaku, who served as the Parliamentary Vice Minister of Foreign Affairs under Premier Giichi Tanaka, Ōkawa Shumei, a civilian ideologist (national socialist), and the instigators of the Mukden Incident itself. These men were critical of newly instituted representative democracy at home and supportive of strong expansionist programs abroad. Their ultranationalist views and militarist sentiments sometimes found expression in political parties, but more often in ultranationalist secret societies and in the armed forces. Ultimately, it was the military that was regarded as being able to solve both national and international problems.

The Japanese reaction against liberalism and democracy was an outgrowth of its authoritarian sociopolitical and military past, but it was also a product of outside influences. For one thing, many Japanese in the 1920's were impressed with the "superiority" of totalitarian regimes in Europe, seeing many points of agreement with traditional Japanese concepts of authoritarian rule. For another, worldwide economic depression and the resultant collapse of international trade had brought unemployment and bankruptcy to Japan. Finally, these difficulties were compounded by the rapid increase in population after World War I, which contributed to the demand for overseas expansion.

All of these problems gave rise to movements aimed at reforming the government and its policies. At the same time, they prompted the Japanese ultranationalists to view colonial expansionism as the solution to many of their problems. Gradually the people gave their support to the military expansionists, and with their support, the military and their sympathizers in the government were able to defy the civilian government and its policies. Military actions such as those in Manchuria were presented to the Emperor and the government as *faits accomplis*. One result of the Mukden Incident was the collapse of civilian cabinets, with the military taking control of the government.

The Mukden Incident had other far-reaching consequences. Between September, 1931, and February, 1932, Japan completed the occupation of Manchuria, which was renamed Manchukuo. Amid mounting tensions between Japan and China and after considerable delay, the League of Nations on February 24, 1933, mildly condemned the Japanese occupation of Manchuria. The failure of the League of Nations to enforce collective security on behalf of China only encouraged the militarist government in Japan, as well as its Fascist counterparts in Germany and Italy, to embark on careers of conquest which merged in the catastrophe of World War II.

## Pertinent Literature

Yoshihashi, Takehiho. *Conspiracy at Mukden: The Rise of the Japanese Military*. New Haven, Conn.: Yale University Press, 1963.

Professor Yoshihashi's study is an outgrowth of his doctoral dissertation at Yale University. Making substantial use of materials derived from the dossiers of the Tokyo War Crimes Trials, as well as diaries, memoirs, and autobiographies of Japanese statesmen, the author admirably presents the background and description of the Mukden Incident. In so doing, he delineates the various currents of development in Japan in the 1920's that paved the way for the rise of the military.

The book is divided into eight chapters of varying lengths. After giving a concise description of the event, the author devotes the next three chapters to the developments, both domestic and international, that led to the outbreak of the Mukden Incident and the collapse of the civilian government under Premier Reijiro Wakatsuki. The fifth chapter focuses on the role played by the major participants in the incident and on the subversive plots that preceded the major event. The next two chapters constitute a detailed analysis of the Mukden Incident itself and the collapse of the Wakatsuki cabinet. The book concludes with an analysis of the significance of the Mukden Incident, explaining, as the author sees it, the reasons why the Japanese military, with the support of the ultranationalists, was able to gain control of the government that ultimately led Japan to defeat.

Marshaling the evidence available to him, Yoshihashi develops the thesis that the Mukden Incident was engineered by civilian as well as by military extremists who took advantage of the difficulties experienced by the Japanese government internally and externally; they implemented what they regarded as a quick solution to Japan's problems. He identifies Mori Kaku, a politician, as the leading exponent of the expansionist policy leading to the incident; and he names Colonel Seishirō Itagaki and Lieutenant Colonel Kanji Ishihara of the Kwantung Army as the chief instigators of the Mukden Incident itself. He also assesses the roles played by other personages, including those of Premier Tanaka, Prince Saionji, and Premier Wakatsuki.

The author makes a significant contribution to the understanding of the domestic background and situation that prepared the way for, if it did not "cause," the Mukden Incident—as well as to an appreciation of its domestic repercussions. In this context, the author reveals the role played by the various attempts at *coups d'état*, such as the March Plot and its successor, the October Plot; the Cherry Society; and other incidents of military defiance of the civilian government that ultimately led to the collapse of the Wakatsuki cabinet.

Ogata, Sadako N. *Defiance in Manchuria: The Making of Japanese Foreign Policy, 1931-1932*. Berkeley: University of California Press, 1964.

This book is based on Ogata's doctoral dissertation and represents his concern for the factors contributing to Japan's defeat in World War II. Concentrating on the question of why Japan followed an expansionist foreign policy that worked to her own destruction, Ogata attempts to answer these questions: Was it the pressure of international rivalry, or the result of domestic needs? Was it the aggressiveness of her imperialistic ideology, or a defect in her political structure?

The book is divided into three parts. Part One deals with the setting or background of the Mukden Incident, focusing on the radical reform movement in Japan and its demand for a strong Manchurian policy. Part Two analyzes the Manchurian Affair and the process of policy formulation. Here Ogata argues that the Manchurian Affair was an outgrowth of the breakdown of the government's policy-making process—the government's inability to insist on standards, resulting in the rise of the military, which either made decisions for itself and presented them to the government as *faits accomplis*, or defied the government's prior decisions. The result was the adoption of the policy of continental expansion. The third and final part deals with the effect of the Manchurian Affair. In retrospect, Ogata concludes that the Manchurian Affair was ". . . a current in the steady stream of Japanese expansion toward the continent of Asia." Because it belonged to the national socialist movement that developed in the late 1920's as a product of the erosion of the process of governmental decision-making, the Manchurian Affair was inevitable.

The author relies on diaries, Kwantung Army documents, and personal papers of former staff officers of the Kwantung Army (for example, Colonel Seishirō Itagaki and Lieutenant Colonel Kanji Ishihara), some of whom were key figures of the Manchurian Affair. Ogata thoroughly evaluates the nature of the turn in Japanese foreign policy, its underlying ideas, and the process by which the change occurred in the course of the Manchurian Crisis. He develops the thesis that in 1931 and 1932, Japan's foreign policy underwent drastic change, signifying a breakdown of the balance between the two major objectives of continental expansion and international cooperation that had traditionally been viewed as almost sacred.

Maintenance and development of Japanese rights and interests in Manchuria had been a national commitment ever since the Russo-Japanese War. The policy of the Wakatsuki cabinet, as formulated by Foreign Minister Baron Kijouro Shidehara, promoted those rights and interests within the limits of international agreements concluded among the great powers, of which Japan was one, as well as between Japan and China. Even the Tanaka "strong" policy, which seemingly gave priority to Manchurian expansion, was hesitant to conduct Japan's external affairs with total disregard of such agreements. But this delicate balance between continental expansion and international cooperation broke down in 1931 as a result of the collapse of the civilian government, which had been undermined by its lack of leadership, growth of the radical reform movement, outbursts of military rad-

icalism, and the government's inability or unwillingness to fight back. The civilian government was too timid to take disciplinary action against the military, when the occasion clearly required it. Like the civilian government, the Emperor, whose power was neutralized by some of the inner court officials, accepted the defiance of the military as *faits accomplis*.

Ogata's study goes beyond a mere description of the Manchurian Crisis. By means of thorough research and convincing argument, the author shows how ideology and decision-making in Japan in the 1920's led to the Manchurian Crisis and the adoption of a new and disastrous foreign policy. This book is an important contribution to a better understanding of Japan in the 1920's and the rise of militarism in the 1930's. — *L.R.M.*

## Additional Recommended Reading

Thorne, Christopher. *The Limits of Foreign Policy: The West, the League and the Far Eastern Crisis of 1931-1933*. New York: G. P. Putnam's Sons, 1972. This and the following two accounts provide thorough analyses of the Manchurian Crisis.

Basset, R. *Democracy and Foreign Policy: A Case History of the Sino-Japanese Dispute, 1931-1933*. London: Longman, Green, 1952.

Smith, Sara R. *The Manchurian Crisis, 1931-1932: A Tragedy in International Relations*. New York: Oxford University Press, 1948.

Storry, Richard. *The Double Patriots: A Study of Japanese Nationalism*. London: Chatto and Windus, 1957. This and the following two books evaluate the nature of Japanese prewar politics and the role of Japanese militarism.

Scalapino, Robert A. *Democracy and the Party Movement in Prewar Japan: The Failure of the First Attempt*. Berkeley: University of California Press, 1953.

Maki, John M. *Japanese Militarism, Its Causes and Cure*. New York: Alfred A. Knopf, 1945.

# THE GENEVA DISARMAMENT CONFERENCE

*Type of event:* Diplomatic: attempt to reach international disarmament agreement
*Time:* February 2, 1932-June 11, 1934
*Locale:* Geneva, Switzerland

### Principal personages:

ANDRÉ PIERRE GABRIEL AMÉDÉE TARDIEU (1876-1945), French War Minister, January 14-February 20, 1932; President of France, February 20-May 10, 1932

HEINRICH BRÜNING (1885-1970), Chancellor of Germany, 1930-1932

ÉDOUARD HERRIOT (1872-1957), President of France, June 4-December 13, 1932

RUDOLF NADOLNY, German delegate to the disarmament conference

SIR JOHN ALLSEBROOK SIMON (1873-1954), British Foreign Secretary, 1931-1935

ADOLF HITLER (1889-1945), Chancellor and Führer of Germany, 1933-1945

KONSTANTIN VON NEURATH (1873-1956), German Foreign Minister, 1932-1938

## Summary of Event

One of the most vexing and seemingly intractable problems of the period between the two World Wars was the question of disarmament. All powers were in one way or another concerned with the limitation of weapons of great destructive power. Nations such as France, concerned with the maintenance of the political balance established after World War I, also sought guarantees against German revanchism through a network of political and military security arrangements. Germany, for her part, wished to have removed the disarmament provisions of the Treaty of Versailles, which had limited the German Army to 100,000 men, with further restrictions on its armaments and its naval strength.

Such questions were considered by the League of Nations. Through a series of invitations, representatives of some sixty nations were gathered at the League's headquarters in Geneva for the opening of disarmament discussions on February 2, 1932. At the commencement of the conference, the French War Minister, André Tardieu, suggested that the most advanced and powerful weapons be strictly reserved for defensive warfare; he also proposed that the League Council establish a standing international peace force, and that members contribute troops from their own armies in connection with the League's peacekeeping mission. The German position, presented by Chancellor Heinrich Brüning, was that to achieve uniform disarmament the other powers would need to reduce their armaments to the levels prescribed for Germany at Versailles. Brüning's views received some support from Italy, and when the conference met again in April, the United States and Great Britain were amenable to a revised version of Brüning's plan. Germany would be allowed any weapons owned by the other signatories of a disarmament convention, and would be permitted to increase its armed forces to 200,000 men by reducing the service term from twelve to six years. Tardieu, though arguing for strengthened security pacts to offset any increase in German military capacities, was also receptive to this project. He was defeated, however, in the French elections of May, 1932; Brüning, who returned to Berlin without an agreement from the League, was dismissed from the Chancellery on May 30, 1932.

The conference recommenced its work in June, and the United States advanced a plan for the abolition of offensive weapons and the reduction of other armaments by one-third; similar reductions in land forces would then bring the other European powers to within range of parity with Germany. President Édouard Herriot of France, however, was unwilling to have France's forces reduced without prior commitments of assistance from her former allies if she were attacked. Britain also held reservations on the proposed dismantling of its advanced weapons, while Japan openly resisted any limitations on its armed forces. While a draft resolution was produced to place some restrictions on offensive weapons such as artillery and tanks, no explicit force levels were specified. The Ger-

man delegate, Rudolf Nadolny, voted against this resolution, and announced further that, unless the principle of military equality were accepted, Germany would not be able to justify its continued participation in the conference. France then put forward a new plan to base troop strengths on uniform periods of short-term conscript duty, while Britain's Foreign Secretary, Sir John Simon, declared his willingness to accept the principle of military equality. On December 11, 1932, a statement was issued by the conference to provide satisfaction for Germany's claims for equal military rights while deferring as well to French interests in a balanced system of European security.

While the implications of Adolf Hitler's accession to the German chancellorship on January 30, 1933, were disquieting to the other European countries, the British delegation moved ahead with a draft convention that stated precisely the number of airplanes, tanks, and artillery pieces each power was to be permitted. In terms of land forces Germany was to be allowed a short-term army equal in strength to its neighbors, and after a five-year transition period these terms would be embodied in a convention that would supersede the Versailles Treaty as an instrument of international arms control.

The conference suffered a setback when Japan, at odds with the other members over its policy of expansion in Asia, abruptly withdrew from the League on March 27, 1933. Nonetheless, in a major policy speech of May 17, 1933, Hitler attempted to improve the international credit of his regime by endorsing the British plan and declaring his commitment to a policy of peace. In June the French proposed yet another plan, which was to reduce armaments in two stages and over eight years; they suggested as well that more extensive means of verification be employed. This project ran into German opposition, and in September, the German Foreign Minister, Konstantin von Neurath, proposed that equality of armaments be granted Germany during the initial period of any arms control plan, before any actual measures of disarmament could be undertaken.

By this time the Nazi program of rearmament had already left German diplomats with little room to maneuver; a rearmament project had been commenced, and further increases were scheduled to begin in October. These developments could not be concealed under any international agreement containing the verification clauses sought by the French. Neurath was recalled to Berlin, and on October 14, 1933, Hitler delivered a public address, in which he argued that Germany, though negotiating for a pact to promote peace and security, had been rebuffed by its former enemies, and thus was compelled to leave the disarmament conference; it would also terminate its membership in the League. In a single unilateral step Hitler had removed his long-contemplated rearmament program from the scrutiny of the League while repudiating the limitations on German armaments set at Versailles. He had also brought about the virtual collapse of serious negotiations at the conference in Geneva. While some efforts were made to revive the talks, notably on the subject of arms manufacture and international trafficking in arms, the governments of the other European powers made their own arrangements to meet German rearmament; the Geneva conference was adjourned indefinitely on June 11, 1934.

## Pertinent Literature

Wheeler-Bennett, John W. *The Disarmament Deadlock*. London: George Routledge & Sons, 1934.

This work by a distinguished British writer on international relations presents a thorough and detailed account of the negotiations in Geneva and their immediate implications for world politics. Written shortly after the actual events, the sense of rapidly changing prospects in the search for an international arms agreement is set against the more alarming possibilities of heightened tensions in Europe, in the wake of the failure of the disarmament conference. Wheeler-Bennett also discusses the political pressures under which the major delegations pursued their negotiations, and the effects of diplomatic events on the political stability of the governments involved.

While all of the major powers involved in the disarmament negotiations are discussed in turn, the central place is assigned to Germany, whose search for military equality occupied most of the first year of the conference, and whose transformation under the Nazi regime ensured the failure of the disarmament talks during the second year at Geneva. Wheeler-Bennett maintains that Brüning's political position was not altogether secure at the opening of the League negotiations, and as the talks progressed, the Nazi Party made appreciable gains in the German elections of April, 1932. Having already committed himself to a policy of cooperation with the League, the fate of Brüning's proposals became intertwined with the political future of his government; when he returned to Berlin without an agreement, or even the prospect of one, he was unable to continue in office. By the lack of a forthright and sympathetic response to Brüning's proposals the Allies had, at least to some extent, made it more likely that the German governments with which they would deal next would be the more intransigent on questions of disarmament.

To be sure, the other governments had their own security interests before them as well. As with Germany, both Great Britain and the United States felt that the increased taxation and public spending necessary for excessive armament posed a liability to their internal financial balance. Moreover, both London and Washington viewed any significant measures of disarmament as having potentially salutary consequences to international peace. French statesmen, however, had to answer to a voting public and a political press that, conditioned by memories of German invasion and destruction during World War I, were openly suspicious of any apparent concessions to the neighboring Germans. France

was further convinced that, whatever professions of peace German representatives might make in Geneva, clandestine rearmament would be an important element of German policy, and, in any case, after the human losses incurred during the World War, France would need to maintain a military establishment that would provide security for the years to come.

Wheeler-Bennett considers the Nazi seizure of power to have been a turning point in international affairs as well as in German politics. Though Hitler at first attempted to reassure the other European nations of his peaceful intentions, the ruthless suppression of political opposition in Germany and the glorification of national militarism provided clear enough evidence of the position the new regime would adopt. While the British arms control proposals made after the installation of the Nazi government were constructive, and indeed might have led to a more satisfactory resolution of the armaments problem, the German attitude by this time was a mixture of obstructionism tempered by Hitler's efforts to cast Germany as pacific in intent, but beset by former enemies determined to perpetuate her military inferiority.

What was particularly disturbing to the other European countries was that the formation of the Nazi government gave state support to large numbers of storm troopers and other paramilitary formations, which, taken together, would have provided much larger manpower reserves even than would have been granted Germany in the event of an international agreement conferring military equality.

Under these conditions it was unlikely that Germany would accept any arms control proposal that could be put before it by the other powers. In domestic policy the Nazi regime was already committed to its program of rearmament; it could appeal to the German people for support on an issue on which Hitler could set himself against the universally despised treaty of Versailles. Hitler had also calculated that the other European powers would not intervene in response to his challenge to the League.

Even so, the disarmament conference did continue for a while without Germany; moreover, both Britain and France prepared proposals to be presented to the German government. Britain was willing to offer additional concessions to Germany, though without accepting in their entirety the steps toward rearmament taken by the Nazi regime. France had insisted, however, that Germany be held to a probationary period, with the suspension of any measures of rearmament, before any obligations for the other powers to respect German military equality should enter into effect. While these proposals were presented both in direct exchanges between the interested nations and before the conference in Geneva, Germany's acceleration of her rearmament program and her calculated defiance of the League had opened the way for a more ominous stage of the armaments race.

Rappard, William E. *The Quest for Peace Since the World War*. Cambridge, Mass.: Harvard University Press, 1940.

This is a useful and scholarly study of international efforts to promote peace and security during the interwar period; the section on disarmament considers in some detail both the background to and the actual proceedings of the Geneva conference, and is based on the reports and public statements issued by participating states at various stages of the conference's work. Rappard does not place emphasis on any single problem, or on the action of any single nation, as having led to the eventual failure of the disarmament conference. Rather, it was a number of issues that divided the various participants and prevented the achievement of an accord, while the withdrawal of Japan and Germany served notice of the weakness of any foundation on which the League may have expected to build its arms control structure.

The difficulties to be expected were evident from the initial sessions of the conference. Britain supported direct, internationally supervised disarmament. While formally committed to international peacekeeping measures, Rappard maintains, France expected more than anything that its military superiority would not otherwise be affected by the action of the League. The American formula for disarmament emphasized the proportional reduction of offensive weapons, which would then contribute to economic recovery as well as to world peace. Germany's proposal for military equality was followed by the plans submitted by Italy and Japan, the last of which supported limitations on weapons not essential to its own military program. The Soviet Union proposed the abolition of all offensive weapons of great destructive power. These attitudes were to remain relatively constant throughout the conference, and major developments arose largely from efforts to determine whether the modification of one or more of these positions could bring the members closer to agreement.

The initial meetings of the disarmament conference had been characterized by presentations by the members in plenary session. Once Germany's claims for equality had been shelved, and the German delegation had left Geneva, direct negotiations between the major powers commenced. By this time the scope of the disarmament controversy had narrowed somewhat, revolving largely around the French contention that international guarantees were a necessary precondition of any accord, and the German insistence that military equality be recognized at the outset of any pact.

The disarmament conference might have reached a turning point in March, 1933; the British plan that had been drafted during the early part of the year was presented before the conference, and was received as the measure that came closest to reconciling France's insistence on generalized means of collective security with Germany's often stated arguments for military equality. France, however, temporized, preferring to defer any grant of possible military advantages to its German rival; moreover, the actual process of the presentation of the British plan and proposed amendments before the full conference delayed any action that could have been taken by the League. Of far graver consequences, in any event, were Japan's decision to leave the League, and the accumulation of evidence of German rearmament. When, in his turn, Hitler decided to withdraw from the conference, the work of disarmament had already been seriously compromised by Japanese acts of war against China and the revival of German militarism.

Rappard is, in a sense, more fatalistic than other writers on the disarmament negotiations of the period. Whatever opportunities the statesmen in Geneva may have had to prevent, or at least forestall, the breakdown of constraints on armaments production, the record would seem to indicate that only fleeting chances for an agreement ever existed, and that no nation was in a position to make significant concessions in order to promote a generalized arms control program. Indeed, in view of subsequent events, and the use of advanced weapons for military conquest, both the large and the small powers represented at the disarmaments conference may have been justified in putting their security interests before any proposed sacrifices of their military establishments. More specifically, Rappard argues that Franco-German distrust was almost certain to surface during the disarmament talks. However persuasive Brüning may have been at the outset of the conference, and however desirable it may have been to deal with him than with his successors, it was unlikely that France could have accepted any changes in the military balance with

Germany that, in the end, might have endangered its own security. Rappard concludes that those nations most in favor of disarmament at the outset in time became the most persistent violators of world peace; this was so not because of any deep-seated flaws in the process of disarmament negotiation, but rather as a result of the fragile and unstable international system that existed during the interwar years. — *J.R.B.*

## Additional Recommended Reading

Temperley, A. C. *The Whispering Gallery of Europe*. London: Collins, 1938. A discussion of the disarmament conference by a British military attaché to the League of Nations from 1926 to 1935; makes some useful points on British military thinking and on the problems of international arms control.

Hillson, Norman. *Geneva Scene*. London: George Routledge & Sons, 1936. Rather breezy first-hand account by a British correspondent.

Simon, John Allsebrook. *Retrospect: The Memoirs of Viscount Simon*. London: Hutchinson, 1952. Memoirs of the former British foreign secretary.

Walters, Francis Paul. *A History of the League of Nations*. London: Oxford University Press, 1952. One of the most thorough overall histories of the League; the chapters dealing with the disarmament conference provide a useful brief analysis of the various plans presented during the negotiations in Geneva.

Scott, George. *The Rise and Fall of the League of Nations*. New York: The Macmillan Company, 1973. Interesting, colorful, but somewhat impressionistic work.

Kimmich, Christopher M. *Germany and the League of Nations*. Chicago: University of Chicago Press, 1976. Solid, scholarly study of Germany's relations with the League; maintains that whatever sincerity Germany may have shown at times, in general terms the Germans viewed the League as a means of reaching their foreign policy goals, and left the League when no further advantages could be expected from it.

Weinberg, Gerhard L. *The Foreign Policy of Hitler's Germany: Diplomatic Revolution in Europe, 1933-1936*. Chicago: University of Chicago Press, 1970. Emphasizes the cynicism of Hitler's relations with the League and the priority rearmament took in Nazi policy.

# CHADWICK DISCOVERS THE NEUTRON

*Type of event:* Scientific: major conception in atomic physics is verified
*Time:* February 17, 1932
*Locale:* Cavendish Laboratory in Cambridge, England

*Principal personages:*
ERNEST RUTHERFORD (1871-1937), Professor of Experimental Physics at the University of Manchester and later at the Cavendish Laboratory, Cambridge University
JAMES CHADWICK (1891-1974), first a student of Rutherford at Manchester and later his assistant at the Cavendish Laboratory

## Summary of Event

By the end of the nineteenth century the notion that matter is composed of homogeneous and indivisible atoms was being challenged by the speculations of physicists. It was beginning to be apparent that there might be still smaller particles. James Chadwick's experimental verification of the existence of one such particle, the neutron, forms an important part of the complex history of the development of modern atomic theory. The links to the past of the emerging subatomic physics can be seen in the way in which the neutron was at first referred to as an uncharged "atom" of one atomic mass unit.

An early turning point from which modern developments in atomic theory follow was provided by the theoretical and experimental work on the electron done by Joseph Larmor and J. J. Thomson in the 1890's. Their work, attempting to explain how electrical charge is ultimately held in matter, by 1897 yielded the conception of the electron as the material unit of electricity associated with an atom, the matter of which was relatively evenly distributed in the space it occupied. While this concept accounted for a variety of experimental effects, others were unexpectedly obtained which it would not explain. When Ernest Rutherford's assistants in 1911 at the University of Manchester in England directed radioactive particles at a thin sheet of platinum or gold leaf and discovered that some of the particles appeared to be deflected backward, he found himself at a loss to explain how this could occur. "It was quite the most incredible event that has ever happened to me in my life. It was almost as incredible as if you fired a 15-inch shell at a piece of tissue paper and it came back and hit you." As a result, Rutherford developed his famous "nuclear atom" concept: the atom was viewed as an entity carrying a positive electric charge counterbalancing the negative charge of electrons circling a dense nucleus. This arrangement made the atom, taken as a whole, electrically neutral, and it concentrated the mass of the atom at the center.

Shortly thereafter, in 1913, Niels Bohr offered a theoretical description

283

of the part of the atom external to the nucleus, but the internal structure continued to offer other problems to which Rutherford and his colleagues turned their attention. One of the first insights was provided by Rutherford himself. In a Bakerian Lecture to the Royal Society of London delivered on June 3, 1920, he spoke about the possible existence of a "kind of neutral doublet"—an electron and a proton in some kind of compound, perhaps an "atom of mass 1 which has zero nucleus charge." It would have

> . . . novel properties. Its external field would be practically zero, except very close to the nucleus, and in consequence it should be able to move freely through matter. Its presence would probably be difficult to detect by the spectroscope, and it may be impossible to contain it in a sealed vessel. On the other hand, it should enter readily in the structure of atoms.

The various factors which led Rutherford to take seriously the possibility of the neutron grew out of his own work on the nuclear atom. He agreed with Bohr that the rather small but massive and positive nucleus "is surrounded at a distance by a distribution of negative electrons equal in number to the resultant positive charge on the nucleus." He also understood that the number of electrons, or atomic number, is about half of the atomic weight. The importance of the atomic number in defining the chemical and physical properties of an element was also beginning to be perceived. Rutherford therefore considered it of the utmost importance to determine if indeed the atomic number is an exact reflection of the nuclear charge. In addition, he knew that in the case of hydrogen, one unit of positive charge is contained in a nucleus of mass one, and that the elements could exist as isotopes—that is, atomic mass could vary without significantly changing the chemical properties of the element.

From these considerations and from experiments that he directed into the collisions of alpha particles with some of the lighter elements, Rutherford developed such speculative alternatives as the idea that the collisions might produce "an atom of mass nearly 2, carrying one charge, which is to be regarded as an isotope of hydrogen," or they might produce his "neutral doublet." None of the alternatives was to be immediately confirmed. It remained to discover physical evidence that might determine both the existence and character of the hypothetical particle. In an attempt to accomplish this task, Rutherford in the early 1920's at the Cavendish Laboratory in Cambridge, England, directed a portion of the research to trying to form a neutral doublet by forcibly combining electrons with protons in a discharge tube. Although all such efforts were unsuccessful, he continued to refer to the idea in some of his papers, and he brought Chadwick in as his collaborator on occasion. Thus, they issued a joint paper in 1929 on "Energy Relations in Artifical Disintegrations," but even as late as this no solid physical evidence of the neutron could be construed.

Then, in 1930, two German researchers, Walther Bothe and H. Becker, were attempting to detect electromagnetic gamma radiation that might be generated from lighter elements under a shower of alpha particles. When they chanced to apply this bombardment to beryllium, they were able to detect a radiation of unaccountable strength. These experiments were confirmed by Irène Curie in Paris in 1931. The following January, 1932, Curie and Frédéric Joliot, who had been pursuing further experiments to find out whether the resulting beryllium radiation could produce disintegrating effects in other elements, discovered evidence of particles that appeared to be unusually energetic protons. While this could have been explained as a collision process involving the nucleus, they interpreted it in terms of an electromagnetic scattering modeled upon the dual nature of light, as developed by Arthur H. Compton in 1923.

It was at this point that Chadwick, with the help of Norman Feather, devised a crucial experiment to test whether the effect observed by Curie and Joliot was indeed electromagnetic scattering or the result of elastic collisions with the nucleus. As Chadwick explained later in his 1935 Nobel Lecture, he developed additional controls on the experimental procedure and he soon became convinced that beryllium radiation could cause other lighter substances, besides those used by Curie and Joliot, to eject particles as a secondary effect. "The experiments showed that the particles are recoil atoms of the element through which the radiation passes, set in motion by the impact of radiation," he said. Chadwick concluded that this beryllium radiation must include particles of a mass like that of the proton, but with a very high penetrating power (sometimes more than ten centimeters into lead). Furthermore, this behavior was consistent with the assumption that such radiation is of particles of one atomic mass but uncharged—*neutrons*, exhibiting the properties Rutherford had speculatively predicted in 1920. Chadwick announced his discovery from the Cavendish Laboratory in a letter to *Nature* written February 17, 1932, and published in the February 27 issue. He received the Nobel Prize in Physics in 1935. The neutron was to become, because of its unique properties of weight and penetrating power, one of the most important research tools in nuclear physics and was to lead to significant practical applications. As the American physicist Donald L. Hughes stated years later, "We need only think of the large scale production of electrical power or the propulsion of giant, swift submarines to realize the spectacular usefulness of the neutron."

## Pertinent Literature

Schonland, Sir Basil. *The Atomists (1805-1933)*. Oxford: Clarendon Press, 1968.

Basil F. J. Schonland (1896-1972) was personally acquainted with many of the principals and witnessed many of the events that are important in the history of atomic theory. He was, for example, a student at Cambridge University until 1923, studying cathode rays with Rutherford and Chadwick at the Cavendish Laboratory.

*The Atomists* begins with a survey of the foundation period of modern atomic physics, from 1805 to the end of the nineteenth century, proceeding from John Dalton's original, indivisible atom to the theoretical ground prepared for the complex models of Rutherford, Bohr, and Werner Heisenberg. The book is one of the few comprehensive works in this area, and it is eminently accessible to the nontechnical reader of history.

Schonland provides an illuminating interpretive framework into which fall the most important events in new ideas and experiments. Dalton's atomic theory, while it remained beyond the reach of experimental demonstration throughout the greater part of the period, still set the tone of future investigations by serving as an attractive (and frustrating) working hypothesis. In chemical theory this influence was quite fundamental, and shows up in many of the theoretical advances. For example, there were Amadeo Avogadro's hypotheses of 1810 concerning the molecular nature of the elementary gases and the volume occupied by gases at standard temperature and pressure; both hypotheses presuppose atomism. So also did William Prout's hypothesis (1815) that "atoms might well be compounded of hydrogen," and Dmitri Mendeleef's periodic classification of the elements (1896). These chemical ideas, in turn, had a profound impact on atomic physics before radioactivity was discovered.

Schonland also considers the impact of electrical studies on atomic theory. In the 1830's Michael Faraday, inspired by the earlier electro-

chemical work of Humphry Davy, developed his experimental laws of electrolysis which introduced the idea of a charged atom or ion. Faraday's experimental work continued until he was able to provide the idea of "lines of force" as the explanatory kernel linking magnetic and electrical phenomena. Following up on this notion, James Clerk Maxwell mathematized and generalized the theory to include light phenomena. Thereafter, experimental and theoretical investigations of the electromagnetic spectra led to Max Planck's quantum theory, and also at the end of the nineteenth century, to J. J. Thomson's discovery of the "atom of negative electricity," the electron.

The author examines most closely the progress of physics after 1890. He tells with great expertise and clarity of the various models of atomic structure proposed in turn by Thomson, Rutherford, Bohr, and Heisenberg. The relationship of these theories to the experimental evidence, as the latter became available, is made clear by Schonland in such a way as to provide the reader with an informed perspective into which the subsequent story of the neutron is seen properly to fit.

Schonland's account impresses the reader with the international nature of the scientific effort, the effect of World War I on the scientists and their productivity, and the special influences of the academic atmosphere and the social milieu in which the investigators moved. These academic and social circumstances prescribed the conditions under which the scientists taught, investigated, informally exchanged information at meetings and in letters, and eventually published their findings. Schonland is careful to bring out the give-and-take relationship between theoretical insight and experimental and instrumental innovation; this is a blurred relationship and often a confused one, yet it is essential to the sharpening of scientific insight into the physical events taking place. *The Atomists* provides an indispensable layman's introduction to the story of how early atomic theory developed.

Massey, Harrie and Norman Feather. "James Chadwick," in *Biographical Memoirs of Fellows of the Royal Society*. XXII (1976), pp. 11-70.

This is the most comprehensive and informative account of Chadwick's professional life (Massey) and work (Feather) yet written. In addition to providing a bibliography of Chadwick's technical papers, the memoir also presents valuable first-hand knowledge, for the authors were personally acquainted with Chadwick, both socially and professionally.

Because Chadwick is recognized for his pivotal discovery of the neutron, a review of the life of this brilliant scientist adds significantly to our understanding of scientific creativity. His beginnings were unexceptional. He was born at Bollington in Cheshire, England, and attended the local municipal schools in nearby Manchester. He went on, at age sixteen, to the University of Manchester where he studied under Rutherford. Chadwick received his bachelor degree with honors in 1911 and proceeded directly into graduate work for the Master's degree during the exciting years when Hans Geiger and Ernest Marsden were carrying on their classic experiments on alpha-particle scattering that had led Rutherford to propose his revolutionary theory of the dense nucleus of the atom. There Chadwick also met many distinguished figures, including Henry Mosely and Niels Bohr. After receiving his Master's degree, Chadwick used a scholarship obtained for him by Rutherford to study in Berlin with Geiger. While he was there, World War I broke out, and he was not allowed to leave Germany. Although Chadwick was more or less a prisoner, Geiger made sure that he met leading German scientists such as Albert Einstein, Otto Hahn, and Lise Meitner.

When the war was over, Chadwick returned to a job with Rutherford at Manchester, and when Rutherford left to direct the Cavendish Laboratory at Cambridge, Chadwick went with him. Eventually he became Rutherford's executive research assistant, with duties that involved him in research and in direction of the laboratory. According to Massey, "Chadwick was always very good with research students. He was sympathetic to their difficulties and was at all times fully up to date with the requirements for adequate research in any of the areas covered."

This article by Massey and Feather is important not only because it tells Chadwick's story, but also because it describes the very important institutional setting that nurtured him. Indeed, the influential role that the immense productivity of the Cavendish Laboratory played in the history of physics is extraordinary. At Cavendish Chadwick not only had access to Rutherford, but also was in close, stimulating contact with the graduate students. His duties as research assistant kept him abreast of new literature, ideas, and experimental developments. As Massey and Feather demonstrate, the discovery of the neutron was indeed "no lucky accident." — *T.M.S.*

## Additional Recommended Reading

Feather, Norman. "A History of Neutrons and Nuclei," in *Contemporary Physics*. I (1960), pp. 191-203 and 257-266. An exhaustive but not too technical treatment of the concept of the neutron in its historical settings.

Hughes, Donald J. *The Neutron Story*. Garden City, N.Y.: Doubleday Anchor Books, 1959. A book for the layman which stresses the theoretical and practical importance of the neutron concept in physics.

Purcell, Edward M., Norman Feather, Emilio Segrè and James Chadwick. "Symposium III: The Discovery of the Neutron and Its Effects upon History," in *Proceedings of the Tenth International Congress of the History of Science*. Paris: Hermann, 1964, pp. 121-162. The four articles in the Symposium cover the history of the discovery of the neutron.

*Nobel Lectures, Including Presentation Speeches and Laureates' Biographies: Physics, 1922-1941*. Amsterdam: Elsevier Publishing Company, 1965. Most of the prizes given in these years were for work in atomic physics.

Rutherford, Ernest. "Bakerian Lecture: Nuclear Constitution of Atoms," in *Proceedings of the Royal Society of London*. XCVII, ser. A (1920), pp. 374-400. The lecture in which Rutherford presented his provocative idea of the "neutron doublet."

Gillispie, Charles Coulson, ed. *Dictionary of Scientific Biography*. New York: Charles Scribner's Sons, 1970-1976. The lives and works of most of the important scientists recounted by reputable scholars; bibliographical references are included.

Trenn, Thaddeus J. "Rutherford and Recoil Atoms: The Metamorphosis and Success of a Once Stillborn Theory," in *Historical Studies in the Physical Sciences*, Vol. VI. Princeton, N.J.: Princeton University Press, 1975, pp. 513-547. A scholarly account of Rutherford's work that led to the discovery of the nucleus.

Bromberg, Joan. "The Impact of the Neutron: Bohr and Heisenberg," in *Historical Studies in the Physical Sciences*, Vol. III. Philadelphia: University of Pennsylvania, 1971, pp. 307-341. A scholarly account of the efforts in 1932 to give a theoretical interpretation of the neutron and its role in atomic structure.

# THE CHACO WAR

*Type of event:* Military: territorial conflict between Bolivia and Paraguay
*Time:* June 15, 1932-June 21, 1935
*Locale:* The Chaco territory, between Bolivia and Paraguay

*Principal personages:*
EUSEBIO AYALA (1875-1942), Paraguayan President during the Chaco War, 1932-1936
JOSÉ FÉLIX ESTIGARRIBIA (1888-1940), Paraguayan military commander
DANIEL SALAMANCA (1869-1935), President of Bolivia, 1931-1934
GENERAL HANS KUNDT (1869-1939), Bolivian military commander
ENRIQUE COSTILLO PEÑARANDA (1892-      ), Kundt's replacement
DAVID TORO (1892-      ), a rebellious Bolivian commander

## Summary of Event

Bolivia and Paraguay are the only two landlocked nations in South America. They are also among the most underdeveloped countries in the world. Their politics have been a discontinuous chain of upheavals, their economic history is one of indelible poverty. What is currently true was doubly the case in the late 1920's and early 1930's, just prior to the outbreak of the Chaco War, in which both countries risked the majority of their young men and the entirety of their meager financial resources in all-out war. Their objective was the territorial acquisition of the Chaco, a wilderness of scrub land, dense forests, and swamps which both countries had long claimed.

Although it is true that "when the war began the Chaco provided one-third of Paraguay's public revenues," this fact testifies more to national poverty than prosperity. And Bolivia had far less of an investment in this area. True, the Mennonite colony managed quite well, indicating that soil cultivation was a long-range possibility and that water, although very scarce in the dry season, might be available from deep wells. However, neither Bolivia nor Paraguay had any plans for development of a territory that lacked any roads, railroads, communications systems, or settlements of great size.

The Chaco had two seasons, rainy and dry. In the rainy season, what roads there were turned muddy and impassable, and rivers swelled beyond their banks. In the dry season "the heat was intense. It beat down from an almost white sky and rose up in thick waves from the hard-baked clay. The tents which the troops used at first were later found to be excellent ovens in which clay bricks were baked." Dust was everywhere; a journalist relates an incident "when all traffic stopped at the approach of

289

the [Paraguayan] General's car, so that he or his guests might proceed without being choked by dust."

In the face of these dismal facts concerning the Chaco, it can only be concluded that Bolivia's motive stemmed merely from aggressive national pride. Stung by its loss of access to the Pacific in its war with Chile (1879-1884) and feeling that its better-trained army would easily defeat Paraguay's meager and poorly equipped legions, Bolivia hoped for easy victory and access to the Paraguay river. Paraguay, on the other hand, felt that it could not give up its sparse colonies in the Chaco without insupportable economic loss and an unacceptable wound to national honor. Thus it was that sporadic breakouts of armed conflict led, by the middle of 1932, to a state of *de facto* war between the governments of Paraguay and Bolivia.

Commanding the Bolivian Army was General Hans Kundt; commanding for Paraguay was José Félix Estigarribia. For both generals, static defense and frontal attack were the preferred tactics, despite the fact that the experience of the Great War clearly showed the vulnerability of frontal attack to machine-gun fire and the vulnerability of static defense to encirclement. Moreover, encirclement in the Chaco was a particularly harrowing experience, since the availability of water was often decisive. More than once the Paraguayans were to defeat the Bolivians and be greeted with the spectacle of Bolivian soldiers:

... insane with thirst, who sucked blood, drank urine and "implored on their knees a little water, urine of the soldiers or gasoline from the [Paraguayan] trucks to appease the thirst that devoured them." Many stumbled away into the bush, staggering, crawling, to collapse and die. Others "marched and marched and marched with their swollen tongues protruding from dry lips, and one by one they fell down and [their fellows] marched on leaving them to die."

It was a war fought without the benefit of modern equipment. Trucks were constantly in short supply, and although both sides had a small air force, little use was made of it by either combatant. The Bolivians maintained control of the air throughout the conflict, but used planes in combat only for occasional, ineffectual strafing. The Bolivians did have daily extensive air reconnaissance, but no use of it was made by officers on the ground.

Although warfare in the Chaco was decidedly conventional, nevertheless it was clear that Estigarribia, the Paraguayan commander, was the better soldier. While his opponent, Kundt, looked to territorial gain, Estigarribia saw his war goal as the destruction of the enemy. One successful Paraguayan offensive followed another, while Bolivian offensives and counterattacks proved more or less ineffectual. In Kundt's great offensive against Nanawa, he lost two thousand men in a frontal attack. In the second Paraguayan offensive alone, Estigarribia captured eight thousand men and rifles and 536 machine guns. In fact, after a year of war, of seventy-seven thousand Bolivian men in the field only seven thousand remained mobilized.

Estigarribia's brillance as a commander was seconded by Paraguayan President Eusebio Ayala, who left military decisions to him. On the other hand, the relationship between Daniel Salamanca, the Bolivian President, and Kundt was never good. His replacement, Enrique Costillo Peñaranda, fared no better and had to contend not only with La Paz but with a contentious subordinate, David Toro.

In June, 1935, the war ended as a defeat for Bolivia and a pyrrhic victory for Paraguay. Bolivia lost sixty-five thousand of her young men in the war, Paraguay thirty-six thousand.

Both countries virtually bankrupted themselves with military expenses. The Bolivian government did not survive the war; that of Paraguay did not survive the negotiations leading to the peace. Finally, after three years of haggling, a peace treaty was signed on July 21, 1938. Bolivia secured the right to use the Paraguay river in order to have access to the sea. Paraguay obtained the Chaco, but both countries had to bear the legacy of a decimated generation of young men and a bankrupt treasury. These conditions led in turn to political and economical instability for years to come.

## Pertinent Literature

Malloy, James M. *Bolivia: The Uncompleted Revolution*. Pittsburgh, Pa.: University of Pittsburgh Press, 1970.

To James Malloy, the Chaco War was not an isolated event in Bolivian history, but a key link in a chain of national politics which finally led to revolution. Professor Malloy adapts to his own purposes Chalmers Johnson's analysis of revolution in *Revolution and the Social System*. According to this theory, there are three preconditions for revolution. The first is that there must be significant dysfunctions in the prerevolutionary society. In the case of Bolivia, these dysfunctions were caused by intractable social and economic problems. Social benefits were distributed with startling inequality. A wide gulf existed between the privileged and the underprivileged, especially the Indian population, and there was little hope of altering the situation, short of revolutionary change. Moreover,

the country's economic health was poor. Lack of resources other than tin and the underdevelopment of manufacturing and agriculture were evident. Equally evident was the impossibility of economic development without first improving the educational system, building roads and railroads, and creating a solid monetary and banking system. Furthermore, this development was made doubly difficult because Bolivia was at the time of the Chaco War a nation totally landlocked and completely divided into a region of high mountains and a region of virtually underpopulated jungle and desert—the Chaco.

To have a revolution, serious dysfunctions, such as Bolivia's deep social rifts and relative economic incapacity, must be supplemented by an intransigent governing elite. In many cases, dysfunctions can be corrected by such elites if they are resourceful enough to create programs to mollify dissatisfied elements. President Franklin D. Roosevelt's social programs to counteract the economic and psychological effects of the Depression are examples of this resourcefulness. Of course, Roosevelt could rely on the nation's essential economic health. Apparently, the Bolivian governing elite generally lacked not only resourcefulness, but also the economic means of exercising any resourcefulness that might have existed. The intransigence of the Bolivian governing elite, and its consequent reliance on coercion and political repression, may have been as much a result of lack of maneuverability as of inflexible ideology.

Even a relatively intransigent governing elite can survive and forestall revolution by waging war to divert the nation's concern with intractable problems. War raises a nation's spirits, subordinates its other concerns to the business of fighting and winning, and makes self-sacrifice popular— providing the war is successful. In the case of Bolivia, what was meant to be a successful diversion in actuality provided powerful accelerators that together comprised the third precondition of revolution. The first was the war. For Bolivia, the Chaco War had a double impact: economic and psychological. It bankrupted the country. Moreover, the humiliating loss to Paraguay confirmed Bolivia as a nation at the bottom of the pecking order, hopelessly landlocked and thoroughly incapable of successful self-assertion. The war had one further consequence: it crystallized the rev-

olutionary spirit of the younger generation while, at the same time, it destroyed the political credibility of the older generation.

Depression was the second powerful accelerator to revolution. It was a *coup de grâce* for an economy already stagnant from its overreliance on tin mining. The depression dramatically emphasized not only the poverty of the poor, but also the unfortunate economic plight of even the moderately affluent. Further, it served to deny the younger generation among these classes what they considered to be legitimate opportunities for advancement. Thus, at the close of the Chaco War, Bolivian society was already dysfunctional, the existing elite was clearly paralyzed and intransigent, and the depression and the loss of the war had brought Bolivia to the brink of revolution.

A revolution by definition topples an existing regime; after a period of chaos and reorganization, another regime emerges, characterized by some stability. Although "Bolivia represents an important example of a recent attempt to wrench a society out of extreme backwardness and propel it into modernity by means of violent revolution," it also is an example of a country whose revolution is incomplete. Since the Chaco War, the nation has had a surfeit of chaos, but little stability. All of its governments, however good their intentions, have been faced with an unresolvable conflict between the need for general economic growth, with its attendant personal sacrifices, and the demand for individual social and economic improvements in an economy characterized by extreme scarcity. In fact, the Bolivian revolution leaves it as an open question whether any change of leadership or political ideology can alter for the better the fate of a country about whose viability as an economic entity such serious questions exist.

Zook, David Hantzler, Jr. *The Conduct of the Chaco War*. New York: Bookman Associates, 1961.

David Zook's book on the Chaco War is a military history in the old style. From it one gets a clear picture of the scale of the conflict and of the largely conventional strategy and tactics involved in its conduct. Although diplomacy is very much a secondary concern of the author, there is adequate coverage of the involuted international negotiations that led up to and away from the actual hostilities. However, the impact of the war on the economics of Bolivia and Paraguay is given scant attention, as are the conditions and the plight of the common soldier. The point of view of this book is very definitely that of the commanders of armies.

To those used to the scale of the world wars and of Korea and Vietnam, the Chaco War seems little more than a skirmish. The start of the war was not a major campaign, but the attack of nineteen Bolivians on a Chaco fort manned by six Paraguayans. A major Bolivian attack involved six thousand men; in ten days' fighting the Bolivians sustained two thousand casualties, the defenders 248. The relatively small scale of operations made relatively small amounts of equipment crucial. The delivery of fifty trucks or the loss of a thousand rifles could turn the tide of war. This was especially true considering the state of the equipment. Although Zook does not touch on this matter,

P. S. Schor in his article on the Chaco paints a vivid picture of an obsolete Paraguayan aircraft manufactured in 1924, flown with a defective rudder wire and equipped with a parachute nicknamed a "suicide umbrella." Schor also speaks of the Paraguayans in 1932 "armed only with knives, axes and obsolete rifles." Despite the small scale of the war, the impact on the two belligerents was a devastating legacy of social and economic instability. Zook, however, limits his examination to the actual cost of the war in men and money.

From *The Conduct of the Chaco War* a clear picture of the strategy and tactics of the conflict emerges, but little is learned about the fate of the common soldier. The war was fought brilliantly by Estigarribia, but largely on conventional lines. Within the limits of available armaments and transportation, he launched campaigns based on the economy of force, the superiority of static defense over frontal attack and the destruction of the enemy through encirclement. Frontal attack was not abandoned, but Estigarribia did not rely on it with the consistency of the Bolivians to whom the bitter experience of failure with large losses taught no lesson. Tanks were little used in the conflict, as they were not available in large numbers and were unsuited to the terrain. Airplanes were used, mostly by the Bolivians, for reconnaissance and ineffectual strafing. Although Bolivia maintained control of the air throughout the war, it made little use of that control.

Zook's war is clearly a battle between the skills of rival commanders. Common soldiers and their problems receive short shrift, though these problems were clearly great; thousands died not of bullets but of thirst and disease. One wonders also about the promptness and adequacy of care for the wounded.

The Chaco War was a classic example of the doctrine that war is an extension of politics by other means. The ineffectual negotiations preceding the conflict are carefully outlined, as are the equally ineffectual negotiations that ended it and finally led to the peace. In the end, the conquests of Paraguay and not any appeal to legality or fairness decided the new borders of the two nations.

— *A.G.G.*

## Additional Recommended Reading

Kain, Ronald Stuart. "Behind the Chaco War," in *Current History*. XLII, no. 5 (August, 1935), pp. 468-474. An economic analysis suggesting ways of dividing the Chaco that would be of equal advantage to both countries.

MacLeod, Murdo, Jr. "Bolivia and Its Social Literature, Before and After the Chaco War: An Historical Study of Social and Literary Revolution." Unpublished Ph.D. thesis, University of Florida, 1962. Before the Chaco War, Bolivia was a European literary colony; afterwards, its literature reflected its own social conditions.

Morris, Robert M. "Economic Progress in the Americas," in *Bolivia*. The Pan American Union, LXX (February, 1936), pp. 169-171. An optimistic article on Bolivian economics after the Chaco War.

Schor, P. S. "Dust in the Chaco," in *The Living Age*. CCCXLIX (October, 1935), pp. 151-159. A personal report on a visit to the Paraguayan front.

Warren, Harris Gaylord. "Political Aspects of the Paraguayan Revolution, 1936-1940," in *The Hispanic American Historical Review*. XXX, no. 1 (February 6, 1950), pp. 2-25. An analysis of the authoritarian-democratic disposition of politics from the fall of Ayala to the death of Estigarribia.

# EMIGRATION OF EUROPEAN INTELLECTUALS TO AMERICA

*Type of event:* Cultural: political conditions on the Continent force European intellectuals to emigrate to the United States
*Time:* 1933-1939
*Locale:* Continental Europe and the United States

*Principal personages:*

ADOLF HITLER (1889-1945), Chancellor and Führer of Germany, 1933-1945

ALBERT EINSTEIN (1879-1955), Nobel Prize-winning physicist, principally known for his Theory of Relativity

THOMAS MANN (1875-1955), author of such novels as *Buddenbrooks*, *The Magic Mountain*, and *Death in Venice*

WALTER GROPIUS (1883-1969), one of the founders of the famed "Bauhaus" school of architecture which promoted the notion that "less is more"

PAUL TILLICH (1886-1965), Lutheran theologian and scholar, known principally as a proponent of situation ethics

## Summary of Event

The history of the United States has been largely written by those immigrants who came to her shores in the hope of eluding old-world taxation, war, and political persecution. From the late 1840's (when the Irish potato famine sent millions of starving people to America) to the first decade of this century when Eastern Europeans poured in, immigration was of massive proportions. The country's vast spaces readily absorbed Europe's "offscourings," and the newcomers fought Indians, cleared the land, built cities, created roads linking the towns and cities, and began an industrial empire the like of which the world had not seen.

However, by the 1920's, the enormous cascade of Irish, Italians, Croatians, Serbs, Lithuanians, Poles, English, Jews, Greeks, and Portuguese declined, largely because of the antiforeign sentiments of native-born Americans who had come to believe the warnings of ultrarightist fellow countrymen about Bolshevists and "treasonous Reds in our midst." World War I had done its part to promote xenophobia, the fear of foreigners that intensified in 1919 when anarchists and leftists threw bombs, struck plants, and agitated for workers' rights. It was this pervasive suspicion of foreigners that induced Congress to pass restrictive immigration laws, such as the Johnson-Reed Act of 1924, designed virtually to halt the flow of Southern Europeans, Asians, and other groups deemed "undesirable" by the Anglo-Saxon/Irish majority.

Certainly, anti-Semitism was widespread in the 1920's. Jews, harassed and humiliated in most parts of America, were a group thought to be

295

distinctly un-American and thus undesirable. Classed with "Reds" and bomb-tossing revolutionaries in the popular imagination, Jews were particularly unwelcome arrivals in the United States.

From 1924, the date of passage of the Johnson-Reed Act allowing only 150,000 immigrants per year to enter the country, to the Crash year of 1929, when the stock market fell apart, many Europeans wanted to come to the United States, but could not. Yet, after the Great Crash, the number of applications for United States visas fell off sharply, in part because Depression-era America was no longer envisioned as a land of milk and honey. Also, enactment of tougher immigration standards by Congress in 1930 (which insured that only those who could readily make a living for themselves could come to the United States) helped to stop the flow of newcomers; the act was law until 1937.

Though America experienced considerable labor unrest during the 1930's, it was stable in comparison with depression-bound Europe, a continent still recovering from the effects of World War I. The deep political and social unrest brought on by the depression helped bring Adolf Hitler's National Socialist movement to power in 1933. True to the vows he set down in his prophetic *Mein Kampf* (1925), a book about Germany's destiny and mission, Hitler as Chancellor and Führer immediately did two things: began rearming Germany in preparation for war, and started planning how best to rid Germany of those minorities deemed undesirable—especially the Jews. Hit-ler, proclaiming that he would give one thousand deutsche marks to any Jew who would leave the country, made certain that Jews were excluded from participating in Germany's economic and social life. Thousands of Jews soon discovered that laws passed in Nazi-run assemblies forbade them to earn a living. After the huge pogrom called *Kristallnacht* ("the night of broken glass") in 1938, it became increasingly evident that their jobs were not the only things they would lose: their very lives hung in the balance.

The period 1933-1939 marked the time when Jewish intellectuals—indeed, persecuted intellectuals from any ethnic group—could flee Europe by heading for those countries that would receive them: Palestine, South Africa, the United States, and a handful of South American nations. Some were refused admittance, but most were able to find refuge of some sort, since they possessed marketable skills. The majority of these refugees took flight immediately after the Nazis came to power, but another sizable segment left in 1935 after the passage of the repressive Nuremberg Laws, and a third group after government-sanctioned persecutions began in 1938.

The Nazi regime, by making life miserable for so many talented Europeans, lost hundreds of creative, even brilliant, persons, including academicians, poets, novelists, clergymen, philosophers, political theorists, doctors, and lawyers. Such people could not endure the militant antiintellectual atmosphere fomented by Hitler and his party members. Stripped of title and respect,

Aryan intellectuals joined with their Jewish counterparts in escaping the death threats and nefarious book burnings. These Europeans made remarkable contributions to their adopted countries; and many are still actively working on behalf of American institutions. In particular, those scientists fleeing from Europe (especially Germany) helped the United States win the war by their part in developing the atomic bomb and other powerful weapons. Moreover, the cultural life of the United States was greatly enriched by the arrival of some of Europe's most accomplished creative artists and performers. American economic life profited, as well, for among those who escaped Europe were many with considerable business acumen.

Prominent among those who chose to emigrate from Fascist Europe were such luminaries as Albert Einstein, the German-Jewish physicist whose Theory of Relativity transformed theoretical physics and man's basic philosophical outlook on his world and whose atomic research led to the Manhattan Project which contributed to the development of the atom bomb. There was also Enrico Fermi, the Italian Nobel Prize-winning physicist and friend of Einstein who was instrumental in devising the world's first self-sustaining nuclear chain reaction at the University of Chicago—an experiment that brought about the Los Alamos, New Mexico, fission experiments. Also emigrating was Ger-

man-born Walter Gropius, an architect and visionary of remarkable gifts, who had reorganized Germany's prewar ducal art school under the name of Bauhaus, which has come to symbolize the sleekness and lack of surface ornament in modern architectural design. Among others leaving the Continent were Thomas Mann, German author of immense talent who gave the world some of its finest twentieth century novels, such as *Buddenbrooks* (1901), *The Confessions of Felix Krull, Confidence Man* (1954), and *The Magic Mountain* (1927); and Paul Tillich, the German-born theologian and philosopher (one of the first academicians to be hounded from Germany by the Nazis), who related Christian teaching to situations which arise in everyday life, using a "Christian existentialist" approach.

Such eminent intellectuals provided the leaven that America needed to keep her in the vanguard of Western thought. Certainly without the presence of these men, America would have not made the cultural and scientific strides it did in the 1930's, 1940's, and 1950's. Not only did the United States become the world's leading political power; the nation was to become a world center of music, dance, painting, and poetry, as well as of science and technology. Such success was achieved because the creative talents of native Americans merged with those of the foreign-born.

## Pertinent Literature

Fleming, Donald and Bernard Bailyn, eds. *The Intellectual Migration: Europe and America, 1930-1960*. Cambridge, Mass.: Harvard University Press, 1969.

This book is without doubt the most important collection of scholarly writings about those European intellectuals who came to the United States in the period 1930-1960 and added so much to the cultural life of the nation. These physicists, theologians, writers, critics, actors, researchers, psychologists, and artists helped to place America at center stage of the world's intellectual community. Without them, American national life would have been very much the poorer. An arbitrary listing of some of their names reveals the splendor of their achievements: Béla Bartók, Rumanian composer and pianist; Bertolt Brecht, German writer; René Clair, French motion picture director; Max Ernst, surrealistic painter from Germany; Erich Fromm, German psychologist; Mies van der Rohe, premier German architect; Saint-John Perse, French poet and diplomat; Rudolf Serkin, Austrian pianist; Yves Tanguy, French surrealistic painter; Stanislaw Ulam, Polish mathematician; Kurt Weill, German playwright; and Carl Zuckmayer, German writer.

The first essay in the book, "Weimar Culture: The Outsider as Insider," sets the stage for the European intellectual migration that would come after Hitler destroyed the democratic Weimar government. Weimar, which was "born in defeat, lived in turmoil, and died in disaster," gave birth to Europe's most amazing cultural rising during the period between the two world wars: the theater of Brecht and Weill, the Bauhaus movement in architecture of van der Rohe and Gropius, the exuberant paintings of Emil Nolde, and the writings of Franz Werfel and Ernst Kirchner. This renaissance was the product of an unstable state, one hovering perilously close to destruction. The excitement arising from the shaky condition of Germany after World War I made Berlin a mecca for intellectuals from all over the Continent. Nevertheless, in the face of massive social discontent, the Weimar enterprise was destroyed when Adolf Hitler assumed power in 1933. After that year, the disappearance of Europe's intelligentsia became a fact as thousands either kept a low profile and gave up their craft or began leaving Europe. They left Germany for many destinations but chief among them was the United States.

Having dealt with Weimar's early promise and later dissolution, the editors present the *émigré* physicist Leo Szilard's "Reminiscenses" about his own and his colleagues' decision to abandon Europe in the early 1930's for a more congenial America. Following Szilard's account are articles dealing with such matters as the work done on the atomic bomb by *émigré* scientists.

The essay, "A New Site for the Seminar: The Refugees and American Physics in the Thirties," by Charles Weiner, director of the Center for History and Philosophy of Physics, discusses the reason behind America's assumption of world scientific leadership after 1930. Nearly one hundred European refugees joined ranks with almost thirteen hundred native American physicists to create a remarkable scientific community. It should be noted that America, far from being a backward scientific outpost, was already a center for physics at the very time that Europe's top physicists were coming to her shores in substantial numbers. This happy linking of American and European talent allowed the Allied powers to develop the atomic bomb before Hitler did.

To be sure, American physics was not the only field to which the talented *émigrés* contributed their abilities. Mathematics, sociology, psychology, literary criticism, and architecture were transformed by the ideas of those fleeing from the Fascists. John von Neumann, contributor to the automata theory and discoverer of new fields of mathematical study, is closely examined; while Paul Lazarfield, an eminent *émigré* social researcher, offers the reader his personal reactions to life in America, a place where "the evolving trends in [social research] broadened, became diversified and refined, and required new institutional forms." Virtually all of the intellectual immigrants found the United States to be not merely an extension of Europe; they discovered that this country offered them an entirely new world in which to work. For some, of course, that world was alien to European sensibilities. Even

those who returned to Europe after the war, however, did not forget the opportunities that America's open society had afforded them.

For Bauhaus architects such as Mies van der Rohe and Walter Gropius, the American city offered the proving ground for radically new architectural modes which, though conceived in Germany, could not have been implemented there because of Nazi philistinism and the Hitlerian hatred of learning. For Gestalt and Freudian psychologists, America, dismissed as an "outpost" of German experimentalism in the 1920's, became a truer center of psychological inquiry than Vienna. To literary critic Eric Auerbach, Yale University offered a faculty as exciting and supportive as he could have hoped for; his masterwork *Mimesis*, one of the most important critical works of the century, testifies to Auerbach's ability to write in America, as well as to the quality of American cultural resources. So it went: scores of major talents who once would never have considered coming to America found that after being forced to emigrate, they were able here to use their creative faculties to the fullest.

Boyers, Robert, ed. *The Legacy of the German Refugee Intellectuals.* New York: Schocken Books, 1972.

As its name implies, Robert Boyer's book is a gathering of essays analyzing the more outstanding revolutionary ideas expounded by those brilliant *émigrés* who chose life in the democracies of the world to intellectual death in Nazi-dominated Europe during the 1930's. From it the reader acquires an appreciation for such

*émigré*-enriched movements as socialist humanism, existentialism, gestalt psychology, and the sociology of knowledge—as well as for those persons who contributed so much to our national cultural life. Among such German refugees were Bertolt Brecht, expressionistic dramatist; Thomas Mann, novelist; and Albert Einstein, physicist.

*The Legacy of the German Refugee Intellectuals* reminds Americans of their enormous debt to those persons of genius who transformed twentieth century American thought; it also reminds them that these geniuses in turn owe much to the United States, their chief port of safety during the Nazi tempest. Speaking for many of his fellow emigrants, social researcher Henry Pachter notes: "America does not absorb or reject a person, but allows many hundred flowers to bloom in its garden."

Pachter's detailed remembrance of his pre-America and post-America existence, "On Being an Exile," is the *pièce de résistance* of the collection, for, unlike many of the essayists represented, Pachter speaks from firsthand experience about what it meant to be a thinking person in Nazi Germany and to leave old ways behind and take one's chances in America's tumultuous intellectual cauldron. He recalls many notable *émigrés*: Heinrich Mann, Alfred Döblin, and André Gide, remembering what the atmosphere was like for them in puzzling America. Because the intellectuals could freely circulate among themselves in the United States, it was a momentous time to have *avant-garde* ideas and the ability to express them.

Following Pachter's introductory piece are essays about some of the more notable movers and shakers among the dispossessed elite. The contributions of Walter Benjamin, author and Marxist economic theorist who died fleeing occupied France, are discussed by Fredric Jameson; Rudolf Arnheim considers the mammoth change in outlook spawned by the psychologist Max Wertheimer, one of the fathers of Gestalt psychology, who taught at the New School for Social Research in New York; and George McKenna focuses on the work of the political theorist Hannah Arendt, who studied American political institutions in order to "recapture the meaning of political action." Thomas Simons, Jr., offers a retrospective look at Karl Kraus, whose journal *Die Fackel*, a satirical masterwork written between 1899 and 1936, savagely attacked "second-rate" Germans and the Nazi state they helped to create; Henry Hatfield discusses novelist Thomas Mann's complex reactions to the America which gave him sanctuary, a country he found alternately inspiring and bitterly disappointing; and Erich Kahler addresses himself to the narrative technique of Hermann Broch, author of the novel known in English as *The Sleepwalkers* (1932) and a man who dared to try to "live death" for his art. George Steiner offers "A Note in Tribute to Erich Kahler," about a humanist-in-exile who established himself at Princeton; Anthony Wilden gives an estimation of *émigré* Herbert Marcuse, author of *Eros and Civilization* (1955), a landmark in psychological theory which attacked certain Freudian concepts of what motivates man; and Iring Fetscher has a splendid discussion of playwright Bertolt Brecht. Edward Sagarin and Robert Kelly, in "Karl Mannheim and the Sociology of Knowledge," consider refugee sociologist Mannheim's reputation to date; John Herz portrays Otto Kirchheimer, the neo-Marxist sociologist whose theories helped Americans better to understand what was transpiring in Fascist Germany. Reuben Abel assesses philosopher Felix Kaufman, a product of pre-Hitler Vienna (and influenced by the phenomenologist Edmund Husserl), who, after emigrating from Germany, fell under philosopher John Dewey's spell during his American sojourn. Finally, Jurgen Habermas discusses the work of Ernst Bloch, an "epic" thinker and the author of *Hope as a Principle*, "a mirror of a philosopher's wanderings. . . ."

Two essays of a general nature have to do with movements heavily influenced by *émigré* German intellectuals. The first, Walter Kaufman's "The Reception of Existentialism in the United States," demonstrates how the Nazi persecution pushed positivistic philosophy into near-oblivion, but unwittingly prompted an increased interest in the philosophical outlook known as "existentialism." Instrumental in introducing existentialism to Europe, then to America, was the French philosopher, Jean-Paul Sartre, who, according to Kaufman, had more of an impact on American philosophy than anyone else in recent times. Also influential in their exile were theologians Paul Tillich and Martin Buber, men often called "existentialistic" in outlook.

The second essay, George Mosse's "The Heritage of Social Humanism," highlights the achievements of those authors—Lion Feuchtwanger, Heinrich Mann, Leonhard Frank, and Alfred Döblin, to name but four—whose belief in reason, justice, and hatred of persecution made them outcasts in Germany. They felt that somehow humanity and civilization would prevail over barbarism; but because of their left-wing sympathies, their ideas went largely unnoticed in America.

Boyer's book offers a fine store of information about the best and brightest products of Weimar Germany—the Germany that Hitler destroyed—and about some of the marvels they helped to engender in their adopted United States. — *J.D.R.*

## Additional Recommended Reading

Fermi, Laura. *Atoms in the Family: My Life with Enrico Fermi*. Chicago: University of Chicago Press, 1954. As the wife of the renowned physicist Enrico Fermi, Laura Fermi tells how she and her husband first tried to live under Italian Fascism, then found themselves forced to flee to London, and finally to America.

Adams, Walter, ed. *The Brain Drain*. New York: The Macmillan Company, 1968. A general discussion of the movements of intellectuals from their native country to their adopted country which disproves the notion that the United States unscrupulously lured intellectuals away from their homes in recent times.

Kulischer, Eugene M. *Europe on the Move: War and Population Changes, 1917-1947*. New York: Columbia University Press, 1948. Discusses the vast internal movements of ethnic subgroups from nation to nation in Europe between the World Wars.

Friedman, Saul S. *No Haven for the Oppressed: United States Policy Toward Jewish Refugees, 1933-1945*. Detroit: Wayne State University Press, 1973. A thorough study of America's initial lack of sympathy toward Jewish victims of Nazi pogroms who sought asylum.

Jones, Maldwyn Allen. *American Immigration*. Chicago: University of Chicago Press, 1960. A general survey giving the two sides of the immigration experience (that is, the new arrival as both emigrant and immigrant) and providing the reader with a viable context in which to understand the phenomenon of immigration in the United States during the 1920's and 1930's.

# NAZI PERSECUTION OF THE JEWS

*Type of event:* Political: development of political, legal, social, religious, economic, and cultural discrimination against Jews
*Time:* 1933-1939
*Locale:* Germany

*Principal personages:*

ADOLF HITLER (1889-1945), Chancellor and Führer of Germany, 1933-1945

HEINRICH HIMMLER (1900-1945), Reichsführer of the SS and Chief of the German Gestapo

HERMANN GÖRING (1893-1946), Interior Minister and Minister of Aviation

REINHARD HEYDRICH (1904-1942), Deputy Chief of the Gestapo, head of the SS Security and Intelligence Service (SD)

ADOLF EICHMANN (1906-1962), head of Austrian Central Immigration Office and Chief of German deportation system during World War II

## Summary of Event

On January 30, 1933, Adolf Hitler took the oath of office making him Chancellor of the German Republic; he was appointed under the Weimar Constitution, which granted President Paul von Hindenberg the authority to invoke dictatorial power to prevent an overthrow of the government. On February 4, 1933, Hitler convinced Hindenberg to authorize prohibition of public meetings and suppression of publications that might endanger the security of the state. From the beginning Hitler utilized that power against his political enemies. On February 27, the Reichstag was set ablaze. Using the pretext of a Communist threat, of which the Reichstag fire was cited as an example, Hitler, with Hindenberg's approval, issued a series of decrees suspending traditional civil rights. Consequently Hitler had, within a few weeks of assuming office, succeeded in accomplishing a "legal" revolution. By July of 1933, the Communists and Social Democrats had been suppressed; and on July 14, the National Socialist Party was declared the only party in Germany. Having consolidated his political authority, Hitler turned his attention to the Jews.

Having advocated anti-Jewish policies for years, Hitler and the National Socialists now had the opportunity to implement those policies. From February, 1933, the Nazis had instituted boycotts against Jewish businesses. Violence against Jews and Jewish stores was intensified after March 11, when Hermann Göring, the Interior Minister, declared that the German police would not protect Jews or their property.

Attacks on Jews continued throughout March. On the 26th of

that month, leaders of various Jewish organizations were called before Göring, accused of spreading abroad false rumors of violence, and forced to promise to contact Jewish organizations around the world to deny reports of brutality and atrocities against Jews in Germany. Another boycott of Jewish business was called for April 1 to April 3, 1933. As government-sponsored anti-Jewish rioting and boycotts occurred all over Germany, wholesale dismissal of Jews from government positions began. After March 1, Jewish lawyers attached to Breslau courts were dismissed. On March 25, Jewish judges in Bavaria were removed from various types of cases. On March 31, a statement was issued mandating the retirement of Jewish judges in Prussia.

The dismissal or forced retirement of judges and lawyers had caused much publicity and raised questions of legality. Therefore, in early April, Hitler's government began enacting a series of laws that changed the legal status of Jews and legalized subsequent persecution. On April 5, Hitler wrote to Hindenberg proposing a "legal" answer to the "Jewish problem." On April 7, the first of what would eventually become some four hundred laws resulting in the destruction of Europe's Jews was enacted. The first law mandated that Jews and enemies of the Nazi state be removed from the Civil Service. A second law, simultaneously enacted, debarred Jewish lawyers. Another law of April 7 excluded Jews from juries and prohibited them from serving as commercial judges. On April 22, Jews were prohibited from practicing as physicians, dentists, or dental technicians in social insurance institutions. On April 25, the number of Jews allowed into German schools was reduced; on May 6, they were removed from positions as honorary professors and university lecturers; in September, 1933, they were excluded from entertainment or cultural occupations; and in October, 1933, they were prohibited from working on German newspapers. Hitler also attempted to deal with Jewish religious practices, for in April, 1933, Jews were prohibited from the ritual slaughter of animals. On July 26 there was a cancellation of the naturalization of Jews who had become German citizens under the Weimar Republic, and in the fall of 1933 Jews were prohibited from inheriting farm property. Reports of murder, assassination, and brutality against Jews continued to reach the non-German world. Some two thousand Jews were killed in 1933 and many were placed in concentration camps. Thus, by the fall of 1933, Hitler had legally excluded Jews from the government and many professions and had instigated a continuing campaign of terror and violence against them. As Jews were losing their rights of German citizenship, the noose of Nazi hostility was being drawn ever tighter around their necks.

No new substantive legislation was passed during 1934, but the Nazis continued to enforce ever more strictly the legislation of 1933. Again, in 1935, the Nazis stepped up their campaign against the Jews. Now Jews were prohibited from going to places of entertainment, such as theaters or swimming pools. However, by late summer, the campaign of harassment abruptly ceased and violence was replaced by an organized, orderly, and bureaucratically administered terror signaled by the promulgation on September 15, 1935, of the Nuremberg Laws. These laws prohibited marriage between Jews and Germans; extramarital relations between Jews and Germans; the employment by Jews of female domestic help under forty-five years of age; the flying by Jews of German flags.

The Nuremberg laws were followed by the promulgation of a new Reich Citizenship Law. Distinguishing between a citizen (*Reichsbürger*) and a state subject (*Staatsangehörige*), Jews were categorized as the latter. This gave Jews a distinctly inferior status, but also redefined citizenship so that it was based upon racial purity and a slavelike obedience, rather than on rights. The same act which deprived Jews of their rights of citizenship and made them subjects of the state also deprived other German citizens of their rights. In time, the Reich Citizenship Law placed Jews under the control of the secret police, with no access to the German legal system. A supplementary act of November 14, 1935, defined the Jew on the basis of a minimum of three full Jewish grandparents; there followed variations of this definition to include many other categories. The enforcement of this law prevented Jewish participation in the 1936 Olympic Games in Berlin.

Within a few years, the Jews came under the authority of SS leaders Heinrich Himmler and Reinhard Heydrich. After promulgation of the Nuremberg Laws, *Entjudung*, or elimination of the Jews from Germany, became the official SS policy. Therefore, Zionism, the desire of Jews to move to Palestine, was encouraged until 1937, when Palestinian Arabs convinced Hitler that a Jewish state would not be beneficial to German interests. In 1937 Adolf Eichmann recommended a policy of forced expulsion of Jews from Germany and Hitler adopted this view. A year later Eichmann set up an office for this purpose in Austria, following its annexation by the Reich.

The increase in the number of Jews which accompanied the absorption of Austria in March, 1938, stimulated anti-Jewish violence throughout the Greater German Reich and resulted in passage of additional discriminatory legislation. For example, effective April 26, 1938, Jews had to report all foreign and domestic property in excess of five thousand marks; this step preceded expropriation. In the summer of 1938, Jewish businesses were defined and Jews were prohibited from engaging in various commercial ventures. In the summer and fall, Jewish physicians and lawyers were denied the right to practice, and Jewish businesses were transferred to Aryans. Identification of Jews became more precise, for Jews were required to obtain official identification cards in 1938; and as of January 1, 1938, all Jews were required to adopt a "Jewish" name as specified by the government. The Nazis were active in other ways, too. Mass arrests of Jews took place in the spring and summer of 1938 and there was an enlargement of various concentration camps, such as those at Dachau and Buchenwald. German annexation of the Sudetenland in October, 1938, and the eventual seizure of all of Czechoslovakia increased the numbers of Jews in German hands. The German response was to intensify their physical attacks.

Emboldened by the marked apathy of the world toward the Nazi program of anti-Semitism and by Hitler's success at Munich, the Germans, in October, 1938, began seizing Polish Jews living in Germany and brutally moving them to the Polish border. When the Polish Government refused to admit them, they were forced to remain throughout the winter in the no-man's land between the Polish and German borders. Meanwhile, on November 9, 1938, in response to the assassination of a Reich diplomat by a Jew, Heydrich organized a massive national uprising against Jews. In this orgy, known as *Kristallnacht*, "the night of broken glass," some two hundred synagogues were destroyed, along with almost a thousand Jewish businesses. About 7,500 Jewish shops were looted, and many Jews were beaten or killed. The Austrians acted even more brutally.

As a result of *Kristallnacht*, a fine of one million marks was imposed on the Jews, and new legislation was passed barring them from all public places, including schools. They were also excluded from the economic life of Germany. On January 24, 1939, Göring placed Heydrich in charge of forced emigration of all Jews. Never again would an outburst such as *Kristallnacht* occur; in the future, Jews would be handled by a rational bureaucracy which would develop a smoothly working system of annihilation.

The prospect of annihilation became clearer in 1939. Increasing unwillingness on the part of the nations of the world to accept Jewish immigration reached the level of irresponsibility; Great Britain, in particular, issued the so-called White Paper in 1939, which severely restricted immigration to Palestine and, thereby, shut off Jewish escape from Europe. The beginning of World War II and Germany's conquest of Poland left the Nazis with more Jews than ever before, none of whom the rest of the world would accept as immigrants.

On January 30, 1939, Hitler predicted the destruction of Europe's Jews. That process began when Heydrich was placed in charge of Ghettoization of all Jews in Nazi-occupied Poland. Heydrich's directive of September 21, 1939, was designed to implement Ghettoization as the first step of "the planned overall measures" (the "final aim")—the eventual destruction of the Jews.

## Pertinent Literature

Morse, Arthur D. *While Six Million Died: A Chronicle of American Apathy*. New York: Hart, 1967.

Focusing on the response of the Government of the United States and other Western democracies to Nazi persecution of the Jews from 1933 to 1945, this is one of the most interesting accounts of the progressive brutality against the Jews prior to World War II. Beginning with the apathetic response of the Allied powers to news of the "final solution" in 1941 and 1942, and describing, as well, the refusal of the Western democracies to take action to prevent the destruction of Jews in 1943 and 1944, Morse turns to a description of the period 1933 to 1939. Here he dramatically recounts the steps taken by the Germans in their organized campaign of persecution of the Jews. Such a campaign was first suggested in two lines from the "Horst Wessel" song, "Wenn das Judenblut vom Messer spritzt, dann geht's nachmal so gut" (When Jewish blood spurts from a knife, things will be much better). Having resolved on a policy of persecution of the 500,000 Jews living in Germany (the total German population was 65,000,000) Hitler and his subordinates initiated a sustained legal, social, political, economic, and physical attack on the Jews.

Carefully detailing the nature of this attack, Morse describes the specific events of 1933, the promulgation of the Nuremberg Laws in 1935, the continuous brutality and violence against the Jews, the German racial discrimination against Jews during the 1936 Olympic Games, the horror of *Kristallnacht* and its effects, and the policies that initiated the destruction of the Jews. Morse also details the reaction of the government of the United States and the Western Allies to each of these events. That reaction was one of unrelieved apathy and indifference.

Morse describes the indifference of the immigration policies of the United States throughout the 1930's. The American quota system, developed through a series of laws passed in 1921, 1924, and 1929, gave American immigration officials the opportunity to prevent Jews from emigrating to the United States. American insistence that Nazi officials provide certification of the good character of potential Jewish immigrants created a barrier to emigration that few German Jews could surmount. Moreover, in the midst of the unemployment of the Great Depression, fear that immigrants would either take the jobs of American citizens or become public charges entailed an overly strict enforcement of requirements that effectively prevented emigration. Immigration laws were strictly enforced under the administration of Franklin D. Roosevelt and quotas remained unfulfilled through the 1930's.

If immigration remained restricted, some Americans hoped that at least the government of the United States might allow Jewish refugee children to enter this country. An organization called German Jewish Children's Aid, directed by Cecilia Razovsky, could only prevail on United States governmental officials to accept one hundred children a year. This may be contrasted with England's willingness to accept nine thousand Jewish refugee children in 1939, prior to the beginning of World War II. Organized labor and patriotic groups such as the American Legion and the women of the Grand Army of the Republic feared the admission into the United States of such children. This was made particularly clear when, in 1939, an effort was made to rescue some twenty thousand Jewish children from impending disaster in Germany. As a result of the lobbying of "patriotic" groups, Congress refused to admit the children.

Even as the Immigration Service and the Congress refused to recognize the crisis in Germany, American and international sports groups made their accommodation with Nazi Germany's racial policies. There was much debate about whether the United States should participate in the 1936 Berlin Olympic Games, in view of Hitler's discrimination against Jewish athletes. The American Olympic Committee could see no reason for nonparticipation by the United States, and this view prevailed.

In 1938, the Evian Conference was held to attempt to resolve the problem of refugees from Nazi Germany through the establishment of an Intergovernmental Conference. Many believed that setting up a committee to deal with this problem was not an effective solution; and indeed, the committee accomplished nothing. Then the British, in the summer of 1939, suggested to the United States the raising of one billion dollars for the resettlement of refugees, but American officials discouraged the idea and it died for lack of support. Thus Hitler's persecution of the Jews continued unimpeded.

Schleunes, Karl A. *The Twisted Road to Auschwitz: Nazi Policy Toward German Jews, 1933-1939*. Urbana: University of Illinois Press, 1970.

Nazi policies toward German Jews and programs for their elimination comprise the subject of this excellent work. Schleunes begins with an analysis of the status of Jews during the Second Reich, together with a general account of anti-Semitism in the nineteenth and twentieth centuries. His conclusion is that prior to World War I anti-Semites represented a lunatic fringe with little influence, while the Jews were thoroughly assimilated into German society.

The situation of the Jew in German society began to change under the Weimar Republic. Jews occupied a middle-class position in society and were successful in establishing themselves in a variety of occupations. Then the false claim began to be made that the Jews dominated the German economy—a claim used by

National Socialist ideology in the 1920's to explain all of Germany's problems after World War I. The forged document *The Protocols of the Elders of Zion* popularized the argument that the world's problems lay with the Jew. In the 1920's, amid the disintegration of the German party system, the views of the National Socialists were increasingly heard. However, Schleunes maintains, Germans were attracted to the Nazi Party not because of its anti-Semitism, but because the Party offered unique answers to the Depression. Eventually Germans were attracted to anti-Semitism because of their support of the Nazis. Schleunes contends that, once in power, the problem for Hitler became that of "unveiling" the assimilated German Jew. While the "Final Solution," the destruction of the Jews, was a major Nazi preoccupation of the 1940's, their major problem of the 1930's was this issue of "unveiling."

Hitler's first attempt at unveiling was through boycotts. Viewing themselves as a revolutionary party, the Nazi revolution was mostly a matter of semantics in all areas except that of the Jews. By March 24, 1933, Hitler had obtained the power to rule by decree, and he used this authority to boycott Jewish business. The boycott failed and was eventually abandoned because Hitler did not at first recognize its overall effects on the German economy. Recognizing the boycott's failure, Hitler moved to enact a series of laws for dealing with the assimilated Jews.

Hitler's first law, in April of 1933, was designed to purge the Civil Service of Jews, particularly lawyers and judges. Hitler then promulgated laws to eliminate Jews from the schools and to prevent Jewish physicians from participating in the national health service. Next, Jews naturalized after 1918 had their citizenship revoked. In September, Jews were excluded from cultural activities. The 1935 Nuremberg laws were involved with legal definitions of Jews and their separation from German society. However, that legislation did not entirely solve the problem of assimilation. Because the boycott had failed, and even legislation was ineffective in "unveiling" the Jews, the Nazis next turned to the policy of Aryanization.

Aryanization was undertaken in 1937 and 1938 as an effort to eliminate Jews totally from the German economy. *Kristallnacht* was, for Schleunes, only one effort among many to rid Germany of her Jewish businesses. But Aryanization failed too; and by 1938 not all Jews had been removed from the economy.

The failure of Aryanization led to the policy of emigration. Emigration required a destination, and, while some Nazis were pleased to support Zionism's Palestine as a destination for Jews, others feared Jewish concentration there, and eventually Hitler rejected the idea. Schleunes finds that every Nazi policy regarding the Jews in the period from 1933 to 1938 failed. The boycott, legislation, Aryanization, and emigration had not achieved the expulsion of the Jews from Germany. Moreover, German policy regarding the Jews seemed, to many leading Nazis, to be without purpose or direction.

As directionless as his policy toward the Jews seemed, by 1938 Hitler had made clear his plans for war, had assumed the role of Commander in Chief, and had filled the most important Reich positions with his loyal supporters. The centralization of his authority and the clarification of his war objectives led Hitler to consolidate his authority over Jewish policy as well. The year 1938 was a turning point. *Kristallnacht* demonstrated that German as well as Jewish property could be destroyed by publicly attacking Jews, and it pointed to the amateurishness and uncoordinated nature of German policy regarding the Jews. Thereafter, German policy toward the Jews hardened under Hermann Göring. Heydrich was placed in charge of the transfer of Jews to Poland after its conquest in 1939. In the words of Schleunes, "The 'experts' were finally in charge of Jewish policy." Under their authority the mechanics of the "final solution" were developed and carried out during the course of World War II. — *S.L.*

## Additional Recommended Reading

Levin, Nora. *The Holocaust: The Destruction of European Jewry, 1933-1945*. New York: Thomas Y. Crowell Company, 1968. Definitive work on the Holocaust that gives considerable attention to the persecution of the Jews prior to 1940.

Dawidowicz, Lucy S. *The War Against the Jews, 1933-1945*. New York: Holt, Rinehart and Winston, 1975. One of the better surveys of the period of persecution of the Jews and the Holocaust.

Cohn, Norman. *Warrant for Genocide: The Myth of the Jewish World Conspiracy and the Protocols of the Elders of Zion*. New York: Harper & Row Publishers, 1969. Excellent intellectual history describing the philosophical and ideological sources of anti-Semitism.

Friedman, Saul S. *No Haven for the Oppressed: United States Policy Toward Jewish Refugees, 1933-1945*. Detroit: Wayne State University Press, 1973. One of the definitive works, along with Morse's *While Six Million Died*, describing American and Allied indifference to the persecution of the Jews.

Schoenberner, Gerhard. *The Yellow Star: The Persecution of the Jews in Europe, 1933-1945*. New York: Bantam Books, 1973. General survey of Nazi persecution of the Jews.

Hilberg, Raul, ed. *Documents of Destruction*. New York: Quadrangle Books, 1961. One of the better collections of documents detailing the persecution and destruction of the Jews under the Nazis.

# HITLER COMES TO POWER IN GERMANY

*Type of event:* Political: Nazism replaces German democracy
*Time:* January 30, 1933
*Locale:* Berlin and the rest of Germany

*Principal personages:*

ADOLF HITLER (1889-1945), Chancellor and Führer of Germany, 1933-1945

FRANZ VON PAPEN (1879-1969), German Chancellor, 1932; and Vice-Chancellor under Hitler, 1933-1934

HERMANN GÖRING (1893-1946), President of the Reichstag, 1932-1933; and Minister in Hitler's cabinet

FIELD MARSHAL PAUL VON HINDENBURG (PAUL LUDWIG HANS ANTON VON BENECKENDORFF UND VON HINDENBURG) (1847-1934), President of the Weimar Republic, 1925-1934

JOSEPH GOEBBELS (1897-1945), Nazi leader of Berlin, eventually Minister for Propaganda and Enlightenment

GENERAL KURT VON SCHLEICHER (1882-1934), last German Chancellor before Hitler, 1932-1933

ERNST RÖHM (1887-1934), Chief of Staff of the Nazi Brown Shirts (the SA)

## Summary of Event

On the morning of January 30, 1933, Adolf Hitler took the oath of office from the venerable President of the Weimar Republic, Field Marshal Paul von Hindenburg. That evening thousands of Nazi Brown Shirts, bearing torches, marched through the Brandenburg Gate past the new Chancellor, celebrating their victory over the forces of German democracy. The Third Reich, which would bring Hitler the fanatical allegiance of the majority of Germans and which would lead to the vast holocaust of World War II, had begun.

Hitler's movement, the National Socialist German Workers' Party (NSDAP), had begun with a handful of malcontents in Munich shortly after World War I. His ruthlessly brilliant leadership differentiated it from the many other racist-nationalist groups of the era. Hitler had tried to grasp power in 1923 at the Beer Hall Putsch, but Weimar democracy had prevailed, and by the time of the 1928 elections, the Nazis appeared to be no more than an annoying inconsequential party of the lunatic fringe radical right. Their combination of nationalism, anti-Marxism, anti-Semitism, anti-big business "socialism," militaristic agitation, and raucous oratory had gained them less than three percent of the popular vote. Yet, in less than five years, Hitler was Chancellor of Germany, placing such key men as Hermann Göring and Joseph Goebbels in charge of the mechanisms of the state. By the time of President Hindenburg's death in August, 1934, Hitler had totalitarian control of the state.

Historians have noted a number of

causes for the Nazi rise. Few will still argue that the German intellectual traditions which venerated the authority of the state, lauded the military virtues, and praised the greatness of the German people, made Hitler's victory inevitable. Nevertheless, this background provided traditions which Hitler could pervert and exploit. The depression, which hit Germany soon after the 1929 stock market crash in the United States, gave Hitler's movement its greatest boost. As business indicators fell and the unemployment lines grew, the Nazis scored impressive electoral gains. Curiously, however, it was not primarily the unemployed who gave their votes to Hitler; most of those were working-class people devoted to Marxism. If moderate, they voted Social Democrat; if radical, they voted Communist. The Nazi voters appear to have come largely from the ranks of the middle classes: shopkeepers, managers, small farmers, white collar workers, civil servants, and others of the *petite bourgeoisie*. They feared the rhetoric of the Marxists and abandoned the traditional bourgeois parties in frustration.

Nationalistic appeals, based on denunciation of the Versailles Treaty imposed on Germany after World War I, excited their support. Hitler, as a humble soldier from the ranks, a man of German "race" although of Austrian citizenship, appealed to their pride with his calls for a Greater Germany. The German people were not as lacking in democratic traditions as some commentators (including Hitler) would have one believe. But their feelings for the Weimar constitution were pragmatic, and when unstable parliamentary coalitions proved unable to handle the economic crisis, they were quite prepared to try more authoritarian solutions.

The Nazis, with their vigor, toughness, and aggressive (if somewhat ill-defined) program, stood out in stark contrast to the modesty and fatigue which characterized the other middle-class parties. Hitler's leadership, amplified by the Goebbels propaganda machine, brought many solid German burghers to his side. Yet, in actual fact, it was the intrigues of reactionary politicians rather than the votes of Germans which put Hitler in power. The Nazis became the largest single power in the German multiparty system, but they never received an absolute majority in a free national election.

The year of the many elections, 1932, shows the dynamics of the Nazi rise. In March, Hitler ran for President against the aging Hindenburg. Hitler received 30.1 percent of the vote to Hindenburg's 49.6 percent, the remaining votes going to the Communist candidate (13.2 percent), and two minor candidates. Clearly, Hitler had lost; but a second ballot was necessary since no one had received an absolute majority. In April, Hindenburg beat Hitler 53 to 36.8 percent. There followed several state legislative elections, the most significant being in Prussia. The Nazis emerged as the largest single party there, with 36.2 percent of the votes. In July, the National Parliament (the Reichstag) was elected. The Nazis won 37.3 percent; they and the Communists—the antidemocratic forces, respectively, of the radical right and the radical left—held a majority of

Reichstag seats between them. A government based on even the broadest coalition of the middle parties was impossible, so in November the German people voted again. This time the Nazi vote totals fell, giving Hitler's brown battalions only 33.1 percent. The Nazi campaign coffers were depleted, and the flood of Nazi votes seemed to have crested and receded. Hindenburg refused to give Hitler the dictatorial powers he demanded as his price for supporting a government with his votes in the Reichstag. Both Hitler and Goebbels became despondent.

The Chancellorship had been held since midyear by a reactionary gentleman once active in the Catholic Center Party, Franz von Papen. After the November elections he found his position undermined not only by the Nazis but by General Kurt von Schleicher, army chief and an inveterate political manipulator. Hindenburg appointed Schleicher Chancellor in December, 1932. The clever general tried to split the Nazi Party and form a coalition of left-wing Nazis, right-wing Social Democrats, and conservatives, in order to keep Hitler from power. Schleicher's plan gathered little support, while Papen worked behind the scenes to unseat Schleicher and create a coalition of Nazis and Nationalists (German National People's Party) in which he would hold a key position. Papen assured Hindenburg and others on the traditional right that Hitler could be controlled by the conservatives in the cabinet. Indeed, only three Nazis, Hermann Göring, Wilhelm Frick, and Hitler himself, would be in the cabinet. Thus Hindenburg agreed to make the fatal appointment.

The first few months of Hitler's rule were crucial to his success, since during that period he accomplished a revolution *after* coming to power. Far from controlling Hitler, Papen and the other conservatives found themselves outmaneuvered by him at every turn. Hitler skillfully dismantled the constitutional guarantees he had sworn to uphold and went on to establish a totalitarian dictatorship in the years that followed. Upon Hindenburg's death in August, 1934, Hitler assumed his powers as President and exacted an oath of personal loyalty from the military.

The Nazi revolution after Hitler's coming to power can be seen as occurring in four phases. First, Hitler prevailed upon Hindenburg to call new elections for the Reichstag. Nazis now controlled the police, so Brown Shirt terrorism went unchecked while the opposition parties labored under severe handicaps. A few days before the election, an ex-Communist Dutch arsonist set fire to the Reichstag building. Quickly, the Nazis fabricated evidence of a Communist uprising and promulgated emergency decrees suspending civil rights. The decrees were never lifted. Even with all the power of the state behind them, the Nazis missed a majority, receiving 43.9 percent of the votes on March 5, 1933.

The second phase was the forcing through the Reichstag of the "Enabling Act," which was written to give Hitler dictatorial powers for a period of four years and required a two-thirds vote of the Reichstag for passage. The Communists had been forcibly excluded and many Social

Democrats had been threatened and did not appear. Nevertheless, Hitler needed the votes of the big Catholic Center Party, so he combined honeyed words and threats to gain its support. When the vote came, only the Social Democratic Party voted "no," all the other parties supporting Hitler. Thus on March 23, 1933, his dictatorship gained its legal basis.

The third phase of the Nazi revolution was the policy of "coordination" (*Gleichschaltung*), which subordinated every organization to the Nazi state. All other political parties were dissolved more or less "voluntarily." The mass media and the arts were coordinated under Goebbels' leadership. Youth organizations, unions, professional societies, and even singing groups and garden clubs found it prudent either to amalgamate with the parallel Nazi organizations or simply to go out of business. Coordination was a process rather than a single action, so it overlapped the other phases in the Nazi takeover chronologically. Its results were uneven. Within the churches, for example, pockets of independence continued to exist, though the vast majority of both Protestants and Catholics formally accepted Nazi dominance. Anyone who actively and publicly opposed coordination faced the prospect of joining the thousands of dissidents in the concentration camps.

The fourth phase included two events in 1934 which placed the capstone on Hitler's control of the state. In late June, rumors of a putsch by Ernest Röhm and certain other "radicals" among the Brown Shirts (the SA) provided an excuse for a bloody purge. Some 150 to 200 potential or real opponents of the regime were shot on Hitler's orders by the SS under the direction of Heinrich Himmler. Not only Röhm, but a number of prominent conservatives including Schleicher, were killed. On August 2, 1934, the eighty-six-year-old Hindenburg finally died. Swiftly, Hitler assumed the powers of the deceased President and had the military swear a personal oath of loyalty to him as "Führer" (leader). Then he arranged for a plebicite in which 89.9 percent of the valid votes cast supported him. Adolf Hitler, the ne'er-do-well Austrian painter, World War I lance corporal, convicted putschist, and fanatic leader of the NSDAP, was the unchallenged Führer of Germany.

## Pertinent Literature

Wheaton, Eliot B. *Prelude to Calamity: The Nazi Revolution 1933-35, with a Background Survey of the Weimar Era.* Garden City, N.Y.: Doubleday & Company, 1968.

Though not a professionally trained historian, Wheaton has done a professional job of reviewing the literature on the Nazi takeover of power and of providing the reader with a clear account of Hitler's victory in Germany. His book demonstrates how Hitler and his cohorts developed their power in the late Weimar Republic, entered office through shrewd political negotiation, and moved aggressively to solidify their position and carry out the Nazification of Germany.

The book has an unusual structure. The heart of it is a day-by-day chronology of the events from the day Hitler was appointed Chancellor through his first six months of power. By setting forth events in this way, Wheaton seeks to draw the reader directly into the whirlwind. Things move incredibly fast: parades and rallies on the one hand, arrests and forcible "coordination" of non-Nazi groups on the other. The approach is very effective. The reader of a standard historical account sees an orderly progression of events which, in reality, has been imposed by the historian after the fact. Wheaton's chronicle keeps the reader off balance, even as the people themselves were in those eventful days.

When the situation calls for it, however, Wheaton suspends his chronicle and engages in traditional historical narrative and analysis. Full chapters are devoted to the controversies over the responsibility for the Reichstag fire and the reasons for the Catholic Center Party's support of the Enabling Act. The entire first section of the book eschews the chronicle approach to provide a background on the problems of German democracy during the Weimar period and an overview of Hitler's origins and early political career. The critical months of the Papen and Schleicher Chancellorships in 1932 are dealt with in narrative style, as are the results of the many 1932 elections.

Some historians see "objectivity" in attempts to avoid judging individual and collective responsibility for events; but not Wheaton. In analyzing the reasons for Hitler's appointment to the Chancellorship, Wheaton assigns much responsibility to Papen and Schleicher. Papen was guilty of severely weakening the struggling prodemocratic forces in the country, particularly when he high-handedly removed the Social Democratic government in the key state of Prussia. Then, after he had lost his Chancellorship because of Schleicher's intrigues, he in turn worked to oust his former colleague. He hoped to manipulate the Nazis and turn Hitler into a kind of figurehead leader. Wheaton sees "no consciously sinister design" in Papen's machinations. Rather, he was victim of his "amateurish" political approach; surely he was neither the first nor the last man to underestimate Hitler.

Among corporate groups, Wheaton sees the responsibility of both the army leadership on the one hand and the Social Democratic Party on the other as primarily sins of omission. The army could have, and should have, acted to limit Nazi terror and protect the constitution it was sworn to uphold. But the aristocratic army leadership had no commitment to democracy. Wheaton castigates the officer corps for its "sheeplike capitulation" to Nazi coordination. The Social Democrats did not lack commitment to the democratic order, but because of "weariness or discouragement" they accepted illegal actions against them and bungled opportunities to work with others to stop Hitler.

Wheaton is far more critical of the Communists than of either the army or the Socialists. They also underestimated the potential power for evil within Nazism, but their "blunders sprang from fixed policies designed to destroy" the Weimar Republic and to replace it with a "Soviet Germany." Thus they not only refused to work with the non-Communist left to save the Republic, but actually became allies of the Nazis in its destruction.

Throughout his book, Wheaton argues that there was no inevitability in Hitler's rise to totalitarian power. Thus he directly confronts the questions of individual and group responsibility for Hitler's victories. He stresses that never in a free election did the Nazis receive a majority of the German votes. Indeed, in the national election just prior to Hitler's appointment to the Chancellorship, two-thirds of the German voters had cast their ballots for non-Nazi parties. Hitler reached and remained on his summit of power "owing to an intricate web of circumstances so tenuous that it would often have been disrupted by the absence or failure of a single strand."

Wheaton's presentation is supported by extensive bibliographical notes which demonstrate his intimate familiarity with the German-language as well as the English-language primary and secondary sources. Though more than a decade old, Wheaton's volume remains a reliably valuable study of the events which brought Hitler to power.

Allen, William Sheridan. *The Nazi Seizure of Power: The Experience of a Single German Town 1930-1935.* Chicago: Quadrangle Books, 1965.

Most of the literature on the Nazi rise to power concentrates quite rightly on events at the top. The key decisions were being made in Berlin by Hitler and his lieutenants, or by Papen, Schleicher, Hindenburg, and the persons with whom they came in contact. But Hitler would never have become Chancellor if his appeal had not found some resonance in Germany as a whole; and he could never have created Nazi totalitarianism had he not had supporters in virtually every town and city who were just as fanatical, ruthless, and ambitious as the men in his immediate entourage.

Allen's book has become a kind of minor classic because it shows the local impact of Nazism, an understanding of which is essential. Thalburg, as Allen calls it, is a real town of ten thousand people with a fictionalized name. Similarly, the author invents names for its inhabitants in order to protect the innocent (and inevitably the guilty as well). The reader comes to know men such as "Walter Timmerlah," a bookstore owner and idealistic Nazi; "Kurt Aergeyz," the ambitious head of the local NSDAP; and "Karl Hengst," the leading Social Democrat of the town. The town's socioeconomic order, its political structure, and its responses to the growing political and economic crisis of the early 1930's are all analyzed.

A careful scholar, Allen takes pains to point out that Thalburg was not "*the* typical German town." There were few Roman Catholics, for example, so the Catholic Center Party played no role. Nor was the Communist Party strong. There were not many Jews, and there was virtually no overt anti-Semitism. Nevertheless, within Thalburg the reader can see a number of developments which were representative of Germany as a whole. In the late 1920's there were few if any Nazis. The Social Democratic Party was very strong, but used its power in moderate and generally unexciting ways. The middle classes, the majority of the people of Thalburg, supported rather unenthusiastically the bourgeois and nationalistic parties of the middle and the traditional right wing. With the coming of the depression, the local government talked a good deal about what ought to be done, but it actually did very little. Indeed, there was little enough that it could do, because the causes of the depression were national and international rather than local. But the depression engendered fear among the good and patriotic citizens of Thalburg, and the handful of local Nazis moved vigorously to exploit that fear.

The NSDAP worked hard for the town's votes. Night after night the Nazis organized rallies, particularly during the seemingly eternal campaigns of 1932. Brown-shirted SA men were imported from adjacent areas to swell their parades. Talking films were shown. Reichstag delegates were brought in for speeches. On one occasion special trains took people from Thalburg to a rally at a neighboring town where Hitler himself spoke. None of the bourgeois parties could match the Nazis for sheer excitement.

The Social Democrats tried to keep up with the Nazis. Though they showed both dogged determination and courage, their Marxist rhetoric scared off more members of the Thalburg bourgeoisie than it attracted, driving them into the arms of the NSDAP. During the 1932 elections Social Democratic vote totals sagged slightly, while the parties of the bourgeois middle and right nearly vanished; the Nazis grew mightily.

Political violence was virtually unknown in Thalburg until the Nazis emerged as a significant force. The Social Democrats dominated the "Reichsbanner," a pro-Republic marching group several hundred strong, but its demonstrations during the late 1920's were no more aggressive than a Fourth of July parade. When the SA began to march in force, however, fights often broke out between the two groups. The middle classes of Thalburg did not approve of the violence, but they tended to blame it on the "Marxists" of the Social Democratic Party. The deep socioeconomic gulf between the middle and the working classes found its parallel in these street battles, and the "good citizens" were forced to choose sides. By the July, 1932, election more than 60 percent of the Thalburg voters chose the Nazis, and the mood of the town reflected a belief that a Nazi victory throughout Germany was inevitable.

When Hitler became Chancellor in Berlin, the Thalburg Nazis rejoiced, while the Social Democrats waited tensely to see whether their national leaders would call a general strike in defense of the Republic. But the call never came. One after another the political and nonpolitical organizations of the town were dissolved or "coordinated."

Allen found that in January, 1933,

there were less than a hundred Nazi Party members in Thalburg, though the Nazis had been receiving about 4,000 of the 6,500 votes cast. By November, 1933, the NSDAP had some 1,200 local members. Thalburg's Nazi leadership took over every significant organization in the town, forcing out not only the Social Democratic and liberal leaders, but the prominent middle-class conservatives as well. Hitler's revolution had come not only to Berlin, but also to the Thalburgs of Germany. — *G.R.M.*

## Additional Recommended Reading

Bullock, Alan. *Hitler: A Study in Tyranny*. New York: Harper & Row Publishers, 1962. Long the standard biography of the Führer, this work shows how he carried out his "revolution after power."

Toland, John. *Adolf Hitler*. Garden City, N.Y.: Doubleday & Company, 1976. A massive and fascinating picture of Hitler and how he came to power, by a highly skilled popular historian.

Bracher, Karl Dietrich. *The German Dictatorship: The Origins, Structure, and Effects of National Socialism*. Translated by Jean Steinberg. New York: Frederick A. Praeger, 1970. A solidly judicious account by the West German scholar who has written in great depth on Hitler's takeover of power.

Tobias, Fritz. *The Reichstag Fire*. New York: G. P. Putnam's Sons, 1964. A detailed and dispassionate investigation by a German Social Democrat, who finds that the Nazis were not implicated in the arson.

Goebbels, Joseph. *My Part in Germany's Fight*. London: Hurst & Blackett, 1935. A view of Hitler's takeover from the Nazi propaganda minister and inveterate diarist.

Dorpalen, Andreas. *Hindenburg and the Weimar Republic*. Princeton, N.J.: Princeton University Press, 1964. A well-documented account by a respected American historian of President Hindenburg's role in the closing years of the Weimar Republic.

# THE UNITED STATES ESTABLISHES DIPLOMATIC RELATIONS WITH THE SOVIET UNION

*Type of event:* Diplomatic: recognition given to Soviet Union by the United States
*Time:* 1933
*Locale:* Washington, D.C. and Moscow

*Principal personages:*
FRANKLIN DELANO ROOSEVELT (1882-1945), thirty-second President of the United States, 1933-1945
JOSEPH STALIN (IOSIF VISSARIONOVICH DZHUGASHVILI) (1879-1953), Dictator of the U.S.S.R., 1924-1953
MAKSIM MAKSIMOVICH LITVINOV (1876-1951), Soviet Commissar for Foreign Affairs, 1930-1939

## Summary of Event

The United States has had a long history of delay in granting diplomatic relations with Communist states. It took Washington three decades to recognize Red China, and a variety of other Communist nations are still denied United States recognition. The reason for this delayed recognition lies in the early history of relations between Washington and the first Communist state—Soviet Russia. The reactions of both the United States and the Soviet Union following the Russian Revolution of 1917 began a long chill in United States-Russian relations which lasted from 1917 to 1933 virtually unabated.

The first incident following the rise of Bolshevism to embitter relations was the military intervention by the Allies in the conflict known as the Russian Civil War. Following the Bolshevik ascendancy to power in November, 1917, foes of the Soviet regime began an attempted counter-revolution in 1918. Centers of these "White" anti-Soviet forces were located in Estonia, Archangel, Siberia, and the Ukraine.

During 1918, the United States and other Allied powers intervened in the Civil War on behalf of the White forces. Because of the sacrifices made by the Soviet government and people during the Civil War, United States and other Allied movements into Russia on behalf of the White forces produced extreme bitterness in the Soviet regime toward the West; and events that followed the Civil War produced bitterness in the United States. By the 1920's, mutual hostility between the United States and the U.S.S.R. was clearly established.

American bitterness was the result of both diplomatic and domestic developments. On the diplomatic front, Soviet Russia had broken ranks with the Allied powers, infuriating President Woodrow Wilson. The Brest-Litovsk agreement concluded by the Soviets and the Germans on March 3, 1918, seemed like a tremendous sellout to the enemy Central Powers. Beyond the world war, the new Soviet regime openly advocated a policy of "world revolution" in the hope that Communist uprisings would quickly follow the Russian inspiration. In Hungary and in Bavaria, there actually occurred shortlived Communist uprisings in 1919. The Communist International, founded in 1919, formalized the Russian commitment to export revolution all over the globe, and world revolution remained a cornerstone for Soviet foreign policy well into the 1920's. This revolutionary objective was in direct opposition to the Wilsonian goal of spreading representative democracy.

Beyond the threat of revolution abroad, Americans in 1919 feared the possibility of revolution at home. Indeed, 1919 was marked by incredible domestic tensions in the United States, highlighted by labor unrest and radicalism. Through the year the nation experienced a strike wave of unprecedented proportions. In Seattle, the American Federation of Labor's local affiliates sanctioned a general strike by all workers in the city to support the demands of shipyard workers. The February Seattle strike was followed by hundreds of strikes through the summer of 1919. But the worst conflict was yet to come: the Great Steel Strike, which began on September 22, was marred by violence, especially in Gary, Indiana, where the United States Army imposed martial law in October. Led by a former radical, William Z. Foster, this strike for a time paralyzed the entire industry before it was eventually defeated. In November, the United Mineworkers led a nationwide coal strike. In the minds of many people, the strike wave of 1919 represented much more than a problem of industrial relations; many people saw the "spector of Communism" in these events.

Beyond the strike wave, the appearance of overtly pro-Communist organizations in the United States helped to poison United States attitudes towards the Soviets. In September, 1919, two Communist groups were formally organized. Both fledgling organizations were offshoots of the more moderate Socialist Party. The new Communist Labor Party represented American-born radicals who supported the Soviet regime, while the Communist Party drew its membership from myriad immigrant groups from Eastern Europe, where sympathy for "Mother Russia" was at a temporarily all-time high. Both Communist groups, though numerically small, attempted to support the strike wave, thus tarnishing labor's image in the process. By January, 1920, the Justice Department, under Attorney General A. Mitchell Palmer, conducted sweeping raids in the country's major cities resulting in the arrests and detention of thousands of suspected radicals. These "Palmer Raids" were followed by the deportation of many immigrants back to Russia.

A final factor in chilling United States-Soviet relations was a series of unsolved bombings, all aimed at conservative, anti-Communist, antiimmigrant government leaders. Given the conservative bent of those attacked, many Americans surmised that the bombers were political leftists inspired by Russia.

Thus, American intervention in the Russian Civil War, labor unrest in the United States, domestic radicalism, and terrorism all effectively led to a lengthy time lag in the establishment of regular diplomatic relations with the Soviet government. Suspicion existed on both sides during the 1920's. But by the 1930's, the situation in both countries was greatly altered, making possible some form of diplomatic compromise.

First, in the Soviet Union the rise of Joseph Stalin to power in the late 1920's was accompanied by a reorientation of Soviet policy. By the late 1920's, it was clear that revolution had not spread to other industrialized nations, and the policy of world revolution—along with its advocates, most notably Leon Trotsky—fell into grave disfavor with the regime. Stalin turned the attention of the Soviet government inward to the ambitious concerns of collectivizing Russian agriculture and building an industrial base. For the time being, then, the Soviet leadership concentrated on domestic problems, rather than on the spread of world revolution.

In the United States, conditions were, of course, altered by the onslaught of the Great Depression. Levels of production and employment fell by fifty percent as the century entered an economic slump of unprecedented proportions. By the 1932 election year, even the conservative corporate community had lessened its opposition to the Soviet regime in one very pragmatic way. While unsympathetic to Soviet socialism, American business viewed the Soviet Union as a potential market of immense size. Business leaders, looking for markets wherever they could be found, began pressing newly-elected President Franklin D. Roosevelt to recognize the Soviet Union. Coming from influential businessmen, the cause of diplomatic recognition gained some cautious momentum. The State Department and the Russians began a series of secret negotiations that culminated with a visit to Washington, D.C., by Soviet Commisar for Foreign Affairs Maxim Litvinov. Arriving on November 7, 1933, Litvinov still lacked official diplomatic status, as reflected in the fact that none of the Americans who greeted him wore the then-traditional top hats. This informal attire, however, was also an action taken in deference to the Communist aversion to aristocratic dress and pomp. Litvinov, who had entered the United States at the invitation of President Roosevelt, began a series of meetings with the President and officials of the State Department. By November 16, 1933, diplomatic relations were formally restored. The Soviet government pledged itself to dampen Communist activities in the United States as part of the agreement.

In recognizing the Soviet regime, the United States had acted much later than other world powers, reflecting a long history of direct United States-Soviet antipathy. In the end, many of the hopes raised by the 1933 agreement were never realized: United States business never really penetrated the Soviet market during the Stalin era; recovery from the Great Depression had to wait for the military spending engendered by World War II; and Communist movements remained active in the United States throughout the 1930's—in fact, the unified Communist Party USA, a Moscow-oriented group, enjoyed unprecedented support in the United States during the Great Depression. Thus, in recognizing the Soviet Union, the United States joined the other nations of the world in acknowledging political reality, but gained few anticipated advantages.

## Pertinent Literature

Kennan, George Frost. *Russia and the West Under Lenin and Stalin*. Boston: Little, Brown and Company, 1961.

George F. Kennan is recognized as one of the foremost scholars in the field of diplomatic history in this century; his area of expertise is the history of Soviet-American relations. The volume under consideration is based on university lectures done by Kennan at Oxford and Harvard in the late 1950's and early 1960's. Prior to his academic activities, Kennan had genuine diplomatic experience as United States Ambassador to the Soviet Union. In this book, Kennan demonstrates the breadth of his knowledge on Soviet-American diplomacy, using an impressive array of Soviet as well as American and West European sources.

This book is excellent as an introduction to the long view of Soviet-American relations. Two-thirds of the chapters cover the reasons for the delay in American recognition. The impact of the Bolshevik Revolution on the Allies is detailed, especially the shock in the West over the Brest-Litovsk agreement. Kennan includes descriptions of the Allied intervention in the Russian Civil War, with an assessment of how these actions embittered the newly established Soviet regime. The Soviet commitment to "export" revolution worldwide was assigned to the Comintern (Communist International), made up of member Communist parties from different parts of the world, including the United States. The brief Communist uprisings in Bavaria and Hungary in 1919 further estranged the Soviets from the West.

Kennan next traces the development of reconciliation between the Soviets and the West. Important in this move was Stalin's abandonment of the policy of world revolution by the 1930's; recognition resulted during the opening year of Franklin D. Roosevelt's presidency.

Kennan's scholarship is of the highest order; his documentation includes both Soviet and Western sources. Of additional importance is Kennan's detailed explanation of all key developments on the diplomatic front. This is an excellent introduction to Soviet-American diplomacy for the general reader.

Carr, Edward Hallett. *A History of Soviet Russia*. Vols. I-III: *The Bolshevik Revolution, 1917-1923*. New York: The Macmillan Company, 1961.

Edward Hallett Carr is a leading British historian, author of the masterful series, *A History of Soviet Russia*, which appeared in Great Britain in the 1950's and in the United States in the 1960's. *The Bolshevik Revolution, 1917-1923* is one section of this series.

Carr's book is essential in documenting the estrangement between Russia and the West following the Bolshevik Revolution. Carr first turns his attention to the Treaty of Brest-Litovsk signed between Russia and Germany. The conclusion of this separate peace drove a deep wedge between the Allied nations and the new Soviet government. Brest-Litovsk led to Allied intervention on behalf of the anti-Soviet White forces that were attempting an active counterrevolution. The intervention guaranteed Bolshevik antipathy toward the West for a long time to follow.

The Bolsheviks also contributed to the chilling of relations with the United States and the West in general through the instigation of subversive activities in the West, as promoted by the Comintern. The author demonstrates a perceptive knowledge of radical movements in the United States, which deepened the Soviet-American rift.

Carr served in British military intelligence prior to his academic career. He makes extremely even-handed accounts of the early troubles between the Soviets and the Americans. This is perhaps the most objective history of the early Soviet period ever written; scrupulously documented, it is an introduction to Soviet-American and Soviet-Western relations that will be of great interest to the general reader. — E.A.Z.

## Additional Recommended Reading

Beloff, Max. *The Foreign Policy of Soviet Russia, 1929-1941.* 2 vols. New York: Oxford University Press, 1947 and 1949. Good, standard account of Soviet foreign policy.

Leuchtenburg, William E. *Franklin D. Roosevelt and the New Deal, 1932-1940.* New York: Harper & Row Publishers, 1963. Includes a good discussion on the establishment of relations with the Soviet Union.

Murray, Robert K. *Red Scare: A Study in National Hysteria, 1919-1920.* New York: McGraw-Hill Book Company, 1964. Details initial impact of anti-Bolshevik feeling in the United States.

# DEVELOPMENT OF RADAR

*Type of event:* Technological: research and development of radar
*Time:* 1934-1945
*Locale:* The United States and Europe

*Principal personages:*
JAMES CLERK MAXWELL (1831-1879), theoretician who explained the nature of electromagnetic radiation
HEINRICH HERTZ (1857-1894), experimenter who demonstrated radio waves could be reflected
LEO C. YOUNG (1926-    ) and
ROBERT M. PAGE (1903-    ), scientists who initiated the research and development of American radar
HENRY THOMAS TIZARD (1885-1959) and
ROBERT ALEXANDER WATSON-WATT (1892-    ), scientists who initiated the research and development of British radar

## Summary of Event

"Radar" is an acronym coined from the phrase "radio detection and ranging." Radar receivers use reflected short-wave radio signals to determine with instant precision the direction and distance of such diverse objects as airplanes, ships, land, thunderstorms, and rain. It has become an essential navigational aid to worldwide commercial shipping and aviation.

Radar came into use during World War II and has been credited with changing the course of history. After Adolf Hitler conquered France in June, 1940, he prepared to invade the British Isles. From August to December he sent fleets of bombers to destroy British factories and soften Britain's resistance before German troops would land. This was the Battle of Britain, which the British won by using radar to direct their limited forces of intercepting fighter planes. When Germany shifted to night bombing raids in 1941, British ground and air-

borne radar enabled their fighters to learn to distinguish friend from foe and zero in on their targets. Thanks to radar, the German threat was foiled, and Britain survived to become the strategic staging area from which American and British forces later attacked and overwhelmed the Nazis.

During the 1930's, radar development was pioneered independently in France, Germany, Great Britain, and the United States. French efforts came to an end when France was conquered by Nazi Germany early in World War II. American and British efforts were pooled in 1940 at British initiative, more than a year before the United States formally went to war against the "Berlin-Tokyo Axis." The origins and development of Japanese wartime radar have still to be determined.

While a number of proposals to build radar-type detection devices were made from late in the nineteenth century onward, none of these launched the development of radar. Neither did the invention in 1925 of the principle of pulse radar; instead, the two American scientists involved were studying the ionosphere. In England scientists were using short-wave radio echoes to track the path of storms, oblivious to the still unperceived possibilities of radar.

But by the end of 1930, the United States Naval Research Laboratory was investigating "radio-echo signals from moving objects," although continuous-beam, rather than interrupted-pulse, signals were employed. It was not until late 1933 that Leo C. Young, who had assisted in the ionosphere studies, recommended that pulse techniques be used, and beginning in January, 1934, Robert M. Page undertook a number of brilliant innovative experimental studies that marked the beginning of the continuous and effective radar program that produced American wartime radar.

Also, in 1934, British authorities were becoming increasingly alarmed at Hitler's arming of Nazi Germany. In response to Nazi propaganda about a "death ray," Scottish scientist Robert A. Watson-Watt wrote a brief technical letter in which he demolished the death-ray fiction but pointed out that the echo of a short-wave pulse theoretically could be used to locate an oncoming bomber. Watson-Watt was acquainted with the radio-wave tracking of thunderstorms. His letter was in reply to a query from a powerful new committee headed by an unusually able scientist-administrator, Henry T. Tizard. Subsequent action by the "Tizard Committee" gave top priority to the systematic research and development of British radar and thereby enabled the English to win the Battle of Britain five years later.

As Page later pointed out, the separate American and British efforts had produced, by the beginning of the war, useful ground-based mobile radar (United States Army), useful naval radar (United States Navy), and useful airborne radar (Royal Air Force), each resting on fundamentally different designs. The further diversification of radar designs and applications during the war by German and Allied research and development outsped the wildest dreams of the pioneers of the 1930's.

Radar was in some ways a typical product of mid-twentieth century scientific technology. It was made possible by two earlier enterprises, neither of which was interested in inventing radar, yet it was not an accidental discovery. The first of these two older enterprises was the scientific basic research tradition, committed solely to understanding phenomena. Two names stand out in this regard: James Clerk Maxwell in Britain, whose mathematical predictions in 1864 regarding the nature of light and electro-magnetic phenomena indicated that the latter, like the former, could be reflected; and Heinrich Hertz, a German physicist, who in 1887 demonstrated experimentally that Maxwell was right.

The second of these two older enterprises upon which radar rested was the sophisticated electronics technology that had accumulated over a third of a century of communication-radio broadcasting. So many names were involved in this development that it must be accepted as a social, rather than a heroic, accomplishment.

Radar likewise was the achievement of dozens of creative men. But it was also a war-oriented enterprise during its first decade, and the creative men were supported in turn by thousands of men and women engaged in the clerical, administrative, manufacturing, training, and maintenance tasks necessary to transform the many needed types of radar systems from concept to experiment to service test to full, practical use as fast as possible. The British (and later the American) radar research, development, and production organizations were staffed by people brought together from all walks of life by the desperate, compelling pressures of a war that they knew offered only two alternatives: total victory or ultimate slavery and death. In contrast to broadcast communication radio, radar was developed under very special and unusual circumstances.

## Pertinent Literature

*Radar, A Report on Science at War.* Released by the Joint Board on Scientific Information Policy for the Office of Scientific Research and Development; the War Department; and the Navy Department. Washington, D.C.: U.S. Government Printing Office, August, 1945.

Radar—the name as well as the equipment—was one of the best-kept secrets of World War II. This fifty-three-page report, available at any repository of federal publications, was the first release to the American public of the story of radar, its wartime development and uses. The report's patriotic emphasis on American achievements tends to obscure equally important British contributions, but it is a useful résumé for the nontechnical reader of how radar was employed in land and sea air defense, against enemy submarines and enemy shipping, in strategic and tactical uses of air power, in naval warfare, and as a new aid to general navigation. The report concludes with a brief technical description of radar systems.

The social, institutional auspices under which radar was developed are set forth in overwhelming detail in sections 3 and 4 of the report. While the names of committees, agencies, laboratories, and their executives make for rather boring reading, they remind us again that thousands of people in the United States and Britain participated in the development and manufacture of wartime radar. It was not a venture dominated by a few heroic creative minds, nor did it have any single "father." One reason for this circumstance lay in the complexity, the design variations, and the number of components in radar systems. Another reason lay in the early commitment by policymakers and scientists to develop radar when the precise design of components was still a matter of speculation and when the solutions to severe technical problems were still unknown. Still another reason is to be found in the unusual conditions and pressures generated by a war emergency that increasingly demanded the total mobilization of a nation's resources.

The fact that for the first time science and scientists became totally devoted to winning a war meant that the organization of radar research and development was without pre-cedent in the history of science and engineering. The general outlines of how United States engineers, scientists, administrators, and military men collaborated to develop radar are set forth in this report.

Rowe, Albert Percival. *One Story of Radar.* Cambridge: Cambridge University Press, 1948.

A crucial reason the British made such spectacular progress in radar development was the unorthodox way they organized teams of scientists and engineers to work on military projects before and during World War II. The author was the administrative head of one such organization, the Telecommunications Research Establishment. His purpose in writing this book, he writes in his preface, was to describe for the general reader how they carried on their affairs in an atmosphere of intellectual freedom and adventure more appropriate to a university laboratory than a governmental or industrial establishment. At the same time there was a unity of purpose, a discipline, and an extraordinary collaboration among the scientists, the military men, and the civil service.

Rowe was not a technically trained man; his talents were managerial and judgmental. He could see how matters were going, act to correct or avert mistakes, and assess the talents of the men under him to elicit their best efforts. Further, he had the confidence of his superiors and knew how to convert their policies to practice. All of these circumstances placed him in a rare position to "watch the whole show" while being directly responsi-ble for managing one part of it.

His account demonstrates how *un-predetermined* their development progress was. They jumped from one technical improvisation to another. They learned to accept second and third best, because they did not have the time to perfect designs to their technical satisfaction. Different teams working on different projects produced results that had to be communicated and coordinated and evaluated as rapidly as possible. When they were seeking desperately in 1940-1941 to develop a reliable airborne radar that fighter pilots could use, Rowe knew they could not expect the quality and reliability of the five-year-old chain of radar coastal towers that gave early warning of massing enemy bombers forty miles or more away during the Battle of Britain. When a group housed at the University of Birmingham came up with the greatest breakthrough in wartime radar, the cavity magnetron transmitter tube, by the middle of 1940, Rowe's group greedily began to apply it to their problems, while Tizard led a delegation to the United States to obtain American collaboration.

Rowe's small book gives an insider's intimate, nontechnical view of how science went to war in Britain to

produce the spectacular research and    in that country. — *T.M.S.*
development progress of early radar

## Additional Recommended Reading

Page, Robert M. "The Early History of Radar," in *Annual Report of the Smithsonian Institution (1962)*. Washington, D.C.: U.S. Government Printing Office, 1963, pp. 315-321. An insightful, somewhat technical résumé by one of the creative pioneers.

Price, Alfred. *Instruments of Darkness: The History of Electronic Warfare*. New York: Charles Scribner's Sons, 1978. An account for "war buffs" of how the Nazis and the Allies used their ever-changing radar and antiradar systems, with two final chapters covering the period 1945-1977.

Ridenour, Louis N., ed. *Radar System Engineering*. New York: McGraw-Hill Book Company, 1947. The first of a projected twenty-eight-volume series produced by the wartime Radiation Laboratory at the Massachusetts Institute of Technology, this technical textbook introducing radar to engineering students is also rich in incidental factual and historical information accessible to the serious lay reader.

Watson-Watt, Robert Alexander. *The Pulse of Radar: The Autobiography of Sir Robert Watson-Watt*. New York: The Dial Press, 1959. An egoistic, highly idiosyncratic account by the gifted British pioneer which includes a perceptive chapter on why the Americans ignored their radar warnings of the Japanese attack on Pearl Harbor.

# ARNOLD TOYNBEE PUBLISHES *A STUDY OF HISTORY*

*Type of event:* Intellectual: analysis of the dynamism of human history
*Time:* 1934-1954
*Locale:* Great Britain

## Summary of Event

Cyclical theories of history have experienced a noteworthy rebirth of popularity in the last century. These theories, which seek to show that events follow an ever-recurrent general pattern, are symptomatic of the Western world's disillusionment in the present century with the liberal belief in unending social progress. The latest and perhaps most popular of these cyclical theories is that propounded by Arnold Toynbee in his multivolume *A Study of History*, published between 1934 and 1954.

Toynbee arrived at his perspective on world history by two routes. The first was an intellectual dissatisfaction with the way history had been written in the nineteenth century; that is, as the history of individual nations. In his view, these nations were not self-contained entities and their histories could be understood only if they were placed within the larger context of the civilizations of which they were each a part. Thus Toynbee arrived at his individual unit of historical study, the civilization. The second route was provided by the outbreak of World War I, which caused Toynbee much emotional travail and led him to question the assumption that European civilization would continue to progress as it seemed to have done for the last hundred years. He suddenly understood what Thucydides must have felt at the beginning of the Peloponnesian Wars—the sensation of standing at the brink of a great civilization's decline. This analogy between Hellenic and modern Western history, which came naturally to the classically trained Toynbee, lies at the very foundation of *A Study of History*; and it led the author to wonder if the stages of Greco-Roman history might be repeated not only in that of Western civilization but in the histories of all civilizations.

What, then, were the stages through which Hellenic civilization passed? According to Toynbee they were four in number. The first was one of growth. All civilizations begin as a consequence of successful response to the challenge of the physical environment, in this case the "hard" environment of the Greek archipelago; then growth results from new challenges stemming from the successful response to the first. This whole process is gradually "etherialized," to use Toynbee's term, or transferred from the material to the spiritual plane, as in Greece the challenge shifted from the difficulties of the natural environment to the problem of political disunity. But the Greeks failed to meet this challenge, for they were unwilling to abandon peacefully their city-states for a pan-Hellenic federation. This failure led to the growing military conflict of the Peloponnesian Wars and the entry of

Hellenic civilization into its second stage, or "time of troubles," which in fact heralded its breakdown. Several temporary recoveries or "rallies" occurred, but the fundamental political problem of Hellenic civilization was left unsolved by the Greeks themselves. A solution had to be imposed from without, this occurring when Augustus founded a "Universal State" in 31 B.C. The founding of the Roman Empire ushered in the third stage of Hellenic civilization, which provided only a brief respite from the classical world's decline. This period was characterized by the maintenance of the *forms* of a civilization's cultural life, the spirit which formerly animated them being dead. The "creative minority" which once inspired the people to follow its lead now ruled only by force. Eventually Hellenic civilization disintegrated into a "dominant minority" (the former "creative minority") and two hostile forces which constantly threatened the civilization's very existence: an "external proletariat" (the barbarian tribes) and an "internal proletariat" (the oppressed people of the empire) who found solace in a religion of foreign origin (Christianity). At last came the "interregnum," the death of the civilization, as the Universal State was increasingly harassed by the barbarians at its borders and torn apart by internal anarchy. The rally that occurred under Diocletian and Constantine, alas, was doomed to failure; and Greco-Roman civilization finally ended with the barbarian invasions of the Western empire.

Toynbee employs this basic model throughout the first six volumes of *A Study of History*, published before World War II. He attempts, with varying degrees of success, to show that all the twenty or so major civilizations he discusses in *A Study of History* conform to this same pattern, or at least would have conformed to it if they had been allowed to complete a full cycle of development. He is especially concerned to show that civilizations decline as a result of internal decay, specifically as a result of the failure to meet moral or spiritual challenges. He goes so far as to maintain that the civilization of the Incas was destroyed not because of diseases brought by Spanish conquerors or the Europeans' military superiority but because the civilization had already decayed within.

In volumes six through ten of his study, however, which were published after a period of personal crisis and the trauma of World War II, Toynbee abandoned this laboriously constructed model. He came to the conclusion that even civilizations were not an adequate basis on which to rebuild his work, and that the only intelligible units of study for world history were the higher religions, of which there are four—Christianity, Islam, Hinduism, and Mahayana Buddhism. Toynbee's system now resembled that of Saint Augustine. While the City of Man is destined to suffer the unchanging cycles of birth and death like that of Hellenic civilization, the City of God attains even greater heights of spirituality; for, as each civilization declines on the secular plane, it gives birth to a "Universal Church." This church embodies the spiritual lessons of the civilization that produced it, lessons which are then incorporated in the civilization that succeeds the now dying one. It forms the crysalis from which this new civilization will emerge, just as the Christian Church provided the basis for medieval Western civilization. Contrary to Gibbon's view, Christianity did not cause the decline of the Roman empire, but rather made possible the preservation of its highest values in the new world that was being born.

All history becomes a revelation of God's will in this new scheme. The only irreversible progress is spiritual progress, since each successive Universal Church contains the wisdom of all the civilizations that have flowed into it. Toynbee now shows us where all history is leading: to the spiritual and political unification of mankind, as the best features of all the major world religions are combined in a grand synthesis that will form the religious basis of a supranational government.

But what is the immediate prospect of Western civilization? Toynbee gives an ambiguous answer to this question. At one point he suggests that the breakdown of our civilization occurred during the age of religious wars in the seventeenth century, which means that we are now in the last stage of our history. But, says the author, the final verdict is not in yet, for it is impossible to determine the stages of a civilization's history until the concluding chapter of that history is written.

## Pertinent Literature

Geyl, Pieter. *Debates with Historians*. New York: Meridian Books, 1958.

Toynbee's work, principally in the form of the two-volume abridgment by D. C. Somervell, was received very favorably by the informed reading public when volumes six through ten were released in 1954. Despite his public acclaim, however, Toynbee has been showered with criticism by his fellow historians, most notably by the respected Dutch scholar Pieter Geyl.

Like most of his critics, Geyl pays tribute to Toynbee's perseverance, vast erudition, and brilliant flashes of insight. His criticism is directed primarily at Toynbee's methodology, particularly at his claim to be using an empirical, scientific approach. Geyl rejects this claim completely. Rather than constructing a hypothesis and then testing it against the available facts, as an empirical approach would dictate, what Toynbee does is to formulate an *a priori* theory of history and then carefully select examples that illustrate rather than prove this preconceived theory. Furthermore, Toynbee uses myths, legends, and virtually any other available material to support his theory, while his extensive reliance on metaphor, simile, and analogy often makes it difficult to pin down his exact meaning. The effect of this method, says Geyl, is to create a mood or atmosphere in which the functioning of the reader's critical faculties is suspended, and illogical or unsupported arguments become plausible. In the end Toynbee stands accused of using the antiscientific, *a priori* method of Oswald Spengler, whose theories and method he claims to oppose.

Besides dismissing Toynbee's empiricism as a sham, Geyl attacks his key notion of a civilization. Not only is it extremely difficult to define what constitutes a civilization, geographically and temporally as well as culturally; it is even harder to compare them once they have been defined, because of their wide diversity. Are such general comparisons as Toynbee makes really useful or informative? Geyl finds presumptuous the idea that a historian can judge when a civilization has reached its peak or begun its decline, for this judgment is based on the particular values held by the historian. Moreover, although Toynbee's theory of history is about civilizations and their development, he uses illustration after illustration from the histories of individual nations. He cannot have his cake and eat it too.

Geyl's final methodological salvo is fired at Toynbee's important concept of "challenge and response," which he uses to explain the origin, growth, and decay of civilizations. According to this concept, civilizations arise as the result of a successful response to the challenge of a difficult environment—the greater the challenge, the greater the response, within certain limits not clearly specified by Toynbee. One of his most striking examples of this phenomenon is Holland, which happens to fall within Geyl's special domain. Toynbee tries to convince us that the constant battle waged by the Dutch against the sea was the stimulus for the creation of one of the most advanced societies in Europe. Geyl's response to this argument is that Toynbee lacks a fundamental understanding of Dutch history. The rise of Holland, he observes, was very late, even within the cultural area of the Netherlands; and this was precisely because of the adverse conditions cited by Toynbee. The conditions were finally overcome, but only with the help of a nearby higher civilization. Furthermore, the continuing growth and high attainment of Holland was due to *favorable* conditions, such as a rich soil and a strategic geographical position, which made her a center of international commerce. Geyl suspects that a close examination of other examples of challenge and response in *A Study of History* would reveal the same distortions of history, a suspicion confirmed by specialists in other areas.

In addition to these largely methodological criticisms, Professor Geyl has also raised some serious doubts about Toynbee's diagnosis of and prescription for Western civilization. One of Toynbee's main motivations for writing *A Study of History* was to answer the question whether the West has entered a period of irreversible decline. That Toynbee feels this decline has begun is suggested by his observation of numerous signs of decay in the West, such as the religious wars of the seventeenth century and the world wars of the twentieth century. Yet he refuses to pronounce the death sentence of our civilization, for this, he says, is not the prerogative of the historians. The phases of a civilization's history become clear to the scholar only when the civilization is dead, a thing of the past. Since the

West is manifestly still alive, it is by his own criterion impossible for Toynbee to answer his initial question. We would be better off, Geyl advises, if we ignored such prophets of doom and went about our business.

Montagu, Ashley, ed. *Toynbee and History*. Boston: Porter Sargent, 1956.

This collection of articles and reviews dealing with *A Study of History* is one of the standard reference works on the subject. Rather than attempting to summarize what each of the contributors has to say about *A Study of History*, the focus here will be on the controversy generated by Toynbee's position on Zionism and Judaism, relating this position to what has been called his "prophetic" vision of the world's future.

No facet of Toynbee's work has stimulated more heated debate than his stand on Zionism and his views on Judaism generally. Toynbee has criticized the state of Israel since its inception and has freely stated his sympathy for the Palestinian cause. He has gone so far as to liken the expulsion of the Palestinians from Israel in 1948 to the Nazi destruction of European Jewry, a comparison that has evoked charges of anti-Semitism from some quarters. Moreover, he even refused in his *A Study of History* to bestow upon Judaism the status of a major world religion.

Toynbee's position on these issues, as Abba Eban has pointed out, must be seen within the general context of his condemnation of nationalism and other "parochial" loyalties as well as his vision of what we must do to avoid the fate of all previous civilizations. The alternative to self-destruction that Toynbee offers us is some form of world government to control the nationalistic passions which have embroiled us in countless wars in past centuries and which threaten us now with thermonuclear annihilation. Furthermore, Toynbee insists that the prerequisite for the attainment of this end, the foundation on which any durable world state must be built, is a return to religious faith.

Toynbee fervently believes that the root cause of the evils of our age is our progressive abandonment of religion and its replacement by neopaganism and secularism or by such secular religions as nationalism. But a simple return to the ancestral faith is no longer sufficient to solve the problems posed by the modern age. What is now called for is a new religion, one combining the best elements of the world's four major religions, and one which will embrace all humanity. This religion has been described as consisting essentially of Christianity with an admixture of Hinduism's toleration for a diversity of beliefs. Only if such a religion takes root will the peoples of the world forsake their blind allegiances to their national governments and devote their energies to attaining universal peace and the political realization of the unity of humanity in a world government.

This religious solution to the problems that beset our civilization has been attacked on several grounds, and not exclusively by religious agnostics. Several critics, while applauding Toynbee's stress on religion, nevertheless chastise him for failing to appreciate the unique contribution made by each of the major religions to world civilization and the appropriateness of each to the people who adhere to it. It has been noted, furthermore, that Toynbee's universal religion bears a striking resemblance to the liberal Protestant Christianity of the late Victorian period of his childhood. A Muslim, Buddhist, or Hindu could be expected to design a quite different religion for the whole of humanity.

Toynbee's passionate advocacy of this new religion and its concomitant world state has made him anathema to many historians, and the prophetic garb in which he has clothed himself carries him beyond the bounds of what historians see as their main function: to describe events and, at the very most, ascribe causes to them. In the opinion of these historians, his obsession with religion has led him to distort history to fit his preconceived opinions. For example, Hans Kohn charges that the ascription of the modern West's problems to the decline of religious faith since the seventeenth century does a major disservice to our civilization and negates what is perhaps our unique contri-bution to world civilization: our positive valuation of freedom of thought and action, as well as our scientific curiosity. These were able to grow only because religion was displaced from the supreme position it had held in the Middle Ages.

Thus, it is Toynbee's concern with the future of the human race and his accent on the necessity for all peoples to abandon the beliefs and institutions that divide them that helps explain his negative attitude toward Judaism and Zionism. His "idolized unity," as Pieter Geyl labels this attitude, leads him to denigrate any parochial allegiance that keeps us from attaining a world religion and world state. In Toynbee's view, Zionism represents a particularly dangerous and artificial revival of the nationalism he wishes us to abandon, while the Jewish people's determined sense of religious identity stands in the way of the religious amalgamation he so desires. As Abba Eban observes, Toynbee's judgment of the Jews is related to his general failure to appreciate the claims of nationality and the importance of group identity, a failure that makes for both bad history and bad prophecy. — *R.E.*

## Additional Recommended Reading

Gargan, Edward T., ed. *The Intent of Toynbee's History*. Chicago: Loyola University Press, 1961. A collection of papers presented by specialists at a symposium on Toynbee in 1955.

Berkowitz, Eliezen. *Judaism: Fossil or Ferment?* New York: Philosophical Library, 1956. An attack on Toynbee's belief that Judaism is a "fossil" religion.

Muller, Herbert J. *Uses of the Past*. New York: New American Library, 1954. A book that, while not primarily about Toynbee, discusses him at some length in a relatively balanced manner.

Ortega y Gasset, José. *An Interpretation of Universal History*. Translated by Mildred

Adams. New York: W. W. Norton and Company, 1973. Charges that Toynbee's work is not a *study* of history, but a *philosophy* of history.

Popper, Karl. *The Open Society and Its Enemies*. 2 vols. Princeton, N.J.: Princeton University Press, 1950. Takes Toynbee to task for failing to offer real solutions to real problems.

Dawson, Christopher. *Dynamics of World History*. Edited by John J. Mulloy. London: Sheed and Ward, 1957. Catholic philosopher and historian Dawson describes Toynbee as a "metahistorian."

# STALIN BEGINS THE PURGE TRIALS

*Type of event:* Political: Stalin's consolidation of power in the Soviet Union
*Time:* December 1, 1934
*Locale:* The Soviet Union

*Principal personages:*

JOSEPH STALIN (IOSIF VISSARIONOVICH DZHUGASHVILI)
(1879-1953), Dictator of the U.S.S.R., 1924-1953

LEON TROTSKY (LEIB DAVYDOVICH BRONSTEIN) (1879-1940),
eminent leader of the Russian Revolution and political
opponent of Stalin

SERGEI KIROV (1886-1934), a member of the Central Committee of Communist Party of the U.S.S.R., 1922-1934

GRIGORI EVSEEVICH ZINOVIEV (HIRSCH APFELBAUM) (1883-
1936), former Chairman of the Communist International,
leader of the left opposition

NIKOLAI IVANOVICH BUKHARIN (1888-1938), leader of right
opposition

NIKOLAI IVANOVICH YEZHOV (1895-1939?), Soviet Minister
of Internal Affairs, 1936-1938

ANDREI VYSHINSKY (1883-1954), Soviet State Prosecutor,
1935-1939

## Summary of Event

By 1934, Joseph Stalin had been leader of the Soviet state for ten years. He had defeated his rivals for the mantle of V. I. Lenin, the first Soviet leader, by a combination of political maneuvering and intrigue and by the skillful use of the Communist Party bureaucracy which he had developed as General-Secretary of the Party's Central Committee. However, his position was still far from secure. Stalin had achieved his preeminent place in Soviet society in large part by opposing the extreme left position of more famous Communists such as Leon Trotsky and Grigori Zinoviev. This popular position gained support both in the Communist Party and among the Soviet populace. Nevertheless, once the left was defeated, he reversed his policies and adopted the very methods he had originally denounced. Furthermore, the failures of some of these policies during the first five-year plan (begun in 1928 and curtailed in 1933) was causing Stalin some difficulties in the highest circles of the Communist ruling elite.

Stalin's political problem was simple—how to get rid of the old Bolsheviks, whose reputations could once again make them his rivals, and, at the same time, to eliminate possible new rivals from the group which he had brought to influence in the 1920's but who were not sullied by the political conflicts of the past decade. To accomplish this, he introduced into revolutionary Russia a bizarre form of political terror and gave a new meaning to the word "purge."

Within the higher circles of the party the most likely source of opposition was the popular Sergei Kirov, whom Stalin himself sponsored in his rise to prominence, and who was regarded as one of the most capable of the country's political leaders. On December 1, 1934, to the dismay of the nation, an obscure assailant (Leonid Nikolayev) shot Kirov to death. It appears probable, though it is not certain, that the assassination was part of a conspiracy; but the extent of the presumed conspiracy and the identities of the participants have been shrouded in some mystery. Many Western historians, buttressing their arguments with an apparent confirmation by Stalin's successor Nikita Khrushchev in 1956, believe that Stalin himself had a hand in the assassination. At the time, Stalin used the occasion of Kirov's murder to reveal to the world the existence of an enormous plot to overthrow his rule, directed, he said, by his archrival, Leon Trotsky (then living abroad). The plot supposedly involved tens of thousands of Soviet political and military personnel, in concert with the Fascist and capitalist foreign enemies of the state.

Kirov's actual assassin and his closest associates accused as accessories were sentenced to death within a few weeks. Shortly thereafter, the state prosecutor arrested two prominent leaders of the former Left Opposition, Grigori Zinoviev and Lev Kamenev, together with a number of their sympathizers, and charged them with maintaining a clandestine and illegal opposition group in Moscow.

The prosecutor's office also charged them with providing ideological support for Kirov's assassins. Although charges of conspiracy against the state were not unprecedented in Soviet history, this was the first time that members of the Communist Party were so charged because of political opposition. The group was quickly tried in secret and sentenced to imprisonment.

For a year and a half there were apparently no more major repercussions from the Kirov assassination. However, behind the scenes, Stalin prepared his full-scale assault on the old Bolsheviks. The allies he would use were concentrated in the Ministry of Internal Affairs, headed by Nikolai Yezhov, and the State Prosecutor's office of Andrei Vyshinsky. In August, 1936, Zinoviev and Kamenev went to trial with fourteen others, accused of the capital crime of conspiring against the Soviet government.

This so-called "Trial of the Sixteen" was the first of three major show trials in the purges and countless scores of other secret and public processes. In January, 1937, seventeen left-wing defendants went on trial for conspiracy, and the next year, in the spring of 1938, twenty-one right-wing opponents of Stalin, including Nikolai Bukharin, were tried on the same charges.

The bizarre nature of the show trials added an eerie, unreal atmosphere to the tragedy of the decimation of the ranks of the Old Bolsheviks. With brazen illogicality, the prosecutors charged life-long socialists with conspiring with their most implacable foes, including Nazi Germany, to overthrow the Soviet government. Easily refutable evidence, including impossible meetings and charges which could be proven false by examining public records and the foreign press, were introduced into court. Confounding matters, the accused almost invariably confessed to these unlikely crimes. Behind all stood the figure of Trotsky, who was accused of master-minding everything, but who in fact was living in exile, his influence in the Soviet Union a faded memory.

All of the accused were found guilty, and most, but not all, were executed. Trotsky himself was assassinated in Mexico in August, 1940, by a man in the employ of the Soviet government. As a result of the purges, almost all of the old political leaders fell from power or disappeared. Ninety-eight of 139 members of the 1934 Central Committee were arrested during the purges. Furthermore, while in 1934 more than eighty percent of the high Communist officials were "long-time" party members (that is, they had joined before 1921), in 1939 only nineteen percent of the party elite fell into that category. Of the whole population, a minimum of seven million persons were arrested and perhaps a half million executed. At the end of the political purges, Stalin turned on the military; throughout 1937 and 1938 continuous waves of arrests decimated well over half of the Red Army command.

The Stalinist purges have remained something of a mystery to the West, whose peoples find them so alien to their own society. First of all, commentators and authors have wondered why the defendants confessed to the absurd accusations. Were they drugged or beaten into submission? Did they believe that the absurdity of their confessions would prove their innocence before the world? Some, perhaps, were promised leniency; or maybe they ignored the question of their own guilt or innocence in the hope of saving the reputation of the Party to which they had devoted their lives.

The question remains whether the purges were an inevitable part of the Communist Revolution or a product of Russia's peculiar history. Similarities to events in the reigns of Ivan the Terrible, Peter the Great, and Alexander I would indicate the latter. One thing seems certain: by means of the purges Stalin was able to secure his position from the threats of potential political and military rivals and rise above all his comrades to become a demigod beyond reproach in the Soviet Union.

## Pertinent Literature

Conquest, Robert. *The Great Terror: Stalin's Purge of the Thirties*. London: Macmillan and Company, 1968.

This volume is the most important English-language work on the purges. Robert Conquest, a historian of the Soviet Union as well as a poet, brings to the study a unique combination of gifts. He not only describes the events but also tries to interpret them for Western readers.

Conquest sees the purges as more a part of the Soviet experience than of Russian history in general and traces their origin to both pre-Revolutionary and post-Revolutionary policies and activities of the Bolsheviks under Lenin. He also believes that the purges left Russia with a continuing heritage of terror, and that hence they were not an isolated instance in Russian jurisprudence but an essential part of the Soviet system.

The author concludes that Stalin was behind the assassination of Kirov, and that the purges thus had as their main purpose the retention of power by the Soviet leader. In this context, the affront to Western conceptions of logic, truth, and justice become comprehensible. The goal of the purges was not to find the true assassins of Kirov and traitors to the state, but to eliminate the rivals of the real assassin. In one of his concluding evaluations, the author relates that in an extraordinary circumstance, the Soviet newspaper *Pravda* in 1951 published a statement in which Herbert Morrison, the British Foreign Secretary, "cogently set forth democratic objections to the Soviet system." The editors answered Morrison, saying that he "was asking for freedom of speech for those it would be wrong to give it to—'the criminals who . . . killed . . . Kirov.' " Conquest comments: "It turns out that it was precisely those people, and no others, who had freedom of speech."

The author also evaluates the economic effect of the purges. He disagrees with the critics who argue that Stalin's methods (both political and economic) were the only way Russia could proceed in the twentieth century, or, as he says, "the only or the best way available—even to a one party-regime—to attain the degree of increased industrialization realized." He sees some parallels between the Soviet economy and what the nineteenth century socialists, including Karl Marx, conceived of as a socialist society, particularly in the collectivization of agriculture and the elimination of private ownership. However, workers' control of the factories was not achieved. This was the "keystone" of socialist economy and in "Stalin's Russia, and for that matter in present-day Russia, there is no sign of any such thing." Furthermore, Conquest insists that the economic benefit supposedly gained by the purges could have been obtained without them. In fact, the elimination of many of the skilled technicians and administrators through the purges proved disastrous for the economy.

Conquest devotes some attention to the strange case of Nikolai Yezhov. As the Minister of the Interior, Yezhov had the main responsibility (along with State Prosecutor Andrei Vyshinski) for administering the purges. Soviet citizens placed the blame at his feet and derisively called the purges the *Yezhovshchina*, recalling the fifteenth century horrors of the era of Tsar Ivan the Terrible. (The suffix "shchina" can be loosely translated as "reign of" and has been applied several times in Russian history to particularly brutal authoritarian periods.) However, in the end Yezhov too disappeared from the scene. Although his exact fate remains unknown, rumors abound. He supposedly committed suicide or was shot. One rumor, which Conquest believes was officially sanctioned to explain the excesses, maintained that he went insane. At any rate, Conquest concludes, the removal of Yezhov did not end the rule by terror he instituted; rather, his successor, Lavrenty Beria, expanded and continued it, making it an integral part of the Russian judicial process. The author believes that the process will not be reversed until Soviet society "comes to a frank confrontation with the past"; namely, recognizing the immorality of the purges themselves.

Deutscher, Isaac. *Stalin: A Political Biography*. New York: Oxford University Press, 1967.

Isaac Deutscher was a Polish Communist and a follower of Trotsky whose biographies of Stalin and Trotsky have earned the respect of the scholarly world. (His planned biography of Lenin was unfinished at the time of his death.) Since Deutscher was a follower of Stalin's archenemy, readers are often astonished at the balanced and sober judgment he presents of Stalin's life and his impact on Russian history and the history of the modern world in general.

Deutscher perceives Stalin as a necessary evil brought about by the forces of Russian and European history. In a passage comparing the effects of the Communist leader on Soviet history with that of Adolf Hitler in Germany, he concludes that while there may have been similarities between the authoritarian rules of the two men, Stalin for all his faults turned a backward nation into a great modern power, while Hitler brought a thriving civilization to the brink of destruction.

Deutscher sees in the purges a similarity to the great Reign of Terror of the French Revolution. His chapter on this aspect of Stalin's rule is entitled "The Gods Are Athirst"—an expression usually applied to those days of the French Revolution when the Jacobin leaders began warring among themselves. Yet Deutscher does note differences between the Russian and French events. The Bolshevik purges occurred at a later stage, when the Bolsheviks had firmly secured power in Russia, while in 1794, when they started their factional party fight, the Jacobins had not yet eliminated all viable opposition. Furthermore, Stalin, unlike Maximilien Robespierre, the chief organizer of the French Reign of Terror, never fell victim to the purges himself. (Yezhov, however, whom the public blamed in large part for the excesses, did.)

Regarding the Kirov assassination, the author hints that Stalin may have been involved; but unlike Conquest, Deutscher does not specifically accuse him. He does believe that Stalin used (or possibly carried out) the assassination in order to eliminate his potential rivals through the purges. Deutscher believes that the illogical confessions at the trials were a very important part of this political process. Relatively few of the accused came to public trial, and their confessions were the strongest, and in some cases the only, real evidence against them.

According to Deutscher, because

of the former internal struggle within the Communist Party these admissions are "far less surprising" than we might suppose. Confessions of real or imagined sins against party discipline had been a routine exercise for loyal Bolsheviks in the 1920's, a device used to explain failures and keep the party intact. Similar methods were introduced in the purges. However, Deutscher believes that party loyalty was only partially behind the confessions. He states that torture and mental anguish were also used to extract admissions of guilt. Hope that relatives would be spared or perhaps even that the accused themselves would survive, as indeed happened in the cases of Karl Radek and Christian Rakovsky, encouraged the prisoners to go through the bizarre rituals. At any rate, Deutscher, like Conquest, morally condemns the era of the purges, though he places the blame on Stalin and not on the Soviet system. — *F.B.C.*

## Additional Recommended Reading

Schapiro, Leonard. *The Communist Party of the Soviet Union*. New York: Vintage Books, 1960. The standard study of the history of the Soviet Communist Party, which contains several chapters on the purges and their effect on the Party.

Fainsod, Merle. *Smolensk Under Soviet Rule*. Cambridge, Mass.: Harvard University Press, 1958. A unique account, based on documents found among captured German archives showing how the purges affected a Soviet provincial city.

Brzezinski, Zbigniew K. *The Permanent Purge*. Cambridge, Mass.: Harvard University Press, 1958. An important study of the effects of the purges on the Soviet system.

Solzhenitsyn, Alexander. *The Gulag Archipelago*. 2 vols. New York: Harper & Row Publishers, 1974-1975. A history of Soviet political prisons both before and after the purges, written by the Soviet Union's most famous dissident.

Orwell, George. *Nineteen Eighty-Four*. New York: Harcourt, Brace, 1949. A famous allegory ostensibly depicting Stalin's Russia.

Koestler, Arthur. *Darkness at Noon*. New York: The Modern Library, 1946. Another famous novel about the purge trials.

341

# GERMANY RENOUNCES THE VERSAILLES TREATY

*Type of event:* Diplomatic: Hitler's decision to rearm Germany
*Time:* March 16, 1935
*Locale:* Germany

### Principal personages:

ADOLF HITLER (1889-1945), Chancellor and Führer of Germany, 1933-1945

GUSTAV STRESEMANN (1878-1929), Chancellor of Germany, 1923; and Minister of Foreign Affairs, 1923-1929

BENITO MUSSOLINI (1883-1945), Fascist Dictator of Italy, 1922-1943

PIERRE LAVAL (1883-1945), President of France, 1935-1936; and Minister of Foreign Affairs, 1934-1936

## Summary of Event

Germany, as the principal leader of the Central Powers in World War I, was the reluctant signatory of the very important Treaty of Versailles ending that conflict. Although Germany did not have to surrender much territory as a result of the treaty, and in fact suffered less in postwar settlements than some of her former allies—for example, Austria-Hungary and the Ottoman Empire—the Germans regarded the settlements as harsh. The nation's leaders had hoped that peace would be concluded on Wilsonian principles of the equality of nations. Instead, a clause in the treaty laid all of the guilt for World War I on Germany and her allies. Germany was required to pay indemnities totaling thirty-three billion dollars. Moreover, and perhaps even more damaging in German eyes, severe restrictions were placed on German military forces—an army of only 100,000 men and a navy of only six capital ships would be allowed. Certain areas of the country were to be demilitarized, in particular, both banks of the Rhine river.

The Germans called the settlement a *Diktat*—a dictated peace—and longed for its overturn. In 1925, while not completely giving up hope of changing the treaty, the Weimar Republic's leading statesman, Foreign Minister Gustav Stresemann, in a series of agreements known as the Locarno Pact, committed his country to abide by Versailles. At the same time, reparation payments were scaled down to facilitate German payment. Furthermore, Stresemann and other leading diplomats of Europe agreed that the nations of the entire Continent should work for a general program of disarmament. If this came about, the military restrictions on Germany would not be so hard to bear.

In fact, hatred for the Versailles Treaty permeated Germany, and Adolf Hitler and the Nazis were able to use this hatred in their rise to power. Yet by the time Hitler did come to power in 1933, Germany was freed from its reparation obligations and only the military clauses of the pact remained as a real restriction. At first Hitler appeared willing to continue the policies of his predecessors, seeking elimination of the Versailles military restrictions through international agreements on mutual disarmament.

At the time of Hitler's assumption of the German chancellorship, a disarmament conference of sixty nations was under way in Geneva. Under the best of circumstances the difficulties of arriving at a mutually acceptable formula for arms limitation made negotiations extremely delicate. With the appearance of Hitler on the scene, success was virtually impossible. German representatives vetoed all efforts at compromise. The German delegates insisted that the paramilitary Nazi storm troopers not be counted among the number of soldiers it was permitted to have. Berlin also rejected as inadequate a proposed timetable providing for German military parity in four years.

In the meantime, Hitler had already begun the clandestine manufacture of German arms. Throughout the summer of 1933 he also waged a propaganda war against the other members of the disarmament conference, maintaining that they and not he were obstructing negotiations. Hitler did succeed in winning over Benito Mussolini, Fascist Dictator of Italy, to some of his proposals; but the French and English delegates remained suspicious. Finally, on October 14, 1933, Germany announced that it was withdrawing from the disarmament conference because the other participants were hindering progress toward a successful conclusion. This startling announcement was followed nine days later by Germany's withdrawal from the League of Nations, which she had entered in the Stresemann period. Hitler justified his leaving the League by declaring it to be merely an instrument of the French in their desire to rule Europe.

Significantly, in these first years of Hitler's rule, the German foreign office, which remained in the hands of the old diplomats and not the new Nazi ideologues, was attempting to isolate France from Great Britain— a policy which Stresemann had also subtly tried to effect. In the end, however, Nazi extremism prevented the Germans from pursuing the traditional path of diplomacy. Polarization of European politics continued in 1934 when the Soviet Union entered the League of Nations and also formed an anti-German bloc with France and her allies.

The disarmament conference ended in failure the following year. At the same time, Hitler had a serious falling-out with Mussolini, his most likely ally in Europe, when the latter objected to Nazi machinations in Austria. German mobilization on the Austrian border with the possible intention of aiding native National Socialists to come to power was nullified when the Italian leader rushed his troops to the area in order to prevent such an occurrence. In January, 1935, Rome and Paris signed an agreement supposedly with the purpose of settling disputes in Africa but clearly directed against the renewed threat from Germany. We see here that despite the new ideologies in Europe, long-standing national diplomatic goals still played an important part in determining the course of events.

With this further isolation of Germany, Hitler officially declared on March 16, 1935, that his country would no longer abide by the disarmament clauses of the Versailles Treaty, and full rearmament began. He cited the failure of the other powers to live up to their promises to disarm. In April, Italian, British, and French delegates met at Stresa in Italy to consider joint action, but nothing more than a mild condemnation by the League of Nations resulted. Great Britain was too concerned with domestic matters; the new President of France, Pierre Laval, was uncertain of the benefits of his country's growing closeness to Moscow; and Mussolini was preparing to launch his war against Ethiopia.

The success of the German defiance of the disarmament clauses and the difficulties between Italy and the other powers over the Ethiopian affair allowed Hitler, in March, 1936, to refortify the Rhineland without foreign opposition. A show of force by France might have caused him to retreat, as he had done in Austria in 1934; but no such demonstration was forthcoming. This act of Hitler not only destroyed the settlement of Versailles but that of Locarno as well. The diplomatic events of the succeeding three years led to World War II.

## Pertinent Literature

Taylor, A. J. P. *The Origins of the Second World War*. New York: Atheneum Publishers, 1962.

A. J. P. Taylor is one of Great Britain's most distinguished historians— a renowned specialist on modern German history and the history of diplomacy. *The Origins of the Second World War* is his most controversial work. Written for a broader audience than professional historians, it attempts to prove (most scholars believe unsuccessfully) that responsibility for World War II lay with the diplomatic failures of England and France rather than with the aggressive policies of Hitler. Thus, while the book is informative for the general reader interested in the "facts" of European diplomacy during the 1930's, the public must be wary of accepting its conclusions without considering opposing arguments.

In this second edition, Taylor answers his critics by stating that he does not approve of Hitler's ideology or methods, but is simply attempting to answer the questions of how and why World War II started in Europe on September 1, 1939. To support his conclusions, the author emphasizes those aspects of Hitler's foreign policy which were a continuation of the traditional aims of Germany. Imperialism and expansionism, in Taylor's view, were characteristic of many European nations. "In principle and doctrine," Taylor writes, "Hitler was no more wicked and unscrupulous than many other contemporary statesmen. In wicked acts he outdid them all."

Taylor writes of Germany's ending

of the Versailles restrictions in two chapters entitled "The End of Versailles" and "The Abyssinian Affair and the End of Locarno." He places the German action in context with the general diplomatic events of the period—for example, Japan's gradual conquest of China already under way in Asia. He also notes the role of the United States in European affairs, maintaining that the advent of Franklin D. Roosevelt to the presidency ushered in a new era of isolationism, leaving England and France to fend for themselves as defenders of the Versailles system. The Republican presidents of the 1920's, Taylor insists, despite America's remaining outside the League of Nations, had not been isolationists.

Hitler came to power during the Geneva disarmament conference, which Taylor portrays as a product of the Locarno accords and hence a result of Stresemann's policies. Furthermore, Taylor lays the principal blame for the failure of the conference on the English and French. After those countries failed to give Germany the arms parity which they had promised, Hitler took the opportunity, granted willingly, to withdraw from the conference.

Afterwards, all the European nations turned to traditional means of diplomacy—bilateral deals, secret treaties, and coalitions. As a result of the Franco-Soviet *rapprochement*, Hitler found himself in alliance with one of Germany's old enemies—Poland. Taylor writes, ". . . in this Polish affair, as in most others, Hitler did not take the initiative." In other words, the Poles came to him when their ally, France, moved closer to another Polish foe, Russia.

The subsequent events in Austria upset Hitler's hopes for diplomatic support from Italy; but he continued on his way to free Germany from the Versailles restrictions with "the certainty of a sleep-walker." Taylor praises the League leaders (Britain, France, and Italy) for showing "signs of resistance" by meeting at Stresa in the wake of Hitler's scrapping of the armament clauses. However, it was just a "mockery" of their former solidarity. Each expected aid from the other two which was not forthcoming. Britain, immediately after Stresa, signed a naval agreement with Germany. Then Italy's involvement in Abyssinia (Ethiopia) signified her virtual severance from League policy and sent Hitler the signal that he could remilitarize the Rhineland—ending Locarno as well as Versailles, as Taylor puts it.

Taylor believes that French resistance to the German army's entrance into the Rhineland, despite the fact that France would have had to act alone, would have been sufficient to drive Hitler back. He declares that the German leader would have turned back at even token resistance, but was confident that none would occur. Hitler was right. French political and military leaders halfheartedly supported the pro-Soviet policies of their country, and very easily found excuses for not opposing Germany. Taylor concludes that March 7, 1936 (the date of the entry into the Rhineland) was a turning point in history; it was the last time that Germany could have been turned back from the path that led to war.

Weinberg, Gerhard L. *The Foreign Policy of Hitler's Germany: Diplomatic Revolution in Europe, 1933-1936*. Chicago: University of Chicago Press, 1970.

Gerhard Weinberg, an internationally known scholar of German diplomacy in the Nazi period, wrote this book as the first in a projected series on the history of Nazi foreign policy. The title, emphasizing "Hitler's Germany," indicates the major thrust of his primary thesis: that the foreign policy of the Third Reich was not a continuation of traditional German goals, as A. J. P. Taylor believes, but a new adventure based on Nazi ideology and, more particularly, on Hitler's dream for a Europe, indeed a world, dominated by the German nation. Most critics agree that Weinberg has successfully proved his argument and rebutted Taylor's thesis.

Hitler's foreign policy, according to Weinberg, had as its ultimate aim the unification of the German peoples in Europe, the acquiring of *Lebensraum*, or "living space," for Germans in Central and Eastern Europe, and the German domination, or the physical elimination, of "racially inferior" peoples. Weinberg contends that Hitler had outlined these aims in his *Mein Kampf* (My Struggle) and his secret second book, both written in the 1920's, and that, despite his actions after coming to power, he never lost sight of his purpose. Nevertheless, in the short run he was flexible enough to take advantage of opportunities as they arose.

Weinberg sees Hitler's foreign policy, in actual practice, as going through three stages: the establishment of his dictatorship, the period of German rearmament, and the planning and carrying out of war. In the first pe-riod, the initial months of his rule, Hitler did not attempt any foreign policy changes while he was consolidating his rule at home. Thus he maintained Germany's old alliances, including those with the West and the Soviet Union. He also achieved a major new diplomatic triumph by signing a concordat with the Vatican in July, 1933. This gave Hitler's government a measure of international respectability.

The period of armament is precisely the time when Hitler went about freeing Germany from the restrictions of Versailles and Locarno. According to Weinberg, Hitler had no intention of allowing Germany to remain unarmed even if the other countries of the Continent agreed to bring their armaments down to the level imposed on the Reich. Therefore, rearmament began in secret as soon as Hitler came to power. There was an internal problem associated with rearmament, as the renewal of the strength of the German military led to rivalry with the Nazi paramilitary storm trooper units—the SS and SA. Hitler took measures to moderate this rivalry so that it would not disturb his future plans. Weinberg believes, with Taylor, that war was inevitable once Germany had overturned the Versailles restrictions.

Weinberg also agrees with most diplomatic historians, including Taylor, that France acting alone in 1936 could have prevented the remilitarization of the Rhineland. However, he thinks that because of international isolation and domestic conflicts, France's leaders did not have the will to act. He believes that no democratic country could have launched a preventive war to stop Hitler in those days, for such a policy of aggression would have been contrary to the very tenets of a democratic society. Hence the nations of the world were forced to wait for Hitler to make the first move.

Weinberg concludes that three factors interacted to bring about the revolutionary change in diplomatic events of the Nazi period. First, the Versailles Treaty did not really leave Germany in a weakened position, and once rearmament occurred the country became a major power again. Second, Hitler's ideology itself broke down the "traditional separation of foreign and domestic policy." The Nazi philosophy and the totalitarian methods Hitler employed within Germany were applied to his diplomacy as well. Third, Hitler faced countries weakened by disunity and short-sightedness. The new nations created in Eastern Europe after World War I were too weak to stand up to a rearmed and reunified Germany; and the Great Powers of Europe were too suspicious of one another, suffered from too many domestic problems, and did not sufficiently realize the danger from Berlin to act decisively against Hitler before he launched World War II. — *F.B.C.*

## Additional Recommended Reading

Rich, Norman. *Hitler's War Aims*. Vol. I: *Ideology, the Nazi State, and the Course of Expansion*. New York: W. W. Norton and Company, 1973. An excellent recent scholarly survey of German foreign policy in the 1930's and 1940's with a hypothesis similar to Weinberg's.

Churchill, Winston S. *The Second World War*.Vol. I: *The Gathering Storm*. Boston: Houghton Mifflin Company, 1948. An account by the great British Prime Minister of "how the English-speaking people through their unwisdom, carelessness, and good nature allowed the wicked to rearm."

Craig, Gordon A. and Felix Gilbert, eds. *The Diplomats: 1919-1939*. Princeton, N.J.: Princeton University Press, 1953. A collection of articles by distinguished diplomatic historians on the men who determined foreign policy in this area.

Robertson, E. M. *Hitler's Pre-War Policy and Military Plans, 1933-1939*. London: Longmans, 1963. Another scholarly analysis of diplomatic events of the 1930's based on unpublished German documents.

—————————., ed. *The Origins of the Second World War: Historical Interpretations*. London: Macmillan and Company, 1971. A collection of essays, principally by British historians, examining the controversies over the interpretations of the origins of World War II.

# GERMANY REMILITARIZES THE RHINELAND

*Type of event:* Military: unilateral abrogation by force of treaties governing a demilitarized zone
*Time:* March 7, 1936
*Locale:* Rhineland area of Germany bordering on France and Belgium

*Principal personages:*

ADOLF HITLER (1889-1945), Chancellor and Führer of Germany, 1933-1945

KONSTANTIN VON NEURATH (1873-1956), Foreign Minister of Germany, 1932-1938

ROBERT ANTHONY EDEN (1897-1977), Foreign Secretary of Great Britain, 1935-1938

PIERRE ÉTIENNE FLANDIN (1889-1958), Foreign Minister of France, 1936

BENITO MUSSOLINI (1883-1945), Dictator and Duce of Italy, 1922-1943

## Summary of Event

At dawn on March 7, 1936, advance units of the German Army entered the demilitarized zones of the Rhineland for the first time since 1918. At 11:00 A.M. German Foreign Minister Konstantin von Neurath notified the ambassadors of the Locarno Pact powers—Britain, France, Belgium, and Italy—that Germany was formally abrogating the Treaty of Locarno. This pact of 1925 had guaranteed the frontier between Germany on one side and France and Belgium on the other, and had affirmed the permanent demilitarization of the Rhineland that had been established by the Versailles Treaty. At noon, German troops crossed the Rhine river bridges and arrived in the Rhine Valley—that part of Germany west of the Rhine bordering on France and Belgium. At that very moment Hitler addressed the Reichstag and justified his violation of the Versailles and Locarno settlements on the grounds that the recent Franco-Soviet alliance invalidated the Locarno agreement and that it was now necessary for German troops to protect the German frontier.

The German military reoccupation of the Rhineland was a flagrantly illegal act; it clearly violated Articles 42 and 43 of the Versailles Treaty. The demilitarization of the Rhineland established by these Articles had been the result of a compromise between France and her Anglo-American allies in 1919. France had initially hoped to detach the Rhineland from Germany, but America and England preferred a demilitarized buffer zone between France and Germany. The English and Americans had given France a security guarantee for this zone in a separate treaty of June 28, 1919. In 1920 and 1923 France had occupied the Rhineland with disastrous results. The Locarno Pact of 1925 sought to stabilize the peace by

348

returning to the idea of a demilitarized zone. Hitler's move of March 7 was clearly in violation of this pact, as well of the Versailles Treaty.

As early as May 21, 1935, Hitler openly stated his opposition to the existence of a demilitarized zone. He considered a demilitarized Rhineland a threat to German living space and an impediment to national prestige. He reached a decision to reoccupy the Rhineland on March 1 of 1936, and issued his preliminary orders to the army on March 2. The highest ranking members of the German General Staff urged caution on the Führer. Hitler chose to ignore their warnings. Though he believed that Britain and France would not offer armed resistance to the reoccupation of the Rhineland, he nevertheless ordered the German Army to fight if the two Western powers resorted to war. The military reoccupation of the Rhineland was the first of Hitler's great gambles: the risk for Germany was great since the German Army was not as powerful as that of Britain and France in 1936. However, Hitler correctly perceived the fears and divisions of the European powers. He was right, and he won; within three days his soldiers were in full control of the Rhineland.

The British and French governments were aware that Hitler coveted the Rhineland area, yet they (as well as most Germans) were surprised by his bold action. Though in retrospect it appears that France and Britain could have defeated Hitler easily in 1936, the two Western powers were unwilling to risk a new war with Germany. Most leading French politicians and generals believed that France was not prepared for war. The French Army concentrated thirteen divisions in the East, but only for the purpose of manning the Maginot Line. Germany sent only nineteen infantry and thirteen artillery units into the demilitarized area.

Although Article 44 of the Versailles statutes regarded a threat to the Rhineland as a "hostile act," the Locarno Pact did not bind England to come to the military aid of France in the case of a threat to the Rhineland. When France called upon her British ally for support in opposing the German move, the British rejected the use of force and economic sanctions, urging negotiation instead. The British Cabinet believed that the remilitarization of the Rhineland was not a "vital British interest." Moreover, the great caution of the British and French governments seems to have had wide popular support in both countries.

With the exception of Czechoslovakia and Rumania, the other European powers in the League of Nations did not strongly oppose the German action. Italy was grateful to Germany for her support in the Ethiopian crisis. Because of that episode, the League itself was in disarray, and this was a primary factor encouraging Hitler to make his move. Poland declared her disinterest in the Rhineland crisis, while the Soviet Union also refused to become involved. The Balkan, Scandinavian, and Latin American countries of the League needed Hitler's good will, since they traded heavily with Germany. When Britain and France called upon the United States to condemn the German action, America refused and retreated farther into isolation.

The Council of the League of Nations met on March 14, 1936, to consider the Rhineland crisis. The members passed a resolution condemning Germany, but proposed no sanctions. Instead, they asked Hitler to propose a new security system for Europe. Hitler and Neurath obliged with ambiguous proposals for peace and non-aggression and renounced any territorial ambitions in Europe. The Rhineland crisis passed and was soon overshadowed by the outbreak of the Spanish Civil War.

The German reoccupation of the Rhineland was an important turning point for several reasons. First, Germany's illegal action resulted in the humiliation of Britain and France and inaugurated the policy of the appeasement of Germany. The lack of any military response to the Rhineland action confirmed Hitler's belief that France, Britain, and the United States could be blackmailed by the threat of war. The Versailles and Locarno Treaties became dead letters, and the policy of "collective security" against aggression fell in ruins. The League of Nations became a shadow.

Second, the remilitarization of the Rhineland altered the balance of power in Germany's favor. It especially weakened the strategic position of both France and Belgium, hampering both countries' security against a surprise attack and limiting the ability of the French to march into Germany in the event of war. The fact that Britain and France sought to call on America for aid was an indication of how Germany had altered the balance of power. The efforts of Britain and France to enlist American help foreshadowed their later dependence on the United States once World War II began.

Third, Hitler's action greatly solidified his power among his generals and diplomats and markedly increased his popularity with the Germans generally. In a plebiscite held on March 29, 1936, 98.7 percent of the Germans gave their approval to the remilitarization of the Rhineland. Hitler consistently viewed his action of March, 1936, as the most daring of all his undertakings.

Finally, and perhaps most important, the Rhineland crisis signaled the end of the post-world War I era and hastened the coming of World War II. Hitler became emboldened to pursue further acts of aggression for hegemony and living space, while Britain and France began to step up their rearmament programs. Thus, the remilitarization of the Rhineland was Germany's first serious territorial bid for European hegemony since the early days of World War I. The failure of the Western powers to act in 1936 helped to set the stage for the next World War.

## Pertinent Literature

Emmerson, James Thomas. *The Rhineland Crisis of 7 March, 1936: A Study in Multilateral Diplomacy*. Ames: Iowa State University Press, 1977.

James Emmerson's book on the Rhineland crisis is the most recent study to appear on the subject. This richly detailed and thoroughly researched work draws on recent volumes of published diplomatic correspondence and on recently released records of the British Foreign Office. Though the Rhineland crisis has been studied in many contexts, Emmerson adds a great number of significant details to fill out the picture of the event. He also provides a number of good insights into the origins and results of the crisis. His goal appears to be to explode a number of myths that have grown up around the German occupation of the Rhineland.

Emmerson clearly shows that it was not only Chancellor Adolf Hitler but also his astute Foreign Minister Konstantin von Neurath who played on the fears and divisions of all the European powers. It was Neurath who helped strengthen Hitler's resolve to oppose any concessions in the Rhineland in the face of possible French and British opposition. The author demonstrates in great detail how the British Cabinet was willing to modify the Locarno Pact by negotiation, and how the other European powers were reluctant to oppose Germany for reasons of trade. Above all, Hitler was able to convince Europe that his aims were peaceful and in line with German territorial and ethnic self-determination.

Emmerson points out that the British and French were surprised by Hitler's action, that Hitler had given orders to the German Army to fight if opposed, and that nothing short of war could have stopped the Rhineland action in 1936. Though all these points have been made in such earlier

works as John Wheeler-Bennett's *The Nemesis of Power*, Emmerson is able to underscore his findings with more authoritative detail than was hitherto generally available.

One of the most valuable features of Emmerson's book is his exploration of the many ironies of the Rhineland crisis. For example, unlike Sir Lewis Namier, who in his *Europe in Decay* (1950) saw the Rhineland crisis as the last great opportunity to stop Hitler before World War II, Emmerson points out that in 1936 the episode never assumed the significance it now enjoys in retrospect. Rather than simply resulting in a diplomacy of appeasement on the part of Britain and France, the Rhineland episode hurt Hitler's credibility and accelerated the arms race, thereby setting the stage for World War II. Perhaps the greatest irony the author finds is that the issue of the remilitarization of the Rhineland might have been settled by negotiation in 1937 or 1938. He agrees, nevertheless, with the retrospective judgment of most historians that with the German entrance into the Rhineland "Europe had lost her last guarantee against German aggression."

Emmerson provides some perceptive applications of the crisis of 1936 to our own time. There are some important lessons to be learned from the process of the Rhineland affair: democratic nations must have resolve, military strength, support of allies and public opinion, and economic well-being to enforce their policies. These elements of strength were lacking in the France and Britain of 1936. Moreover, democratic countries are not inclined to intervene in what they regard as the "internal affairs" of other states. For example, many British felt that the Rhineland action of 1936 was a legitimate attempt of the Germans to regain their own territory.

Weinberg, Gerhard L. *The Foreign Policy of Hitler's Germany: Diplomatic Revolution in Europe, 1933-1936.* Chicago: University of Chicago Press, 1970.

This well-balanced work on the foreign policy of Nazi Germany puts the Rhineland crisis into needed perspective. Weinberg effectively argues that the remilitarization of the Rhineland completed the 1933-1936 phase that witnessed a "diplomatic revolution" in Europe. Hitler's success in the Rhineland captured the diplomatic initiative for Germany. The result was the substitution of international anarchy for collective security. "Once this phase had been completed, Germany's determination for war became the central issue in world diplomacy."

Weinberg shares the views of many historians of the Nazi period that the key to Hitler's diplomacy was the desire for living space (*Lebensraum*). The first aim of the Nazi regime from 1933 to 1934 was the job of domestic consolidation. Hitler was therefore conciliatory for the most part in the field of foreign policy. He needed to neutralize and possibly isolate France. From 1933 to 1934, Germany concluded treaties with Poland and the Vatican, maintained a degree of cooperation with the Soviet Union, and stepped up trade with other countries.

By 1935, however, Hitler felt sufficiently confident to embark on a cautious program of military and territorial expansion, while attempting to avoid war. For example, Germany worked for the return of the Saar territory, and in 1935 instituted a system of military conscription. Hitler was not yet ready to remilitarize the Rhineland, however, for fear that France would claim a violation of the Locarno Pact and resort to war. What encouraged him was the disarray of the League of Nations and the weakening of the alliance of the Locarno powers brought on by the Italian war with Ethiopia.

For Weinberg, the demilitarization of the Rhineland was a crucial aspect of the post-World War I settlement, for it left Germany open to invasion in the West and made her incapable of aggression in any other direction. In the German view, a demilitarized Rhineland complicated rearmament, hurt national prestige, and above all prevented the acquisition of living space—the "main aim" of Nazi diplomacy. Weinberg makes the important point that a German move into the Rhineland would also divert the attention of the German public from the economic difficulties of the winter of 1935-1936. Such illustrations of the intimate links between domestic and foreign policy are always most welcome in works dealing mainly with diplomacy.

As early as 1935 the French Ambassador to Berlin, André François-Poncet, warned his government that Germany might confront France with a *fait accompli* in the Rhineland, but this was an exaggeration of German military strength. Belgium was similarly frightened by Germany, while England professed her willingness to come to an agreement over the issue.

Hitler's plans to occupy the Rhineland on a Saturday increased the element of surprise, since the French and British diplomats were away for the weekend. Weinberg finds that the Germans ordered a tactical fighting withdrawal in the event of French and British military opposition. He maintains that the French could have acted alone to contain Germany, but the French government, and especially the army, lacked the determination to resist the German moves. The French Foreign Minister Étienne Flandin prophesied to the American Ambassador in Paris that the Germans would first fortify the Rhineland and then turn east. Nevertheless, the French failed to act.

Weinberg's account of the outcome of the Rhineland events is refreshingly less deterministic than most accounts of the affair. For him, the inaction of the British was not a foregone conclusion; for a while it looked as if the British government would stand with France and threaten military action against Germany. Weinberg provides us with three important reasons why this did not happen. First, the British Dominions, particularly South Africa, refused to support England in a military action against Germany. Second, the British did not deem the Rhineland occupation sufficiently dangerous to warrant the risk of war. Most important, the British public and press supported negotiation with Germany, since they felt that the Germans were merely reoccupying their own territory.

With the successful occupation of the Rhineland, the post-World War I security system collapsed, and, Weinberg argues, a "diplomatic revolution" ensued as the European powers were forced to reorient their policies toward Germany. Hitler was now confident that with the absence of collective security he could take even greater risks to achieve the ultimate German aim of living space. It is ironic that only one major observer of the European scene—Pope Pius XI—counseled his French Ambassador to send 200,000 French soldiers into the Rhineland to counter Germany's actions. But the pontiff's advice was given on March 16, when the Rhineland occupation had become a *fait accompli*. In any case, the French Army would probably have ignored the Pope's words.

Weinberg's conclusions on the significance of the remilitarization of the Rhineland are shared by most historians of the period. He sees the event as a great military and diplomatic success for Hitler's Germany and as a crucial power shift in Germany's favor in the direction of European hegemony. The events in the Rhineland inaugurated the second phase of the diplomacy of Nazi Germany that would last from 1936 to 1939. This phase would be marked by German expansion without war in Austria and Czechoslovakia, employing some of the methods Hitler had used so successfully in the Rhineland. — *L.S.*

## Additional Recommended Reading

Namier, Sir Lewis B. *Europe in Decay: A Study in Disintegration, 1936-1940*. London: Macmillan and Company, 1950. Argues that the Rhineland crisis resulted in the Western appeasement of Germany, and that 1936 represented the last chance of the Western powers to stop Hitler without resorting to a world war.

Wheeler-Bennett, John W. *The Nemesis of Power: The German Army in Politics, 1918-1945*. New York: The Viking Press, 1949 and 1967. A major study of the German Army from 1918 to 1945, maintaining that Hitler overruled the reservations of the German generals with regard to the remilitarization of the Rhineland, and holding that his control over the army was strengthened by his great diplomatic and military success of 1936.

Taylor, A. J. P. *The Origins of the Second World War*. New York: Atheneum Publishers, 1962. This strongly revisionist work tends to blame the inconsistencies of British and French diplomacy rather than German actions for the origins of World War II.

Robertson, E. M. *Hitler's Pre-War Policy and Military Plans, 1933-1939*. London: Longmans, 1963. A concise survey of German territorial ambitions before World War II, showing that Hitler planned to remilitarize the Rhineland as early as February 14, 1936.

George, Margaret. *The Hollow Men: An Examination of British Foreign Policy Between the Years 1933 and 1939*. Foreword by A. L. Rowse. London: Leslie Frewin, 1965. This study of the motives behind the British government's policy of appeasement in the 1930's shows that both fear of war and sympathy for Germany motivated the attitudes of conservative British politicians in the Rhineland crisis.

Hildebrand, Klaus. *The Foreign Policy of the Third Reich*. Translated by Anthony Fothergill. London: B. T. Batsford, 1973. A survey of Nazi foreign policy that stresses the continuities between Bismarck and Hitler and views Nazism as the culmination of "caesaristic" traditions in Prussian-German history.

# INVENTION OF THE JET ENGINE

*Type of event:* Technological: development and building of an efficient jet engine
*Time:* April and September, 1937
*Locale:* Rugby, England; Marienehe, Germany

### Principal personages:

R. E. LASLEY, American designer of steam turbines

FRANK WHITTLE, British inventor of the turbojet

W. G. CARTER, British chief designer of the Gloster Aircraft Company and designer of the first British jet plane

HANS-JOACHIM PABST VON OHAIN, German inventor of the turbojet

ERNST HEINKEL (1888-1958), German aircraft designer and owner of the Heinkel aircraft factory

## Summary of Event

The idea of using gas turbines for the jet propulsion of airplanes took shape in men's minds in the 1920's. Initially, it seemed premature. In 1922, at the request of the United States Army, Edgar Buckingham of the National Bureau of Standards compared the best theoretical performance of a jet propulsion system with that of existing engine propeller systems and concluded that "propulsion by the reaction of a simple jet cannot compete, in any respect, with airscrew propulsion at such flying speeds as are now in prospect." As the speeds envisaged were 200-250 miles per hour, there was little reason to develop jet propulsion engines until airplanes were capable of speeds approaching five hundred miles per hour, for conventional piston engines were more efficient at lower speeds and altitudes. By the end of the decade, however, a few inspired persons chose to pursue the idea.

In 1930, R. E. Lasley, a designer of steam turbines for the Allis-Chalmers Manufacturing Company, took

out patents and established a corporation in Waukegan, Illinois, to develop a gas turbine for airplanes. After bench tests in 1934, the United States War Department and Lasley himself judged the engine hopelessly inefficient when compared with piston engines. His funds exhausted, Lasley abandoned his tests.

Royal Air Force flight cadet Frank Whittle was more determined and more fortunate. In 1928, as part of his required science thesis at the RAF College in Cranwell, England, he discussed the possible use of jet propulsion and gas turbines to propel aircraft at five hundred miles per hour at high altitude where such speeds were feasible. He won the college's prize for the aeronautical sciences, and eighteen months later, on January 16, 1930, applied for a patent on the use of the gas turbine for such a purpose. The patent unequivocally stated that the planned invention would provide a large thrust in proportion to its weight; would perform at greater altitudes than were then attainable; would effect greater speeds than were previously possible with a reasonably low fuel consumption; and would possess a simple and convenient external form.

Whittle was unable to interest either the British Air Ministry or private engine manufacturers in what seemed to them an impractical idea, given the state of aerodynamics and metallurgy. However, the RAF was so impressed with Whittle's abilities that it sent him to Cambridge University in 1934. By 1935 he was so depressed about his chances for having the engine developed that he was prepared to allow the basic patent to lapse rather than pay the renewal fee. Salvation appeared that year in the form of two former RAF officers who helped Whittle form the company Power Jets, Ltd., in March, 1936, with the financial backing of the London investment banking firm of O. T. Falk and Partners. Whittle graduated with first class honors in the Mechanical Sciences in 1936, and the RAF allowed him to remain at Cambridge for postgraduate research in engineering while he continued work on the engine. Detailed design and construction were contracted with the British Thomson-Houston Company in Rugby, which built steam turbines for electricity generating plants. The engine was completed in 1937, and bench tests from April to August were sufficiently successful to encourage major reconstruction and the further interest of the Air Ministry.

The engine was rebuilt twice, the second time at the expense of the Ministry, which assumed responsibility for all future developmental costs in 1939 after its Director of Scientific Research had observed the engine in operation. The Air Ministry, now convinced that the gas turbine was practical, placed a contract with Power Jets for a flight engine, and with the Gloster Aircraft Company for an experimental jet fighter. Whittle designed the engine; the Gloster chief designer, W. G. Carter, together with his team, designed the airplane. On May 15, 1941, with Flight Lieutenant Philip E. G. Sayer at the controls, the Gloster E 28/39 flew for seventeen minutes, and by May 28 it had completed a series of seventeen flight tests in which it had exceeded the top speed of the Spitfire, England's standard piston engine fighter, at all heights.

The Gloster was a successful jet airplane, but it was not the first. The first flight of a jet aircraft occurred in Germany on August 27, 1939, almost two years before the Gloster's maiden flight. Hans-Joachim Pabst von Ohain, a former student of aerodynamics at the University of Goettingen, took out several gas turbine patents in 1935, but German engine manufacturers showed no interest. In their opinion the lack of suitable heat-resistant, light metal alloys would result in an excessively heavy engine. Ernst Heinkel, however, one of the most versatile of German aircraft designers and entrepreneurs, had been interested in the possibilities of jet propulsion for high altitude and high speed craft since 1930. He hired Ohain to develop a test gas turbine engine, which first ran successfully in September, 1937. After completing a second small test engine, the two men began work on a flight engine and test airframe. Five days before the outbreak of World War II, on August 27, 1939, a second version of the flight engine powered the experimental He 178 V1, with Erich Warsitz at the controls, in the first flight of a jet plane. By April, 1941, a month before the Gloster craft flew, the prototype of a Heinkel twin-jet fighter, the He 280 V1, had flown successfully. In the fall of 1939, German Air Ministry officials refused to support the He 178 because they believed that their piston-engine craft would suffice to win the war; so the small plane was relegated to a Berlin museum, where it was destroyed in an Allied bombing raid in 1943. By that time the German Air Ministry had thrown its support to more advanced jet engine enterprises at BMW, Junkers, and Heinkel.

The British and German efforts were shrouded in the utmost secrecy; consequently, when an Italian jet-propelled plane, the Caproni-Campini CC2, first flew in August, 1940, and then made a widely publicized flight from Milan to Rome in 1941, many believed it to be the first successful jet airplane. But the CC2 was actually powered by an ordinary reciprocating liquid-cooled aircraft engine driving a fan within its fuselage, not by a turbojet.

Both Whittle's and Ohain's engines were turbojets, operating essentially in the following manner. They inducted air, compressed it to three to five times its original pressure, and then forced it into a combustor, or combustion chamber, where it was allowed to expand slightly while fuel was sprayed in by a high pressure pump and ignited. The combustion greatly expanded the air, which proceeded through a turbine wheel fixed to the same shaft as the compressor. The air rushing out turned the turbine, which in turn ran the compressor and pulled in more air at the front of the engine. Since not all the power thus generated was required to run the turbine, the excess energy exiting rearward through the exhaust nozzle formed the jet, which provided the forward thrust.

As Whittle had discerned in 1930, once planes were designed that were aerodynamically capable of speeds in the 400-500 miles per hour range, the turbojet became the preferred engine because of its relative simplicity, low engine weight, and high air flow. Lightweight, high-quality, heat-resistant metal alloys, the absence of which had initially deterred the participation of engine manufacturers, were developed to meet the needs of the engine. The financial support of government and industry was ultimately what enabled Whittle and Ohain to bring their near-parallel efforts to fruition, thus illustrating the maxim that complex modern invention is the product of the sustained vision and efforts of individual genius supported by institutions capable of amassing resources unavailable to the individual. In this case the end result, the gas turbine, has proven to be a flexible source of power for aviation capable of driving not only the jet but also a propeller in the turboprop configuration, or a ducted fan in the turbofan version. It led first to a revolution in military aviation during the latter part of World War II, which had provided the impetus for its speedy evolution, and then to a revolution in commercial air transportation, the effects of which are so much in evi-    dence today.

## Pertinent Literature

Neville, Leslie E. and Nathaniel F. Silsbee. *Jet Propulsion Progress: The Development of Aircraft Gas Turbines*. New York: McGraw-Hill Book Company, 1948.

There is a paucity of literature for the general reader on the jet engine, its history and operation. In the light of its significance, this absence is unfortunate, but not surprising, given the rather technical nature of the subject. Most of the works on aviation history concentrate on the evolution of the airplane and relegate the discussion of aircraft power plants to a distinctly secondary position, although airplane and engine development go hand in hand. While most of the material on jet propulsion is contained in more general works on aviation history, there is some literature on the subject suitable for laymen written in the 1940's, soon after the development of the aircraft gas turbine. Historical works on contemporary topics often suffer from excessive bias and lack of information. This problem is not evident in the book on jet propulsion by Leslie E. Neville and Nathaniel L. Silsbee, of the Institute of Aeronautical Sciences. The authors have written a history of aircraft gas turbines which concentrates on American developments but ably discusses in detail the prior evolution of the turbojet by the British and Germans in the 1930's. They do not attempt a comprehensive history of the subject; instead, they seek "to present simply and accurately the fundamentals of the gas turbine as applied to aircraft, with an outline of the development of such units in Germany, Great Britain, and the United States," where the major strides in jet propulsion occurred in the 1930's and 1940's. Using sources that range from military intelligence reports to interviews with participants in the actual events, they have admirably succeeded.

Beginning with a short general description of the turbojet, the book discusses Nazi Germany's development of the first operational jet fighter, the Messerschmidt Me 262, together with its power plants. It slights the early developments that led to the first jet flight of the Heinkel He 178 in favor of those that culminated in the plane that threatened to disrupt the Allied air offensive against Germany in the later stages of World War II. Neville and Silsbee then explain how Whittle and Rolls-Royce developed operational turbojets, after which they devote three chapters to American efforts—one to those of the Army Air Force and American industry, one to the Navy and industry, and a final one to the role of research by the National Advisory Committee on Aeronautics (NACA). The book concludes with two chapters on unsolved problems, such as the development of heat resistant metals and jet fuel, and the future of jet propulsion. The authors chronicle the roles of inventors, the military, and industry in the development of turbojets and turbojet powered craft, with detailed discussion and descriptions of important engines, such as the Junkers Jumo-004, the Rolls-Royce "Nene," and the General Electric I-16. The work is liberally illustrated with pictures of important American and British participants in jet development and with diagrams, charts, tables, and cutaway drawings of the engines. Of particular interest to the American reader is the story of the cloak-and-dagger secrecy surrounding the development of America's first jet airplane, the Bell XP-59A, and of the critical role in American jet engine development played by the British, who disclosed to American authorities all of their information on jet planes and engines in July, 1941, as a result of a mutual aid agreement.

Although the book contains much technical material, it generally avoids formulas, calculations, and highly technical discussions. Where such data are necessary, the authors explain them in clear, concise language. For the reader's further enlightenment, the authors have included a glossary, a chronology of the principal events in turbojet development in England, Germany, and the United States, and a comprehensive bibliography that cites not only relevant books and articles but also lists of the gas turbine patents in Germany, Switzerland, and the United States. This book is a basic introduction to the history of turbojet development in the 1930's and 1940's and constitutes a most valuable reference resource.

Smith, G. Geoffrey. *Gas Turbines and Jet Propulsion for Aircraft*. London: *Flight*, 1946.

Leslie Neville and Nathaniel Silsbee credit G. Geoffrey Smith with pioneering writings on the subject of aircraft gas turbines and, in this work, with providing a complete history of the subject. G. Geoffrey Smith was editorial director of the prominent aviation journal *Flight* and a long-standing expert on aircraft engines whose interest antedated World War I. The first edition of this work appeared in December, 1942, and despite wartime restrictions, the first three editions dealt knowledgeably with the fundamentals of jet propulsion, metallurgical problems, and early projects and patents; the fourth edition brought the information up to date.

The author explains the types of jet propulsion systems, their construction and operation, and the aerodynamic problems involved in high speed flight; he also compares gas turbines with other forms of aircraft propulsion. After tracing the origins of the jet as far back as the ancient Greeks, he elaborates on twentieth century accomplishments in Sweden, Switzerland, Italy, England, Germany, and the United States, with emphasis on the last three countries. He shows particular interest in the use of the gas turbine to drive propellers (the turboprop), seeking to demonstrate their worth as an efficient alternative to the piston engine. (Future developments would prove his judgment to be correct.) Smith also includes provocative chapters on the future prospects of tailless aircraft and flying wings and on the prospects of applying the steam turbine to aircraft propulsion. In the case of the latter, he cautions against accepting as final the NACA conclusion that the steam turbine would be far too heavy and uneconomical for use in aircraft. Although the NACA diagnosis ultimately proved to be correct, his argument is nonetheless stimulating in its advocacy of the improbable, which, in the larger sense, is what invention and genius are all about. After a short biographical chapter on Englishmen who made significant contributions to aircraft turbine development, the author concludes with transcriptions of British Broadcasting Company programs in 1944 explaining the operation of the jet engine, and of lectures given by various experts on such topics as military and civilian usage of turbine powered aircraft and the possibilities of combining turbine and piston engines.

Smith's work can be viewed not only as a historical account but also as a historical source, as it discusses current ideas about the future development and use of the gas turbine in aviation. Although the book is valuable as a basic primer in jet propulsion with abundant explanatory illustrations and charts, it is disjointed in its organization and occasionally repetitive and hard to follow. Its approach to the subject is also more complex than that of Neville's and Silsbee's study; consequently, the general reader will profit more from Smith's expertise if he reads the book by Neville and Silsbee first. — *J.H.M.*

## Additional Recommended Reading

Finch, Volney C. *Jet Propulsion Turbojets*. Millbrae, Calif.: The National Press, 1948. A very technical study by a professor of engineering, which includes a useful introduction on the history of the gas turbine in aviation.

Gray, George W. *Frontiers of Flight: The Story of NACA Research*. New York: Alfred A. Knopf, 1948. A discussion of the role of NACA in flight development which contains a solid chapter on jet propulsion, its problems and research.

Hildreth, C. H. and B. C. Nalty. *1001 Questions Answered About Aviation History*. New York: Dodd, Mead, and Company, 1969. An interesting compilation of facts, including some on jet propulsion, presented in the form of questions and answers.

Ley, Willy. "Jet Propulsion: From Fancy to Fact," in *Aviation*. XLIII, no. 1 (January, 1944), pp. 147-149, 309-311, and 313; no. 2 (February, 1944), pp. 121-125. Ley concentrates on rocketry, his specialty, and neglects the gas turbine almost entirely.

*The Lore of Flight*. New York: Time-Life Books, 1970. This comprehensive treatment of all facets of aviation has an excellent, well-illustrated chapter on gas turbines that is especially illuminating on more recent developments.

Miller, Ronald and David Sawers. *The Technical Development of Modern Aviation*. New York: Frederick A. Praeger, 1970. This history of the development of the commercial airliner includes a long and informative chapter on the application of the gas turbine to commercial aviation.

# JAPANESE MILITARY CAMPAIGNS IN CHINA

*Type of event:* Military: armed invasion into China
*Time:* July 7, 1937-August, 1945
*Locale:* China

*Principal personages:*
CHIANG KAI-SHEK (1887-1975), Chinese Nationalist leader
HASHIMOTO GUN, Chief of Staff of the North China Army
GENERAL IWANE MATSUI, Commander of the Shanghai expeditionary force
PRINCE KONOYE FUMIMARO (1891-1945), Prime Minister of Japan
MAO TSE-TUNG (1893-1976), Chinese Communist leader
WANG CHING-WEI (1884-1944), Chinese collaborator
GENERAL CH'IN TEH-CH'UN, Mayor of Peking

## Summary of Event

On July 7, 1937, shots were exchanged between Chinese and Japanese soldiers stationed near the Marco Polo Bridge thirty miles outside Peking. This minor incident soon brought war in China, a conflict that led to Japanese-American confrontation and the Pacific War. For China, Japanese invasion was a major factor in the rise and eventual victory of Communism.

To many observers, the Marco Polo Bridge incident appeared to be a repetition of the Mukden Incident of 1931, in which a group of military conspirators had staged a railroad attack that became a pretext for Japanese occupation of Manchuria. To protect its holdings in Manchuria, Japan gradually extended political control to North China. Under the 1901 Boxer Protocol, Japan had the right to maintain a legation guard at Peking, and to protect communication to the seaport of Tientsin. About seven thousand troops guarded the Peking-Tientsin railway and the Peking-Hankow line to the south. The

Chinese 29th Army controlled the strategic area around the Marco Polo Bridge.

After 1931, expansion of Japanese influence in North China and growing Chinese nationalism under Nationalist leader Chiang Kai-shek made conflict almost inevitable. Diplomatic attempts to give the Nanking-based Nationalist government control of North China in exchange for recognition of the Japanese puppet state of Manchukuo broke down by January, 1936. Nevertheless, Japanese policy in China was to avoid war, because of Japan's fear of war with Russia.

After the initial fighting of July 7, 1937, local military commanders on both sides arranged a ceasefire and investigation. General Ch'in Teh-ch'un, the Mayor of Peking, and General Hashimoto Gun, the *de facto* commander of the Japanese troops, arranged a local armistice on July 11. The disposition of Japanese troops and other evidence suggest that the incident was not planned, but both sides quickly sent reinforcements. Although the field armies reached a settlement, the cabinet of Prime Minister Konoye Fumimaro in Tokyo put pressure on Nanking. Public xenophobia arose on both sides. On the night of July 25, skirmishes broke out near Peking; and on July 27, full-scale fighting occurred near the Marco Polo Bridge. Diplomatic negotiations continued, but the attempt to localize the conflict failed when Chinese troops opened fire on Japanese troops at Shanghai on August 13 and bombers attacked Japanese naval forces on August 14. The long and bitter Sino-Japanese War had begun, not as the result of a plot by Japanese army officers, but because the Chinese government made a stand against further Japanese encroachment in the North.

The Japanese Shanghai garrison was heavily outnumbered, but it held off German-trained Chinese troops until relieved by an expeditionary force under General Iwane Matsui. On November 5, the Japanese landed in Hangchow Bay, south of Shanghai, and attacked the rear of the Chinese force besieging the city. By November 8, Shanghai was under Japanese control. The Japanese then pushed rapidly west towards the Nationalist capital of Nanking. Defying Japanese demands for a negotiated settlement, Chiang Kai-shek moved his capital far beyond the gorges of the Yangtze to Chungking, where he held out until 1945. Following the capture of Nanking on December 12, 1937, local Japanese military commanders permitted their troops to wreak havoc on the populace in days of looting, burning, rape, and mass murder.

The "Rape of Nanking," as it came to be called, failed to terrorize the Chinese; in fact, it strengthened their resolve to resist Japanese control. Overseas sympathy for China created an anti-Japanese sentiment that eventually led to economic embargoes, diplomatic confrontation, and finally war in December, 1941. President Franklin D. Roosevelt had already called for a "quarantine" of aggressive nations in a speech delivered on October 5, 1937, although American policy was to avoid direct pressure. On October 6, the League of Nations, responding to an appeal by Chiang Kai-shek, censored Japanese actions in China. Western powers, however, were not willing to support China militarily. Even when the British warship *Ladybird* was damaged and the American gunboat *Panay* was sunk in the Yangtze by Japanese forces on December 12, the two governments accepted apologies and indemnities from Tokyo.

In January, 1938, Japan decided to begin a major military campaign to conquer the vastness of China. To cut off supplies to Chungking, an expeditionary force was landed near Hong Kong, capturing Canton on October 21, 1938. Japanese forces on the Yangtze captured Hankow on October 25. In the North, Japan began a campaign to take Shantung by seizing Tsingtao on January 10, 1938, although they suffered a defeat by Chinese troops at Taierchwang on April 9. The Chinese were soon again on the defensive, halting the Japanese advance by destroying the Yellow river dikes.

By the end of 1938 a military stalemate was reached in China, with Japan occupying the North, much of the coastal areas, and the major cities and railroads which linked them. Chiang remained in Chungking, supplied by long routes through Indochina until June, 1940, and by the Burma Road until May, 1942. He had been forced into a reluctant alliance with the Chinese Communists, led by Mao Tse-tung, whose guerrilla forces increased their power in rural areas behind Japanese lines. Chiang hoped to husband his forces for a future showdown with the Communists, thinking that the United States would eventually declare war and defeat Japan.

For their part, the Japanese were forced to tolerate a stalemate because of a renewed Russian menace to the north and insufficient military power to control all of China. On July 11, 1938, troops of the Kwantung Army fought with Soviet frontier guards on the Siberia-Manchuria border. Both sides reinforced infantry with tanks, artillery, and aircraft. The Russians won a clear victory. The next year hostilities again broke out in Outer Mongolia in May, continuing until an armistice was reached on September 16, 1938. At the battle of Khalka, July 2 to August 23, 1938, Russian units inflicted serious losses on Japanese troops.

Having averted war with Russia, Japan began plans for a southward advance designed in part to isolate Chiang Kai-shek. In March, 1940, Wang Ching-wei, a former Nationalist rival of Chiang, agreed to head a puppet government in Nanking. During the Pacific War years the Japanese were forced to adopt a defensive posture as Mao Tse-tung's Communist forces consolidated their power in occupied areas and attacked isolated Japanese garrisons and lines of communication. Never seeking full-scale war in China, Japanese forces were confronted by a new sense of Chinese nationalism, symbolized by Chiang's refusal to accept colonial status, and by a "no-win" military situation.

## Pertinent Literature

Johnson, Chalmers A. *Peasant Nationalism and Communist Power: The Emergence of Revolutionary China, 1937-1945*. Stanford, Calif.: Stanford University Press, 1962.

This book analyzes Japanese military campaigns in China and the guerrilla warfare that frustrated their goals. The author focuses on the nineteen areas behind Japanese lines that were controlled by Communist forces. Abundant evidence supports Johnson's argument that Communism did not really succeed until Japanese invasion stimulated nationalism among the peasant masses.

Japanese brutality and attempts to pacify the population by terror backfired. In many areas of China the only force fighting the Japanese was Communist, as Chiang Kai-shek was isolated in central China. Japan did not have enough manpower to control a country of China's size and population. Traditional urban and rural elites sympathetic to the Nationalist government were forced to flee, leaving the peasantry for eight years under nominal Japanese control. Communist cadres could work in the villages of China free from their Nationalist enemies with whom they had fought bitterly from 1927 to 1937. Drawn deep into China by Chiang's courageous refusal to accept humilating treaty terms in 1937-1938, the Japanese overestimated the area they could effectively control. Driving out the Nationalist government and failing to create a viable client state, the Japanese army left a favorable environment for Communist growth. Japanese aggression was thus an important factor in the ultimate Communist victory in 1949.

The author begins by showing the modest success of Communist efforts to mobilize the peasantry before 1937, although he perhaps underplays the Kiangsi period in order to make a stronger case. For example, the Communists achieved success in Shansi as early as 1935. Chapter Two illustrates the negative role Japan had in arousing the national consciousness of the peasants, and Chapter Three discusses how the Communists adopted policies, programs, and propaganda that took advantage of the political situation. It was not Marxist-Leninist ideals that appealed to the masses, Johnson contends, but an anti-Japanese nationalist ideology. Class-conflict issues were played down, especially during the so-called "United Front" from 1937 to 1941, and "national salvation" was stressed.

Mao's followers grew most rapidly in the occupied areas. Japanese forces repeatedly made futile forays from the cities and railways in "mop-up" campaigns aimed at destroying Communist base areas, but their efforts only solidified local support. Three types of Communist units emerged: regulars, guerrillas, and militia. The local militia provided essential intelligence and sabotaged Japanese communications. Until the last years of the war, Communist forces followed Mao's rules for guerrilla warfare, choosing when and where to engage the enemy. When Japanese units were stronger, the guerrillas retreated temporarily. Resistance warfare was coupled with firm measures against collaborators so that Japanese units found scant indigenous support and no legitimacy other than coercive force.

In Chapter Four, Johnson describes the growth of Communist-controlled territory in North China. Japanese and Communist forces contended for the area after the Nationalists were eliminated early in the war. By the time the war ended, Mao could claim a loyal constituency of 100,000,000 peasants mobilized during the conflict.

Chiang Kai-shek's political power, by contrast, was based on the urban middle and upper classes. Social and political reforms were often spoken of in Chungking, but seldom carried out. In addition, the Nationalists were reluctant to commit their forces fully against Japan, especially after the American entry into the war. They hoped that a quick victory over Japan would follow, permitting them to renew their attack on Communism. Unfortunately, this temporizing policy favored the Communists. With their economic and social reforms in the villages, the Communists were able to build a strong base while they were fighting Japan.

Ironically, one of Japan's avowed goals in China was to destroy Communism; but they unwittingly favored it by discrediting the Nationalists. What had begun in 1937 as a conflict between two elitist governments became a people's war of liberation under the Communist flag.

Johnson's research is thorough and his book is well documented in both Western and Japanese sources. The one weakness is the lack of extensive Chinese sources: perhaps a slightly different view would emerge from examining the Chinese side. However, Japanese frustration and failure in the occupation of China are well represented.

Bunker, Gerald E. *The Peace Conspiracy: Wang Ching-wei and the China War, 1937-1941*. Cambridge, Mass.: Harvard University Press, 1972.

This study reveals how Japan unsuccessfully tried to extricate herself from the "China Incident" through complex and devious negotiations with various Chinese political factions. The central subject is Wang Ching-wei, an important Nationalist official and rival of Chiang Kai-shek who agreed to head the most important of several puppet regimes established by the Japanese.

The author carefully guides the reader through the intricate labyrinth of Chinese and Japanese politics before and during the China War. It is clear that Japan had neither unified leadership nor a coherent policy toward China which would define her ultimate aims. While certain political leaders, and even some military factions, sought an end to the costly China War through negotiation, they had a naïve view of the power of Chinese nationalism. They also had little control over Japanese field commanders who pressed for further military action and final victory over the embattled Chungking government of Chiang Kai-shek. By 1941, Japanese involvement in China had aroused the West. Prime Minister Fumimaro tried to reconcile the expansionism of militarists in his own country, Chiang Kai-shek's nationalism, and President Roosevelt's increasingly firm support of the Nationalist government. Bunker notes that "the imperial mystique would not allow Japan to retreat." Occupation of China was to lead to direct economic confrontation with the United States and Japan's desperate attempt to resolve the China War by attacking the West in December, 1941.

Bunker agrees with most scholarship that the outbreak of war in July, 1937, was not planned by Japanese military schemers. A full-scale military involvement was not desired at a time when Russia posed a grave threat; so the military force that Japan put in China was small. Its continued presence in China, now nationally awakened, was precarious, depending on "prestige"; and many Japanese felt that a partial retreat would become a withdrawal, even from Manchuria. Chiang and Fumimaro held tenuous control over their respective countries: they both looked to nationalistic victories to win broader political support.

Wang Ching-wei became an important pawn in the struggle. He was idealistic, and felt that the only escape from destruction would be to appease the Japanese. While Chiang Kai-shek held out in his Chungking fastness, Wang agreed to form a government in the spring of 1940. It soon became apparent that Wang was a tool of the Japanese seeking to divide the Nationalist cause. His hopes for Japanese concessions to give his regime legitimacy were not realized. This was due in part to fragmentation of Japanese authority: regional military commands in North, Central, and South China had some autonomy. They competed with one another to the extent of organizing rival client governments. Decisions made in Tokyo could not always be implemented in China. As more and more of China came under Japanese military control, the field armies were less and less willing to recognize the minimal demand of Chinese nationalism: that is, complete withdrawal of all Japanese troops after peace was established.

After Canton fell on October 21, 1938, the Nationalists became landlocked in a remote province, isolated from foreign aid. Bunker suggests that Fumimaro, under military pressure, made a fundamental mistake on January 16, 1938, when he announced that Japan would no longer negotiate with the Nationalist regime. This limited future attempts to extricate troops from China to tricky secret negotiations and dealings with prominent Chinese who had no real power base. Wang Ching-wei was an example. Not until 1942, when the Pacific War began turning against Japan, did Tokyo make real concessions; but by then it was too late. Japanese demands amounted to complete control of China, "a political, economic, and strategic stranglehold." Unwillingness to compromise undermined the attempts of Wang Ching-wei to bring peace to his war-torn country. Wang died in a Nagoya hospital on October 10, 1944, his peace movement a failure. He was considered a traitor by most Chinese.

Wang's efforts were undermined by Japanese duplicity. In January, 1940, when a conference was held at Ch'ingtao to announce the formation of his government, a close associate made public the humiliating terms demanded by Japan. On the very eve of inauguration of the Nanking regime, Wang was revealed as a puppet. Secret Chiang-Japanese negotiations were held behind Wang's back, but Chiang Kai-shek proved as firm as Wang was conciliatory. Frustrated, Japan belatedly recognized Wang Ching-wei's government on November 30, 1940. This signaled a final decision for a lengthy war in China. Inchoate political goals, insensitivity towards Chinese nationalism, and fragmented military control all prevented Japan from extricating herself from China. — *R.R.*

## Additional Recommended Reading

Boyle, John Hunter. *China and Japan at War, 1937-1945: The Politics of Collaboration.* Stanford, Calif.: Stanford University Press, 1972. An excellent study arguing that

Japan did have a consistent China policy during the war, but one that did not recognize Chinese nationalism.

Crowley, James B. "A Reconsideration of the Marco Polo Bridge Incident," in *Journal of Asian Studies*. XXII (May, 1963), pp. 277-291. Presents evidence to support the view that the outbreak of the China War was not a conspiracy by the Japanese military.

Lindsay, Michael. *The Unknown War: North China 1937-1945*. London: Bergstrom and Boyle Books, 1975. A vivid personal account and photographic history of life in Communist-held areas during the war.

Lu, David J. *From the Marco Polo Bridge to Pearl Harbor: Japan's Entry into World War II*. Washington, D.C.: Public Affairs Press, 1961. A scholarly study of Japan's entanglement in China, primarily from the perspective of diplomatic history.

Peattie, Mark R. *Ishiwara Kanji and Japan's Confrontation with the West*. Princeton, N.J.: Princeton University Press, 1975. An essential book portraying the development of Japanese perceptions towards China through the thought of a Japanese who played a leading role.

Snow, Edgar. *The Battle for Asia*. New York: Random House, 1941. A fascinating journalistic account of the China War before Pearl Harbor, including many firsthand observations of the Chinese side of the conflict.

Tuchman, Barbara W. *Stilwell and the American Experience in China, 1911-1945*. New York: The Macmillan Company, 1971. A very readable study which focuses on Stilwell, Military Attaché to Nationalist China until 1939, with a good deal of material on the China War presented with a strong anti-Chiang Kai-shek bias.

# THE UNITED STATES ESTABLISHES
# A TWO-OCEAN NAVY

*Type of event:* Political: shift in role of the United States in the world
*Time:* 1938-1941
*Locale:* The United States

Principal personages:
> FRANKLIN DELANO ROOSEVELT (1882-1945), thirty-second
> President of the United States, 1933-1945
> CARL VINSON (1883-    ), Chairman of the House Naval
> Affairs Committee
> ADMIRAL HAROLD RAYNSFORD STARK (1880-1972), Chief of
> Naval Operations, 1939-1941
> PARK TRAMMEL (1876-1936), Chairman of the Senate Naval
> Affairs Committee

## Summary of Event

The goal of establishing a two-ocean fleet was a powerful if elusive force in determining the nature of the United States Navy before Pearl Harbor. In the late 1930's that standard became the latest in a succession of rallying cries designed to gain popular support for naval expansion. Its appeal originated in a growing recognition that vital American interests were being threatened simultaneously by Germany and Japan. In this unprecedented circumstance the necessity of creating fleets capable of fighting independently in widely separated theaters seemed evident. Congress, responding to the change in popular attitude, passed legislation between 1938 and 1941 designed to translate the ideal of a two-ocean fleet into reality.

United States naval policy in the twentieth century has been a mirror of national ambition. In the 1890's, and especially after the Spanish-American War, the horizon of that ambition increased measurably. At a

single stroke the United States became both a Caribbean and a Pacific power. The addition of the Philippines was especially exciting. Together with Hawaii, which was annexed in 1898, the Philippines provided American commerce with a toehold in the fabled China trade. For better or worse, expanded interests called for expanded responsibilities, and President Theodore Roosevelt, an enthusiastic convert to American imperialism, led the movement to secure those interests. Between 1905 and 1909, Congress authorized the construction of sixteen new battleships. Meanwhile, work on the Panama Canal, which was intended to provide much-needed flexibility for the fleet, continued toward its ultimate completion in 1914.

By the time of Roosevelt's presidency, Japan, and especially Germany, were seen as the most important potential threats to American commerce and possessions. Tension caused by the treatment of Japanese

368

nationals living in the United States was the primary reason for Congressional approval of the last six new battleships authorized during Roosevelt's administration. But the attention of most American naval experts was fixed on Germany, where an ambitious twenty-year naval construction program was announced in 1900. While the German fleet law was intended as a challenge to British naval supremacy, it was also perceived as a threat to American interests by a host of United States Congressmen and naval authorities. That traditional German concerns were continental seemed to make no difference. Those guiding American naval policy believed that it would be a mistake for the United States to allow itself to be surpassed in naval power by any nation that also maintained a great standing army. This growing American fear of Germany was also reflected in the concentration of the fleet. Long a dictum of America's most distinguished naval authority, Captain A. T. Mahan, the concentration of naval forces was adopted by Roosevelt as a cardinal principle of fleet deployment. Throughout his presidency, and Taft's as well, the main fleet remained posted in the Atlantic.

After 1914 the prewar desire to improve the United States Navy to second place behind the British fleet was replaced by a determination to build "a navy second to none." This challenge to British naval superiority, the first ever by the United States, took the form of two great construction bills passed by Congress in 1916 and 1918. As a result, in the three years that followed the signing of the armistice ending World War I, the United States built more warships than all of the rest of the world combined. There is little doubt that in taking dead aim at British naval superiority the United States also revealed apprehension concerning Japan. Between 1917 and 1921 Japanese naval appropriations tripled, clearly revealing that despite its limited resources Japan was not intimidated by the upsurge in American construction. It is therefore not surprising that with the demise of German naval power in 1919 concern in the United States shifted from the Atlantic to the Pacific. In the summer of that year the battle fleet was divided, with the newer and heavier units being sent to the West Coast.

Fear of a costly all-out naval race in the immediate postwar period served to induce a certain amount of moderation. At Washington, in 1921-1922, the five leading naval powers adopted a system of restrictions on individual capital ships (battleships, battle cruisers, and aircraft carriers) as well as on the aggregate tonnages of capital war fleets. By the terms of the Five-Power Treaty, Britain and the United States were to share the first rank of naval power, Japan was assigned the second rank, while France and Italy were relegated to the third rank. In 1930 this agreement was augmented by the London Treaty, which established similar kinds of restrictions on the noncapital construction (cruisers, destroyers, and submarines) of Britain, the United States, and Japan. Thus, from 1922 through 1936, the size and nature of the United States war fleet was restricted by international agreement.

The Five-Power and London Treaties expired at the close of 1936, thereby ending a distinctive era in the history of recent international relations. While a variety of rivalries within the treaty structure produced growing dissatisfaction with the existing restrictions, Japan's unequivocal demand for naval equality with Britain and the United States was the most conspicuous reason for the collapse of naval limitation. Japan's subsequent penetration of China in 1937 and Hitler's annexation of Austria and absorption of the Sudetenland in 1938 seemed to provide ample proof for the proposition that unilateral restraint by the United States was a dangerous policy. The issue of naval preparedness became correspondingly less controversial.

Already by 1934, with the breakdown of naval limitation likely, Congress had moved to improve the status of the war fleet. Spearheaded by the very supportive chairman of the House Naval Affairs Committee, Carl Vinson, and the chairman of the Senate Naval Affairs Committee, Park Trammel, this movement had as its objective the replacement of all obsolete warships, or "floating coffins," to use Vinson's words, in the fleet. The resulting Vinson-Trammel bill, which became law in March of that year, envisioned the replacement of almost a third of the existing tonnage of the Navy, including practically all of the destroyers and submarines. The clear intention of this action was the establishment of a fighting force that would be in fact as well as on paper the equal of any in the world.

By 1938 this goal was no longer considered adequate to guarantee national security. Isolationists, hemispherists, and internationalists were in widespread agreement that a powerful navy was an indispensable adjunct to a free America. Thus, another authorization bill was swiftly passed by Congress. The second Vinson-Trammel bill sought the creation of a navy twenty percent larger than that permitted by the former limitation treaties. As Europe plunged into war, the last restraints on full-scale naval construction disappeared. On June 14, 1940, the day that Paris fell to the German *Blitzkrieg*, President Roosevelt signed into law a naval expansion bill that authorized an eleven percent increase in appropriations. Three days later, Admiral Harold R. Stark, Chief of Naval Operations, asked Congress for an additional four billion dollars in order to bring the fleet up to the two-ocean standard. This bill, which was passed the following month, was the largest single naval construction program ever undertaken by the United States or any other country. It provided for a seventy percent increase in combat tonnage to be constructed over a period of six years.

Despite this flurry of activity, American naval power was insufficient to protect the Atlantic and Pacific interests of the United States in the wake of Pearl Harbor. A full year prior to that catastrophe, the Navy, together with the President, had arrived at the conclusion that in any future war that included both Germany and Japan the fleet would take the offensive in the Atlantic while assuming a defensive posture in the Pacific. Even this severe modification of the strategy implicit in the two-ocean standard did not achieve satisfactory results for a disconcertingly long period of time. While the success of Japan's surprise attack on Pearl Harbor might well be considered the result of a failure of specific rather than general preparedness, the inability of American naval resources to provide adequate protection against the onslaught of Germany's U-boat attack during all of 1942 provides convincing evidence that the Atlantic fleet had not acheived a "one-ocean" capability at that time. It was not until early 1943 that American naval forces began to gain the upper hand in the Atlantic and Pacific theaters of the war.

## Pertinent Literature

Tuleja, Thaddeus V. *Statesmen and Admirals: Quest for a Far Eastern Naval Policy.* New York: W. W. Norton and Company, 1963.

The rise of American naval power from the time of Theodore Roosevelt to the outbreak of World War II was an impressive achievement. As late as the 1890's it was not certain that the United States enjoyed naval supremacy even within the Western Hemisphere; half a century later the American claim to a "navy second to none" had won recognition throughout the world. Yet, as events after Pearl Harbor were to demonstrate, the achievement of first rank naval power did not necessarily assure the protection of the nation's farflung interests. Thus, American naval development prior to 1942, while impressive, was inadequate to achieve its intended purpose. From this perspective, the record is one of failure rather than success.

In tracing the course of American expansionism since the close of the nineteenth century, many writers have noted the persistence of the national reluctance to face up to the consequences of abandoned isolationism. Thaddeus Tuleja believes that the failure of the United States to adjust to these new realities is particularly well illustrated in Japanese-American naval relations between World War I and World War II. From 1922 through 1936 this relationship was largely defined by the terms of the Five-Power Treaty, an agreement that Tuleja believes was especially prejudicial to American security. In order to persuade Japan to accept second-rank status for its capital fleet, the Harding Administration conceded that, with the exception of Hawaii, the United States would refrain from further fortifying its Pacific possessions. Inasmuch as Japan at the Versailles Conference had been given mandates over the former German islands in the North Pacific, this self-denying pledge jeopardized the future defense of American outposts such as Guam, Midway, Wake, and the Philippines. The expectation that these possessions could not be protected in the event of war with Japan was an important factor in determining a military strategy for the Pacific. By the late 1930's the Army and Navy had reluctantly concluded that in any future war that included both Japan and Germany the defensive perimeter in the Pacific would not extend beyond Hawaii. Thus Tuleja concludes that from the perspective of World War II, United States acceptance of the terms of the Five-Power Treaty was a huge mistake. The adoption of the Treaty, he claims, was largely the result of pressures exerted by misguided pacifists and isolationists.

American naval preparedness, trapped in a system of treaty restrictions, was further affected by internal discord. The Republican presidents of the period, Harding, Coolidge, and Hoover, were cool to proposals to build the Navy up to treaty strength in modern units. Relations between the Hoover Administration and the General Board of the Navy were, in fact, downright hostile. Nor was there a concensus on policy within the Navy itself. While the General Board consistently opposed limitations of any kind on United States naval construction, several ranking admirals, including William V. Pratt and William H. Standley, took a more generous view of the Five-Power and London Treaties. Since the fleet had not been built up to Treaty limits in modern units, Pratt and Standley believed that the Treaties were valuable in that

they provided a certain legitimacy for expanded naval construction. Finally, tactical considerations also divided professional opinion within the Navy. The General Board, traditionalist in its thinking, consistently championed the battleship as the mainstay of the fleet against the challenge of those who believed that the future of naval warfare rested with carrier-based aircraft.

Although President Franklin D. Roosevelt's support for naval construction prior to 1937 was motivated to a large extent by a desire to counter the harsh economic effect of the Depression, the status of the fleet received close attention beginning in 1934. By 1938, the announced intention of naval bills was the creation of a two-ocean fleet, an objective that had not been reached by the time of Pearl Harbor. Once again the United States entered a war that it was not fully prepared to fight. Tuleja laments the persistence of the American tradition that holds, "Declare and then prepare." The lack of a sustained effort to balance naval power against the expansion of national interests created a situation that only invited aggression.

Davis, George T. *A Navy Second to None: The Development of Modern American Naval Policy*. New York: Harcourt Brace, 1940.

United States naval policy in the twentieth century has been subject to a constant tug of war between the expansionists, who complain that Americans have been reluctant to support a navy capable of defending recognized interests, and the critics of expansionism, who contend that

American naval policy has been unnecessarily provocative. While Tuleja represents the former position, Davis typifies the thinking of the latter school. Although a generation older than Tuleja's work, Davis's study remains a model of scholarship as well as a forceful statement of a point of view that continues to enjoy support.

Both Davis and Tuleja emphatically agree that American naval policy between the Spanish-American War and World War II was neither clearly defined nor consistently supported. They would, however, disagree on the reasons for this indecisiveness. While Tuleja lays the blame on national myopia, Davis ascribes the reason to the close balance between "big navy" and "small navy" forces. The record demonstrates, Davis claims, that the disposition of a particular president was often sufficient to tip the balance in Congress from one group to the other. Hoover, to cite one example, was able to prevent the authorization of a single new ship during his term in office, whereas Franklin D. Roosevelt as early as 1934 won approval for the largest peacetime naval construction bill passed to that time.

Davis, in sharp contrast with Tuleja, believes that the Five-Power and London Treaties, for all of their imperfections, represented a noble experiment. That the limitations imposed by these Treaties were reasonably fair to all parties is suggested by the fact that naval interests in each of the countries involved complained bitterly of discrimination. After 1930 the delicate balances created by the limitation treaties were increasingly threatened by the rise of Japanese militarism. Once it became clear that meaningful limitation would cease at the end of 1936, a full-scale naval race broke out, each country pitting its resources against the other in a costly and largely vain effort to improve its relative position. Davis is convinced that rapid unilateral armament constitutes dangerous folly. Unusual naval construction by one power inevitably leads to reaction in kind by another, and hence forward the cycle is repeated at a more intense and threatening level with little change in the relative status of power relationships. As far as Davis is concerned, a two-ocean fleet was a phantom that was deliberately exploited by naval enthusiasts to win uncritical support for ever-increasing naval appropriations.

Davis not only writes the history of modern American naval expansion; he is also interested in testing key assumptions that undergirded that expansion. He doubts that any important correlation exists between seapower and trade. Cooperation, he contends, is often more important than coercion in determining trade relations between sovereign states. Thus, a reciprocal trade agreement act will open more commercial doors than a strong navy. Davis finds it significant that Switzerland, with no merchant fleet at all, in 1940 had one of the highest levels of per capita trade in the world, and that the Scandinavian countries, which possessed the highest per capita merchant tonnage in the world, did so without the benefit of a powerful navy. Davis concludes that an expansionist naval policy is not only costly and risky; it is also unnecessary in order to assure national security and guarantee American trade. — *M.W.B.*

## Additional Recommended Reading

Roskill, Stephen W. *Naval Policy Between the Wars*. Vol. II: *The Period of Reluctant Rearmament, 1930-1939*. Annapolis, Md.: United States Naval Institute Press, 1976. A study of the movement from naval disarmament to rearmament with excellent use of unpublished United States, and especially British, sources.

Wheeler, Gerald. *Prelude to Pearl Harbor: The United States Navy and the Far East, 1921-1931*. Columbia: University of Missouri Press, 1953. A discussion of the disparity of attitudes between the Navy and the American public and Congress during the most important period of naval limitation.

Pelz, Stephen E. *Race to Pearl Harbor: The Failure of the Second London Naval Conference and the Onset of World War II*. Cambridge, Mass.: Harvard University Press, 1974. A tracing of the naval policies of the great sea powers from the close of the period of limitations to Pearl Harbor, using United States, British, and Japanese sources.

Tate, Merze. *The United States and Armaments*. Cambridge, Mass.: Harvard University Press, 1948. A monograph summarizing United States participation in various disarmament proposals from the turn of the century to 1947.

Brodie, Bernard. *Sea Power in the Machine Age*. Princeton, N.J.: Princeton University Press, 1941. A highly informative discussion of the development of naval technology and tactics from the advent of the steam engine to World War II.

# HITLER ESTABLISHES CONTROL
# OF THE DIPLOMATIC AND MILITARY HIERARCHY

*Type of event:* Political: Nazi coordination of traditional German governmental elites
*Time:* January-February, 1938; announced February 5, 1938
*Locale:* Berlin

*Principal personages:*
ADOLF HITLER (1889-1945), Chancellor and Führer of Germany, 1933-1945
FIELD MARSHAL WERNER VON BLOMBERG (1878-1946), War Minister of the German Reich, 1933-1938
GENERAL WERNER VON FRITSCH (1880-1939), Commander in Chief of the German Army, 1934-1938
COLONEL FRIEDRICH HOSSBACH (1894-    ), Military Adjutant to Hitler, 1934-1938
KONSTANTIN VON NEURATH (1873-1956), German Foreign Minister, 1932-1938
HERMANN GÖRING (1893-1946), Chief of the Luftwaffe, promoted to Field Marshal in 1938
JOACHIM VON RIBBENTROP (1893-1946), German Ambassador to London, 1936-1938; and German Foreign Minister, 1938-1945
HEINRICH HIMMLER (1900-1945), Reichsführer of the Nazi SS and Chief of the German Gestapo
GENERAL HEINRICH ALFRED HERMANN WALTHER VON BRAUCHITSCH (1881-1948), appointed Commander in Chief of the German Army in 1938
CARL GOERDELER (1884-1945), Lord Mayor of Leipzig and anti-Nazi opposition leader

## Summary of Event

On February 5, 1938, the German press announced a major shake-up in the military and diplomatic elites of Adolf Hitler's Germany. In 1933 Hitler had become Chancellor as part of a cabinet which included representatives of the traditional German conservative power structure. Throughout 1933 and 1934, Hitler and the Nazi leadership "coordinated" most of the institutions of Germany to create a totalitarian state. By late 1937, the only significant governmental units which were not under absolute Nazi control were the military and diplomatic hierarchies. Through a series of machinations known as the "Blomberg-Fritsch affair," Hitler, Herman Göring, and Heinrich Himmler discredited the traditionalist leadership and replaced key leaders with men subservient to Hitler. Thus the Führer cleared the way for his attacks on Austria and Czechoslovakia in 1938 and for the beginning of World War II in 1939.

On November 5, 1937, Hitler held a top-secret briefing for his Foreign Minister, Konstantin von Neurath, his War Minister, Werner von Blomberg, and the chiefs of the army, navy, and air force, Werner von Fritsch, Erich Raeder, and Göring respectively; Hitler's military adjutant, Colonel Friedrich Hossbach, took notes. Hitler elaborated on how he would soon be ready to start the policy of aggressive expansion he had outlined in *Mein Kampf*. Austria and Czechoslovakia would be annexed when conditions appeared favorable. A major war to win *Lebensraum* (living space) for Germany would come no later than 1943-1945; the military and diplomatic leaders must make ready. Neurath, Blomberg, and Fritsch raised several objections: such a war, they argued, was impractical and could lead to disaster. But Hitler was adamant, and as he observed their responses, he doubtless became convinced that these men must be removed and their subordinates brought to heel before he could proceed with his plans.

Werner von Blomberg, the War Minister and then the only Field Marshal in Germany, was the first to go. Perhaps Hitler might have been willing to keep him on since he had enthusiastically supported Nazism since coming to power with Hitler in 1933. But in doing so, Blomberg had alienated some of the traditionalists in the officer corps, thus limiting his value to Hitler. Moreover, Hermann Göring, always ready to put another feather in his cap, wanted to take Blomberg's place as War Minister. By chance, Blomberg, a widower, was anxious to marry an attractive young woman

who lacked the social standing expected of the spouse of so high an officer. Blomberg solicited and received the support of Göring and Hitler for the unusual marriage; but after it had taken place, a police file surfaced indicating that the new "Frau Field Marshal" was not simply of humble origins, but that she had a record of prostitution and pornographic modeling. Göring, supported by Himmler, feigned indignation and protested to Hitler that Blomberg's indiscretion must be punished by removal from office. The officer corps, which disliked Blomberg's pro-Nazism, was in no mood to defend him. During the closing days of January, 1938, therefore, Hitler called for Blomberg's resignation.

The natural choice to succeed him would have been Fritsch, but Hitler disliked the firmly nonpolitical soldier who had so recently expressed misgivings about the Führer's aggressive plans. Himmler's Gestapo conveniently came forward with a dossier purporting to prove that Fritsch had engaged the services of a male homosexual prostitute. The charges were utterly false, based upon a case of intentionally mistaken identity, but Hitler demanded Fritsch's resignation pending the outcome of a special court martial. The court, led by Göring, found the "evidence" so absurd that Fritsch was completely exonerated. But the ruse had already accomplished its intended task by casting doubt on Fritsch's reputation and removing him from office. Hossbach, a staunch traditionalist and loyal supporter of Fritsch, was fired as Hitler's adjutant.

Though Göring would have liked

to take Blomberg's position, Hitler did not trust his long-time paladin with so important a post; instead he fed Göring's ego by promoting him to the exalted rank of Field Marshal. Then he took Blomberg's job for himself, appointing Blomberg's chief of staff as his own. Hitler's new office was called the High Command of the Armed Forces ("Oberkommando der Wehrmacht," or OKW). Another general with marital problems, Brauchitsch, was given von Fritsch's old position at the High Command of the Army ("Oberkommando des Heeres," or OKH). To ease Brauchitsch's domestic situation and make the new army chief beholden to him, Hitler arranged for a very generous alimony settlement for Brauchitsch's first wife, paid from the Führer's private funds. The new army chief quickly agreed to a complete reorganization of the military leadership. More than a dozen top generals were suddenly retired and some forty others were transferred to new posts.

At the same time, Hitler pulled in the reins on the foreign office. The traditionalist Foreign Minister, Baron Neurath, had just turned sixty-five and had heart trouble. No lurid subterfuges were necessary to remove him from office; Hitler simply "promoted" him to a meaningless position as head of a "Secret Cabinet Council," and the compliant Neurath accepted without demur. Joachim von Ribbentrop, Hitler's personal foreign policy adviser who had been serving as ambassador in London, took over the foreign office. Several ambassadors were transferred, and pressure was put on all diplomats to join the Nazi Party. Little else was necessary;

foreign policy was set by Hitler himself and the diplomats were simply informed after the fact.

The sordid background of the military reorganization had been kept entirely secret from the public, but most high officers and those close to them in other ministries were well aware of what had happened. Among the traditionalists still within the government and the military, bitter words were privately exchanged on the shoddy treatment of individuals by Göring, Himmler, and by Hitler himself. Little by little influential traditionalists began to perceive the disasters to which the Nazis were bringing Germany. Men such as Carl Goerdeler, who eventually would become heavily involved in the opposition conspiracy which resulted in the abortive assassination attempt of July 20, 1944, began to work together and to seek allies among anti-Hitler elements.

For the Führer, however, the housecleaning seemed an unadulterated success. His move against the army leadership had run the potential risk that disaffected officers would stage a mass resignation or even attempt a military *coup*. In fact, there were whispers that both courses had been considered. But no action was taken by the military men. The shift at the foreign office involved less risk for the Nazis, and it too was accomplished without embarrassment. Neither the diplomatic nor the military officers were now in a position to act as significant brakes to Nazi aggressiveness. Hitler was ready to move, and move he did. Austria was annexed on March 12, 1938, five weeks after the shake-up had been announced. At the Munich Conference of September 29, Hitler took the Czech Sudetenland and liquidated the rest of that country the next March. The attack on Poland, September 1, 1939, began World War II.

## Pertinent Literature

Deutsch, Harold C. *Hitler and His Generals: The Hidden Crisis, January-June 1938.* Minneapolis: University of Minnesota Press, 1974.

Harold Deutsch has spent half a lifetime investigating the opposition conspiracies against Hitler. Since his days with the Office of Strategic Services in France and Germany in 1944-1945, he has collected materials and systematically interviewed numerous persons on virtually every aspect of the military opposition in Nazi Germany. His previous book, *The Conspiracy Against Hitler in the Twilight War*, dealt with 1939-1940. Another volume is planned on the period of the Munich crisis.

This careful, detailed, and extraordinarily judicious investigation of the reorganization which culminated in the announcements of February 5, 1938, avoids the sensationalist approach to which the events might lend themselves. German police officials and military officers passed around the file of pornographic pictures of the new Frau Blomberg; an underworld figure identified General Fritsch as the man whom he had blackmailed after having caught him in a homosexual encounter; Hitler made a substantial payoff to the first wife of General Brauchitsch so that she would allow him a divorce to marry a younger woman. Deutsch deals with all these topics forthrightly, following the historian's dictum that the story should be told as it actually happened. He compares conflicting accounts of the events, sometimes minute by minute, drawing on all the standard sources plus many which have been made available exclusively to him. Skillfully, he has interrogated and interviewed the survivors. Deutsch's greatest interest is in the potential for opposition to Hitler and the Nazi hierarchy within the ranks of the traditional conservatives. He recognizes that in spite of the indignation of many high officers at the treatment of Fritsch, no significant group of officers was prepared to act to preserve the army chief and the relatively autonomous position of the German army at that point. But the shock of the Fritsch case, and the fact that those who wanted to see him exonerated through the due process of law were forced to work together clandestinely, "crystallized a number of Opposition nuclei that might otherwise have taken months or years to evolve." Carl Goerdeler, for example, the conservative and moralistic former Lord Mayor of Leipzig, warned Fritsch of the coming Gestapo frame-up. Goerdeler was in contact with General Ludwig Beck, Fritsch's chief of staff; with Hans Bernd Gisevius, a German civil servant; with Admiral Canaris at Military Counter Intelligence; and with General Olbricht, a local troop commander. All of these men were later to play key roles in

378

the plots against Hitler.

Occasionally the reader may find the story a bit complicated, but Professor Deutsch is as skillful an instructor as an investigator. A comprehensive list of "dramatis personae" and a time chart help the reader to keep the story straight. Deutsch shows that

Hitler, Göring, and Himmler were immediately successful in their "virtual *coup d'état*" against the army. But their success forced their opponents among the German traditionalists into a position from which meaningful anti-Nazi opposition developed.

Seabury, Paul. *The Wilhelmstrasse: A Study of German Diplomats Under the Nazi Regime.* Berkeley: University of California Press, 1954.

Paul Seabury's study of the German foreign office, nicknamed the "Wilhelmstrasse" because of its address, has proven to be a durable book. Its emphasis is not upon the content of Nazi foreign policy, but rather upon the institution of the foreign office. Thus, although many significant volumes on Nazi foreign policy have been written since the appearance of this concise book, it has not really been superseded.

When Hitler came to power in 1933, Konstantin von Neurath, a respectably conservative career diplomat and a holdover from previous cabinets, was sworn in with him. Neurath was seen by many as the guarantee that Hitler would not engage in rash or aggressive foreign adventures. Similarly, most diplomats remained at their posts, carrying out their day-to-day business with decorum even while the brown-shirted Führer ruled in Berlin.

Joachim von Ribbentrop, a successful international wine merchant and a relative newcomer to Nazi ranks, set up an office of his own across the street from the Wilhelmstrasse in 1933. He edged out the other Nazi claimants to foreign policy expertise at Hitler's court and be-

came Ambassador-at-Large in 1935. There was no love lost between the traditionalist diplomats of the Wilhelmstrasse and this Nazi "poacher" on their preserve. In 1936 von Ribbentrop wanted the appointment as State Secretary, a position second only to Neurath's, but the latter blocked him. As a consolation prize, von Ribbentrop became ambassador in London. Conservatives at the Wilhelmstrasse sent him a young career diplomat, Erich Kordt, as liaison officer; Kordt eventually developed into a key operative in the anti-Nazi opposition.

While Hitler was arranging to rid himself of the military leadership, he went after Neurath with similar, though less lurid, duplicity. The conservative Foreign Minister had been a loyal enough tool for Hitler's initial moves to cast off the bonds of the Treaty of Versailles. He had little to say about the content of foreign policy; he and the other career diplomats simply carried out Hitler's instructions. But the misgivings he openly expressed to Hitler after the secret conference of November 5, 1937, as well as his generally old-fashioned demeanor, convinced Hitler that it was time for a change. On February

2, Neurath was feted on his sixty-fifth birthday, and Hitler praised him extravagantly. Three days later he replaced him with Ribbentrop. To keep up appearances, Neurath was appointed "President of the Secret Cabinet Council," a suddenly created body which never held a meeting. Neurath, whose heart was giving him trouble, accepted the new situation with formal good grace and continued to serve the Third Reich in a variety of capacities until its demise.

Seabury points out that Hitler's coordination of the Wilhelmstrasse, announced February 5, 1938, was not as revolutionary a step as it might seem at first. Ribbentrop, once in office as Foreign Minister, drew most of his staff and his ambassadors from the career service rather than from his own Nazi "experts." The "poacher," commented Wilhelmstrasse pundits, had been made the "gamekeeper" and defended his new territory against outside encroachments. Most of the ambassadors called home in the shake-up were soon reassigned, though doubtless with a new understanding of their orders. Finally, it was Hitler himself who continued to make foreign policy, and the men of the Wilhelmstrasse—now even including Ribbentrop—had little to say about what the Führer's next moves would be.

Seabury looks at the institution of the German foreign office in comparison with that of other major nations. He sees a general tendency during the period toward taking the major decisions of foreign policy out of the hands of the traditional diplomatic elite and placing it in the hands of domestic political leaders and their political appointees. If Nazi Germany were not the only country plagued by the phenomenon of the "vanishing diplomatist," however, it was in Germany that this change was the most dramatic and the most catastrophic. — *G.R.M.*

## Additional Recommended Reading

Bullock, Alan. *Hitler: A Study in Tyranny*. New York: Harper & Row Publishers, 1962. Long the standard biography of the Führer, this book demonstrates how the winter of 1937-1938 was the turning point in Hitler's foreign policy.

Toland, John. *Adolf Hitler*. Garden City, N.Y.: Doubleday & Company, 1976. A massive and fascinating popular history of Hitler, how he took control within Germany, and how he nearly conquered Europe.

Craig, Gordon A. *The Politics of the Prussian Army, 1640-1945*. New York: Oxford University Press, 1955. The historical background of the complex relationship between the elite officer corps and the Nazi leadership, ably set forth by a distinguished American historian.

Wheeler-Bennett, John W. *The Nemesis of Power: The German Army in Politics, 1918-1945*. New York: The Viking Press, 1949 and 1967. A detailed account of the political follies of the German military leadership by a highly critical British scholar.

O'Neill, Robert J. *The German Army and the Nazi Party, 1933-1939*. London: Cassell & Company, 1966. A straightforward description by an Australian military officer based upon an Oxford University doctoral thesis.

Taylor, A. J. P. *The Origins of the Second World War*. New York: Atheneum Publishers, 1962. The product of an often brilliant and sometimes outrageous British scholar, this book shocked many historians by suggesting the revisionist thesis that Hitler's aims and policies differed little from those of the German traditionalists, and that it is thus unfair to blame the Führer for World War II.

Rich, Norman. *Hitler's War Aims*. Vol. I: *Ideology, the Nazi State, and the Course of Expansion*. New York: W. W. Norton and Company, 1973. Rich cogently argues that Hitler's foreign policy, though devious and opportunistic, was firmly rooted in his ideology of racist expansionism.

# INVENTION OF XEROGRAPHY

*Type of event:* Technological: development of electrophotography
*Time:* October 22, 1938
*Locale:* Astoria, New York

*Principal personages:*
CHESTER F. CARLSON, physicist and patent attorney who invented the process of electrophotography
OTTO KORNEI, engineer who assisted in the earliest experiments on electrophotography
ROLAND MICHAEL SCHAFFERT, scientist at the Battelle Memorial Institute in Columbus, Ohio
JOSEPH C. WILSON, President of Xerox Corporation, Rochester, New York
JOHN H. DESSAUER, scientist and Director of Research and Engineering at Xerox Corporation, Rochester, New York

## Summary of Event

In Astoria, New York, stands an unpretentious building with a bronze plaque on the wall commemorating an event that occurred on October 22, 1938: Chester F. Carlson and Otto Kornei produced the first dim copy of an image by a process called "electrophotography." The text of the copy was simply "10-22-38 Astoria." Carlson patented the process, and after considerable additional work, also patented a working model of a copying machine based on electrophotography. Carlson had come to New York from California, where he had earned his bachelor's degree in physics at the California Institute of Technology in 1930, and was employed by the patent department of P. R. Mallory Company. His experimental work was carried out in his spare time and entirely at his own expense; he hired Otto Kornei, an unemployed engineer recently arrived from Germany, to assist him.

Carlson's invention may be contrasted with ordinary photography, in which an image is produced by the effect of light on a film or plate coated with a silver compound. In electrophotography, the light-sensitive element is a reusable plate of metal coated with a layer of sulfur and electrostatically charged before exposure. When the plate is exposed, electrical charge leaks away from the illuminated areas in proportion to the light that falls. The image is trapped as an invisible pattern of static charges which may be rendered visible by dusting the plate with fine powder which adheres to the charged areas. The copying process ends when the powder pattern is transferred to paper and permanently bonded by heat or solvent vapors. In conventional photography, the image is developed by bathing the film in successive chemical liquids which darken the exposed areas and remove unexposed silver compounds. The advantage of electrophotography lies in the speed and convenience of dry developing, and in the economy resulting from having a reusable plate, thus avoiding the consumption of expensive silver compounds.

In modern xerographic equipment, most of the technical details are different from the ones used by Carlson and Kornei, but the principles are essentially the same. The light-sensitive plate is usually coated with a thin layer of selenium, which is much more sensitive than the original sulfur; and electrostatic charging is accomplished by a corona discharge instead of by simply rubbing the plate with cloth or fur, as was the practice in 1938. The corona discharge is generated in a shielded wire maintained at a high voltage and moved across the selenium-coated plate prior to exposure. The clinging powder image was formerly transferred to paper by pressing, thus causing the powder to stick to the paper. A superior method is now used in which the paper is given an electrical charge opposite to that of the powder, causing the image to be transferred as the powder clings preferentially to the paper.

For six years Carlson was unable to obtain financial backing for further research and development on his invention, despite repeated attempts. In 1944, he demonstrated his process in Columbus, Ohio, at the Battelle Memorial Institute. When asked for his opinion of the demonstration, Dr. R. M. Schaffert, then head of the Graphic Arts division at Battelle, wrote a memorandum favoring the new idea, and support was granted. In the years that followed, Battelle scientists, including W. E. Bixby, R. M. Schaffert, L. E. Walkup, C. D. Oughton, J. F. Rheinfrank, and E. N. Wise, improved the process and patented further inventions related to it. The work attracted additional support from the United States Signal Corps and from the Haloid Company of Rochester, New York, a small company that needed a new product to bolster earnings in the period following World War II. During this time many other companies were approached and offered a share in the new process in exchange for their support of the research at Battelle, but none was interested.

After 1947, research began to be directed towards the production of a practical copying device that could be sold commercially. In 1948, work had progressed far enough for a demonstration to be held at a meeting of the Optical Society of America in Detroit. The date was October 22, 1948, the tenth anniversary of Carlson's first copy, and for the occasion a new word, "xerography" (from the Greek, meaning "dry-writing"), was coined to replace the more technical term "electrophotography." The demonstration was a success, but Haloid could not immediately benefit from the publicity. Two more years of developmental work was necessary before the "Model A" copier, the first commercial xerographic copier, could be brought out in 1950. "Model A" was successful mainly for preparation of multilith masters; it was not particularly successful as a document copier.

It was not until 1960, after a long, expensive, and difficult period of development, that the Xerox model 914 copier became available ("Xerox" and "914" are registered trademarks

383

of the Xerox Corporation, Stamford, Connecticut). Many people contributed to the success of model 914 (so-called because it used 9 x 14 inch paper), but prominent mention should be made of Dr. John H. Dessauer, Haloid's Vice-President in charge of research and product development, and Joseph C. Wilson, the company president. Soon after the introduction of the new copier, Haloid adopted a new name: Xerox Corporation.

Model 914 weighed about six hundred pounds and could make up to four hundred copies an hour. It was reliable and simple to operate. These virtues soon made it very popular: so much so that people began to speak and write of a "copying revolution." Soon many other companies began to develop and market competitive models, and in the latter part of the 1960's, copiers became smaller and boasted increased copying rates. By 1975 it was estimated that seventy-eight billion copies were being made annually in the United States, and that 2.3 million copying machines were in use. Extrapolation of the growth of the copying led to the expectation that the volume would double within five years.

The easy availability of multiple copies of documents, periodicals, and books led to many benefits, and also to some problems. In a government study of photocopying, 21,280 libraries were surveyed with regard to their copying practices. It was found that in 1976, a total of 114 million copies were made, of which 54 million were of copyrighted materials. Authors and publishers were becoming concerned about their rights, while libraries, always desirous of providing service at low cost, found copying irresistible. Eventually there were lawsuits, including the case of *Williams and Wilkins* (a publisher) v. *the United States*. The United States Supreme Court reached a tie vote on the case, in which the publisher sought royalties from a library which had reproduced copyrighted material. In 1976, President Gerald Ford signed into law a new copyright bill that went into effect January 1, 1978. Under the new law, publishers will receive royalties for some of the copies made in libraries, but limited royalty-free "fair use" library copying will still be allowed.

The technical development of xerography continues to the present time. Color copying is now possible, though it is not widespread, and copying on both sides of the paper has also been achieved. Problems concerning copyright conflicts and other societal impacts remain.

## Pertinent Literature

Dessauer, John H. *My Years with Xerox: The Billions Nobody Wanted*. Garden City, N.Y.: Doubleday & Company, 1971.

Dr. John H. Dessauer was employed by the Haloid Corporation of Rochester, New York, in 1935, and continued on with Haloid and its successor, the Xerox Corporation, until his retirement in 1970. At various times he was Executive Vice-President and head of the Research and

Engineering division. Although trained as an organic chemist, Dessauer has nevertheless written a nontechnical account of the growth of the corporation of which he was a part, including material on the development of xerography and the people who made it possible. He has perhaps understated the importance of his own contributions to the science and practice of xerography, but his record speaks for itself.

The subtitle of the book is *The Billions Nobody Wanted*. It is ironic that many of the same corporations that now sell or lease office copiers were not interested in buying a share in xerography in the 1940's and 1950's when they were offered the opportunity. The onerous costs of developing the process were borne by Battelle Memorial Institute and by Haloid. Many people, including the author, committed large amounts of their own funds to the purchase of Haloid stock in those early days. Of course they were eventually rewarded with riches, and Chester Carlson, the original inventor of xerography, became a millionaire many times over, from the enormous growth in value of his Haloid stock and from the patent royalties he was paid.

Such a success story is very close to the heart of the free enterprise system. In the years 1938-1968, it was again proved, as it had been years before with men like Edison, that an individual inventor with enough talent, persistence, and luck could still achieve enormous personal success from his invention. The society in which he lived allowed Carlson the opportunity to raise capital, allowed him the protection of patent laws, and rewarded him with an ample share of the resulting profits. The rewards made the risks tenable, not only for Carlson, but for all the others who put down hard-earned cash to buy shares in Haloid.

The commercial exploitation of xerography was made possible not only by good scientific and technical work, but also by some brilliant and farsighted business decisions. An important event was the renegotiation of the patent agreement with Battelle, in which Sol Linowitz was cited as Haloid's attorney. Haloid gained the right to license or sublicense patents owned by Battelle. Haloid exploited this right, not by charging heavy fees to the licensees, but by reserving the right to share in the fruits of future research done by the licensee. Also crucial to the success of Xerox was the decision that copiers would not be sold, but would be leased to the user for a monthly rental plus a charge for each copy made. Thus the increased volume of copying that accompanied the growing popularity of the method resulted in increased revenues. The manufacturer could also afford to build a high-quality product requiring little servicing, and was repaid by depreciation charges that reduced the corporation's taxes. The late Joseph C. Wilson, then President of Xerox, led the corporate "team" which was responsible for these decisions.

The author recognizes that technological change can cause problems for society, and acknowledges that the mass application of xerography has done harm in some areas. He prefers, however, to stress the benefits that have come from the improved communication made possible by xerography, and from the generosity of the Xerox Corporation in supporting cultural and public service media events. A good example of the latter was the controversial television series in 1964 on the United Nations, sponsored by Xerox at a cost of four million dollars.

The entry of Xerox Corporation into the education field is said by the author to have resulted from a combination of pragmatism and idealism. In the 1960's, classrooms were bulging with students born in the "baby boom" of the post-war years, holding out the promise of great profits to be made from educational media and equipment. Through the acquisition of companies such as R. R. Bowker, American Education Publications, and University Microfilms, Xerox Corporation became the publisher of *Weekly Reader*, *Dissertation Abstracts*, *Paperbound Books in Print*,

and other publications used mainly in libraries and schools. The copying process was viewed as only one step in the flow of information, and there were those who felt that the corporation could become an integrated information company, with storage, retrieval, transmission, and copying and duplication systems all available. This vision was not destined to come true, at least not completely. After an unsuccessful attempt, Xerox has withdrawn from the main-frame computer business.

The technological part of the "copying revolution" has probably reached its peak, and society must now adjust. As Dessauer says in the last chapter of his book, "As new scientific discoveries and new technologies become available at an ever faster pace, finding ways of applying them for the welfare of society will be the greatest opportunity that awaits man in the future."

Schaffert, Roland Michael. *Electrophotography*. New York: Halsted Press, 1975.

Dr. R. M. Schaffert has been closely associated with research in electrophotography since the 1940's; he was one of the original team of scientists at Battelle Memorial Institute during the critical early development stages of xerography. This book is concerned largely with technical matters, with only about seven pages out of a total of nearly a thousand being devoted to introductory and historical material. It is interesting to find Carlson's original term "electrophotography" used as the title of the book. In the introduction, the author explains that electrophotography is now used as a generic term covering

not only xerography but also several other related, but not identical, processes for forming images. A section on process terminology discusses the use of standardized terms in place of the more familiar but less scientific trade names.

Xerography is discussed in the second chapter. Here one finds exceptionally lucid descriptions of the six phases of the process, augmented by drawings and graphs, with frequent references to the technical literature, including patents. Seven other chapters follow, which, together with the chapter on xerography, comprise the first part of the book.

The second part of the book treats the theory of electrophotographic processes. Here the subject matter is solid state chemistry and physics, and becomes highly mathematical in places. This section can be recommended for anyone who intends to specialize in the area and could possibly be used as material for a graduate engineering course.

The third part of *Electrophotography* is entitled "Applications and Reference Material in Electrophotography." There are forty pages of schematic diagrams of commercial copying equipment of various makes and models, including descriptions of their operating characteristics. Not only office copiers, but also microfilm copiers, reader-printers, electronic printers, and facsimile systems are treated. Some photographs of older equipment are included in this section, and the trend towards smaller and more convenient devices is evident by comparison. (There is no photograph of Carlson's original patent model, which now resides in the Smithsonian Institution in Washington, D.C.) Products of eight different manufacturers are mentioned in detail, but the author stresses that many other manufacturers produce copying equipment. This part of the book ends with over seven hundred literature references, about half of which are cited in the text, and a list of over four thousand patents with brief notes on the subject of each. The coverage extends to patents issued up until the end of 1972. It may be of interest to note that C. Carlson appears as inventor or coinventor on thirty-seven different patents, and R. M. Schaffert on fourteen. A few of the patents predate Carlson's earliest patent, notably those issued to P. Selenyi and W. Huebner in the early 1930's; but their inventions have not been commercially significant.

Color copiers are discussed only briefly in the book. The Xerox System 6500 is not shown, and the diagrams of the SCM "Color-in Color" system, which are referred to in the text, have been omitted, possibly through an oversight. Also not mentioned are the use of lasers in xerography, and the integration of computers with xerographic printers is referred to only briefly. Thus the coverage of new technology and new devices extends approximately to 1973. — *J.R.P.*

## Additional Recommended Reading

Dessauer, John H. and H. E. Clark, eds. *Xerography and Related Processes*. London: Focal Press, 1965. Notable mainly for a chapter by Chester F. Carlson entitled "History of Electrostatic Recording," including a picture of his first xerographic recording, as well as drawings from his earliest patents.

Morrison, Donald M. "What Hath Xerox Wrought?," in *Time Magazine*. CVII (March 1, 1976), p. 69. Statistics on the growth of copying and commentary on the impact of copying upon business, government, and life in general.

Kelley, Neil D. "Xerography: The Greeks Had a Word for It," in *Infosystems*. XXIV, part 2 (January 1, 1977), pp. 4-6. Informal historical survey of xerography and the Xerox Corporation.

Lehmbeck, Donald R. "Electrophotographic Processes and Systems," in *Neblette's Handbook of Photography and Reprography*. Edited by John M. Sturge. New York: Van Nostrand Reinhold, 1977, pp. 331-387. Largely technical and of less scope than R. M. Schaffert's "Electrophotography," but somewhat more up-to-date on color xerography.

*Williams and Wilkins* v. *the United States. Supreme Court Review*. (1975), pp. 355-417. A case illustrating the conflict between the rights of publishers and authors and the need for libraries to distribute copies.

# DECISION BY THE UNITED STATES TO CONSTRUCT AN ATOMIC BOMB

*Type of event:* Political: conscription of science for military purposes
*Time:* 1939-1942
*Locale:* The United States

### Principal personages:

FRANKLIN DELANO ROOSEVELT (1882-1945), thirty-second President of the United States, 1933-1945

VANNEVAR BUSH (1890-        ), Director of the Office of Scientific Research and Development

ALEXANDER SACHS, a financier and occasional presidential adviser

JAMES BRYANT CONANT (1893-        ), President of Harvard University and Director of the National Defense Research Council

LEO SZILARD (1898-1964), a refugee scientist from Hungary

## Summary of Event

The building by the United States of an atomic bomb was not the result of a single decision, but of a series of decisions taken over more than two years. Although President Franklin D. Roosevelt held the ultimate responsibility, his attitudes were shaped by scientific advisers whose reasoned conclusions and best guesses convinced him that it was possible to construct a nuclear fission device "of superlatively destructive powers," as a 1941 report termed it.

Research had been going on in the 1920's and 1930's, primarily by European physicists including Enrico Fermi and Emilio Segré in Italy; Lise Meitner and Otto Frisch, who in 1938 fled Austria for Denmark where Niels Bohr was working; Hungarians such as Leo Szilard; and Otto Hahn and Fritz Strassmann at the Kaiser Wilhelm Institute in Berlin. Their research indicated the possibility of bombarding the nucleus of the uranium atom, splitting it into lighter fragments, and releasing tremendous amounts of energy. A significant number of these scientists fled Fascism for the United States or England. Many of them gathered with American physicists in January, 1939, at the Fifth Washington Conference on Theoretical Physics to hear Bohr recount the exciting atomic discoveries. Within the year, nearly one hundred papers had been published in scholarly journals expanding and confirming this new work.

Those who had escaped the Nazis and feared the possibilities of the German research began a lengthy effort to arouse in their American colleagues and in the United States government some sense of their own urgent concern. Fermi's failure to generate any active interest from the Navy in March, 1939, was followed closely by the German halting of the export of uranium ore from the newly seized mines in Czechoslavakia. Hungarian refugee Leo Szilard and others, convinced that only the name of Albert Einstein would be heeded, prevailed on him to sign a letter to the President warning of the dangers and possibilities of atomic energy. To assure that the letter would reach him, they enlisted the aid of financier and occasional presidential adviser Alexander Sachs, who presented the letter to Roosevelt in early October, 1939.

Sachs and the Einstein letter convinced the President that the situation ought to be explored. Accordingly he established the Advisory Committee on Uranium, headed by Lyman Briggs, Director of the National Bureau of Standards with military and scientific representation. This attempt to draw federal support into scientific research for the national defense saw few early results. The committee met infrequently and its financial support involved only a $6,000 research grant.

Research on the explosive potential of uranium, which was being carried on at some twenty university laboratories scattered across the country, pointed in two main directions. One involved the separation of the fissionable isotope U-235 from the much more common U-238 by a variety of methods including gaseous or thermal diffusion, electromagnetic separation, and the centrifuge. The other sought the transmutation of uranium into a new fissionable element, plutonium (U-239), as a result of a controlled chain reaction in an atomic pile. It would not be until 1942 that either a chain reaction or the separation of more than a few micrograms of U-235 would be accomplished.

As the Germans drove into France in the spring of 1940, others in the scientific community grew increasingly concerned. Responding to that concern in June, 1940, President Roosevelt established the National Defense Research Council (NDRC) under the leadership of Vannevar Bush, president of the Carnegie Institute. Creative and highly capable, Bush and his able deputy, Harvard President James Conant, played key roles in the decision to make the bomb.

While support for the Uranium Committee and other scientific defense research grew during the next year, Bush believed that the work lacked the necessary urgency. In June, 1941, acting on Bush's advice, Roosevelt created the stronger Office of Scientific Research and Development (OSRD) with Bush as the head. Conant moved up to head the NDRC, and the Uranium Committee, strengthened and enlarged, became the S-1 Section of OSRD.

Scientists in Britain and the United States were becoming certain that a fission bomb could be built. The very small group within the United States government that was informed about this mainly secret scientific work, however, still had to be convinced. Roosevelt, Vice-President Henry Wallace, Secretary of War Henry L. Stimson, and Army Chief of Staff George C. Marshall were not yet ready to make the industrial and financial commitment to move toward full production.

Just prior to our entry into World War II, the work to date was reviewed by a committee from the National

Academy of Sciences headed by a Nobel Prize winner, Arthur Compton. He reported in November, 1941, that, at an estimated cost of $100 million, fission bombs could be produced in three or four years. Thus, at the time of the Japanese attack on Pearl Harbor, a large scale exploration had been begun but no final commitment had been made.

With our sudden entry into the war, the President had to chose between two different roads. The United States could decide that it must have this bomb that might win the war in the long run since the Germans were working on one of their own. Or, because of the dangerously inadequate state of our defenses, we could cut back on this unproven program and concentrate our resources on the more immediate goal of not losing the war in the short run. In the face of these conflicting pressures, Roosevelt and the OSRD moved toward the bomb.

In May, 1942, the S-1 Section heard reports that their researchers were unable to settle on which method would give the quickest path to the bomb since at least four seemed to be at nearly equal levels of development. The S-1 recommendations were bold. Rather than lose time exploring a single method that might prove to be a dead end, we must have an all-out effort on four fronts: gasseous diffusion, the centrifuge, electromagnetic separation, and one or more uranium piles. Bush and Conant convinced Marshall and received the President's approval in June, 1942. The Army Corps of Engineers created the Manhattan Engineer District (MED) in that month, and work began on facilities in Oak Ridge, Tennessee, Los Alamos, New Mexico, and Hanford, Washington, that would cost nearly two billion dollars by 1945. The appointment of Brigadier General Leslie R. Groves to head the Manhattan Project in August provided the necessary driving leadership.

The United States would lead the world into the Atomic Age. The nation's leaders had made the decision out of fear that Nazi Germany might win the race for the atomic bomb. It was a race in which they did not want to run, but one which they believed the United States had to enter.

## Pertinent Literature

Hewlett, Richard G. and Oscar E. Anderson, Jr. *A History of the United States Atomic Energy Commission*. Vol. I: *The New World, 1939-1946*. University Park: Pennsylvania State University Press, 1962.

There is no single book which deals exclusively with the decision by the United States to construct an atomic bomb. Without question, the best study of this series of decisions is found in the first four lengthy chapters of this excellent work, which is part of a broader survey of the Manhattan Engineer District and the Atomic Energy Commission. Although employed by the AEC, the authors constructed an objective, independent, and sound appraisal of events. Mining a vast amount of material, much of which would not be available to other scholars for some years because of national security restrictions, Hewlett and Anderson have written the standard work on the topic. It is a careful blending of scientific information, political and military considerations, and individuals, both well-known and little-known.

Beginning with a summary of the work of European and American physicists and chemists in the 1930's, the authors convey the excitement that knowledge of nuclear fission brought to the scientific world. They recount the early attempts to gain governmental support of this research, attempts which were disappointing to men vitally concerned with the threat of Hitler and the Nazis. Since the scientists themselves were divided over the possibility of whether a bomb could be constructed, however, leadership from President Roosevelt's Advisory Committee on Uranium was halting and conservative. With the entry of Vannevar Bush as the head of the newly formed National Defense Research Council in 1940, the authors show a change in the level of intensity. Bush was plainly a major driving force.

Hewlett and Anderson write clearly on complex scientific matters and give even the lay reader a necessary understanding of what was involved in the separation of the fissionable uranium isotope, U-235, and in the creation of plutonium, the other means of building a fission bomb. These explanations are coupled with the authors' ability to provide a strongly human picture of the individuals involved. The reader is awed by the incredible difficulties faced by these scientists in pushing forward the limits of knowledge. Standing out especially clearly is the figure of Ernest O. Lawrence, director of the Radiation Laboratory at the University of California at Berkeley. A brilliant scientific investigator in his own right, he was also a dynamic leader, capable of making others share his enthusiasms. He believed that the United States had to develop the atomic bomb before the Germans and was convinced that his method of electromagnetic separation could provide at least one good way of reaching that goal.

Although the book is primarily concerned with events in the United States, it does not slight the British contribution. Facing a national threat from Germany earlier than had the United States, the British had mobilized their scientific community for the war effort by 1940. Their conviction that it was possible to build a fission bomb in time to be useful in the present war nudged the National Defense Research Council and the Office of Scientific Research and Development at crucial times and began a fruitful collaboration between the two nations for the duration of the project.

President Roosevelt appears in this book from time to time as the man who bore the ultimate responsibility of the decision and without whom it would not have been possible, but his decisions are plainly conditioned by the advice of Bush, James Conant, Arthur Compton, and other scientists. The President remains a somewhat shadowy figure, however. Emphasis is on science and engineering rather than politics.

Once Roosevelt decides to make the full effort to produce the bomb, the authors must describe the plans being made for large-scale production plants. Excellent photographs and drawings, especially of the electromagnetic separation facilities, aid their efforts. The decision to bring in the Army, the early tensions between the officers and the scientists over priorities, plans, and technical details, and the involvement of large and small business are all carefully documented.

The reader, finally, is most impressed by the intellectual courage of the men who had to make the scientific-political leap into the unknown on the basis of unproven theories. They moved from laboratory to massive production facilities without the heretofore nearly mandatory steps of extensive experimentation and pilot plants. The decision to construct an atomic bomb was, among many other things, an act of faith.

Smyth, Henry DeWolf. *Atomic Energy for Military Purposes: The Official Report on the Development of the Atomic Bomb Under the Auspices of the United States Government, 1940-1945*. Princeton, N.J.: Princeton University Press, 1945.

*The Smyth Report*, as it is generally known, was released less than a week after the explosion of the atomic bomb over Hiroshima in August, 1945. Henry DeWolf Smyth, Chairman of the Department of Physics at Princeton University, came early to the bomb project, appointed by Vannevar Bush to the S-1 (Uranium) Section of the Office of Scientific Research and Development in August, 1941, as part of Bush's plan to strengthen that section. He was brought to Chicago by Arthur Compton to direct the research program of the Metallurgical Laboratory, where he remained for the duration of the project.

When General Leslie Groves felt the need for a report that would summarize the technical work done by the Manhattan Engineer District, he chose Smyth to compile it. Completed prior to the dropping of the bomb, it contained a substantial amount of heretofore highly secret material. James Conant and Groves met with Secretary of War Henry L. Stimson to consider whether the report should be published. The question was answered in the affirmative by Groves, Stimson, and ultimately by President Truman, but apparently not for the reasons originally envisaged by Smyth. The War Department approved publication to set some kind of limit on the material to be released since there would be a great clamor for technical information on nuclear fission from scientists the world over. Smyth, however, had a somewhat different point of view. He hoped to explain to the large numbers of scientists and engineers in this country the facts of bomb development and construction. They would, he believed, help to explain it to their fellow citizens. Thus could the mass of Americans begin to make the intelligent decisions relating to the social, political, and military implications of atomic power, as they must in a democracy. No longer would a small number of leaders have exclusive knowledge.

Although security considerations limited some of the materials, a surprisingly large amount of information is presented. The report is not a "popular" account, but one to be understood by scientists, engineers, and those with a solid background in college physics and chemistry. While not written for the average reader, it provides an understandable, chronological framework of the scientific advances. Written with a step-by-step organization with each paragraph numbered, it is an essential reference tool for anyone seeking an account of the history of nuclear fission. Summary sections at the end of each chapter help the reader to keep track of the events covered therein, and sections giving the state of knowledge at a particular time show how much was known and how much had yet to be learned.

Beginning in the 1930's, Smyth summarizes the physics necessary to understand atomic matters and the work of the men and women in their laboratories. He deals extensively with the scientific problems of isotope separation and chain reaction. Not concentrating exclusively on technical matters, he also relates the organization of the research and the approaches to the government for support in his account of the developments.

Appendixes cover certain technical aspects and include a dramatic War Department release on the New Mexico test of July 16, 1945, which ushered in the Atomic Age. Two useful indexes give a complete list of the persons involved and the chief subjects covered in the report. Taken with Hewlett and Anderson's study, this book combines to make a coherent, detailed scientific and political history of the decision to construct an atomic bomb. — *C.W.J.*

## Additional Recommended Reading

Laurence, William L. *Men and Atoms*. New York: Simon and Schuster, 1962. Twice a Pulitzer Prize winner and Science Editor of the *New York Times*, the author was the only reporter with full access to the MED program during the war, and his section on the early years of bomb development gives an excellent, clear exposition for the layman.

Schoenberger, Walter S. *Decision of Destiny*. Athens: Ohio University Press, 1969. Although the decision which mainly concerns the author is the one to drop the bomb on Japan, he begins with a significant introductory section on the 1930's and early 1940's.

Compton, Arthur Holly. *Atomic Quest: A Personal Narrative*. New York: Oxford University Press, 1956. A leader of the project, Compton traces the decision made among his friends from the viewpoint of one of the earliest of the "insiders."

Groueff, Stephane. *Manhattan Project: The Untold Story of the Making of the Atomic Bomb*. Boston: Little, Brown and Company, 1967. A journalist for the *Paris-Match Magazine*, the author conducted extensive interviews with leaders of the MED project and gained valuable insights into the personalities of many of the people involved.

Lamont,Lansing. *Day of Trinity*. New York: Atheneum Publishers, 1965. Dealing primarily with the first atomic bomb test at Alamogordo, New Mexico, Lamont introduces his book with a lengthy study of the scientific background and some of the key people involved.

Brown, Anthony C. and Charles B. MacDonald. *The Secret History of the Atomic Bomb*. New York: The Dial Press, 1977. Based on the multivolume "Manhattan District History" compiled by personnel engaged in the project, this work deals primarily with the technical side of the decision.

# NAZI EXTERMINATION OF THE JEWS

*Type of event:* Sociological: perpetration of genocide on the Jews
*Time:* 1939-1945
*Locale:* Europe

*Principal personages:*
ADOLF HITLER (1889-1945), Chancellor and Führer of Germany, 1933-1945
HEINRICH HIMMLER (1900-1945), Reichsführer of the SS and Chief of the German Gestapo
HERMANN GÖRING (1893-1946), German Interior Minister and Minister of Aviation
REINHARD HEYDRICH (1904-1942), Deputy Chief of the Gestapo and head of the SS Security and Intelligence Service (SD)
ADOLF EICHMANN (1906-1962), head of the Austrian Central Immigration Office and Chief of German deportation system during World War II

## Summary of Event

The Nazi extermination of European Jews during World War II was the outgrowth of Adolf Hitler's violent persecution of Germany's Jews that began with his ascent to power in 1933. Deprived of their political rights, occupations, and property, the Jews in Germany suffered physical violence, mental anguish, exile, and death at the hands of the Nazis. On January 30, 1939, Hitler predicted that the coming world war would bring "the annihilation of the Jewish race throughout Europe." World War II began seven months later when, on September 1, Hitler's armed forces invaded Poland. Simultaneously, the Nazis initiated policies and programs that would bring about the extermination of the Jews.

At the time of the Nazi invasion of Poland, Reinhard Heydrich was placed in charge of German actions affecting the Jews in Poland, who comprised about two million of the Polish population in 1939. They had, during medieval and early modern times, been driven to Poland because of persecution and expulsion from Western Europe. Moreover, Polish borders as redrawn after World War I included many Jews. Heydrich first began to deal with them in his September 21, 1939, directive. This order was issued to the heads of the *Einsatzgruppen*, or mobile killing squads. First, Jewish property was to be "Aryanized" or expropriated. Second, Jews were to be forced into ghettos in the large cities. Over each ghetto, Jews were required to establish a Council of Elders, or *Judenrat*, which was to administer the ghetto in conformity with Nazi orders. Heydrich's directive was regarded as the preliminary step to "the Final Aim," which eventually accomplished the destruction of European Jewry.

If ghettoization was one of Hitler's policies toward the Jews in 1939, another was murder, even at that early date. The *Einsatzgruppen* which accompanied the German armies in Poland and elsewhere were given orders to massacre Polish civilians, but especially the Jews. The *Einsatzgruppen* constituted an elite of carefully selected Nazis with academic degrees whose task was to plan and accomplish the mass murder of civilians. Eventually, members of *Einsatzgruppen* operated throughout Eastern Europe and with the assistance of some 200,000 collaborators tortured and murdered about one and a half million Jews by the end of World War II. However, two difficulties arose with the *Einsatzgruppen*. First, as efficient as they were in murdering Jews, they were not efficient enough to accomplish the destruction of all of Europe's Jews. In just two days at Babi Yar in Russia, thirty-five thousand Jews had been shot, but, given a Russian Jewish population of four to five million, obviously something more was needed. Second, there was some concern about the ability of members of this Nazi elite to retain their sanity as they went about their duties. "The unlimited brutalization and moral depravity," wrote German General Johannes Blaskowitz, "will spread like an epidemic through the most valuable German human material" and "brutal men will soon reign supreme."

In order, then, to help solve these two problems, a more efficient means of murder was devised that would have a less brutalizing effect on the Nazi murderers. Ghettoization had concentrated the Jews into a rather small area, including the central Polish cities of Radom, Lvov, Lodz, Lublin, Warsaw, and Cracow, which were then sealed. Jews from all over Europe, including Germany, were deported to the Polish ghettos. Concentrated in the worst parts of cities and required to subsist on a few calories a day, many Jews fell ill or starved. However, since starvation was too slow for the Nazis, other means of extermination were being prepared; in the meantime, the Jews were exploited as a natural resource.

The largest form of exploitation was forced labor for large-scale projects of various sorts. Soon the Jews were being literally worked to death constructing concentration and labor camps. Once the labor camps were in operation, major German industrial corporations, such as Krupp and I. G. Farben, continued the brutal process of killing forced labor with overwork. At the I. G. Farben synthetic rubber works at the Auschwitz extermination camp, it was estimated that the life expectancy of workers was three to four months. The ghettos were also centers of labor where Jews were required to produce a variety of manufactured goods for the Nazis. Even though Jews were, by their labor, contributing significantly to the German war effort, Hitler's implacable objective, regardless of the impact on the German economy or the war, remained the destruction of their race.

By the winter of 1942, rumors of the Nazi determination to destroy the Jews utterly began to circulate. Actually, that decision had already been made and was being carried out. Since the mass shootings of the *Ein-*

*satzgruppen* had certain drawbacks, as had the program of starvation, German technical skill solved the problem by devising a very orderly technology of murder. Facilities for extermination by gas were constructed in six extermination camps—Auschwitz, Treblinka, Sobibor, Maidanek, Belzek, and Chelmno—and the Nazi bureaucracy was now skillfully organized to undertake mass murder and process the corpses as efficiently as possible. Top Nazi officials coordinated the entire procedure at a conference held near Berlin on January 20, 1942. As a result of the decisions made there, Jews from all over Europe began to be sent by rail to the extermination camps. To illustrate the efficiency of the camps, in two months of the summer of 1942, three hundred thousand Jews from the ghetto of Warsaw were gassed at Treblinka, the *Judenrat* of the Warsaw ghetto, for example, being forced to furnish six thousand Jews a day for transportation there. From all over Europe, Jews were sent to Polish extermination camps until one and three-quarter million had been exterminated in Auschwitz, one and a half million had died at Maidanek, and hundreds of thousands had been killed elsewhere by 1944.

About fifty thousand people were engaged in carrying out the extermination process. Two types of gas were employed: carbon monoxide and hydrogen cyanide (Zyklon B), which was regarded as much quicker than carbon monoxide. The procedure was very much the same in the various death camps. Jews would arrive jammed into railroad boxcars. Forced out of the cars, they would be sent to barber shops where their heads were shaved and the hair carefully retained for various manufacturing purposes. Then they would be required to surrender all their clothing, valuables, spectacles, and everything else they possessed—even artificial limbs. Those Jews not spared for forced labor were then marched to large open areas in front of gas chambers, where they were forced to wait, often for hours, until smaller groups were "processed." These smaller groups were marched into the gas chambers, which were filled so full that there was no room even to fall down. The doors were sealed, and while the remainder waited the gas was turned on for about half an hour. When all were dead, doors at the opposite end from the entrances were opened and the corpses removed. Gold fillings and valuable dental bridges were salvaged, and the bodies were burned while the next group entered the chamber. By 1944 this process had become so efficient that tens of thousands of Jews were being slaughtered daily. Auschwitz held the record: in July of 1944, thirty-four thousand people were killed there in a single day.

In addition to efforts at extermination, the Nazis also undertook medical experiments on the Jews. Regarding them as potential research animals, the Germans were ready to test literally any drug or attempt any experimentation on the Jews. All segments of the German scientific community took part in the experiments, for reasons that were frequently obscene and sadistic as well as scientific. Almost all of the experiments involved torture, and resulted in the deformity or death of the victims. In short, such "research" was little more than one aspect of the extermination process. Altogether, by the end of World War II, the combined activities of the *Einsatzgruppen*, the medical experimenters, and the extermination camps had brought death to approximately six million Jews.

## Pertinent Literature

Hilberg, Raul. *The Destruction of the European Jews*. Chicago, Ill.: Quadrangle Books, 1961.

Hilberg's book, the definitive study of the extermination of European Jews from 1939 to 1945, is a magnificent scholarly effort and is the source from which all subsequent studies of the Holocaust have derived much of their substance and orientation. Even those works, such as L. Davidowicz's *The War Against the Jews, 1933-1945*, which reject Hilberg's description of the motives and actions of the Jews, have in the orientation of their denials been strongly influenced by Hilberg's book.

What Hilberg presents is a study of the process and the machinery of destruction; in the coldest possible terms he describes the technology and mechanics of extermination and the administrative bureaucracy through which they functioned.

Hilberg divides his book according to the two phases of destruction. First, in considering the early treatment of the Jews, he traces Nazi efforts to define the Jew legally. Beginning with a description of the dismissals of Jews from the professions and governmental positions, Hilberg next identifies the various aspects of the process of Aryanization, which involved the expropriation of Jewish property through prohibitive taxation, and the subsequent transfer of that property to Aryans. Having impoverished the Jews, the Nazis next imposed upon them programs of forced labor and starvation. These measures were all aspects of a systematic expropriation of all Jewish property which eventually reduced the Jewish population to destitution. Soon after the start of World War II, the Jews were expelled from the countryside of Poland and forced into ghettos. Hilberg documents the confiscation of Jewish property, exploitation of Jewish labor, and the use of starvation to control the Jews in the ghettos, ending his description of the first phase of the destruction process with an analysis of ghettoization in Poland in 1939 and 1940.

The second and most disastrous phase of the destruction of the Jews comprises the heart of the book. Here Hilberg describes in minute detail the actual process of the extermination program, first through the use of the *Einsatzgruppen*, or mobile killing units; second, through the deportations of Jews from all over Europe to the extermination camps; and third, through the actual operation of the extermination camps. All aspects of the technology and administration of destruction are analyzed in great detail.

The controversial aspect of Hilberg's study is his analysis of the role of Jews in their own destruction. In response to the question of why six million Jews allowed themselves to be slaughtered like sheep, Hilberg replies that the Jews were totally unprepared for the Holocaust. Jewish resistance was almost nonexistent, the Warsaw ghetto uprising being the sole notable exception. Hilberg maintains that Jewish refusal to resist reflected the two-thousand-year-old tradition, or habit, of appeasement of their enemies in order to avoid disaster. He reasons that Jews had tragically learned from centuries of persecution that nonresistance was the key to their salvation. This lesson "could not be unlearned," and consequently the Jews were rendered helpless.

Hilberg notes that the Jews were of course deceived by the Germans regarding their extermination, but more important, he holds that the Jews practiced *self*-deception, even in such extermination camps as Auschwitz. He describes two arguments which they used to justify their nonresistance and self-deception. First, many held that some Jews were being saved through the sacrifice of others. For example, Jacob Gens, head of the Vilna *Judenrat*, said, "With a hundred victims, I save a thousand people. With a thousand, I save ten thousand." When this proved to be untrue, nonresistance was justified as being a way to avoid suffering, pain, and torture. Thus straitjacketed by their own history and tradition, the Jews "plunged themselves physically and psychologically into catastrophe."

Hilberg's picture of the role of the Jews in their own destruction is unacceptable to Jewish historians and writers. The heavy emphasis of Jewish writers on resistance has partly been an attempt to provide an answer to Hilberg's accusations and to place full responsibility for the destruction of the Jews where it belongs: on Adolf Hitler and the Nazis.

Des Pres, Terrence. *The Survivor: An Anatomy of Life in the Death Camps*. New York: Oxford University Press, 1976.

This is one of the most interesting and sensitive works on life in Nazi concentration camps available. Although focusing on those few prisoners who survived Nazi concentration camps rather than on the actual destruction of the Jews, Des Pres describes conditions in the camps with so much accuracy and poignancy that the reader begins to understand something of the true nature of the Holocaust.

Des Pres focuses on the concentration camp experience in the Soviet Union and Nazi Germany, emphasizing the latter. A survey of fiction, such as *The Plague*, by Albert Camus; *The Fixer*, by Bernard Malamud; and *One Day in the Life of Ivan Denisovich*, *Cancer Ward*, and *The First Circle*, by Alexander Solzhenitsyn, leads Des Pres to conclude that survivors of concentration camps "*chose* life" and that positive choice made life possible.

Choosing life presupposed other

characteristics, such as the will of the survivor to bear witness. One of the very reasons for staying alive was to tell the truth or bear witness to the evils of the camps. The survivor represented those who did not survive, and his duty to reveal the truth on behalf of the dead was a heavy obligation. To convey the endless scream of the Holocaust gave the survivor a purpose for living. Des Pres states that "the final horror is that no one will be left," that no one would tell what happened, that no one would know. The fear was that the past would be obliterated. Thus the duty of the survivor to describe the past became all the more important.

The need to testify was based on a sense of obligation to the dead on the part of survivors. In the camps, despite the ever-present brutality and terror, a system of mutual aid existed. Having received the benefits of such aid, the survivor was obliged to act on behalf of the dead who had provided support; the survivor deeply felt the need to discharge his debt. Moreover, a sense of guilt at having survived was another motive for testifying. Finally, the testimony of the survivor was a moral statement to the world, an appeal to the world's conscience. There were many motives for bearing witness, but the most important for Des Pres is that the survivor, an ordinary person, had the courage to persist in publicizing to the world a statement of conscience and morality, a statement of the survival of humaneness in the midst of the inhumanity of the concentration camp.

Some of those inhuman aspects of life in the concentration camp are described by Des Pres as an orga-nized and deliberate "excremental assault." By this, he means that inmates in Nazi concentration camps were systematically and continuously subjected to filth in order to increase their anguish, to debase them, and to shame and humiliate them. Human dignity for Des Pres is based on a belief in the human soul: it is a form of spirituality. The Nazis sought utterly to destroy that spirituality, to replace it with self-disgust, and to undermine all feelings of mutual support by creating a pervasive loathing. In trying to make inmates feel subhuman, the excremental assault was important. The survivor had to overcome his disgust and cultivate a concern for his appearance. Such concern was a form of resistance, a way of preserving human dignity and life itself.

The horrors of the excremental assault left many prisoners feeling that they were immersed in a nightmare. The shock of life in the Nazi concentration camp was so traumatic that prisoners went through a time of "initial collapse," which was like a terrible dream; most prisoners could not survive this initial shock. Those who were eventually able to overcome it, reintegrate their lives, face the horror of the concentration camps, and begin to resist were a very small minority. Those who could not regain the will to live soon died for "lack of information, because they did not know what to do or how to act"; or they died of grief over the deaths of loved ones. Des Pres believes that the real reason for early death in most cases was "the horror and irreparable hurt felt by the prisoner when he or she first encounters the spectacle of atrocity." Such overwhelming hurt eventuated in the wish to die, "to have done with such a world."

Those prisoners who were able to overcome the wish to die, to overcome the trauma and shock of the concentration camp, experienced the feeling of awakening from a nightmare. The survivor "turns back to life," and then he began a process of inner healing. Frequently this awakening took the form of a desire to bear witness, which led to a reintegration of personality and a feeling of purpose in life.

Having slowly pulled the strands of life together, the survivor would begin a process of life in the midst of the constant presence of death in the camps. If death characterized the environment, the survivor had to keep himself separate from the environment: he was obliged to "be in the world but not of it." Those engaged in such passive resistance constituted an underworld, or underlife, involving trickery, theft, bribery, smuggling, and so forth to support life. Food was stolen or purchased to sustain life a bit longer, and arms, whenever possible, were purchased. Most of all, the underworld provided a means to enhance decency in the camps. To help preserve life, the underground used any and all means.

The underworld united prisoners in a common resistance and shared efforts to save and sustain lives; and, in sustaining others, members of the underworld found a key to their own survival. Rarely was the underground successful, but with difficulty and much hardship, in small efforts to sabotage the efficient bureaucratic administration, death was cheated and life was shared. Out of the destroyed society of the camps, there slowly emerged a rudimentary new society based on sharing, giving, and receiving; on needing to bear witness and to support one another; and on spreading life-giving power amid the death of the Nazi concentration camps.

The survivor ultimately sustained himself in the agony of his living death and his environmental hell only through his desire to live. Divested of everything but agony, he still persisted in his commitment to life; he was testimony to the fact that life alone matters. That concentration on life oriented the survivor to the present. The past had been totally obliterated, and to look to the future from the concentration camp was impossible. Living required day-to-day endurance. Thus the past and the future ceased to have meaning, as survivors lived only for the present, only to get through another day. That effort to endure, to invest life with dignity, and to bear witness, was a way of "saying NO" to the inhumanity and death surrounding them.

That "NO" for Des Pres constituted heroism. Here was the heroic understanding that "life, the earth in its silence, is all there is." Along with the works of authors such as Lucy Dawidowicz (*The War Against the Jews, 1933-1945*) and Michael Elkins (*Forged in Fury*), who, in order to oppose Hilberg's interpretation of the role of the Jews in their own destruction, focused their attention on overt examples of Jewish resistance, Des Pres' book is a superb endorsement of survival, of life as a heroic and ultimate form of resistance to Nazi extermination of the Jews. — *S.L.*

## Additional Recommended Reading

Levin, Nora. *The Holocaust: The Destruction of European Jewry, 1933-1945*. New York: Thomas Y. Crowell Company, 1968. An excellent description of the destruction of the Jews which not only covers the machinery of destruction but also deals with Jewish resistance and the reaction of the Jewish community to Nazi efforts at extermination.

Dawidowicz, Lucy S. *The War Against the Jews, 1933-1945*. New York: Holt, Rinehart and Winston, 1975. A very well-written account of the Holocaust that emphasizes Jewish resistance and the activities of the Jewish community of the ghettos during the period 1939 to 1945.

Trunk, Isaiah. *Judenrat: The Jewish Councils in Eastern Europe Under Nazi Occupation*. New York: The Macmillan Company, 1972. The definitive study of the operation and functioning of the *Judenrat*, or Councils of Jewish elders, as they tried to provide leadership under Nazi direction in the ghettos.

Elkins, Michael. *Forged in Fury*. New York: Ballantine Books, 1971. An extremely well-written and poignant account of Jewish underground and resistance efforts against Nazis in the ghettos and death camps.

Ainszstein, Reuben. *Jewish Resistance in Nazi-Occupied Eastern Europe: With a Historical Survey of the Jew as a Fighter and Soldier in the Diaspora*. New York: Barnes & Noble, 1975. One of the more important treatments of Jewish resistance to the Nazis in Eastern Europe.

Feingold, Henry L. *The Politics of Rescue: The Roosevelt Administration and the Holocaust, 1938-1945*. New Brunswick, N.J.: Rutgers University Press, 1970. The definitive study of the actions of the Roosevelt Administration with regard to the Holocaust, emphasizing the indifference and apathy of the United States to the plight of the European Jews.

# THE BATTLE OF THE ATLANTIC

*Type of event:* Military: decisive battle waged between Allied and German navies
*Time:* September, 1939-May, 1945
*Locale:* North Atlantic

*Principal personages:*

FRANKLIN DELANO ROOSEVELT (1882-1945), thirty-second
President of the United States, 1933-1945

SIR WINSTON LEONARD SPENCER CHURCHILL (1874-1965),
Prime Minister of Great Britain, 1940-1945

ADOLF HITLER (1889-1945), Chancellor and Führer of Germany, 1933-1945

ADMIRAL HAROLD RAYNSFORD STARK (1880-1972), United
States Chief of Naval Operations, 1939-1941

ADMIRAL ERNEST JOSEPH KING (1878-1956), Commander in
Chief of the United States Fleet and Chief of Naval Operations, 1941-1945

ADMIRAL KARL DÖNITZ (1891-    ), Commander of the
German submarine fleet and successor to Erich Raeder as
Commander in Chief of the German fleet

## Summary of Event

In the West it is widely believed that the Battle of the Atlantic was decisive in bringing about the defeat of Nazi Germany. Had Hitler been successful in denying his adversaries access to American men and materials, the outcome of World War II might have been much different. Yet, when hostilities began in September, 1939, neither Britain nor Germany properly understood the nature of the impending struggle for control of the Atlantic. Despite lessons taught by World War I, Hitler's strategy for winning the conflict ignored the advice of his admirals until it was too late. Control of the Continent, he believed, was the key to victory. Consistent in his deprecation of the value of naval weapons, until 1943 Hitler provided little support for submarine construction. As a result, only forty-three U-boats were ready for combat when war broke out. The knowledge of this fact, combined with the development of asdic (sonar), in turn caused the British to underestimate the impact of the submarine on war fleet operations and merchant shipping.

The deadliness of the German submarine assault on Allied shipping did not become evident until the spring of 1940. With the fall of France, submarine pens were constructed in the Bay of Biscay, which increased both the range and flexibility of U-boat operations. Just as important, Admiral Karl Dönitz, the resourceful commander of the German submarine fleet, developed new techniques of attack. Instead of operating singly, U-boats began to hunt in wolf packs which operated on the surface at night. Catching prospective targets in moonlight or silhouetted against coastal lights, surfaced submarines maneuvered into torpedo-launching position at speeds superior to those of most victims, only to submerge and escape in the resulting confusion. The success of these techniques is eloquently expressed in statistics on tonnage sunk. For the first seven months of the war, the toll of Allied merchant shipping lost to German submarines averaged about 110,000 tons per month. For the month of June alone, however, that figure jumped to 300,000; by October it had reached almost 450,000 tons. With U-boats sinking Allied ships at a faster rate than they could be replaced, the Battle of the Atlantic was in grave danger of being lost.

In desperation, Winston Churchill, who became Prime Minister in May, turned to the United States for help. The amount of American resources that eventually found their way to Britain constitutes a tribute to the skill and persistence of Churchill's representations; it also reflects the growing conviction in the United States that Britain was vital to the defense of the Western Hemisphere. In September, President Franklin D. Roosevelt authorized the transfer of fifty overage destroyers to Britain in exchange for leases to British territory in the western Atlantic. Two months later, Churchill's plea that Britain could no longer afford to purchase American products caused Roosevelt to propose the Lend-Lease bill to Congress. This bill, which was passed in March, 1941, over the vociferous objections of congressional isolationists, opened the American storehouse to all countries whose defense the President deemed vital to the defense of the United States.

As the isolationists had predicted, the passage of Lend-Lease led to a shooting war with Germany. In April, Roosevelt warned all belligerent warships to stay out of the western half of the Atlantic; those vessels intercepted by American patrols would have their locations transmitted in English. While couched in neutral language, this policy was especially helpful to British convoys seeking to avoid German submarines. Three months later the United States negotiated a friendly occupation of Iceland, which was considered important to the security of both Britain and the United States. From this point it was only a short step to the adoption of a policy of convoying ships from North America to Iceland. In practice, British merchant ships were allowed to sail in the protection of American convoys, a move that was especially provocative.

Despite the outrage of his military advisers at these violations of traditional neutrality, Hitler remained cautious. He repeatedly ordered his U-boat commanders to avoid hostile contact with American vessels. But incidents, both accidental and deliberate, were bound to occur. In October the destroyer *Kearny* was torpedoed with the loss of eleven men; six weeks later the *Reuben James* was sliced in two with the loss of ninety-six men. On December 11, in an action that defies easy explanation, Hitler declared war on the United States, thus formalizing what was already a fact.

As far as the Battle of the Atlantic

was concerned, the first year of America's entry into the European war proved kinder to Germany than it did to the United States. While most of the German surface fleet remained bottled up in Baltic and Norwegian ports, U-boats became an awesome threat to Allied shipping. Admiral Dönitz continually shifted his submarines to positions where they were least expected. Unescorted merchantmen were especially easy prey, and they were vulnerable all along the western Atlantic, from Newfoundland to Brazil. From January through November, 1942, more than 500,000 tons of Allied merchant shipping were lost each month. Until August, replacement tonnage did not match the tonnage destroyed. By the end of the year, however, it had become evident that, despite these discouraging results, time was on the side of the Allies. In December, Allied merchant tonnage sunk declined to 400,000 tons, while the construction of replacement tonnage hit 1,000,000 tons for the first time. After March, 1943, the disparity between these figures widened still further.

The reversal of fortunes in the Battle of the Atlantic was the result of a combination of factors. Most important and most obvious, the United States was simply richer than Germany in essential materials and manpower. Thus, at the outset of hostilities merchant shipping was thinly protected, even on the crucial runs to Iceland and the British Isles. By the end of the war, however, most convoys were escorted by destroyers, while the use of aircraft carriers had become much more common. Less conspicuous, but almost as decisive,

was the fact that the deployment of American resources was skillfully coordinated by Chief of Naval Operations Admiral Harold R. Stark and his successor, Admiral Ernest J. King. For all of their differences of personality, the courtly Stark and the acerbic King shared a deep conviction that the convoy was the only way to ferry troops and materials over an ocean crisscrossed by submarines. This conviction proved increasingly correct as the Battle of the Atlantic wore on to its final resolution. Meanwhile, improved training and increased experience of crews promoted the more effective use of available equipment.

Consequently, merchantmen sailed with greater precision within the tricky confines of the convoy, while escorts learned the fine arts of sonar detection, extended sweeps, and saturation depth charge attacks. Technology also contributed to the outcome of the Battle of the Atlantic. Planes equipped with microwave radar, which submarines could neither detect nor jam, combined with the powerful Leigh searchlight, made submarine surfacing at night almost as dangerous as it was during the day. It is interesting to note that both Dönitz and Hitler believed that microwave radar was the main cause of Germany's defeat in the Atlantic. Snorkels, which allowed submarines to recharge their batteries while submerged, partially neutralized the advantage enjoyed by planes equipped with undetectable radar and powerful searchlights, but their widespread use came too late to have an important impact.

The Battle of the Atlantic is also the story of individual courage and cowardice. It is to the credit of both

Allied and German crews that the instances of gallantry predominate. In fairness to the record, it should be pointed out that Admiral Dönitz, together with most of his officers and crews, continued the fight with resourcefulness and tenacity to the bitter end. On May 8, 1945, when Dönitz finally ordered his remaining submarines to surrender, forty-nine were still at sea.

## Pertinent Literature

Morison, Samuel Eliot. *History of United States Naval Operations in World War II.* Vol. I: *The Battle of the Atlantic, September 1939-May 1943.* Boston: Little, Brown and Company, 1947.

Samuel Eliot Morison was a distinguished American historian who maintained a lifelong interest in the exploration of the North Atlantic. In 1942, at his own suggestion, he was commissioned by the Naval Reserve for the sole purpose of preparing a history of United States naval operations in World War II. All relevant materials were made available to him, and he frequently augmented his formal research by visits to military fronts. The resulting comprehensive work is nothing short of monumental. Its fifteen volumes constitute the most massive study in existence of naval operations during the war.

Morison's introductory volume, *The Battle of the Atlantic, September 1939-May 1943*, is indispensable reading for those wishing a clear understanding of the subject. There are, of course, understood limitations. The American orientation tends to minimize, if only by the extent of the coverage, the role played by the Canadian and British fleets. The terminal point of this volume, May, 1943, neglects the final two years of the war, a deficiency which is filled by Volume X of the series. The essential dynamics of the conflict, however, were well established by the spring of 1943. Finally, as the title clearly states, Morison's account is basically a history of naval operations. He discusses policymaking hardly at all and devotes only slightly more attention to problems of administration. His focus throughout is on the development of tactics designed to neutralize the devastating impact of the U-boat, and on the men who ultimately made those tactics work.

The year 1942 was by any standard one of great disappointment for American naval operations in the north Atlantic. The great vulnerability of merchant shipping to U-boat attacks in United States coastal waters was especially shocking. Lack of experience in dealing with submarine warfare offers only a partial explanation for this defensive failure. Even though the United States had two years in which to learn from the belligerents before entering the war herself, she was woefully deficient in a variety of auxiliary craft that were crucial to effective antisubmarine warfare. The fact that provision for the construction of these ships was not included in proposed budgets places responsibility for the neglect squarely on the Navy itself. The unwillingness of the Army and Navy to coordinate their air operations further contributed to the ineffectiveness of antisubmarine warfare in its early stages.

Like most writers who have examined the naval campaigns in the Atlantic during World War II, Morison is intrigued by the activities of Admiral Dönitz, who not only directed the submarine campaigns throughout the war, but also served as Commander in Chief of the fleet from 1943 until 1945. Dönitz was brilliant and controversial. His wolf pack and surface attack techniques were both innovative and highly successful. When he was put on the defensive later in the war, Dönitz ordered U-boat captains to stand and fight it out with enemy aircraft, a daring tactic that met with indifferent results. But Dönitz mainly invites criticism for his decision to concentrate on the sinking of tonnage rather than cargoes. His belief that the Battle of the Atlantic would be won only if Germany succeeded in sinking more ships than could be built caused him to order attacks on empty ships if they provided easier targets than loaded ships. Although his strategy has its defenders, Morison believes that the failure to concentrate on cargoes headed for the war zones was a major mistake in judgment.

The American reaction to the unpredictable and often disconcerting activities of the U-boat was sensible and ultimately triumphant. It was early decided that all of the Navy's resources should be devoted to protecting the convoys. The record of this operation, especially after 1942, was outstanding. Only when convoys were adequately secured did the Navy embark upon search and destroy operations. The carrier-based "hunter-killer" groups that in the later stages of the war ferreted out and destroyed U-boats in record numbers constituted a terrifying new ingredient in the antisubmarine campaign. It is a tribute to the success of these operations that from 1943 to the close of the war Dönitz found his best hunting in the Indian Ocean.

Abbazia, Patrick. *Mr. Roosevelt's Navy: The Private War of the U.S. Atlantic Fleet, 1939-1942*. Annapolis, Md.: United States Naval Institute Press, 1975.

Although the titles would suggest close similarity between Abbazia's study and Morison's earlier work, such comparison would be misleading. While Morison concentrates on battles and the men who fought them, Abbazia is primarily interested in the policy decisions that paved the way for United States involvement in the Battle of the Atlantic. The incidents that occurred as a result of these decisions, while fully described, are important mainly insofar as they demonstrate the nature and consequence of policy.

Abbazia's inquiry is linked generically to that body of historical literature that questions the process by which the United States became involved in World War II. Unlike most revisionist writers, however, Abbazia does not take issue with the desirability of the final result. Roosevelt's launching of an undeclared war against

Nazi Germany, while perhaps not in the most honored of American traditions, is judged to have been necessary. Moreover, Abbazia is convinced that the decision to take the initiative against Hitler was a slow evolutionary process that involved the best thinking of presidential advisers.

Abbazia argues that as early as 1937 Roosevelt had reached the conclusion that it might become necessary for the United States to adopt some of the techniques employed by aggressor nations in order to combat their evil influence. As he suggested to his cabinet in December of that year, "If Italy and Japan have evolved a technique of fighting without declaring war, why can't we develop a similar one?" This vague but tantalizing proposition came into sharper focus in the fall and winter of 1940-1941. In early September, Roosevelt announced the creation of a "neutrality patrol" designed to keep belligerent ships away from American shores. Over the protests of Navy officers who felt that manpower and equipment were already badly strained, Roosevelt steadily broadened the zone of the patrols. There is no question that Germany was the object of concern. In November, Chief of Naval Operations Admiral Harold R. "Betty" Stark recommended to the President a redefinition of American naval priorities in the event of a two-front war. Plan D ("Dog"), which Roosevelt subsequently adopted, proposed the establishment of an offensive capability in the Atlantic while maintaining only a defensive capability in the Pacific. After the passage of Lend-Lease, which has been described as an economic declaration of war against Germany, Roosevelt waited for Hitler to react. In March, he told Secretary of the Interior Harold Ickes that decisive action by the United States in the Atlantic probably depended upon a future German "incident."

For the remainder of 1941, German-American relations became a sparring match between two seasoned performers. The strategies were complex and the stakes were high. Roosevelt needed his "incident" in order to justify more overt aid to Britain. At the same time, he was reluctant to goad Hitler too far for fear of possible repercussions at home. It was supremely important that Hitler be made to appear the aggressor rather than the victim of aggression. For his part, Hitler treated the United States with caution and even deference. He steadfastly resisted the advice of his admirals to retaliate against unneutral American behavior. Hitler was determined to avoid providing the incident that Roosevelt seemed to need and want. In the meantime, he hoped that Japanese aggression would divert American attention to the Far East.

Germany's ill-considered decision to join in the war against the United States after Pearl Harbor suggests a quality of intemperance which was, in fact, uncharacteristic of Hitler's previous treatment of the United States. Although Abbazia finds no direct evidence that Roosevelt wished for war with Germany, circumstances indicate that he was not averse to additional incidents that would reduce the political risk of assuming a more active role in behalf of British interests in the Atlantic. Confrontations between American and German warships—grave incidents, indeed—did not occur until late 1941. By that time, however, the United States had already become an integral part of the Battle of the Atlantic. As Abbazia shows, a close examination of American policy before Pearl Harbor contributes greatly to an understanding of the reasons for eventual Allied victory in the Atlantic. — *M.W.B.*

## Additional Recommended Reading

Morison, Samuel Eliot. *History of United States Naval Operations in World War II*. Vol. X: *The Atlantic Battle Won, May 1943-May 1945*. Boston: Little, Brown and Company, 1956. Completes Morison's treatment of United States naval operations in the Atlantic.

Roskill, Stephen W. *The Navy at War, 1939-1945*. London: Collins, 1960. A study by Captain Roskill, the official historian of British naval operations during World War II, complementing Morison's narratives.

Leutze, James R. *Bargaining for Supremacy: Anglo-American Naval Collaboration, 1937-1941*. Chapel Hill: The University of North Carolina Press, 1977. The latest scholarship on the reorientation of United States naval policy toward closer cooperation with Britain in the immediate prewar period.

Ruge, Friedrich. *Sea Warfare, 1939-1945*. London: Cassell, 1957. An able and concise examination of German naval operations during World War II by a German naval officer.

King, Ernest J. and Walter M. Whitehill. *Fleet Admiral King: A Naval Record*. New York: W. W. Norton and Company, 1952. An insider's perspective on naval operations; somewhat slow reading.

# GREAT BRITAIN ISSUES THE 1939 WHITE PAPER RESTRICTING JEWISH EMIGRATION TO PALESTINE

*Type of event:* Diplomatic: response to Arab and Zionist expectations
*Time:* 1939
*Locale:* Palestine

*Principal personages:*

THEODOR HERZL (1860-1904), Austrian Jewish author of *The Jewish State* and the father of modern political Zionism

ABDUL-HAMID II (1842-1918), Sultan of the Ottoman Empire which included Palestine until the end of World War I

LORD (WILLIAM ROBERT WELLESLEY PEEL) EARL PEEL (1867-1937), head of the British Royal Commission investigating the Palestine question in 1936

SIR JOHN ACKROYD WOODHEAD (1881-1973), head of the British Commission reporting on the Palestine question in 1938

LORD ARTHUR JAMES BALFOUR (FIRST EARL OF BALFOUR) (1848-1930), Secretary of State for Foreign Affairs of Great Britain, 1916-1919; and the author of the Balfour Declaration

## Summary of Event

The rise of Jewish nationalism was sparked by a combination of factors. First, there were Jews who for centuries had dreamed and written about returning to their "Promised Land" in Palestine. Second, there were Russian Jews who fled the pogroms of the late nineteenth century. Many came to America, but some decided to set up Jewish colonies in Palestine organized on socialist principles. By 1882, Sultan Abdul Hamid II outlawed this type of colonizing experiment in the Ottoman domains. Third, the Zionist movement united the ancient Jewish dream of returning to Zion with actual Jewish emigration to Palestine. In 1896, Theodor Herzl, a brilliant Austrian journalist, became the father of modern Zionism by writing his famous book *The Jew-* *ish State* as a response to the anti-Jewish sentiment he had witnessed in Western Europe. In this book, he hypothesized that Jews and non-Jews could never really live together in peace and concluded that a Jewish state should be created. Others with equal passion joined him in the struggle toward building a Jewish state, in Palestine if possible, elsewhere if necessary. Herzl's vision was assumed by the World Zionist Organization, which pursued the idea of Palestine as the only natural site for a Jewish homeland.

The rise of modern political Zionism coincided with the rise of European colonialism. Zionist leaders went to European capitals seeking support for their goals in Palestine. The German Kaiser was unreceptive, but

411

Britain proposed that a section of her own East African empire (Uganda) should be considered. Finally, in 1917, as part of British strategy in World War I, the Secretary of State for Foreign Affairs, Lord Arthur James Balfour declared British support for the idea of a "national home for the Jewish people" in Palestine, "it being clearly understood that nothing shall be done which may prejudice the civil and religious rights of existing non-Jewish communities in Palestine, or the rights and political status enjoyed by Jews in any other country."

Palestine remained under British mandate between the two world wars, and Zionists were led to believe that Britain was serious about increasing Jewish settlement there. Palestinian Arabs reminded Britain, on the other hand, that the Balfour Declaration guaranteed their rights as a community still representing over two-thirds of the total population in spite of increasing Jewish immigration. As World War II approached, refugees from Nazi Germany exerted extreme pressure for more Jewish settlement. The British, caught between increasing pressure from both Zionists and Palestinians, were paying the price for making conflicting promises to both parties. Each of the three groups saw the other two as conspiring against its own aims. The period between the two world wars was punctuated by many study commissions, reports, and recommendations on the part of Great Britain, but none was successful in resolving the dilemma. The Arab revolt of 1936 was followed by a commission under Lord Earl Peel which reported no alternative to partition. Totally rejected by the Arab

majority, the Peel Commission was followed by Sir John Woodhead's Report (November, 1938), which reduced the Jewish share of Palestine under Peel's plan to about four hundred square miles around Tel Aviv—the only part where Jews were then a majority. This plan was totally rejected by the Zionists.

Having arrived at a political impasse, Britain convoked a conference in London (February-March, 1939) with Zionist and Palestinian leaders, together with some Arab leaders from other countries. British diplomats conferred with both groups separately, but no settlement appeared possible. Therefore, in May, eager to settle the issue or put it on the shelf before direct confrontation with Germany, Britain issued the 1939 White Paper imposing its own terms: Britain would continue to rule Palestine for a ten-year period during which time Arabs and Zionists would be given increasingly responsible roles in government if they were able to work together. *With joint cooperation* independence would be a reality in ten years—otherwise it would be postponed; seventy-five thousand Jewish immigrants could enter Palestine over a five-year period, future immigration being dependent on Arab acceptance; restrictions on land sale to Jews would prevail in some areas, while in other areas no land could be bought by Jews.

The two-thirds majority Arab population responded in varying ways to Britain's White Paper. Remembering past British vacillation on the Palestine question and holding a strong bargaining position with the Allies in the deteriorating world political situation, the majority of Arabs officially rejected the White Paper. The Zionists not only rejected it; they assailed it as a breach of mandate. In a statement by the Jewish Agency, as the Zionist leadership in Palestine was called, the policy spelled out in the White Paper was termed "a breach of faith and a surrender to Arab terrorism. . . . It is in the darkest hour of Jewish history that the British Government proposes to deprive the Jews of their last hope and to close the road back to their Homeland." The Jewish Agency refused to help Britain apprehend the Jewish terrorists who were convinced more than ever after the 1939 White Paper that violence was the only way to secure Palestine as a Jewish state. Further-

more, the Jewish Agency increased its support for illegal immigration of Jews into Palestine.

The 1939 White Paper affirmed the impossibility of a peaceful settlement and totally alienated the Zionists, who were now in an awkward situation. Their guerrillas fought British soldiers in Palestine while supporting Britain internationally in the struggle against Nazi Germany. Yet the White Paper did not win the support of the most important Arab factions. It did appear to shelve temporarily the Palestine question during the years of the war; but the scene was now set for violence, partition, and the withdrawal of Great Britain from Palestine after World War II.

## Pertinent Literature

Laqueur, Walter Ze'ev. *The Israel-Arab Reader*. New York: Bantam Books, 1970.

In this volume, a professor of the history of ideas has compiled a documentary history of the Middle East conflict. In his introduction to this massive compilation of pertinent literature, Laqueur explains his rationale for choosing the forty-two documents and twenty-eight articles or statements by scholars and leading figures in the Middle East.

*The Israel-Arab Reader* is the most complete record available of the long and bitter struggle between Hebrew and Palestinian nationalism. Each document has a brief introduction. Part I covers the period from the first stirrings of the Zionist and Arab movements to 1917, the date of the Balfour Declaration. The tie between Jewish communities in the *diaspora*

(areas outside of Palestine) survived in the traditional prayer, "Next year in Jerusalem." The political expression of this hope is found in the rise of modern Zionism documented here in the Manifesto of Bilu (1882), excerpts from Herzl's *The Jewish State*, the Basle Declaration, the Balfour Declaration, and others. The rise of Arab consciousness begins with the Program of the League of the Arab Fatherland (1905). The famous McMahon Letter of 1915, the Feisal-Weizmann Agreement, and the Feisal-Frankfurter Letters of 1919 are also included.

Part II deals with the problems of the British Mandate from the end of World War I to the British decision to return the Mandate to the United

Nations. Included is the UN resolution on the partition of Palestine (1947). In this section are many of the suggestions and study reports on the Palestine question that proved unworkable, including, of course, the 1939 White Paper and Zionist reactions to it.

Part III covers materials from the emergence of Israel after the 1947 war to the aftermath of the third Arab-Israeli war in 1967. Included is Israel's Proclamation of Independence and her Law of Return. The draft constitution of the Palestine Liberation Organization (1963) and numerous statements by leaders of both sides make up the bulk of this section, which closes with the resignation broadcast of President Gamal Abdel Nasser on June 9, 1967.

Part IV looks at the Arab-Israeli conflict with comments from those most closely involved. Most of the comments have to do with the prospects for war or peace since the 1967 war. The analysis and opinions of outside observers such as Arnold Toynbee, Hal Draper, I. F. Stone, and Bernard Lewis are presented. Laqueur himself closes this section with a piece entitled "Is Peace in the Middle East Possible?" He concludes that the problems that persisted in 1939 continue to plague the leaders of both sides.

The last section of this reader is pessimistically but perhaps realistically entitled "From War to War." It begins with the crucial UN Security Council Resolution on the Middle East immediately after the November 22, 1967 war. The next eight documents cover the covenants and platforms of various new and old Palestinian Liberation groups, including the Seven Points of Al Fatah. Documents from neighboring Arab countries are also included, such as the Syrian Ba'th Party Congress Resolutions of April, 1969. The last six documents are by Israelis or outsiders looking at the Middle East and Israel's role in the conflict. An interview with Jean-Paul Sartre is part of the collection.

This volume, which contains the complete text of Great Britain's 1939 White Paper, as well as documents explaining the situation before and after its issuance, is important not only for understanding the importance of the White Paper but also for a comprehensive understanding of the complex events that surrounded it between the wars. Furthermore, those interested in looking at the whole issue of the Arab-Israeli impasse will find this collection an excellent place to begin. The more closely one looks at the situation in 1939 and Britain's response to it in the White Paper, the more one may see parallels in the impasse that persists to this day. Now, as in 1939, the heart of the dilemma remains the claim of two people to the same land.

Goitein, S. D. *Jews and Arabs: Their Contacts Through the Ages.* New York: Schocken Books, 1974.

S. D. Goitein, an eminent professor at the School of Oriental Studies of the Hebrew University in Jerusalem, provides a scholarly approach to

Jewish-Arab relations from the earliest times. Many common stereotypes associated with the faiths founded by Moses and Mohammed are challenged and even shattered in this well-written account of an ancient problem that has immediate relevance.

Many will be surprised to learn that Jews fared much better under Arab Muslim hegemony than they had previously done under the Christian Byzantines and later under European kingdoms in the Middle Ages. It is no coincidence that at the birth of Zionism, ninety percent of the world's Jews lived in Europe and Russia and most of the remainder were spread from Morocco to Iran. It was Jewish confrontation with the predominantly Christian West that gave rise to the Zionist idea that Jew and non-Jew ultimately could not live together in peace.

Goitein provides a historical summary of the origins of Arabs and Jews, discussing the numerous myths (such as "the Semitic race") that emerged from ignorance and conjecture. Regarding common origins, he notes:

> The idea that Jews and Arabs are "cousins" through Ishmael and Isaac, the sons of Abraham, was not an indigenous tradition, either in the Bible or among the ancient Arabs. However, as it was accepted as a fact in the whole of Jewish literature since the time of the Second Commonwealth, and as it was incorporated by Muhammad into the Holy Book of Islam itself, this idea of close relationship was accepted by the two peoples throughout the long period of their symbiosis in Islamic times.

Provable fact or not, as far as common origins are concerned, Goitein points to the many similarities between the two peoples. The most common ancient factor was their "primitive democracy" or self-governing lineages in which the *lex talionis* made no distinction between the rich and the poor. Domestic slavery, the role of women, and religious ideas are discussed in their historical context as yet other factors indicating close affinity between the Arabs and Jews. Most important, Goitein states, is that ancient Israel and the Arabs alone preserved their primitive democracy, and the moral attitude implied by it, at the decisive hour in their history—that is, when both peoples became the bearers of religions which were destined to mold the development of a great part of the human race.

The domestication of the camel (about 2000-1000 B. C.) was closely associated with the beginnings of the Arab people, who were primarily nomadic traders. Jews, on the other hand, had become agriculturalists. Goitein describes the consequences of the Arab devotion to their language and Jewish devotion to their ideas. He describes Islam as much closer to Judaism than to Christianity and notes that the influence of Judaism on early Islam must have been considerable. The role of Judaism on post-Koranic Islam was even greater. A large part of the book shows how Islam paid back its debt to Judaism. Under Arab Islamic rule, Jews were not treated differently from members of other non-Muslim religions. Indeed, the disappearance of Christianity in areas where Judaism thrived under Islam (North Africa and Yemen, for example) may suggest some favoritism toward Judaism. While some Jews and Christians attained high posts under Islamic rule, their positions as minorities remained precarious and sometimes even dangerous. But the economic and social institutions of Jews during the first five centuries of Islam worked toward the revival and gradual unification of the Jewish people inside the Muslim world.

In the last two chapters, Goitein discusses the cultural development of the Jewish people inside Arab Islam, their contribution in the medieval period in the Middle East, and the linguistic aspects of Jewish Arabic symbiosis which reached its peak with Hebrew poetry in the Middle Ages. He also treats the rise of Jewish philosophy under Islam and Jewish and Islamic mysticism. A brief section is devoted to comparing Jewish and Muslim law and ritual, customs, folk literature, and art.

The last chapter moves into the modern period with a discussion of the reemergence of Arab nationalism and the creation of the modern state of Israel. It is no coincidence that Zionism and Arab nationalism should emerge on the world scene at the same time, even though circumstances differed. The State of Israel, Goitein concludes, is simply a patch of Europe transplanted to the eastern shore of the Mediterranean, but a future symbiosis of Arab and Jewish cultures and traditions could occur. Israel has become a laboratory for the world where East meets West through two peoples with very ancient ties.

Goitein does not speak directly to the White Paper of 1939, but the entire book is crucial to understanding the historical, cultural, ideological, and religious roots of the confrontation between Jews and Arabs. Goitein places the conflict surrounding the 1939 White Paper in a broad historical perspective spanning four millennia. This work appears to confirm that the Arab-Israeli impasse is at its roots a civil war between brothers. Civil wars can be the worst kind of wars, but once peace is achieved, the foundations for reconciliation are there, waiting in hope for the full structure to be built. — *H.H.B.*

## Additional Recommended Reading

Khouri, Fred J. *The Arab-Israeli Dilemma.* Syracuse, N.Y.: Syracuse University Press, 1976. A professor of political science explores the complex issues and isolates the facts from partisan propaganda in analyzing the conflict.

Mansfield, Peter. *The Arab World: A Comprehensive History.* New York: Thomas Y. Crowell Company, 1976. A thorough study of Arab history and the Arab world from the past to the present.

Chouraqui, André. *A History of Judaism.* Translated by Yvette Wiener. New York: Walker, 1962. A concise introduction to four millennia of Jewish history in a clear and simple style.

Saint John, Robert. *Ben-Gurion: A Biography.* Garden City, N.Y.: Doubleday & Company, 1971. A well-written account of the life of the Russian-born Zionist pioneer who led the war for Israel's independence and became the first Prime

Minister in 1948.

Ward, Richard J., Don Peretz and E. M. Wilson. *The Palestine State: A Rational Approach*. Port Washington, N.Y.: Kennikat Press, 1977. After discussing the historical background, the authors offer forms and projections of a Palestinian entity, with a political and economic framework for the future.

Hadawi, Sami. *Bitter Harvest: Palestine Between 1914-1967*. New York: New World Press, 1967. The author, who served the Mandate Government of Palestine with distinction and became a Palestinian refugee after 1948, chronicles the major events of the Israeli-Palestinian impasse for half a century.

Antonius, George. *The Arab Awakening*. New York: Capricorn Books, 1965. This first study of Arab nationalism is a classic; Palestinian dreams of a homeland are considered within the broader perspective of Arab aspirations, particularly in the twentieth century.

# JOHN STEINBECK PUBLISHES *THE GRAPES OF WRATH*

*Type of event:* Sociological: publication of a novel that portrays the life of the dispossessed tenant farmers of the Midwest
*Time:* 1939
*Locale:* New York City

Principal personages:
> JOHN ERNST STEINBECK (1902-1968), an author of social fiction who was awarded the Nobel Prize for Literature in 1962
> FRANKLIN DELANO ROOSEVELT (1882-1945), thirty-second President of the United States, 1933-1945

## Summary of Event

As a soul-sickened Europe faced inevitable war in 1939, many Americans were beginning to pull themselves out of the economic quagmire of the Great Depression which had begun shortly after the 1929 Wall Street stock market crash. It was a tragedy of mammoth proportions, affecting all Americans in various ways. Apart from Southern blacks, perhaps no group of people was as ravaged by the Depression as the dispossessed tenant farmers of Kansas, Oklahoma, Arkansas, and Texas (collectively branded by the pejorative term "Okies"). The topsoil of their farms had been literally blown away by a combination of erosion and high winds. As a consequence, these farmers were ruined financially. The designation "Dust Bowl" refers to the devastated region where Okies once lived before the banks and land companies had foreclosed their mortgages and taken away their homes and farms.

With their ancestral holdings seized, the Okies set their sights on the Golden State—California. There they hoped to be able to start farming again; unfortunately, however, most of them were bitterly disappointed by the pitiful opportunities offered them in this purported "land of milk and honey." Their exodus from their former homes to the far West inspired John Ernst Steinbeck to see at first-hand the extent of their defeat and suffering. Out of his experiences with the migrants on the long road west, Steinbeck created his most notable novel, *The Grapes of Wrath*, published in 1939. No stranger to the miseries of poor rural and urban folk, Steinbeck was already the respected author of several novels, including *Tortilla Flat* (1935), *In Dubious Battle* (1936), and *Of Mice and Men* (1937). All stressed themes of man's cruelty toward his fellow men and the considerable spiritual resources of those most down on their luck.

*The Grapes of Wrath* chronicles the fortunes of a typical Okie family, the Joads, who, as critic Joseph Fontenrose observes, were much like the Israelites fleeing from Pharaoh (Pharaoh in this case being the Shawnee Land and Cattle Company of Oklahoma and the Growers' Asso-

418

ciation of California). An official of the Land and Cattle Company tells the Joads that they must vacate their little farm, which has been in the family for some time, because they lack the money to keep up their mortgage payments. When the Joads question the decision, they, like so many others, are told that there is no one to whom they can turn for help. The company is a faceless beast of prey: there is no John D. Rockefeller or Jay Gould to blame or hate—only an anonymous Board of Directors.

The Joads and their neighbors, simple people knowing only their land and the ways of tilling it passed on by their forebears, are at first awestruck by the bank's verdict, then dumbstruck by the foreclosure of their land, then finally horrorstruck by the cool, callous way in which the company knocks down a farmhouse with a monstrous tractor. With what little money they have left, they decide to do what so many others in the Southwest had done: buy an overpriced jalopy from the local crooked used car dealer, pile mattresses, personal items, dogs, and as many people as possible onto its sagging cutout rear end, and head west on U.S. Route 66, the "highway of the Okies."

Hardships awaited these dispossessed Okies at every point on the journey, the most trying of which were created by fellow men: the border patrollers, the store owners, ranchers, grandees, state and local police, and antimigrant goons in the small towns along the way. Added hazards were the hard-to-negotiate mountains, as well as the nearly unendurable wastes of the deserts. As Steinbeck discovered, the Okies

were a thoroughly despised lot, hated because they did not fit into the established order either in their native region or in California; footloose, ignorant, and often nearly penniless, they were feared as potential "Reds" (that is, Communist dupes) who would do battle against society simply because they had nothing to lose.

As for the "promised land" of California, most migrants discovered that if the state were in fact as lovely a place as people had said, it was not home. Almost all of the productive land in California had long since been appropriated by big landholders, leaving migrants no choice but to hire themselves out as workers on melon, peach, apple, orange, and cotton orchards and farms, in order to survive. As Steinbeck demonstrates, the most fortunate of the Okie migrants camped out in government-operated facilities offering hot running water and other amenities; in such camps, surrounded by friendly people of their own "kind," migrants led a decent, though hardscrabble, existence.

However, as Steinbeck also learned on his journey with the migrants, few camps were so equipped; most had rude pit-type toilets and few if any cooking places. Since many camps were maintained by the very people who owned the land on which the migrants worked, there was always a company store in which high-priced goods of inferior quality were offered to workers in exchange for the pittance that they earned picking lettuce, oranges, or cotton.

Steinbeck further observes that the migrants' lives were made even more miserable by those they encountered in the gas stations, grocery stores, and main streets along their migration path—people in the same situation as themselves, who would cheat and abuse them at any opportunity. For their own salvation, then, the migrants had to turn inward toward their own people.

*The Grapes of Wrath*, in part, created the considerable controversy that it did among Americans because of the graphic language which the characters customarily used. Shockingly vivid descriptions of people in dire circumstances, as well as the antiestablishment "message" Steinbeck sought to convey, was enormously disturbing.

Certainly, American readers were not unacquainted with obscenities in novels (Ernest Hemingway and William Faulkner had used them in their novels and stories); yet Steinbeck jolted them with the rawest language imaginable—the actual language of the downtrodden.

Particularly startling to readers were frequent references to sexual organs and bodily functions; some of these readers roundly and publicly denounced the "utter filth" found in the novel and petitioned their local libraries to avoid purchasing it. As a result, a number of libraries failed to order *The Grapes of Wrath*, and the book was rejected for use in many high school literature classes.

Nonetheless, by employing the actual language of the Okies, Steinbeck pushed American realism a step farther than it had ever gone before. His crusading in this respect made it possible for other writers who wished to depict life "in the raw," such as Norman Mailer and Truman Capote, to gain a wider acceptance than might

otherwise have been possible. Steinbeck's poignant descriptions of Okie life are often referred to as "earthy," and many passages have little appeal for the prudish or squeamish.

However, what really touched off the political controversy was the way Tom Joad, a young parole-jumper from Sallisaw, Oklahoma, and his mentor and friend, Jim Casy, joined together to fight for migrant rights rather than passively accepting a pitiful existence in worker camps run by big landowners. Steinbeck clearly identifies Joad and Casy as heroes—heroic participants in a just cause. Casy's martyrdom at the hands of the police and strike breakers, coupled with his bold assertions about workers joining together, made Steinbeck the target of accusations of being a socialist (or even a Communist) out to demean American businessmen.

By so exposing the practices of those California landowners who exploited migrants by holding out promises of easy money in the Golden State, Steinbeck's *The Grapes of Wrath* made millions of Americans conscious of a tragic situation heretofore overlooked. While people could handily ignore the plight of faceless thousands toiling away in fields and orchards, it was much harder to do after encountering the problems of such arrestingly portrayed characters as Rose of Sharon, Ma Joad, Tom Joad, the Wilsons, and Jim Casy.

The book's message was not lost upon President Franklin D. Roosevelt, who was in the White House during the Dust Bowl years; he subsequently paid much attention to the problems of dispossessed farm workers through such federal programs of assistance as the Works Progress Administration (WPA). Better housing and working conditions became a reality for many Okies because of Roosevelt's concern.

Like any truly great novel, *The Grapes of Wrath* made an indelible impression upon those who read it.

While some dismissed the book out of hand as "trash" and "filth," as many others found in it a sublime and simple truth: that mankind is an indivisible whole and that men are, in fact, very much their brothers' keepers, no matter how different those brothers may be.

## Pertinent Literature

Donohue, Agnes McNeill, ed. *A Casebook on* The Grapes of Wrath. New York: Thomas Y. Crowell Company, 1968.

In her Preface, editor Donohue likens the publication of *The Grapes of Wrath* to an earthquake which "has dwindled down to an occasional tremor," the book having been "inordinately praised and inordinately damned." Her purpose in this compendium of the best critical writing about the novel is to "follow its turbulent history . . . to make an excursion into American literature, history, myth, culture, and dream."

What distinguishes this anthology of critical writing from most others is its insistence upon being not only a literary study, but also a sociopolitical study. The first sixty pages comprise a historical account of the varied reactions to the publication of *The Grapes of Wrath*. These reactions, written between the novel's publication in 1939 and 1944, treat it as a social and political document. The second half of the book, on the other hand, deals with the literary aspects of Steinbeck's novel and includes (among others) the opinions of Steinbeck's fellow novelist, Christopher Isherwood, as well as those of critics Maxwell Geismar, Chester Eisinger, and Warren French. In all, the view-

points of twenty-nine writers are represented.

All of the writers included in the first half of *A Casebook on* The Grapes of Wrath—Frank J. Taylor, Malcolm Cowley, Lyle Boren, Carey McWilliams, Martin Shockley, and Leo Gurko—try to answer the question of whether *The Grapes of Wrath* is an accurate assessment of the social conditions found in migrant camps and other way stations, or whether it is mere fabrication and distortion. As might be expected, there is much disagreement about Steinbeck's accuracy.

Liberals were delighted by Samuel Sillen's article "Censoring *The Grapes of Wrath*," a piece assailing those who attacked the book, calling them Fascists and fools. ("Are your libraries making an effort to meet the demand for the book? Is an attempt being made to hinder its circulation? Let us know.") Conservatives rallied to the side of such essayists as Frank Taylor, whose *Forum* article, "California's Grapes of Wrath," termed the book "inaccurate" and misleading. Moreover, Lyle Boren's piece, "The Grapes of Wrath," a congressional address filled with fulminations and various charges, sums up the attitude of those who found the book both decadent and subversive: "I cannot find it possible to let this dirty, lying, filthy manuscript go heralded before the public without a word of challenge or protest."

Carey McWilliams came out on the side of Steinbeck in his "California Pastoral," published in *The Antioch Review*, which presented three actual histories of labor mistreatment included in the LaFollette Committee Report submitted to the United States Congress. Because there were many of the same sort of antimigrant incidents in the study as those narrated by Steinbeck, McWilliams believed that what the novelist said about conditions in the camps was true and faithfully recorded.

The articles comprising the second half of the book deal with a variety of matters: Jeffersonian agrarianism and *The Grapes of Wrath*, religious symbolism, the juxtaposition of the grotesque and the commonplace, pervasive motifs, and Steinbeck's ambivalence, to name but a few of the most significant. Noted critics expound upon the richness of language, characterization, and message to be found in a novel often patronized as "overly simplistic" and "transparent."

Most striking are the articles by Thomas Dunn, Edwin Moseley, Gerald Cannon, and Charles Dougherty in which the Biblical lore found in *The Grapes of Wrath* is examined, and in which parallels are established between such figures as Tom Joad and Moses, Ma Joad and Deborah, and Jim Casy and Jesus Christ.

*A Casebook on* The Grapes of Wrath, possibly the most complete anthology of Steinbeck criticism, is a valuable guide. It enables the general reader and scholar alike to delve more deeply into the sociopolitical and literary concerns of Steinbeck's epic novel.

Fontenrose, Joseph. *John Steinbeck: An Introduction and Interpretation*. New York: Barnes & Noble, 1963.

For those wishing to know how John Steinbeck used myth and biology to create his best-known novels, this book by a professor of classical mythology is a fascinating study. And to those with a particular interest in *The Grapes of Wrath*, Fontenrose has much to say. His chapter dealing with the novel is one of the classic pieces of Steinbeck criticism.

Fontenrose believes that *The Grapes of Wrath* has as its thesis the notion that "all life is one and holy" and that, in the words of Jim Casy, every man has "jus' got a little piece of a great big soul." Surely it is true that members of the Joad family, who at first only seek the company of one another, learn by the novel's end that what is important is not individuals or even the family: it is the whole of mankind that really matters. Thus, Rose of Sharon's loss of her baby is not allowed to be the book's concluding event; rather, she offers her milk to a dying man, thereby participating in the life of all men. Moreover, as the fortunes of the Joad family decline during their long journey across plains, mountains, and desert, "the communal unit of united workers, which came to birth in the roadside camps . . . grows stronger, and this upward movement is accompanied by the growth of Casy and Tom Joad in understanding the forces at work."

What Fontenrose is saying is of historical significance, for at the time that Steinbeck was writing *The Grapes of Wrath*, anyone advancing the idea that poor people ought to band together to seek better wages and working conditions was likely to be called a "red" agitator. Steinbeck dared to speak out eloquently for the dispossessed.

The realities of tenant farmer life in California wayside camps demanded that someone remind the general public that the migrants were not the scum of humanity which growers often portrayed them to be, but, instead, ordinary people who needed to work and live. Their fight would be the fight of anyone faced with similar circumstances: eviction, bankruptcy after a crop's complete failure, and the necessity of traveling thousands of miles to find work. To fight the banks, land companies, and ranchers was difficult, requiring the oppressed to stay together and not allow themselves to be treated like slaves.

The main conflict in the novel becomes that between "organisms" (as Steinbeck saw them), a conflict which is "necessarily an ecological struggle, a disturbance of an ecological cycle." In Fontenrose's estimation, the battle that raged between migrants and those who use them has a biological parallel. For like a large ecosystem that has been disturbed by a new element entering into it, the California ranch is disturbed by the coming of a mass of landless, penniless people in search of a better existence. The ranch is transformed by the new arrivals, and to deal with the threat to stability the ranch owner calls in police so that order might be restored. But the invasion has already changed California society and there is no returning to the past.

Fontenrose treats the novel's mythic aspects by expanding upon critic Peter Lisca's comparison of portions of the novel to the Hebrews' exodus from Egypt in the Old Testament, finding, among other things, that the name Joad is derived from Judah, the land in which the Israelites peacefully dwelt until a new Pharaoh arose in Egypt, ushering in an era of plague and hunger. Like the Israelites, the Okies had to leave their Egypt (Oklahoma) for the Promised Land (California), where they were met by hostile Canaanites (antimigrant Californians). Once in Canaan, they learned to live with their own people, severely punishing those who disturbed the community's peace. Tom Joad, in turn, is seen as the new Moses, leading his followers out of the land of famine, and the twelve Joads become the twelve apostles of Christ (represented by Jim Casy, the definitive humanitarian).

What Fontenrose says about *The Grapes of Wrath* is not based upon idle speculation or on "scissors and paste" scholarship; many parallels do actually exist between characters and incidents in the Bible and those in Steinbeck's novel. Fontenrose's ideas, because they add new dimensions to an already gripping modern-day trag- edy, are well worth examining. — *J.D.R.*

## Additional Recommended Reading

Hoffman, Frederick John. *The Modern Novel in America, 1900-1950*. Chicago: Henry Regnery, 1963. Insights into *The Grapes of Wrath*, showing how it fits into the continuum of modern American literature.

Tedlock, Ernest Warnock. *Steinbeck and His Critics: A Record of Twenty-five Years*. Albuquerque: University of New Mexico Press, 1957. One of the better studies of Steinbeck's critical reputation.

Howard, Leon. *Literature and the American Tradition*. Garden City, N.Y.: Doubleday & Company, 1960. Offers a short assessment of *The Grapes of Wrath* as a significant contribution to American letters.

French, Warren. *John Steinbeck*. New York: Twayne, 1975. A good introduction to the Steinbeck canon; discusses the theme, characterization, and general coherence of *The Grapes of Wrath*.

Kazin, Alfred. *On Native Grounds: An Interpretation of Modern American Prose Literature*. New York: Harcourt, Brace, 1942. Discusses how *The Grapes of Wrath* helped to shape contemporary American fiction.

# THE SYNTHESIS OF DDT FOR USE AS AN INSECTICIDE

*Type of event:* Scientific: discovery and eventual application of DDT as an insecticide
*Time:* 1939
*Locale:* Switzerland

*Principal personages:*

OTHMAR ZEIDLER, German scientist who first synthesized DDT

PAUL HERMANN MUELLER (1899-1965), Swiss scientist who discovered the use of DDT as an insecticide

RACHEL LOUISE CARSON (1907-1964), American biologist whose book *Silent Spring* (1962) led to the ban of DDT

## Summary of Event

The scientific discoveries and expertise of the twentieth century have revolutionized man's ability to control his environment by helping him to understand and manipulate many of the key elements of his world. Much of this new understanding was applied to technological breakthroughs that have proven to be of tremendous benefit to mankind. Some aspects of the new technology were immediately recognized as a grave danger to man's existence, while still other discoveries that began positively have proven over time to be far more complex and negative than was originally imagined.

DDT (dichloro–diphenyl–trichloro-ethane) is a grayish-white powder manufactured from chlorobenzene and chloral which kills insects by affecting their nervous systems. It differs from other insecticides in that it decays very slowly, and consequently can remain in the environment long after its use. It is insoluble in water, but soluble in many other substances such as acetone, ether, benzene, and carbon tetrachloride.

DDT had first been prepared in 1873 by Othmar Zeidler, who published a description of it in *Berichte der Deutschen chemischen Gesellschaft*. Zeidler, however, had not indicated that it could have any physiological action, and so the discovery was forgotten for more than half a century until unearthed by Paul Mueller.

Mueller was a research chemist who had been hired by J. R. Geigy, a Swiss company, in 1925, shortly after earning his doctorate, to develop tanning agents for the Basle dye factory. Because of his academic interest in botany, he began with a study of plant pigments. He also began working on a corollary problem, that of the preservation and disinfection of animal skins, which naturally led him to a study of pesticides. By 1935 he had narrowed his field of search to contact insecticides and had established what he considered to be the characteristics of the ideal contact insecticide. It should have great toxicity for insects, little or no toxicity for plants and animals, and no odor, and should be rapid, long-lasting, and low-priced. Stability and decompos-

425

ability were two characteristics which the researcher failed to consider.

Mueller began a painstaking study of many different types of compounds on many different insects, culminating in his discovery of DDT in 1939; he soon applied for a patent on it. The following year the insecticide was used with dramatic success to squelch a plague of the Colorado beetle which threatened the potato crop in Switzerland at a time in world history when all food crops were of utmost importance. It was first sold to the Allies in 1942 under the trade name Gesarol.

During these early years of World War II (as had been the case during other wars), as many soldiers were dying of typhus, malaria, and other disabling diseases carried and spread by insects as from wounds suffered in action. The United States Army was frantically attempting to boost production of the best insecticides available and to push for new chemicals to fight these old problems, when Gesarol became available. Preliminary tests showed that the new insecticide would kill the lice that carried typhus as well as the mosquitoes that carried malaria. Moreover, the residual effect on surfaces sprayed with the chemical could last for weeks, giving continuing protection.

Having by this time analyzed Gesarol and discovered that it was DDT, the Allies went into large-scale production and application of it. The shirts of British and American troops were impregnated with DDT as a routine precaution. Entire islands were sprayed with it in the Asian theater of war before or immediately after troops landed. The entire population of Naples, Italy, was dusted with DDT in early 1944, effectively stopping a serious typhoid epidemic. The insecticide was hailed as a mercy weapon that could save lives during the war and improve the country's health thereafter, and Paul Mueller was awarded the Nobel Prize for Physiology and Medicine in 1948.

However, two of the properties of DDT that made it so valuable as an insecticide—its great toxicity, and its persistent residual effect—have also been found to cause problems with its use. Although published reports indicate that there was concern in these areas even during its dramatic triumphs in the 1940's, production of DDT rose steadily from seventy-five tons in 1943 to 64,000 tons in 1962 as more and more uses were found for it.

In 1962 Rachel L. Carson, an American biologist, brought attention to the undesirable effects of DDT in her highly influential book, *Silent Spring*. She pointed out that because DDT is not soluble in water, it can persist in water and the soil, where it can contaminate beneficial insects and wildlife. Moreover, DDT can be stored in the fatty tissues of animals, including man, and build up to toxic levels.

Because of a growing concern over the harmful effects of DDT, the United States Environmental Protection Agency conducted a seventeen-month investigation and finally banned almost all uses of DDT in 1972, describing it as "an uncontrollable, durable chemical that persists in the aquatic and terrestrial environments" that "may have a serious effect" on human beings. Exemptions were made to the ban in the case of a sudden epidemic when DDT is the most effective means of combatting disease-carrying insects, for use on onions, green peppers, and sweet potatoes in certain areas that have particular pest problems with these crops, and for shipment to countries where malaria is a problem.

## Pertinent Literature

West, T. F. and G. A. Campbell. *DDT: And Newer Persistent Insecticides*. New York: Chemical Publishing Company, 1952.

This handbook was prepared for use by those who were desirous of using the new insecticide DDT but did not have access to more extensive written information. Although other persistent chemical insecticides are discussed, the main concern of the authors is to summarize the body of practical knowledge about DDT that was available within the decade after it became prevalent as a commercial preparation.

West and Campbell begin with a short history of the synthesis of DDT and the discovery of its potential as an insecticide. They include an amazing photographic series on the de-lousing project in the control of the typhoid epidemic in Naples in 1944 with accompanying text, and in this, as well as other examples which they cite, they are tremendously enthusiastic over the marvels of the new chemical.

The first section of the work contains straightforward scientific information on the chemical structure of DDT, its manufacture, and the principle of formulation. There follows a chapter on various studies of its toxicity to man. While West and Campbell cite several studies showing that dangerous levels are not difficult to reach, their viewpoint reflects the many other reports from the first decade of use which assume that DDT will be used very carefully, therefore, they do not include strong warnings on its use. They detail numerous studies indicating that DDT would have no detrimental effect on fish or wildlife, but do suggest that, used carelessly, it could present a danger to beneficial insects.

The authors devote the next three hundred and fifty pages to instructions on how to use DDT in paints to kill flies, in household fabrics to kill cockroaches and bedbugs, in clothing to prevent lice, as a fog in orchards and warehouses, and as a direct spray against dozens of insects which they list.

Benzene hexachloride, DDD, and chlordane are the subjects of fairly limited discussion at the end of the work, as they were considerably newer insecticides as well as less dramatic than DDT.

It is probably through such enthusiastic spreading of the word as represented in handbooks such as this for the layman that the chemical crisis described by Rachel Carson in *Silent Spring* (1962) grew to dangerous proportions.

# The Synthesis of DDT for Use as an Insecticide

Carson, Rachel Louise. *Silent Spring*. Boston: Houghton Mifflin Company, 1962.

Although the insecticide DDT was known from the earliest days of its use as a potentially dangerous chemical, the true cumulative effect that it was having on man and his environment was not thoroughly investigated until Rachel Carson, an American biologist, brought the question before the public in this controversial work.

The two characteristics that made DDT such a desirable and dramatically successful insecticide when it was first introduced during World War II, namely, its great toxicity and its residual persistence, were investigated by the Department of Agriculture before it was used extensively by the Army. These early reports all warned, however, that toxicity could become a real problem with extensive exposure and that contamination of food should be avoided. These early warnings, however, were ignored as more and more postwar uses were enthusiastically found for DDT, and its production had risen from seventy-five tons in 1943 to 64,000 tons by 1962, when *Silent Spring* burst upon the American consciousness.

Carson begins her book by describing an idyllic American town ravaged by the negative side-effects of insecticides: domestic animals and wildlife sicken and die, vegetation withers, people have puzzling illnesses and sometimes sudden unexplained deaths. Although the occurrence of all of these disasters in one community is a fictional example, the author does claim that many real communities are suffering substantial numbers of such disastrous side-effects.

Carson continues with a very clear explanation of the chlorinated hydrocarbons used commonly as insecticides, some five times more toxic than DDT, and a second major group of insecticides, the organic phosphates. She explains how they affect humans and other animals and at what level of contamination poisoning can be considered to have occurred, and cites numerous appalling and quite real examples.

Carson's next section deals with ground and surface water pollution, especially by insecticides, but also from industrial wastes and other chemicals. Tied closely to this discussion is that of soil contamination. The author explains how soil must contain bacteria, earthworms, and other life forms and how contamination from pesticides alters the balance of the populations, which can in turn allow an unchecked growth of harmful organisms. Soil can also contain insoluble insecticides which can contaminate plant tissues for years after the original contamination, presenting a particular problem with food crops.

Although Carson rhapsodizes briefly about sagebrush and roadside landscapes, the bulk of the work contains careful explications of specific cases of acute and chronic poisoning by insecticides. The experiences of Detroit, Michigan, and Sheldon, Illinois (where ninety percent of the cat population died after a general aerial application of an insecticide), are all too similar to the grim fable with which she begins the book. Although Carson spends many pages discussing the danger to and inadvertent destruction of various bird, fish, and insect populations, her more interesting discussions center on daily household chemical poisoning hazards and health problems linked with chemicals. The book's numerous grim examples are documented in fifty pages of bibliographic citations which are listed at the end of the work.

Although *Silent Spring* was greeted by many at its publication as a hysterical overstatement of a possible problem, it was read by many laymen, who, during that decade of social unrest, insisted that the government act to control the dangerous substances cited by Carson. As a result, the Environmental Protection Agency banned the use of DDT in 1972. — *M.S.S.*

## Additional Recommended Reading

Bloom, Sandra C. and Stanley E. Degler. *Pesticides and Pollution*. Washington, D.C.: The Bureau of National Affairs, 1969. A short but well-researched overview of the state of pesticide research and monitoring at the time of writing as well as the state and federal legislation on the subject prior to the 1972 EPA decision.

Henkin, Harmon, Martin Merta and James Staples. *The Environment, the Establishment, and the Law*. Boston: Houghton Mifflin Company, 1971. An account of a hearing conducted by the Wisconsin Department of Natural Resources in response to a petition filed by two citizen groups to determine whether DDT was an environmental pollutant.

Whorton, James. *Before* Silent Spring: *Pesticides and Public Health in Pre-DDT America*. Princeton, N.J.: Princeton University Press, 1975. A background paper published shortly after the EPA ban on DDT which shows that similar regulation has occurred after a period of indiscriminate use of other substances in the past when new information about their danger has come to light.

# THE BATTLE OF BRITAIN

*Type of event:* Military: fight for control of the skies over Britain in World War II
*Time:* Late summer, 1940-1941
*Locale:* England and the English Channel

*Principal personages:*

AIR MARSHAL SIR HUGH DOWDING (1882-1970), Commander in Chief of the Fighter Command with the Royal Air Force

AIR VICE MARSHAL KEITH R. PARK (1892-1975), Commander of No. 11 Group in the Fighter Command with the Royal Air Force

GENERAL SIR ALAN FRANCIS BROOKE (1883-1963), General Officer and Commander in Chief of the Southern Command

FIELD MARSHAL HERMANN GÖRING (1893-1946), Commander in Chief of the German Luftwaffe

FIELD MARSHAL ALBERT KESSELRING (1887-1960), Commander of Luftwaffe Air Group II

FIELD MARSHAL HUGO SPERRLE (1885-1953), Commander of Luftwaffe Air Group III

GRAND ADMIRAL ERICH RAEDER (1876-1960), Commander in Chief of the German Navy

## Summary of Event

With the German conquests of the Low Countries and France completed by June, 1940, Britain now stood alone to confront Hitler's forces. Winston Churchill spoke to his countrymen: "Hitler knows he will have to break us on this Island or lose the war." Most British military leaders assumed that a German invasion of Britain from across the Channel was likely to come soon.

British chances of throwing back any invasion during the summer of 1940 were questionable. While the Royal Navy did control the seas immediately around Britain, its forces were being strained by the need to protect the Atlantic supply routes from America against U-boat attacks. Some fifty-five army divisions could be mustered to defend the island, but many of those divisions were only at half strength, and the bulk of British army weapons had been abandoned in the evacuation at Dunkirk earlier in June.

Therefore, as an army general observed at the time, the defense of Britain would rest primarily on the Royal Air Force (R.A.F.), particularly on the Fighter Command planes. Since 1936, Sir Hugh Dowding, head of the Fighter Command, had tried to convince the Cabinet and the Air Council that, in the next war, Britain would undoubtedly be on the defensive. For that reason, priority in aircraft planning and production should be given to a build-up of fighter plane strength, not bombers as the Air

Council wanted. Dowding also stressed the need for improved detection and early warning of approaching enemy aircraft. Over much opposition and after much delay, Dowding persuaded the Air Council of the correctness of his views. In 1939 the Air Council ordered stepped-up production of more fighters, as well as the construction of an early warning system.

British designers came forth with two types of improved fighter planes: the Hurricanes and the Spitfires. Both flew at speeds of three hundred miles per hour maximum (fast for the time), had heavy armor, constant speed propellers, and self-sealing fuel tanks, and were armed with eight machine guns. Those were the planes, together with the pilots who flew them, that won the Battle of Britain.

During 1937, British physicists had worked on aircraft detection by means of radio wave signals, and what later would be known as radar was developed. Work began on building a linked system of radar stations, ground observation units, and Fighter Command sector control bases which would enable the Fighter Command to anticipate and intercept enemy bombers. Hundreds of barrage balloons and antiaircraft artillery added to the British defensive shield.

Since the fall of France, Hitler had sought to persuade the British that they should negotiate a settlement and end the fighting between their nations. His peace overtures were rejected by Churchill, and with much reluctance—believing it "technically unfeasible"—Hitler approved Operation Sea Lion, the plan for the invasion of England, and tentatively set September 21, some two months hence, as the day for the first crossings. Ninety thousand German troops would make up the initial assault force, building to ten divisions within two weeks. Preparations for Operation Sea Lion went forward rapidly. More than twelve hundred boats and barges were assembled at ports across the Channel from England, troops were trained in landing procedures, and bases were built for the aircraft which would provide cover for the landing.

Serious disagreement then arose between the German naval and army high commands as to whether the landings should be made along a broad front in southern and eastern England as the army wanted, or on a more concentrated front in Kent and Sussex. Admiral Raeder insisted that his ships could not assure protection of the assault forces over the broad front, while the generals feared that the narrow front would enable the British to place their full force in one locality and so more effectively contest the invasion. Raeder finally won his point, and the narrow front plan was adopted; but the delay had further shortened the time margin for implementation, and logistic revisions had to be made with dangerous haste to get Operation Sea Lion under way before autumn storms closed the Channel.

On their side, British ground and air defense preparations proceeded also. Under General Alan Brooke, the Home Guard was increased to 500,000 men; mobile field guns, antitank weapons, and small arms were provided in ever larger amounts; more than two million bomb shelters

431

were built and distributed; and plans to resist German landings from the sea, or by parachutes from the air, were laid out.

It was apparent to both sides that control of the air over southern England would be the vital factor determining the success or failure of Operation Sea Lion. Göring had no doubt that his Luftwaffe could gain that control. Indeed, he believed that his bombers would so pulverize British defenses within a month's time that the islanders would have to surrender and a cross-Channel invasion would be rendered unnecessary. Göring had cause for his optimism. With more than thirteen hundred bombers and twelve hundred fighter planes, the Luftwaffe in Western Europe greatly overmatched the R.A.F. The Luftwaffe squadrons were organized into three air groups (Luftflotten); of these the largest were Luftflotte Two (Kesselring) and Luftflotte Three (Sperrle) stationed in France and the Netherlands. They would spearhead the German air offensive.

To confront the German air power, Dowding's Fighter Command had only about seven hundred front line fighter aircraft, with another 350 in reserve. And those were, of necessity, deployed all over the island. Even the heaviest concentration of fighter planes—those in Group No. 11 (Park) in the southeast—would probably be outnumbered by as much as ten to one by the attacking German planes. Dowding's most serious shortage, however, was of men to fly the planes. There were only a few more than fourteen hundred fully trained fighter pilots and almost no reserves available to replace them if they were disabled or killed.

The Battle of Britain for air supremacy cannot be said to have taken place on any one specific day. Rather, the fighting consisted of a number of bomber attacks and fighter plane encounters, increasing in size and intensity from July into September, 1940. During July and into early August, the Luftwaffe carried out intermittent strikes, mostly on British shipping in the Channel and on the port of Dover. Some 150 civilians were killed and twenty ships sunk in those strikes, but the Luftwaffe also lost dozens of its planes to R.A.F. fighters and to antiaircraft fire.

The next phase of the German air offensive was directed at the radar stations and airfields in the southeastern counties of England. Here the bombers of Kesselring and Sperrle were very successful. British losses of men and machines were heavy, and the prospects of clearing the area for the Sea Lion landings were enhanced. But the airfields were quickly patched up, the radar stations were rebuilt, and by mid-August the Fighter Command had operationally recovered. In fact, because of the energetic efforts of the Minister of Aircraft Production, Lord Beaverbrook, Dowding more than made up his losses in fighter aircraft. The pilot shortage was being somewhat rectified by a speed-up of graduation from the Training Schools, the retraining of bomber pilots, and shifting pilots from other branches of the military.

Göring meanwhile had been planning Operation Eagle, a massive saturation of the southern ports and airfields. Operation Eagle had to be postponed several times in early August because of bad weather. Then on August 13, British radar stations picked up signals of very large formations of approaching aircraft: Operation Eagle had begun. The attackers came in several waves, and Park's fighters rose to meet them. Some of the German bombers got through and did further damage, but the Hurricanes and Spitfires shot down forty-seven of the enemy planes at the cost of thirteen British craft.

Bad flying weather returned, causing a two-day suspension of the operation. By August 15, favorable weather prompted Göring to order the renewal of the bombings. He declared that the objective was to obliterate the Royal Air Force planes and facilities. On that day, and into August 16, four successive waves came across the Channel and across the North Sea from bases in Norway. Luftflotte Two and Luftflotte Three bombers got past Park's fighters and the antiaircraft guns in sufficient numbers to destroy four aircraft factories and five airfields in the vicinity of London. But the bombers from Norway had been sent with insufficient fighter escort and they were brought down in large numbers. In those two days, the Luftwaffe had seventy-six planes shot down, the worst damage in a short period the German Air Force would ever suffer. In all, between August 8 and August 26, the British fighters destroyed 602 German aircraft—mostly bombers, especially the Stuka dive bombers, which proved very vulnerable. In that same period, 259 British fighter planes were shot down.

Yet, despite their losses, the Luftwaffe attacks intensified. Göring was convinced that, weather permitting, Britain could be brought to its knees in about two weeks. During the last week of August and the first week of September, 1940, there were over thirty major attacks, averaging more than one thousand planes each time. Most of the bombs fell on the airfields and sector stations of Group No. 11. Vice Marshal Park admitted that the damage was extensive and that the fighting efficiency of his command was being seriously impaired. Dowding saw the mounting loss of fighter pilots as critical; in those two weeks, 103 R.A.F. pilots were killed or missing. By September 6, the Fighter Command (and therefore all of Britain) was on the verge of defeat. Across the Channel, Operation Sea Lion preparations were stepped up with the news of the Luftwaffe successes.

Then, in early September, Göring made a serious tactical mistake. He ordered the Luftwaffe to shift its attacks from the R.A.F. facilities to terror attacks on London and other cities. Göring had received intelligence reports that the Fighter Command had been neutralized and no longer had sufficient strength to stop his bombers. Those reports were wrong, as the events of the following week would show. If Göring had pursued his objective of smashing the Fighter Command, he might have won the Battle of Britain.

On September 7, the British government sent out the code signal "Cromwell," signifying that the expected invasion was now at hand. On that same day, nearly four hundred German bombers hit East London, killing more than one thousand civilians and doing extensive damage to houses, docks, and warehouses. That night, another 250 bombers, guided by the light of the extensive fires, did more damage to the British capital. Park sent up his fighters to intercept, and in the air battles another thirty-eight German planes went down, as did twenty-eight British. But what was most important, Park had demonstrated that the Fighter Command was still functioning and lethal. London was again bombed on September 9, but with less effect than on September 7 because only about half of the attacking planes got through to their targets. The Royal Navy and R.A.F. Bomber Command, meanwhile, had increased their shelling and bombing of the German invasion ports. It was obvious that the Germans did not yet control the Channel or the air space over England. Faced with that knowledge, Hitler postponed Operation Sea Lion to September 27.

What proved to be Göring's last effort to clear the way for the invasion came on September 15, 1940. He threw everything he had into that day's fighting. One hundred twenty-three bombers with five fighter escorts each went out from the continental bases. Park's squadrons, reinforced by planes from other British Air Groups, went to meet the Luftwaffe. The air battle began about noon and lasted until the evening of September 15. When that day ended and the Luftwaffe streaked back to its bases, sixty German planes had been destroyed, with British losses of only twenty-six aircraft. September 15, 1940, would later be identified as the day the R.A.F. won the Battle of Britain. "We still keep this day, and I hope we will always keep it," Harold Macmillan would write, "in commemoration of our victory."

Two days later, realizing that the Luftwaffe could not gain air supremacy and that it was now too late for favorable weather, Hitler ordered the indefinite postponement of Operation Sea Lion. His interest turned eastward instead, and German plans for the invasion of Russia commenced.

Britain would still have to endure repeated pounding by German bombers in the later so-called "Blitz" of 1940-1941, but in the summer of 1940 the "gallant few" of the R.A.F. Command had saved Britain from invasion. Adding up the final cost, it appears that six to seven hundred British fighter planes had been destroyed between July and September, 1940, as against some fourteen hundred German aircraft of all types.

**Pertinent Literature**

Spaight, James M. *The Battle of Britain, 1940*. London: Geoffrey Bles, 1941.

This book has the value and immediacy of primary source material because it was written in early 1941 while the Battle of Britain was still raging. At that time, the author held the position of Principal Assistant Secretary to the Air Ministry, which gave him an excellent opportunity to observe the lengthy Battle of Britain as it unfolded.

Spaight, unlike most later historians, regards the battle as having commenced with the first large German air raids on June 18, 1940, when some one hundred Luftwaffe bombers hit towns in eastern and southern Britain, as well as coastal shipping. Those raids continued into July, 1940, killing or wounding more than eight hundred people.

He then traces the major incidents in the British defense of their island into the winter of 1940-1941: August 8 when the Germans lost sixty aircraft and had their "first defeat off our shores," August 15-16 which saw 180 enemy planes shot down, and then the first terrible raids on London of August 24. The attacks on London continued through that autumn, while the cities of Coventry, Birmingham, Southampton, Portsmouth, and Manchester also received heavy blows from German planes. All brought grievous civilian casualties and heavy property damage. Between August and December, 1940, 22,500 civilians were killed and 32,000 seriously wounded. During the Battle of Britain civilian casualties ran as high as those of the military. Despite all that, Spaight observes that the German air attacks did not seriously dislocate or interrupt armaments production; in fact, by early 1941 the output of war materials had steadily mounted.

All that summer, the threat of invasion remained. Spaight assumes that September 15, 1940, was the date the Germans set for their first invasion launchings. But that was the day the Fighter Command "shot the Luftwaffe out of the sky" to blunt the projected invasion, while the Bomber Command in those weeks struck at the invasion ports in France, Belgium, and the Netherlands, sinking barges, damaging ships, igniting docks. Smoke from the bombing, he writes, could be seen across the Channel, and many dead German bodies washed ashore on the British coast.

Now, as the threat of invasion lifted, Spaight most feared a blockade of Britain by the German Navy. German control of the Channel ports and the presence of a large fleet of U-boats seemed to indicate the real possibility that a blockade which could strangle Britain by stopping the flow of vital supplies from America was in the offing. Therefore, as he saw it, the most important task of the war would be to destroy the submarines and prevent a blockade.

A second important task had already begun when R.A.F. bombers attacked the continental ports and then went on to hit petroleum plants in Germany itself. Berlin itself had been bombed thirty-five times in the summer and autumn of 1940, and numerous other cities were also hit. Spaight admits that undoubtedly civilians were killed by British bombs, although he piously declares that "British airmen do not deliberately attack non-combatants."

Even as Spaight writes, the "callous ham-fisted" night bombings by the Luftwaffe are going on, and he speaks of further devastation ahead. But Britain will carry the war to the "Herrenvolk," and, by a combination of British sea and air power, the mighty German armies ultimately will be defeated.

Middleton, Drew. *The Sky Suspended: The Battle of Britain*. London: Secker and Warburg, 1960.

Drew Middleton, an American journalist working in London at the time of the German attacks, wrote this fine account on the basis of his own immediate experiences and from materials later available.

As he points out, the Battle of Britain is important for two major reasons: it was the first decisive defeat of German armed forces in World War II, and it was the greatest encounter of manned aircraft during the war. With the coming of rocketry and ballistic missiles after 1945, air power in terms of fighters and bombers drew to an end, so there will never be another encounter quite like the Battle of Britain.

Focusing on the composition and strength of the Luftwaffe, Middleton provides some useful statistics. As of August 10, the German Air Force had 4,295 aircraft, of which 3,242 were operational combat planes. Of those, 2,355 were deployed in the three Luftflotten (Air Fleets) stationed in Western Europe for service against the United Kingdom. Broken down as to type, the three air fleets had 998 long range bombers, 316 dive bombers, 702 single engine, and 261 twin engine fighters and fighter bombers. Of all of these, the most valuable craft were the Junker 88 heavy bombers, and their escorts, the Messerschmitt 109 and 110 fighters; those were the planes that nearly gained victory for Germany. The famed and feared Stuka (Junker 87) dive bombers which had wreaked havoc in Poland and the Low Countries earlier proved almost useless against the British fighters and were withdrawn midway through the Battle of Britain.

When speaking of British preparations, two decisions stand out in Middleton's estimation: the construction of the heavily armored and armed Hurricane and Spitfire fighters, and the development and building of the radar detection system. The Germans had also worked on a technique similar to radar but it was used only at sea. Never fully appreciating the value of the British radar, Göring failed to knock out the radar stations in the United Kingdom, and that failure may be counted as a major factor in the German defeat.

Middleton thinks of the Battle of Britain as beginning in May, 1940, and ending in April, 1941, during which there were three phases. The first and most important phase came with the daylight air battles. His descriptions of the aerial dogfights in the skies over Britain are stirring. He was an eyewitness to a number of those encounters and spoke to the pilots afterward, or took from their flight logs their feelings and reactions. He also offers vignettes of the life of ordinary British people during the bombings of the first phase. The second phase came with the day and night bombings of London—the Blitz—and the third phase was the bombing of the provincial cities which ended the battle in the spring of 1941.

In his concluding chapter, Middleton explains the significance of the Battle of Britain. Suppose, he writes, that the Germans had won the battle, either by invasion or by collapse and surrender after the bombing. Then Hitler, utilizing British industrial output, could have turned eastward much strengthened, and might well have conquered Russia. The German General Runstedt is quoted as saying that the Battle of Britain was the decisive battle of the war. If Britain had gone down, Germany could have defeated Russia in the next year. The British victory, furthermore, destroyed the myth of the invincibility of the Luftwaffe; British radar showed that Germany was not technically superior in all respects; and the victory not only gave heart to Britons but also convinced others—particularly Americans—that the defeat of Germany was possible. — *J.W.P.*

## Additional Recommended Reading

Churchill, Winston S. *The S cond World War.* Vol. II: *Their Finest Hour.* Cambridge, Mass.: Houghton Mifflin Company, 1949. The wartime Prime Minister devotes a chapter of his history, *The Second World War*, to the Battle of Britain. Particularly valuable for his recollections of conversations with military leaders and for tables of battle statistics.

Wilmot, Chester. *The Struggle for Europe.* New York: Harper & Row Publishers, 1952. Probably the best brief discussion of the preparations for Operation Sea Lion and of the fighting of the Battle of Britain. Clearly and succinctly written.

Fleming, Peter. *Operation Sea Lion.* New York: Simon and Schuster, 1957. A thorough narrative of the military and moral elements that went into the German invasion plans and the British response. Excellent analysis of the reasons for the German failure.

Ansel, Walter. *Hitler Confronts England.* Durham, N.C.: Duke University Press, 1960. An exceptionally detailed study of Operation Sea Lion plans and preparations, with many maps, diagrams, and illustrations. Very difficult to read because of the author's convoluted style.

Collier, Basil. *The Battle of Britain.* London: B. T. Batsford, 1962. A balanced, well-written study. Finds that the British victory can be attributed primarily to two factors: the superior system of early warning and control, and the fact that Dowding and Park were better tacticians than their German counterparts. Contains a twelve-page chronology of events relating to the Battle of Britain.

Panter-Downes, Mollie. *London War Notes, 1939-1945.* New York: Farrar, Straus and Giroux, 1971. A collection of correspondence to the *New York Times* by a woman living in London during the Battle of Britain and the Blitz which tells how the bombings affected people in the capital.

Taylor, A. J. P. *The Second World War.* New York: G. P. Putnam's Sons, 1975. Includes an account of the background of Operation Sea Lion and of the Battle of Britain. Taylor, unlike most historians, finds that Göring's Operation Eagle campaign had "nothing in common" with Operation Sea Lion. He also states that Hitler took almost no interest in the invasion of England.

# JAPAN OCCUPIES INDOCHINA

*Type of event:* Military: armed expansion and diplomatic response
*Time:* September, 1940-July, 1941
*Locale:* French colony of Indochina

### Principal personages:

YASUKE MATSUOKA (1880-1946), Japanese Foreign Minister, 1940-1941

CORDELL HULL (1871-1955), United States Secretary of State, 1933-1944

FRANKLIN DELANO ROOSEVELT (1882-1945), thirty-second President of the United States, 1933-1945

## Summary of Event

It took Japan two bites to swallow Indochina: the first, in September 1940, devoured the northern half of that French colony; the second, in July, 1941, consumed what was left. While these events were of the utmost importance to the people involved, and while they triggered international responses of far-reaching consequences, they have been all but forgotten in the global drama of World War II.

Indochina was a French colony and thus under the protection of the French Republic. Unfortunately for Indochina, however, France was not in a position to defend its colonies. By June, 1940, the efficient German armies had conquered France. Territory which Germany did not occupy was organized into a collaborationist government located at the French town of Vichy. Though more than fifty thousand French troops remained in Indochina, they could expect little help from the mother country. Indochina was vulnerable.

Meanwhile, Japan sought to make Asia its economic and military preserve. Japan called it the "Greater East Asia Co-Prosperity Sphere." However, in 1940 Japan was having difficulty in persuading China to follow the scenario. Japanese armies had been waging war in China since 1937, with considerable military success but without any political success. China would not surrender. Guerrilla warfare tied down large numbers of Japanese troops, causing considerable strain on the Japanese economy. Japanese occupation of Indochina would help the war effort by cutting off the Chinese supply line which ran from Haiphong in Indochina to Chungking in China. Also, French Indochina would have to be taken before Japan could move into other, richer portions of Southeast Asia.

The United States disapproved of Japan's actions. Since the start of the Sino-Japanese War in 1937, America had expressed its dislike for Japanese expansion. Initially, protests were reserved in tone; but with the rapid German military victories in the spring of 1940, the likelihood of Japan moving into Southeast Asia increased and the United States became more vehement in its opposition. Most notable of the American actions was the transfer of the United States Fleet from San Diego to Pearl Harbor in the Hawaiian Islands. By stationing the fleet on the Japanese flank, President Franklin D. Roosevelt and Secretary of State Cordell Hull were warning Japan that the United States would not stand idly by while Japan pushed into Southeast Asia and the oil-rich Netherlands East Indies.

This was the situation when Japan decided that the time had come to occupy the northern half of French Indochina. Diplomatic negotiations looking toward the occupation began in June, 1940, but were stalled by French officials who hoped that the United States would come to the aid of their beleaguered colony. In addition, the French troops in Indochina were quite willing to resist. The United States was not prepared to confront Japan over northern Indochina, and by themselves the French forces were no match for the Japanese Army. Thus, when the Japanese declared that they were coming in either with or without an agreement with the French authorities, France capitulated.

The United States responded by embargoing the export to Japan of all iron and steel scrap. This mild form of economic sanction was designed to persuade Japan that any further expansion would not be tolerated. The scrap embargo was a nuisance to Japan, but it did not seriously hinder its ability to wage war. Had Secretary Hull sought a real confrontation, he could have employed his major weapon, an oil embargo; but oil was such a crucial commodity that Hull feared that such an action would provoke Japan to make a dash for the oil reserves in the Netherlands East Indies. In addition, it was possible that the Japanese move into northern Indochina was merely connected with the war against China and was not part of a general southern expansion. Since Hull had no intention of provoking a confrontation with Japan over China, September, 1940, did not seem an appropriate time to employ meaningful economic sanctions against Japan.

The American scrap embargo did not deter Japanese expansion. In fact, it provided a rationale for further Japanese southern expansion. The Japanese had complained that they needed to establish their "Co-Prosperity Sphere" because the Western powers, notably the United States and Great Britain, controlled access to critical raw materials. Without a secure supply of such raw materials, Japan would always be vulnerable to the whims of the West. The scrap embargo supported this interpretation, so, rather than being dissuaded, Japanese leaders decided to accelerate their southern expansion.

The opportunity to strike farther south came in June, 1941. Germany had turned its war machine toward Russia. With Russia involved in a war with Germany, Japan had to decide whether to strike at its age-old enemy to the north or take advantage of Russian weakness to concentrate Japanese military power in a major push to the south. Japan decided to go south, and on July 27 occupied the remainder of French Indochina. This time there were no mixed signals. Japan was clearly moving to attack the Indies and probably knock out the American-owned Philippines and the

British naval base of Singapore. Roosevelt responded with full economic sanctions, meaning an embargo on oil. The British and the Dutch did the same. Japan had a choice: it could either give up or it could push forward toward the oil in the Indies. Japan decided to strike out for the oil. Before it could do so, however, Japan had to remove the American fleet poised on its flank, which it did at Pearl Harbor on Sunday morning, December 7, 1941.

## Pertinent Literature

Feis, Herbert. *The Road to Pearl Harbor*. Princeton, N.J.: Princeton University Press, 1950.

The American response to Japan's occupation of French Indochina is well described in this older but still valuable book. Though Feis writes primarily about the American government and the persons in it, he includes enough background material concerning Japanese motives to provide a total picture. His emphasis is upon the Department of State; but here, too, there is enough reference to other parts of the Roosevelt Administration to give a balanced picture.

Feis emphasizes that Japanese southern expansion divided the American policymakers. Some, notably Secretary of War Henry L. Stimson and Secretary of the Treasury Henry Morgenthau, Jr., wanted to confront Japanese expansion and bring a halt to the Asian war. Secretary of State Cordell Hull, on the other hand, was more cautious. Hull was, of course, equally opposed to Japanese southern expansion, but, according to Feis, was intent upon avoiding a confrontation with Japan if it was at all possible. These differing attitudes resulted in conflict within the Roosevelt Administration which was most clearly shown in the debate over embargoing exports to Japan.

Japan bought many important commodities from the United States, and Morgenthau and Stimson sought to use this economic leverage to compel Japan to give up its aggression. The crucial commodity was oil, for without it the Japanese war machine could not operate. Secretary Hull fought the advocates of a strong embargo, especially including oil, because he feared that the consequences of economic warfare would be military warfare. Feis agrees with Hull's analysis of the situation, especially the Secretary's fear that an oil embargo would push Japan into a quick drive south.

While describing Hull as cautious, Feis also depicts him as approving a gradual but consistent increase in economic pressure on Japan. The scrap metal embargo of September, 1940, was among the first of these economic measures which Hull advocated. During the following winter the list of embargoed items grew. Feis contends that the growth of the embargo was part of a plan which had Hull's approval. (More recent scholarship has questioned how systematic this process was and even whether the embargoing was directed against Japan or in favor of stockpiling badly needed commodities in the United States.) Whatever the precise nature of the embargo program, oil was not included; and as long as oil flowed freely to Japan, Japan would not be brought to her knees.

The crisis came in July, 1941, when Japanese soldiers marched into southern Indochina. Feis describes how the United States Navy did not want war with the Japanese at that time; but the President believed that something had to be done. Roosevelt's retaliation was to freeze all Japanese assets in the United States. Without money the Japanese could not purchase oil. However, Roosevelt too did not want a war over French Indochina, so he offered a concession: the release of a moderate amount of oil to Japan. As long as Japan was receiving some oil from the United States, Roosevelt believed, there would be no war. But when the plan was put into operation, no oil flowed to Japan. Feis is not able to explain why the carrot was never offered.

After nearly three decades, Feis's book stands as the best study of the subject, although in some respects it has not worn well with age. Students of American foreign policy who read Feis today will note that his book is a product of the World War II era: it was written shortly after the end of the war by a man who had been a State Department officer in the years prior to the Pearl Harbor attack. Feis's experiences in the State Department gave him valuable insights into how the government functioned, but those same experiences left him unsympathetic to Japan's justification for its actions. Feis is aware of one of the Japanese justifications—that Japanese expansion was only a defensive response to a threatening combination of Western powers—but he rejects this with the comment that "it was only because Japan was pursuing threatening aims, that it was opposed and impeded." To Feis, it was Japan that forced the issue of expanding through Asia, and it was Japan that made the crucial decision to move into southern French Indochina. Feis does not consider that so long as Japanese military aggression was contained in China there was no war with the United States. But when Japanese armies pushed into southern Indochina in July, 1941, they threatened territory conquered and ruled by French, Dutch, British, and American forces. In this context the conflict between Japan and the United States can be viewed as a great-power rivalry over the riches of Southeast Asia rather than as a simple case of Japanese aggression.

Lu, David J. *From the Marco Polo Bridge to Pearl Harbor: Japan's Entry into World War II*. Washington, D.C.: Public Affairs Press, 1961.

Perhaps because the United States won and Japan lost World War II, the Japanese side of the events leading to that war has not been given much consideration. David Lu sets out to examine the decision-making process in Japan and ends writing a narrative history not only of the political problems confronting Japan but of the military and diplomatic ones as well. Lu begins with the state of Japanese politics prior to the beginning of the Sino-Japanese war in 1937 and traces events to the Pearl Harbor attack.

Lu explains how Indochina was important to Japan with respect to the war in China. By 1940, Japanese armies had pushed the Chinese troops deep into southern China and away from the coastal cities, and as a result, foreign sources of supply had to enter China through routes such as that provided by northern Indochina. In addition, if Japan sought to move farther south, it would have to secure French Indochina in order to protect the Japanese flank and to provide a staging area for military operations against the British, Dutch, and American colonies.

Lu recognizes that the expansionists were present long before the Sino-Japanese war, but he also demonstrates that American hostility toward Japanese expansion in China pushed Japanese leaders toward a policy of southern expansion in order to avoid dependence upon American-supplied strategic raw materials. This policy existed in 1939, and the opportunity to implement it came in 1940 when German military victories in Europe forced the European powers to abandon Asia, leaving that region vulnerable.

The situation was complicated by the German conquest of the Netherlands and the resulting flight of the Netherlands government into exile. Secretary of State Cordell Hull feared that Japan might take advantage of this situation to extend Japanese control over the Netherlands East Indies,

and he warned Japan against any such move. Japanese leaders took this warning as evidence of American (or possible British) interest in acquiring the Dutch colony. As a result, the fall of the Netherlands both created an opportunity for Japanese expansion and increased Japan's fear of encirclement by Western powers.

To break this encirclement and force the United States to remain neutral in the Asian war, Foreign Minister Yasuke Matsuoka urged an acceleration of the program of southern expansion and an alliance with Germany. Matsuoka hoped that the provocation which the southern expansion would cause would be offset by the alliance with Germany, and that the United States would remain neutral. Since he was a graduate of the University of Oregon Law School, few people in Japan questioned Matsuoka's judgment concerning the American government.

However, Matsuoka was wrong. Both the southern expansion and the alliance with Germany hurt Japanese-American relations. As the United States became more hostile toward Japan, Japanese leaders saw the need for a secure supply of raw materials as the most important problem facing them. Lu does not justify Japan's drive into Southeast Asia in search of oil, but neither does he adopt the usual view that Japan was simply another Fascist state bent upon conquest. Lu explains that Japan first tried to negotiate an agreement with the Netherlands East Indies which would permit Japan to buy the oil it needed. The Indies government, fearing the Japanese designs on Southeast Asia, refused to sell oil in the quantities Japan wanted. Unable to buy what they needed and correctly assuming that American oil could not be considered dependable, the Japanese leaders decided that it would be necessary to take what they could not obtain through peaceful negotiations.

Lu's thesis is that the failure to negotiate an oil agreement with the Indies discredited diplomacy as a solution. Military leaders who had always thought that diplomacy was a futile gesture now argued that military force was the only solution to Japan's problems. Matsuoka had failed to gain the required goals through diplomacy, and he fell from power. It is Lu's thesis that Matsuoka was actually a moderate who was not at all anti-American. His failure, however, brought Hideki Tojo into power. Under Tojo's leadership, the two nations went to war. — *J.G.U.*

## Additional Recommended Reading

Anderson, Irvine H., Jr. *The Standard Vacuum Oil Company and United States East Asian Policy, 1933-1941.* Princeton, N.J.: Princeton University Press, 1975. An account of how a major United States corporation coped with Japanese expansion.

Burns, Richard Dean and Edward M. Bennett, eds. *Diplomats in Crisis: United States-Chinese-Japanese Relations, 1919-1941.* Santa Barbara, Calif.: ABC-CLIO, 1974. A series of essays on the prominent diplomats involved in interwar diplomacy.

Langer, William L. and S. Everett Gleason. *The Undeclared War, 1940-1941.* New York: Harper & Row Publishers, 1953. The basic study of pre-Pearl Harbor diplomacy covering both Asia and Europe.

Morison, Samuel Eliot. *History of United States Naval Operations in World War II.* Vol. III: *The Rising Sun in the Pacific, 1931-April 1942.* Boston: Little, Brown and Company, 1947. The naval aspects of Japanese expansion.

Schroeder, Paul W. *The Axis Alliance and Japanese-American Relations, 1941.* Ithaca, N.Y.: Cornell University Press, 1958. A controversial interpretation which concentrates on the influence of the Japanese-German alliance on United States policy.

Utley, Jonathan G. "Upstairs, Downstairs at Foggy Bottom: Oil Exports and Japan, 1940-41," in *Prologue, the Journal of the National Archives.* VIII (Spring, 1976), pp. 17-28. An examination of the program of economic pressure applied against Japan.

# GERMANY INVADES THE BALKANS

*Type of event:* Military: expansion of war into Southeast Europe
*Time:* April 6, 1941
*Locale:* The Balkan Peninsula

*Principal personages:*

ADOLF HITLER (1889-1945), Chancellor and Führer of Germany, 1933-1945

BENITO MUSSOLINI (1883-1945), Fascist Dictator of Italy, 1922-1943

JOSEPH STALIN (IOSIF VISSARIONOVICH DZHUGASHVILI) (1879-1953), Dictator of the U.S.S.R., 1924-1953

PRINCE PAUL (KARAGEORGEVICH) (1893-    ), Yugoslav Regent, 1934-1941

PETER II (KARAGEORGEVICH) (1923-1970), King of Yugoslavia, 1934-1945

GENERAL DUŠAN SIMOVIĆ (1882-1962), leader of Yugoslav *coup* in 1941; and Prime Minister of Yugoslavia, 1941-1942

BORIS III OF SAXE-COBURG (1894-1943), King of Bulgaria, 1918-1943

BOGDAN FILOV (1883-1945), Prime Minister of Bulgaria, 1940-1943

CAROL II OF HOHENZOLLERN-SIGMARINGEN (1893-1953), King of Rumania, 1930-1940

## Summary of Event

On the morning of April 6, 1941, German planes and troops attacked Yugoslavia and Greece. Following its *Blitzkrieg* pattern employed elsewhere, the Wehrmacht defeated these Balkan states in a matter of days and Germany with her Allies—Italy, Bulgaria, and Hungary—occupied the countries until they were driven out in 1944. Superficially it appeared that these small Balkan nations had fallen victim to Hitler's insatiable appetite for world domination. In fact, the matter was more complicated because bringing the hot war into the Balkans had not been the German leader's plan.

By the summer of 1940 the Axis dominated the European continent. France lay defeated and England isolated. The Soviet Union was an uncertain friend in the East, but nevertheless still allied to the German Reich by their mutual defense pact of 1939. The smaller countries of Europe were either occupied by the Axis or firmly neutral. The latter was the case of the nations of Southeast Europe.

Even before the war began, these countries had fallen into the economic sphere of Germany as most of their foreign trade involved the Central European power. Politically, the parliamentary regimes of the 1920's became royal or military dictator-

444

ships, all of which aped at least part of the Fascist programs and ideologies of Italy and Germany. By agreement Hitler recognized the Balkans as the Italian sphere of influence; and indeed, when the Germans occupied Czechoslovakia in the spring of 1939, Mussolini soon followed suit by incorporating Albania into the Italian kingdom.

Events, however, in the first year of the war changed the situation. Germany's victories were so rapid that they dismayed her friends and foes alike. Shortly after the fall of France, the Soviet Union demanded the Rumanian province of Bessarabia which had belonged to the Russian empire before the 1917 revolution. Rumania's King Carol II asked Hitler for advice, but the Führer, not ready to go to war against Stalin told the Balkan monarch to acquiesce.

Moscow's maneuvers in the Balkans presented a new problem for Berlin. Spheres of influence in this area had not been clearly defined by the German-Soviet agreement. If Bulgaria fell under the Kremlin's influence, German strategic interests would be imperiled. Now, after occupying Bessarabia, the Soviets suggested to Sofia that they could help Bulgaria regain the Dobrudja region which the nation had lost to Rumania in 1913. Hitler at this point in the summer of 1940 decided to invade the Soviet Union the following spring. He wished to settle both Bulgaria's and Hungary's *irredenta* questions with Rumania by diplomatic means in order that the Balkan peninsula might remain in a state of friendly neutrality while Germany was at war in the East, and indeed, by September, he successfully brought all parties to agreement on territorial adjustments.

Nevertheless, there was yet another impediment to Hitler's plans. Mussolini had joined the war during the French campaign, in part because he felt that Hitler's military successes were detracting from his own prestige. Now with the Rumanian settlements Germany had even entered into the Italian sphere—Southeastern Europe. The Italian dictator decided to undertake a military campaign in the Balkans without German participation. Mussolini's natural object of attack in the region was Yugoslavia; but Hitler objected to any adventures in that country, so Mussolini planned an invasion of Greece, scarcely informing his German ally of his intentions. On October 28, 1940, the Italian army crossed the Albanian border into Greece. After some immediate Italian successes, the Greeks, stoutly defending their nation, drove their foe back, and Mussolini was humiliated. He now had to ask an angry Hitler for aid in his Balkan campaign.

The German army which had entered in force into Rumania in preparation for the planned Russian invasion was now to be used first to bail out the Italians. On December 13, Hitler ordered "Operation Marita," the rapid defeat of Greece. The plan required that German troops invade Greece through Bulgaria while Yugoslavia remained neutral. The Führer asked both Bulgaria and Yugoslavia to join the recently formed Three-Power Pact (Germany, Italy, and Japan) to affirm their commitment. The Bulgarian monarch, Boris III, agreed, and at the beginning of March, 1941,

Prime Minister Bogdan Filov traveled to Vienna to sign the pact. German troops entered Bulgaria in force shortly thereafter. On March 26, the Yugoslav Prime Minister and Foreign Minister also signed the Three Power Pact. However, the next day a military *coup d'état*, led by air force General Dušan Simović, seized power in Belgrade and dismissed the pro-German regent Prince Paul. His young nephew King Peter was declared to have reached his majority. Crowds in Belgrade were jubilant and openly anti-Nazi.

The new Yugoslav government assured Hitler that they would nevertheless remain neutral in the upcoming campaign; but the German dictator was outraged at the behavior of the Yugoslavs and decided that, along with Greece, the South Slav kingdom would be invaded and destroyed. Thus in the wake of the invasion Yugoslavia disappeared. Two small states—an occupied Serbia and an independent Croatia with an Italian monarch and Fascist (Ustashi) government—replaced the central part of the kingdom. The remainder was divided among Germany's allies.

## Pertinent Literature

Van Creveld, Martin. *Hitler's Strategy 1940-1941: The Balkan Clue*. Cambridge: Cambridge University Press, 1973.

Using new materials, including detailed diplomatic and military documents, and reconsidering past assumptions, Van Creveld develops in this volume a new interpretation of the war in the Balkans. While past accounts took literally Mussolini's statement that Hitler would read about his Greek campaign "in the newspapers," Van Creveld convincingly demonstrates that the two dictators conferred on the matter during their historic meeting at the Brenner Pass on October 4, 1940.

Van Creveld's main thesis, in fact, is that Hitler had more interest in the initial undertaking of the Greek campaign than had hitherto been supposed. According to the author, Hitler distinguished between Balkan Yugoslavia, which he required to be neutral for support of his 1940 policy, and Mediterranean Greece. At first, in the summer, he expressed to Mussolini a disinterest in his plans to invade Greece. However, in late September when the Führer called off his plans to invade England, the situation changed.

Van Creveld asserts that Hitler now favored a Greek invasion to implement his new peripheral strategy against the British Empire. His former indifference to an Italian invasion of Greece now turned to encouragement, and when the two dictators met at the Brenner Pass, the Führer gave his Italian counterpart his approval. Since Van Creveld does not believe that Hitler had yet decided to invade Russia, he does not consider this as a reason for the change in strategy. His portrayal of Hitler as the chief instigator of the Greek adventure, or at least as a partner with responsibility equal to Mussolini's is a controversial conclusion arrived at largely through speculation.

Van Creveld conveniently divides the war in Southeast Europe into two stages—a Mediterranean campaign, that is, the peripheral strategy against Great Britain, and the Russian campaign. He concludes that Hitler did not decide to invade the Soviet Union until after December of 1940. As evidence he points to the offer that German Foreign Minister Joachim von Ribbentrop made to his Soviet counterpart, Vyacheslav Molotov, during the latter's visit to Berlin in November. The Germans offered the Soviets a chance to join the Three Power Pact if they turned their attentions away from Europe. Stalin refused. It was at this point, Van Creveld says, that Hitler decided to go to war against the Soviet Union. Then the purpose of the Balkan campaign changed to

protect the German flank during the Eastern invasion. Unfortunately, Van Creveld does not refute the overwhelming evidence that Hitler planned the invasion of the U.S.S.R. several months earlier. The offer to Molotov was merely a ruse which the Nazis did not seriously expect Stalin to take up. However, neither the actual overlapping of the two military goals nor the question of who actually initiated the Greek campaign (Hitler or Mussolini) seriously damages Van Creveld's main thesis that events in the South Balkans influenced German strategy both against England and the Soviet Union.

On another question the author demonstrates that the German campaign did not in itself delay the German timetable in its Eastern invasion. Communication and supply difficulties would have postponed the proposed Soviet operation in any case.

Miller, Marshall Lee. *Bulgaria During the Second World War*. Stanford, Calif.: Stanford University Press, 1975.

Marshall Miller, a Washington attorney, wrote this book based on research he carried out as a postgraduate student at Oxford, using original Bulgarian and German documents gathered in Sofia, Washington, London, and elsewhere. He was even able to gain access to Bulgarian archives which were closed for public use. Miller also incorporated material he collected in interviews from surviving participants of the events he describes. The chief value of the volume is that it presents a comprehensive history of Bulgaria's participation in World War II, including domestic as well as foreign policy.

Thus he enables the English-reading public to see how Bulgaria fit into German plans.

According to Miller, Bulgaria's leaders—both King Boris and Prime Minister Filov—wished to keep the country neutral in World War II. He describes Prime Minister Filov as pro-German but maintains that King Boris was neutral in attitude as well as intention. Sofia's major goals were to preserve domestic tranquillity and obtain Bulgarian *irredenta* through peaceful means. Bulgaria became more pro-German after World War II began because Nazi military victories made it the dominant power in the region. After the Soviet Union annexed Bessarabia, King Boris found it very difficult to turn down Moscow's offer to help the Balkan kingdom regain Dobrudja. It was under these circumstances that King Boris asked Hitler to arrange the return of that disputed area. The successful German resolution of the problem placed Bulgaria in the Reich's debt. However, when King Boris made a state visit to Hitler in November, 1940, he was still reluctant to join the Three Power Pact. He did promise to allow the Germans to use Bulgaria as a staging ground in "Operation Marita." Several months later, "yielding" to German pressure, Bulgaria joined the pact.

Miller also believes that fear of the Soviet Union and the internal Bulgarian Communist movement had a significant bearing on the relationship of Sofia to Berlin. In the period of the Nazi-Soviet accord (1939-1941), the Bulgarian Communist Party enjoyed an unaccustomed measure of freedom of action. Some Communists even won election to the overwhelmingly government-dominated Parliament.

In the fall of 1939, the Soviet Union began applying diplomatic pressure on Bulgaria to get the kingdom to sign a mutual defense treaty similar to the one the U.S.S.R. had with Germany, but which in fact was directed against the Third Reich. The special Soviet ambassador, Arkadi Sobolev, came to Sofia for this purpose. At the same time, Miller asserts, the Soviet embassy leaked news of the secret Sobolev negotiations to the Bulgarian Communist Party and helped them organize a public campaign for the signing of a pact. Miller concludes, that the effect of this activity was just the opposite of that which Moscow hoped to achieve, for Hitler's argument that "as long as the Russians knew that Bulgaria was not a member of the Tripartite [Three Power] Pact, Russia would try to blackmail Bulgaria in every conceivable way" carried much weight in Bulgaria's decision to move closer to Germany.

Miller shows that the strengthening of ties between Germany and Bulgaria because of international events was reflected in domestic policies which introduced institutions and laws similar to those in Nazi Germany into the Balkan kingdom. For example, late in 1940 the Parliament authorized labor and youth organizations similar to the German "Strength Through Joy" and "Hitler Youth." At the same session the legislative body also passed restrictions against Bulgaria's Jews and international organizations associated with Western Europe, such as the Masons and Rotarians. (These laws were hitherto unheard of in Bulgaria.) In brief, Miller's book allows us to see how German policies at the beginning of World War II affected the fate of a small Balkan country. — *F.B.C.*

## Additional Recommended Reading

Barker, Elizabeth. *British Policy in South-East Europe in the Second World War.* London: Macmillan and Company, 1976. A British view of the war in the Balkans, based on foreign office documents, by a respected wartime correspondent of the region.

Weinberg, Gerhard L. *Germany and the Soviet Union, 1939-1941*. Leiden: E. J. Brill, 1954. The classic diplomatic study of the events leading up to the German invasion of the Soviet Union, including activities in the Balkans.

Filov, Bogdan. "The Diary of Bogdan Filov," in *Southeastern Europe*. Vols. 1-4, 1974-1977. A five-part series of extracts from the daily wartime diary of the Bulgarian Prime Minister, the first part containing the record of the German entrance into the Balkans.

Ciano, Galeazzo. *The Ciano Diaries, 1939-1943*. Edited by Hugh Gibson. New York: Howard Fertig, 1973. A record of events including Italian-German relations in the Balkans by the Italian Foreign Minister, Mussolini's son-in-law.

Ristić, Dragiša N. *Yugoslavia's Revolution of 1941*. University Park: Pennsylvania State University Press, 1966. A scholarly monograph on Yugoslavia's role in the Balkan invasion.

# GERMAN INVASION OF RUSSIA

*Type of event:* Military: surprise attack by one nation on another
*Time:* June 22, 1941
*Locale:* The Soviet Union

*Principal personages:*

ADOLF HITLER (1889-1945), Chancellor and Führer of Germany, 1933-1945

JOSEPH STALIN (IOSIF VISSARIONOVICH DZHUGASHVILI) (1879-1953), Dictator of the U.S.S.R., 1924-1953

FIELD MARSHAL HEINRICH ALFRED HERMANN WALTHER VON BRAUCHITSCH (1881-1948), Commander in Chief of the German Army

FIELD MARSHAL WILHELM JOSEPH FRANZ VON LEEB (1876-1956), German Commander of Army Group North on the Russian Front

FIELD MARSHAL FEDOR VON BOCK (1880-1945), German Commander of Army Group Center on the Russian Front

FIELD MARSHAL KARL RUDOLF GERD VON RUNDSTEDT (1875-1953), German Commander of Army Group South on the Russian Front

## Summary of Event

The German invasion of Russia in June, 1941, abruptly terminated the uneasy friendship that had existed between Nazi Germany and the Soviet Union since their conclusion of the Nazi-Soviet Pact in August, 1939. Under the terms of this treaty, the two powers promised not to make war on each other and agreed to divide Eastern Europe into German and Soviet spheres of influence. Adolf Hitler, the German Dictator, was thus assured of Russian neutrality when he touched off World War II by launching his attack on Poland on September 1, 1939; two days later Great Britain and France declared war on Germany when she failed to respond to their ultimatum demanding an immediate withdrawal from Polish soil. Within a month, a defeated Poland was partitioned between Nazi Germany and Soviet Russia.

As World War II steadily expanded into a global conflict, serious strains developed in Russo-German relations. During June of 1940, while the German Wehrmacht was completing its conquest of France, Joseph Stalin, the Soviet Dictator, took further steps to consolidate his sphere of influence allotted him under his agreement with Hitler by absorbing the Baltic states of Latvia, Lithuania, and Estonia, and by occupying the Rumanian territories of the Northern Bukovina and Bessarabia. Hitler, however, refused to accept Stalin's interpretation of the Nazi-Soviet Pact as allowing him to occupy and annex all those areas which the agreement referred to as part of the Soviet sphere of influence. The Führer, moreover, was disturbed by the hurried character of the Soviet occupation of the Balticum and Rumanian territories—the latter so perilously close to Germany's main oil supply in Rumania—at the very moment when German forces were still tied down in the West. Consequently, in late July, 1940, just as the Battle of Britain was about to begin, Hitler informed Field Marshal Walther von Brauchitsch, Commander in Chief of the German Army, and his other military chiefs of his intention to invade and destroy the Soviet Union. At last, Hitler would be able to realize the dream he had expressed many years before in his political autobiography *Mein Kampf*, namely that of destroying the citadel of Communism and acquiring *Lebensraum* (living space) in Eastern Europe at its expense.

The planning of the Russian campaign consumed much of Hitler's attention throughout the remainder of 1940 and early 1941. Great Britain's refusal to come to terms convinced Hitler that only with the defeat of Russia would the British will to fight be broken and the Battle of Britain, then raging, finally be won. By early October, Hitler had moved large contingents of German forces into Poland and Rumania. On December 18, he christened the Russian operation "Barbarossa" (after the twelfth-century German Emperor Frederick Barbarossa of Hohenstaufen) and ordered his military planners to be ready by May 15, 1941, "to crush So-

viet Russia in a quick campaign even before the end of the war against England." Hitler, in other words, was committing Germany to fighting a two-front war. The rout, meantime, of the Italian invasion of Greece in late 1940 and early 1941 by the combined efforts of the Greek army and British reinforcements obliged Hitler to shore up his right flank opposite Russia before invading that country. In April, the German Wehrmacht launched a massive *Blitzkrieg* against Yugoslavia and Greece, breaking all organized resistance in both countries by the end of the month. Significantly, however, Hitler's heavy commitment of troops in the Balkans obliged him to postpone the scheduled date for the invasion of Russia by five weeks.

Hence, when at dawn on Sunday, June 22, 1941, a German invading force of three million men launched a surprise attack on the Soviet Union, five valuable weeks of campaigning time had already been lost. The German invasion forces comprised three army groups, each supported by elements of the Luftwaffe. Army Group North, commanded by Field Marshal Ritter Wilhelm von Leeb, was assigned the task of pushing the Soviets out of the Baltic states and then taking Leningrad. Army Group Center, under Field Marshal Fedor von Bock, was to take Smolensk, the gateway to Moscow. Finally, Army Group South, commanded by Field Marshal Karl von Rundstedt was to strike into the Ukraine. Together, these armies inflicted catastrophic losses on the Red Army in the opening months of the campaign.

Nevertheless, a number of factors

prevented Hitler from ever realizing his dream of conquering the Soviet Union. First and perhaps foremost, the size of the Soviet Union afforded the retreating Red Army the opportunity to trade space for the time it needed to recover from its initial setbacks. Second, Hitler could not concentrate on a single objective; his switching of forces back and forth between those army groups moving on Leningrad and Moscow resulted in his capturing neither. Third, poor German intelligence underestimated the fighting spirit of the Red Army and, above all, its strategic reserves. Fourth, the German army for all of its mechanization lacked adequate numbers of tracked vehicles with which to move men and matériel over such a vast country with poor roads. Other important factors which doomed Hitler's efforts included his brutal treatment of the Russian people in keeping with Nazi racial theories and the onset of one of the worst winters in years, thus underscoring the significance of the five-week postponement of the invasion.

By the fall of 1941, the Germans had invested Leningrad and had captured major Russian cities including Smolensk and Kiev. Only now did Hitler allow his forces in Army Group Center to drive on Moscow, the battle for which raged throughout October and November. The Russians, however, taking advantage of the bitter winter weather and the overstretched German supply lines, blocked the Nazi advance less than twenty miles from the Soviet capital. By early December, the Germans had lost more than 800,000 men, killed, captured, and wounded, while the Russian losses in these categories totaled in excess of five million. The Soviets, nevertheless, were able to offset some of these losses by moving in reserve forces from the Far East to positions in front of Moscow. There, the Red Army launched a powerful counterthrust against the faltering Germans that reached its peak on December 6, 1941. On the following day, the Japanese surprise attack on Pearl Harbor brought the United States into what was now a genuinely global war which Hitler could no longer win.

## Pertinent Literature

Seaton, Albert. *The Russo-German War, 1941-1945.* New York: Frederick A. Praeger, 1970.

Albert Seaton, a leading authority on the German Wehrmacht and the Red Army, has written the most comprehensive study to date on what was the bloodiest battlefront of World War II. He devotes well over a third of his book to the antecedents of the Nazi invasion of Russia in June, 1941, and the period of the early German triumphs down to the Battle of Moscow. Throughout this part of the book, Seaton carefully examines several of the major problems which ultimately frustrated the Germans in their attempt to conquer Russia. These included, among others, the failure of German intelligence to gather accurate information on the Soviet Union and its ability to wage war, the nature of Hitler's strategy and his contemptuous attitude toward the German High Command, and, finally, in relationship to this problem, the grave difficulty which the German armed forces had in dealing with the sheer physical enormity of the country which it was trying to defeat and subjugate.

Between the two World Wars, the intelligence interests of Germany, unlike those of other great powers, had largely ignored the Soviet Union. Hence, when war broke out between Germany and Russia in 1941, the depth of German military intelligence on the Soviet Union paled by comparison with the information which other nations had gathered, in particular Great Britain. Seaton points out that in 1939 and 1940, during the period of the Nazi-Soviet Pact, Hitler had even forbidden the collection or evaluation of material on the Red Army. Furthermore, the officer who, at that time, was in charge of Foreign Armies East, one of the two main subdivisions of German military intelligence that included the Red Army in its area of coverage, had no real knowledge of the Soviet Union or its military establishment; in fact, he could not even speak Russian. The Germans gleaned most of their battle intelligence from agents, border-crossers, and from their Finnish, Hungarian, and Japanese allies. Consequently, the Germans developed a reasonably adequate picture of the Soviet troop formations in the border regions but had a very poor idea as to the number of Red Army reserves in the hinterland. Indeed, as Seaton observes, the Germans were to remain poorly informed throughout the war on the depth of the Soviet strategic reserves. Stalin's effective use of these reserves in front of Moscow in 1941 and a year later at Stalingrad go far toward explaining how the Russians managed to turn the tide against the Nazi invaders.

If more accurate intelligence information on the Red Army had been available to Hitler, one has to wonder how much consideration he would have given to it in the planning of his grand strategy against the Soviet Union. According to Seaton, Hitler's accurate assessment of the complex political and ethnic structure of the Soviet Union only enforced his confident belief that one good kick would bring down what he regarded as the tottering Bolshevik regime. Hitler, in his contempt for the Slavs, refused to give any consideration to enlisting the support of the Great Russians and the other nationalities which comprised the Soviet Union. Instead, he called upon his senior commanders to wage a race war without pity, which in practice meant the extermination of Jews, Communist commissars, and the enslavement of the Soviet peoples. Another mistake that Hitler made, in Seaton's opinion, was his insistence on capturing the Baltic states and the Ukraine before driving on Moscow. Hitler believed that the economic resources of these two areas outweighed the importance of taking the Soviet capital as soon as possible after the beginning of the Russian campaign. Seaton concurs with senior officers of the German High Command that a successful thrust on Moscow would not only have inflicted on the Soviet Union the loss of control and communications but by drawing the main enemy forces toward the capital it would have torn a great hole in any form of continuous Red Army front. In this way, the destruction of Soviet military power might have been realized. Hitler, however, sneeringly overruled his military chiefs who voiced this opinion in a conference held on December 5, 1940. Two weeks later Hitler signed a directive of the operation against Russia, which embodied his muddled priorities; at the same time, he changed the name of the operation from *Fritz* to *Barbarossa*.

Another problem which disturbed Hitler's military chiefs was the sheer size of the country which the German army was expected to conquer. They pointed out that because of the funnel shape of the Russian hinterland, the deeper an army penetrated the wider became the frontage. Thus, the initial front of some 1,300 miles would rapidly extend to 2,000 and even 2,500 miles by the time the German army reached its projected winter holding line stretching from Archangel on the White Sea to Astrakan on the Caspian Sea. Indeed, as Seaton points out, when the campaign did get under way, the axes of the rapidly moving infantry divisions spread out like the ribs of a fan so as to create large gaps between the formations. The military commanders also expressed concern before the start of the campaign as to how a force of three million men and half a million horses could be supplied in so vast a country where there were few good roads and where the wide railroad gauge would impede through-running military trains from Germany. Ultimately, the failure of Hitler to resolve the problems which his military planners foresaw contributed to his defeat in Russia.

Whaley, Barton. *Codeword Barbarossa*. Cambridge, Mass.: MIT Press, 1973.

In his book, Barton Whaley provides an answer to one of the most intriguing questions to come out of World War II: how was it that Joseph Stalin, forewarned of the German invasion by the U.S. State Department, British Prime Minister Winston Churchill, and his own agents, allowed himself to become the victim of a surprise attack by Nazi Germany? Whaley's study is one of a number of books to appear in recent years dealing with the subject of espionage and counterespionage during World War II. It covers the activities of various intelligence networks during the period July, 1940 to June, 1941, when Hitler was actively formulating his plans to invade Russia.

Whaley explains at the beginning of his book that, previously, all authorities had ascribed Stalin's total disregard of the warnings about the German attack either to his authoritarian rule or to his personal paranoid tendencies. In other words, they had presumed that Stalin alone of the world's informed leaders refused to accept the fact in June, 1941, that Hitler was about to invade Russia. Whaley, however, refutes this notion; he shows, instead, that the great majority of world leaders and intelligence services miscalculated Hitler's intention just as badly as did Stalin. All writers, Whaley notes, cite Churchill, President Roosevelt, U.S. Secretary of State Cordell Hull and his

Under-Secretary Sumner Welles as the only statesmen who knew for some time that Hitler intended to strike at Russia. To this list, Whaley adds several other leaders, including the Czechoslovak President-in-exile Eduard Beneš and Pope Pius XII. The inability of Churchill and others to convince Stalin of the threat to his country poses for Whaley the double question not only of *why* the Soviet leader was surprised when the attack came but also of *how* Hitler managed to inflict the surprise.

Hitler, in formulating his plans for the invasion of Russia during 1940 and 1941, realized that the numerous highly visible preparations for such a large campaign would not go unnoticed by the enemy. Indeed, the enemy could rush to judgment by assuming that the preparations themselves constituted a signal that the invasion was imminent. An informed Stalin could presumably take necessary countermeasures which would spoil the chances for the success of Barbarossa once it began. Hence, in order to mask their true intentions, the Germans deliberately launched what they themselves termed the "greatest deception operation in the history of war." The German objectives, Whaley observes, were to mislead the enemy about their very intentions to invade Russia and to conceal the time, direction, and strength of the blow.

According to the author, the German deception operation, which was conducted for eleven months prior to the invasion, consisted mainly of four distinct deception themes. These themes, he points out, overlapped in time, were mutually supporting, and were designed to fit the preconceptions of the enemy at each stage of the operation. The first deception theme was that the German military buildup on the eastern frontier was mainly part of the preparations for Hitler's invasion of Great Britain, known under the code name of Operation Sea Lion. Whaley flatly asserts that "Barbarossa was Sea Lion" and that Sea Lion was nothing but a hoax, an elaborate deception which served as a cover story for Barbarossa. The Germans made this cover story work, in part, by explaining that their troop maneuvers were conducted in the east so as to be out of range of British bombers and reconnaissance aircraft. As the second major deception, Hitler allowed information to leak that his troop buildup in the east was also designed as a defensive measure against a possible Russian attack. The third deception made use of the Nazi *Blitzkrieg* against Yugoslavia and Greece in April, 1941, to explain the large numbers of German troops pouring into the Balkans.

Finally, and most importantly, just a month before the invasion, the Reich Foreign Ministry circulated a cover story that German actions in the east were determined by increasingly unsatisfactory Russian conduct. In this way, the Nazis were able to convince Stalin right up to the moment of the invasion that Germany would send Russia an ultimatum before launching any attack. Numerous other statesmen around the world also expected an ultimatum. Churchill and a few others, as noted earlier, were aware that Hitler intended to invade Russia. But the British leader was puzzled that Stalin failed to believe his warnings, for he did not understand, in Whaley's words, *"how Hitler was masking his unqualified decision to attack."* This was because British intelligence and other contemporary intelligence services had failed to recognize the deceptive nature of Operation Sea Lion and to perceive that Hitler had completely duped Stalin into thinking that war was not imminent. — *E.P.K.*

## Additional Recommended Reading

Werth, Alexander. *Russia at War, 1941-1945*. New York: E. P. Dutton, 1964. An absorbing account of the events of June 22, 1941, and the opening months of the Russo-German War as viewed from the Russian side of the front by a British correspondent stationed in the Soviet Union during World War II.

Clark, Alan. *Barbarossa: The Russian-German Conflict, 1941-1945*. New York: William Morrow and Company, 1965. Examining the Russo-German conflict mainly from the German side of the front, Clark offers a detailed treatment of Hitler's invasion of Russia and his failure to take Moscow.

Dallin, Alexander. *German Rule in Russia, 1941-1945: A Study of Occupation Policies*. New York: St. Martin's Press, 1957. A scholarly study of the Nazi attempt to organize and exploit the conquered Russian territories.

Reitlinger, Gerald. *The House Built on Sand: The Conflicts of German Policy in Russia, 1939-1945*. New York: The Viking Press, 1960. Covers the same ground as Dallin's book but in a more readable fashion.

Liddell Hart, B. H. *History of the Second World War*. New York: G. P. Putnam's Sons, 1971. Liddell Hart, one of the greatest military thinkers of the twentieth century, devotes two informative chapters to Hitler's invasion of Russia in 1941.

Salisbury, Harrison E. *The 900 Days: The Siege of Leningrad*. New York: Harper & Row Publishers, 1969. Contains a vivid portrayal of the reaction of German and Soviet officials to the Nazi attack on Russia.

# JAPAN OCCUPIES THE DUTCH EAST INDIES, SINGAPORE, AND BURMA

*Type of event:* Military: invasion and occupation of Asian territories
*Time:* December 8, 1941-August, 1945
*Locale:* Southeast Asia

*Principal personages:*

SIR WINSTON LEONARD SPENCER CHURCHILL (1874-1965),
   Prime Minister of Great Britain, 1940-1945

LIEUTENANT GENERAL TOMOYUKI YAMASHITA (1885-1946),
   Commander of the Japanese 25th Army in Malaya

LIEUTENANT GENERAL ARTHUR ERNEST PERCIVAL (1887-
   1966), British General in command of Malaya

COLONEL MASANOBU TSUJI (1902-      ), head of Operations
   with Japanese 25th Army in Malaya

GENERAL SIR ARCHIBALD PERCIVAL WAVELL (1883-1950),
   Supreme Allied Commander in the Southwestern Pacific,
   December 29, 1941

REAR ADMIRAL KAREL W. F. M. DOORMAN (1889-1942),
   Allied Naval Commander of Eastern striking force, Battle
   of Java Sea

LIEUTENANT GENERAL HEIN TER POORTEN (1887-   ), Commander of Dutch land forces in Java

LIEUTENANT GENERAL SHOJIRO IIDA (1888-      ), Commander of the Japanese 15th Army in Burma

GENERAL SIR HAROLD RUPERT LEOFRIC GEORGE ALEX-
   ANDER (1891-1969), Commander of Burma Army, March
   5, 1942

## Summary of Event

On the night of December 7-8, 1941, an invasion force of 27,000 Japanese troops landed at Singora and Patani in southern Thailand, and at Kota Bharu in northern Malaya. Their objective was the conquest of Malaya, which produced about forty percent of the world's rubber and sixty percent of its tin, as well as iron and bauxite. Four hundred miles to the south lay Singapore, the "Gibraltar" of Asia and key to British plans for defense of its Asian empire. Loss of Singapore would be not only a military disaster, but also a lasting political blow to the concept of white imperialism in Asia.

From the very beginning, the 25th Japanese Army had the initiative. It was led by Lieutenant General Tomoyuki Yamashita, who had served in North China. Yamashita was Japan's most able general, inspiring almost hero-worship among his men. Most of his soldiers were seasoned, especially the 5th Division, one of the

457

best in the army. Although the Japanese had acquired little jungle training in China, the head of operations, Colonel Masanobu Tsuji, had studied jungle warfare in Taiwan since early 1941. Tsuji's innovations were invaluable. Bicycles were to replace the cavalry of China, and about two hundred light tanks were to support the infantry. Intelligence gathered by Japanese agents revealed the weakness of British preparations and the vulnerability of the land approach to Singapore.

The British were well aware of the Japanese threat by 1941, but European operations prevented the rapid build-up of air power needed to protect Malayan airfields and to prevent a mass landing. As early as 1938, Major-General William Dobbie pointed out that the defense of Singapore required protecting Malaya, as the great guns at the naval base pointed seaward. By 1941 it was too late. On the eve of invasion, British leaders seriously underestimated the military ability of the Japanese, thinking they were hopelessly bogged down in China.

Japanese troops numbering 125,000 were more than a match for British forces. The British had about 88,000 troops: 37,000 Indians, 19,600 British, 15,200 Australians, and 16,000 local recruits. Many of these, however, were poorly trained and only recently assembled. Air cover was also inadequate, and Japanese pilots flying the new Zeros soon had command of the sky. Virtually the only naval defense was the battleship *Prince of Wales* and the battle cruiser *Repulse*, but they were destroyed by air on December 10. Japan thus had control of the sea as well as the sky. The campaign became a matter of time as the British tried unsuccessfully to impede the rapid southward advance of the Japanese until Singapore could be reinforced. Yamashita continually pressed his troops to attack. They carried only light equipment and rice rations, using bicycles to cover ground quickly and pass destroyed bridges. Tanks were used to breach fixed defenses, often panicking Indian troops not trained in antitank tactics. The British had considered tanks unsuited for jungle warfare. Major battles were fought at Jitra, Slim river, and Muar river, but one ill-prepared defense line after another fell, with great loss of men, supplies, and morale. On January 31, 1942, the last British forces crossed to Singapore island and hastily prepared for a final onslaught.

Singapore had long been called a "fortress," which lulled its defenders into false security. A flat island separated from the mainland by the Johore Straits, it was not a natural fortress like Gibraltar and Corregidor. On the night of February 8, 1942, Japanese troops in small boats gained a foothold and repaired the causeway which had been inadequately demolished. Artillery and tanks crossed over, and on February 15, Lieutenant General Arthur Percival surrendered. Unknown to Percival, Japanese supply lines were stretched thin and Yamashita was on the verge of halting the attack on the city. The tired and dispirited Commonwealth operational forces of 85,000 had been defeated by 30,000 troops Yamashita had left at Singapore. Singapore had fallen in only seventy days, thirty days ahead of the Japanese schedule. The British holding action was a failure. Including the capitulation, British losses were 38,496, Indian 67,340, Australian 18,490, and volunteers 14,382. Official Japanese casualties were 9,824.

The fall of Singapore helped speed the conquest of the Dutch East Indies, which had already begun with landings on Northeast Borneo and the Celebes on January 11, 1942. The vast area of the Dutch East Indies was lightly defended. The Dutch Army totaled about 100,000 men, and few had adequate equipment. Only two hundred aircraft were available, and advancing Japanese forces met little effective resistance. On January 23, 1942, they landed at Balikpapan, and on February 14, they seized Palembang on Sumatra. This latter action, coupled with landings on Bali and Timor, created a vast pincer movement around the important island of Java. Java contained valuable oil fields and the largest population in the Indies, producing a significant rice crop. General Archibald Wavell, Supreme Commander of Allied forces in the Southwestern Pacific, had established his headquarters in Java, but with invasion imminent he moved to India on February 25, leaving the defense of Java to the Dutch General Poorten.

The only hope was to forestall invasion by naval action. Although he commanded a mixed Allied force lacking even a common signal code, Rear Admiral Karel W. F. M. Doorman valiantly engaged Japanese naval forces in the Battle of Java Sea on February 27-28. Aided by three spotter planes, Rear Admiral Takeo Takagi won a onesided victory in the greatest surface battle since Jutland in 1916. Doorman lost two light cruisers, the *Java* and *De Ruyter*, and three destroyers. The *Houston* and *Perth* escaped, but were subsequently sunk while trying to slip through the Sunda Straits. Command of the Java Sea allowed Japanese troop transports to land on the night of February 28. Once ashore, Dutch and Australian forces were no match for the Japanese, who reached Tjilatjap on the south coast of Java on March 6, 1942. General Poorten surrendered on March 8, followed by the formal surrender March 12, 1942.

The oil fields of the Dutch East Indies were Japan's main strategic goal, but the need for a defensive perimeter led to the conquest of Burma. Control of Burma would close the 750-mile Burma Road to Nationalist forces in Chungking and weaken Chinese resolve. Burma was defended by an Indian and Burmese division under Lieutenant General Thomas J. Hutton, but they were unable to halt the Japanese 15th Army under Lieutenant General Shojiro Iida. A small force entered southern Burma on December 11 and seized Tavoy eight days later. On January 20, with the Malaya campaign going well, troops moved into Burma in strength using envelopment and infiltration tactics. On January 30-31 they took Moulmein at the mouth of the Salween river, putting pressure on Rangoon. The lack of training of British forces led to a general rout, and the Japanese entered Rangoon March 8, capturing substantial supplies intended for China. They then turned north, seizing the terminus of the Burma Road, Lashio, on April 29, and Mandalay on May 2, 1942. British forces were forced to evacuate Burma over difficult jungle tracks with considerable losses, and in June the intense monsoon weather halted all operations, with Japan firmly in control of Burma.

British forces in Burma had been intended for internal police duties, and the loyalty of many Burmese to the colonial government was nominal. General Harold Alexander replaced Hutton on March 5, but a shift in command could not remedy basic deficiencies in troop training and size. As in Malaya and the Indies, the Japanese attack revealed a colonial power too weak to defend its territory.

## Pertinent Literature

Kirby, S. Woodburn. *Singapore: The Chain of Disaster.* London: Cassell, 1971.

There are many books about the military disaster in Malaya and Singapore, but Kirby, who also edited the official British version of the campaign, has written one of the best. It is detailed enough for the general reader and analytical, but written in a somewhat dry style. Adequate maps are included at appropriate places so the reader can visualize battles described in the text.

Kirby does not avoid criticizing military decisions when he sees a mistake, but he avoids the "witch-hunt" approach which would seek to put the blame for Singapore upon individuals or single events. His basic thesis is that twenty years of British neglect of security requirements in East Asia put those in command on December 8, 1941, in an untenable position. When battle was joined, the attempt to guard dispersed air fields prevented Percival from massing troops along the vital western corridor in Malaya. Plans for defending Malaya and Singapore came far too late, despite obvious signs indicating that Japan was on the verge of attack.

The author considers the total war effort in order to put Singapore's defense in the proper perspective. Britain was facing Hitler's armies in Europe, and after June 22, 1941, she had to aid her new Russian ally. East Asia was necessarily low on Churchill's priority list, and England optimistically believed that Japan would not go to war. Not only did Japan attack, but she did so with considerable planning, based on extensive intelligence work. Japanese troops were battle-tested, well-trained, and supported by superiority in the air and at sea.

With his stress on long-term factors, Kirby devotes half of his book to matters leading up to the Japanese attack. Changes in strategy and the assessment of Singapore's vulnerability over the years show that clear warnings went unheeded. In 1937, British commanders had noted that Malaya would have to be included in Singapore's defense. Major General William Dobbie and his senior staff officer Percival projected a scenario that was almost a blueprint for the 1941 invasion. Men in the colonial civil service such as Governor Sir Shenton Thomas did not understand defense requirements nor trust military men.

When the war began in 1939, London saw the role of Malaya in economic, not military terms. Increased output of tin and rubber to gain credits to fight in Europe was the primary goal. Within the Commonwealth only Canada was a larger dollar earner. Little manpower was left to prepare for the possibility of attack. Although Australia and those in charge of defending Singapore appealed to Churchill in 1941 for air and naval power to destroy an invasion fleet before it landed, spare tanks and planes were sent to the Russian front. The only defensive action taken was the politically symbolic dispatch of the *Prince of Wales* and *Repulse* to Singapore. Churchill's naval advisers, including Admiral Phillips, who was to command the British Asian fleet, argued against exposing the ships to air attack. Their vulnerability was complete when an accompanying aircraft carrier ran aground en route to Singapore and was left behind for repairs. Adequate air cover could not be provided by the Air Force in Malaya, and the early sinking of two capital ships was a blow to both civilian and military morale.

Percival was an able staff officer, but lacked the strong personality needed to unite the diverse forces under his command. Many of the Indian and Australian troops were hastily organized and untrained. By the time he retreated to Singapore, Percival's badly mauled units were only thirty to seventy percent effective. No reserves of any strength were available, and the island was too small for effective counterattack.

While defeat was almost inevitable given the lack of defensive preparation, a more effective delaying action and orderly retreat was possible. Following initial battle for north Malaya at Jitra, the 11th Division repeatedly bore the brunt of Yamashita's aggressive campaign. The men were forced to retreat 220 miles in twenty-nine days, fighting a rear-guard action most of the way. They were exhausted at the battle of Slim river, when Japanese tanks broke through the lines of tired defenders, creating a rout that opened up central Malaya. Fresh troops from the 9th Division would have been more effective at Slim river, but Percival did not employ them.

Before the invasion, British leaders tended to underestimate Japanese military power, pointing to their failure to conquer China. The Japanese soldier was seen with contempt, but by the time Yamashita reached the Johore Straits, Japanese troops were considered supermen. Neither view was accurate, but both were damaging. The cost of complacency was the "greatest national humiliation suffered by Britain since Yorktown." Britain regained her empire in 1945, but colonial peoples throughout Asia were no longer willing to be ruled by the nation defeated at Singapore.

Lebra, Joyce C. *Japanese-Trained Armies in Southeast Asia: Inpendence and Volunteer Forces in World War II*. New York: Columbia University Press, 1977.

This well-researched study focuses on an important but neglected aspect of Japanese military conquest in Southeast Asia: the training of native armies. When Western colonial powers returned to their former colonies in 1945, they found their former subjects unwilling to return to colonial status. As Professor Lebra notes, ". . . nationalism and aspiration for independence had been stimulated to a point of no return." Japanese occupation and military training had a long-term impact in postwar Asia. It was an essential factor in the struggle for political independence in the region, perhaps the most important legacy of Japanese imperialism.

To a large degree this was not planned by the Japanese military, for no coherent policy had been devised for Southeast Asia. With the unexpectedly rapid fall of British and Dutch colonial regimes, the Japanese suddenly found themselves faced with the problem of governing and defending a vast region of great cultural diversity. There was little coordination between Tokyo and armies in the field, and the services disagreed over objectives.

The result was the appearance of widely different policies throughout the region, as the author clearly shows in Chapter One. The indigenous military forces created in Asia ranged from mere puppets to quasiindependents, depending on the degree of control and Japanese strategic interests. Chapters Two to Four deal with the political and military training of Indians, Burmese, and Indonesians (Java). Chapter Five briefly analyzes smaller military units formed in Malaya, Sumatra, Indochina, Borneo, and the Philippines. The last two chapters describe the revolt of independence armies at war's end and the long-term significance of military training.

The Indian National Army (INA) was formed with volunteers captured in the Malaya campaign. It was the only volunteer army that was battle-tested and well-trained in the British school. It was given cohesion and political legitimacy by the Bengali nationalist leader, Subhas Chandra Bose. Bose was the most prominent of the wartime collaborators. Like other Asian nationalists, he saw cooperation with the Japanese as the path to independence. Japan's "Greater East Asia Co-Prosperity Sphere," and "Asia for the Asians" political programs had an appeal that the West failed to realize. Bose was given a good deal of support because India was still under British control, and it did not figure in Japanese plans for permanent colonial possession: the Co-Prosperity Sphere stopped at the Indo-Burma border. The INA was the only volunteer force that fought side-by-side with Japanese units during the abortive Imphal campaign inside the Indian frontier in 1944. All other volunteer units were intended for domestic control and defensive purposes. After 1943, coastal defense became the main function of native troops.

Unlike the Indian Army, the Burma Independence Army, Peta (the Indonesian Army), and all other volunteer forces were built from the ground up. More than 175 Southeast Asians were trained as officers at the Military Academy in Japan, while lower ranks were trained in their locale. As many as 153,000 Asians received such training before Japan's defeat in August, 1945.

By 1944 prolonged Japanese rule, harsh economic exploitation, and postponed promises for independence led to increased friction and revolt in Java and Burma. Because Indonesia had vital petroleum resources, Japanese authorities avoided using the term and concept of Indonesia, and divided the islands administratively. In the case of Vietnam, a *coup* deposed Vichy forces on March 9, 1945, and Bao Dai was made head of a nominally independent Vietnam.

The war and the weakness of the West revealed by Japanese victories in early 1942 would in themselves have caused great changes, but certain Japanese policies added to the impact of the war. Leaders and men for the volunteer armies were deliberately picked from ethnic segments ignored by colonial regimes, while former elites (except in the INA case) were ignored. This had a great impact on social and political change. Many postwar leaders such as Sukarno and Ne Win gained experience in volunteer forces. In contrast to colonial army training, Japanese military training emphasized guerrilla warfare, an experience that proved valuable in postwar independence struggles. Japanese stress on *seishin* (spirit) and self-discipline over technology was also a useful lesson for postwar revolutionaries. Although it was not a conscious goal, volunteer armies stimulated endemic revolutionary forces in Asia.

Lebra's book contains an extensive and useful bibliography on the subject and Southeast Asian history in general. A glossary helps identify the many terms and organizations mentioned in the text. Although perhaps intended for the specialist, this book is indispensable for understanding the meaning of the Japanese occupation of Southeast Asia. — *R.R.*

## Additional Recommended Reading

Aziz, M. A. *Japan's Colonialism and Indonesia*. The Hague: Martinus Nijhoff, 1955. A study of prewar Japanese policy towards the Dutch East Indies and the conquest and occupation of the islands.

Benda, Harry J. *The Crescent and the Rising Sun: Indonesian Islam Under the Japanese Occupation, 1942-1945*. The Hague: W. van Hoeve, 1958. Reveals how the Japanese mobilized support in the Dutch East Indies by utilizing the indigenous religion.

Collier, Basil. *The War in the Far East, 1941-1945: A Military History*. New York: William Morrow and Company, 1969. Although not limited to the Japanese Southeast Asia campaign, this well-written account is one of the best books on the war for the general reader.

Churchill, Winston S. *The Second World War*. Vol. IV: *The Hinge of Fate*. Boston: Houghton Mifflin Company, 1951. Contains interesting insights into attitudes towards East Asia and the fall of Singapore.

Kirby, S. Woodburn. *The War Against Japan*. Vol. I: *The Loss of Singapore*; Vol. II: *India's Most Dangerous Hour*. London: Her Majesty's Stationery Office, 1957 and 1969. Extremely detailed official histories based on original documents, essential reading intended for the military history specialist.

Leasor, James. *Singapore: The Battle That Changed the World.* Garden City, N.Y.: Doubleday & Company, 1968. A readable journalistic account with human interest elements, although somewhat biased in interpretation.

Percival, General Arthur E. *The War in Malaya.* London: Eyre and Spottiswoode, 1949. An account by the leading British participant.

Simson, Brigadier Ivan. *Singapore: Too Little, Too Late: Some Aspects of the Malayan Disaster in 1942.* London: Leo Cooper, 1970. A bitter account by the former Chief Engineer in Malaya relating his frustrating attempts to prepare defenses in Malaya and Singapore.

Tsuji, Masanobu. *Singapore: The Japanese Version.* Translated by Margaret E. Lake. New York: St. Martin's Press, 1961. One of the few firsthand accounts available in English, detailing the fascinating story of the man who planned the campaign that brought about the fall of Singapore.

# GERMANY AND ITALY DECLARE WAR
# ON THE UNITED STATES

*Type of event:* Military: German and Italian decision to support Japan
*Time:* December 11, 1941
*Locale:* Berlin, Rome, and Washington D.C.

*Principal personages:*

FRANKLIN DELANO ROOSEVELT (1882-1945), thirty-second
President of the United States, 1933-1945

ADOLF HITLER (1889-1945), Chancellor and Führer of Germany, 1933-1945

BENITO MUSSOLINI (1883-1945), Dictator and Duce of Italy,
1922-1943

CORDELL HULL (1871-1955), United States Secretary of
State, 1933-1944

HENRY LEWIS STIMSON (1867-1950), United States Secretary
of War, 1940-1945

## Summary of Event

On December 11, 1941, four days after the Japanese attack on Pearl Harbor, the governments of Germany and Italy issued declarations of war against the United States of America. Though the Germans especially had pledged Japan their aid in the event of a conflict between Japan and America, no mention of Japan was made in the German and Italian declarations. The Germans claimed that the Americans had committed open acts of war against Germany in the Atlantic. Congress unanimously passed a joint resolution affirming a state of war with Germany. The American entry into the war linked the conflicts in Europe and the Pacific and rendered World War II a truly global affair.

That the United States would become involved in a war in Europe seemed highly unlikely in the period from 1936 to 1940, since during these years the American government and

people were strongly isolationist. Moreover, Nazi Germany was preoccupied in Europe and not primarily interested in American and the Western Hemisphere. Though most Americans were opposed to Mussolini's invasion of Ethiopia in 1935, the United States government responded with the first of the Neutrality Acts. This act included an arms embargo designed to weaken Italy. By 1936 it became clear that Germany and Italy were bent on territorial revisions. The Rome-Berlin Axis was formed in 1936, and Japan joined Germany and Italy in an anticomintern pact in 1937. In response the United States government extended the Neutrality Act in 1937.

Despite the American desire to stay out of a European war, President Franklin Delano Roosevelt and his advisers became concerned about the danger of foreign aggression in Europe and the Pacific by 1937. In 1938

America's opposition to German persecution of the Jews led to a replacement of the American ambassador in Berlin by a *chargé d'affaires*. By 1939, the outbreak of war in Europe increased the Roosevelt Administration's belief that Germany posed a real threat to American security.

The turning point that led to the confrontation between the United States and the Rome-Berlin Axis occurred in 1940. The crisis was precipitated first in Europe by the fall of France and the Battle of Britain, and second in the Pacific by Japanese ambitions. The fall of France seriously alerted Americans to the might of Nazi Germany, while the dogged resistance of the British to Germany resulted in increased American aid toward England. By the summer and fall of 1940, America responded to the Nazi *Blitzkrieg* in Europe with billions of dollars for defense, destroyers for England, and the first peace-time Selective Service Act in American history. Roosevelt was re-elected in November of 1940, an indication that most Americans understood the Axis threat to national security. The United States proclaimed itself an "arsenal of democracy" while still hoping to stay out of war.

American aid to England resulted in increased tensions with Germany, especially in the Battle of the Atlantic. In early 1941 the Joint Chiefs of Staff of the American armed forces met with their British opposite numbers and held meetings on how to coordinate military actions in the event of American entry into the war. It was decided that the defeat of Germany be given top priority. In a speech of May 27, 1941, Roosevelt stressed the German danger to the Western Hemisphere and declared a state of national emergency. In August, Roosevelt and British Prime Minister Winston Churchill issued the Atlantic Charter against the Axis powers. Serious naval incidents began in September and October when German submarines torpedoed the American destroyer *Greer* and sank the *Reuben James*. Congress repealed the Neutrality Act and permitted the arming of American merchant ships. America also promised to aid the Soviet Union after the German attack of June 22, 1941. In June of 1941 German consulates in the United States were closed. It is clear that by the fall of 1941 Roosevelt and his policymakers believed that Germany was bent on world domination, that she was a great threat to the Western Hemisphere, and that war with her was a strong possibility.

In spite of the increased American presence in the European conflict, the ultimate initiative for war lay with Germany and her Japanese ally. Hitler did not intend to go to war with the United States, but he nevertheless contributed enormously to the American entry into the war. In an unpublished sequel to *Mein Kampf* written in 1928, Hitler expressed the possibility of a future collision with the United States after Germany completed her hegemony over Europe. Particularly after the Depression of 1929, Hitler's attitudes toward the United States were those of contempt for what he believed was a culturally and racially decadent country. He also underestimated America's industrial capacity and her willingness and ability to fight a war. In this connection he was impressed by the strength of American isolationism. Thus, unlike many German diplomats, Hitler failed to grasp the implications of American power. In contrast to the Americans, the Germans developed no military plans in the event of war with the United States. Hitler was able to convince the Italians in 1939 that America would not fight. Germany's contempt for America turned to hostility when Americans expressed their opposition to Nazi totalitarianism and aided Britain and the Soviet Union.

In spite of his attitude toward the United States, Hitler realistically tried to avoid any incidents with American ships in the Atlantic, being aware that German submarine warfare had brought America into World War I. By September of 1941, however, he gave in to the demands of the German Navy that wished to sever American supply lines to the British.

Germany's short-lived caution in the Atlantic was offset by her recklessness in her support of Japanese ambitions in the Far East. In 1940 Japan and the United States began their collision course that would lead to Pearl Harbor. Germany hoped that Japan would be a counterweight to the Soviet Union in the Far East and would help check the United States commitment to Europe. On September 27, 1940, Germany and Japan concluded a mutual assistance pact, and on April 4, 1941, Hitler assured the Japanese of his full support in the event of a Japanese-American conflict.

The Japanese attack on Pearl Harbor on December 7, 1941, took the Germans and Italians by surprise. On December 9, President Roosevelt announced that he considered Germany just as guilty as Japan for the surprise attack. Secretary of War Henry L. Stimson wanted an American declaration of war against Germany, but was overruled. Instead of gaining time, the Germans chose to gamble on Japanese power. Hitler took the initiative for war by ordering all-out submarine attacks on American ships, and along with his Italian ally declared war on the United States.

The Nazis were pleased by the Japanese attack on Pearl Harbor, for they believed that Japan would weaken the British, Soviet, and especially American war efforts. But by declaring war on America at the very time his armies were becoming bogged down in the Soviet Union and his navy halted in the Battle of the Atlantic, Hitler made the most fatal blunder of his career. When he said that his declaration of war on the United States would be "decisive not only for the history of Germany, but for the whole of Europe and indeed for the world," he was right. With their declaration of war, Germany and Italy sealed their fate and guaranteed their own ultimate defeat. The events of December 11, 1941, also signaled the ascendancy of America to the status of a superpower.

## Pertinent Literature

Divine, Robert A. *The Reluctant Belligerent: American Entry into World War II*. New York: John Wiley and Sons, 1965.

In addition to this major book, Robert A. Divine has published two other works dealing with the American entry into World War II—*American Diplomacy During the Second World War* and *Roosevelt and World War Two*. In his study of the coming of war between America and the Axis powers, Divine focuses primarily on American attitudes and policies.

In strong contrast to such revisionist historians as Charles Callan Tansill, who maintains that Roosevelt provoked Germany and Japan to go to war, Divine is critical of the Roosevelt Administration for quite different reasons. His major argument is that American foreign policy between 1936 and 1941 was formulated in reaction to decisions reached in Rome and Berlin. These American reactions were strongly isolationist at first and had the effect of making the United States Hitler's "silent partner" in disturbing the peace of Europe.

Divine maintains that the American response to Axis aggression was inconsistent for the most part. The American government and people desired both to stay out of war and to see Germany and Italy defeated. The United States went to war in 1941 only reluctantly and mainly because of the initiatives and miscalculations of Germany and Japan.

Franklin Delano Roosevelt was primarily concerned with domestic problems during his first term (1933-1937). Congressional isolationists were able to have their way in this period. European appeasement of Hitler during the late 1930's simply reinforced American isolationist policies of neutrality toward Axis aggression. By 1937 the "cash and carry" policy of trade with countries at war was a compromise between the needs of peace and prosperity.

By 1938 and 1939, however, the Roosevelt Administration became concerned with the Axis threat to European security and sought to revise the Neutrality Act to the benefit of England and France. America nevertheless clung to the illusion that she could protect her security by measures short of war.

Divine's arguments and illustrations confirm the widely shared opinion that it was in the summer of 1940 that America took sides in the European conflict. The Battle of Britain was an important turning point, for it resulted in American aid to England, increased friction with Germany, and unprecedented measures for national defense at home. The author makes the important point that Hitler's victories in Europe in 1940 emboldened the Japanese in their ambitions toward Southeast Asia. The treaty of mutual aid between Germany, Italy, and Japan of September 27, 1940, was clearly directed against the United States, says Divine. Japan threw in its lot with Germany to compel the United States to withdraw its opposition to Japanese expansion. The Germans joined Japan to discourage American opposition to German expansion. Divine shows how both these strategies backfired, for the United States would agree neither to the Japanese domination of Asia nor to the German domination of the Atlantic.

By 1941 the Roosevelt Administration adopted a hard line regarding both German and Japanese ambitions. Divine might appear to agree with the revisionists in his statement that "Roosevelt had led the nation to the brink of war in the summer of 1941. . . . The United States moved inexorably toward war in the fall of 1941." Yet he nevertheless maintains that the major initiatives for war remained in German and Japanese hands. On September 4, 1941, German-American conflict in the Atlantic began when a German submarine torpedoed the destroyer *Greer*. Divine neglects to point out that who initially attacked whom has never been established. The German attack on the *Kearney* and the sinking of the *Reuben James* in October of 1941 led to the repeal of the Neutrality Act. American public opinion moved away from isolationism as a result of such incidents.

Divine argues that Roosevelt and close advisers such as Harry Hopkins believed that war with Germany was inevitable, but he does not imply that they actively sought to go to war. Divine skillfully emphasizes this point by posing the question whether war with Japan meant an immediate shooting war with Germany as well.

Divine finds that though Roosevelt and his advisers believed that Germany had encouraged Japan to attack the United States, America chose to ignore the Axis alliance even after Pearl Harbor and waited for Germany and Italy to make the next move.

Thus, according to Divine, the United States refused to act against Japan and Germany until forced into war. The author judges American foreign policy in the 1930's to have been "sterile and bankrupt." Although it was the most powerful nation in the world, the United States abdicated its responsibilities and became a tool rather than a molder of events. America surrendered the initiative to Germany and Japan and finally took action only because of German and Japanese recklessness and miscalculations. The Germans came to the aid of their Japanese ally in the hope that the Japanese would prevent America from aiding Europe. The President and Congress had no alternative but to affirm the state of war initiated by Germany and Italy.

Compton, James V. *The Swastika and the Eagle: Hitler, the United States, and the Origins of World War II*. Boston: Houghton Mifflin Company, 1967.

This ably written and well-documented study traces the confrontation between Germany and the United States primarily from the vantage point of German attitudes and actions. Throughout his book Compton emphasizes the role of Hitler's views toward the United States in shaping German policy on the eve of World War II. Hitler's judgments of Amer-

ica were based on subjective social and racial criteria rather than on economic and military realities. In an unpublished essay on German foreign policy aims written in 1928, Hitler viewed America as a serious future threat to a German-dominated Europe. But in the years of the Depression, the Führer became convinced that the United States was beset by cultural decadence, economic and social strife, and racial intermingling. He concluded that America had neither the will nor the means to fight a new war, and the strong isolationist movement in the United States confirmed his prejudices. Moreover, Hitler developed an intense dislike of Ambassador William Dodd and President Franklin Roosevelt when the two American statesmen expressed their dislike of the Nazi regime.

The interests of Nazi Germany were centered around Europe. Hitler believed that because of her distance and her lack of interest in Europe, America was geopolitically negligible as a world power, and this attitude prevented his realistic appreciation of the American character and American power. His views were shared by some influential officials in the Third Reich, such as Foreign Minister Joachim von Ribbentrop and General Friedrich von Boetticher, the German Military Attache in Washington. Compton maintains that many German diplomats in Washington and Berlin had a more realistic understanding of American power. But their views and dispatches were not reported to Hitler, for the Führer characteristically preferred to have his prejudices confirmed rather than contradicted.

It was because of the Battle of Britain and the ambitions of Japan that Germany became entangled with the United States, a power that was negligible by German standards. Compton offers the now-conventional interpretation that Hitler and the Germans totally miscalculated when they believed that the invasion of the Soviet Union, the Battle of the Atlantic, and the power of Japan would discourage American entry into the war.

Compton declares that American impact in German foreign relations was greatest in the Far East. The Germans had no initial desire to be at war with the United States, and until the fall of 1941, German submarines were ordered not to attack American merchant ships. But Hitler attempted to intimidate the United States by encouraging Japanese ambitions in the Far East. By late 1941 Germany was willing to gamble on a quick victory over the Soviet Union and an America too weakened by the Japanese threat to aid Britain.

Compton argues that the Germans did their best to discourage the Japanese from reaching an agreement with the United States. Still, Hitler and Mussolini were genuinely surprised by the Japanese assault on Pearl Harbor. According to Compton, Hitler's reasons for declaring war on the United States so quickly after Pearl Harbor are not easy to explain, for the German declaration of war on the United States was contrary to everything Hitler practiced and preached. Compton shows that the Germans never planned a military attack on America. German agents committed acts of sabotage in the United States, attempted economic penetration of Latin America, and tried some heavy-handed and largely ineffective efforts at propagandizing the American people; but these actions were not sufficient in themselves to lead to war.

The author's explanations of why Germany and Italy declared war on the United States are balanced and judicious. Though the Germans did not intend to go to war with America, says Compton, they contributed greatly to bringing about a conflict with the United States. Hitler the realist practiced caution in the Atlantic, but Hitler the illusionist recklessly encouraged the Japanese in the Pacific. He failed to understand that the Americans believed Germany was bent on world domination. As Roosevelt put it, "If Germany wins, the world is lost." The Americans were quick to implicate Germany in the Japanese attack on Pearl Harbor.

Compton also concludes that Hitler was unable to rise above his prejudices toward an America he characterized as weak and lacking in resolve. In his final days in the Berlin bunker, Hitler said, "The war with America is a tragedy, illogical, devoid of fundamental reality." Yet, it was his own fatal misjudgment of America that rendered Nazi policies toward the United States "devoid of fundamental reality." The inability of the Germans to grasp the war as a strategic whole led to the hasty declaration of war against the United States in December of 1941. — *L.S.*

## Additional Recommended Reading

Tansill, Charles Callan. *Back Door to War: The Roosevelt Foreign Policy, 1933-1941*. Chicago: Henry Regnery Company, 1952. One of the first strongly revisionist works on German-American relations to appear after World War II; argues that Roosevelt sought a pretext for war with Germany and maneuvered Japan into war.

Langer, William L. and S. Everett Gleason. *The Undeclared War, 1940-1941*. New York: Harper & Row Publishers, 1953. A richly detailed nonpartisan account of America's entry in World War II.

Schroeder, Paul W. *The Axis Alliance and Japanese-American Relations, 1941*. Ithaca, N.Y.: Cornell University Press, 1958. An important revisionist work that attributes the coming of war with Germany and Japan to a hard line of the Roosevelt Administration caused by misguided moralism.

Williams, William Appleman. *The Tragedy of American Diplomacy*. New York: World Publishing Company, 1962. An influential revisionist economic interpretation of American diplomacy which suggests that American economic expansion helped lead to war with Germany and Japan.

Friedlaender, Saul. *Prelude to Downfall: Hitler and the United States, 1939-1941*. Translated by Aline and Alexander Weerth. New York: Alfred A. Knopf, 1962. This analysis of German policy toward the United States during the outbreak of World War II maintains that Hitler believed that war with the United States was inevitable as early as 1940 and allied with Japan as a result.

Rich, Norman. *Hitler's War Aims*. 2 vols. New York: W. W. Norton and Company, 1973. A detailed, well-balanced study of the theory and practice of Nazi ambitions, a work that, in contrast to most commentaries on the subject, claims that Hitler's attitudes and policies toward America were more realistic than fanciful.

# THE BATTLE OF MIDWAY

*Type of event:* Military: decisive naval battle in the Pacific
*Time:* June 3-6, 1942
*Locale:* The Pacific Ocean in the vicinity of Midway Island

*Principal personages:*

ADMIRAL CHESTER WILLIAM NIMITZ (1885-1966), Commander in Chief of the United States Pacific Fleet

ADMIRAL ISOROKU YAMAMOTO (1884-1943), Commander in Chief of the Japanese Combined Fleet

REAR ADMIRAL RAYMOND AMES SPRUANCE (1886-1969), Commander of the United States Naval Task Force 16

REAR ADMIRAL FRANK JACK FLETCHER (1885-    ), Commander of the United States Naval Carrier Striking Force

VICE ADMIRAL CHUICHI NAGUMO (1887-1944), Commander of the Japanese First Carrier Striking Force

COMMANDER JOSEPH J. ROCHEFORT, JR., Commander of the United States Naval Combat Intelligence Unit at Pearl Harbor

## Summary of Event

All who have written about the Battle of Midway agree that it was a turning point in the Pacific war. Victorious wherever they had gone, the Japanese naval planners believed that the next battle would be a decisive defeat of the United States Pacific fleet.

Admiral Isoroku Yamamoto, Commander in Chief of the Combined Fleet, who dominated Japanese naval planning, attempted to accomplish several things at Midway. The island was a thousand miles from Hawaii, close enough to serve as a base and outpost in that direction. It could provide an anchor in the ribbon defense which the Japanese intended to stretch from the Aleutians in the north all the way to Australia. Those in the Japanese Navy who felt that holding Midway would overextend their supply and fighting capacities were un-

done by Lieutenant Colonel James Doolittle's raid on April 18, 1942, on Tokyo and other Japanese cities. To protect the nation and the Emperor, Midway was obviously necessary.

More basic to Yamamoto's plan was the need to destroy the American fleet in a decisive engagement before the overwhelming United States production could make itself felt. What was left of the U.S. fleet had to be drawn into battle. The Americans would have to fight for Midway.

Yamamoto put together the largest fleet the Japanese had ever assembled; it included eleven battleships headed by the *Yamato*, Japan's newest and the world's largest battleship, four heavy and four light carriers, twenty-one cruisers, sixty-five destroyers, more than fifty support and smaller craft, and nineteen submarines. In a serious strategic error Yamamoto dispersed these vessels in many groups so widely scattered that they could not be mutually supporting. To capture Kiska and Attu in the Aleutians, he diverted the Northern Force of two light carriers, eight cruisers, thirteen destroyers, and six submarines; the Force was scheduled to attack slightly earlier, divert the Americans, and occupy the islands. Although the Japanese succeeded in the landings, they were a sideshow. The islands were too remote to be valuable and the American ships committed there did not weaken the United States fleet significantly.

The main event, farther south, also saw badly divided Japanese forces. From the southwest came the Midway Occupation Group, supported by the Second Fleet with two battleships, eight cruisers, a light carrier, and a dozen destroyers. Approaching Midway from the northwest was Yamamoto with the Main Body and the Carrier Striking Force. His main force was organized around three battleships and a light carrier. Split off to the north to move either to the Aleutians or Midway, but in actuality too far from either, was the Guard Force of four battleships and a screen of cruisers and destroyers. In the van was the First Carrier Striking Force under Vice Admiral Chuichi Nagumo with the four heavy carriers, *Akagi*, *Kaga*, *Soryu*, and *Hiryu*, with their screen and support vessels.

Nagumo's carriers would attack Midway on June 4 and destroy the United States airfields and planes preparatory to the landings; when the Americans sortied from Pearl Harbor, the Main Body would move in and destroy it. Success had made the Japanese arrogant. They made no plans for what to do if the Americans did not cooperate.

They did not. The intelligence unit at Pearl Harbor under Commander Joseph J. Rochefort, Jr., had broken the Japanese naval code and had decided on the basis of incomplete information and brilliant analysis that Midway was the primary target. Admiral Chester W. Nimitz, Commander in Chief of the Pacific Fleet called in all his available carriers and could come up with only three: *Enterprise* and *Hornet*, commanded by Rear Admiral Raymond A. Spruance, and the wounded *Yorktown* under Rear Admiral Frank Jack Fletcher. Screened by a total of eight cruisers and fourteen destroyers, these were all that Nimitz could scrape together. He ordered the extensive reinforcement of Midway to a total of 120 planes, antiaircraft guns, and 3,632 defenders. The three carriers lay in wait for the Japanese, northeast of Midway, as ready as forewarning could make them.

Confirmation that the intelligence guesses were correct came early on June 3 when a scout plane sighted the invasion force six hundred miles to the southwest. Army and Marine pilots attacking from Midway scored no significant hits. Unaware that American ships were anywhere around, Nagumo launched an attack with half his planes (108) before dawn on June 4; the other half he held back in case the United States fleet threatened. Searches by Nagumo's own planes were inadequate.

The Midway defenders put all their planes in the air and took heavy punishment, but were not knocked out.

Defending planes were totally outclassed, but they and the antiaircraft guns still inflicted losses on the Japanese Zeros. By 7:00 A.M. the first raid was over and the Japanese flight leader radioed Nagumo, "There is need for another attack."

Before the second attack could be launched the Japanese carriers were scattered repeatedly by Marine and Army pilots from Midway, none of whom scored hits and nearly all of whom died trying. In the midst of these attacks, a Japanese scout plane at 8:20 reported an American carrier within range. Rather than immediately launching the second wave of planes which were being rearmed for another attack on Midway, Nagumo decided to recover his first wave and re-rearm the second for fleet action. By 9:18 all was ready, although the haste meant that bombs and torpedoes were piled around the carrier decks.

At that point, unprotected American carrier torpedo planes began nearly suicidal attacks. Of the forty-two committed, thirty-eight were lost. None scored hits, but the defending Zeros were drawn down to low levels to attack them. At the end of these attacks, SBD Dauntless dive bombers located and hit the *Kaga*, *Akagi*, and *Soryu*. American bombs as well as explosions on board turned them into flaming wrecks within five minutes.

The Japanese attacked with planes left on the *Hiryu*, damaging the *Yorktown*, while American planes sank *Hiryu*. (*Yorktown* would be sunk on June 6 by Japanese submarine I-168.) Spruance refused to be drawn into night action with Yamamoto's battleships. With Midway still in United States hands and facing two carriers, Yamamoto withdrew, losing a heavy cruiser.

With overwhelming superiority in numbers and quality of weapons, the Japanese had lost four great carriers, the battle, and ultimately the war.

## Pertinent Literature

Lord, Walter. *Incredible Victory*. New York: Harper & Row Publishers, 1967.

In *Incredible Victory*, Walter Lord combines high dramatic skills with a deeply rooted respect for historical evidence. Although in some of his points he differs with Samuel Eliot Morison's three chapters on Midway in Volume IV of the *United States Naval Operations in World War II*, *Incredible Victory* takes the careful, accurate framework of the official history and fleshes it out with further research and investigation. Lord interviewed nearly four hundred men who were there. The result is a happy combination of event and personality that demonstrates how popularly written history can be sound scholarship.

Lord's Foreword makes clear the thrust of the book. At Midway, the American fleet was hopelessly outclassed in equipment, weapons, and experience. It had no right to win, but it did. Accurately calling Midway a battle that changed the course of the war, Lord ranks it with Marathon, the Armada, and the Marne. The book is a tribute to the human spirit, to that special "magic blend of skill, faith, and valor that can lift men from certain defeat to incredible victory." But the book is not only drama. Facts are not bent nor events modified to provide excitement. The author is careful in his conclusions, judicious in his use of opinion, and almost always clear in his explanation. The narrative skips back and forth between American and Japanese forces at sea and on land, revealing the thoughts and actions of the leaders and the led.

Beginning with Admiral Yamamoto's understanding that the United States fleet had to be destroyed before new ships could be added to it, Lord shows the careful, if sometimes myopic, shaping of the Japanese leader's plans. To counter this assault, American naval intelligence had to discover Japanese intentions. With the breaking of the Japanese naval cipher, Commander Joseph J. Rochefort, Jr., could make some shrewd guesses as to where and when they were coming. Admiral Chester Nimitz, Commander in Chief of the Pacific Fleet, accepted the assessment and tried to be as ready as possible with the men and tools at hand.

One of Lord's contributions in this work is his study of the forces on Midway itself. He shows the mix of tension, exhilaration, doubt, fear, and chilling urgency of those who had to try to make the island invulnerable to assault, frequently having to make bricks without straw. The reader is left with the impression that, had the Japanese tried to land, they would have been driven off. Midway's 120 airplanes were far from the best, but they were all that could be crowded onto the island. Lord describes the planes, mainly the antique Vindicators and Brewster Buffaloes, which Marine pilots flew with a kind of resigned anger.

The author's account of the battle is clear, although the book needs maps beyond those on the endpapers. The battle is a complex one and those maps merely give an overview of it. Having to switch back and forth between the Japanese and the United States sides, the reader is occasionally confused as to the course of events; but that is probably unavoidable. The story is generally very well and precisely told, concentrating on the decisive morning of June 4.

A particular strength of the work lies in the thumbnail sketches of the men involved on both sides. Leaders such as Admirals Spruance and Fletcher, Captain Buckmaster of the *Yorktown*, Admirals Yamamoto and Nagumo, come alive. Lord's characterizations of Spruance and the other leaders do not differ significantly from accepted judgments. Spruance, careful as well as bold, could have lost the battle by pursuing the badly hurt Japanese First Carrier Striking Force into a night engagement with Yamamoto's huge Main Force battle fleet, as the Japanese Admiral wanted him to do. Vice Admiral Nagumo lost his part of the battle through indecision as to the timing of the raid on the American carriers and lack of careful searching by his scout planes. Yamamoto, the architect of the victory at Pearl Harbor was the architect of defeat at Midway. His wide dispersal of ships and his misuse of both carriers and battleships set the stage for disaster.

Beyond the plans and actions of the admirals, the reader is also left with vivid impressions of many others who fought and often died at Midway. There was Commander John C. Waldron, who led the doomed Torpedo Squadron 8 from the *Hornet* in an attack in which all fifteen planes were lost and all the airmen except Ensign George Gay died. On the Jap-anese side there was Lieutenant Jo-ichi Tomonaga from the *Hiryu*. With the *Hiryu* the only Japanese carrier left afloat, Tomonaga led his torpedo bombers against the *Yorktown* flying a plane with only one undamaged gas tank, knowing that he would not have enough fuel left to return. The glory of the incredible victory is dimmed by the sadness that men must die in war.

Fuchida, Mitsuo and Masatake Okumiya. *Midway: The Battle That Doomed Japan.* Menasha, Wis.: United States Naval Institute Publication, 1955.

Captain Mitsuo Fuchida, the primary author of this work, was an eyewitness of much of the action at Midway. Senior air wing commander aboard the *Akagi*, flagship of the Nagumo Force, he would have led the air assault on Midway and, in all likelihood, on the U.S. carriers as well, had he not undergone an operation for appendicitis just after the fleet left Japanese home waters. Burned, and with both ankles broken during a climb from the burning bridge of the *Akagi*, he was transferred to the Naval War College after his wounds healed. His special assignment was to make a report on the Battle of Midway. This report forms the heart of the book, the most complete Japanese study of the battle.

Fuchida and Okumiya lay a solid background for their work with a lengthy analysis of the history of Japanese naval thinking. The reader senses their frustration with the foolishness of the military and political leaders in their acceptance of war with the United States without a full awareness of the dangers. Okumiya says in his Preface that "the Pacific War was started by men who did not understand the sea and fought by men who did not understand the air." It is this lack of understanding of the air forces that forms the basis of their criticism of Yamamoto, Nagumo, and other admirals who led Japan to defeat. They make a good case.

In general agreement with American writers, the authors are critical of Japanese plans for Midway. The Aleutian adventure, in which Okumiya was involved, served no good purpose. The forces approaching Midway were so badly dispersed that they could not be mutually supporting. But in addition to these strategic mistakes, the authors see other and more critical flaws underlying the defeat. Since they were present at the deliberations and throughout the action, they can speak with personal knowledge of the state of mind of the Japanese naval planners.

It is in this state of mind that they find one of the most serious problems: profound overconfidence verging on arrogance. Six months of startlingly easy victories in the Pacific and Indian oceans led many to believe that the Japanese navy was invincible. Hence, no real plans were made for contingencies. If the Americans refused to act as they were supposed to act, a possibility that few even considered, they could be handled without difficulty. The authors give credit to American intelligence but criticize its Japanese counterpart at all levels. Intelligence gathering and interpretation in Japan and on the scene were both faulty.

The authors' criticism of Yamamoto's fleet dispersal is standard. They see the basic fault in Yamamoto's (and other Japanese admirals') inability to understand that World War II was a carrier war. The battleship, which for generations had been the heart of the fleet, had lost primacy to the airplane. Rather than using the battleships in their most effective role as gunfire and antiaircraft support for the carriers, as the Americans did, they were to be used to provide the knockout punch after Midway had been neutralized and the American fleet lured out to sea. In actuality, none of the huge ships fired its main batteries at enemy ships during the battle.

Nagumo and his First Carrier Striking Force had a double mission that, at best, complicated their role. They were tied to the Midway invasion by the demand that they neutralize the air power on the island by a given time. But they also had to be ready to meet the enemy fleet. No clear working priority was ever established between the two responsibilities. Nagumo bears a large share of the blame for the loss of his carriers. His search for the U.S. fleet was plainly inadequate. He was indecisive when the fleet was discovered. Caught with all of his planes on board, gassed and fully armed, he gave the Americans their perfect opportunity.

The authors' description of the battle is clear and dramatic. An excellent appendix lists all the Japanese ships and their commanders. Finally, they share with the reader the deep sense of loss that sailors of any nation feel when a great ship goes down. For anyone attempting to understand the Battle of Midway, this is an essential work. — *C.W.J.*

## Additional Recommended Reading

Morison, Samuel Eliot. *History of United States Naval Operations in World War II.* Vol. IV: *Coral Sea, Midway and Submarine Actions, May 1942-August 1942.* Boston: Little, Brown and Company, 1950. The classic three chapters on Midway, written with a sailor's love of the sea and ships and the historian's need for order and clarity, remain the standard against which other books on Midway are judged.

Smith, William Ward. *Midway: Turning Point of the Pacific.* New York: Thomas Y. Crowell Company, 1966. Commander of the *Yorktown*'s cruiser screening force, Smith knew all the other American admirals personally. He writes as an eyewitness with insights of a professional sailor.

Loosbrock, John F. and Richard M. Skinner, eds. *The Wild Blue.* New York: G. P. Putnam's Sons, 1966. Among these articles taken from the *Air Force Magazine* is one written shortly after the action by Lieutenant Colonel Walter C. Sweeny, Jr., who led the Army B-17 raids against the Japanese around Midway.

Dull, Paul S. *A Battle History of the Japanese Navy (1941-1945)*. Annapolis, Md.: United States Naval Institute Press, 1978. Making extensive use of both Japanese and American sources, the author writes clearly and carefully of each action and has a very complete section on Midway.

Belote, James H. and William M. Belote. *The Titans of the Sea: The Development and Operations of Japanese and American Carrier Task Forces During World War II*. New York: Harper & Row Publishers, 1975. Provides a contrast of United States and Japanese carrier doctrine.

Tuleja, Thaddeus V. *Climax at Midway*. New York: W. W. Norton and Company, 1960. A careful study which provides an excellent treatment of the battle; clear and accurate in its conclusions.

Frank, Pat and Joseph D. Harrington. *Rendezvous at Midway:* U.S.S. Yorktown *and the Japanese Carrier Fleet*. New York: The John Day Company, 1967.

Stafford, Edward P. *The Big E: Story of the* U.S.S. Enterprise. New York: Random House, 1962.

Griffith, Alexander. *A Ship To Remember*. New York: Howell, Soskin, 1943.

These three works study respectively the three American carriers (*Yorktown*, *Enterprise*, and *Hornet*) which fought at Midway.

# SOVIET INVASION OF EASTERN EUROPE

*Type of event:* Military: expansionism in response to invasion
*Time:* Mid-1944 to mid-1945
*Locale:* Eastern Europe

*Principal personages:*

JOSEPH STALIN (IOSIF VISSARIONOVICH DZHUGASHVILI) (1879-1953), Dictator of the Soviet Union, 1924-1953

ADOLF HITLER (1889-1945), Chancellor and Führer of Germany, 1933-1945

GENERAL HEINZ GUDERIAN (1886-1954), Chief of the German General Staff, 1944-1945

FIELD MARSHAL ERIC VON MANSTEIN, German Army Group Commander in the Ukrainian regions

MARSHAL GEORGI KONSTANTINOVICH ZHUKOV (1895-1974), Commander of all Soviet field armies in the Ukrainian regions

## Summary of Event

By late summer of 1943, the German war on the Soviet Union had reached yet another crossroads in what had been a succession of fluctuations. The recently concluded Battle of Kursk (July, 1943) had put an end to whatever dreams still lingered in the minds of Adolf Hitler and his General Staff that the war in Russia could be brought to a victorious end. While the brutal Battle of Stalingrad in late 1942 had guaranteed that the Germans could not win the war in Russia, the vicious tank battle at Kursk had virtually assured that they would lose it. Sizable reserves of panzer units and experienced combat troops had been squandered in an attempt to regain the initiative and slice off the huge Russian salient which had resulted from the Soviet counteroffensive of early 1943.

For Hitler and his decisionmakers, the question had now become one of how best to conduct a defensive struggle against the inevitable resumption of Soviet attacks. To be sure, the German forces in Russia remained sizable and the terrain occupied substantial. However, the tide of the war in the East had clearly turned by late 1943 and the prospect of a prolonged war there now depended largely upon the nature of the German response. With victory no longer a realistic prospect, a form of stalemate was sought until perhaps unforeseen events might occur to help alter the situation.

In many respects, the last eighteen months of the war in the East, from late 1943 until the fall of Berlin in 1945, were marked by serious differences of opinion between Hitler and his commanders on how to deal with the increasingly threatening Russian recovery. As the German commanders in the field saw it, the problem was one of regaining operational freedom. A more fluid military situ-

479

ation was sought in which vital areas would continue to be defended while the less tenable ones were abandoned. Local reserves would be rebuilt in order to provide for the possibility of localized counterattacks in the event of Soviet breakthroughs. Both General Heinz Guderian, appointed Chief of the General Staff in 1944, and Field Marshal Eric von Manstein, the latter being in command of the seriously threatened southern sectors, advocated strongly the adoption of such a mobile defense and appeared confident that a response of this type could indefinitely harass any and all Russian assaults.

Unfortunately, from the German General Staff viewpoint, Hitler remained adamantly opposed to such a defensive policy. Although Hitler too had to admit that offensive operations were now no longer feasible, he was determined to cling to whatever terrain his armies still possessed regardless of the extent of the Soviet pressure. When the German armies lay outside Moscow in late 1941, Hitler had first espoused his policy of no withdrawals. It had met with broad opposition from virtually all of his field commanders, but the decision not to retreat was enforced with impressive results. The German front before Moscow was successfully held, thus convincing Hitler that his judgment was clearly superior to that of his trained and decorated officers.

Now, in the face of a similar but more serious challenge from the Soviets, Hitler once again was reluctant to trust his commanders' judgments. General Guderian in his *Panzer Leader* wartime memoirs offered the telling evaluation that

. . . if Hitler heard the word "operational," he lost his temper. He believed that whenever his generals spoke of operations they meant withdrawals; and consequently Hitler insisted with fanatical obstinacy that ground must be held, all ground, even when it was to our disadvantage to do so.

The result was the loss of any stalemated situation during 1943, and by the spring of 1944 such a condition was no longer possible to create from the German point of view. By April of 1944, the Soviets were at the foothills of the Carpathian Mountains on the Hungarian frontier and controlled the extensive Odessa-Warsaw railroad line. In addition, the Soviet forces were near Brest-Litovsk and the Bug river where Hitler had launched his invasion in 1941. The halt in the Russian offensive at these lines was due not so much to the credibility of the Axis defenses, as to the muddy ground conditions and the drastically overstretched supply and communications lines.

With the Rumanian oil fields clearly within the Soviet's reach, Hitler anticipated additional attacks upon his forces in that area. Instead, the Russian assault, timed roughly to coincide with the D-Day landings in Normandy in June of 1944, fell upon Hitler's Army Group Center. Approximately 300,000 German casualties resulted and a 250-mile breach was cut into the German front. East Prussia and the Baltic area were now open to Russian penetration, and both Belorussiya and northeastern Poland had already been seized.

July of 1944 showed further evidence of the extent of the German collapse. By the 26th the Vistula river was reached, and by the 31st of July Soviet troops had reached the outskirts of Warsaw. The month of July alone had cost the German command two hundred miles of terrain, and early August saw Russian bridge-heads across the Vistula some 130 miles south of Warsaw.

The mastermind behind the Soviet successes had been Marshal Georgi Zhukov. More than any other single Russian commander, Zhukov had been responsible for turning the tide of the war with his surprising counteroffensive launched at Stalingrad. From late 1942 until mid-1944, Zhukov had systematically chased the Axis armies out of southern Russia, and now was poised for a penetration of the Eastern European countries.

With the destruction of the German Army Group Center, genuine resistance to the Soviet offensives was no longer really viable. By the fall of 1944, a lull of sorts had set in partly because of the sheer exhaustion of the Russian spearheads, and also in part (because of) what would appear to have been political considerations in the mind of Joseph Stalin. The Russians controversially delayed their attack on Warsaw in the midst of a local uprising in the city against the German occupation forces. Without Soviet assistance, the uprising failed after two months of brutal street fighting with German SS troops. The rationale for the Soviet stance here remains subject to debate, although a weakened Warsaw may have appealed to Stalin with a view to his intentions to dominate Poland totally after the war.

As early as 1942, Stalin had made it clear to British Prime Minister Winston Churchill that Russia intended to press for major revisions in Eastern Europe upon the war's completion. While such a futuristic view may have seemed presumptuous in 1942, Stalin was in a position by the fall of 1944 to realize such an ambition. Clearly, the messianic designs of the Communist ideology played a part in his strategy, but at least as noteworthy was the consideration of Russian national security. In preceding centuries, Russia had experienced invasions by both the Swedes and the French who had entered Russia via the unstable regions of Eastern Europe. In both World Wars I and II, German armies had also invaded Russia by the same route. As such, Stalin's interest in an Eastern Europe under some form of Russian control was clearly motivated by a traditional Russian feeling of insecurity.

Beginning in August of 1944, Stalin began the process of driving the Germans from the Balkans with the conquest of Rumania. On the 27th, Galatz fell, on the 30th the Ploesti oil fields of Rumania were seized, and on the 31st Bucharest was taken. The German command had retreated some 250 miles in a twelve-day period of August, and in the next six days had pulled back another two hundred miles as the Soviets moved to the Yugoslavian border at Turnu Severin.

During the remaining four months of 1944, the Balkans were absorbed into the Russian sphere of control. Budapest managed to hold out until mid-February of 1945 because of the commitment of a potent force of Hitler's dwindling panzer reserves, but Belgrade had been lost in October.

The opening of 1945 saw the Soviet armies within approximately three hundred miles of Berlin itself, and, if past offensive advances could be used as a yardstick, this distance could conceivably be covered by a further Russian assault in about five weeks.

Certainly the ability of the Germans to continue resistance in Eastern Europe in early 1945 was due largely to the myriad range of options which lay open to the Soviet High Command. By 1945, Soviet forces outnumbered the German defenders eleven to one in infantry, seven to one in tanks, and twenty to one in heavy guns and artillery. Curiously, Hitler continued to dismiss such statistics as "rubbish," and, as Heinz Guderian again notes in his *Panzer Leader* memoirs, Hitler told Guderian at the end of 1944 that "the Eastern Front must take care of itself."

During April of 1945, Soviet forces occupied the rest of Hungary, Czechoslovakia, and roughly half of Austria, including the capital, Vienna. Berlin fell to the Red Army on May 2 and the war in Europe formally ended several days later. The military casualty listings for the entire Eastern Front wars since 1941 attest to the severity of the fighting. The Germans alone suffered 1,015,000 dead, 4,000,000 wounded, and 1,300,000 missing, while Russian figures are estimated at 14,000,000 casualties, of whom some 10,000,000 died.

## Pertinent Literature

Liddell Hart, B. H. *The German Generals Talk*. New York: William Morrow and Company, 1948.

Originally titled *The Other Side of the Hill*, this work by Captain B. H. Liddell Hart was something of a first of its kind. During the immediate aftermath of World War II, Liddell Hart spent considerable time personally interviewing a variety of high-ranking German officers on their impressions of the war years. The result is this highly absorbing text which, as the original title implies, offers a first-hand account of the military operations from the vantage point of German generals who participated in them.

Under normal circumstances, such interviews could be expected to be somewhat wooden affairs in which stock answers are given to equally mundane inquiries. Such is not the case here. Liddell Hart was a figure well-known to most German officers because of his prewar writings in England on the possibilities of employing mechanized forces in a thoroughly integrated fashion. Noted German generals including Rommel, Guderian, Manstein, and Manteuffel had all become familiar with Liddell Hart's ideas and incorporated them into the German strategic concept known as *Blitzkrieg* or "lightning warfare." As such, the officers here are discussing the critical battles of World War II with a man whose own military visions and judgments they clearly respect. Indeed, both prior to the war and afterwards, Liddell Hart became known as the captain to whom generals listen.

The nature of Liddell Hart's work here is to capture the impressions of the German commanders regarding decisions made, opportunities lost, and evaluations of the various opposing armies. In conducting such an inquiry, Liddell Hart offers a survey of the entire European theater of operations from 1939 to 1945. However, while the German generals are forthcoming on many subjects, there seems to be a particular willingness on their part to recount their impressions of the Eastern Front and the Russian opponent.

While numerous chapters in the book deal with the Russian Front, two in particular are relevant to the closing months there: "After Stalingrad" and "The Red Army." In the former, the generals expound in some detail on the frustrations they faced in dealing with the onslaught of Soviet offensives from 1943 to 1945. Although experiences differed somewhat, all of the commanders agreed that Hitler's policy of no unauthorized withdrawls prevented them from practicing the notion of elastic defense. Many officers adamantly maintained that the war in Russia, even after the Stalingrad debacle, could have been fought indefinitely had resources not been squandered away by the rigidity of Hitler's position that no retreats could be undertaken without his personal consent. There is considerable bitterness in the tone of the responses given to the author by these generals, not so much because the war was lost, but because Hitler had prevented them from conducting the kinds of operations they would have preferred if left alone to practice their craft.

Particularly revealing also are the views given on the nature of the Russian Army. Here the analysis extends from an evaluation of Soviet weaponry to the fighting qualities of the individual Russian soldier. With respect to the Soviet war matériel, the German generals offered considerable praise for the T-34 tank and the "Stalin" model which appeared in 1944, the latter being felt to be the best tank design of the war by any belligerent. What makes such a commentary particularly noteworthy is the fact that on the eve of the German invasion of Russia in 1941, the quality of Soviet equipment elicited derisive remarks from German intelligence agencies.

With regard to the Russian soldier, the German generals offer somewhat more graphic opinions. All seem to agree that the Russian proved to be a tenacious fighter, particularly on defense, and perfectly willing to follow directives regardless of the logic or practicality involved. Generally, though, it was felt that the Soviet combat troops were not technically well-trained nor were they especially well-led, particularly by lower level officers. Yet a grudging admiration seems to emerge for the fact that the typical Russian soldier appeared to be impervious to nature's discomforts and the absence of adequate support facilities.

Since the appearance of Liddell Hart's book in 1948, many of the surviving German generals have written memoirs and accounts of the war years. But the frankness expressed here and the freshness of their memories offer an excellent source of impressions that many subsequent writings cannot eclipse.

Guderian, Heinz. *Panzer Leader*. New York: E. P. Dutton, 1952.

With the possible exception of Field Marshal Erwin Rommel, a figure considerably popularized by his amazing exploits in the desert campaigns of North Africa, no single German commander in World War II was more celebrated by friend and foe alike than Heinz Guderian. Even more so than Rommel, Guderian exhibited an expertise in the potentials of tank warfare as early as the 1930's. In the prewar years, it was Guderian who helped to direct and coordinate the development of the German panzer formations which during the war provided the army with a highly integrated strike force capable of making the most carefully structured defensive position obsolete.

Originally written in German and translated by Constantine Fitzgibbon, *Panzer Leader* is Guderian's personal memoir on his career in the German Army and his observations on the war in Europe. Although Guderian first made a name for himself during the Germans' startlingly rapid overrunning of France in 1940, most of his wartime experience was spent in the East as part of the Russian campaign. In exacting detail, the author outlines the vast scope of the battles between 1941 and 1945, focusing most particularly upon his involvement with the constantly reduced panzer divisions. As might be expected, the more dynamic aspects of the book tend to deal with Guderian's role in the initial extensive thrust into the Soviet Union in 1941.

Considerable attention is given to Hitler's highly controversial decision to shift the focal point of the invasion away from Moscow and toward the Ukraine in late summer and early fall of 1941. Guderian, who could quite possibly have been the first invader of Russia to seize Moscow since Napoleon Bonaparte, leaves no doubt as to his opposition to the southern strategy adopted.

Attention to the decision before Moscow in 1941 carries a wider importance, however. Beginning in mid- to late- 1941, Guderian notes an ever-increasing tendency on Hitler's part to waver in the face of future objectives. It is suggested here that from this point in the Russian campaign until the bitter end in 1945, Hitler and his commanders increasingly differed on the style and direction of the war effort. Ironically, after the abortive Moscow assault in 1941, the war itself became nearly anticlimactic for Guderian.

After the Stalingrad reversal in 1942 and the subsequent Soviet counteroffensive lasting into 1943, Guderian was removed from the scene of the battles and ordered to devote his time to a reorganization of the battered panzer forces. However, as critical conditions emerged both on the Western and Eastern Fronts of Europe, Guderian was placed in the position of Chief of the General Staff. Normally a highly significant command post, Chief of the General Staff now had become confined to a virtual errand boy's role which allowed Guderian little more than an occasional opportunity to confer with Hitler on strategic decisions. In most instances, though, decisions had already been made by Hitler in advance and the best Guderian could hope for was the chance to ask openly for reconsiderations. Time and again Guderian found this a useless exercise and a source of considerable frustration, especially in view of the fact that the prospects for victory were being squandered away by senseless policies.

Like many other German officers familiar with the deteriorating military situation on the Eastern Front from 1943 to 1945, Guderian was convinced that a more appropriate defensive posture could have substantially altered the success of the Russian offensives. His bitterness at being denied the opportunity, along with his fellow commanders, to practice their military skills even at this late date in the war is not hidden.

Interestingly, however, Guderian's staff position during the late years did enable him to observe closely Hitler and the manner in which decisions were made. The concluding chapter of the book, entitled "Leading Personalities of the Third Reich," offers an especially telling portrait of Hitler from the vantage point of one who was not only representative of the military's perspective, but who was also actually present in Hitler's High Command circle. This series of observations, coupled with Guderian's encounters with Hitler as a military commander during the war itself, provide a remarkable portrait which would certainly appear to have influenced later authors attempting to discern Hitler's personality.

Throughout this work, it is Guderian's style to comment on events in a completely unemotional manner. This is not to suggest that his own feelings are absent, but is meant to imply that the events largely speak for themselves. The hopeless frustration felt by Guderian during the period of late 1944 and 1945 with regard to the conduct of operations in Eastern Europe against the Russian onslaught is made all the more vivid by the quiet desperation of his literary style. Having left his mark upon history, both as a military commander and as an innovator in strategy and tactics, Guderian clearly transcended the grim politics of Nazism. — *T.A.B.*

## Additional Recommended Reading

Ryan, Cornelius. *The Last Battle*. New York: Simon & Schuster, 1966. Deals with the final days of Hitler's Third Reich. While the emphasis is on the Battle for Berlin in 1945, the full collapse in the East is also depicted.

Toland, John. *The Last 100 Days*. New York: Random House, 1966. Covers a broad range of events during the last few months of the war including the utter hopelessness of German commanders attempting to conduct meaningful operations in the East in the waning weeks.

Clark, Alan. *Barbarossa: The Russian-German Conflict, 1941-1945*. New York: William Morrow and Company, 1965. Rather than placing the full burden of defeat upon Hitler's interference with the General Staff, Clark suggests that a great many of the German defeats were attributable to the German officers themselves and their own various ambitions, petty rivalries, and miscalculations.

Mellenthin, Friedrich Wilhelm von. *Panzer Battles: A Study of the Employment of Armor in the Second World War*. Translated by H. Betzler. Edited by L. C. F. Turner. Norman: University of Oklahoma Press, 1956. A panzer officer's depiction of the last days on the Eastern Front focuses upon the insurmountable problems which Germany faced in trying to parry the massively superior Russian offensive thrusts with severely limited resources.

Gilbert, Felix, ed. *Hitler Directs His War: The Secret Records of His Daily Military Conferences*. New York: Oxford University Press, 1950. A collection of actual transcripts of Hitler's private conferences with his personal staff, including dialogue conversations between Hitler and General Heinz Guderian during the last days of the Eastern Front battles.

Majdalany, Fred. *The Fall of Fortress Europe*. Garden City, N.Y.: Doubleday & Company, 1968. An account of the Allied regaining of Europe from the Axis Powers which vividly portrays the designs of the Soviet Union with respect to the future of the Eastern European countries overrun by its armies.

Seaton, Albert. *The Russo-German War, 1941-1945*. New York: Frederick A. Praeger, 1970. Numerous chapters of this thorough study are devoted to the Soviet drive into Eastern Europe.

# THE FIRST SUPERFORTRESS BOMBING RAID ON JAPAN

*Type of event:* Military: beginning of the B-29 bombing of Japan
*Time:* June 15, 1944
*Locale:* Chengtu, China; and Yawata, Japan

*Principal personages:*
FRANKLIN DELANO ROOSEVELT (1882-1945), thirty-second
    President of the United States, 1933-1945
GENERAL HENRY HARLEY (HAP) ARNOLD (1886-1950),
    Commander of the United States Army Air Corps
MAJOR GENERAL KENNETH B. WOLFE (1896-1971), Com-
    mander of the Twentieth Bomber Command
BRIGADIER GENERAL LAVERNE (BLONDIE) SAUNDERS (1903-
    ), Commander of the 58th Bombardment Wing (VH)

## Summary of Event

The Doolittle raid on Tokyo in April, 1942, was the first air raid by United States bombers on the Japanese home islands and the only one for the next two years. The rapid Japanese advance in the Pacific and the Japanese hold on the Asian mainland drove the Americans from any bases close enough to carry out air raids on Japan. The available heavy bombers, the B-17 Flying Fortress and the B-24 Liberator, did not have adequate range. The B-29 Superfortress, however, brought new technology to bear.

The Army had shown interest in the new long-range, high-altitude bomber which the Boeing Company had begun to develop in 1938. Although the XB-29 was not test flown until September, 1942, the Air Corps had already authorized Boeing to begin production as soon as possible. Far larger than the B-17, the Superfortress measured ninety-nine feet in length with a wing span of 141 feet. It weighed more than sixty tons fully loaded and had a top speed of 363 miles per hour. Powered by four 2,200-horsepower Wright "Double Cyclone" engines, it had a combat radius of some 1,600 miles fully armed. Three separate pressurized compartments meant that its crew of eleven could cruise at the plane's service ceiling of 33,000 feet without the necessity of oxygen masks. The aircraft was armed with ten .50 caliber machine guns in five turrets in the fuselage, which could be centrally directed, and had two more .50's and a 20mm cannon in the tail. Under ideal conditions it could carry a bomb load of ten tons.

Plans by the Air Force for the plane's use had taken various forms including its commitment in Europe. By the time significant numbers of the planes could be ready, however, British and American bombers flying from England had made the B-29 less than essential for the war against Germany. By the end of 1943, the Air Force Chief, General Henry H. (Hap) Arnold, was committed to its use against Japan.

United States air bases in the Aleutian Islands, however, were too far from Japan. The islands in the Mariana group which could provide bases (Saipan, Tinian, and Guam) were not projected to be in American hands until the winter of 1944. Thus, Air Force planners looked to China.

The plan for bases in China combined with President Franklin D. Roosevelt's desire to "do something" for that nation. China was last to get priorities, supplies, and support. Roosevelt feared that unless the Chinese leader, Chiang Kai-shek, received some tangible help, he might quit the war. When the Air Force suggested basing the new B-29's in India but staging them through fields in China as visible evidence of United States support, it found a receptive audience in the President. He approved this plan, known as Operation Matterhorn, in November, 1943.

The idea of an independent, powerful, strategic bombing force had long been a dream of American flyers. Supplying itself with all the necessities of war, this command could, it was hoped, bludgeon any enemy into surrender by strategic bombing without the necessity of invasion. Perhaps the Superfort was the weapon.

The United States Joint Chiefs of Staff, with General Arnold as their agent, retained command of the newly created Twentieth Bomber Command. Neither the British commander in the area, Lord Louis Mountbatten, nor United States Army commander Lieutenant General Joseph W. Stilwell would decide on the deployment and use of the B-29's in their theater. They would, however, see a significant amount of the very limited tonnage that was flown over the Hump into China diverted to the B-29 bases at Chengtu.

The Twentieth Bomber Command under Brigadier General Kenneth B. Wolfe was originally made up of the 58th Bombardment Wing and the 73d Bombardment Wing. The 73d was detached in April, 1944, to go to the Mariana Islands whose date of capture had advanced to June, 1944. A Wing contained 112 bombers plus replacement ships and slightly over three thousand officers and eight thousand enlisted men. Support, service, and engineer personnel brought total strength of the Twentieth Bomber Command to approximately 20,000 men.

Since all supplies for Chinese bases had to be flown in, stockpiling was difficult. B-29's from India had to fly seven round trips to bring enough gasoline and other necessities to make possible one mission over Japan. With the loss of the 73d Wing, the 58th Wing could not supply itself for raids of one hundred planes or more, the hoped-for number, more than a few times each month. This, combined with the high rate of engine failures and loss of planes because of inexperienced crews and the other faults to be expected in a new weapon, meant that the first raid on Japan could not be launched until June 15, 1944.

The AAF's Committee of Operations Analysts had suggested that an appropriate strategic target for B-29's would be the coke ovens that supplied Japan's steel mills. The first strike would be at the coke ovens of the Imperial Iron and Steel Works at

Yawata on the island of Kyushu, which was at the edge of the bomber's combat range.

Beginning on June 13, ninety-two planes left the Bengal fields in India, seventy-nine of which reached the Chengtu bases. Each came loaded with two tons of five-hundred-pound bombs and needed only to refuel in China. Washington, which had picked the target, ordered a night mission with bombs to be dropped from between eight thousand and eighteen thousand feet. On June 15, the same day that the Marines went ashore on Saipan, sixty-eight planes, led by Wing Commander Brigadier General LaVerne (Blondie) Saunders, left the fields. Four were forced back by engine trouble and one crashed immediately after take-off. Forty-seven Superforts bombed Yawata that night, most using radar because of a very effective blackout of the city compounded by haze and smoke. The other planes had not made it over Yawata for a variety of reasons, mostly mechanical. Five planes were lost, one to enemy fighters on the return trip. Fighter opposition over the target and antiaircraft fire had been light.

Photo reconnaissance showed very little damage, with only one hit on a shop at the plant and none on the coke ovens. This was not a massive fire-bomb raid of the type that would begin in May, 1945, from the Mariana Islands. The AAF was still concentrating on high-altitude, precision strategic bombing. The 58th Wing would average two raids a month until March, 1945, when it was moved to Saipan. Operating under a very difficult logistical situation, Matterhorn had been a stimulant for Chinese morale and had provided a necessary shakedown for the new bombers and crews. Matterhorn was not a success nor was the first raid on Japan; but both presaged a more destructive future for the Superfortress.

## Pertinent Literature

Craven, Wesley Frank and James Lea Cate, eds. *The Army Air Forces in World War II*. Vol. V: *The Pacific: Matterhorn to Nagasaki, June 1944 to August 1945*. Chicago: The University of Chicago Press, 1953.

Nearly the first two hundred pages of this valuable study of the Army Air Forces in World War II deals with the Matterhorn project. Making extensive use of the large body of manuscript materials available and the reports of the United States Strategic Bombing Survey, the authors have presented what will probably remain the definitive history of the Twentieth Bomber Command.

Beginning with a section on the development of the B-29 Superfortress, the authors describe and analyze the early plans for using the new bomber. Although production of the B-29 was a full year faster than originally planned because of close cooperation between Boeing and the Air Force and some daring chances taken by both, it appeared to the planners that Germany might well be defeated before the plane could play a significant role in Europe. But British failures in Burma, Japanese successes in China, and a deteriorating situation in the East generally called for a more active policy in the China-Burma-India Theater.

To do anything there, however, meant trying to deal with a complex national and command situation involving prickly personalities and divergent national interests. This history clarifies and delineates the personalities and interests, sometimes with a fairly clear bias toward those interested in strategic bombing.

Policies and personalities overlapped in a most difficult way. Theater Commander Lieutenant General Joseph W. Stilwell, who was also Chief of Staff to Chinese leader Chiang Kai-shek, wanted to concentrate on building up the Chinese Army, regaining north Burma, and opening a road into China which would allow this large, reinvigorated Chinese Army to drive out the Japanese. Major General Claire L. Chennault, nominally Stilwell's subordinate but often more nearly independent as commander of the Fourteenth Air Force in China, wanted to increase the tonnage flown across the Hump. With this, he believed, he could harass Japan's land and sea routes, winning the war from the air. Added to this were Chiang's fears of the Communists in the north and British needs to regain prestige and retain India. None of these interests would welcome a new and independent bomber force, especially since it would divert supplies and be controlled from Washington. The United States Joint Chiefs of Staff and General H. H. Arnold, however, believed that the potential of this strategic offensive

weapon might well be siphoned off into immediate tactical needs of whoever would control it in Asia.

A strong point of the book is the exposition of the massive transportation problems faced by anyone who would fly out of India and China. Half a world away from the United States, India's port and transportation facilities were inadequate at best and primitive at worst. Since no road was available into China, B-29's had to carry in their own supplies. While this gave some flying time to the crews, it was not the kind of formation, high-altitude flying necessary for bombing raids, and morale dropped. The crews of these new planes looked on themselves as "a goddam trucking outfit." Losses were incurred as the Superforts fell to mechanical failure and inexperienced crews. Even with this commitment of B-29's to carry supplies, the hard-pressed Air Transport Command had to divert tonnage to Chengtu.

Using battle reports, the authors cover each raid in detail from the first at Yawata to the last against Singapore in March, 1945. The reader is struck by the difficulties faced and, at least partially, overcome. Mechanical failures caused far more losses than did the Japanese. Accidents, such as two bombs in a stick hitting and detonating in the air, took their toll. While generally not a book with a dramatic style, some of the events are by their nature dramatic. Bad weather and heavy clouds, smoke from fires started by bombs dropped from earlier planes, winds with velocities up to two hundred miles per hour, and inexperienced bombardiers and navigators combined to make the effectiveness of the early raids spotty at best. The problems also pointed to a possible solution, however, one that General Curtis LeMay would use beginning in May, 1945: the massive fire-bomb raids that would devastate nearly all major Japanese cities.

When General LeMay took command of the Twentieth Bomber Command in the late summer of 1944, training and demands on crews were intensified and the raids had greater weight and effectiveness. But the concentration remained on high-altitude precision bombing. The "lab testing" of this new weapon from China continued until focus shifted to the Mariana Islands in late 1944. At this point, also, some of the Twentieth Bomber Command's work would be shifted from strategic bombing of Japan to support of efforts in the Dutch East Indies and Burma.

The authors end their work on Matterhorn with a number of careful conclusions. The Chengtu operation was not a decisive factor in the Japanese surrender, but the planners did not intend it to be. The diversion of the 73d Wing to Saipan doomed an already shaky logistical system to failure: two combat sorties per plane per month was not an enviable record. The Chinese people were enthusiastic about their role in the raids and the fact that a powerful new weapon was helping them in their fight against Japan. Protection of the B-29's in China did tie down fighters and aviation gasoline that the Fourteenth Air Force might well have used elsewhere. Combat testing of the B-29 and its crews led all concerned to recognize what a superb plane it was. When it moved to Saipan, the 58th Wing was a very effective combat organization. Whether it could have been more effectively used elsewhere, the authors conclude, will remain a debatable matter. But in the summer of 1944, China was the only location from which the United States could strike at Japan's home islands.

Chennault, Claire Lee. *Way of a Fighter.* New York: G. P. Putnam's Sons, 1949.

Approaching the B-29's in China from an entirely different point of view from that of the official Air Force history is the work of General Chennault, Commander of the Fourteenth Air Force in China until the summer of 1945. In this very personal and often bitter memoir of his war years, Chennault tells of his long struggle to build an Air Force in China. Operation Matterhorn, for him, was wrong for many reasons.

From his experience with B-24 heavy bombers in the 308th Bomb Group, Chennault was convinced that bombers had to have fighter escort, without which they would suffer unacceptable losses from enemy fighters. However, the B-29's could not have fighter escort over the target because the distances were too great. In this judgment, he was incorrect. The losses over Japan were never found to be "excessive."

Matterhorn would concentrate on steel mills and other strategically important targets in Japan. Chennault believed that shipping constituted the Japanese jugular vein, and the United States Strategic Bombing Survey Reports after the war supported his conclusions. The Japanese were operating at only two-thirds of capacity in 1944 because of a shortage of imported iron ore. More than five million tons capacity would have to be destroyed in order to cut into production. Concentration on shipping, docks, and other port facilities would probably have been more effective.

Promised ten thousand tons of supplies a month over the Hump in 1943, Chennault was not receiving even close to that amount, so it is not surprising that he was angry about the diversion of Hump tonnage to the independent Twentieth Bomber Command. He was especially upset that he was also saddled with six squadrons of P-47 Thunderbolt fighters which were to be used, on orders from Washington, only to protect the B-29 bases around Chengtu. The B-29's themselves were inefficient in their role as transports, and although some were converted to gasoline tankers, much of the Twentieth Bomber Command's supplies had to be carried by the Air Transport Command. The original Pentagon promise to Chennault and his commander, Lieutenant General Joseph W. Stilwell, that the Bomber Command would not draw off any Hump tonnage could not be kept.

Chennault's complaint that the men of the Twentieth Bomber Command lived lush, luxurious lives with too many people and too much in the way of supplies does not seem to be borne out by the writings at the time by the Bomber Command's historian. This record maintains that in mid-1944 there was only one surface vehicle per base, no PX rations, no shipment of clothing, no hospital rations or supplies, and less than twenty-five percent of the mail flown in.

According to Chennault, the "bomber radicals" in the Pentagon were determined to keep a tight hold on the B-29's. In this he was correct. There seems to be no doubt that if he had gained command over them, they would have been diverted to tactical support in China. During the Japanese assaults in the early summer of 1944, Chennault appealed personally and unsuccessfully to the 20th's commander and to Air Force Chief General H. H. Arnold to use the B-29's to bomb the major Japanese supply base at Hankow. He was plainly pleased with the recall of the first Commander of the Twentieth Bomber Command, Brigadier General Kenneth B. Wolfe, whom he dismisses as a "Pentagon Planner" who "struck out with a large swish of his briefcase."

Chennault's view of Wolfe's replacement, Major General Curtis LeMay, however, was far different. A fighter from the European Theater of Operations, LeMay made the B-29's into the force which they were meant to be. Chennault takes credit for the raid on Hankow which finally took place in December in which planes filled with incendiary bombs burned the heart out of the city. This was the first mass fire-bomb raid that the B-29's attempted and it was extremely effective. The author was pleased with the possibility of "burning the guts out of Japan," and saw the Hankow raid as showing LeMay the way.

Challenging, highly personal, and occasionally insistently wrong-headed,

*Way of a Fighter* is an apt description    of this work. — *C.W.J.*

## Additional Recommended Reading

The United States Strategic Bombing Survey. *Air Campaigns of the Pacific War.* Washington, D.C.: U.S. Government Printing Office, 1947.

——————— . *The Strategic Air Operations of Very Heavy Bombardment in the War Against Japan (Twentieth Air Force).* Washington, D.C.: U.S. Government Printing Office, 1946.

——————— . *Summary Report: (Pacific War).* Washington, D.C.: U.S. Government Printing Office, 1946. These three works with their impressive statistics, excellent charts, and great detail provide the reader with both facts and evaluation of the first raids on Japan.

Fine, Lenore and Jesse A. Remington. *The United States Army in World War II: The Technical Services; The Corps of Engineers; Construction in the United States.* Washington, D.C.: Office of the Chief of Military History, 1972. In its chapter "Airfields for Very Heavy Bombers," the work traces the problems that the engineers faced in China and elsewhere in providing air fields for the new planes which, at 140,000 pounds fully loaded and with a wheel-load of 60,000 pounds, broke through or broke up normal runways.

Romanus, Charles F. and Riley Sunderland. *The United States Army in World War II: China-Burma-India Theater; Stilwell's Command Problems.* Washington, D.C.: Office of the Chief of Military History, 1956. Looking at the B-29 from the point of view of the foot soldier, the authors deal well with the material on Operation Matterhorn and its impact on Stilwell and his problems.

Haugland, Vern. *The AAF Against Japan.* New York: Harper & Brothers, 1948. A readable survey of the air war in the Pacific and in Asia which gives an accurate description of operations, the personalities of officers in command, and the difficulties they faced.

Goldberg, Alfred, ed. *A History of the United States Air Force: 1907-1957.* Princeton, N.J.: D. Van Nostrand Company, 1957. Rich in photographs, this overview of the Air Force has a brief but clear exposition of the Twentieth Bomber Command.

*Pedigree of Champions.* Seattle, Wash.: The Boeing Company, 1977. Fits the B-29 into the broader picture of plane production over the years at Boeing, contains some excellent color photographs, and gives the specifications and a brief history of the development of the Superfortress.

# FORMATION OF THE ARAB LEAGUE

*Type of event:* Diplomatic: agreement to form regional cooperation organization
*Time:* September 25, 1944-March 22, 1945
*Locale:* Alexandria and Cairo, Egypt

*Principal personages:*

ROBERT ANTHONY EDEN (1897-1977), British Secretary of
State for Foreign Affairs, 1940-1945

MUSTAFA EL-NAHAS PASHA (1876-1965), Prime Minister of
Egypt, 1942-1944

NURI AS-SAID (1888-1958), Prime Minister of Iraq

ABDULLAH IBN-HUSEIN (1882-1951), Amir (Ruler) of Transjordan

SHUKRI AL-KUWATLI (1891-1967), President of Syria

## Summary of Event

During World War II two fundamental forces were at work for the formation of unitary organizations in the Middle East: Arab leaders were strongly inclined to press for the achievement of the Arab unity that had been frustrated by the Anglo-French occupation of the Levant and the Fertile Crescent after World War I, while British policy sought to encourage Arab aspirations toward unity by supporting regional organizations through which Britain could exercise a guiding influence. This process began with the reduction of French power in the region as a result of its defeat by Germany in 1940, the Axis appeal to Arab nationalist circles intent on independence from Britain and France, and British overtures aimed at the conciliation of Arab desires for national independence and unification. The threat posed to Britain's position in the area by a brief pro-Axis putsch in Iraq led to a reformulation of British Middle Eastern policy. On May 29, 1941, Anthony Eden, Britain's Secretary of

State for Foreign Affairs, pointed to Britain's "long tradition of friendship with the Arabs" and offered British support for the independence of the French mandatory states of Syria and Lebanon. He concluded that, "It seems to me both natural and right that the cultural and economic ties between the Arab countries, and the political ties too, should be strengthened. His Majesty's Government for their part will give their full support to any scheme that commands general approval."

This declaration was well received by Arab leaders, but only after the retreat of German and Italian forces from the Egyptian desert were further measures considered. In November, 1942, Mustafa el-Nahas Pasha, the Prime Minister of Egypt, called on the Arabs to form a "powerful and cohesive bloc." The following month the Iraqi Prime Minister, Nuri as-Said, visited Cairo and declared that he was also fully committed to working for Arab unity. In February, 1943, Eden again signaled Britain's interest by stating that, while no concrete proposals had been received, Britain was once more prepared to support Arab efforts to achieve regional unification. In response, Amir Abdullah of Transjordan advanced a plan by which a United Syrian State was to be formed comprising Syria, Lebanon, Palestine, and his own country; a variation of this project envisioned the inclusion of Iraq in an Arab Federation with the proposed Greater Syrian State. These proposals were sent to British authorities in the Middle East, but no official response was communicated by Britain. Other Arab leaders reacted coolly to Abdullah's project, while the President of Syria, Shukri al-Kuwatli, rejected any schemes that fell short of full Arab unification by declaring, "Syria will refuse to have raised in her sky any flag higher than her own, save that of an Arab Union."

Egypt also hoped to take the lead in the Arab unity movement, and in the spring of 1943 invitations were issued for Arab leaders interested in unification to come to Cairo. In July and August, Nuri of Iraq visited the Egyptian capital after brief talks with Arab leaders in Syria, Lebanon, Transjordan, and Palestine; on further consultation with Nahas, a joint statement was issued on the possibility of arranging a conference on Arab unity to be held in Egypt. During the fall of 1943 Nahas also received representatives of Transjordan and Saudi Arabia. In January, 1944, Lebanon indicated its interest, though (because of in part its large Christian community) Lebanese spokesmen insisted on the retention of a maximum degree of national independence.

Moreover, as Nuri as-Said reported in March of the same year, representation for the Palestinian Arabs was expected to pose problems owing to disagreements within the leadership of that national group.

The next step was the convocation of a General Arab Conference in Alexandria, which was opened on September 25, 1944, and was attended by the Prime Ministers of Egypt, Transjordan, Syria, Iraq, and Lebanon; delegates from Saudi Arabia and Palestine and an observer from Yemen also arrived after the talks had begun. The widely divergent views expressed by the participants ruled out any comprehensive resolution of the question of Arab unity. While the conference considered proposals for a unitary state with central political authority and for a federated state with a central parliament to decide inter-Arab questions, several states expressed reservations on the merging of their sovereignty in a larger body. Syria was again suspicious of plans like that of Amir Abdullah for the fusion of several Arab states, though the Syrian delegation did support the ideal of a union of all Arab countries. Lebanon preferred a loose confederation without political or military obligations; this point of view was also adopted by Yemen. Egypt attempted to reach a compromise by proposing that no changes be made in the *de facto* sovereignty of the respective Arab states, and that resolutions for inter-Arab cooperative action be taken only by unanimous vote, with the exception that inter-Arab disputes be resolved by majority vote of the other League members. This point of view was ac-

495

cepted by Iraq, though with slight modifications, and by the conclusion of the Alexandria conference on October 7, 1944, a protocol was agreed to by the participating states. This document recorded the intentions of the conference members to form a League of Arab States having a Council on which each state was to be equally represented. The Council was to mediate disputes between member states, and means of cooperation on economic, cultural, and other matters were to be provided.

The Dumbarton Oaks conference of 1944, which outlined the framework for the United Nations, provided Arab leaders with some guidance on regional organizations; Egyptian leaders also studied the Union of American Republics for instruction on analogous regional pacts. After the Alexandria conference, however, the Prime Ministers of Egypt, Syria, and Transjordan were all relieved of their positions, and some Egyptian spokesmen sharply criti-cized the proposed League. Leaders of the Lebanese Christian community attacked the League as an infringement of Lebanese sovereignty. Thus the Arab leaders who met in Cairo in the early spring of 1945 did not consider any arrangements more extensive than a loose confederation. The Arab League Pact signed on March 22, 1945, confirmed the terms stated in the Alexandria protocol and established a permanent Secretary-General for the organization; provisions were also made for biannual meetings. In contrast to the previous protocol, however, no mention was made of eventual Arab unity; rather, the Arab League Pact emphasized even more strongly the independence and sovereignty of member states. In this form the Arab League has remained the symbol of the common national ties of the Arab peoples and a forum by which matters of regional and international importance could be discussed among the Arab states.

## Pertinent Literature

Abdullah ibn-Husein, Amir of Transjordan. *Memoirs of King Abdullah of Transjordan*. Edited by Philip P. Graves. Translated by G. Khuri. London: Jonathan Cape, 1950.

This work has the value of being the personal recollections of one of the more persistent advocates of one form of Arab unity. Abdullah traces his career from the beginning; a substantial portion of his memoirs deal with the Arab revolt of 1916 and the subsequent military and diplomatic events that replaced Ottoman rule with the British mandatory system. As the son of one of the most im-portant leaders of the Arab independence movement, Abdullah acted for some time as his country's foreign minister and thus had to deal with the inter-Arab and external forces that contributed to the division of the Arab peoples after World War I. In 1923, he was recognized as ruler of Transjordan.

In those portions of his book concerning political questions during

World War II, Abdullah discusses his views on Arab unity and his talks with other Arab leaders. For the most part his own proposals dealt with the possibility of a fusion of Transjordan, Syria, Palestine, and Lebanon into a single Arab state, which Abdullah wished to become a constitutional monarchy, with himself as King. His claims to the throne of the projected Greater Syria were based on Transjordan's historical record of service to Britain and the allies, Transjordan's guardianship of Syrian interests, and the effective collapse of French mandatory rule in Syria. Upon the formation of the Greater Syrian monarchy special administrative regimes were to be established on behalf of the Christian minority in Lebanon and the Jewish minority in Palestine. This done, further measures to secure the adherence of Iraq to the Syrian state were to be undertaken in order to create an Arab federation, the federal government of which was to be entrusted with matters relating to common defense, cultural advancement, and economic cooperation; this federation could then be prepared to accept further members from other states in the Arab world. Abdullah also outlines an alternative proposal that differs from the first largely in that it was to provide for greater autonomy in the administration of its constituent states and was to have an elected federal legislature. As before Abdullah expected to be the head of this proposed Syrian federation.

In most of his memoirs Abdullah is relatively favorable to the British and he does not question the strategic claims by which Britain justified its control of much of the Middle East. One of the few reproaches he directs at British policy concerns the proclamation he issued on April 8, 1943, to the people of Syria, calling upon them to discuss his proposals for union or federation. British authorities in the Middle East banned the publication or broadcast of this proclamation; when he inquired on this matter Abdullah received only evasive responses from British representatives. With respect to inter-Arab talks a summary is provided of Abdullah's instructions to his personal representatives for use at their meetings with other Arab leaders and at the Cairo conference at which the Arab League negotiations were concluded. While willing to accept if necessary a loose federation of the Arab states, Abdullah emphasized the need for a resolution of the Syrian question, preferably along the lines of his earlier proposals. Abdullah also declared that Transjordan should play a leading role in the work of Arab unity in view of its prominent part in the Arab nationalist movement; he believed that his country was better prepared to assist in the promotion of Arab union than such states as Syria or Saudi Arabia, neither of which had been conspicuously active in the arrangements for the Alexandria and Cairo conferences on Arab unity.

As has been seen, Abdullah's memoirs are in part an attempt to justify the assertion of his national and dynastic ambitions during the negotiations for Arab union; the insights provided on Transjordan's position are useful though rather tendentiously presented. Abdullah does not comment on the activity of other Arab leaders before or during the Arab League negotiations, and the actual formation of the Arab League is mentioned only in passing.

Macdonald, Robert W. *The League of Arab States. A Study in Regional Organization*. Princeton, N.J.: Princeton University Press, 1965.

This is the most systematic and frequently used study of the formation and operations of the Arab League. It is the work of a political scientist; as a general proposition Macdonald is concerned with the efficacy and limitations of regional organizations in the post-World War II world. Hence he commences his work by examining the provisions made in the United Nations Charter for regional organizations between states. As the Arab League is one of the few existing examples of such an arrangement, its establishment and functions are instructive from the point of view of the application of international law to the resolution of questions of common interest to neighboring states, the more so since the instruments establishing the Arab League were modeled on United Nations and League of Nations documents. The United Nations Charter explicitly recognizes the formation of legally constituted regional organizations for purposes of mutual security; an implied function of such organizations is the promotion of regional cooperation and national integration.

In one of his opening chapters, Macdonald deals with the events leading to the establishment of the Arab League. He traces its origins to the confused political atmosphere of the wartime Middle East and the proliferation of proposals for political organization by Arab leaders. He dis-cusses briefly British encouragement for Arab unity, and then deals in somewhat more depth with the various proposals advanced by Arab leaders. The political and administrative features of each projected form of Arab union are weighed against the practical difficulties of implementation. Thus he distinguishes between the proposals for the political fusion of several Arab states offered by Amir Abdullah of Transjordan and the less comprehensive plans to which the other Arab leaders eventually agreed. Given the differences between Arab leaders on the proper means of unification, Macdonald argues that a loose confederation was the only realistic form of unitary organization available to the Arabs.

As a result, the Alexandria protocol of 1944 and the Arab League Pact of 1945 were more concerned with practical measures for inter-Arab cooperation than with political unification; indeed, the latter document referred entirely to administrative questions and made none of the allusions to eventual unity that had appeared in the Alexandria protocol and that had figured prominently in earlier projects for Arab unification. In Macdonald's view, one of the basic achievements of the 1945 Cairo conference was the provision for committees by which some of the more mundane matters of inter-Arab cooperation might be arranged. On the

498

whole he gives the Arab League high marks for its performance in the fields of economic, cultural, and scientific cooperation.

Work in this area of regional interaction has also been enhanced by collaboration with the specialized agencies of the United Nations. He also discusses in detail the administrative framework of the Arab League, in particular the office of the Secretary-General, and the means by which League decisions are taken and enforced. The Arab League has also been of some service in the conciliation of states involved in inter-Arab disputes, much as its authority has not been sufficient to ensure complete tranquility in the Arab world.

Macdonald concludes that the continued existence of the Arab League, in spite of seemingly chronic social and political upheaval in the Middle East, is indicative of the underlying soundness of its original pact and administrative structures. Indeed, he feels that it compares reasonably well with other regional organizations, such as the Organization of American States. While many Arab writers have been inclined to criticize the Arab League for not having done more to promote Arab unification, Macdonald is rather more optimistic on its role in dealing with regional and external problems. Writing from the vantage point of some twenty years after the formation of the Arab League, Macdonald states that it was remarkable that the charter member states, many of which had little experience in independent self-government and some of which still seemed to be semimedieval societies, could have established a regional organization that has endured and that has performed useful functions.

Macdonald's work is based on published official documents and secondary sources on his subject, including some materials in Arabic; he refers as well to the pertinent literature on international law and regional organizations. The appendixes include the founding documents of the Arab League; tables and figures illustrating the organizational structure and decision-making processes of the Arab League are also provided. The style is somewhat technical and relies in part on the terminology and expressions characteristic of writing on legal and political subjects. — *J.R.B.*

## Additional Recommended Reading

Ansari, Mohammad Iqbal. *The Arab League 1945-1955.* Aligarh, India: Institute of Islamic Studies, 1968. Solid, systematic study based on many of the Arabic sources for this question.

Kirk, George. *The Middle East in the War.* New York: Oxford University Press, 1952. Comprehensive study of Middle Eastern politics during World War II that deals extensively with British and European interests in the area; the Arab League is discussed on pp. 333-344.

Khadduri, Majid. "Towards an Arab Union," in *American Political Science Review.* XL (1946), pp. 90-100. Useful short survey that deals directly with the wartime inter-Arab negotiations.

Anabtawi, M. F. *Arab Unity in Terms of Law*. The Hague: Martinus Nijhoff, 1963. A study of Arab unification movements in terms of international law which criticizes the Arab League as insufficiently devoted to working for permanent Arab unification.

Sayegh, Fayez A. *Arab Unity: Hope and Fulfillment*. New York: Devin-Adair, 1958. Discussion of Arab unity movements and organizations from the point of view of a committed Arab nationalist; considers the Arab League a first step of limited usefulness in the direction of Arab unification.

Foda, Ezzeldin. *The Projected Arab Court of Justice*. The Hague: Martinus Nijhoff, 1957. Concerns judicial mediation within the Arab League; argues that more effective measures should be provided for the arbitration of inter-Arab disputes.

Hassouna, Hussein A. *The League of Arab States and Regional Disputes*. Dobbs Ferry, N.Y.: Oceana, 1975. A study of the functions and performances of the Arab League with regard to regional questions, written from the point of view of the international lawyer.

# CELLULAR RESEARCH

*Type of event:* Scientific: modern developments in cellular biology
*Time:* 1945 to the present
*Locale:* Worldwide, but principally the United States

*Principal personages:*

ALBERT CLAUDE (1899-　　), a Luxembourg-born biologist who has developed cell fractionation and electron microscopy techniques, and is the discoverer with K. R. Porter of endoplasmic reticulum; won Nobel Prize, 1974

CHRISTIAN RENE DE DUVE (1917-　　), a Belgian biologist who has developed cell fractionation techniques, and is the discoverer of lysosomes; won Nobel Prize, 1974

GEORGE EMIL PALADE (1912-　　), a Rumanian-born biologist who has developed electron microscopy techniques, and equated endoplasmic reticulum of intact cells; won Nobel Prize, 1974

KEITH R. PORTER (1912-　　), an American biologist who has developed techniques in transmission and scanning electron microscopy, and is the discoverer with A. Claude of endoplasmic reticulum

## Summary of Event

The cell theory, one of the central concepts of biology, was formulated in 1839 by botanist M. J. Schleiden and zoologist Theodor Schwann. These German scientists, synthesizing a number of observations dating from Robert Hooke's description of cork in 1665, defined cells as the basic unit of life. In 1858 Rudolf Virchow advanced another significant postulate: all cells come from preexisting cells. During the next seventy years the cell doctrine became firmly entrenched, so that by 1925 E. B. Wilson wrote in his classic volume *The Cell in Development and Heredity*, "Long ago it became evident that the key to every biological problem must finally be sought in the cell."

Biochemistry also had its birth in the nineteenth century with the application of physics and chemistry to the study of living organisms. By the early twentieth century cell biologists and biochemists had begun to integrate their discoveries. Cytochemical stains for various cellular entities were developed, and gradually information about the structure and function of cells accumulated.

The extraordinarily rapid growth of cell biology, however, began in the mid-1940's principally as a result of powerful new tools: the electron microscope, the analytical centrifuge, X-ray diffraction, and radioactive biochemical tracers. Modern cell biology has established a commonality of biological organization from the molecular level up through cellular organelles to the cell itself. This universality of cellular organization was neither assumed nor predicted, but has emerged from the past twenty-five years of molecular and cell research. The descriptive period in cell biology is almost over; in the 1970's interest has begun to shift to regulatory mechanisms integrating the activities of cellular organelles with the overall function of the cell. It is difficult or impossible, and frequently inappropriate, to delineate the boundaries of cell biology, molecular biology, and biochemistry. The current body of knowledge about cell structure and function is a product of contributions from these several biological disciplines.

Of prime importance among the instrumentation of cell biologists is microscopy. By about 1880 the light microscope had reached its maximum potential development of about $0.2\mu m$ resolution. Phase-contrast microscopy, developed in the 1940's, permitted the observation of living, unstained and therefore highly transparent cells; interference microscopes, employing similar optic principles, are useful for quantitative measurements. The most valuable technology of the era, however, is transmission electron microscopy. The transmission electron microscope (TEM), developed in Germany and the United States during the 1940's, "illuminates" cells by passing high speed electrons through the specimen; as a result of density differences, cellular entities differentially absorb, transmit, or scatter electrons, forming an image on an electron-sensitive photographic plate or a fluorescent screen.

Sample preparation for TEM, pioneered by George Palade, Keith Porter, and Albert Claude during the 1950's, involves multistep processes of fixation, embedding, thin sectioning with an ultramicrotome, and staining. Heavy metal shadowing is employed to enhance contrast in some specimens, especially microorganisms and isolated organelles. In a more recently developed technique, freeze fracture and freeze etching, the sample is frozen rapidly and sectioned in a vacuum at $-100°C$. The specimen, which tends to fracture along lines of natural weakness, is left in the vacuum long enough to allow some of the water to evaporate from the exposed surface, which is subsequently shadowed and treated with acid, leaving a metal replica to examine in the TEM. This technique has provided valuable information about membrane structure.

Since the late 1960's, scanning electron microscopy (SEM) has become available for biological application. A fine stream of electrons scans the surface of the specimen, generally intact cells, releasing from the specimen secondary electrons, which are collected by a photomultiplier and displayed on a television picture tube. Specimens are prepared for SEM by fixation or freeze drying and shadowing with a heavy metal. A vast amount of information about cell surfaces has been obtained with this instrument.

Cell fractionation, developed and refined during the 1940's and 1950's by Claude, Palade, and Christian de Duve, is one of the most useful techniques of modern molecular and cell biology. Tissue gently homogenized to rupture cell membranes is centrifuged in a vacuum at high speed with a concentrated solution of sucrose or cesium chloride. The solution forms a density gradient within which the various molecular fractions become layered at positions corresponding to their own density. The centrifuge tube is then punctured at the bottom and fractions are collected and analyzed appropriately for content or chemical activity.

Radioactive isotopes are widely employed for the study of reaction pathways in cell fractions, where emitted radiation may be measured by a scintillation counter. Labeling of intact cells is usually monitored by radioautography, in which a thin layer of photographic emulsion is spread over the cells. Radioactive rays or particles produce silver grains in the emulsion, which after development can be seen along with the cells in the light microscope; a similar procedure has been developed for TEM.

Cell culture is used in biochemical work and in the study of cellular interactions. Cells in culture may be manipulated by microsurgery, treated with chemicals, irradiated, and caused to hybridize with cells of another species.

X-ray diffraction, although not used widely in biology, provided data with which James D. Watson and Francis Crick resolved the molecular structure of DNA (1953), undoubtedly the most significant biological discovery of the twentieth century.

It is known that cells exist in a great variety of sizes and shapes as a consequence of their evolutionary adaptation to different environments. Cells have, however, very many characteristics in common: all are surrounded by a cell membrane, all pos-sess genetic information necessary for the synthesis of cellular components, and all have the ability to obtain energy from the environment and to use it for the support of life processes.

The organelles of eukaryotic cells (all organisms save viruses, bacteria, and blue-green algae) are composed of the following elements: membranes, chromatin, and microtubules or microfilaments. By current interpretation, membranes appear universally to consist of proteins (of varying identity) suspended in a fluid matrix of lipid molecules. The permeability of membranes is dependent upon specific molecular composition, particularly protein. Membranous organelles include the cell (plasma) membrane, the nuclear membrane, mitochondria, chloroplasts (in plants), lysosomes, vacuoles, endoplasmic reticulum, and Golgi apparatus.

Chromatin is found dispersed within the nucleus except during cell division when it becomes condensed into chromosomes. Chromatin is composed of a DNA core, large amounts of chromosomal proteins of several types, and small amounts of RNA. The packaging of these molecules is still a topic of intense debate and study, as is the precise functional role of each molecular species.

Microfilaments and microtubules are proteinaceous structures found free in the cytoplasm (the cell content outside the nucleus) or as components of organelles such as myofilaments (in muscle cells), centrioles, basal bodies, cilia, and flagella. They function in both cellular and intracellular movement.

## Pertinent Literature

Swanson, Carl P. and Peter L. Webster. *The Cell*. Englewood Cliffs, N. J.: Prentice-Hall, 1977.

This book, authored by two outstanding scientists, is an introductory text in cell biology. It is brief (three hundred pages) and easily understandable to the reader who has a rudimentary knowledge of biology. Although not truly historical in approach, it does treat chronologically the "classic" experiments in a number of important areas of this relatively young discipline. The book emphasizes the biochemical aspects of cell biology, particularly the cell's activity as an energy-transforming unit.

Following a general introductory chapter, the authors discuss cellular information and its organization in the nucleus. Experiments in 1934 by Joachim August Hämmerling on the green alga *Acetabularia* firmly established the fundamental role of the nucleus as control center of the cell. Modern genetics is based upon the assumption that the chromatin of the nucleus, which condenses into chromosomes for distribution to daughter cells during cell division, contains coded information essential for directing cellular activity. A number of experiments in the 1940's and 1950's identified DNA as the informational molecules within the chromosomes. Watson and Crick published in 1953 their Nobel Prize-winning discovery of the structure of the DNA molecule, including a prediction, verified experimentally within a few years, of the mechanism of its replication and distribution to daughter cells. The packaging of DNA, histone chromosomal proteins, and nonhistone chromosomal proteins into the chromatin of eukaryotic cells has occupied the attention of cell biologists for many years. Current evidence suggests that chromatin is organized into strands of nucleosomes, or "beads," containing DNA and histones, which are frequently coiled upon themselves. Histones and nonhistone chromosomal proteins, which are also associated with chromatin but in a much more variable way, apparently play an important role in regulating transcription, the process in which DNA directs the synthesis of proteins in the cytoplasm and thereby controls the function of the cell.

Completing the chapter is a discussion of the nature of the genetic code (residing in the sequence of nucleotides comprising the DNA molecule), its transcription by RNA (ribonucleic acid), and translation into the vast numbers of specific proteins characteristic of each cell. Some of these proteins function as structural elements, while others are enzymes, or biological catalysts, which control the synthesis of a variety of cell products.

Chapter 3 deals with the structure and function of cell boundaries. The plasma membrane is a highly specialized, selectively permeable structure, composed of a bimolecular layer of lipid molecules interspersed with proteins. This "fluid mosaic model," based principally upon evidence from freeze fracture and freeze etch preparations, accounts for many of the properties of the plasma membrane. Proteins extending through the lipid bilayer facilitate the transfer of materials into and out of the cell. Associated surface molecules are involved in recognition of and response to the extracellular environment; for example, blood types are determined by the surface glycoproteins and glycolipids of erythrocyte plasma membranes. Membranes from different cells and organisms vary widely in the chemical composition of their membrane proteins and lipids, which explains in part the variation in physiological activities of different membranes.

Energy capture and conversion by chloroplasts and mitochondria are discussed in Chapter 4. Following a brief description of photosynthesis by green plants, the authors describe the ultrastructure of chloroplasts and relate to it the function of the membrane fraction (capture of solar energy by chlorophyll) and the soluble fraction, or stroma (reduction of atmospheric carbon dioxide to form glucose). The function of mitochondria is to perform cellular respiration, the stepwise conversion of chemically stored energy (glucose) into ATP, a molecule used to perform the cell's work. Mitochondria are composed of an outer membrane similar in molecular composition to the plasma membrane, and an inner membrane folded into cristae projecting into a matrix. Fractionation experiments have revealed specific enzymatic activities associated with each of the mitochondrial components; for example, the formation of ATP molecules is associated with "respiratory assemblies," stalked particles attached to the inner mitochondrial membrane.

In Chapter 5, Swanson and Webster outline structure and function of the other cytoplasmic organelles. The endoplasmic reticulum (ER) is a network of interconnecting tubules whose major function is synthesis and transport within the cell. Rough ER has attached ribosomes, 200Å particles where amino acids are assembled into proteins under the direction of messenger RNA which has been transcribed from the DNA code. Smooth ER, having no ribosomes, is implicated in carbohydrate metabolism and the synthesis of lipids. The Golgi apparatus, a stack of flattened membranous sacs, packages and transports certain cellular materials, especially proteins and polysaccharides, for transport out of the cell. Lysosomes are membrane-bound vesicles containing enzymes which digest intra- or extracellular material. Apparently there is a temporal continuity between the nuclear membrane, the ER, the Golgi apparatus, lysosomes, and the plasma membrane. Evidence suggests that the cell uses this dynamic membrane system for the distribution of materials.

Since the refinement of high resolution electron microscopy, two non-membranous, proteinaceous structures, microtubules and microfilaments, have been recognized as important cellular components. Microtubules, each about 150Å in diameter, are arranged in a characteristic and remarkably uniform pattern to form cilia and flagella of motile cells; aggregates of microtubules also comprise the spindle upon which the chromosomes move to daughter cells during cell division. 40 to 80Å micro-filaments, well-known in muscle, are now commonly described in a wide variety of other cells; they are involved in changes in cell shape during growth and movement.

The remaining chapters of the book cover comparative cytology; cellular reproduction, development, and death; gamete formation; and evolutionary trends.

Brinkley, B. R. and Keith R. Porter, eds. *International Cell Biology, 1976-1977.* New York: Rockefeller University Press, 1977.

This seven-hundred-page volume is a compilation of papers presented at the First International Congress on Cell Biology, held in Boston, Massachusetts, in 1976. The symposia topics at this historic meeting rank among the most important in cell biology at this period of its development and are authored by world authorities in their specialized fields. For this reason the book is a most valuable resource for scholars of cell biology.

The papers are divided into twenty-two sections on such topics as cell surface phenomena, endoplasmic reticulum-Golgi apparatus and cell secretion, molecular basis for cell motility, cytoplasmic control of nuclear expression, chromatin and chromosome organization and function, gametogenesis, and viral gene function in host cells. In many, but not all, cases, introductory or concluding remarks provide background information or summarize developments in the field. Nevertheless, the material would be difficult for persons unfamiliar with cell biology in general.

The breadth of content of the book illustrates the interdigitation of cell biology with molecular biology, biochemistry, and virology. Although methodology is not particularly emphasized, information developed from most of the techniques currently applicable to cell biology is included. — *J.R.S.*

## Additional Recommended Reading

Allen, Garland E. *Life Science in the Twentieth Century*. New York: John Wiley and Sons, 1975. A history of selected areas of biology: development, heredity, evolution, physiology, biochemistry, and molecular biology.

Becker, Wayne M. *Energy and the Living Cell: An Introduction to Bioenergetics*. Philadelphia: J. B. Lippincott Company, 1977. A brief introductory text on energy flow, energy sources, and cellular work.

Goldsby, Richard A. *Cells and Energy*. New York: The Macmillan Company, 1977. A short treatment of cellular energy production and utilization.

McElroy, William D. and Carl P. Swanson. *Modern Cell Biology*. Englewood Cliffs, N. J.: Prentice-Hall, 1976. A text on cell biology for beginning students.

# CHANGING ATTITUDES TOWARD RELIGION IN AMERICA

*Type of event:* Religious: shift towards secularization in postwar America
*Time:* 1945 to the present
*Locale:* The United States

*Principal personages:*
> PAUL MATTHEWS VAN BUREN (1924- ), a theologian and the author of *The Secular Meaning of the Gospel*
> HARVEY GALLAGHER COX, JR. (1929- ), a theologian and the author of *The Secular City*
> THOMAS JONATHAN JACKSON ALTIZER (1927- ), a theologian and the author of *The Gospel of Christian Atheism*
> MARTIN LUTHER KING, JR. (1929-1968), a Baptist minister and civil rights leader
> JOHN FITZGERALD KENNEDY (1917-1963), thirty-fifth President of the United States, 1961-1963
> HUGO LAFAYETTE BLACK (1886-1971), Associate Justice of the United States Supreme Court, 1939-1971
> JOHN COURTNEY MURRAY (1904- ), a historian and the author of *Religion in America* (1958)
> HELMUT RICHARD NIEBUHR (1894-1962), a historian and the author of *The Shaping of American Religion* (1961)
> SIDNEY EARL MEAD, a historian and the author of *The Lively Experiment* (1963)
> POPE JOHN XXIII (1881-1963), leader of the ecumenical movement who convened Vatican II
> PAUL TILLICH (1886-1965), a philosopher and theologian

## Summary of Event

The changing attitudes toward religion in America since the end of World War II contrast sharply with the religious values of an earlier age which stressed individualism in matters of piety, personal salvation, worship, and expression of religious doctrine. Since 1945, one of the dominant themes in American religious thought has been that of secularization. This theme strongly influenced the writing of a number of leading theologians during the 1960's, including Paul Van Buren (*The Secular Meaning of the Gospel*), Harvey Cox (*The Secular City*), and Thomas Altizer (*The Gospel of Christian Atheism*). Collectively, these writings reflect changing American attitudes toward religion and have helped to make the United States a major center of theological discourse.

Secularization, as the dominant process of the period, had already

507

begun, even as a religious phenomenon, with the social encyclicals at the beginning of the century and the various social reform movements that sought to come to grips with phenomena of pluralism, urbanization, and "Americanization." World War II, of course, contributed in a dramatic way to the process. It initiated relationships between religious bodies that before were conceived as impossible. It challenged the values of the religious bodies themselves, especially insofar as they were based on the traditional interpretations of more doctrinal and pietistic approaches. It produced a sudden and painful feeling of alienation and loss of the securities of the past. The war experience generated distinctly different attitudes. Faith itself became questionable; the best theologians had to begin to struggle with the meaning of the secular city and the "death of God." It was uncertain whether the events pointed to a period of decline or a period of growth. In 1948, Emmanuel Cardinal Suhard of Paris issued a sober pastoral letter entitled "The Church Today: Growth or Decline." The question is still with us today as we approach the 1980's.

A new generation of Americans with new attitudes toward religion produced broad movements indicative of the creative activity of the period: the ecumenical movement, particularly as pursued by the Roman Catholic Church; the Civil Rights movement led by Martin Luther King, Jr., a Baptist minister; and the peace movement. These movements are but reflections of a new attitude which demanded that a greater social consciousness be incorporated into religious doctrine and practice, and which demanded "relevancy" as a kind of ultimate criterion of the authenticity of religion itself. Some of these changes were demonstrated in concrete ways, such as the election of John F. Kennedy, as President in 1960, the first Roman Catholic to be elected to the office.

Changing attitudes also found expression in two other broad areas of American life—education and democracy. The question of the relationship between Church and State figured heavily in the literature of the 1950's. Theoretical questions became practical questions when Associate Justice Hugo Black delivered the majority opinion of the U.S. Supreme Court when it ruled in the case of *McCollum* v. *Board of Education* (1948) that "released" or "dismissed" time for religious instruction in public schools was unconstitutional. Further, in the *Engel* v. *Vitale* case (1962), the Supreme Court found the Regent's Prayer in New York unconstitutional. Such issues arose spontaneously out of the process of growing secularization in the educational system; they represent the growing pains of an open, pluralistic society trying to come to grips with the meaning of faith in the light of new experiences.

Writers such as John Courtney Murray, S. J. (*Religion in America*, 1958), Helmut Richard Niebuhr (*The Shaping of American Religion*, 1961), and the noted historian of religion Sidney E. Mead (*The Lively Experiment*, 1963) continued to struggle in a positive way with the problem of the "Americanization" and "democratization" of religion in America, showing the positive effects of America's religious heritage on its democratic way of life. At the same time there occurred an amelioration of relationships between religion and those who represented the more radical philosophy of secular humanism. At least on the theoretical plane, if not always on the practical plane, there were significant efforts at dialogue. Elements of this change in attitude are reflected, for example, in the World Council of Churches (meeting in Amsterdam in 1948) and the theology of the Vatican Council (1962-1965) which was convened by Pope John XXIII.

Behind these developments are dramatic changes in the philosophical foundations of religious thinking. In America, writers such as Paul Tillich and Reinhold Niebuhr, as well as a host of more popular writers, have been influential in applying, for example, the principles of contemporary European existential philosophy and psychology in the overall challenge to rethink the foundations of faith in a way more compatible with the spirit of the age. Each theological system of the main religious bodies in America has been deeply affected by the "new theology."

On the social and political plane, the Civil Rights movement, the Vietnam War, and the peace movement contributed as much as the experience of World War II itself to draw religious consciousness in the direction of social reform. In addition, the focus of attention on moral problems in our times—nuclear war, euthanasia, abortion, genetics, technology—seem to indicate that religion in America is at a crossroads.

The crossroads present both a challenge and a danger. The danger is inherent in the process of secularization: religion may become so caught up with "this world" that it will lose sight of its spiritual foundations. Just as in the past religion's exclusively spiritual approach without sufficient involvement in problems of the real world led to a loss of faith in the churches, so today religion's immersion in the social problems and cultural issues of the day may lead to oversecularization. In essence, America's challenge is as old as religion: how to be in the world but not lost in it.

## Pertinent Literature

Gaustad, Edwin Scott. *A Religious History of America*. New York: Harper & Row Publishers, 1966.

*A Religious History of America* is a thorough and comprehensive historical work which offers a general framework within which one can examine postwar developments in American religion. We gain a better understanding of the present state of religion in the United States when we see it in the light of the past. This volume was written with the firm conviction that the role of religion has been a significant and at times even critical one in the overall history of America. Through the eyes of America's religious history one can look at the history of America itself, just as a grasp of social, political, and cultural developments can aid our understanding of the unique phenomenon of religion in America.

During the age of exploration and colonization, well-documented by the author with sources from the times, the melting pot of religious ideals and feelings was prepared. In the beginning America preserved a particular religious heritage and life style, still insulated from the state of mind that was to come, in which the challenges of a pluralistic and increasingly secular society would force religion to deepen itself or perish.

In Part Three of a *A Religious History of America*, entitled "The Age of Expansion," we see the beginnings of a changing order from which the present age was born. Americans began to move from the immediate problems that first confronted settlers—religious freedom and tolerance—to the broad scope and transformations brought on not merely by problems of personal salvation and relationship with one's neighbor, but also by the complex social problems of urbanization. Examination of the nation's early religious history leads to an understanding of the tension that seems to characterize the present day: tension between the transcendent religious freedom of individual piety so characteristic of America's earliest religious underpinnings and the present need for relevancy in an open society, which forces the individual out of himself and into the world.

For the most part Gaustad lets the narration of events and original sources speak for themselves. He shows us how a self-confident, pioneering America brought the same utopian feelings of progress and perfection to its religion as it brought to its other activities. We see the seemingly endless opportunities for expansion reflected in America's feeling that it was chosen, that it had a "manifest destiny" to be God's instrument. In spite of all the hardships that life involved, Americans nevertheless shared a kind of spiritual feeling, exaggerated and naïve, perhaps, but nonetheless in sharp contrast to the modern postwar period with its cynicism and loss of faith. The important turning point between early and present religious America is described in a chapter entitled "Immigration and Assimilation," in which Gaustad talks about the process of "Americanization."

In the last two parts of the book, the author examines religion in America up to the end of Vatican II and discusses the writers who in one way or another brought the "new theology" to the fore. The age begins with the social encyclicals and ends with the "God is dead" theology; it is the age of two World Wars, of the Ecumenical movement and the Civil Rights movement, of a reexamined relationship between Church and State, of released time for parochial schools, the election of a Catholic president, and the Vatican Council. Yet these are only the outward manifestations of a more radical kind of change taking place. After the Civil War, a quiet revolution began; America became secularized, and the long-range effects of that change are still to be seen.

McLoughlin, William G. and Robert N. Bellah, eds. *Religion in America*. Boston: Houghton Mifflin Company, 1968.

The question "how is America religious?" is the leading question posed by this book in relation to postwar America. The authors' assumption is that no interpretation of the particularly unique phenomenon of "America's religion" is possible without at the same time understanding the nation's evolving culture, history, and social behavior. They are convinced that the evolution of religion in the postwar period has not been haphazard, but logical and traceable. The last thirty-year period is seen as a critical time during which America's religious heritage has been at stake. The future is still uncertain— it can become either an age of new freedom and creativity or an age which suffers the loss of its faith.

The events of the present day can also be viewed as further manifestations of the perennial dialogue between pietist movements and the secular; this dialogue can even be said to constitute the basic context in which Western culture has evolved in the modern period since the rise of science and the Industrial Revolution. Nevertheless, the American religious experience has been unique, for no other group of people has become such a melting pot of religious feelings as America has. No other people have experienced quite like America such a tension between the desire to be religious and the temptation to pursue materialism and "worldliness." Nowhere else has the unique problem of religion today— the relation between social and reform movements and the experience of the transcendent freedom of individual piety—been so sharply lived. The paradoxical nature of these feelings, more than anything else, forms America's challenge as far as religion is concerned. But the challenge comes at a time when the country has barely completed its growth; this is one of the main reasons for the marked difference between a European view of the same questions and the way America experiences them. America's youth and naïveté add a unique dimension to the questions themselves. Hopefully, American pragmatism will accept the challenge of reconciling opposites in a creative new form.

What comes out of a reading of *Religion in America* is an optimistic view of America's religious future. The painful awareness of present confusion over the temporary loss of the securities of the past—both on the institutional and intellectual levels— can be seen as part of a developing process of maturity. Efforts at ecumenical exchange propose a deeper sense of brotherhood than the isolationism of the past could have imagined. Our real pluralism is becoming a state of mind in which a healthy granting of validity to other forms of faiths is possible. There is a willingness to work for the future without having all the answers in advance, to rediscover and adapt to the secular experience the perennial validity of the essential religious symbols.

The authors have no illusions, however, about the inevitability of the future. Alongside the new efforts to transcend the limits of the past there is the ever-present desire on the part of many others for the simple securities of the past. If any one feeling is generated by this book as a whole, it is the feeling that a dialogue has begun and that dialogue is the only way open to us. Religion in America, as anywhere else, participates in the dynamism of social, cultural, and political change. In the melting pot of change, religion may lose some of its more obvious externality. But it may also become more real in the process. — *T.R.K.*

## Additional Recommended Reading

Brauer, Jerald C., ed. *Essays in Divinity*. Vol. V: *Reinterpretation in American Church History*. Chicago: University of Chicago Press, 1968. An important work in the study of religion in America stressing the historical and cultural dimensions, along with theological development, of religious history in America.

Burr, Robert N. *A Critical Bibliography of Religion in America*. Princeton, N.J.: Princeton University Press, 1961. An excellent and authoritative guide to the subject matter.

Cogley, John, ed. *Religion in America: Original Essays on Religion in a Free Society*. New York: Meridian Books, 1958. Essays which cover the main problems confronting postwar religion in America: dialogue in a pluralistic society, religious freedom and the separation of Church and State, the parochial school question, and the rise of secularism.

Herberg, Will. *Protestant-Catholic-Jew: An Essay in American Religious Sociology*. Garden City, N.Y.: Doubleday & Company, 1955. An interpretation of the religiosocial situation in contemporary America with emphasis on the overriding tension between religiousness and secularism.

Marty, Martin E. *The New Shape of American Religion*. New York: Harper & Row Publishers, 1959. Stresses the need for dialogue between America's religious past and present, arguing that a realistic approach must come to grips with pluralism and the overriding factors of urbanization and secularization in American social life.

Mead, Sidney E. *The Lively Experiment. The Shaping of Christianity in America*. New York: Harper & Row Publishers, 1963. One of the classic interpretations of religion in America.

Zaretsky, Irving I. and Mark P. Leone, eds. *Religious Movements in Contemporary America*. Princeton, N.J.: Princeton University Press, 1974. A comprehensive work which examines contemporary religious movements, underlining the reciprocal relationship between them and modern social and cultural patterns in America.

# CHANGING PATTERNS IN EDUCATION

*Type of event:* Educational: growth and turmoil in American schools
*Time:* 1945 to the present
*Locale:* The United States

*Principal personages:*
EARL WARREN (1891-1974), Chief Justice of the United States Supreme Court in *Brown* v. *Board of Education of Topeka*
WARREN EARL BURGER (1907-    ), Chief Justice of the United States Supreme Court when states were urged to speed up integration
RICHARD MILHOUS NIXON (1913-    ), thirty-seventh President of the United States, 1969-1974
GERALD RUDOLPH FORD (1913-    ), thirty-eighth President of the United States, 1974-1977

## Summary of Event

There have been many changing patterns in education from 1945 to the present, such as the growth of teacher unions, the increasing dominance of public over private universities, the movement toward equal opportunity for women, minority groups, and the handicapped, and the virtual replacement of scholarships for merit by scholarships for need. All of these trends are important. More important, however, are the general growth of education in the United States and the problem of desegregation in the elementary and secondary schools.

The tremendous growth of the American education system from 1945 to the present day is largely, though not entirely, a function of demographic change. The population simply expanded, and, with a system of universal elementary and secondary schooling already in effect, education—kindergarten through twelfth grade—had to expand accordingly. In 1939-1940 there were 25,400,000 pupils in elementary and secondary education; by 1973-1974, there were 45,400,000. This increase in total pupils understates the even more rapid increase in numbers of high school graduates—from 1,143,000 in 1939-1940 to 2,762,000 in 1973-1974.

Higher aspirations on the part of Americans in general and employers in particular probably account in great part for the tremendous increase in collegiate enrollments from a mere 2,287,000 in 1950 to 9,731,000 in 1975. In 1950 only 14.2 percent of the eighteen- to twenty-four-year-old population enrolled; in 1975 it was an amazing 35.2 percent. Two interesting factors are hidden in this composite change. In the first place there is the growth of the public comprehensive two-year community colleges. In 1947 there were 250 of them, with an average per-college enrollment of less than a thousand students. By 1975 their number had increased over threefold and their average size was nearly five times what it had been. This growth represented one quarter of enrollments: one freshman in four was attending a public community college. The growth in enrollment in these institutions was in fact phenomenal—from 163,000 in 1947 to 2,400,000 in 1975—a fifteenfold increase. This enormous growth repeats itself at the Masters and Doctoral levels. In 1939-1940, 26,731 Masters degrees were conferred; this rose to 277,033 in 1973-1974. Only 3,290 Doctorates were awarded in 1939-1940; in 1973-1974 the number was 33,816.

Tremendous growth in the number of students at both elementary and secondary levels and in higher education entailed tremendous increases in expenditures. Public elementary and secondary school revenues rose from just over two billion dollars in 1939-1940 to more than fifty-eight billion in 1973-1974. Of this, by far the largest shares came from state and local sources; still, the federal government contributed nearly five billion. Moreover, the federal government's share had increased from a mere $2,500,000—an increase of two thousand percent. This phenomenal increase was accompanied by equally phenomenal increases in federal monitoring and control. Parallel increases were also experienced in higher education. Here the current fund income rose from $715 million in 1939-1940 to thirty-six billion dollars in 1974-1975; however, the size of this increase is dwarfed by the size of the increase of its federal share: from thirty-nine million to five billion dollars.

The growth of American education has, it seems, reached its virtual peak and is now due for a downturn. Between now and 1985 kindergarten through twelfth grade enrollments are expected to drop eight percent; higher education enrollments are expected to slow down with a cumulative rise of nineteen percent. Moreover, there is every indication that even this modest increase will result in an overproduction of higher education degrees.

The second major pattern of change in education since 1945 was desegregation. The Supreme Court decision against segregation in *Oliver Brown* v. *Board of Education of Topeka* is nearly a quarter of a century old. When it was pronounced on May 17, 1954, during the incumbency of Earl Warren, the South was running a segregated school system, from elementary grades through college, which was said to be separate but equal. The Court made it clear that separate was inherently unequal. This landmark decision had little effect, however, in the first decade of its implementation. At the end of ten years, half of the biracial school districts in the Deep South were officially desegregated, but this desegregation was only token: less than two percent of the black children actually attended integrated schools.

Such token compliance was brought to an end by a Supreme Court decision of October 29, 1969, under the new Chief Justice, Warren Burger. This decision insisted that it was "the obligation of every school district . . . to terminate dual school systems at once and to operate now and hereafter only unitary schools." This decision had an immediate effect in the South. Between 1968-1969 and 1970-1971, the percentage of black children in schools having a white majority rose from eighteen to thirty-nine. More significant, perhaps, the percentage of blacks in totally non-white schools fell in the South from sixty-eight to fourteen. In 1968-1969 there were two million blacks in such schools; in 1970-1971 there were only 443,000.

Although problems of integration in the South were hardly solved, the 1970's have been dominated by problems of integration in the North, where there had never been dual school systems set up by law, but where school segregation had resulted from segregation in housing. The remedy most widely used to resolve this problem was forced busing; use of this remedy stripped away the complacency of the North and of Northerners who felt that segregation was the "South's problem." Fierce controversy and violence burst forth in Boston, and other Northern cities—Detroit, Baltimore, Chicago, Cleveland—felt the tremors of this racial earthquake. The issue reached the halls of Congress and the desks of Presidents Richard Nixon and Gerald Ford, and is still not solved today. In all likelihood problems in integrating school systems—North and South—will continue to challenge Americans in the decade to come.

## Pertinent Literature

Hechinger, Fred M. and Grace Hechinger. *Growing Up in America*. New York: McGraw-Hill Book Company, 1975.

Literature on American education tends to be partisan and parochial. The reader is asked to concentrate on one small aspect or to endorse the author's views about some sweeping educational reform. The Hechingers' study is neither partisan nor parochial. It is a synthesis of existing studies, an attempt to put controversy in perspective and narrow works in a broad context. Such a book can always be attacked for its presumption in standing above the battle or be treated with contempt because it contributes nothing new. But *Growing Up in America* stands up well to such criticisms. It earns its right to stand above the battle and, while it lacks in new knowledge, it has useful new perspectives in abundance. Thus the most recent events in American education—the push for ethnic pluralism, the radical movement toward deschooling, desegregation, the effects of the G.I. Bill, student radicalism—are seen in three contexts: historical, cultural, and social.

When recent events are seen in a historical context, they can be better understood. Thus, the long-term ineffectuality of student radicalism had been demonstrated well before Berkeley. In addition, nothing happens in American education outside the context of American culture as a whole. The progressively respectful attitude of the school toward children must be seen in the context of society's change of heart and mind as children were transformed from eco-

515

nomic assets into the hope of the future. Finally, education cannot be elevated above its relatively subordinate place in the initiation of social change. Education does not initiate change; rather, it institutionalizes change already given the stamp of approval by the political process. Those, therefore, who have hoped to use the schools as instruments of radical politics have invariably failed.

*Growing Up in America* is organized thematically and the first theme is Americanization. In this chapter, the Hechingers chronicle the schools' enthusiastic execution of their mission to weld the disparate elements of emerging America—especially the hordes of new immigrants—into "one nation under God." It was a task to which the schools were ideally suited. Enormous and efficient bureaucracies could deliver large doses of patriotism disguised as American history and eradicate, not without a certain pleasure, the Jewishness of Jews and the Polishness of Poles. It is no wonder a reaction took place by those who felt that not only nations, but people, had rights—to be Jewish or Polish, not to pray to God, not to salute the flag. Moreover, these rights were constitutionally guaranteed. However, it took the Supreme Court more than 150 years to make such a statement as "in this country, it is no part of the business of government to compose official prayers for any group of Americans to recite."

The Hechingers concern themselves next with the organization of schools. At first schools were highly decentralized in accordance with the dictates of the ward system. As the corruption of this system became in-

creasingly evident, bureaucratic centralization seemed like the best solution. As was customary in America, this solution was greeted with overwhelming enthusiasm. Educators searched endlessly for "the one best way"; there was "one best way" for everything from penmanship to posture. This enthusiastic and in many ways misguided search led to a uniformity that gradually lost touch with the minds and hearts of children. The move for decentralization, evident in the 1960's and 1970's, can be seen as a reaction to the excesses of a system not in itself deleterious when followed by those with balanced views.

In their next two chapters, "American Childhood: The Utopian Myth" and "The Black Ordeal," the Hechingers deal with two kinds of oppression: that of children generally and that of black children in particular. The chapter on childhood is perhaps the most original in the book. It effectively undermines the myth that Americans have always put children on a pedestal. Quite the contrary; until very recently, large numbers of children were exploited as economic assets. For black children, of course, the situation was even worse since they were systematically excluded from the social benefits of education. Their long struggle, which led to Chief Justice Warren's unforgettable words—"We conclude that in the field of public education the doctrine of 'separate but equal' has no place. Separate educational facilities are inherently unequal"—is carefully chronicled.

The last two substantive chapters of *Growing Up in America* concern the history of collegiate education:

516

the colleges themselves and college students. Two great events in this area were the Morrill Act and the G.I. Bill. Both were proposed as conservative measures; both had radical consequences in expanding the audience for higher education. But the colleges—especially the older, elitist colleges—resisted this tendency toward expansion. Such reactionary tendencies led occasionally to student revolt, culminating in the revolts of the 1960's. The results of these student movements were uniformly meager.

The Hechingers are bullish on American education. For all its troubles, American education has fostered egalitarianism and class mobility. Energized by a constant flow of reformers from Dewey to Bruner and supported by timely interventions of the Supreme Court, American education has imperfectly but worthily embodied the educational and political idealism of Jefferson and Franklin.

Jenks, Christopher and David Riesman. *The Academic Revolution.* Garden City, N.Y.: Doubleday & Company, 1968.

The central thesis of Jenks's and Riesman's scholarly but subjective study of American higher education is that since World War II there has been a revolution in academia: the graduate school model has become the only model for higher education as a whole to emulate. With few exceptions—community colleges and general education colleges are two—all institutions of higher learning have striven to meet the standards of the graduate school. In the first place, these standards are meritocratic, attempting to judge on objective rather than subjective criteria. Second, they are focused on the award of the Ph.D., a degree which certifies workmanlike competence in a narrow specialty. Third, graduate school standards eschew applied knowledge. Fourth, although many of those they prepare become teachers, graduate schools do not teach pedagogy. Lastly, as in all professions, graduate school professors reserve the right to judge other graduate professors. This right, which they share with the medical and legal professions, along with the monopoly they possess on certification, are truly amazing prerogatives for graduate schools because there is little correlation between what is learned in them and later professional success.

The graduate school model dominates all graduate schools without exception. Not only is this rigidity disturbing in itself; it is disturbing because it influences the four years that a student goes to college to obtain his baccalaureate. Virtually all four-year colleges try to follow the university college model in which the four undergraduate years are specifically a preparation for graduate school, one's major presumably being apprentice work for one's Ph.D. specialization. This system has serious defects: most importantly, not all graduates go on to Ph.D. programs. In any case, those who come from more imaginative general education programs do at least as well in grad-

517

uate school as standard college students.

It is indeed unfortunate that neither the black colleges, the Protestant colleges, nor the Catholic colleges provide alternate models for undergraduate education. There are, however, two kinds of institutions that do provide such models: community colleges and colleges specializing in some version of general education. The authors' controversial view is that community colleges are not an adequate alternate model. Despite their rhetoric of service to the disadvantaged, they are designed to convince most students who attend them that college is not for them. Therefore, rather than providing an alternate path for such students, they merely provide a safety valve for the universities which do not want to be bothered. The authors are more optimistic about colleges specializing in a form of general education. These are not numerous, but they do have a vigorous countercultural existence that may have some positive effect on the more prevalent model.

Since alternate models for colleges hardly exist and do not seem probable in the near future, the authors suggest some modest reforms in graduate education itself. In the first place, they suggest the addition of some practical experience akin to the clinical experience in medical schools. Second, they hope that Ph.D.'s can be made more flexible by encouraging new interdepartmental mixes of subspecialties. Third, they feel that the year after the doctorate might be devoted to an internship in teaching.

The authors' delineation of the academic revolution is as true today as it was ten years ago when their book was published. The reforms they suggest are largely unimplemented, but most still make sense. Their work serves a real purpose in making clear what the academic revolution is not. It is not a social revolution. The number of elite slots in society has been unchanging in recent years. Higher education is instrumental only in providing new under-class candidates for the upper-class slots that open up through downward mobility.

— A.G.G.

## Additional Recommended Reading

Bird, Caroline. *The Case Against College*. New York: David McKay Company, 1975. Attacking the national myth that every eighteen- to twenty-year-old should go to college, the author feels that in many instances parents and students have been wrongly oversold.

Glazer, Nathan. *Remembering the Answers: Essays on the American Student Revolt*. New York: Basic Books, 1970. A reasoned analysis and critique of the impulses behind and the consequences of student revolt based on radical assumptions.

Kohl, Herbert. *36 Children*. New York: New American Library, 1967. An impassioned account of one man's successful encounter with a class of thirty-six black children in an East Harlem school.

Silberman, Charles E. *Crisis in the Classroom: The Remaking of American Education*.

New York: Random House, 1970. A disturbing picture of current practice along with a program for reform.

# THE CRISIS IN RAILROAD TRANSPORTATION

*Type of event:* Economic: decline of an important American industry
*Time:* 1945 to the present
*Locale:* The United States

*Principal personages:*
> BEN WALTER HEINEMAN (1914-    ), innovative chairman and chief executive officer of the Chicago and North Western Railway from 1956
> ROBERT YOUNG, President of the New York Central who engineered the 1968 merger with the Pennsylvania Railroad
> STUART THOMAS SAUNDERS (1909-    ), President of the Pennsylvania Railroad who was active in the 1968 merger with the New York Central

## Summary of Event

The lyrics of "City of New Orleans," a widely popular folk song of the 1970's, are based on the dramatic and depressing saga of the declining American railroads and reflect the degree to which railroad travel has become yet another object of romantic recollection and nostalgia. Yet, the situation since 1945 abounds with paradox. In particular, the country's transportation network still has a vital need for railroad freight service. Threatened strikes by railroad workers are subject to maximum federal intervention because rail shutdowns would quickly cripple major industries. Clearly, railway freight service remains important for the United States' economy. Also, in the passenger business, where rail service has generally deteriorated most rapidly, the need for passenger railroads remains a social and economic necessity. For example, if commuter service into the nation's great cities were discontinued, the cost to society would be immense. Already overcrowded freeways and parking facilities would be clogged beyond capacity, to say nothing of the increase in wasted gasoline and additional environmental pollution. In short, the need for both freight and passenger railroading exists today, but societal need must be balanced by examining historical reality. The decline of the American railroads is clearly discernible and probably will continue.

The decline of railroads after World War II was foreshadowed by events before 1945. In a very real sense, the Wright Brothers and Henry Ford laid much of the groundwork for rail decline. In 1918, the United States Post Office Department began its air-mail service, and in subsequent years, the railroads lost the bulk of the country's mail service and consequently lost an important source of government subsidies. The booming prosperity of the 1920's brought further competition for the railroad industry as the automobile industry grew and prospered. Ford marketed his Model T, a car with a price low enough to capture wide sales. Government, espe-

520

cially on the state and city levels, spurred programs for highway construction, furthering the use of automobiles. The convenience of the "door-to-door" service obtained by automobile passengers, along with the privacy of the family car, began to deprive railway passenger service of potential customers. Competition to the railroad in the private sector was matched by that in public transportation when in 1929, on the eve of the Great Depression, the Greyhound bus system inaugurated service. The buses would command a larger and larger share of the low-priced intercity passenger traffic in the years to come. Like the automobile, the buses enjoyed government aid indirectly through increased highway appropriations and construction. Finally, by the late 1920's, air passenger service operated regularly on a modest scale. The budding airline service was a harbinger of further competition in the passenger field. Airlines had one crucial advantage—speed.

Not only railroad passenger traffic was threatened with decline before 1945; freight traffic also seemed in store for a downturn. By the mid-1930's the trucking industry was emerging as a growing form of transportation. Interstate trucking achieved the same boost from highway construction that the automobile and bus had, and offered the potential of "door-to-door" service to freight customers. Beyond trucking competition, the railroads began to lose the freight business of several energy-related industries, such as the petroleum industry, which was relying increasingly on interstate pipelines to meet their particular needs.

World War II brought increased business, both passenger and freight, to the nation's railroads, but recovery for the industry seemed less likely when one considers the competitors already in action by the 1940's. A key development for the railroads themselves was the increased use during wartime of the efficient diesel locomotive. Diesels proved superior in all ways to steam locomotives, and the days of the "iron horse" were numbered by 1945. Nonetheless, by the end of the war, indications of the postwar decline of railroads were evident.

A key development in the decline since 1945 has been the drop in railway mileage: the extent of track has fallen steadily since the end of World War II. As a result, fewer communities enjoy railroad service of any type. Decline in passenger service has been most obvious; one reason is that, after 1945, very few innovations in the service were forthcoming. Vista-domed passenger cars were first used in 1945, but much of the passenger rolling stock remained outmoded until the 1970's. In addition to creaky equipment, the quality of passenger service was notoriously poor. Trains frequently ran behind schedule. Long layovers occurred for passengers at transfer points such as Chicago. Passenger operations became a drag on the total operations of key lines, and many rail companies simply permitted passenger service to deteriorate while concentrating on more profitable freight service. By 1957, airline passenger traffic exceeded the railroads' passenger traffic for the first time.

Passenger service continued to dwindle through the 1960's. The obvious need for commuter service, which only occurred during two peak periods on weekdays, could not sustain the overall losses in the passenger field. In 1970, RAILPAX—now called AMTRAK—marked the effective nationalization of interstate passenger railroading in the United States. New equipment, particularly the Turbo engine, has been introduced, along with modern passenger coaches. Still, AMTRAK faces deficits and meets these with schedule cuts. It remains to be seen how the system will fare in the future.

Commuter railroads servicing the big cities have received government subsidies as well, especially for the equipment necessary to modernize. Some lines, such as the Long Island, have been taken over by the government, while other commuter lines fall under the authority of regional transportation systems. Still, service has been cut during nonpeak periods and the future of commuter lines, such as the South Shore, an electronic railway that services Chicago and industrial northwest Indiana, is very dubious. Commuter lines need more executives like the Chicago and North Western's Ben Heineman, whose ef-

ficient, courteous service turned his commuter line into a profitmaker.

In the freight field, decline has not been so great as in the passenger operations. Many railroads have diversified, acquiring their own trucking firms to coordinate truck and rail efficiency. The "piggy-back" cars that haul truck trailers have been a success, and there have been innovations in freight car size that may prove profitable for freight operations. Mergers have been a clear trend, with the biggest single merger involving the New York Central and the Pennsylvania Railroad in 1968. President Robert Young of the New York Central engineered the merger with the active support of President Stuart Saunders of the Pennsylvania Railroad. As railroads diversify, they have often obtained conglomerate holdings, such as Heineman's Northwest Industries, which have helped to offset rail losses in other fields. Despite all of this, however, decline continues. The Penn Central gained little strength from the 1968 merger and continues to experience financial difficulties. In all operations, then, American railroads face an uncertain financial future. The nation, nevertheless, cannot do without them.

## Pertinent Literature

Stover, John F. *The Life and Decline of the American Railroad.* New York: Oxford University Press, 1970.

John F. Stover, a History professor at Purdue University, is a leading scholar specializing in the field of railroad history. In addition to the volume under consideration, he has

written two other major works on railroad history, *American Railroads* (1961) and *The Railroads of the South, 1865-1900* (1955). He has had direct experience with railroad corporations, serving in 1962 as an exchange fellow with the Illinois Central Railroad.

One of the major difficulties in trying to investigate railroad history lies in the sources available to the general reader. Since railroads remain a romantic memory for many Americans, the literature of American railroading abounds with oversized picture books focusing on the steam locomotive era. Often written by self-styled railroad "buffs," these pictorial volumes are decidedly lacking in historical narrative, and instead often have texts filled with technological details and speed records. Unfortunately, the pictorial nostalgic volumes leave key questions undiscussed. What role has railroading played in the tremendous economic success of the United States? How did the railroads spur economic development? What has government done to aid and to regulate the nation's railroads? Why have twentieth century railroads suffered such a marked decline? Though the early years of railroading have been ably described by Robert Fogel, the entire sweep of railroad history has fallen to Stover for scholarly examination. Stover's excellent narrative in this volume covers the whole of railroad history through to the Penn Central merger of 1968. His concluding chapters are particularly important in explaining the reasons the railroads have declined.

Stover sees the decline as beginning after World War I. He acknowledges the new modes of transportation developed in this century, and gives statistics that demonstrate the impact of these new forms on the rail-roads. Beyond alternative means of transportation, he also details the crucial role of government in supporting these newer modes of transportation. The factor of government support of highways and airports is somewhat ironic, since the railroads experienced their own heyday of government aid in the mid-nineteenth century in the form of huge subsidies for additional mileage and extensive land grants. The late nineteenth century, however, saw the beginnings of regulation with the creation of the Interstate Commerce Commission. Throughout the twentieth century, government has regulated and taxed the railroads while extending tax aid to newer forms of transport. Once the exclusive beneficiaries of government aid, the railroads now watch other industries obtaining similar aid.

Stover provides a complete account of the drastic decline in passenger service, but since the volume was written previous to the creation of AMTRAK, readers must go elsewhere to study the most recent events affecting passenger service. Still, the author's account does extend to the "eve" of AMTRAK, and in a very real sense describes the malaise that led directly to AMTRAK's creation. The discussions of recent freight service, its decline, and its shifting technology are thoroughgoing and clear. Stover also chronicles the trend toward merger and conglomerate investments by the railroads. His description of the Penn Central merger of 1968 is well executed. Because there are so few scholarly books on American railroad history, this volume is highly recommended.

## The Crisis in Railroad Transportation

Southerland, Thomas C., Jr. and William McCleery. *The Way to Go: The Coming Revival of U.S. Rail Passenger Service.* New York: Simon and Schuster, 1973.

This volume is perhaps the most informed of the books written by the railroad "buffs." Both authors possess credentials outside of history, but impressive nonetheless. Southerland has served as Assistant Dean of the School of Architecture and Urban Planning at Princeton University and has chaired that University's Environmental Advisory Committee. He holds a degree from the United States Naval Academy. McCleery is a playwright, editor, and author.

Readers will obtain an accurate description of the reasons for the passenger service decline that has occurred since 1945. Chiefly to blame, according to the authors, are a legacy of popular mistrust of the railroad corporations; the concentration of railroads on more solvent freight investments and their neglect of passenger service; labor unions with outdated work rules; and government aid to automobile and air traffic. The authors also describe the creation of AMTRAK and its early problems. More than anything else, however, the book is marked by advocacy, although of a quite informed type. The authors are active environmentalists and hence support a revival of passenger railroading on environmental grounds. They carefully document the pollution and safety hazards of auto traffic, along with the major question of fuel economy. Railroads prove superior in all areas. The authors also present a fascinating discussion of new technological developments in the passenger field, focusing on the "great trains of Europe." They present the reader with descriptions of how passenger railroading is thriving in other parts of the world and conclude that it will enjoy a revival in the United States out of environmental and economic necessity. Given current problems with AMTRAK, the authors may not have made their point. But, given repeated Arab threats to our country's petroleum supplies, their prognosis for the future may prove correct.
— *E.A.Z.*

## Additional Recommended Reading

Stover, John F. *American Railroads.* Chicago: University of Chicago Press, 1961. An excellent though earlier work by Stover from the excellent series, *The Chicago History of American Civilization.*

The American Assembly, Columbia University. *The Future of American Transportation.* Englewood Cliffs, N.J.: Prentice-Hall, 1972. The authors call for the pruning of existing track mileage, which is overextended with few trains—a condition that has resulted in poor maintenance.

Tyler, Poyntz. *Outlook for the Railroads.* New York: H. W. Wilson, 1960. The author supports large-scale, regional consolidations, with Interstate Commerce Commission approval, to strengthen the railroads.

Carper, Robert S. *Focus: The Railroad in Transition.* South Brunswick, N.J.: A. S.

## The Crisis in Railroad Transportation

Barnes, 1968. The author focuses on the decline of railroads as a result of economic change, centering his discussion on the World War II years.

Daughen, Joseph R. and Peter Binzen. *The Wreck of the Penn Central.* New York: Little, Brown and Company, 1971. The authors detail the merged line's recent difficulties.

# THE DEMISE OF THE PURITAN ETHIC IN AMERICA

*Type of event:* Sociological: reassessment of ethical standards
*Time:* 1945 to the present
*Locale:* The United States

## Summary of Event

Despite the obvious difficulties inherent in seeking national identities, man has attempted to define such characteristics since the time of Aristotle; and this preoccupation has been especially tempting in the United States with its diverse, heterogeneous population. Although there are almost as many classifications of the American character as there are theorists, the myriad definitions usually fit into two broad categories: that of the rugged individualist, or conversely, that of the materialistic conformist. While the evidences of conformity had been observed and commented upon as early as the time of Alexis de Tocqueville, the predominant myth of the American temper has been that of the individualist. Closely allied with this concept has been the pervasive influence of the Puritan heritage and its concomitant ethic.

The Puritan ethic gave the individualist a social sanction for his self-interest by its insistence that what was best for the individual was best for society at large. Thus, the Puritan ethic's stress on hard work, deferred gratification, and thrift justify the excesses of laissez-faire capitalism. The rigid application of this ethic to the American situation is still debated, but there is no doubt that such an ethic not only inspired our Puritan ancestors, but has also played an important role in the educational system, and in the various media which have formed the social values of generation after generation, from Benjamin Franklin's maxims to the Horatio Alger stories to modern self-help books and popular columnists.

Periodically, the applicability of the Puritan ethic is attacked and critics decry a turning away from basic values; but never was such a belief in its demise so forceful as in the period following World War II. The opening salvo in the attack was sounded by David Riesman in his 1950 book, *The Lonely Crowd*. In this book Riesman introduced the terms "inner-directed" and "other-directed" to our vocabulary. It was his thesis that America was turning away from the norm of the self-made man (or "inner-directed") to that of the conformist. Basically, his "other-directed" man was the one whose values are determined from without, from his peers, as opposed to the inner-directed person, who internalizes a value system garnered from his family and ancestors.

Shortly after Riesman's book, in 1956, William H. Whyte described in more detail what he considered the modern American prototype in *The Organization Man*. Whyte's thesis was that the Puritan, or Protestant, ethic was being replaced by what he called "the social ethic," which he defined as the moral legitimization of society's pressures on the individual.

It was Whyte's view, and the view of many others, that this discernible turning away from the Puritan ethic was a more decisive and definitive change in the basic American character than any of the temporary pendulum swings of the past. The rejection of the Puritan ethic, he felt, was caused by basic changes in the American scene which unalterably changed all aspects of life, and consequently of the basic American character.

The primary influence in the change of modern life in the United States was the technological revolution which began during World War II. When American industry converted from producing war matériel, these technological advances affected all areas of society. Besides the great availability of new consumer goods and a relatively large and affluent working class to produce and purchase them, there was a large population of children, the "war babies" who would soon present the manufacturers with ever-increasing customers for their products and a work supply force which in turn depended upon a growth economy for its livelihood. The burgeoning population turned to mass-produced communities, the suburbs, where life was more comfortable but more regimented. At about this same time, the number of white-collar workers (those middle-class "service occupations" as opposed to the producers of goods) began to swell, so that by 1956, they outnumbered blue-collar workers. With this explosion in the work force came massive changes in work conditions; the modern office utilized amenities previously enjoyed only in the upper-class residence, with its spaciousness, air conditioning, and soothing lighting and color combinations.

The enjoyment of this material prosperity opposed the Puritan ethic's emphasis on hard work and gratification deferral, so the ethic was subtly modified to stress the value of working with others, getting along with others. White-collar workers, no longer being independent producers of goods, were more and more controlled by the large corporations for which they labored. The concept of hard work and competitiveness leading to material success as in the old agrarian and industrial ages of the United States had to be altered to working within an organization for the good of the corporation, and ultimately, society. President Eisenhower's designated Secretary of Defense, Charles Wilson, summed up the new "corporation ethic" when he stated that "what was good for our country was good for General Motors, and vice versa." Somehow, most people remembered the gist of what he said as, "What is good for General Motors is good for the country."

More significant, perhaps, is the personal life of the typical American. Besides the exodus to the suburbs and the increase in the white-collar work force, the postwar years brought television, the most pervasive medium of communication man has ever seen. Television's ability to mold opinions and sell products was soon recognized and the advertising industry supplied the means of disposing of the great supply of consumer goods being turned out. The selling of products which had not existed a few years previously, and more importantly, the creation of desires in the minds of the consumers, depended upon a reversal of the Puritan ethic's stress on frugality, self-denial, and saving. Advertisers turned to motivational research to discover the inner workings of the consumers' psyches in order to convince them that they "deserved" all these material comforts.

In the 1950's also came another subtle revolution, that of rising consumer credit. Beginning with the Diners Club Credit Card in 1950, the average American began living beyond his means, so that by 1958, the Diners Club numbered 750,000 members. Other credit cards soon began competing, including those of major stores and their "revolving credit" in which consumers became accustomed to constant monthly payments. Consumer debt in the decade rose from $73 billion to $196 billion. With the emphasis on home buying in the suburbs, the graduated income tax, and easy credit, personal savings decreased. The later addition of inflation further decreased the few incentives for thrift which might have remained. No little part of this greater consumer spending was due to the virtual necessity of automobile ownership necessitated by greater commuting distances between the suburbs and the inner cities where jobs were located, and the general neglect of public mass transportation.

A third disincentive to personal thrift in addition to the massive advertising and easy credit indebtedness was planned obsolescence, most notable in the automobile industry, which began to change models yearly. Part of the innate obsolescence of consumer products, of course, is due to rapid technological advances, but advertisers, eager to create a demand for rival products, began stressing new improvements, real or imaginary, in items as indistinguishable as detergents, cigarettes, and beers.

Another natural consequence of the technological revolution was an increase in leisure time for a greater proportion of the population and a new emphasis on consumption in the pursuit of leisure activities. In this realm, once again, television was the foremost influence. Because of the great competition for leisure-time spending, the movie industry explored previously taboo themes of drug addiction, miscegenation, homosexuality, and blatant sexuality, ending years of voluntary self-censorship. Literature soon followed suit. After protracted legal battles, *Lady Chatterley's Lover* was exonerated of the charge of obscenity by the courts in 1960. This greater freedom in subject matter in the various media provided the matrix for the overt attacks on the Puritan ethic of the Beat generation of the late 1950's and the hippies of the 1960's.

Illustrative of the difficulty in interpreting the effects of greater freedom in sexual conduct and frankness in its discussion upon the nation's mores was the release of the Kinsey Reports in 1948 and 1954. The reports shocked the public in their open discussion of sexual practices which had already been prevalent among Americans. Kinsey's message was that most Americans had not been living according to the more rigid Victorian moral codes still represented by many laws on the books. Nonetheless, Kinsey's report and the greater freedom among the media brought the subject of sex into polite conversation, bombarding the public with more sensual stimuli suggesting a revised code of behavior to match reality. The term "situational ethics" was coined to indicate shifting ethical values dependent upon specific circumstances rather than an unchanging moral code handed down from one generation to the next.

Most crucial to the question of a changing Puritan ethic is the effect of all these changes on the youth of America who no longer passively accepted the mores of their families and church. This "post-affluent" generation did not remember a depression and was inclined to take material possessions for granted. From grade school on, the emphasis turned more and more to the values of socializing. By 1953, thirty-five percent of third grade readers emphasized the importance of "winning friends" rather than the old success-oriented individualism of the readers of the early decades of the twentieth century. On college campuses, under the barrage of student activists' demands for students' rights, most colleges gave up the old concept of *in loco parentis*, making college life much more permissive. It has been suggested that this more sheltered existence in the schools is one of the causes for larger enrollments in graduate schools which have become more attuned to the social ethic, especially in the areas of the humanities and social sciences.

In spite of these apparent attacks upon traditional values, it should be pointed out that the 1950's showed a revival of interest in religion. In 1957, a census report indicated that ninety-six percent cited a church af-

filiation of some sort. However, this religious feeling did not go deep; the church was not looked upon as an agent of social reform. The popular religion of the 1950's was the type such as that preached by the popular Norman Vincent Peale, who stressed the social values of peace of mind and emotional security, cautioning against the evils of overtrying and emotional stress. There was a brief flurry of controversy over the "God is dead" theory of Thomas J. J. Altizer and others. This controversy referred more to a change from a belief in a transcendent deity to an immanent God rather than to a disbelief in any deity. The overall trend was to a more personal and mystical experience of religion instead of to a traditional denominational affiliation. This trend, too, had the effect of negating traditional values.

There is little question of whether modern America's emphasis on gross national product, mass consumption, and time payments is opposed to the Puritan ethic of hard work, deferred gratification, and thrift. What may be questioned is whether this change is just another reaction to past restrictions from which the country will return to a more restrictive moral and ethical code, or whether it is a permanent change. Those who espouse the theory that the economy dictates mores, that a surplus economy stresses consumption, and that a return to a scarcity economy will reawaken the old competitive, individualist work ethic, see little chance for such a return, given the increased government regulation which restricts the older free interaction among competing forces. It seems, indeed, that the old

Puritan ethic, as it relates to society as a whole, is currently dormant, and if it is to return, it will have to be modified drastically to fit the present-day United States.

## Pertinent Literature

Whyte, William H., Jr. *The Organization Man*. New York: Simon and Schuster, 1956.

The first large-selling book to bring up the question of the changing American character was David Riesman's *The Lonely Crowd*, which appeared in 1950. Riesman's hypothesis was that population and technological changes bring about changes in the social character of a nation. He believed that the United States had reached a point of decreasing population which in turn led to a switch from an "inner-directed" to an "outer-directed" population; that is, people were now dependent on their peers for the development of inner qualities and feelings rather than internalizing adult authority as the inner-directed person does. While the strict correlation Riesman saw with population has been shown lacking, the change of the national character he related was seized upon by others. One of the most popular writers who built on Riesman's earlier work was William H. Whyte.

It is Whyte's idea that in the industrial era people realized that success was often due more to birth and personal connections rather than to the old virtues of hard work and sacrifice. At the same time, the constraints of mass production opposed the thrift ethic, and self-reliance in most endeavors gave way to the committee method, thus making it necessary to devise a new ethic or rationale to justify or legitimize these pressures placed on individuals by society. This new ethic is what Whyte calls the "social ethic." It consists of three main tenets: the belief in the group as the center of creativity, a belief in the need of mankind to belong to a group, and the faith in science to achieve that sense of belonging.

Whyte goes on to analyze the ramifications of his thesis. He points out that advertisers have turned to the advances of sociology and psychology in the new field of motivation research to find out what motivates consumers and to assuage their guilt feelings about their over-consumption of goods previously considered luxury items. He points out that the old ethic of hard work and success has been replaced by the warnings against overwork and ulcers, shifting guilt feelings to overstriving and hard work.

The change is traced to the turn of the century, when the intellectual groundwork was laid by the philosophers of pragmatism, ethical relativism, and Freudianism who switched from looking for the perfectibility of man to the improvement of society. This has led in a natural progression to "social engineers" who attempted the creation of an exact science of man. These efforts, Whyte feels, have been unsuccessful, and the real impact this "scientism" has had on our value system is a return to a Middle Ages mentality with its need to belong to any one of myriad groups.

These changing values are permeating the school curriculum. Whyte points out that schools have often vacillated between practical, vocational education, and the liberal arts, but he cites figures showing that the swing to vocationally oriented schools has been long and consistent until business schools have grown to be among the largest, and there is no evidence of any reversal of the trend. Even the formative influence of popular fiction is shown to foster the ideas of the social ethic.

Whyte relates this new social ethic to America's traditional sense of democracy, which stresses freedom for all. The social ethic gives more freedom and power to those less capable of handling it to the detriment of the more gifted, or the self-made man of the past. It leads to a denigration of leadership, stressing group decisions and actions. The well-rounded man of the social ethic is one who has a "passive" ambition: he is a conformist above all. In a section entitled "The Executive: Non-Well-Rounded Man," Whyte points out that the top executives of companies still adhere to the Protestant ethic, but the true

entrepreneurs who still remain are found in small businesses and primarily in service industries.

Whyte also analyzes suburbia and what it has done to the traditional patterns of American life. The suburbs are supposedly classless societies; yet, that classlessness itself becomes a kind of goad and incentive to changing life styles. At first, not keeping up with the Joneses justifies the lack of money of the young middle class when they are starting out. But eventually, as individuals within that close-knit society of suburbia acquire new possessions, what once was considered a luxury item now becomes a necessity. Whyte gives the example of clothes dryers which were relatively new items at the time; the two- and three-car families of today's suburbs are a natural progression in this acquisitive society.

Although Whyte is chronicling a movement near its beginning, many of the trends he notes have continued and become more marked, although some reactions have also occurred. In some cases he exaggerates the extent and importance of some of the changes, but subsequent history has shown many of his analyses to be accurate.

Hacker, Andrew. *The End of the American Era*. New York: Atheneum Publishers, 1970.

Hacker's book is primarily concerned with America's declining position in world affairs, a decline he attributes largely to the demise of the principles associated with the Puritan ethic. In his pessimistic look at American life, Hacker tries to relate the internal changes of the basic Ameri-

can character to America's role as a world power. It is his belief that the Puritan ethic has an economic basis. Such an ethic occurs only in eras of scarcity or with the advent of revolutionary regimes, and he forsees no reversion to such times for the United States. Therefore, he sees the end of the era of America's influence in world affairs. He warns that Americans must either recognize this reality or continue foreign intervention at the risk of wearing themselves down.

The Puritan ethic, in Hacker's view, kept people in their place. He views its demise in this country, however, as more apparent than real. It is his opinion that it never applied to the great mass of the American public which now makes up the middle class. This new middle class, he claims, is descended from the older peasants, the proletariat which never was guided by the Puritan ethic.

The overall change of the national character is traced to World War II. Prior to the war, the relatively affluent middle class was a more traditional one. The war was a time in which soldiers drawn from the poorer class, just emerging from a serious depression, were fed and clothed in better fashion than ever before. In civilian life war jobs were plentiful— so plentiful, in fact, that blacks and women for the first time were able to earn good wages and raise their standard of living.

At the close of the war things improved even more. Technology, turning to civilian markets, produced more opportunities for a wider base of the public. These opportunities brought greater freedom and democracy for a larger proportion of the population than ever before, and also inevitably brought greater expectations. Hacker warns that "Tensions and frustrations are bound to arise when 200 million human beings demand rights and privileges never intended for popular distribution." This enlarged middle class included blacks and women, who had won a new status during the war, as well as the returned soldiers themselves, who had become accustomed to a higher standard of living in the military service and who were now receiving college degrees under the benefits of the G. I. Bill.

The economic boom following the war produced more profits for corporations. These profits, Hacker believes, went to hiring more white-collar workers rather than to lowering prices, thus building up a "new managerial temperament" of salaried men whose concern was not rapacious profits for the company, as had typified industry's leaders of the past, but the perpetuation of the bureaucracy they had built up.

The corporation is one of Hacker's villains. Though corporations are central to the nation's economy, they have no "theoretical rationale linking power, purpose, and responsibility," as did such power bases of the past as the church and guild. Since almost one-half of the stockholdings in the United States are held by other corporations, Hacker claims that their power is that of machines rather than men. These corporations dictate what possessions the public will buy, exert undue influence over our increasingly vocational educational systems, affect the growth and deterioration of communities, and, finally, affect public morality through what technology makes available. An example of the latter is the development of the birth control pill.

Under these influences, Hacker believes life in the United States is characterized by an identity crisis, a sense of rootlessness and alienation.

He sees the new majority as very ordinary unambitious people who seek security above all else. Even college graduates, coming largely from the older lower class, he sees as attempting to become what others expect them to be rather than self-determined individuals.

Hacker says that the youth of America, the "post-affluent generation," take abundance and material possessions for granted. They have thus shucked off the Puritan ethic's need for "internalized repressions that have burdened the lives of their elders," and they also have escaped from the influence of the older generation.

It is Hacker's view that the nation as a whole is no longer guided by the Puritan ethic because the new middle class, being largely composed of what used to be the lower class, never was very influenced by it. The rapid technological changes which have brought new abundance to the American economy and new power to American corporations have also combined to ensure the demise of the Puritan ethic's influence over the nation as a whole. — R.A.G.

## Additional Recommended Reading

Riesman, David, Revel Denney and Nathan Glazer. *The Lonely Crowd: A Study of the Changing American Character*. New Haven, Conn.: Yale University Press, 1950. A seminal work in the technique of sample interviewing in an attempt to analyze the character of typical Americans; Riesman's thesis is that the Americans have changed from being "inner-directed" to being "other-directed."

Hartshorne, Thomas L. *The Distorted Image: Changing Conceptions of the American Character Since Turner*. Cleveland, Oh.: The Press of Case Western Reserve University, 1968. A survey of the views of the American character as interpreted by scholars and intellectuals from the late nineteenth century to the 1950's.

Cawelti, John G. *Apostles of the Self-Made Man*. Chicago: University of Chicago Press, 1965. A study of the American ideal of success as purveyed by the popular media of success manuals and guides and popular novels through the ages.

Higham, John, ed. *The Reconstruction of American History*. New York: Humanities Press, 1962. A collection of essays which surveys the trends in historical interpretation; Potter's "Quest for the National Character" summarizes the various views.

Miller, Douglas T. and Marion Nowak. *The Fifties: The Way We Really Were*. Garden City, N.Y.: Doubleday & Company, 1977. Reviews all aspects of American life in the 1950's, illustrating the various trends and events which helped shape the American character.

O'Neill, William L. *Coming Apart: An Informal History of America in the 1960's*. Chicago: Quadrangle Books, 1971. Traces the changes in American character during the decade of the 1960's.

Manchester, William. *The Glory and the Dream: A Narrative History of America, 1932-1974*. A massive study of the major historical events of four decades showing the influences on American character through a generation.

Brinton, Crane. *A History of Western Morals*. New York: Harcourt, Brace & Company, 1959. A study of the morals of Western society from early times to the 1950's, based on the author's belief that the change in American character emerging in the 1950's was a temporary one which would soon give way to a new era.

Ahlstrom, Sydney E. *A Religious History of the American People*. New Haven, Conn.: Yale University Press, 1972. A study of the religious life and affiliations of the American people which is helpful in showing the relationship between religious feelings and the Puritan ethic.